# ¡TRATO HECHO!

## *Spanish for Real Life*

**Second Edition**

**Annotated Instructor's Edition**

**John T. McMinn**
Austin Community College

**Patricia Rush**
Ventura College

**Patricia Houston**
Pima Community College

**Rosa María Acero**
Ventura College

**Prentice Hall**
Upper Saddle River, New Jersey 07458

*Library of Congress Cataloging-in-Publication Data*

McMinn, John T.
¡Trato hecho! : Spanish for Real Life / John T. McMinn ... [et al.]. —
2nd. ed.
p. cm.
English and Spanish.
Rev. ed. of: ¡Trato hecho! / John T. McMinn, Robert A. Hemmer,
Virginia D. Vigil. Combined ed. c1996.
Includes Index.
ISBN 0-13-021515-5
1. Spanish language Textbooks for foreign speakers—English.
I. McMinn, John T. II. McMinn, John T. ¡Trato hecho!
PC4129.E5M44 1999
468.2'421—dc21 99-40603
CIP

*Editor-in-Chief:* Rosemary Bradley
*Acquisitions Editor:* Kristine Suárez
*Development Editor:* Mariam Rohlfing
*Associate Editor:* Heather Finstuen
*Editorial Assistant:* Amanda Latrenta
*AVP, Director of Production and Manufacturing:* Barbara Kittle
*Executive Managing Editor:* Ann Marie McCarthy
*Editorial/Production Supervision:* Nancy Stevenson
*Executive Marketing Manager:* Ilse Wolfe
*Marketing Coordinator:* Don Allmon
*Manufacturing Manager:* Nick Sklitsis
*Buyer:* Tricia Kenny
*Creative Design Director:* Leslie Osher
*Interior and Cover Design:* Carole Anson
*Photo Researcher:* Diana Gongora
*Image Specialist:* Beth Boyd
*Manager, Rights & Permissions:* Kay Dellosa
*Director, Image Resource Center:* Melinda Reo
*Line Art Coordinator:* Guy Ruggiero
*Electronic Line Art Creation:* Michelle Logerfo
*Formatting Manager:* John J. Jordan
*Electronic Page Layout:* Wanda España/Wee Design Group
*Electronic Art Creation:* Maria Piper

Photo Acknowledgments appear on p. 492, which constitutes a continuation of the copyright page.

This book was set in 10.5/12.5 Minion by Wee Design Group and was printed and bound by World Color. The cover and endpapers were printed by The Lehigh Press, Inc.



Printed in the United States of America
10 9 8 7 6 5 4 3 2 1

Student text: ISBN 0-13-021515-5
Annotated Instructor's Edition: ISBN 0-13-021596-1

Prentice-Hall International (UK) Limited, London
Prentice-Hall of Australia Pty. Limited, Sydney
Prentice-Hall Canada Inc., Toronto
Prentice-Hall Hispanoamericana, S.A., Mexico
Prentice-Hall of India Private Limited, New Delhi
Prentice-Hall of Japan, Inc., Tokyo
Pearson Education Asia Pte. Ltd., Singapore
Editora Prentice-Hall do Brasil, Ltda., Rio de Janeiro

# BRIEF CONTENTS

LECCIONES

# SCOPE AND SEQUENCE

## TEMA 3

### En mi clase
**22–29**

- Los estudiantes
- Los números de cero a cien
- El artículo definido: género y número
- El artículo indefinido

## TEMA 4

### Las clases y los horarios
**30–37**

- Los horarios
- ¿A qué hora es tu clase de...?
- Los verbos que terminan en *-ar*
- Las preguntas

### ¡TRATO HECHO!
**40–43**

- Rincón profesional: Educación bilingüe
- A escuchar
- El buzón de Doña Rosa
- A leer
- A escribir

## TEMA 3

### De compras
**64–71**

- De tienda en tienda
- La comida
- Preposiciones de lugar
- Expresiones afirmativas y negativas

## TEMA 4

### La ropa
**72–79**

- La moda personal
- Problemas con las compras
- *Me/te/le gusta(n)*
- Pronombres y adjetivos demostrativos

### ¡TRATO HECHO!
**82–85**

- Rincón profesional: De compras por el Internet
- A escuchar
- A leer
- A escribir

## TEMA 3

### Los quehaceres domésticos
**106–113**

- Hay que limpiar
- ¿Qué pasa?
- Los comparativos
- Los superlativos

## TEMA 4

### La guardería infantil
**114–121**

- De visita en la guardería
- Fabiola y Elvira en la guardería
- Los verbos *tener* y *venir*
- Los verbos irregulares: *-er* e *-ir*

### ¡TRATO HECHO!
**124–127**

- Rincón profesional: Decoradores de interiores
- A escuchar
- A leer
- A escribir

## LECCIÓN 7

# La vida cotidiana

234–275

### TEMA 1

**La ciudad y el campo**
236–243

- La vida urbana
- La vida rural
- El imperfecto
- Más sobre el imperfecto

### TEMA 2

**Un accidente con el coche nuevo**
244–251

- ¿Cómo funciona?
- Un accidente
- El pretérito y el imperfecto
- La narración en el pasado

## LECCIÓN 8

# Vámonos de viaje

276–317

### TEMA 1

**¿Adónde vamos?**
278–285

- De vacaciones
- En el aeropuerto
- Los complementos directos
- Más sobre los complementos directos

### TEMA 2

**En el hotel**
286–293

- En la recepción
- En la habitación
- Los complementos indirectos
- Los verbos como *gustar*

## LECCIÓN 9

# La salud y el bienestar

318–359

### TEMA 1

**El ejercicio**
320–327

- El cuerpo
- La importancia del ejercicio
- Los mandatos (*tú*)
- Los mandatos (*nosotros*)

### TEMA 2

**La dieta**
328–335

- Comer bien es importante
- El buen comer significa buena salud
- Introducción al subjuntivo
- Más sobre el subjuntivo

# Preface

***¡Trato hecho!*** is a modular beginning Spanish program for students who want to put Spanish to immediate use in their personal lives, communities, or workplaces. The central goals of ***¡Trato hecho!*** are to build proficiency in and appreciation for the Spanish language, to develop students' understanding of Hispanic cultures and their growing importance in the world, and to provide contexts that reinforce the usefulness of Spanish in today's economy, particularly in North America.

Students today recognize the important role Spanish plays and will continue to play in North America. The global economy and community, NAFTA, and opportunities in international business have sparked a renewed interest in language study. ***¡Trato hecho!*** responds to this surging interest by stressing the features of Spanish needed for everyday communication and applying them immediately to realistic settings around the world.

Its "hands-on" style brings the learner into direct contact with Spanish as it is used in everyday living, from the classroom to the home, from the bank to the hospital, from the restaurant to the airport, from shopping to leisure activities. Packed with dynamic realia from the United States and Spanish-speaking countries, it encompasses the idea of Spanish for the Real World. Communication is the key, and the logical, concise grammar explanations are organized to enhance language acquisition. The totally new ***¡Trato hecho!*** section that concludes each chapter directly connects the student with the Hispanic world and reinforces its importance in today's global society.

## Approach and Organization

At the heart of ***¡Trato hecho!*** is its flexible, modular approach. The text is divided into ten regular *lecciones* and two review chapters. The logical overall design is shown by the well-balanced scope and sequence and the carefully controlled vocabulary list. Each group of exercises progresses smoothly from mechanical through meaningful to open-ended. Directions begin in English and change into Spanish at the midpoint of the text, while grammatical explanations remain in English to aid student comprehension.

The main theme of each of the ten regular *lecciones* is divided into four interrelated topics or *temas*, each of which corresponds to a language function that comprises four two-page modules. Each *tema* comprises two vocabulary modules and two grammar and activity modules. *Temas* 1 and 2 and *Temas* 3 and 4 are followed by vocabulary and a *Reunión* section that combines the themes and structures of the previous two *temas.* The *Reunión* sections include listening practice and activity sections such as *Lo sabía*, largely based on realia, *A conversar*, and *A buscar*, encouraging technology use in the classroom.

The two review chapters (6 and 12) recombine vocabulary, structures, functions, and cultural information in applied settings to offer cumulative real-world practice as well as a systematic review of all material covered. While these chapters offer a communicative focus, a solid grammatical core is presented. Further practice of all vocabulary and structures is provided in the workbook, website, and in the CD-ROM accompanying this text. The lab manual and accompanying audio program reinforce the listening skills developed through the text.

The modular approach of ***¡Trato hecho!*** has been enthusiastically received by instructors and students. Students who work full- or part-time in addition to attending college benefit from compact modules, because material is more manageable when learners can test their abilities and apply new material in one module before continuing to the next one. Students find smaller chunks of material better suited to their fragmented schedules. Instructors say they also prefer modules because they afford flexibility in planning and personalizing a course and tailoring it to the needs of their audience.

With *¡Trato hecho!*, instructors have the option of customizing material by selecting modules to emphasize. For example, in a course that meets three hours per week and focuses on grammatical accuracy, an instructor might decide to emphasize the grammar modules. Other instructors might elect to cover fully the vocabulary and synthesizing modules and assign the grammar modules a secondary role. The flexibility offered by the modular design allows instructors to tailor materials to the specific goals and needs of their students.

## Chapter Organization

The material in the ten regular *lecciones* is divided into four interrelated color-coded *temas* that emphasize skill-getting. Each *tema* comprises two vocabulary modules and two grammar and activity modules. This modular, color-coded format provides an extremely focused and flexible framework for presenting and learning new material within the limited blocks of time available to today's students and instructors. After every two *temas* are a list of new vocabulary, presented by *tema* and color, and *Reunión* activities designed to combine material from the previous two *temas.*

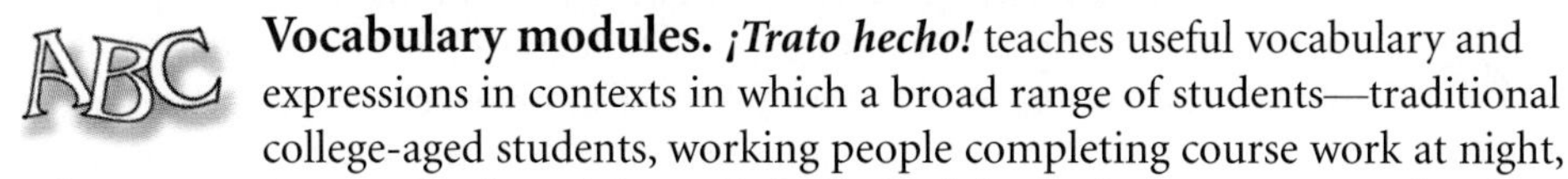

**Vocabulary modules.** ***¡Trato hecho!*** teaches useful vocabulary and expressions in contexts in which a broad range of students—traditional college-aged students, working people completing course work at night, retirees returning to school—might realistically find themselves or someone they know. The use of lively illustrations, realia, and vivid photographs in the vocabulary modules makes it possible to present new language entirely in Spanish while building a rich cultural framework. Presentation of new material is interwoven with contextualized and personalized activities that give students immediate practice. A limited number of new structures are previewed in each vocabulary module, laying the groundwork for their formal presentation in the grammar modules that follow. The dialogs introduce a varied cast of characters who become the students' friends and tie together the sequence of themes as they move through the book.

**Grammar modules.** Each grammar module of ***¡Trato hecho!*** presents and puts to use one new structure. Grammar explanations are extremely simple and direct; they facilitate study at home, if necessary, as well as review. In addition, self-check questions (*Para averiguar*) appear in the margins of the text to help students focus on essential points of each explanation and to enable them to verify that they have understood an explanation after they have read it.

We encourage students to look over these self-check questions before reading the explanations or proceeding to the exercises and activities (*A lo personal*), which provide immediate reinforcement of new structures.

**Vocabulary summary.** A cumulative list of new active vocabulary appears in a module that follows every two skill-getting modules (*temas*) and precedes the skill-using module (*Reunión*). New words and expressions, all of which are recorded in the audio program, are divided into four color-coded sections that correspond to the *tema* in which they appear. The color-coded format of the chapter vocabulary list makes it easy for students to study for exams and for instructors to create them.

***¡Trato hecho!* module.** In recognition of the increased interest in Applied Spanish courses across the country, each of the ten regular *lecciones* of ***¡Trato hecho!*** concludes with a task-based module in which students use Spanish in a realistic, applied way. Modules focus on a variety of fields where students may be likely to seek their future careers, including: education, music and entertainment, the retail industry, law enforcement and emergency assistance, the restaurant business, the hotel and travel industries, the media and communication industries, banking and commerce, and medicine. The ***¡Trato hecho!*** modules make use of dynamic art, articles, and other documents to emphasize the usefulness and vitality of Spanish in today's world.

Each ***¡Trato hecho!*** module is a recap of the material in the chapter and provides an opportunity for students to pull together and use what they have learned in a series of reading, writing, listening, and speaking activities, all within an industry-specific context related to the chapter theme. The *Rincón profesional* uses authentic materials in the target language to explore a different professional field in each chapter, allowing students to recognize the importance of Spanish in today's marketplace, and providing an insider's look at each profession. The very popular *Doña Rosa* feature, in the format of an advice column, presents students with readers' questions about personal, professional, and social situations, and asks them—alone or in pairs—to come up with real or humorous solutions for the "readers'" problems. Furthermore, each ***¡Trato hecho!*** module winds up with an industry-specific group activity requiring students to work in teams to find creative solutions to simulated "real-world" professional projects. Students who participated in classroom tests of these group activities were overwhelmingly positive in their comments. "Fun" and "helpful" were frequent responses.

**Reading and writing activities.** Each ***¡Trato hecho!*** module also includes a reading and writing section. Students become independent readers and writers by acquiring a mix of flexible techniques and strategies. Each reading section focuses on one new reading strategy that students put to immediate use as they read an authentic text carefully selected to tie together or expand the chapter topics. Authentic texts include articles from magazines and newspapers, as well as brief literary texts. Pre-reading activities and post-reading comprehension checks assure students' growth and success. Writing activities, contextualized with the chapter theme, offer students opportunities to apply their steadily growing base of vocabulary and structures to situations that require practical and creative expression.

## Program Components

The essential goal of each component of ***¡Trato hecho!*** is simple: to make teaching and learning Spanish a successful experience. Each component is carefully and logically woven into the program. Each brings the language, culture, and people of the Spanish-speaking world alive for instructors and students.

### Annotated Instructor's Edition

Marginal annotations in the Annotated Instructor's Edition include warm-up and expansion exercises and activities and additional cultural information. It also includes tips and ideas designed specifically for graduate teaching assistants or adjunct faculty who may have limited course preparation time. Answers to discrete point activities and the tapescript for the in-text listening activities are also provided for the instructor's convenience.

### Instructor's Resource Manual

In addition to sample syllabi and lesson plans, the scripts for the audio program and the video, the Instructor's Resource Manual includes an array of extra in-class activities and strategies for integrating the multimedia into the course.

### Student Audio CD

The Student CD contains the recordings for the in-text *A escuchar* listening activities. This component helps students to acquire and review vocabulary, become more accustomed to hearing spoken Spanish, and understand it better.

### Audio Program

The Audio Program contains six CDs for the lab that provide the listening material for the lab manual, one student CD that contains the dialogs for the in-text *A escuchar* sections, and two vocabulary CDs with recordings for all the text's active vocabulary. The Audio Program is also available on cassette.

## Workbook/Lab Manual

The workbook section provides review exercises for each lesson segment and offers a variety of opportunities for additional grammar and vocabulary practice. Instructors may choose to assign these activities as homework or use them to reinforce class lessons. Authentic materials in the ***¡Trato hecho!*** sections corresponding to these sections in the textbook provide additional practice of the language in a natural context. The lab manual section provides structured listening practice for each lesson. It reviews vocabulary and grammar introduced in each *tema* while recycling and reinforcing language functions in a variety of contexts, to maximize student exposure to the use of the target language in real-life settings.

## Answer Key

A separate optional Answer Key to the workbook activities is provided so students may check their own work if the instructor wishes.

## Testing Program

The Testing Program for ***¡Trato hecho!*** uses a variety of techniques to evaluate students' skills in listening, speaking, reading, writing, and culture. This testing program consists of alternative tests for each chapter, mid-term and final examinations, and oral proficiency tests. It has been carefully crafted so the tests reflect the teaching methodology used in the text. The Testing Program is available in paper, IBM, and Macintosh formats. Dialogs for the listening component are available on cassette.

## *¡Trato hecho!* CD-ROM

Created specifically for ***¡Trato hecho!***, the CD-ROM features interactive Spanish practice through engaging vocabulary, grammar, listening, speaking, reading, and writing practice. Chapter topics are presented through audio, video, and visual means; students can practice their pronunciation through voice-recording technology. Interactive games provide students with a fun way to review material. Each chapter also includes cultural activities and a path to the ***¡Trato hecho!*** website, which provides further related activities and resources.

## *¡Trato hecho!* Website

The website has been specifically created to accompany ***¡Trato hecho!*** and contains a wealth of activities and cultural resources. Students can practice and review their vocabulary and grammar through self-testing exercises, the results of which they can communicate to their instructor through e-mail. Students can communicate with "key pals," offering them the opportunity to engage in *real-life* communication with a person or persons of their choice in a Spanish-speaking country or with Hispanics in the United States. Students may also do *guided* research on topics related to the chapter themes, answering brief essay questions, which give them further writing practice. Also, *Resource Areas* for the instructor and for the student provide access to daily events and issues throughout the Spanish-speaking world, bringing absolute currentness and relevance to the classroom.

## *¡Trato hecho!* Video

Created especially for ***¡Trato hecho!***, the video features semi-scripted interviews with Spanish speakers employed in the fields discussed in the ***¡Trato hecho!*** section of each chapter.

## Transparencies

A set of 50 full-color text-specific transparencies of maps, readings, and illustrations to facilitate internalization of new vocabulary provides visual support for the student text.

## Photo File

A beautifully crafted photo file of 50 color photographs mounted on cardboard and indexed by theme also accompanies ***¡Trato hecho!*** It can be used to aid instructors who conduct their lessons fully in the target language, to provide comprehensible input of vocabulary themes such as family life, or to stimulate conversation when discussing topics such as jobs, sports, and travel.

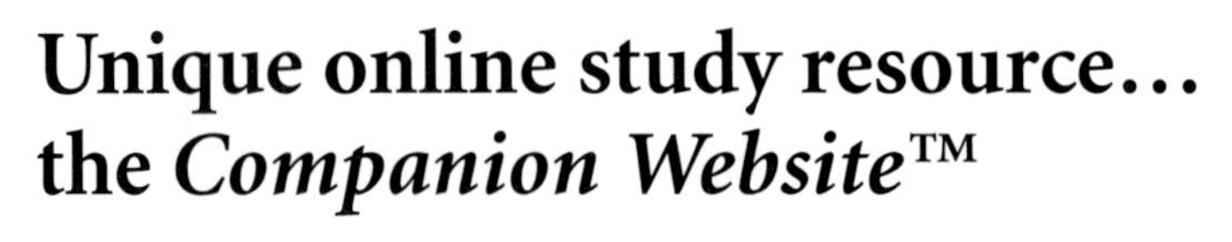

# Unique online study resource… the *Companion Website*™

**www.prenhall.com/trato**

Prentice Hall's exclusive *Companion Website*™ that accompanies ***¡Trato hecho!*** offers unique tools and support that make it easy for students and instructors to integrate the website materials with the text. The site is a comprehensive resource that is organized according to the chapters within the text and features a variety of learning and teaching modules:

### *For students:*

- **Study Guide Modules** contain a variety of exercises and features designed to help students with self-study. These modules include:

  —*chapter objectives* that help students organize key concepts to be learned

  —*activities* based on carefully selected Spanish-speaking websites that give students the opportunity to perform a variety of tasks to strengthen their reading and writing skills and improve their proficiency in language and culture.

  —*web destinations/modules* that provide web links and guidance on Spanish search engines to support the *A buscar* activities found in each *Reunión.*

  —*tutorial* modules that test the grammar and vocabulary of each chapter with instant scoring and feedback.

  —*built-in e-mail* routing option that gives students the ability to forward essay responses and graded quizzes to their instructors.

  —"*key-pal*" section where students can select a pen pal from the Spanish-speaking country of their choice and enjoy exchanging e-mail with them.
- **Reference Modules** contain resources for students, including on-line vocabulary and grammar support and cultural resources such as Spanish newspapers and country-specific information.
- **Communication Modules** include tools such as *Live Chat* and *Message Boards* to facilitate online collaboration and communication.
- **Personalization Modules** include our enhanced **Help** feature that contains a text page for browsers and plug-ins.

### *For instructors:*

- **The Faculty Module** includes resources for teaching. This includes links to sites that provide professional resources for language teachers and additional cultural resources.
- **Syllabus Manager**™ tool provides an easy-to-follow process for creating, posting, and revising a syllabus online that is accessible from any point within the Companion Website™. This resource allows instructors and students to communicate both inside and outside of the classroom at the click of a button.

The Companion Website™ makes integrating the Internet into your course exciting and easy. Join us online at **http://www.prenhall.com/trato** and enter a new world of teaching and learning possibilities and opportunities.

# Acknowledgments

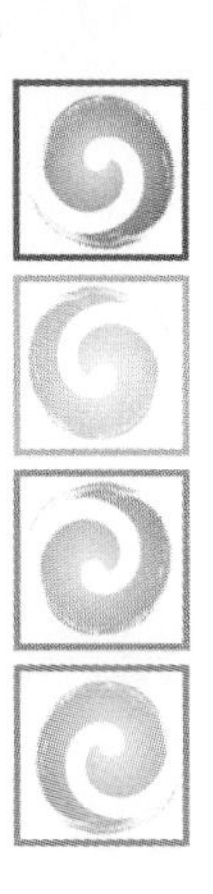

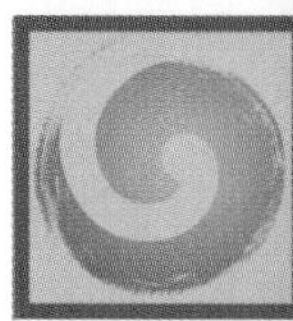

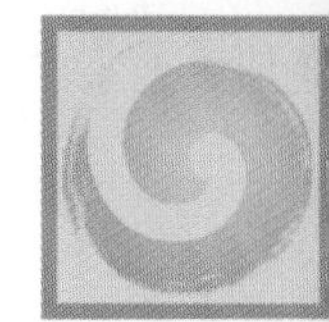

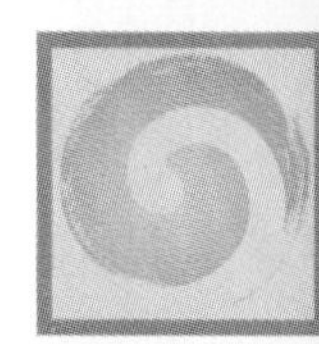

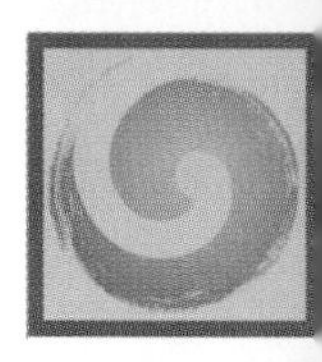

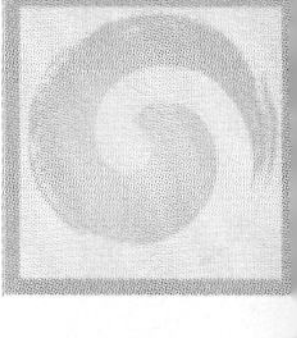

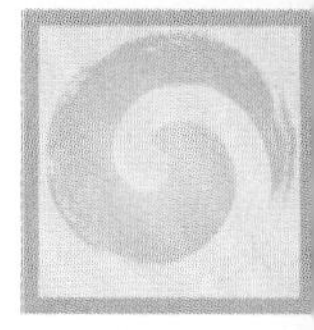

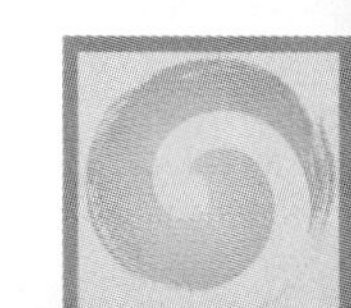

First, a very profound *gracias* to all who have helped us to bring ***¡Trato hecho!*** even closer to our ideal of a "dream" text for both teachers and students of first-year Spanish.

Many thanks are due to our colleagues and students for their patience, insight, and good humor as they helped us to classroom-test and refine the exercises and activities for "real-world" communication. Many more thanks are due to them for their continuing support and encouragement.

Special thanks go to Darrell Dernoshek for writing the Workbook and Instructor's Resource Manual that follow through on ***¡Trato hecho!***'s goals of step-by-step activities to take our students from mechanical practice to "real world communication", and to Mercedes Vallé of the University of Massachusetts, Amherst, for the testing program; and to Mark Davies of Illinois State University for the website activities.

We are truly grateful to the members of the Spanish teaching community whose comments and suggestions helped us to shape, reshape, and fine-tune the broad vision of the book, the sequence of material, and the final versions of the lessons. We would particularly like to thank the following reviewers of the second-edition manuscript and page proofs: Enrica Ardemagni, *Indiana University at Purdue*; Daniel Chaney, *Columbus State Community College*; Darrell Dernoshek, *University of South Carolina*; Dianne Hobbs, *University of North Carolina, Wilmington*; Laurie Huffman-Hasbun, *Los Medanos College*; Kim Jackson, *Belmont University*; Carol Kuznacic, *Longview Community College*; Purificación Martínez, *East Carolina University*; Sonia Nalon, *Florida State University*; Michele Shaul, *Queens College*; James Sutherland, *Clemson University*; Anita Tedesco, *Union County College*; Germán Torres and Carmen Schlig, *Georgia State University*; and Timothy Wilson, *Parkland College*.

To our Prentice Hall partners in adventure: First, we thank you for the opportunity to be part of the new ***¡Trato hecho!*** Rosemary Bradley, we thank you for your vision and for the determination to keep it—and us—on track. To Mariam Rohlfing and Glenn Wilson, intrepid guides and amazing editors, who have an uncanny sense of what works in a classroom and in the real world, thank you for your fierce dedication to making this dream book come true. To Kristine Suárez, Acquisitions Editor; Heather Finstuen, Associate Editor; Nadejda Rozeva and Amanda Latrenta, Editorial Assistants; Ilse Wolfe, Executive Marketing Manager; Don Allmon, Marketing Coordinator; Ann Marie McCarthy, Executive Managing Editor; Nancy Stevenson, Production Editor; Michele Logerfo and Maria Piper, Electronic Line Art Creation; Guy Ruggiero, Line Art Coordinator; Carole Anson, Associate Creative Director; Leslie Osher, Creative Director; and Wanda España, Wee Design Group—thank you, thank you, thank you for your magic in shaping and crafting ***¡Trato hecho!*** and introducing it to the "real world."

To Kira Vargas, a wise young woman with extraordinary talents, thank you for sharing so many of your gifts and so much of your time to make ***¡Trato hecho!*** work—"*¡ya mero!*"

Most importantly, we extend a big hug and thanks and *cariños* to our friends and families for their love and support through it all, especially Bud, Alison, Mark, George, Guillermo, Bernie, Bob, Greg, and the always-present Tink.

P.S. *To our friends, colleagues, and family members who might recognize themselves in the characters in* ***¡Trato hecho!****, anything you like is really based on you; what you don't like is purely coincidental.*

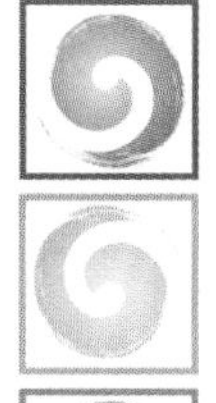
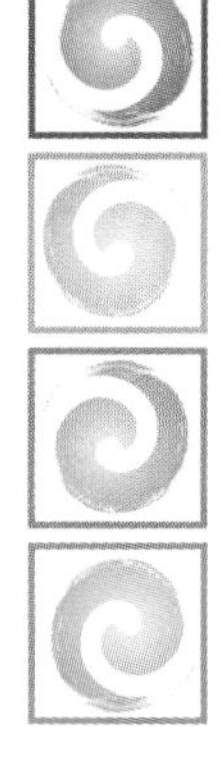

# Our Characters

**Lázaro Frankel Rodríguez:** Born in the United States, he is 30 years old and works as a bilingual teacher in an elementary school. He teaches third grade. His grandfather is from Argentina and his grandmother from Uruguay; they emigrated to the United States shortly after they married. Lázaro is dating Isabel López.

**Isabel Fukiyama López:** She is a 24-year-old student of business administration at the university. She was born in Perú, but her parents came to the United States when she was three. She lives with her parents, her brother, and her grandparents. She is dating Lázaro.

**Alberto Yuja Fournier:** He is a Spanish professor at the university. He is 50 years old and fully bilingual. His parents and two sisters came to the United States from México in 1956, when Alberto was eight years old. He has two children: Elenita and Beto.

**Carlos Montoya:** He is a 26-year-old graduate student in business administration. A third-generation Colombian, he had to learn Spanish in high school, as his parents spoke only English. He is Lázaro's roommate.

**Mary Lancaster:** She is a 25-year-old student teacher enrolled in the teaching credential program. She is student teaching in Lázaro's class. Her parents lived in Spain when she was a child and she learned the language there. She dates Carlos and takes classes with Professor Yuja.

**Ana Castro Rossi:** She is a 27-year-old businesswoman. She was born in the United States to Costa Rican parents. Her parents retired to Costa Rica and she manages their travel agency. She lives with her sister, Lucero.

**Lucero Castro Rossi:** She is 25 years old and works at the travel agency with her sister, Ana. She is also Ana's roommate.

**José Galván Rossi:** He is the eight-year-old son of Lucero and Ana's aunt and uncle, who are deceased. He is now Ana and Lucero's adoptive son. He is fully bilingual and is a student in Lázaro's third grade class.

**Raúl Espinoza Saldívar:** He is another eight-year-old student in Lázaro's class. He is a recent emigrant from El Salvador. He lives with his parents and his brother, Miguel.

**Fabiola Reyes Alexander:** She is an eight-year-old student in Lázaro's class. She is originally from Panamá but moved to the United States with her parents four years ago. She is fully bilingual and has one sister, Elvira.

**Jeanne Girardot:** She is eight years old and a student in Lázaro's class. She is French-Canadian but has lived in the United States since she was one year old. She is fully bilingual in French and English and is now learning Spanish.

¡TRATO
HECHO!

# 1 En clase

LECCIÓN UNO

CHECK OUT THE *¡TRATO HECHO!* WEBSITE AND CD-ROM FOR ACTIVITIES, GAMES, SELF-TESTS, AND MUCH MORE!

TEMA 1

## Las presentaciones

- Saludos
- Los compañeros
- *Ud.*, *tú* y *yo*
- *Estar* + adjetivo

TEMA 2

## La clase de Lázaro

- Situaciones
- Hablando por teléfono
- Más sobre *estar* y los pronombres personales
- Adjetivos plurales

TEMA 3

## En mi clase

- Los estudiantes
- Los números de cero a cien
- El artículo definido: género y número
- El artículo indefinido

TEMA 4

## Las clases y los horarios

- Los horarios
- ¿A qué hora es tu clase de...?
- Los verbos que terminan en *-ar*
- Las preguntas

# ¡TRATO HECHO!

- Rincón profesional: Educación bilingüe
- A escuchar
- El buzón de Doña Rosa
- A leer
- A escribir

# TEMA 1 Las presentaciones

## Saludos

Buenos días

Buenas tardes

Buenas noches

**¡ojo!**

You use **¿Cómo se llama Ud.?** when talking to someone to whom you want to show respect, such as a professor, your boss, or a person you do not know well. **¿Cómo te llamas?** is used to ask the name of a classmate, a child, or another person with whom you have a casual relationship.

**Follow up for dialog.** Model *me llamo* by pointing to yourself and saying your name. Then write *me llamo* on the board and repeat the sentence. Now ask individual students for their names, using *¿Cómo se llama Ud.?* Ask a student to ask another student his/her name, using *¿Cómo te llamas?* Expand the conversation by adding *mucho gusto.*

**Note.** Point out the use of inverted question marks at the beginning of a question. Mention that the same is true for exclamation marks. Provide an example on the board.

### Saludos en la universidad

*Isabel visits Dr. Yuja's office....*

ISABEL: Buenos días. Disculpe, ¿es usted el profesor Alberto Yuja-Fournier?
PROF. YUJA: Sí, a sus órdenes.
ISABEL: Mucho gusto, profesor Yuja.
PROF. YUJA: Encantado.
ISABEL: Yo soy la estudiante nueva. Estoy en su clase de español a las dos de la tarde.
PROF. YUJA: ¿Cómo se llama?
ISABEL: Me llamo Isabel Fukiyama.
PROF. YUJA: ¿Cómo se escribe su apellido?
ISABEL: Se escribe efe, u, ka, i, i griega, a, eme, a.
PROF. YUJA: Encantado, Isabel.
ISABEL: Igualmente, profesor.

**A. Identificación.** Complete the following sentences based on the dialog.

1. El profesor se llama __________.
2. Isabel es la estudiante __________.
3. Es estudiante en la clase de __________.
4. Su nombre completo es __________.

- The Spanish alphabet is listed below. It has two more letters than the English alphabet: **ñ** and **rr**. Notice that the pronunciation of the letter **r** varies according to its position. If it appears at the beginning of a word, **r** is pronounced as **rr**.

| | | | | | | | | | |
|---|---|---|---|---|---|---|---|---|---|
| **a** | a | **g** | ge | **m** | eme | **r** | ere | **w** | doble ve/uve doble |
| **b** | be | **h** | hache | **n** | ene | **rr** | erre | | |
| **c** | ce | **i** | i | **ñ** | eñe | **s** | ese | | |
| **d** | de | **j** | jota | **o** | o | **t** | te | **x** | equis |
| **e** | e | **k** | ka | **p** | pe | **u** | u | **y** | i griega |
| **f** | efe | **l** | ele | **q** | cu | **v** | ve/uve | **z** | zeta |

The letters **b** and **v** are pronounced alike, so when spelling, people often say **be grande** (*big*) for the letter **b** and **uve** or **ve chica** (*small*) for **v**.

**B. ¿Cómo se escribe?** Spell the names in Spanish of your favorite people or things. Your classmates should try to name them.

1. su actor favorito
2. su actriz favorita
3. su restaurante favorito
4. su grupo musical favorito
5. su auto favorito

Un **jaguar** toma **jugo** en la **jungla**.

**Note.** Mention that until recently *ch* and *ll* were separate letters of the alphabet with their own dictionary entry. Stress that *h* is a silent letter. Emphasize the sounds of other letters as they occur in examples, e.g., the sound of *c* as *k* except in front of *e* or *i*, when it is spelled by *qu*.

**C. ¿Formal o informal?** How would you ask each of the following people his or her name?

1. your history professor
2. a young child
3. a customer at your job
4. a classmate

**D. Respuestas.** Respond using the expressions in the box.

| | | | |
|---|---|---|---|
| Me llamo… | ¿Qué tal? | ¿Cómo estás? | Soy… |
| Igualmente. | Chao. | Mucho gusto. | ¡Hola! |

1. Mi nombre es…
2. ¿Cómo te llamas?
3. Soy Alberto Yuja.
4. ¡Buenas noches!
5. ¿Cómo se llama Ud.?
6. Me llamo Isabel, ¿y tú?
7. Mucho gusto.
8. ¡Buenas tardes!

**Follow up for D.** Compare the use of *¿Cómo se llama Ud?* and *¿Cómo te llamas?* by showing pictures of people of various ages. Tell students to use the *tú* form when addressing each other. Have them practice greeting one another, adding expressions such as *Igualmente, Encantado/a* to their conversation.

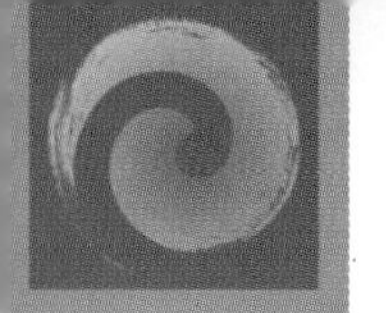

# ABC Los compañeros

—Hola, Ana.
¿Cómo estás?
—Bien, gracias Mary.
¿Y tú?
—Regular, gracias.

—Muchas gracias, profesor.
—De nada, Carlos. Nos vemos en clase.
—Sí, hasta luego.

—Chao, Isabel.
—Adiós, Lázaro.

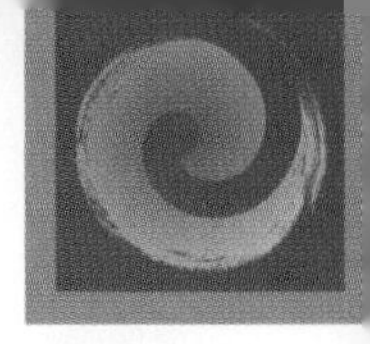

## La estudiante nueva

*It is Isabel's first day of classes....*

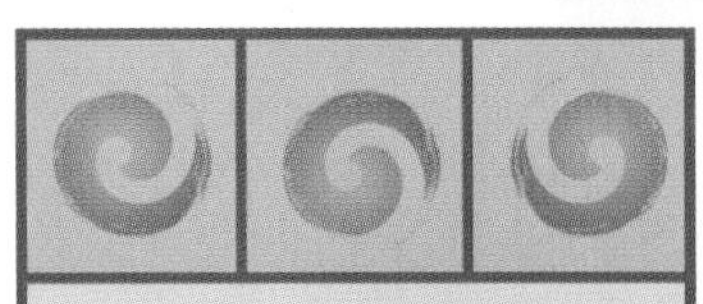

**¡ojo!**

In Spanish, there are different forms of *you*, showing your relationship to the person/s with whom you're speaking. In introductions, use **Quiero presentarte a**... if introducing someone to a friend of yours or to a child, **Quiero presentarle a**... if introducing someone to an adult or in a business-type environment, and **Quiero presentarles a**... if the person is being presented to a group of others.

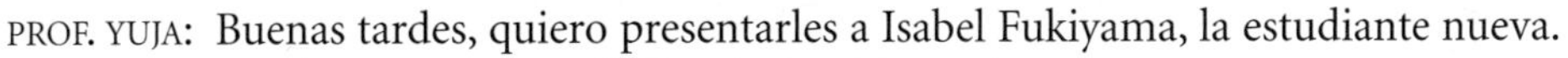

PROF. YUJA: Buenas tardes, quiero presentarles a Isabel Fukiyama, la estudiante nueva.
CARLOS: Mucho gusto, yo me llamo Carlos Montoya.
ISABEL: Encantada.
CARLOS: Igualmente. Tú estás también en la clase de contabilidad, ¿verdad?
ISABEL: Sí, estamos juntos en dos clases.
MARY: Yo me llamo Mary Lancaster y mi amiga se llama Ana.
ISABEL: Mucho gusto.
MARY: Igualmente.
ISABEL: Ana, ¿cúal es tu apellido?
ANA: Es Castro-Rossi.
ISABEL: Encantada, Ana.
ANA: Igualmente, Isabel.

**Follow up for dialog.** Point out the feminine forms of the adjective, contrasting them on the board with examples, e.g., *Isabel es la estudiante nueva. ¿El profesor es nuevo?*

**A. Una conversación.** Role-play the following conversation with a classmate.

—Buenos días (Buenas tardes, Buenas noches).
—____________________.
—¿Cómo te llamas?
—Me llamo ______________.
—¿Cómo se escribe tu apellido?
—Se escribe ______________.

**Expansion for A.** Write vocabulary words on the board or on flashcards, asking students to spell them.

**B. ¿Quién eres tú?** Walk around the room, greeting students and asking their names, first and last. As they spell their names, write them on a separate piece of paper. Ask them to verify by saying, **¿Está bien así?**

**C. Una sopa de posibilidades.** Choose the correct form of introduction. Select from **Quiero presentarte a...**, **Quiero presentarle a...**, or **Quiero presentarles a....**

1. introducing a new student in class to other students
2. introducing a new student to the professor
3. introducing one adult to another at a business meeting
4. introducing two children to one another

**Expansion for C.** Role-play additional presentation situations in class, presenting *Quiero presentarte* and *Quiero presentarle* introductions.

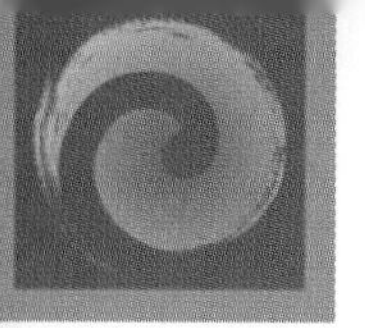

# Usted, tú y yo
## (Formal/informal pronouns)

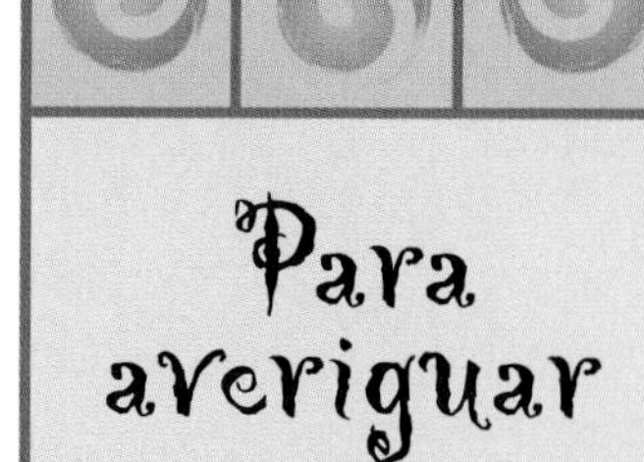

**Para averiguar**

1. When do you address someone with **tú**? And with **Ud.**?
2. How do you say *I*? Do you generally use subject pronouns in Spanish?
3. **Tú eres** means *you are.* What does **eres** mean?
4. Literally, what does **(yo) me llamo** mean?

- There are two ways to say *you* (singular) in Spanish. Use **tú** when talking to a classmate, a friend, a family member, or a child. Use **usted** to address another adult you don't know or someone to whom you wish to show respect. Although in many situations **tú** is used among peers regardless of age difference, when in doubt, use **usted** unless both people are college age or younger. **Usted** is often abbreviated **Ud.** or **Vd.**

- **Yo** means *I*. **Yo, tú,** and **usted** each have a different form of the verb. Do you see any patterns in the endings of the first two verbs in the lists?

| Yo | Tú | Usted |
|---|---|---|
| (Yo) me llamo | ¿Cómo te llamas (tú)? | ¿Cómo se llama Ud.? |
| (Yo) estudio | (Tú) estudias | (Ud.) estudia |
| (Yo) estoy | (Tú) estás | (Ud.) está |

- In Spanish, the verb ending contains the information about who the subject is. Therefore, the subject pronouns **yo**, **tú**, and **Ud.** are frequently omitted because the subject is clear from the verb ending. However, if there is a subject change within a sentence the subject pronoun is retained for clarity.

**Ud.** estudia y **ella** trabaja. — *You study and she works.*

- **Estudio** and **yo estudio** both mean *I study* in English; **estudias** and **tú estudias** mean *you study* in English. As you can see, you should not expect to be able to translate word for word from English to Spanish. To communicate, use an equivalent expression, not a literal translation. The lack of a one-to-one correspondence between Spanish and English can also be seen in the phrases used to ask for and give names.

**¿Cómo te llamas?** — *What is your name?* (literally, *What do you call yourself?*)

**Me llamo Patricia.** — *My name is Patricia.* (literally, *I call myself Patricia.*)

## A lo personal

**A. ¿Y tú?** Ask a classmate you don't know questions about himself/herself, changing the questions below from the **Ud.** form to the **tú** form.

MODELO: ¿Cómo se llama Ud.?
E1: *¿Cómo te llamas?*
E2: *Me llamo María.*

1. ¿Está Ud. en la clase de español?
2. ¿Cómo está Ud.?
3. ¿Qué estudia Ud.?
4. ¿Dónde estudia Ud.?
5. ¿Estudia Ud. matemáticas?
6. ¿Estudia Ud. mucho?

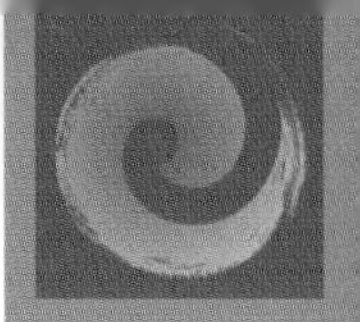

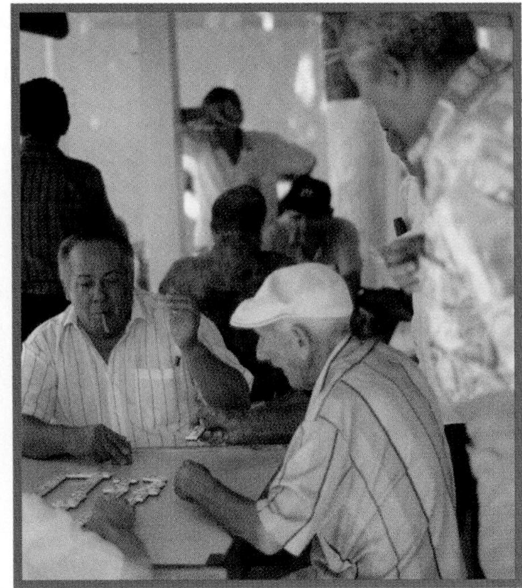

**B. ¿Tú o Ud.?** Who would be more likely to say the following while getting acquainted, the people on the left or those in the photo to the right?

1. ¿Cómo te llamas?
2. ¿Cómo se llama Ud.?
3. Me llamo Alicia, ¿y tú?
4. Me llamo Pablo Zamora, ¿y Ud.?
5. ¿Cómo está Ud.?
6. ¿Cómo estás tú?
7. ¿Estás bien?
8. ¿Está Ud. bien?

**C. ¿Cómo se llama usted? ¿Cómo te llamas?** How would you ask these people their names?

MODELO: an elderly neighbor
*—¿Cómo se llama Ud.?*

1. a professor
2. a classmate
3. your classmate's younger brother
4. your roommate's grandmother
5. a salesclerk
6. your roommate's girlfriend/boyfriend
7. your father's boss
8. your mother's secretary

**D. ¿Cómo está usted? ¿Cómo estás tú?** How would you ask the people in Activity C how they are?

MODELO: an elderly neighbor
*—¿Cómo está usted?*

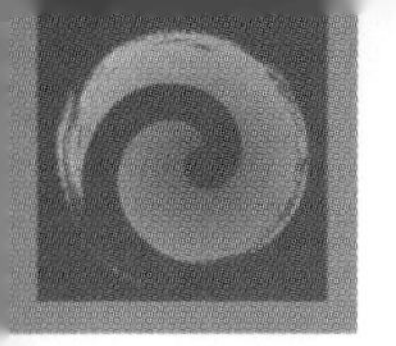

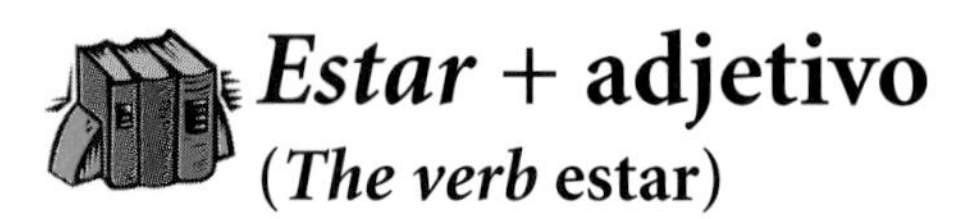

# *Estar* + adjetivo
## (*The verb* estar)

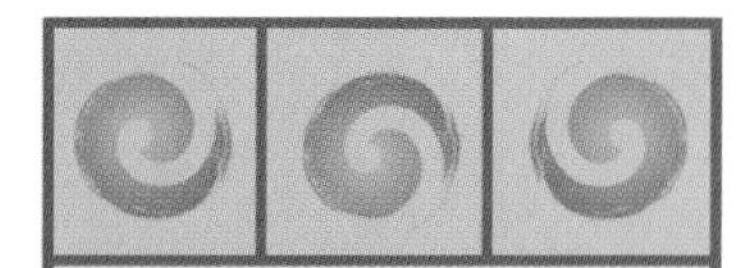

### Para averiguar

1. What form of **estar** should you use with **yo**? with **tú**? with **Ud.**? What form should you use to talk about a third person, such as Carlos or Ana?
2. If an adjective that describes a male ends with **-o**, what will it end with when it describes a female?

- **Estar** is one equivalent of the verb *to be* in English. Its singular forms are:

| | | |
|---|---|---|
| **yo** | **estoy** | *I am* |
| **tú** | **estás** | *you are* |
| **él/ella/Ud.** | **está** | *he/she/you (formal sing.) is/are* |

- To say how you or another person is doing, use an adjective with the verb **estar**.

—¿Cómo **estás**? — *How are you? (familiar)*
—**Estoy contento/a.** — *I'm happy.*

—¿Cómo **está** Ud., Sra. Ortiz? — *How are you, Mrs. Ortiz? (formal)*
—**Estoy** un poco **cansada**. — *I'm a little tired.*

—¿Cómo **está** Carlos? — *How is Carlos?*
—Carlos **está** muy **ocupado**. — *Carlos is very busy.*

- Many adjectives end with **-o** when describing characteristics of men and with **-a** when describing characteristics of women.

| **Male** | **Female** | |
|---|---|---|
| aburrid**o** | aburrid**a** | *bored* |
| cansad**o** | cansad**a** | *tired* |
| confundid**o** | confundid**a** | *confused* |
| content**o** | content**a** | *happy* |
| nervios**o** | nervios**a** | *nervous* |
| ocupad**o** | ocupad**a** | *busy* |
| preocupad**o** | preocupad**a** | *worried* |

- Most words that end with any letter other than **-o** or **-a** have only one form for both men and women.

| **Male or Female** | |
|---|---|
| triste | *sad* |
| regular | *so-so* |
| bien | *fine* |
| mejor | *better* |
| mal | *bad* |

## A lo personal

**A. ¿Cómo está Ud.?** Do the following words describe you at this moment?

MODELO: cansado/a
*Sí, estoy (un poco, muy) cansado/a.* o *No, no estoy cansado/a.*

1. ocupado/a
2. nervioso/a
3. triste
4. aburrido/a
5. regular
6. preocupado/a
7. confundido/a
8. contento/a

**B. En clase.** Which words best describe how you feel in the following courses? If you have never taken the course, imagine how you would feel.

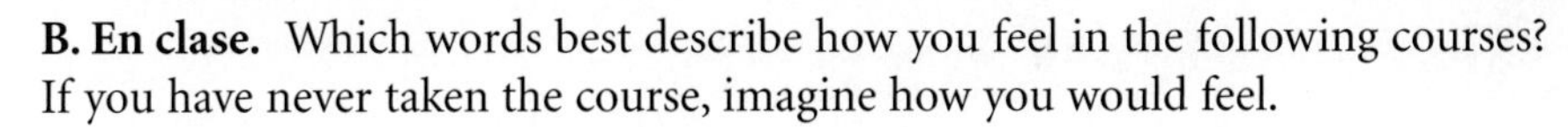

nervioso/a bien confundido/a aburrido/a mal ocupado/a contento/a

MODELO: en la clase de inglés
*En la clase de inglés, estoy aburrido/a.*

1. en la clase de literatura
2. en la clase de música
3. en la clase de informática
4. en la clase de arte
5. en la clase de matemáticas
6. en la clase de español

**C. ¿Familiar o formal?** Would the people in the illustrations use familiar or formal greetings? Role-play each scene with a classmate.

MODELO: E1: *¿Cómo estás?*
E2: *Estoy enferma.*

1

2

3

4

5

**D. Compañeros de clase.** Prepare a conversation in Spanish in which you introduce two classmates to each other. Each asks how the other is doing and what he/she is studying. Then, you all say goodbye with an expression of your choice.

# TEMA 2 La clase de Lázaro

## Situaciones

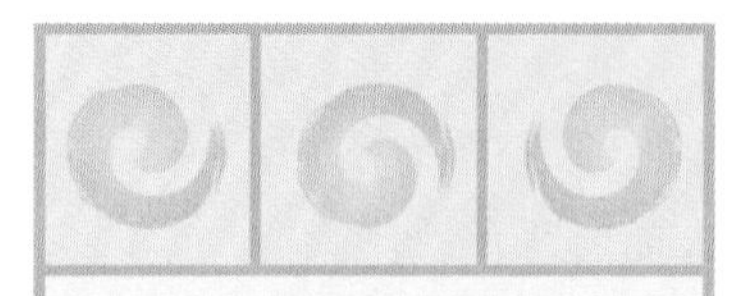

**¡ojo!**

Forms of the verb **estar** (**yo estoy, tú estás, él/ella/Ud. está…**) are used to tell someone's current condition or their location. The verb **ser**, which also means *to be* in English (**yo soy, tú eres, él/ella/Ud. es…**), describes characteristics of a person, such as physical description. You will learn more about **ser** in Lesson 2.

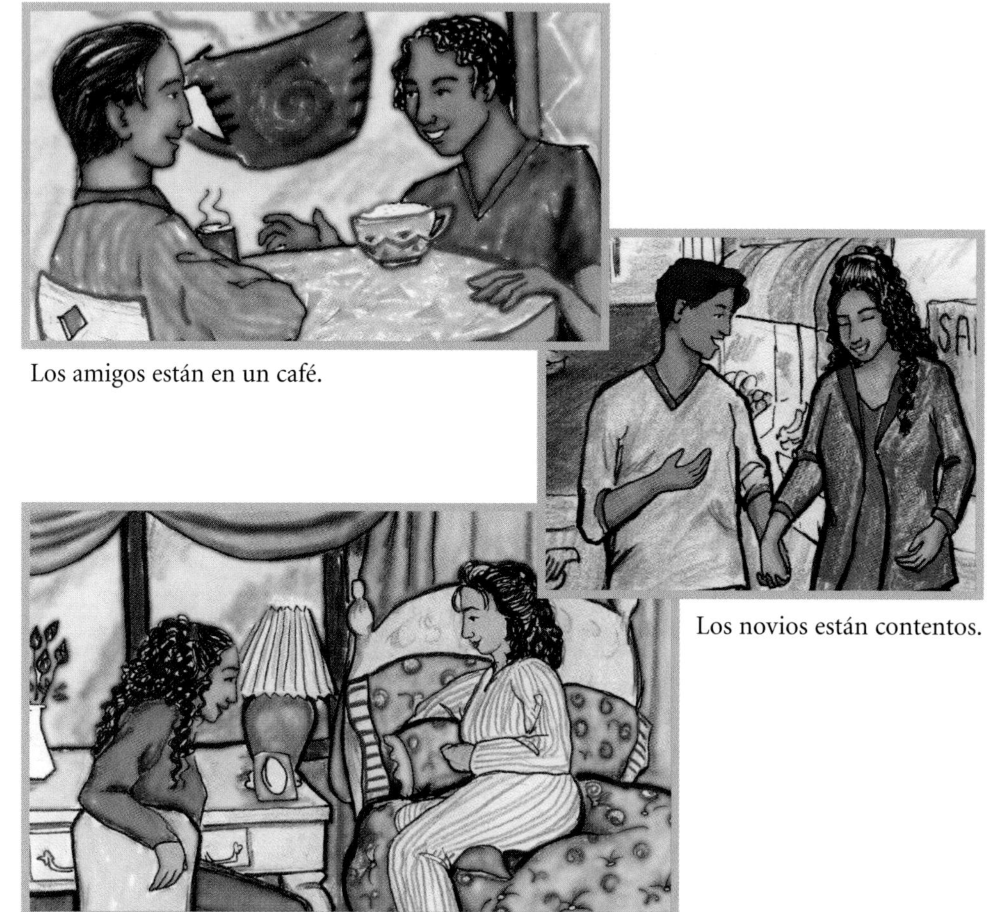

Los amigos están en un café.

Los novios están contentos.

Las compañeras de cuarto están en su dormitorio.

### La nueva maestra

*Mary runs into Lázaro at the school where he teaches third grade….*

MARY: Buenos días, Lázaro. ¿Cómo estás?
LÁZARO: Hola Mary, yo estoy bien. ¿Y tú?
MARY: Bien, gracias.
LÁZARO: ¿Estás aquí para tus prácticas de maestra?
MARY: Sí, mañana es el primer día. ¡Estoy muy nerviosa!

*The following morning Lázaro introduces the new student teacher to his third grade students…*

LÁZARO: Buenos días, Mary, ¿cómo estás?
MARY: Estoy muy contenta, Lázaro. Soy la nueva maestra en prácticas en tu clase.
LÁZARO: ¡Qué bien! ¡Atención, estudiantes! Quiero presentarles a la señorita Mary Lancaster. Ella estudia para maestra y va a estar con nosotros dos días a la semana.
TODOS: Mucho gusto, señorita Lancaster.
MARY: Encantada. ¿Cómo están todos?
TODOS: Estamos muy bien, gracias. ¿Cómo está usted, señorita Lancaster?
MARY: Estoy bien, gracias.

**A. ¿Quién es Mary? ¿Cómo está?** Answer the following questions based on the dialog.

1. ¿Quién es Mary?
2. ¿Cómo está Mary?
3. ¿Mary es estudiante?
4. ¿Mary es amiga de Lázaro?

**Suggestion for A.** Using paired sentences in a comprehensible-input environment, contrast *ser* and *estar*, e.g., *Soy profesor/a. Estoy en clase. Estoy contento/a.*

**B. ¿Y tú?** Ask your classmate the following questions. He/she will then ask you.

1. ¿Cómo te llamas?
2. ¿Cómo estás?
3. ¿Eres estudiante o maestro/a?
4. ¿Estás cansado/a?
5. ¿Estás ocupado/a?
6. ¿Estás contento/a?

**C. Una entrevista.** Interview a classmate, greeting him/her and introducing yourself, finding out his/her name, asking how he/she is, requesting as much information as possible as to whether he/she is busy, happy, tired, sick, well, etc. Introduce your friend to another group of students, sharing information from their group.

## Hablando por teléfono

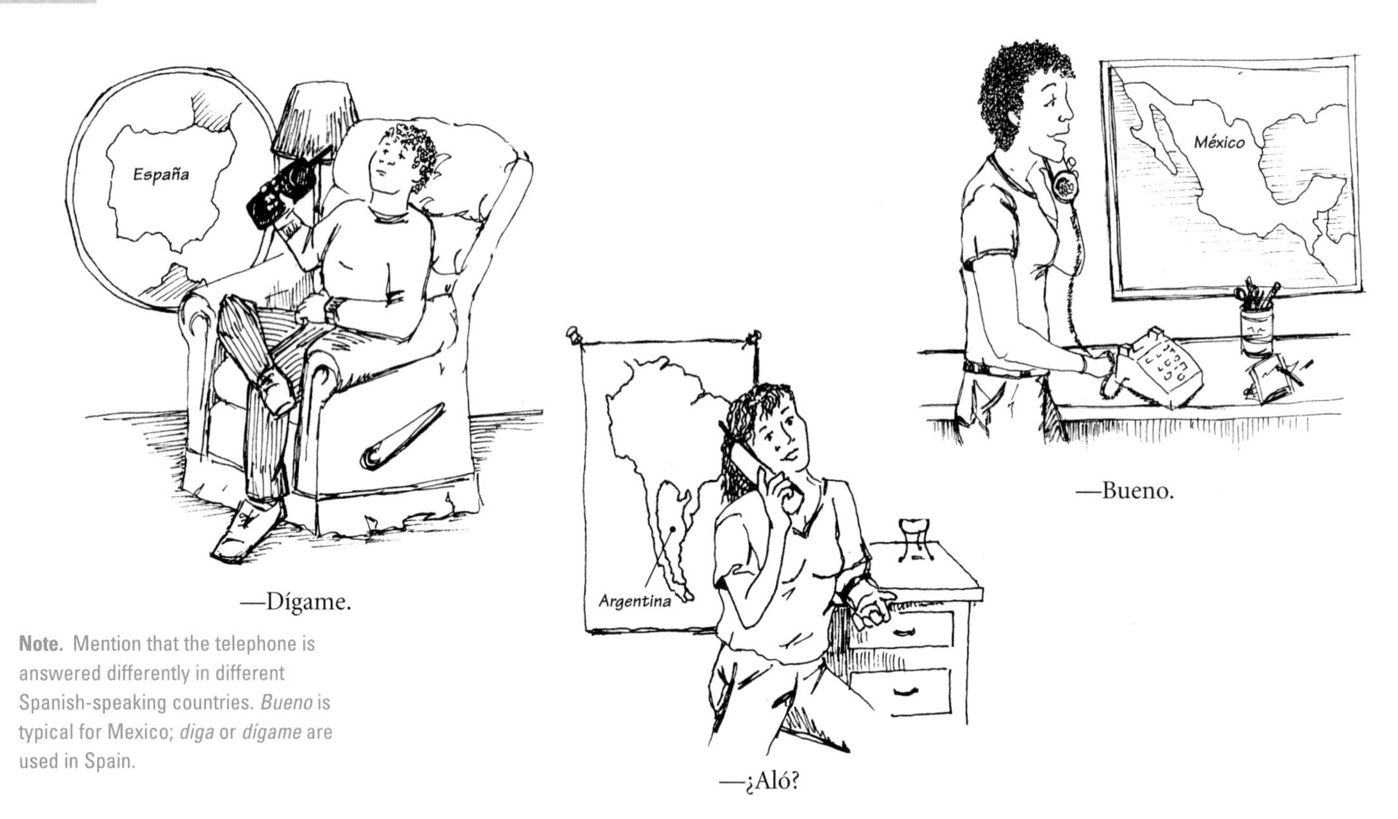


—Dígame.

—¿Aló?

—Bueno.

**Note.** Mention that the telephone is answered differently in different Spanish-speaking countries. *Bueno* is typical for Mexico; *diga* or *dígame* are used in Spain.

### Carlos llama a Mary

*Mary talks to her boyfriend Carlos on the phone....*

MARY: ¿Aló?
CARLOS: Hola, Mary, ¿cómo estás?
MARY: Bien, Carlos.
CARLOS: Te invito a tomar un café.
MARY: No puedo ahora porque estoy muy ocupada. Tengo mucha tarea.
CARLOS: ¡Qué pena!
MARY: ¿Tú no estás ocupado?
CARLOS: No, ahora no estoy muy ocupado porque no tengo tarea.
MARY: ¡Qué bien, Carlos!
CARLOS: Bueno, nos vemos mañana en la escuela.
MARY: Hasta mañana.

**A. Hablando por teléfono.** Complete the following telephone conversation with your classmate.

—Hola, (1) ________, ¿cómo estás?
—(2)________________________. ¿Cómo (3)________ tú?
—(4)________________________. Tengo muchas clases y mucha tarea.
—(5)________________________. Yo estoy (6)__________________ porque no tengo tarea.
—Bueno, hasta (7) ______________________.
—(8)________________________.

**B. ¿Cómo están los estudiantes?** Look at the students below and choose an adjective from the box below to match their current conditions.

**¡ojo!**

Adjectives become plural in Spanish if they describe more than one person or thing.
**Los estudiantes están contentos.**
**Las maestras están ocupadas.**

| nerviosa | ocupada | cansado | alegres | contenta | enfermo |
|---|---|---|---|---|---|

**C. ¿Es posible?** Match the adjective with its appropriate noun. ¡OJO! Is the noun singular or plural, masculine or feminine?

1. los estudiantes
2. el maestro
3. las amigas
4. la compañera de clase
5. los novios
6. el compañero de cuarto

a. contentos
b. preocupado
c. ocupada
d. cansados
e. furiosas
f. aburrido

**Expansion for C.** Provide additional cognates, using them in masculine/feminine and singular/plural situations.

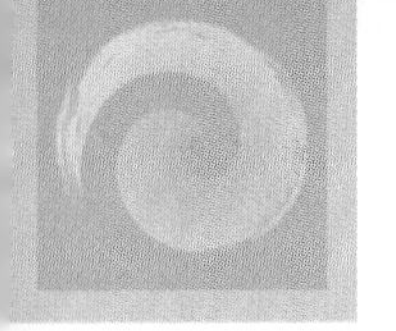

# Más sobre *estar* y los pronombres personales

## (*More on* estar *and subject pronouns*)

**Para averiguar**

1. What does the verb **estar** mean? What are its forms?
2. How do you say *I, you, he, she, we,* and *they* in Spanish? Why are *I, you,* and *we* generally dropped? Which three pronouns have the same verb form in the singular? in the plural?
3. What does **vosotros** mean? In what part of the Spanish-speaking world is it used? What do you use for both formal and familiar plural *you* in American Spanish?

- To say how *more than one person* is doing or where *they are*, use a plural form of **estar**.

| **estar** *(to be)* | | | |
|---|---|---|---|
| **Singular forms:** | | **Plural forms:** | |
| yo **estoy** | *I am* | nosotros/as **estamos** | *we are* |
| tú **estás** | *you are (familiar)* | vosotros/as **estáis** | *you are (familiar)* |
| usted **está** | *you are (formal)* | ustedes **están** | *you are (formal)* |
| él **está** | *he is* | ellos **están** | *they are (m.)* |
| ella **está** | *she is* | ellas **están** | *they are (f.)* |

- In Spain, the pronoun **vosotros** is used as the plural of familiar **tú**, but in Latin America, the plural of both the formal **usted** and the informal **tú** is **ustedes** (usually abbreviated **Uds.** or **Vds.**).

**Vosotros estáis** aburridos. — *You (plural) are bored.*

- Remember, the subject pronouns are generally not used because each has a unique verb ending that tells you who the subject is. But **usted**, **él**, and **ella** have the same verb form, as do **ustedes**, **ellos**, and **ellas**, and are therefore used when needed for clarity.

¿**Estás** en casa? — *Are you at home?*
¿**Está Ud.** en casa? — *Are you (formal) at home?*
¿**Está él** en casa? — *Is he at home?*
¿**Está ella** en casa? — *Is she at home?*

- The feminine pronouns **nosotras**, **vosotras**, and **ellas** are used to describe all female groups. For mixed groups use **nosotros**, **vosotros**, and **ellos**. To say how more than one person is doing, use a plural form of **estar** with an adjective that also reflects the plural.

—¿Cómo **están** ustedes? — *How are both/all of you?*
—**Estamos** content**os**/**as**. — *We are happy.*

—¿Cómo **están** Mary y Ana? — *How are (they) Mary and Ana?*
—**Están** cansad**as**. — *They are tired.*

—¿Cómo **están** los profesor**es**? — *How are the teachers?*
—Ellos **están** preocupad**os**. — *They are worried.*

## A lo personal

**A. ¿Quiénes?** To whom might the following sentences refer? Insert names of people you know.

MODELO: Estamos en casa.
*Mi compañero de cuarto y yo estamos en casa.*

1. Está en la clase de literatura.
2. Están contentas.
3. Está aburrido.
4. Estamos en la clase de español.
5. Están ocupados.
6. Está nerviosa.
7. Estoy preocupado.
8. Estás en Estados Unidos.

**B. Los amigos.** Tell where you or your friends are or how you are doing using the correct form of **estar**.

MODELO: Yo_____ en la clase de literatura.
*Yo estoy en la clase de literatura.*

1. Ana _____ en casa.
2. La señorita Lancaster _______ en la universidad.
3. Ustedes _______ contentos.
4. Tú _________ en Nueva York.
5. Nosotros _________ cansados.
6. Mary _______ muy ocupada.
7. Usted _________ bien.
8. Los amigos __________ en la cafetería.
9. Lázaro __________ en la escuela (*school*).
10. Yo __________ muy nerviosa.

**C. ¿Cómo están?** It is the beginning of the semester, and you and all of your friends have different reactions to your classes. Tell how each one feels using the form of **estar** that corresponds to the subject of the sentence.

MODELO: (Yo) contento/a en la clase de español.
*Yo estoy contento/a en la clase de español.*

1. (Nosotros) aburridos en la clase de historia.
2. (Ellos) confundidos en la clase de matemáticas.
3. (Ellas) interesadas en la clase de literatura.
4. (Ustedes) preocupados/as en la clase de economía.
5. (Tú y yo) contentos/as con todas las clases.
6. (Usted y yo) cansados/as en la clase de educación física.
7. (Nosotras) nerviosos/as en la clase de geografía.
8. (Él y ella) furiosos en la clase de política.
9. (Tú y él) tristes en la clase de japonés.
10. (Ud. y yo) ocupados en la clase de biología.

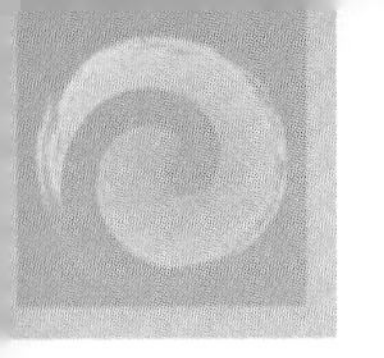

# Adjetivos plurales
## (*Plural adjectives*)

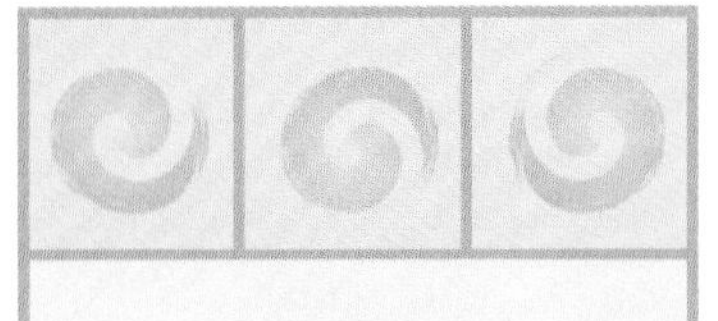

**Para averiguar**

1. If an adjective ends in a vowel, how do you make it plural?
2. How do you make an adjective plural if it ends in a consonant?

**Note.** Point out to students that *z* → *c* in front of *e* or *i*.

- Spanish adjectives match the nouns that they describe in number and gender. If a noun is plural, the adjective will also be plural. Adjectives that end in vowels are made plural by adding **-s**.

| | |
|---|---|
| Lázaro está content**o**.<br>Lázaro y sus amigos están content**os**. | *Lázaro is happy.*<br>*Lázaro and his friends are happy.* |
| Carlos está preocupad**o**.<br>Carlos y yo estamos preocupad**os**. | *Carlos is worried.*<br>*Carlos and I are worried.* |
| María está cansad**a**.<br>María y Lucero están cansad**as**. | *María is tired.*<br>*María and Lucero are tired.* |
| Isabel está furios**a**.<br>Isabel y Ana están furios**as**. | *Isabel is furious.*<br>*Isabel and Ana are furious.* |

- If the adjective ends in a consonant, it is made plural by adding **-es**.

| | |
|---|---|
| Pablo está débil.<br>Pablo y sus compañeros están débil**es**. | *Pablo is weak.*<br>*Pablo and his mates are weak.* |
| Carlos está feliz.<br>Carlos y Mary están felic**es**. | *Carlos is happy.*<br>*Carlos and Mary are happy.* |

- Adjectives referring to all feminine groups are feminine and plural while adjectives referring to mixed groups are masculine and plural.

| | |
|---|---|
| Patricia y Rosa están content**as**.<br>Patricia, Rosa y Carlos están content**os**. | *Patricia and Rosa are happy.*<br>*Patricia, Rosa, and Carlos are happy.* |
| Laura y María están preocupad**as**.<br>Laura, José y María están preocupad**os**. | *Laura and María are worried.*<br>*Laura, José, and María are worried.* |

## A lo personal

**A. Adjetivos.** Make the following sentences plural by modifying the adjective in italics so that it agrees with the rest of the sentence.

1. Las nuevas maestras están *nervioso.*
2. Los maestros están *ocupado.*
3. Las universidades están *cerrado.*
4. Las estudiantes están *enfermo.*
5. Los estudiantes están *cansado.*
6. Los amigos están *aburrido.*
7. Las profesoras están *contento.*
8. Los compañeros de clase están *confundido.*
9. Los directores están *feliz.*
10. María y Ana están *preocupado.*

**B. ¿Cómo está/n?** Is this a typical classroom? Use the correct form of **estar** and one of the adjectives in the box below to describe how various members of the class are feeling.

MODELO: José y Elena
*José y Elena están contentos.*

| contento | cansado | confundido | aburrido | preocupado | ocupado |
|---|---|---|---|---|---|

**C. ¿Cómo están tus compañeros?** Look around your classroom and describe how some of your classmates are doing, using the list of adjectives in Activity B. Then ask the people you describe to tell you whether or not your description of how they are doing is accurate.

**D. ¿Cómo están estas personas?** Using the information provided below, choose the most logical adjective from the list to describe how the following people are feeling. Remember to change each adjective as necessary so that it agrees with the subject of the sentence.

| triste | ocupado | confundido | contento | nervioso | cansado |
|---|---|---|---|---|---|

1. Carlos y Mary no tienen clase de español. Ellos están ____________.
2. Lucero y Ana tienen un examen de matemáticas mañana. Ellas están ____________.
3. José y Raúl están en Estados Unidos y no hablan inglés. Ellos están ____________.
4. Elena, Patricia y Juan tienen mucha tarea hoy. Ellos están muy ____________.
5. Rosa y Alejandro no tienen amigos en la universidad. Ellos están ____________.
6. Los compañeros de Rosa están en una clase muy interesante. Ellos están ____________.

# Vocabulario

## TEMA 1
### Las presentaciones

| Saludos y despedidas | |
|---|---|
| **Adiós** | *Goodbye* |
| **Buenos días** | *Good morning* |
| **Buenas tardes** | *Good afternoon* |
| **Buenas noches** | *Good evening, good night* |
| **Chao** | *Ciao* |
| **¿Cómo estás?** | *How are you? (familiar)* |
| **¿Cómo está Ud.?** | *How are you? (formal)* |
| **Estoy…** | *I am…* |
| **Hola** | *Hello* |
| **Hasta luego** | *See you later* |
| **Hasta mañana** | *See you tomorrow* |
| **Nos vemos** | *Be seeing you* |
| **¿Qué tal?** | *How's it going?* |

| Presentaciones | |
|---|---|
| **¿Cómo te llamas?** | *What's your name? (familiar)* |
| **¿Cómo se llama Ud.?** | *What's your name? (formal)* |
| **Me llamo…** | *My name is…* |
| **Mi nombre es…** | *My name is…* |
| **Mucho gusto** | *Pleased to meet you* |
| **Encantado/a** | *Pleased to meet you* |
| **Igualmente** | *Likewise* |
| **Quiero presentarte a…** | *I want you to meet…(familiar)* |
| **Quiero presentarle a…** | *I want you to meet…(formal)* |
| **Quiero presentarles a…** | *I want you to meet…(formal, plural)* |

| Adverbios | |
|---|---|
| **bien** | *fine* |
| **mal** | *bad* |
| **regular** | *so-so* |

| Otras expresiones | |
|---|---|
| **A sus órdenes** | *At your service* |
| **De nada** | *You're welcome* |
| **Disculpe** | *Pardon me (formal)* |
| **Gracias** | *Thank you* |
| **Lo siento** | *I'm sorry* |
| **puedo** | *I can* |
| **tengo** | *I have* |
| **tienes** | *you have (familiar)* |
| **tiene** | *he/she has, you have (formal)* |

## TEMA 2
### La clase de Lázaro

| Sustantivos | |
|---|---|
| **el/la amigo/a** | *friend* |
| **el/la compañero/a** | |
| **de clase** | *classmate* |
| **de cuarto** | *roommate* |
| **la contabilidad** | *accounting* |
| **el día** | *day* |
| **el dormitorio** | *bedroom* |
| **la escuela** | *school* |
| **el español** | *Spanish* |
| **el/la estudiante** | *student* |
| **el/la maestro/a,** | *teacher* |
| **— en prácticas** | *student teacher* |
| **el/la novio/a** | *boyfriend/girlfriend* |
| **el/la profesor/a** | *professor, teacher* |
| **la semana** | *week* |
| **el/la señor/a** | *Mr./Mrs., sir/madam* |
| **la señorita** | *Miss* |
| **la tarea** | *homework* |
| **la universidad** | *university* |

| Adjetivos | |
|---|---|
| **alegre** | *happy* |
| **cansado/a** | *tired* |
| **contento/a** | *happy* |
| **furioso/a** | *furious* |
| **inteligente** | *intelligent* |
| **juntos/as** | *together* |
| **nervioso/a** | *nervous* |
| **nuevo/a** | *new* |
| **ocupado/a** | *busy* |
| **popular** | *popular* |
| **preocupado/a** | *worried* |
| **religioso/a** | *religious* |
| **serio/a** | *serious* |

| Otras expresiones | |
|---|---|
| **ahora** | *now* |
| **porque** | *because* |
| **¿Quién?** | *Who?* |
| **sí** | *yes* |
| **tarde** | *late* |
| **todos** | *all/everybody* |
| **verdad** | *true* |
| **y** | *and* |

# Reunión A

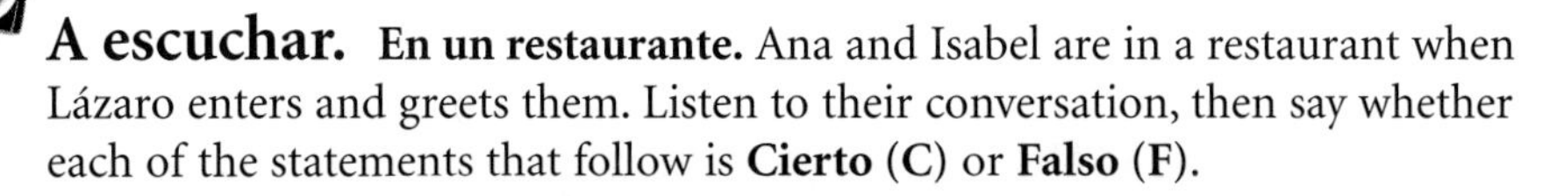

**A escuchar.** **En un restaurante.** Ana and Isabel are in a restaurant when Lázaro enters and greets them. Listen to their conversation, then say whether each of the statements that follow is **Cierto (C)** or **Falso (F)**.

1. ______ Ana está muy bien.
2. ______ Lázaro es estudiante en la universidad.
3. ______ El profesor Yuja es un buen profesor.
4. ______ Isabel y Ana tienen clase.

**Tapescript for A escuchar. En un restaurante.**
LÁZARO: Hola, Ana, ¿cómo estás?
ANA: Estoy muy bien, gracias. ¿Cómo estás tú, Lázaro?
LÁZARO: Bien, gracias.
ANA: Lázaro, te presento a mi amiga Isabel Fukiyama. Isabel, te presento a mi amigo Lázaro Frankel.
LÁZARO: Mucho gusto.
ISABEL: Encantada. ¿Eres estudiante en la universidad?
LÁZARO: No, soy maestro en la escuela primaria. ¿Eres compañera de clases de Ana?
ISABEL: Sí, soy compañera de Ana en la clase de español del Profesor Yuja.
LÁZARO: ¡Qué bien! El profesor Yuja es un buen profesor.
ANA: Sí, y además es muy simpático.
ISABEL: Ana, tenemos clase con el profesor Yuja a las dos de la tarde y faltan diez minutos.
ANA: ¡Es verdad! Adiós, Lázaro.
LÁZARO: Nos vemos, Ana. Mucho gusto, Isabel.

**Answers for A escuchar.** 1) *C.* 2) *F.* 3) *C.* 4) *C.*

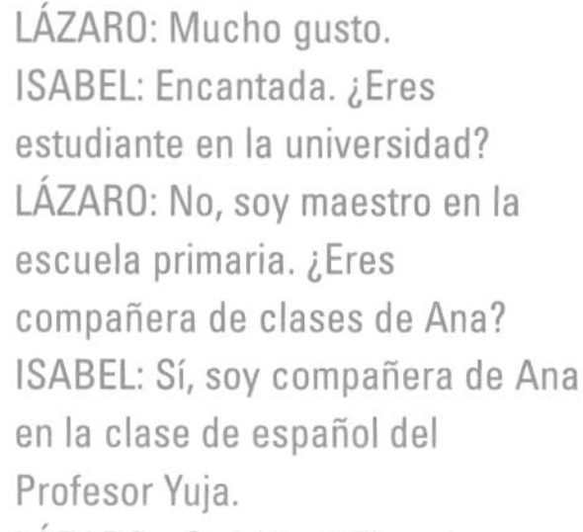

**A conversar.** With a classmate, prepare a conversation greeting one another, asking each other's name, spelling your own name, asking how the person is, and saying farewell. Present your conversation to another group of students. Then, listen to theirs.

**¿Lo sabía?**

**Quiero presentarle a Luis Miguel.**
Nació en San Juan, Puerto Rico. Él es muy famoso y muy guapo. A Luis Miguel también se le llama "El Ídolo". Ahora vive en México. Es un cantante muy popular. Sus discos venden 20 millones de copias. Él es joven, menor de treinta años. Es feliz. El es amigo de Daisy Fuentes, pero es soltero. Canta en español y en inglés. Su mamá es una modelo italiana y su papá, Luisito Rey, era (*was*) un cantante español que (*that*) murió en 1992. Luis Miguel da conciertos en los Estados Unidos. ¿Le gustaría ir a un concierto?

**¿Comprende Ud.?** Mark **Sí** or **No** for each of the following statements based on the information presented.

1. ______ Luis Miguel nació en Montevideo, Uruguay.
2. ______ También se le llama "El Ídolo".
3. ______ Es un actor muy popular.
4. ______ Sus discos venden 20 millones de copias.
5. ______ Canta en español y en alemán.
6. ______ Luis Miguel da conciertos en los Estados Unidos.

**A buscar.** Using the Internet and other sources (magazines, newspapers, etc.), search for the titles of at least three popular albums by Luis Miguel and share your findings with the rest of the class.

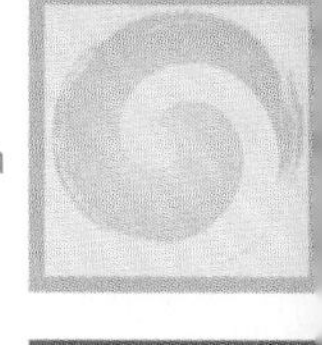

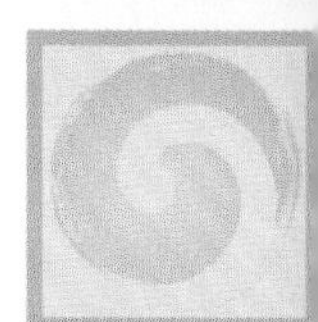
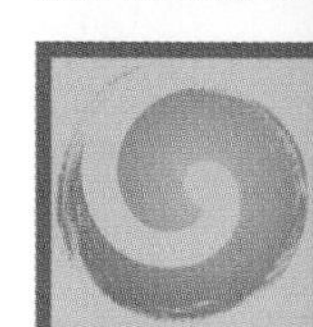

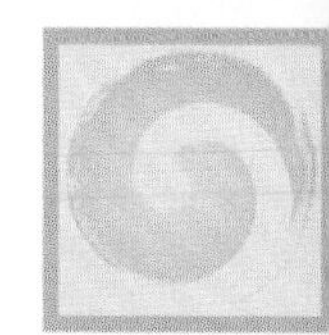
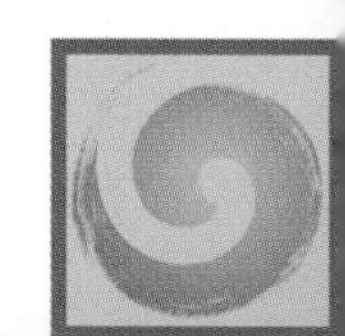

# TEMA 3 En mi clase

## Los estudiantes

Expansion. Before beginning this section, provide comprehensible input by pointing out objects in your classroom. You may include objects not mentioned in the dialog, such as *la puerta, las luces, el televisor, la videocasetera, la grabadora, la mochila.* Students could create a model classroom with magazine/newspaper photos, labeling each item in Spanish.

### ¿Dónde están las cosas?

*Lázaro and Mary in the classroom….*

LÁZARO: Hola, Mary. Mira, esta es la clase de tercer grado.
MARY: ¡Es muy bonita!
LÁZARO: Sí, la clase tiene muchas cosas interesantes.
MARY: ¿Cuántos estudiantes hay en tu clase?
LÁZARO: Hay veinticinco.
MARY: ¿Dónde están los libros de texto?
LÁZARO: En el estante. En el escritorio hay una computadora, una calculadora, papel, unos cuadernos, bolígrafos y lápices. También hay dos pizarras.
MARY: ¡Hay dos ventanas grandes!
LÁZARO: Sí, hay mucha luz (*light*) en mi salón de clase.
MARY: Bueno, nos vemos mañana y ¡gracias!
LÁZARO: De nada, Mary. ¡Hasta mañana!

**A. ¿Sí o no?** Read the following sentences based on the dialog and decide whether each is **Cierto** (C) or **Falso** (F). Correct any false statements.

1. _____ El escritorio es muy pequeño.
2. _____ Hay dos pizarras en el salón.
3. _____ Los libros de texto están en el estante.
4. _____ Hay mucha luz porque hay ventanas.

**B. ¿Dónde está?** Match each item on the left with its logical place in the classroom.

New words: *tiza, pizarra.*

1. los libros de texto
2. la tiza
3. la computadora
4. la silla

a. el escritorio
b. la pizarra
c. la mesa
d. los estantes

**C. ¿En qué tienda?** In which store would you most likely find each of the items listed below?

MODELO: una mesa
*en Carsa*

1. un escritorio
2. papel
3. una silla
4. un cuaderno
5. una calculadora
6. una computadora
7. bolígrafos
8. un estante

**D. Una lista de compras.** First look at the items in Activity C and check whether you can find at least one of each in your classroom. Then, with a classmate, prepare a list of school supplies needed for the new semester.

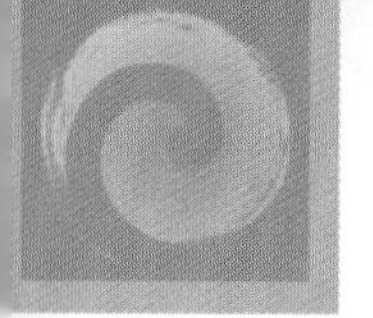

# ABC Los números de cero a cien

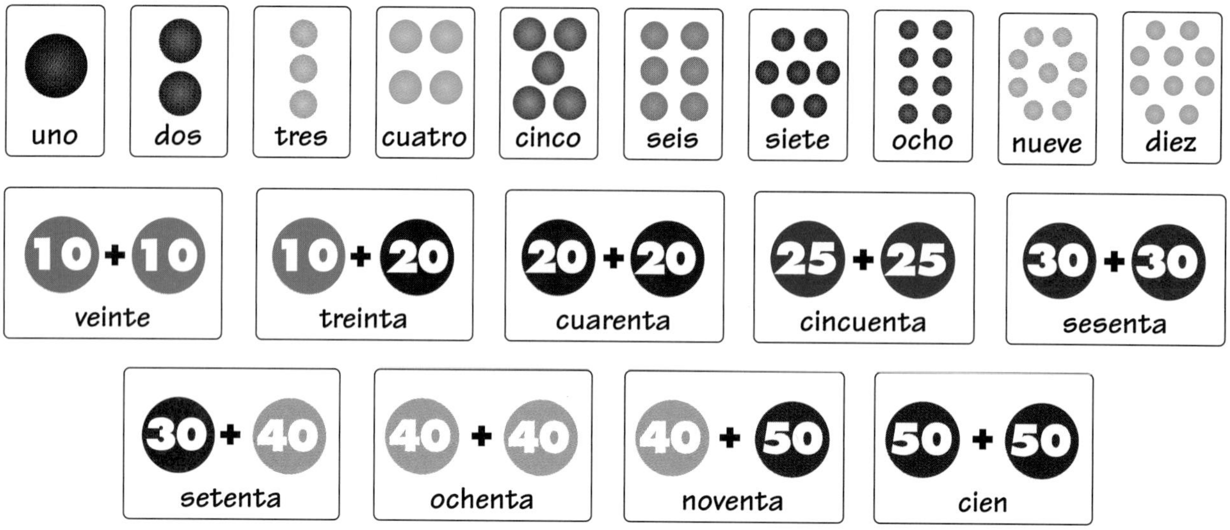

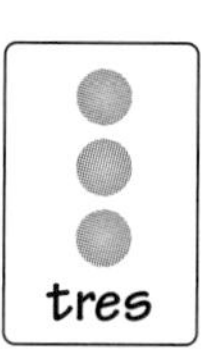

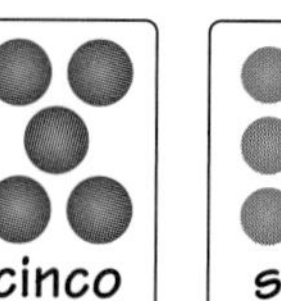

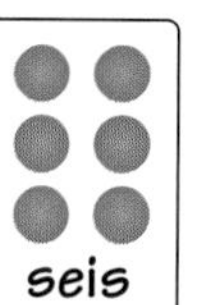

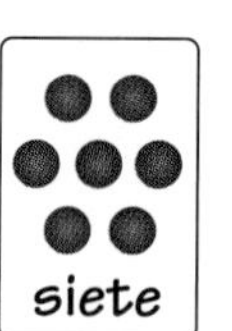

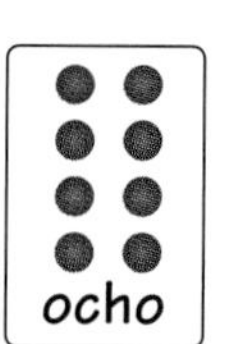

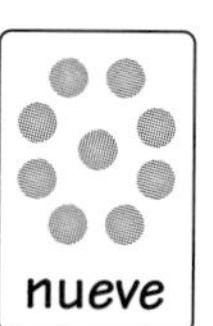

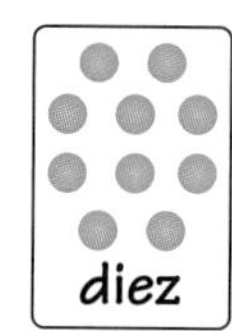

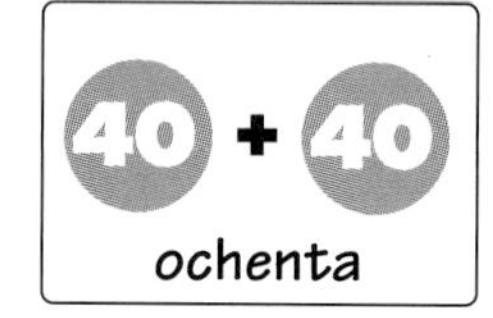

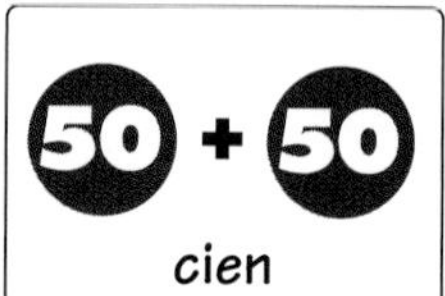


**Note.** Explain that 16–19 and 21–29 will also be seen spelled as 3 separate words. Provide examples showing the use of *cien/ciento*, and the use of *y* between numbers of tens and ones, as in *cuarenta y dos*. Ask questions about math problems, telephone numbers (mention they are often read in pairs in Hispanic countries), number of students in class, prices of classroom items, etc. Write prices on board, emphasizing that the comma and decimal are reversed in Spanish using examples such as 1.000 and $14,99.

0. cero
1. uno
2. dos
3. tres
4. cuatro
5. cinco
6. seis
7. siete
8. ocho
9. nueve

10. diez
11. once
12. doce
13. trece
14. catorce
15. quince
16. dieciséis
17. diecisiete
18. dieciocho
19. diecinueve

20. veinte
21. veintiuno
22. veintidós
23. veintitrés
24. veinticuatro
25. veinticinco
26. veintiséis
27. veintisiete
28. veintiocho
29. veintinueve

30. treinta
31. treinta y uno
32. treinta y dos …
40. cuarenta
50. cincuenta
60. sesenta
70. setenta
80. ochenta
90. noventa
100. cien

## Mary en el salón de clase

*It is Mary's first day as a student teacher….*

MARY: Por favor abran el libro de gramática en la página 32. Vamos a hacer los ejercicios 1 y 2.

ESTUDIANTE 1: ¡Yo quiero pasar a la pizarra, señorita Lancaster!

ESTUDIANTE 2: ¡No, yo!

MARY: Silencio, por favor. Levanten la mano. Raúl, pasa a la pizarra, por favor.

JEANNE: Son las tres, señorita Lancaster.

MARY: ¿Son las tres de la tarde? Terminen los ejercicios en su casa. Nos vemos el jueves.

TODOS: Adiós, señorita Lancaster.

**A. ¡A adivinar!** See if you can match each of the following classroom instructions with its English equivalent. ¡OJO! A command has a final **-n** when it is directed to a group.

1. Abra(n) el libro en la página...
2. Cierre(n) el libro.
3. Escuche(n) los casetes.
4. Repita(n) cada palabra, por favor.
5. Vaya(n) a la pizarra.
6. Lea(n) la oración.
7. Levante(n) la mano.
8. Saque(n) papel y un lápiz.
9. Escriba(n) la respuesta.
10. Conteste(n) la pregunta.
11. Haga(n) los ejercicios en el cuaderno.
12. Aprenda(n) el vocabulario.
13. Siénte(n)se.

a. Learn the vocabulary.
b. Repeat each word, please.
c. Write the answer.
d. Open the book to page...
e. Listen to the cassettes.
f. Raise your hand.
g. Sit down.
h. Answer the question.
i. Read the sentence.
j. Close the book.
k. Go to the board.
l. Do the exercises in the workbook.
m. Take out paper and pencil.

**B. ¿Qué número?** Figure out the following patterns and supply the correct numbers. Alternate reading each group with your classmate.

1. 2, 4, 6, __, 10, __, 14, __
2. 1, 2, 4, 8, 16, __, __
3. 100, 90, __, 70, __, 50, __, 30, __, 10
4. 1, __, 9, 27, 81

**C. El horóscopo.** You are calling the service in the ad to get your horoscope. Tell what number you dial and a classmate will guess your sign.

MODELO: —*El 34.*
E1: *Tú eres Leo.*
E2: *Sí, soy Leo.*

TODOS LOS DÍAS

TU HORÓSCOPO TELEFÓNICO

SÓLO MARCA EL

91-801-510+□□

*y luego el número junto a tu signo*

*¡Este número puede cambiar tu vida!*

**D. ¿Cuál es tu teléfono?** Ask five of your classmates their phone numbers and write them down as they would be written by Spanish speakers. Then, practice saying the numbers aloud.

MODELO: You hear: 781-5563
You write: 7-81-55-63
You say: *siete, ochenta y uno, cincuenta y cinco, sesenta y tres.*

**Variation for D.** Bring in pages from a phone book, classified or display ads with telephone numbers for students to practice in groups.

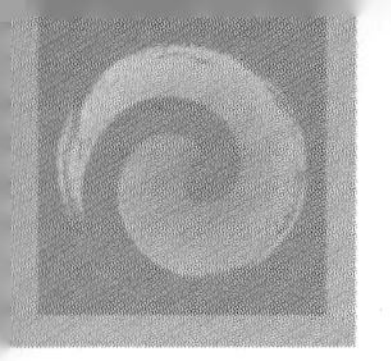

# El artículo definido: género y número
## (*Definite articles*)

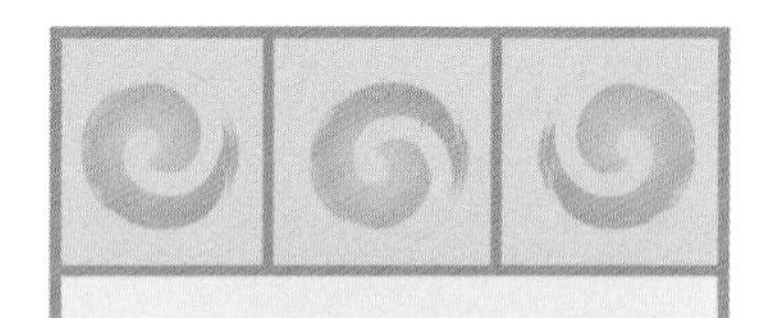

**Para averiguar**

1. What are the four forms of the Spanish word for *the*? When do you use each one?
2. Are the following nouns masculine or feminine: **diccionario, biología, sociedad, composición**?
3. When do you make a noun plural by adding **-s**? By adding **-es**?

- All nouns in Spanish have gender. This means that they are classified as masculine or feminine. In grammar, the terms masculine and feminine have little to do with being male or female, unless they refer to sexed beings. You cannot guess the gender of a word from its meaning. For example, the word for dress (**vestido**) is masculine and the word for necktie (**corbata**) is feminine.

- There are four different ways to say *the* in Spanish. The form you use depends on whether the following noun is masculine or feminine, and whether it is singular or plural.

| The definite article | | | | |
|---|---|---|---|---|
| | **Masculine** | | **Feminine** | |
| **Singular** | **el** libro | *the book* | **la** silla | *the chair* |
| **Plural** | **los** libros | *the books* | **las** sillas | *the chairs* |

**Note.** Explain that *-ción* equals *-tion* (*conversación* = conversation) and *-dad* equals *-ity* (*universidad* = university).

- Generally, nouns ending in **-o** or **-l** are masculine and those ending in **-a, -dad, -tad** or **-ción, -sión** are feminine. There are exceptions, such as **el día** (*day*) and **la mano** (*hand*). The gender of nouns ending in other vowels or consonants is not always predictable, so you should learn them with the article in order to help you remember whether they are masculine or feminine. Here are some nouns you might use in class. Can you fill in the blanks with **el** or **la**?

| | | | | | | |
|---|---|---|---|---|---|---|
| 1. | ___ tarea | *homework* | | 7. | ___ vocabulario | *vocabulary* |
| 2. | ___ pregunta | *question* | | 8. | ___ ejercicio | *exercise* |
| 3. | ___ respuesta | *answer* | | 9. | ___ cuaderno | *notebook* |
| 4. | ___ palabra | *word* | | 10. | ___ libro | *book* |
| 5. | ___ página | *page* | | 11. | ___ bolígrafo | *pen* |
| 6. | ___ oración | *sentence* | | 12. | ___ español | *Spanish* |

**Note.** Point out that *el hombre/la mujer* is an exception to this rule.

- Nouns referring to males are masculine and those referring to females are feminine. Nouns ending in **-e** generally have the same form for a man or a woman.

  el señor / la señora
  el profesor / la profesora
  el estudiante / la estudiante

- To make a noun plural, use the plural form of the article and add **-s** to nouns ending with a vowel or **-es** to those ending with a consonant.

  el libro / los libro**s** — la mesa / las mesa**s**
  el papel / los papel**es** — la universidad / las universidad**es**

- Note that a final **-z** becomes **-c** when **-es** is added: **el lápiz → los lápices**, and the accent on words ending with **-ión** disappears in the plural: **la oración → las oraciones**.

## A lo personal

**A. ¿El artículo definido?** Which item is "in" or "on" the other item? Use **está** after a singular noun and **están** after a plural noun.

MODELO: mesa/mochila
*La mochila está en la mesa.*
libros/estante
*Los libros están en el estante.*

1. lápices/mesa
2. tarea/pizarra
3. cuaderno/papel
4. respuestas/pizarra
5. ejercicio/página 31
6. libros/mochila
7. libro/preguntas
8. sillas/estudiantes
9. profesor/salón de clase
10. estudiantes/universidad

**B. ¿Cuánto cuesta?** Say how much each of these items costs.

MODELO: *La calculadora cuesta treinta y cuatro dólares con noventa y cinco centavos.*

1

2

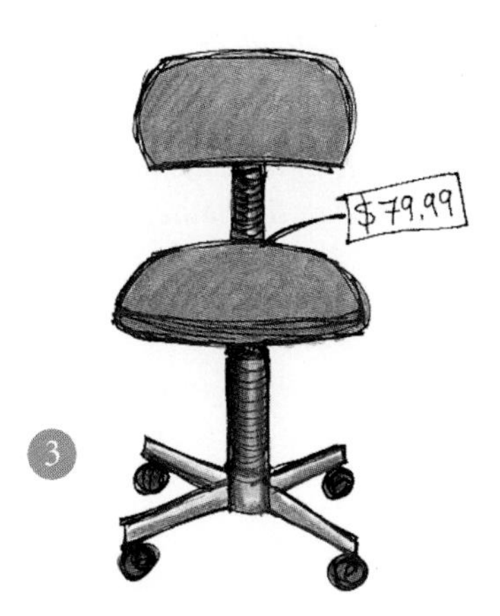


3

4

5

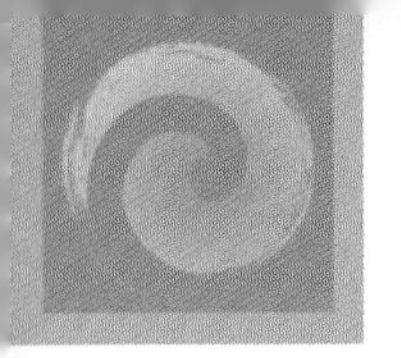

# El artículo indefinido
## (*Indefinite articles*)

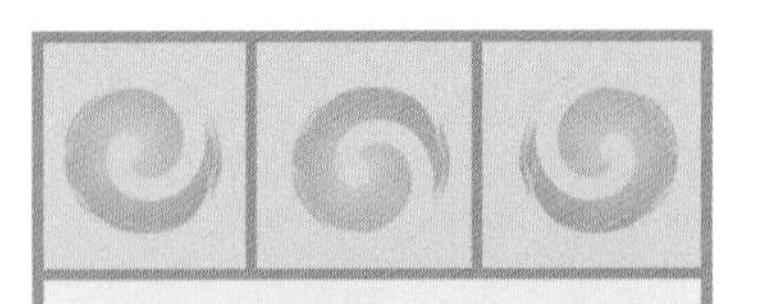

**Para averiguar**

1. What are the two forms of the Spanish word for *a*?
2. How do you say *some*?
3. What word means *there is* and *there are* in Spanish?

- Like the word for *the*, the words for *a* and *some* have different forms, depending on whether the following noun is masculine or feminine, singular or plural.

| The indefinite article | | | | |
|---|---|---|---|---|
| | Masculine | | Feminine | |
| **Singular** | **un** libro | *a book* | **una** silla | *a chair* |
| **Plural** | **unos** libros | *some books* | **unas** sillas | *some chairs* |

- As in English, the word for *some* can be omitted in Spanish. Do not use the indefinite article when forming a question with the verb **hay** in Spanish. Instead, use **algún/as/os/as** (*any*). **Algún** is the only equivalent form of *any* that carries an accent.

Hay (unos) libros en la mesa. — *There are (some) books on the table.*
¿Hay (algunas) mochilas en clase? — *Are there any bookbags in class?*

- The word for *one* is the same as the word for *a*. When counting, use **uno** to say one, but before a noun, use **un** or **una**.

**uno**, dos, tres, cuatro... — *one, two, three, four...*
**un** libro — *a book, one book*
**una** mesa — *a table, one table*

- Use the verb **hay** to say that something exists or to tell how many there are.

**Hay** libros interesantes en el estante. — *There are interesting books on the shelf.*
**Hay** una ventana en la clase. — *There is one (a) window in the classroom.*

— ¿**Hay** algún lapiz en la mesa? — *Are there any pencils on the table?*
— **Hay** tres lápices. — *There are three pencils.*

- **Hay** has only one form for both singular and plural and is also used to form questions: *Is there...? Are there...?* = **¿Hay...?**

**Hay** un libro en el estante. — *There is a book on the shelf.*
**Hay** sillas en el salón de clase. — *There are chairs in the classroom.*

¿**Hay** estudiantes en la clase? — *Are there students in the classroom?*
¿**Hay** una ventana en la casa? — *Is there a window in the house?*

## A lo personal

**A. ¿Qué compro?** You need three of each of the following supplies for your room or school. Tell which you have and how many you have to buy.

MODELO: Tengo dos libros.
*Necesito un libro más.*

1. Tengo dos bolígrafos. Necesito _______ más.
2. Tengo dos cuadernos. Necesito _______ más.
3. Tengo dos lápices. Necesito _______ más.
4. Tengo dos mesas. Necesito _______ más.
5. Tengo dos borradores. Necesito _______ más.
6. Tengo dos sillas. Necesito _______ más.

**B. ¿Qué cosas?** Complete these sentences with all appropriate words. Use the plural when necessary.

MODELO: En mi mochila, hay (libro, lápiz, calculadora, bolígrafo, cuaderno).
*En mi mochila, hay unos libros, unos lápices y un bolígrafo.*

| | | | | | |
|---|---|---|---|---|---|
| ejercicio | respuesta | palabra | computadora | escritorio | profesor |
| profesora | estudiante | libro | cuaderno | pizarra | silla |
| estante | reloj | ventana | puerta | pregunta | oración |

1. En mi libro hay...
2. En la clase de español hay...
3. En el salón de clase hay...
4. En la pizarra hay...
5. En la universidad hay...
6. En mi casa hay...

**C. ¿Qué hay aquí?** Tell how many of the following items there are in your classroom.

MODELO: profesores
*Hay un profesor en la clase.*

estudiantes ____________________
ventanas ____________________
pupitres ____________________
pizarras ____________________
profesores ____________________
lápices ____________________
mochilas ____________________
escritorios ____________________

**D. ¿Los artículos definidos o indefinidos?** After completing the following sentences with a form of the definite or indefinite article, use the questions to interview a classmate.

1. ¿A qué hora es ____ clase de español?
2. ¿Hay ____ profesor o ____ profesora en ____ clase de español?
3. ¿Quién es ____ profesor/a?
4. ¿Estás ____ poco nervioso cuando estás en ____ clase de español?
5. ¿La tarea está en ____ cuaderno o en ____ libro?
6. ¿Hay ____ computadora en tu salón de clase?
7. ¿Tienes ____ clase de literatura este semestre?
8. ¿Hay ____ estudiante en la universidad?

# TEMA 4 Las clases y los horarios

## Los horarios

| HORARIO | LUNES | MARTES | MIÉRCOLES | JUEVES | VIERNES | SÁBADO | DOMINGO |
|---|---|---|---|---|---|---|---|
| 9-10:00 | Contabilidad | | Contabilidad | | Contabilidad | | |
| 10-11:00 | | | | | | | |
| 11-12:00 | | | | | | | |
| 12-1:00 | | Informática | | Informática | | | |
| 1-2:00 | | | | | | | |
| 2-3:00 | | | | | | | |
| 3-4:00 | Trabajo | | Trabajo | | Trabajo | | |
| 4-5:00 | | | | | | | |
| 5-6:00 | | | | | | | |
| 6-7:00 | | | | | | | |

### ¿Cuándo es la clase?

*Isabel and Carlos talk about their classes....*

ISABEL: ¿Qué estudias, Carlos?
CARLOS: Estudio administración de empresas.
ISABEL: Yo también, ¿qué clases tomas este semestre?
CARLOS: Tomo español, informática y contabilidad. ¿Y tú?
ISABEL: Tomo contabilidad también y además tomo matemáticas, español y psicología. ¿Cuándo es tu clase de contabilidad?
CARLOS: La clase de contabilidad es los lunes, los miércoles y los viernes.
ISABEL: ¿Y la clase de informática?
CARLOS: La clase de informática es los martes y los jueves. El martes de esta semana hay examen.
ISABEL: ¡Huy! Estás en clase todos los días. ¿Hay tarea para todas las clases?
CARLOS: Sí, ¡y trabajo tres días por semana también!

**Note for A.** You may wish to write the Spanish name for some different courses on the board to promote the use of cognates: *geografía, historia, geometría, filosofía, ciencias políticas,* etc.

**A. ¿Qué necesita Ud. para las clases?** Check off the items you need for each of the following classes.

1. para biología ___ una calculadora ___ un microscopio ___ un diccionario
2. para informática ___ un borrador ___ un microscopio ___ una calculadora
3. para contabilidad ___ un lápiz ___ un cuaderno ___ una calculadora
4. para español ___ un libro ___ una calculadora ___ un diccionario
5. para literatura ___ un diccionario ___ una computadora ___ un libro

## LA HORA Y EL HORARIO

- To ask what time it is use **¿Qué hora es?** To answer use **Son las...** for all hours except one o'clock, which takes **Es la...** To ask at what time something occurs use **¿A qué hora...?** and to answer use **...a las...** or **...a la....**

| | |
|---|---|
| —**¿Qué hora es?** | *What time is it?* |
| —**Son las** diez./**Es la** una. | *It's ten o'clock./It's one o'clock.* |
| —**¿A qué hora es** la clase? | *At what time is class?* |
| —La clase es **a las** diez. | *Class is at ten.* |

- To indicate how many minutes *past* the hour use **y**. To indicate how many minutes *to* the hour use **menos**. The half-hour is expressed as **media** and the quarter-hour as **cuarto**. For A.M. and P.M. use **de la mañana**, **de la tarde**, or **de la noche** when giving a specific time. Otherwise use **por la mañana**, **por la tarde**, or **por la noche**.

| | |
|---|---|
| —¿A qué hora es el concierto? | *At what time is the concert?* |
| —Es a las diez **y media de la noche**. | *It's at ten thirty P.M.* |
| —¿A qué hora tienes la clase? | *At what time do you have class?* |
| —Tengo clase a la una **menos cuarto.** | *I have class at a quarter to one.* |
| —¿Cuándo estudias? | *When do you study?* |
| —Estudio **por la mañana.** | *I study in the morning.* |

- To express that something happens on a specific day use **el.** Use **los** to express that something happens on a day of the week regularly.

| | |
|---|---|
| Hay un examen **el lunes.** | *There is an exam on Monday.* |
| La clase de química **es los sábados.** | *Chemistry class is on Saturdays.* |

**B. ¿Cómo son las clases?** Decide how you feel about each of these classes, then exchange information with a classmate.

MODELO: E1: *¿Estás contento/a en la clase de biología?*
E2: *Sí, estoy contento/a en la clase de biología.* o
*No. ¡En la clase de biología estoy confundido/a!*

contento/a aburrido/a confundido/a cansado/a nervioso/a ocupado/a

1. biología
2. informática
3. cálculo
4. historia
5. inglés
6. contabilidad
7. geometría
8. psicología

**C. Entrevista.** Interview a classmate about the classes he/she is taking this semester.

1. ¿Qué estudias? ¿Qué clases tomas? ¿Qué clases son interesantes? ¿Qué clases son aburridas? ¿Hay mucha tarea en las clases? ¿Estás nervioso/a cuando hay un examen?
2. ¿Qué días estás muy ocupado/a? ¿Qué días no hay clase? ¿Trabajas? ¿Dónde? ¿Qué días trabajas? ¿Estás ocupado/a en el trabajo?

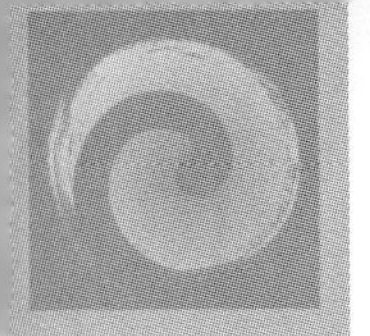

# ABC ¿A qué hora es tu clase de...?

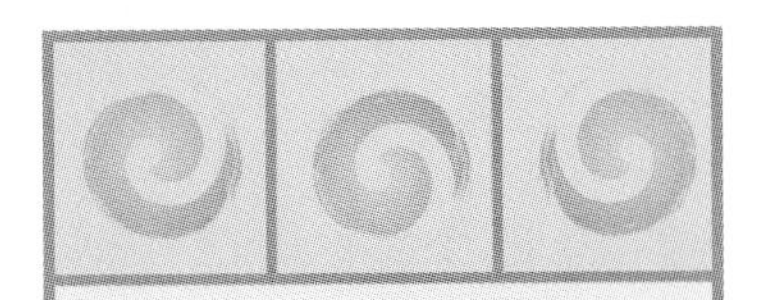

## ¡ojo!

To express the idea of *from...to/through...* with days of the week, use **de... a....** To express *from...to/until...* with time, use **desde... hasta....**

Trabajo **de** lunes **a** viernes **desde** las nueve y media **hasta** las tres.
*I work from Monday to Friday from 9:30 to 3:00.*

## Y tú, ¿qué haces?

*Ana tells Mary about her schedule....*

MARY: Ana, ¿tomas solamente la clase de español?
ANA: No, también tomo psicología.
MARY: ¿A qué hora es tu clase de psicología?
ANA: Es los sábados a las diez de la mañana. No tomo la clase durante la semana porque trabajo de lunes a viernes.
MARY: ¿Dónde trabajas?
ANA: Soy la gerente de la agencia de viajes de mis padres.
MARY: ¡Trabajas mucho!
ANA: Sí, siempre estoy muy ocupada. También tengo un hijo de ocho años. Y tú, ¿qué clases tomas, Mary?
MARY: Tomo español, pedagogía y hago mis prácticas para maestra en la escuela primaria.
ANA: ¿Qué días haces prácticas?
MARY: Dos días a la semana: los martes y los jueves desde las ocho de la mañana hasta las tres de la tarde.

**Answers for A.** 1) *A.* 2) *A.* 3) *M.* 4) *A.*

**A. ¿Ana o Mary?** Place an **A** next to the sentences which refer to **Ana**, **M** for those associated with **Mary**.

1. ___ ¿Quién toma clases de psicología?
2. ___ ¿Quién trabaja en una agencia de viajes?
3. ___ ¿Quién practica en una escuela?
4. ___ ¿Quién tiene un hijo de ocho años?

## ¡ojo!

Some Spanish-speaking areas of the world use the twenty-four-hour clock in official schedules. To convert from the twenty-four-hour schedule, subtract twelve hours. 18:00 = 6:00 de la tarde.

**B. Mi horario.** Fill in the chart with your class and work schedules. Then compare classes and work hours with other students.

| HORARIO | LUNES | MARTES | MIÉRCOLES | JUEVES | VIERNES | SÁBADO | DOMINGO |
|---|---|---|---|---|---|---|---|
| 9-10:00 | | | | | | | |
| 10-11:00 | | | | | | | |
| 11-12:00 | | | | | | | |
| 12-1:00 | | | | | | | |
| 1-2:00 | | | | | | | |
| 2-3:00 | | | | | | | |
| 3-4:00 | | | | | | | |
| 4-5:00 | | | | | | | |
| 5-6:00 | | | | | | | |
| 6-7:00 | | | | | | | |

**C. ¿Qué hora es?** Your classmate will ask you what time it is on each clock. Respond by saying the hour. He/she will then say where he/she is at that time and ask you the same question.

MODELO: E1: *¿Qué hora es?*
E2: *Es la una.*
E1: *Yo estoy en clase a la una. ¿Y tú?*

**D. ¿Están abiertos los restaurantes?** Use the ads for restaurants from the Monterrey, México, Yellow Pages to ask your classmate when each restaurant is open.

MODELO: E1: ¿Singapur Express *está abierto (open) a las diez de la mañana?*
E2: *No, no está abierto. Está cerrado (closed).*

1. ¿*Singapur Express* está abierto a las tres de la tarde?
2. ¿*El Fundado*r está abierto los lunes a las diez de la mañana? ¿los lunes al mediodía?
3. ¿*Showbiz Pizza Fiesta* está abierto los viernes a las once y media? ¿los sábados a las once y media?
4. ¿*Sólo Faltas Tú* está abierto los martes a las cinco menos cuarto? ¿los domingos a las cinco menos cuarto?

**E. Entrevista.** Interview a classmate and write down the answers to these questions.

1. ¿Qué día es hoy? ¿Qué hora es?
2. ¿Qué días tienes clase? ¿A qué hora es tu primera clase? ¿y tu última clase?
3. ¿A qué hora es tu programa de televisión favorito? ¿Qué día es? ¿Cómo se llama el programa?
4. Los viernes a la medianoche, ¿dónde estás por lo general? ¿Estás en casa? ¿con amigos? ¿en el trabajo?

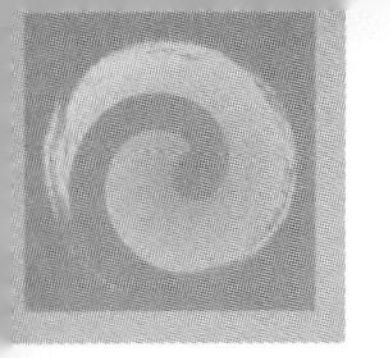

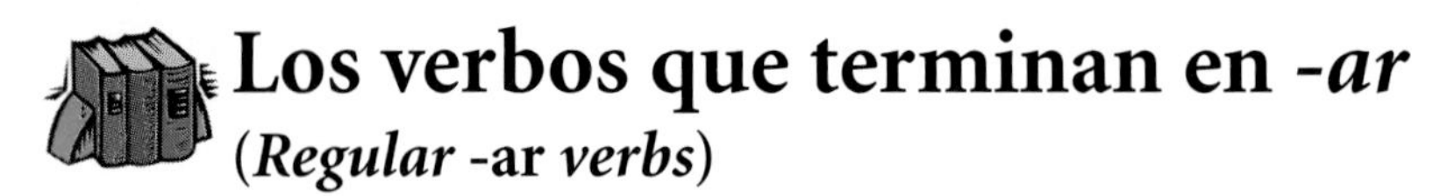

# Los verbos que terminan en *-ar*
## (*Regular* -ar *verbs*)

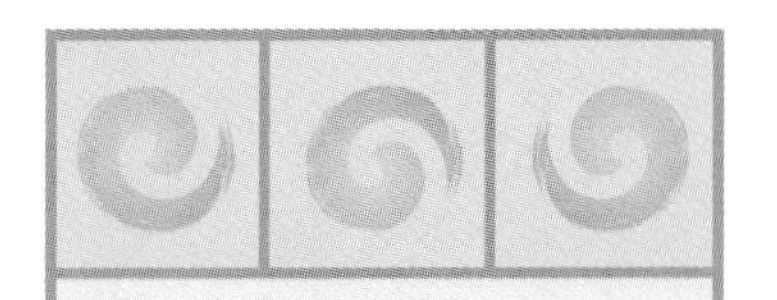

**Para averiguar**

1. What is an infinitive?
2. What are the three infinitive endings in Spanish?
3. What are the regular endings for conjugating **-ar** verbs in Spanish?

- ***Infinitives.*** The basic form of the verb that you find in dictionaries or vocabulary lists is called the infinitive. Some examples of infinitives in English are *to play, to eat,* and *to go.*

  In Spanish, infinitives consist of single words that end in **-ar, -er,** or **-ir:** estudi**ar,** com**er,** viv**ir**. The part of the verb that carries the meaning is called the stem and the part that expresses the subject of the verb is called the ending.

  Ex: **Estás → Est** is the stem and **ás** is the ending.

- **-ar *verbs.*** To indicate the subject of a verb, you must use different verb endings. This is called conjugating the verb. To conjugate an **-ar** verb, drop the final **-ar** and add the endings below.

| **Trabajar** *(to work)* | | | |
|---|---|---|---|
| yo trabaj**o** | *I work* | nosotros/as trabaj**amos** | *we work* |
| tú trabaj**as** | *you work* | vosotros/as trabaj**áis** | *you work* |
| él/ella trabaj**a** | *he/she works* | ellos/ellas trabaj**an** | *they work* |
| usted trabaj**a** | *you work* | ustedes trabaj**an** | *you work* |

—¿**Trabajas** en la biblioteca? *Do you work in the library?*
—No, **trabajo** en una tienda. *No, I work in a store.*

—¿**Miras** la televisión? *Do you watch television?*
—No, no **miro** la televisión. *No, I don't watch television.*

These **-ar** verbs follow the pattern above.

| | | | |
|---|---|---|---|
| **ayudar** | *to help* | **ganar** | *to earn, win* |
| **bailar** | *to dance* | **hablar** | *to speak* |
| **caminar** | *to walk* | **lavar** | *to wash* |
| **cantar** | *to sing* | **limpiar** | *to clean* |
| **descansar** | *to rest* | **necesitar** | *to need* |
| **mirar** | *to watch, look at* | **escuchar** | *to listen* |
| **desear** | *to desire, wish* | **preparar** | *to prepare* |
| **estudiar** | *to study* | **regresar** | *to return* |
| **fumar** | *to smoke* | **tomar** | *to drink/to take* |

**Note.** Point out that when *a* is followed by the definite article *el,* they contract to *al.*

- Note that the word **a** must precede human direct objects. In this context it is called the *personal* **a.** Direct objects are people, animals, and objects to whom something is being done. In the following examples, **Lázaro**, **el profesor**, and **el estudiante** are the direct objects because they are being invited and listened to.

—¿Por qué no **invitas a** Lázaro? *Why don't you invite Lazaro?*
—**Escucho al** profesor. *I listen to the professor.*
—¿**Ayudas al** estudiante? *Do you help the student?*

## A lo personal

**A. Para practicar.** Write the missing subject pronouns indicated by the verb. Some may have more than one possibility.

1. ________ estudias contabilidad.
2. ________ estudio español y literatura.
3. ________ /________ /________ trabajan en la oficina.
4. ________ /________ estudiamos en esta universidad.
5. ¿Dónde estudia ________ /________ /________?
6. ________ /________ trabajamos con Carlos.
7. ¿Qué clases toman ________ /________ /________?
8. ¿Cómo está ________ /________ ?

**B. Las actividades.** Complete the sentences with the appropriate form of the verb.

1. Ana y Carlos ________ (estudiar) español.
2. Tú también ________ (tomar) clases.
3. Ellos no ________ (hablar) mucho español, pero ________ (practicar) todos los días.
4. Lázaro ________ (trabajar) en la escuela.
5. ¿Qué clases ________ (tomar) ustedes?
6. Nosotros ________ (escuchar) a la profesora y ________ (practicar) español.
7. Ellas ________ (cantar) en la clase de música.
8. Yo ________ (caminar) a la universidad.

**C. El horario de Alejandro.** Complete the following note that Alejandro wrote you about his schedule with the appropriate form of the verb in parentheses.

*Hola, yo soy Alejandro. Hoy yo (1) ____________ (estar) muy contento porque no tengo clases los sábados y hoy es sábado. Los sábados yo (2) ____________ (trabajar) en un restaurante por las mañanas. Por las tardes, mi novia y yo (3) ____________ (descansar) en casa y (4) ____________ (mirar) la televisión. Los domingos, mi novia (5) ____________ (ayudar) a sus padres en casa y yo (6) ____________ (limpiar) mi apartamento y (7) ____________ (preparar) las cosas para toda la semana. Durante la semana, mi compañero de cuarto y yo (8) ____________ (estudiar) mucho. Nosotros también (9) ____________ (practicar) deportes los lunes y los miércoles. Los martes y los jueves yo (10) ____________ (caminar) por el parque con mi novia. Los viernes mis amigos (11) ____________ (bailar) en un club. Mi novia y yo también (12) ____________ (bailar) a veces, pero nosotros (13) ____________ (regresar) temprano a casa.*

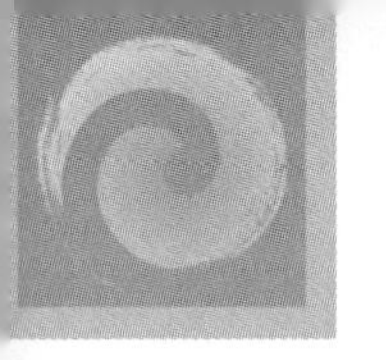

# Las preguntas
## (*Asking questions*)

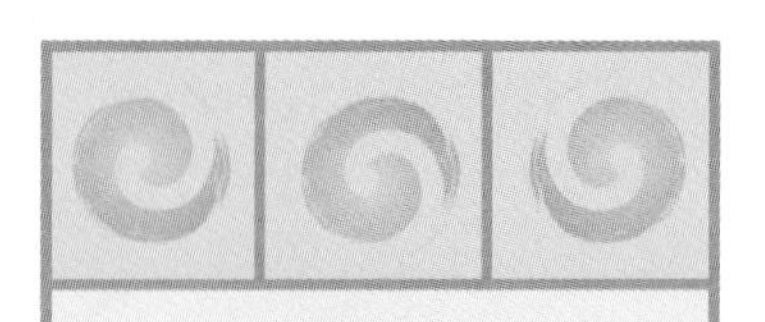

**Para averiguar**

1. Where do you generally place the subject of a question?
2. How do you express tag questions like *isn't he?*, *can't she?*, and *don't they?*
3. Which question words have written accents? Which ones have plural forms?
4. What does **cuál** mean? What does **qué** mean? When do you use **cuál** instead of **qué** to say *what?*

- To ask a question that may be answered *yes* or *no*, use rising intonation. Notice that the word *do*, used to ask questions in the present tense in English, is not translated in Spanish and that answers in the negative often use **no** twice.

| | |
|---|---|
| —¿**Hablas** español? | *Do you speak Spanish?* |
| —Sí, hablo un poco. | *Yes, I speak a little.* |
| —¿**Está** Ana en casa? | *Is Ana at home?* |
| —**No, no** está en casa. | *No, she is not at home.* |

- When the subject of the verb is stated, it is generally placed after the verb in a question.

| **Statement** | **Question** |
|---|---|
| **Daniel** estudia todos los días. | ¿Estudia **Daniel** todos los días? |

- In English, when you think you already know the answer to a question and you are just asking to be sure, you end your question with a tag such as *can't you?*, *isn't he?*, *doesn't she?*, or *right?* In Spanish, use **¿verdad?** (*true?*) or **¿no?** with rising intonation.

| | |
|---|---|
| Hablas español, **¿verdad?** | *You speak Spanish,* **don't you?** |
| Puedes estudiar con nosotros, **¿no?** | *You can study with us,* **can't you?** |

- To ask questions that will be answered with new information, such as *where, when,* or *with whom,* use the following question words. Note that several question words have plural forms and all have written accents. Remember that many times question words will have more than one single meaning.

| | | | | | |
|---|---|---|---|---|---|
| **¿cuál(es)?** | *which? what?* | **¿cómo?** | *how?* | **¿por qué?** | *why?* |
| **¿cuándo?** | *when?* | **¿dónde?** | *where?* | **¿quién(es)?** | *who?* |
| **¿cuánto/a?** | *how much?* | **¿adónde?** | *to where?* | **¿con quién(es)?** | *with whom?* |
| **¿cuántos/as?** | *how many?* | **¿de dónde?** | *from where?* | **¿qué?** | *what? which?* |

- **¿Qué?** and **¿Cuál?** The interrogatives **¿qué?** and **¿cuál?** may mean *what* or *which* in different circumstances. When **¿qué?** is used alone, it is a request for a definition and it means *what*? in English. When followed by a singular or plural noun, **¿qué?** means *which*? and requests information about *one* or *some among many*.

| | |
|---|---|
| ¿**Qué** es un infinitivo? | *What is an infinitive?* |
| ¿**Qué** clase(s) prefieres? | *Which class(es) do you prefer?* |

- **¿Cuál?** generally implies selection from a group and generally does not precede a noun directly.

| | |
|---|---|
| ¿**Cuál** es tu película favorita? | *What is your favorite movie?* |
| ¿**Cuál** es tu número de teléfono? | *What is your telephone number?* |

## A lo personal

**A. Más preguntas.** Ask your partner the following questions using the question words in parentheses to obtain as much information as you can.

MODELO: tus clases (cuántos/as, qué, cuándo, por qué)

E1: *¿Cuántas clases tomas este semestre?*
E2: *Tomo tres clases.*
E1: *¿Qué clases son?*
E2: *Son literatura, informática y español*
E1: *¿Cuándo es la clase de español?*
E2: *Es los lunes y los martes.*
E1: *¿Por qué estudias español?*
E2: *Porque me gusta hablar español.*

1. bailar (dónde, con quién, cuándo)
2. mirar la televisión (cuándo, qué, por qué)
3. escuchar música (qué, cuándo, dónde)
4. comprar (qué, cuándo, dónde, con quién/es)

**B. El día de Carlos.** Read about Carlos's day below. Then write five questions to ask one of your classmates about it.

Hoy es jueves. Tengo muchas clases hoy. Tengo la clase de matemáticas a las 9:00 de la mañana. Es una clase muy difícil. Prefiero la clase de literatura hispanoamericana. Es interesante y la profesora es muy buena. Después de la clase de literatura, estudio por una hora en la biblioteca con mi amigo Alejandro. A la 1:30 Alejandro y yo vamos a la cafetería para comer. Prefiero comer en mi casa porque la comida de la cafetería es muy mala, pero tengo una clase a las 2:00. Es una clase de química y el profesor es viejo y aburrido. Después de la clase de química regreso a mi casa para descansar.

**C. ¿Qué? o ¿Cuál?** Supply the appropriate question word.

MODELO: ¿_________ es tu restaurante favorito?
*¿Cuál es tu restaurante favorito?*

1. ¿ _________ es un elefante?
2. ¿ _________ es esto?
3. ¿ _________ quieres hacer este fin de semana?
4. ¿ _________ es tu mochila?
5. ¿ _________ es tu clase favorita?
6. ¿ _________ hora es?
7. ¿ _________ estudias?
8. ¿ _________ hay en la mesa?

# Vocabulario

## TEMA 3
### En mi clase

**Sustantivos**

| | |
|---|---|
| **la administración** | *administration* |
| **la agencia** | *agency* |
| **la biblioteca** | *library* |
| **la biología** | *biology* |
| **el bolígrafo** | *pen* |
| **el borrador** | *eraser* |
| **la calculadora** | *calculator* |
| **la computadora** | *computer* |
| **el cuaderno** | *notebook* |
| **el dinero** | *money* |
| **la empresa/el negocio** | *business* |
| **el escritorio** | *big desk* |
| **el estante** | *shelf* |
| **el/la gerente** | *manager* |
| **el lápiz** | *pencil* |
| **la librería** | *bookstore* |
| **el libro** | *book* |
| **la mesa** | *table* |
| **el papel** | *paper* |
| **la pizarra** | *chalkboard* |
| **la psicología** | *psychology* |
| **el pupitre** | *student desk* |
| **el restaurante** | *restaurant* |
| **el salón de clase** | *classroom* |
| **la silla** | *chair* |
| **el teléfono** | *telephone* |
| **el texto** | *text* |
| **la tiza** | *chalk* |
| **el total** | *total* |

**Adjetivos**

| | |
|---|---|
| **grande** | *big* |
| **gratis** | *free (of cost)* |
| **pequeño/a** | *small* |

**Adverbios**

| | |
|---|---|
| **difícil** | *difficult* |
| **fácil** | *easy* |

## TEMA 4
### Las clases y los horarios

**Sustantivos**

| | |
|---|---|
| **el domingo** | *Sunday* |
| **el horario** | *schedule* |
| **la informática** | *computer science* |
| **el jueves** | *Thursday* |
| **el lugar/sitio** | *place* |
| **el lunes** | *Monday* |
| **la luz** | *light* |
| **la mañana** | *morning* |
| **el martes** | *Tuesday* |
| **la medianoche** | *midnight* |
| **el mediodía** | *noon* |
| **el miércoles** | *Wednesday* |
| **la práctica** | *practice* |
| **la programación** | *programming* |
| **el sábado** | *Saturday* |
| **el semestre** | *semester* |
| **la ventana** | *window* |
| **el viaje** | *trip* |
| **el viernes** | *Friday* |

**Verbos**

| | |
|---|---|
| **estudiar** | *to study* |
| **hay** | *there is/are* |
| **practicar** | *to practice* |
| **tomar** | *to take* |
| **trabajar** | *to work* |

**Adverbios**

| | |
|---|---|
| **primero/a** | *first* |
| **siempre** | *always* |
| **solamente** | *only* |
| **suficiente** | *sufficient* |
| **temprano** | *early* |
| **tercero/a** | *third* |
| **último** | *last* |

**Otras expresiones**

| | |
|---|---|
| **¿A qué hora?** | *At what time?* |
| **¿Cuántos/as?** | *How many?* |
| **cuarto** | *quarter* |
| **de** | *from* |
| **desde** | *from* |
| **medio/a** | *half* |
| **¿Qué?** | *What? Which?* |
| **¿Qué hora es?** | *What time is it?* |
| **también** | *too, also* |

# Reunión B

**A escuchar. Mary habla con Isabel.** Listen to the conversation between Mary and Isabel and then circle the correct answer.

1. Isabel tiene muchas/pocas clases.
2. Su clase de contabilidad es fácil/difícil.
3. Isabel trabaja/no trabaja.
4. Mary hace sus prácticas de maestra en el tercer/primer grado.
5. El maestro de la escuela California es José/Lázaro.
6. Isabel tiene que ir a la biblioteca/a la escuela.

**Tapescript for A escuchar. Mary habla con Isabel.**

MARY: ¿Cómo estás, Isabel?
ISABEL: Regular, tengo muchas clases y siempre estoy muy ocupada.
MARY: ¿Son muy difíciles tus clases?
ISABEL: La sociología, la historia y el español son fáciles, pero tengo mucha tarea. La contabilidad es difícil y tengo que estudiar mucho.
MARY: Isabel, ¿también trabajas?
ISABEL: No, porque no tengo tiempo. ¿Cómo son tus clases, Mary?
MARY: La pedagogía no es ni fácil, ni difícil; el español es muy fácil, pero mis prácticas de maestra son difíciles, y tengo que trabajar mucho.
ISABEL: ¿Dónde haces tus prácticas?
MARY: En la escuela California, en el tercer grado con el profesor Lázaro Frankel.
ISABEL: ¡Qué coincidencia! ¡Lázaro es mi novio! Bueno, adiós, Mary, tengo que ir a la biblioteca.

**Answers for A escuchar.**
1) *Muchas.* 2) *Difícil.* 3) *No trabaja.* 4) *Tercer.* 5) *Lázaro.* 6) *Biblioteca.*

**A conversar.** With a classmate, prepare a conversation in which one of you is **el/la profesor/a**, the other **el/la estudiante perdido/a** (*the lost student*). You may wish to use the following expressions.

| | |
|---|---|
| **Hable más despacio, por favor.** | *Speak slower, please.* |
| **¿Qué significa...?** | *What does...mean?* |
| **¿Cómo se dice...en español?** | *How do you say...in Spanish?* |
| **¿Cómo se pronuncia esta palabra?** | *How do you pronounce this word?* |
| **No comprendo.** | *I don't understand.* |
| **No sé.** | *I don't know.* |

## ¿Lo sabía?

Read the ad and answer the following questions.

1. ¿La clase es para adultos?
2. ¿Cuesta mucho dinero la clase?
3. ¿Qué día de la semana es?
4. ¿A qué hora es?
5. ¿Cómo se llama la maestra?
6. ¿Cuál es el número de teléfono?

*Cerámica Para Niños*

*Clases Informales*

*Gratis—Para todas las edades*
*Viernes—De 3 a 5 de la tarde*

*Ensúciense las manos con obras fantásticas de cerámica con la maestra Sally Spiro.*

**El Centro para la Comunidad el Parque Oeste**
**C/ Harrison, 450**
**Para más información llamen al 648-1895**

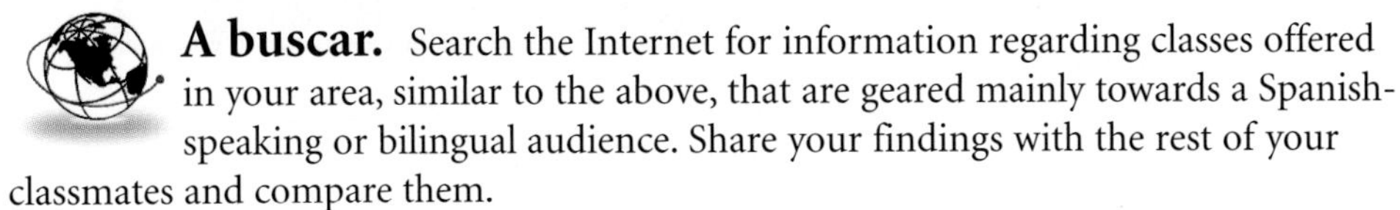

**A buscar.** Search the Internet for information regarding classes offered in your area, similar to the above, that are geared mainly towards a Spanish-speaking or bilingual audience. Share your findings with the rest of your classmates and compare them.

# ¡TRATO HECHO!

## Rincón profesional: Educación bilingüe

### La educación bilingüe

Si usted lee este artículo, usted probablemente estudia español. ¿Estudia Ud. español porque es obligatorio en su universidad, o estudia Ud. español porque comprende que es un privilegio—profesional y personal—tener la posibilidad de comunicarse con personas que hablan uno de los idiomas más importantes del mundo?

Para la mayoría de las personas, la importancia de hablar más de un idioma es obvia. Si yo sólo hablo un idioma, sólo tengo mi cultura. Si hablo dos idiomas, puedo moverme entre dos culturas. Si hablo tres idiomas, estoy cómodo (*comfortable*) entre muchas culturas. Es irónico que en los Estados Unidos, famosos por abrir sus puertas a inmigrantes de todas partes del mundo, todavía haya quienes luchen contra la educación bilingüe y a favor del movimiento *English only*.

Sin embargo (*However*) muchas personas en Norteamérica entienden ya la necesidad de estudiar otras lenguas. Al hablar otros idiomas tenemos muchas más oportunidades a varios niveles: en el mundo (*world*) profesional podemos encontrar trabajos con compañías y negocios internacionales; en el ámbito social, una segunda lengua nos permite comunicarnos con personas de otras partes del mundo y aprender sobre otras costumbres y modos de vida. Además, cuando estudiamos otro idioma, estudiamos también nuestra propia lengua, viendo las diferencias y similaridades entre nuestro idioma natal y el idioma extranjero (*foreign*).

Los expertos recomiendan aprender un segundo idioma cuando uno es muy joven, y la edad ideal según muchos estudios realizados oscila entre los tres y los trece años. Por esta razón, la educación primaria en una escuela bilingüe puede ser de gran beneficio, si no para nosotros, al menos para nuestros niños.

La verdadera educación bilingüe, como existe en Europa o en América del Sur, no es solamente para los estudiantes que necesitan aprender el idioma oficial de su nueva patria. La verdadera educación bilingüe es para enriquecer la vida de todos los niños. Por ejemplo, la educación bilingüe en Suiza (*Switzerland*) quiere decir que los niños—todos los niños—desde la escuela primaria, estudian las clases de la mañana en francés y las clases de la tarde en alemán, en italiano o en inglés. En Perú, Colombia y Argentina muchos estudiantes asisten a escuelas bilingües español-inglés, español-alemán o español-japonés. Cuando terminan sus estudios, estos estudiantes ya están preparados para trabajar en una economía internacional.

¡Piénselo Ud! Con el sistema europeo de educación bilingüe, ¡Ud. no tendría que tomar estas clases obligatorias de español!

**¿Comprende Ud.?**

1. What are two reasons for studying Spanish mentioned in the article?
2. What are the obvious benefits of speaking two languages?
3. How do students in the European or South American system of bilingual education spend their school day?
4. From your vantage point as an adult today, which system makes more sense to you?

**A escuchar.** **Una fiesta en el Club Hispano.** Answer the following questions based on the dialog that you will hear between Débora and Christopher.

**¿Comprende Ud.?**

1. ¿Dónde están Christopher y Débora?
2. ¿De dónde es Christopher?
3. ¿De dónde es Débora?
4. ¿Cuántas lenguas habla Christopher?
5. ¿Qué estudia Débora?

**Tapescript for A escuchar. Una fiesta en el Club Hispano.**
CHRISTOPHER: ¿Quieres bailar esta salsa?
DÉBORA: Sí. Tú no eres hispano, ¿verdad?
CHRISTOPHER: No, soy alemán, pero me gusta mucho el español. Además, estudio negocios internacionales y necesito hablar dos o tres lenguas.
DÉBORA: ¡Hablas muy bien el español!
CHRISTOPHER: Gracias. ¿De dónde eres tú?
DÉBORA: Yo soy norteamericana, pero mis padres son nicaragüenses. Estudio medicina y necesito comunicarme con los pacientes en varias lenguas.
CHRISTOPHER: ¿Qué lenguas hablas?
DÉBORA: Hablo inglés y español. También tomo clases de alemán porque quiero trabajar en Alemania en el futuro.

**Answers for A escuchar.**
1) En el Club Hispano. 2) Es alemán. 3) Es norteamericana. 4) Dos. 5) Medicina.

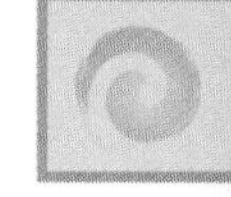

## El buzón de Doña Rosa

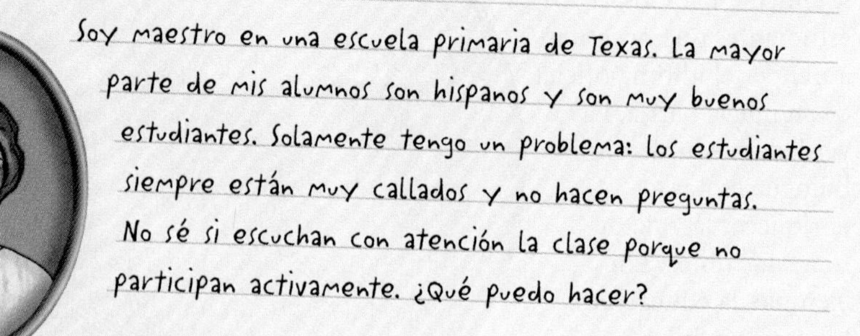

Querida Doña Rosa:

Soy maestro en una escuela primaria de Texas. La mayor parte de mis alumnos son hispanos y son muy buenos estudiantes. Solamente tengo un problema: los estudiantes siempre están muy callados y no hacen preguntas. No sé si escuchan con atención la clase porque no participan activamente. ¿Qué puedo hacer?

Un maestro solitario

**¿Qué dice Doña Rosa?** Help Doña Rosa write the answer for *Un maestro solitario*. With your classmate write a list of questions that you feel would entice children to participate more actively in class.

**Somos profesores.** You are a group of new teachers in a bilingual elementary school. Some of the students in your class will speak no English, some will speak no Spanish. Discuss how each group might feel and how to make your students more comfortable in the new setting. Make Spanish labels for different items in the classroom and put them up.

## A leer

**How to read in a new language**

As you begin to read in Spanish, you will realize very quickly that you are learning more than the content of the words and sentences. Reading is one of the best and fastest ways to internalize the structures, rhythms, and patterns of your new language. As you read, do not try to translate the sentences. That will only help you to practice English. You really want to practice Spanish. You will not need to know every word to get the sense of what you are reading. Here are some tips to remember as you begin to develop this very important skill.

1. Pay close attention to the titles and headings. They will set the stage and give good clues to what you are looking for.
2. Skim the entire passage for a quick sense of the content.
3. As you begin to read the first paragraph, look for cognates—words that you recognize from English.
4. Look for the new words in Spanish that you have learned earlier in the lesson.
5. Read for ideas, not for word meanings.
6. If you feel you are guessing a lot, you probably are. And that's good!
7. As you get the gist of a sentence or paragraph, make a little note in the margin to refresh your memory.
8. Don't forget. You promised not to translate!

**Antes de leer.** Make a list of all the words that you can identify in this article. Then, compare your list with a partner's and with the help of a dictionary, determine how many of those words are cognates.

*Hollywood is bilingual. American producers are hiring more and more Hispanic actors. Being bilingual is important in order to attract a wider audience.*

A los hispanos les gusta mucho el cine. A pesar de que representan sólo el 10% de la población total en los Estados Unidos, ellos compran más del 15% de los boletos. Por eso, los productores de cine contratan ahora a más artistas hispanos. Ellos buscan a los artistas hispanos bilingües, para atraer a más hispanos a los teatros. Esto es importante porque el español es la segunda lengua que más se habla en los Estados Unidos: aproximadamente 17.345.000 personas[1] lo hablan. Ahora hay muchos artistas hispanos que hablan inglés y español y llegan a audiencias hispanas y a otras culturas. Entre los más populares tenemos a Anthony Quinn, Salma Hayek, Paul Rodríguez, Antonio Banderas, Marc Anthony, Ricky Martin, Jennifer López, Andy García, Cameron Díaz, Chayanne, Edward James Olmos y Hector Elizondo. ¿Conoces a estos artistas?

[1] En tercer lugar está el francés con 1.930.404, en cuarto el alemán con 1.547.987, en quinto el italiano con 1.308.648 y en sexto el chino con 1.219.462 de personas.

**¿Comprende Ud.?** Answer the following questions according to the reading.

1. ¿Qué porcentaje de hispanos hay en los Estados Unidos?
2. ¿Qué porcentaje de hispanos compran boletos para el cine?
3. ¿Cuál es la lengua que más hablamos en los Estados Unidos?
4. ¿Cuál es la segunda lengua?
5. ¿Por qué es necesario contratar a actores bilingües?

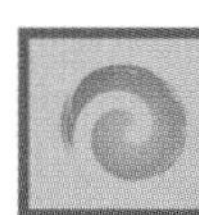

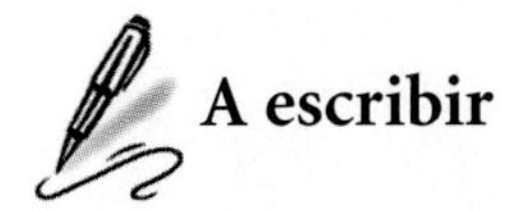

## A escribir

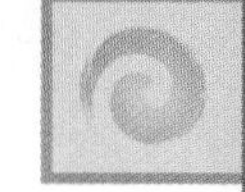
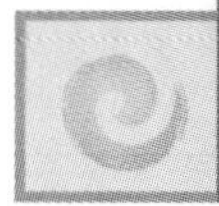

Write a list of some of the advantages of being bilingual in the current job market. Then, compare it with a classmate's and discuss the differences. What other fields, aside from those mentioned here, may be open to you because of bilingualism? You may conduct the discussion in English but try to write the items in your list in Spanish.

# 2 De compras

LECCIÓN DOS

CHECK OUT THE *¡TRATO HECHO!* WEBSITE AND CD-ROM FOR ACTIVITIES, GAMES, SELF-TESTS, AND MUCH MORE!

TEMA 1

## Las tiendas

- En la librería
- En la zapatería
- El verbo *ser*
- Los adjetivos

TEMA 2

## En el centro comercial

- ¿Dónde está…?
- En la perfumería
- Más sobre el verbo *estar*
- *Ser* y *estar*

TEMA 3

## De compras

- De tienda en tienda
- La comida
- Preposiciones de lugar
- Expresiones afirmativas y negativas

TEMA 4

## La ropa

- La moda personal
- Problemas con las compras
- *Me/te/le gusta(n)*
- Pronombres y adjetivos demostrativos

# ¡TRATO HECHO!

- Rincón profesional: De compras por el Internet
- A escuchar
- A leer
- A escribir

# TEMA 1 Las tiendas

## En la librería

El estéreo es para mi hijo José porque le gusta la música.

El teléfono celular es para mi novia Mary. ¡Qué habladora es!

La mochila es para mi novio Lázaro. Es muy trabajador.

El reloj es para mi hermana Lucero. Ella siempre es puntua

**Expansion.** Mention several items that could be given as gifts and ask students to describe a person for whom the item would be appropriate. For example, *¿Un libro de ciencias?* Possible answer: *Un/a estudiante serio/a.*

**Note.** Point out that *y* becomes *e* in front of words beginning with *i* or *hi.*

### De compras

*Lázaro talks to a salesperson at the bookstore....*

VENDEDOR: Buenas tardes, ¿en qué puedo servirle, señor?
LÁZARO: Deseo comprar un regalo para una amiga.
VENDEDOR: ¿Cómo es ella?
LÁZARO: Es joven, romántica e inteligente.
VENDEDOR: ¿Qué tipo de libros le gustan?
LÁZARO: Le gustan las novelas románticas.
VENDEDOR: Esta novela es romántica y muy interesante. Es del escritor peruano Mario Vargas Llosa y se llama *La tía Julia y el escribidor.*
LÁZARO: Muy bien, la compro. ¿Cuánto es?
VENDEDOR: Son quince dólares. ¿Cómo va a pagar?
LÁZARO: Al contado. Aquí tiene un billete de veinte dólares.
VENDEDOR: Gracias. Aquí tiene su cambio, cinco dólares.

**A. Buscando información.** Answer the following questions based on the dialog.

1. ¿Qué busca Lázaro?
2. ¿Para quién es?
3. ¿Cómo es ella?
4. ¿Cómo se llama el libro?
5. ¿Quién es el escritor?
6. ¿Cómo paga Lázaro?

**Answers for A.** 1) *Un regalo.* 2) *Para una amiga.* 3) *Joven, romántica e inteligente.* 4) *La tía Julia y el escribidor.* 5) *Vargas Llosa.* 6) *Al contado.*

**B. ¿Para quién?** Match the personality listed with the appropriate book title.

| | |
|---|---|
| 1. una niña de cinco años | a. *Don Quijote* |
| 2. un profesor de ciencias | b. *Star Trek* |
| 3. una joven romántica | c. *La historia de México* |
| 4. un estudiante de español | d. *La biología de Costa Rica* |
| 5. una estudiante de historia | e. *Don Juan Tenorio* |
| 6. un niño de diez años | f. *Los Beanie Babies en fotos* |

**Follow up for B.** Explain the work of Cervantes and its importance in literature. Also comment on the figure of *Don Juan.*

**C. De compras.** You are traveling on business in Costa Rica and forgot to bring a book. With a classmate playing the part of the salesperson at the **Librería Internacional,** prepare a dialog selecting the type of book, its price, and the purchase.

**Follow up for C.** Discuss Gabriel García Márquez and other famous writers in Spanish as time allows. Addresses in this part of Costa Rica are listed by how many meters away from a recognized landmark. 100 meters=1 block (of any length). The bookstore is 300 meters west of Taco Bell. You may translate *cocina, estacionamiento.*

**LIBRERÍA INTERNACIONAL**

· ***Noticia de un secuestro*/**
**Gabriel García Márquez**
· ***El punto crucial*/Fritjof Capra**
· ***Reingeniería*/Charles Champy**
· **Internet Páginas Amarillas**
· **Música/Biografías**
· **Arquitectura/Cocina/Literatura**

Horario: 9:30 A.M. a 7:00 P.M.
De lunes a sábado. Jornada Continua.
Amplio estacionamiento.
**San Pedro, 300 m oeste de Taco Bell, contiguo a Óptica Rivera. Tel: 233-3309**

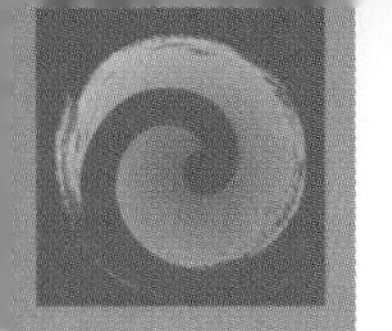

# En la zapatería

**Note.** Mention that *jgo.* in the ad refers to *juego*, used here as matching set for bed linens.

**Expansion.** Bring photos from newspapers/magazines of merchandise available in a department store. Present items with comprehensible input, mentioning prices. Ask students to figure out the price if a *descuento de 10%, 20%, 30%, 50%* were subtracted.

## Las rebajas

*Ana talks to an employee at the mall....*

ANA: Disculpe, señor, ¿en qué tienda puedo comprar unos zapatos bonitos?
INFORMACIÓN: Hay una zapatería muy grande en el segundo piso. Está junto a la farmacia.

*En la zapatería...*

VENDEDORA: ¿Puedo ayudarla en algo?
ANA: Sí, gracias. Deseo unos zapatos negros de tacón alto del número siete y medio.
VENDEDORA: Tengo solamente estos dos modelos de plataforma.
ANA: No me gustan los zapatos de plataforma. ¡Son muy incómodos! Gracias, pero voy a mirar en otros lugares. ¿Dónde hay otra zapatería?

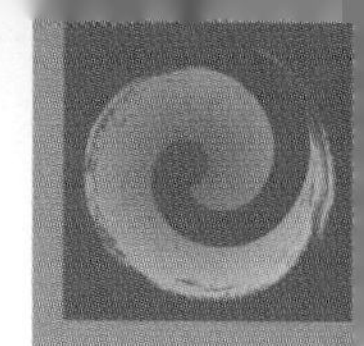

VENDEDORA: En el primer piso hay una zapatería y también hay zapatos muy elegantes en el almacén Samson.
ANA: ¿Dónde hay mejores precios?
VENDEDORA: El almacén Samson tiene zapatos bonitos, pero son muy caros. La zapatería del primer piso tiene zapatos baratos, pero no son elegantes. Nosotros tenemos zapatos bonitos a precios moderados.
ANA: Bueno, muchas gracias.

**A. ¿Comprende Ud.?** Answer the following questions based on the dialog.

1. ¿Qué busca Ana?
2. ¿Qué número de zapato necesita ella?
3. ¿Cuántas zapaterías hay en el centro comercial?
4. ¿Cómo son los zapatos del almacén Samson?

**Answers for A.** 1) *Zapatos.* 2) *El siete y medio.* 3) *Tres.* 4) *Bonitos pero muy caros.*

**B. De compras.** With a classmate, role-play a shopping situation in a department store. One of you is the salesperson, the other a customer wishing to buy something.

MODELO: E1: *Yo busco unos zapatos de tenis.*
E2: *Tengo varios estilos. ¿De qué número?*
E1: *Número ocho.*
E2: …

**C. Entre todos.** In groups of four, discuss your favorite shoe type, size, and price. Look for magazine or newspaper photos to assist you. Name the store(s) you shop at and where they're located.

**D. El arte del regateo.** While traveling in Mexico, you see some **huaraches** (*sandals*) that you must have, at an open-air market. With another student as **el/la vendedor/a,** practice bargaining until you agree on a price. Use expressions like **caro/a** (*expensive*), **barato/a** (*cheap*), **buen precio** (*good price*), etc.

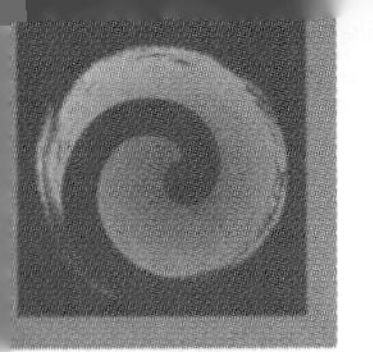

# El verbo *ser*
## (*The verb "to be"*)

**Para averiguar**

1. What does the verb **ser** mean?
2. How do you ask where a friend is from?

- Use the verb **ser** to tell where people are from, what they do, or what they are like.

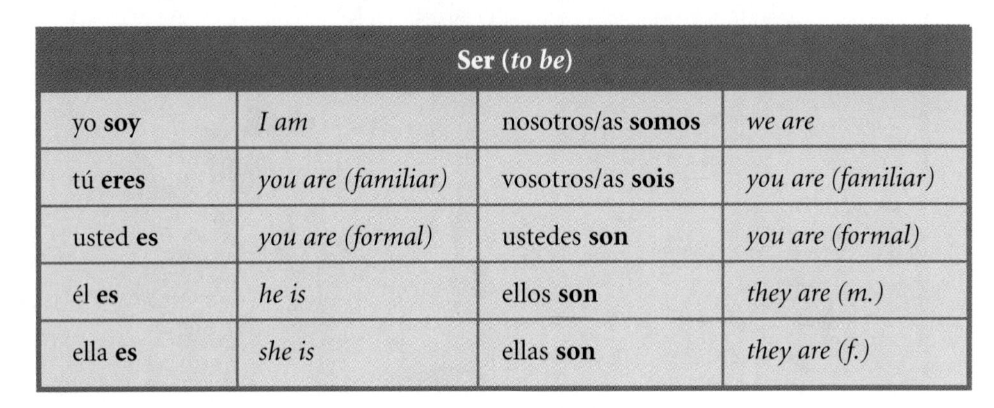

| **Ser** (*to be*) | | | |
|---|---|---|---|
| yo **soy** | *I am* | nosotros/as **somos** | *we are* |
| tú **eres** | *you are (familiar)* | vosotros/as **sois** | *you are (familiar)* |
| usted **es** | *you are (formal)* | ustedes **son** | *you are (formal)* |
| él **es** | *he is* | ellos **son** | *they are (m.)* |
| ella **es** | *she is* | ellas **son** | *they are (f.)* |

—¿De dónde **son** Uds.? — *Where are you from?*
—**Somos** de Miami. — *We're from Miami.*

—¿**Son** estudiantes? — *Are you students?*
—Yo **soy** estudiante pero ella **es** profesora. — *I'm a student but she is a professor.*

—¿Cómo **es** Mary? — *What is Mary like?*
—Mary **es** joven y romántica. — *Mary is young and romantic.*

- Use **ser** with adjectives denoting nationality. Note that Spanish does not capitalize these adjectives.

Marta **es** argentina. — *Marta is Argentinian.*
Pierre **es** francés. — *Pierre is French.*

- Use **ser** with **de** to tell what something is made of or to whom it belongs.

La mochila **es de** piel. — *The backpack is (made) of leather.*
Ese teléfono celular **es del** (de + el) profesor. — *That cell phone belongs to the professor.*

### A lo personal

**A. ¿Quiénes son?** To whom might the following sentences refer? Insert names of someone you know or someone who is famous.

MODELO: Somos estudiantes.
*Mi compañero y yo somos estudiantes.*

1. Es profesor/a.
2. Son conservadores.
3. Es muy tímido.
4. Somos compañeros/as de clase.
5. Son de aquí.
6. Son románticos.

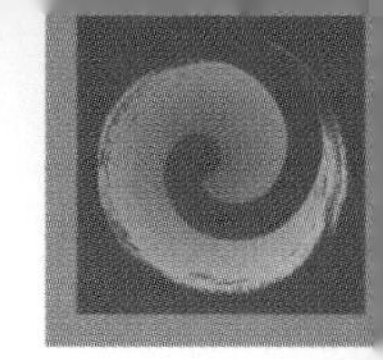

**B. Nacionalidades.** You are at a meeting of international students where all participants are from their nation's capital. Give their nationality and tell where they are from.

| Caracas | Bogotá | La Paz | Buenos Aires | Madrid | Managua | Tegucigalpa |
|---|---|---|---|---|---|---|

MODELO: yo/boliviano
*Yo soy boliviano. Soy de La Paz.*

1. nosotras/colombianas
2. Javier/argentino
3. ellos/españoles
4. ustedes/hondureños
5. María/nicaragüense
6. tú/venezolano

**C. La clase de español.** Describe your Spanish class using the correct form of the verb **ser**. Negate the verb when appropriate.

MODELO: La clase________difícil.
*La clase no es difícil.*

1. La clase________grande.
2. Los estudiantes________simpáticos.
3. Nosotros________estudiantes trabajadores en la clase.
4. El/La profesor/a________muy inteligente.
5. El salón de clase________bonito.
6. Todos nosotros________serios.
7. Yo________perezoso/a.
8. Los libros________interesantes.

**D. Regalos.** Fill in the form of **ser** and an appropriate description to explain why you and your friends need these gifts.

MODELO: Compro un diccionario para Lucía porque ella...
*Compro un diccionario para Lucía porque ella es estudiante de español.*

1. Mi amigo Roberto necesita un reloj porque...
2. Compro un teléfono para Mary porque ella...
3. Gregorio y Daniela necesitan una computadora porque ellos...
4. Alicia desea un libro porque ella...
5. Yo deseo muchas rosas y música suave porque...

**E. ¿Y sus compañeros de clase?** Ask a classmate about himself/herself. Then describe your classmate to the rest of the class.

1. ¿De dónde eres?
2. ¿Eres trabajador/a o perezoso/a?
3. ¿Eres serio/a o cómico/a?
4. ¿Eres tímido/a o extrovertido/a?
5. ¿Eres romántico/a?

Now summarize your similarities and differences. Write down your answers.

MODELO: *Tú eres de Chicago, pero yo soy de Atlanta.* o
*Nosotros somos tímidos/as.*

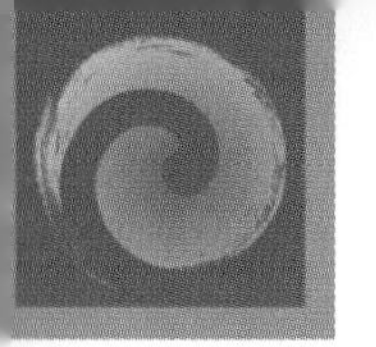

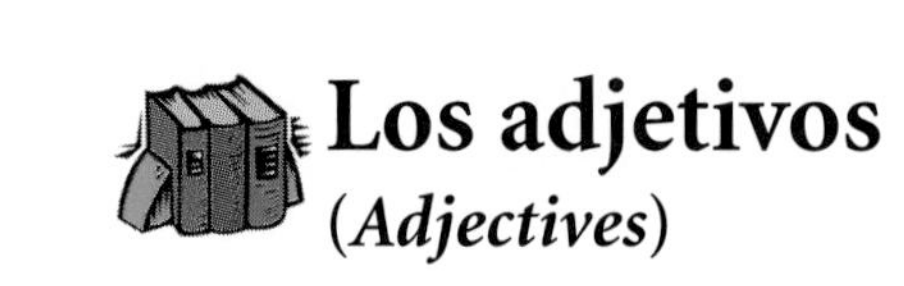

# Los adjetivos
## (*Adjectives*)

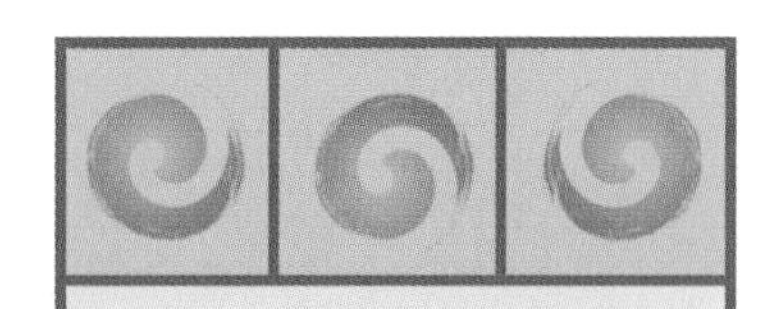

### Para averiguar

1. If the masculine form of an adjective ends in **-o**, what is its feminine form? Which adjectives do not have different masculine and feminine forms?
2. How do you make an adjective plural?
3. Where are most descriptive adjectives placed in relation to the noun they describe?
4. Where do you place adjectives of quantity?

**Follow up.** Have students change the verb and adjective to plural in the following sentences. MODELO: *Soy trabajador. Somos trabajadores.*
1) *Soy serio.* 2) *Eres liberal.*
3) *Ud. es pesimista.* 3) *Ella es rebelde.*
5) *Ella es simpática.* 6) *Soy tímido.*
7) *Ella es generosa.* 8) *Eres tonto.*
Then, have students change the following sentences from plural to singular.
1) *Somos religiosas.* 2) *Uds. son egoístas.* 3) *Ellos son pesimistas.*
4) *Ellas son rebeldes.* 5) *Somos extrovertidos.* 6) *Ellas son interesantes.*
7) *Uds. son inteligentes.*
8) *Somos realistas.*

- In Spanish, adjectives have different forms depending on whether they describe a masculine or a feminine noun, and whether the noun is singular or plural.

| | **Masculine** | **Feminine** |
|---|---|---|
| **singular** | El profesor es **aburrido.** | La clase es **aburrida.** |
| **plural** | Los profesores son **aburridos.** | Las clases son **aburridas.** |

- Generally, as with nouns, adjectives ending in **-o** in the masculine end with **-a** in the feminine. However, adjectives ending in **-ista** have only singular and plural forms.

Mi novi**o** es muy romántic**o**, pero también egoíst**a**.
Mi novi**a** es muy romántic**a**, pero también egoíst**a**.
Mis amig**os** son egoíst**as**.
Mis amig**as** son egoíst**as**.

- Adjectives ending in a consonant or **-e** generally have the same masculine and feminine forms, except for adjectives ending in **-dor, -dón, -ón,** and adjectives of nationality, which add **-a** in the feminine.

Mi profeso**r** es intelectua**l**, pero también pacient**e**.
Mi profesor**a** es intelectua**l**, pero también pacient**e**.

Mi profeso**r** es españo**l** y muy trabaja**dor**.
Mi profesor**a** es españo**la** y muy trabaja**dora**.

- Add **-s** to pluralize adjectives ending in a vowel and **-es** to adjectives ending in a consonant. Possessive adjectives like **mi** (*my*) and **tu** (*your*, familiar) are also made plural by adding **-s**.

—¿Tu**s** clase**s** son buena**s**?
—Mi**s** clase**s** son interesant**es**, pero difícil**es**.

- In Spanish, descriptive adjectives are usually placed after the noun they describe rather than before the noun as in English.

| | |
|---|---|
| Me gustan las clases **fáciles.** | *I like easy classes.* |
| Hay una librería **grande** en la ciudad. | *There is a big bookstore in the city.* |

- Adjectives indicating number or quantity precede the noun.

| | |
|---|---|
| Hay **una** cafetería en el campus. | *There is a cafeteria on campus.* |
| Tengo **muchos** amigos en mis clases. | *I have many friends in my classes.* |

## A lo personal

**A. Novios diferentes.** Isabel and Lázaro are opposites. Describe Isabel based on these statements about Lázaro.

MODELO: Lázaro es tímido.
*Isabel no es tímida; es extrovertida.*

Lázaro es...

1. conservador
2. realista
3. serio
4. muy pesimista
5. conformista
6. aburrido

**B. Los padres y los hijos.** With a classmate, read the article and list all the cognates that you find. Then, discuss whether you agree or disagree with each point by saying: **estoy de acuerdo** or **no estoy de acuerdo**. Finally, try to come up with at least three more items to add to the chart. Then, share your results with other students in your class.

**Warm-up for B.** Ask students to find cognates for *submissive, antisocial, immature, hostile, obsessive, capricious, frustrated.* Then, ask students to explain what parents do to cause these behaviors, according to the article. Introduce *estoy de acuerdo* and *no estoy de acuerdo* as you ask students their opinions about statements made in the article.

### ¿EN QUÉ NOS EQUIVOCAMOS?

Quizás usted no sepa por qué su hijo actúa de determinada manera. Averígüelo con esta tabla. Busque primero la conducta que más se parezca a la de su hijo y luego, revise cuál es su actitud como padre. La clasificación es muy amplia y general, por eso téngala en cuenta sólo como referencia.

| SI LOS PADRES SON | LOS CHICOS PUEDEN SER |
|---|---|
| Muy permisivos | Antisociables. Caprichosos. Incapaces de afrontar responsabilidades y problemas. |
| Sobreprotectores (ansiosos) | Inmaduros. Obsesivos. Angustiados. |
| Incoherentes | Hostiles. Dominantes. |
| Celosos | Agresivos. |
| Despreciativos | Tímidos. Agresivos. Mentirosos, irónicos. Con tendencia a estar a la defensiva. |
| Golpeadores | Agresivos. Hostiles. |
| Muy ambiciosos (Hiperexigentes) | Frustrados. Inmaduros. |
| Rígidos | Excesivamente dóciles. Tímidos, sumisos. |
| Poco afectivos | Pesimistas. Agresivos. Retroceden en su crecimiento. |

**C. Una entrevista.** Use the following questions to interview a classmate.

1. ¿De dónde eres? ¿Cómo eres? ¿Eres extrovertido/a? ¿Eres perezoso/a o trabajador/a? ¿Eres optimista o pesimista? ¿Eres atlético/a?
2. ¿De dónde es tu mejor amigo/a? ¿Cómo es? ¿Es estudiante? ¿Son ustedes muy diferentes? ¿En qué son diferentes?

| | | | | | | |
|---|---|---|---|---|---|---|
| aburrido | inteligente | serio | realista | cómico | trabajador | rebelde |
| perezoso | tímido | simpático | cariñoso | rico | feo | antipático |
| pesimista | liberal | ambicioso | estudioso | optimista | atractivo | |

**D. Yo soy.** From the previous list of words put together three sentences that describe you.

MODELO: *Yo soy optimista, serio y cariñoso.*

**Expansion for D.** Ask the students to use the same list of words to describe the characteristics of a person they would not want for a mate! MODELO: *Ella es pesimista, fea y antipática.*

**E. ¿Quién soy yo?** Write a short description of a famous person, telling where he/she is from, what he/she is like, and what he/she looks like. Then read your description aloud and your classmate will try to guess who it is.

# TEMA 2 En el centro comercial

## ¿Dónde está...?

Suggestion. Explain that ordinal numbers match their noun, e.g., *segundo, segunda, primeros, primeras*. Mention that *primero, tercero* drop *-o* before a masculine, singular noun.

### Necesito información

*Ana asks for directions at the mall....*

ANA: Disculpe, ¿dónde están los baños?
INFORMACIÓN: Están en el primer piso, enfrente de los restaurantes.
ANA: ¿Enfrente del restaurante japonés?
INFORMACIÓN: Sí, exactamente.
ANA: ¿Sabe dónde hay una perfumería?
INFORMACIÓN: Hay una perfumería muy buena en el tercer piso, enfrente del almacén Samson. Tiene que tomar las escaleras eléctricas hasta el tercer piso, doblar a la izquierda y caminar por el lado derecho hasta encontrar la perfumería.
ANA: Muchas gracias.

**A. ¿Qué dice el diálogo?** Answer the following questions based on the dialog.

1. ¿En qué piso está el baño?
2. ¿Qué almacén hay enfrente de la perfumería?
3. ¿En qué piso está la perfumería?
4. ¿Qué tipo de comida hay en el centro comercial?

**Answers for A.** 1) *En el primer piso.* 2) *Almacén Samson.* 3) *En el tercer piso.* 4) *Comida japonesa.*

**B. Un mapa.** Draw a map of your favorite **centro comercial,** labeling the stores by title, such as **zapatería.** Exchange maps with a classmate and ask him/her to give you directions to a particular store.

MODELO: E1: *¿Dónde está la tienda de Disney?*
E2: *Está junto a la zapatería, enfrente del almacén Sears.*

**C. Busco un regalo.** Fill in the blanks according to a gift you wish to buy for a friend.

UD.: Buenos días. Busco un regalo para ____________.
VENDEDOR: ¿Cómo es ____________?
UD.: Es ____________ y ____________.
VENDEDOR: Esto cuesta ____________.
UD.: Bien, me llevo____________.
VENDEDOR: ¿Desea pagar al contado, con cheque o con ____________?
UD.: ____________.

**D. Un viaje a España.** Your aunt, **Tía Juana,** is going to visit relatives in Spain. She wants to take some gifts along. Think of five of your family members and describe a gift for each. Include at least one reason for your choice.

MODELO: Para José… *un libro de automóviles, porque le gusta la mecánica.*

**E. Los libros son buenos regalos.** Prepare your Christmas shopping list for four friends. As you're working in a bookstore, you want to buy books because you receive an employee discount. List the names of four friends, describe their personalities, then write a book title and author that would make the perfect gift. You may wish to include bilingual works—go to the library, a bookstore, or search the Internet for Hispanic authors.

| Nombre | Descripción | Título | Escritor/a |
| --- | --- | --- | --- |
| | | | |
| | | | |
| | | | |
| | | | |

# ABC En la perfumería

**La nueva imagen de la belleza**

**Nueva línea de cosméticos y tratamientos para la piel. Además de estar bella vas a ganar dinero perteneciendo a nuestro selecto grupo de representantes de ventas.**

*Línea Metálica*
*¡25%*
*de descuento con compra al contado!*

## Ana va de compras

*Ana buys perfume for Isabel....*

ANA: Buenos días, señorita.
VENDEDORA: Buenos días. ¿En qué puedo servirle?
ANA: Deseo comprar un regalo para una amiga.
VENDEDORA: ¿Cómo es su amiga?
ANA: Es joven, alegre y bonita.
VENDEDORA: Tengo un perfume de un diseñador francés.
ANA: ¿Qué precio tiene?
VENDEDORA: Cuesta setenta dólares la onza.
ANA: Es muy caro. ¿No hay nada más barato?
VENDEDORA: Los perfumes nacionales son más baratos. Éste cuesta treinta dólares la onza.
ANA: Me lo llevo.
VENDEDORA: ¿Desea pagar al contado, con cheque o con tarjeta de crédito?
ANA: Con mi tarjeta de crédito.
VENDEDORA: ¿Puede firmar aquí, por favor? Gracias. Aquí tiene su recibo.
ANA: Gracias, hasta luego.
VENDEDORA: Adiós, señorita.

**Answers for A.** 1) *Un regalo.* 2) *Joven y bonita.* 3) *Porque es caro.* 4) *30 dólares.* 5) *Con tarjeta de crédito.*

**A. ¿Qué compra Ana?** Answer the following questions based on the dialog.

1. ¿Qué desea comprar Ana?
2. ¿Cómo es la amiga de Ana?
3. ¿Por qué no compra Ana el perfume francés?
4. ¿Cuánto cuesta el perfume nacional?
5. ¿Cómo paga Ana?

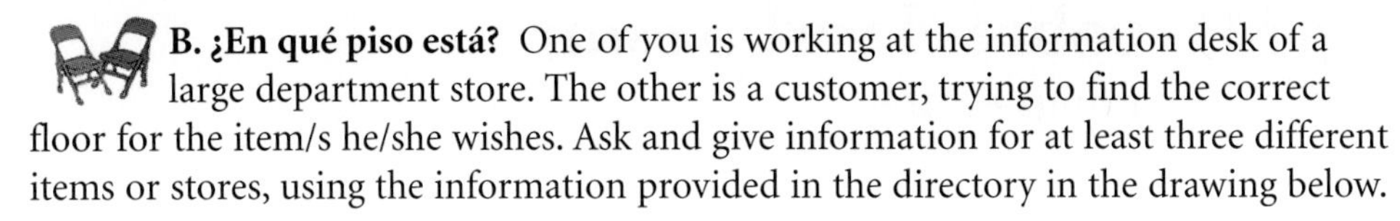

**B. ¿En qué piso está?** One of you is working at the information desk of a large department store. The other is a customer, trying to find the correct floor for the item/s he/she wishes. Ask and give information for at least three different items or stores, using the information provided in the directory in the drawing below.

MODELO: E1: *Por favor, busco un vestido elegante para una fiesta.*
E2: *Los vestidos están en el tercer piso, señorita.*

**C. ¡No se puede regatear aquí!** One of you is a salesclerk at a department store, the other a tourist from Perú. The tourist wants to buy an expensive bottle of perfume, but offers the salesclerk less money than it's worth. Explain that bargaining is not allowed in this store, but that you do have perfumes that are on sale (**de rebajas**). Mention:

- the original price of the perfume
- the amount of the discount
- the price difference between imported and domestic perfumes
- the products currently on sale
- whether or not the tourist purchases the perfume

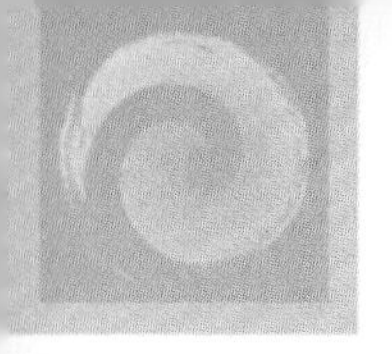

# Más sobre el verbo *estar*
## (*More about* estar)

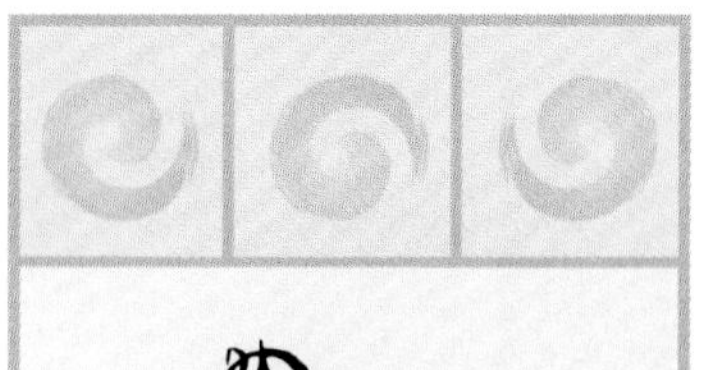

**Para averiguar**

1. What are two ways to say *to be* in Spanish?
2. Which forms of **estar** have written accents?
3. What are two uses of **estar**?

- As you have seen, both **ser** and **estar** mean *to be*. However, these two verbs cannot be used interchangeably in Spanish. Here are some rules that will help you determine when to use **estar**.

- In Lección 1, you learned to use the verb **estar** to describe how someone is feeling.

| | |
|---|---|
| —¿Cómo **estás**? | *How are you?* |
| —**Estoy** un poco cansado. | *I'm a little tired.* |

- Use **estar** to describe mental and physical conditions.

| | |
|---|---|
| —¿Cómo **están** ustedes? | *How are you?* |
| —**Estamos** muy ocupados. | *We are very busy.* |
| —¿**Estás** cansada? | *Are you tired?* |
| —No, **estoy** bien. | *No, I'm fine.* |

- **Estar** is also used with the following words to denote variable conditions.

| | |
|---|---|
| **solo/a** | *alone* |
| **limpio/a** | *clean* |
| **sucio/a** | *dirty* |
| **listo/a** | *ready* |
| **abierto/a** | *open* |
| **cerrado/a** | *closed* |

| | |
|---|---|
| El apartamento **está limpio.** | *The apartment is clean.* |
| La tienda **está cerrada.** | *The store is closed.* |
| Los estudiantes **están listos.** | *The students are ready.* |
| Las mesas **están sucias.** | *The tables are dirty.* |

- Use **estar** to tell where someone or something is.

| | |
|---|---|
| —¿Dónde **están** los baños? | *Where are the bathrooms?* |
| —**Están** enfrente del restaurante. | *They are across from the restaurant.* |
| —¿Dónde **estás** ahora? | *Where are you now?* |
| —**Estoy** en el jardín. | *I am in the garden.* |
| —¿Dónde **está** Amparo? | *Where is Amparo?* |
| —Amparo **está** en Valencia. | *Amparo is in Valencia.* |

## A lo personal

**A. ¿Cómo están?** Use **estar** with a logical adjective from the list below to describe the people or items located in parentheses.

solo/a, contento/a, cerrado/a, sucio/a, listo/a, enfermo/a, ocupado/a, nervioso/a, cansado/a

MODELO: Quiero descansar un poco. (yo)
*Yo estoy cansado.*

1. Trabajamos mucho en este momento. (nosotros)
2. Hay un examen hoy. (Uds.)
3. El examen no es muy difícil. (los estudiantes)
4. Necesitas ir al hospital. (tú)
5. Mi compañera de cuarto no tiene familia. (ella)

**B. ¿Dónde está? ¿Cómo está?** Say where the person is and how he/she feels in the following circumstances. Watch the verb forms for clues to the subject. You can use some adjectives more than once.

MODELO: Compro perfume. El perfume es barato.
*Estoy en la perfumería. Estoy contenta.*

1. Tomas un examen de español. El examen es difícil.
2. Miran la televisión. No tienen energía.
3. Bailamos y conversamos. Hay muchos amigos.
4. Siempre escuchas a la profesora, pero el álgebra es imposible de comprender.
5. Miro zapatos, anillos y libros que deseo. No tengo dinero.

**C. Estamos...** Complete each of the following sentences so that they reflect how you feel in different situations and at different times. Be as creative as possible!

1 Estoy muy triste cuando...
2. Mis amigos y yo estamos muy contentos cuando...
3. Yo estoy un poco nervioso/a cuando...
4. Yo estoy furioso/a con mis amigos cuando...
5. Mis amigas están aburridas cuando...
6. Mis padres y yo estamos preocupados cuando...
7. Estoy muy confundido/a cuando...
8. Mi novia/o y yo estamos ocupados cuando...

**D. Entrevista.** Interview a classmate using the following questions, then switch roles.

1. ¿Cómo estás hoy? ¿Qué días estás muy ocupado/a? ¿Cuándo tienes tiempo libre?
2. ¿Estás nervioso/a cuando estás solo/a? ¿Estás triste cuando no estás con tus amigos?
3. ¿Dónde está tu restaurante favorito? ¿Está cerrado los domingos? ¿Cuándo está abierto?
4. ¿Hay un centro comercial cerca de tu casa/apartamento? ¿Siempre estás en el centro comercial en tu tiempo libre? ¿Cuándo estás en el centro comercial?
5. ¿Hay una cafetería en tu campus? ¿Dónde está? Cuando estás en la cafetería, ¿normalmente estás solo/a o con amigos?

# Ser y estar
## (Meanings of "to be")

**Para averiguar**

1. What does **¿Cómo están tus padres?** mean?
2. What are four uses of **ser**?
3. What does **¿Cómo son tus padres?** mean?

- Although **ser** and **estar** both mean *to be,* the two verbs are not interchangeable. Each verb has its own meaning.

You have just learned to use **estar**:

- to describe mental and physical conditions

¿Por qué **estás** triste? — *Why are you sad?*
**Estoy** nervioso. — *I'm nervous.*

- to describe variable conditions

¿La tienda **está** abierta o cerrada? — *Is the store open or closed?*
El agua **está** sucía. — *The water is dirty.*

- to tell where something or someone is

Mi apartamento **está** cerca de aquí. — *My apartment is near here.*

Use **ser**:

- to identify people or things

—¿Quién **es** tu profesora? — *—Who's your teacher?*
—**Es** la profesora López. — *—It's Professor López.*

- to describe general characteristics such as personality and physical traits

—¿Cómo **es** Alicia? — *—What does Alicia look like?*
—**Es** bonita y joven. — *—She's pretty and young.*

- to tell/ask the time or say/ask when something occurs

¿Qué hora **es**? — *What time is it?*
¿A qué hora **es** la clase? — *At what time is the class?*

- to tell where someone is from

—¿De dónde **eres**? — *—Where are you from?*
—**Soy** de los Estados Unidos. — *—I'm from the U.S.*

- to tell to whom something belongs or what it is made of

—¿De quién **es** el libro? — *—Whose book is it?*
—**Es** el libro del profesor de español. — *—It's the Spanish teacher's book.*

—¿De qué **son** los zapatos? — *—What are the shoes made of?*
—**Son** de piel. — *—They're made of leather.*

- Some adjectives change meaning depending on whether they are used with **ser** or **estar**. Here are some examples:

| | | | |
|---|---|---|---|
| **estar** aburrido | *to be bored* | **ser** aburrido | *to be boring* |
| **estar** listo | *to be ready* | **ser** listo | *to be clever* |

- Compare these sentences.

| | |
|---|---|
| ¿Cómo **está** tu padre? | *How is your father doing?* |
| ¿Cómo **es** tu padre? | *What is your father like?* |
| Tu madre **está** bonita. | *Your mother looks pretty. (on a specific occasion)* |
| Tu madre **es** bonita. | *Your mother is pretty. (She's a pretty woman in general.)* |

## A lo personal

**A. ¿Dónde está? ¿Cómo es?** A new friend has invited you to visit and then to go shopping. Complete each question with the correct form of **ser** or **estar**.

**Follow up for A.** Have students work in pairs to create a role-play using the questions. One student calls the other about going shopping.

1. ¿Dónde ________ tu apartamento?
2. ¿ ________ cerca o lejos del centro comercial?
3. ¿ ________ un centro comercial grande o pequeño?
4. ¿Cómo ________ las tiendas, interesantes o aburridas?
5. ¿ ________ tú en el apartamento ahora?
6. ¿Qué hora ________?
7. ¿Hasta cuándo ________ abiertas las tiendas?
8. Puedo ________ en tu casa en una hora.
9. ¿ ________ tú listo ahora?

**B. ¿Dónde? ¿De dónde? ¿Cómo?** Use the correct form of **ser** or **estar** to finish these thoughts.

1. Estos perfumes ________ de Francia.
2. Nosotras ________ en una perfumería cara.
3. Mañana ________ el cumpleaños de mi amiga Isabel.
4. Yo ________ preocupada porque necesito un regalo especial para ella.
5. Ella ________ una mujer muy inteligente y alegre.
6. Hoy, ella ________ enferma y ________ en casa.
7. El novio de Isabel ________ muy romántico.
8. Él compra rosas que ________ rojas y bonitas.
9. El regalo de cumpleaños ________ un anillo.
10. El anillo ________ de oro.
11. ¡Isabel ________ muy contenta!

**C. ¿Ser o estar?** Read the question and determine why **ser** or **estar** is used. Then interview a classmate using the questions.

1. ¿De dónde eres? ¿Cuántos son Uds. en tu familia? ¿Cómo son tus padres? ¿Cómo están?
2. ¿Quién es tu mejor amigo/a? ¿De dónde es? ¿Cómo es? ¿Cómo está? ¿Dónde está ahora?
3. ¿Qué días estás en clase? ¿Cómo son tus profesores?
4. ¿Está tu apartamento/casa/cuarto cerca de aquí? ¿Es un lugar cómodo? ¿Es agradable?

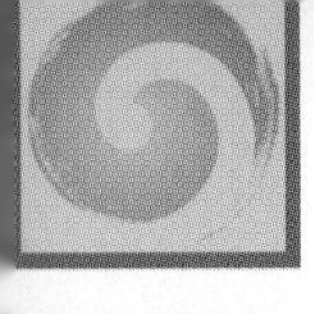

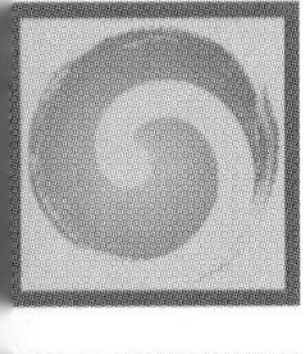

# Vocabulario

## TEMA 1

### Las tiendas

**Sustantivos**

| | |
|---|---|
| **el almacén** | *department store* |
| **el anillo** | *ring* |
| **el billete** | *bill (currency)* |
| **las botas** | *boots* |
| **los calcetines** | *socks* |
| **el cambio** | *change* |
| **las compras** | *purchases* |
| **el/la dependiente/a** | *salesperson* |
| **el dólar** | *dollar* |
| **el/la escritor/a** | *writer* |
| **el estilo** | *style* |
| **las medias** | *stockings* |
| **el piso** | *floor* |
| **la pulsera** | *bracelet* |
| **las rebajas** | *sales* |
| **el regalo** | *gift* |
| **el reloj** | *watch, clock* |
| **las sandalias** | *sandals* |
| **el tacón** | *heel* |
| **la talla** | *size* |
| **la tienda** | *store* |
| **la zapatería** | *shoe store* |
| **el zapato** | *shoe* |

**Verbos**

| | |
|---|---|
| **ayudar** | *to help* |
| **buscar** | *to look for* |
| **comprar** | *to buy* |
| **desear** | *to wish* |
| **ir** | *to go* |
| **mirar** | *to look (at)* |
| **pagar** | *to pay* |

**Adjetivos**

| | |
|---|---|
| **alto/a** | *tall* |
| **barato/a** | *inexpensive* |
| **bonito/a** | *pretty* |
| **hablador/a** | *talkative* |
| **incómodo/a** | *uncomfortable* |
| **joven** | *young* |
| **negro/a** | *black* |
| **puntual** | *punctual* |
| **trabajador/a** | *hard-working* |

**Otras expresiones**

| | |
|---|---|
| **aquí** | *here* |
| **¿Cuánto/a?** | *How much?* |
| **al contado** | *in cash* |
| **¿En qué puedo servirle?** | *How can I help you?* |
| **éste/a** | *this one* |
| **éstos/as** | *these ones* |

## TEMA 2

### En el centro comercial

**Sustantivos**

| | |
|---|---|
| **el baño** | *bathroom* |
| **la calle** | *street* |
| **el centro** | *center* |
| **el cheque** | *check* |
| **el cumpleaños** | *birthday* |
| **el deporte** | *sport* |
| **la dirección** | *direction, address* |
| **el/la diseñador/a** | *designer* |
| **la escalera** | *stairs* |
| **la fiesta** | *party* |
| **el lado** | *side* |
| **el motivo** | *motive, purpose* |
| **los muebles** | *furniture* |
| **la mujer** | *woman* |
| **el/la niño/a** | *child* |
| **la oficina** | *office* |
| **la peluquería** | *beauty salon* |
| **el perfume** | *perfume* |
| **el/la primo/a** | *cousin* |
| **el recibo** | *receipt* |
| **el refresco** | *soda* |
| **la ropa** | *clothing* |
| **la tarjeta de crédito** | *credit card* |
| **el televisor** | *television set* |

**Verbos**

| | |
|---|---|
| **caminar** | *to walk* |
| **costar (ue)** | *to cost* |
| **doblar** | *to turn* |
| **encontrar (ue)** | *to find* |
| **firmar** | *to sign* |
| **llevar** | *to take along, carry* |
| **saber** | *to know* |

**Adjetivos**

| | |
|---|---|
| **alegre** | *happy* |
| **blanco/a** | *white* |
| **deportivo/a** | *sport* |
| **derecho/a** | *right* |

**Otras expresiones**

| | |
|---|---|
| **a la izquierda (de)** | *to the left (of)* |
| **cerca de** | *near* |
| **enfrente de** | *in front (of), across from* |
| **junto a** | *next to* |
| **por favor** | *please* |
| **tu** | *your* |

# Reunión A

**A escuchar.** **La fiesta de cumpleaños de Isabel.** After listening to the conversation, complete the following sentences.

1. La fiesta de cumpleaños es para __________.
2. Mary vive en la calle ____________.
3. Su casa es ____________ y ____________.
4. El teléfono de Mary es el 5-_________-42-________.

**Tapescript for A escuchar. La fiesta de cumpleaños de Isabel.**
MARY: Lázaro, el sábado hay una fiesta en mi casa. Es el cumpleaños de Isabel.
LÁZARO: ¡Qué bien! ¿Dónde está tu casa?
MARY: En la calle Margarita número ochenta y cinco. Está cerca del almacén Samson.
LÁZARO: ¿Cómo es tu casa?
MARY: Mi casa es blanca y pequeña.
LÁZARO: ¿Cuál es tu teléfono?
MARY: Cinco, veintitrés, cuarenta y dos, treinta y uno.
LÁZARO: Gracias, ¿puedo llevar algo?
MARY: Sí, ¿puedes comprar los refrescos?
LÁZARO: Con mucho gusto. Nos vemos el sábado.

**Answers for A escuchar.**
1) *Isabel.* 2) *Margarita.* 3) *Blanca, grande.* 4) *23, 31.*

**A conversar.** You and two classmates are planning a birthday party for a friend. Discuss where the party will take place (address, description of house), the date and time and possible gifts.

**¿Lo sabía?** Look at the following brochure on establishing credit. Can you find any cognates? Can you identify the main points of this brochure? Who is it for? What type of person may benefit from this type of advice? How much information can you understand without consulting your dictionary?

## CÓMO ESTABLECER BUEN CRÉDITO

**El buen crédito es importante**

Le ayuda a:

- solicitar un préstamo
- comprar artículos importantes a crédito
- alquilar un apartamento
- financiar un automóvil
- conseguir una hipoteca
- establecer cuentas con compañías de servicios públicos
- y hasta a conseguir un empleo

**Cuatro Pasos Para Establecer Buen Crédito**

**1.** Comience con una cuenta de cheques. Esto ayuda a probar su responsabilidad financiera y es una forma conveniente de pagar sus deudas.
**2.** Si tiene ingresos seguros y vive en la misma zona desde hace un año o más, trate de solicitar crédito con los comerciantes locales.
**3.** Consiga una tarjeta de crédito asegurada. Estas tarjetas son respaldadas por el dinero que Ud. tiene en el banco. Después de un año, puede pedir una tarjeta no asegurada.
**4.** Solicite que un amigo con buen crédito sea co-firmante de su solicitud de crédito. Después de un año, Ud. puede solicitar crédito sólo a su nombre.

**A buscar.** Can you find any information (in Spanish) on the Internet regarding bank, loan, or credit card applications? You can look for this type of application printed in Spanish at your bank or at local stores and bring them to class to compare with your classmates' findings. Look also in magazines and newspapers.

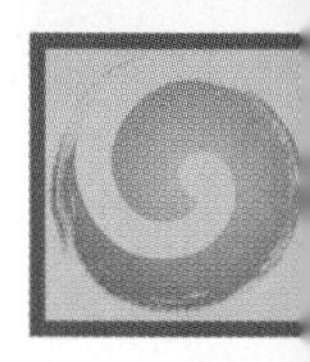
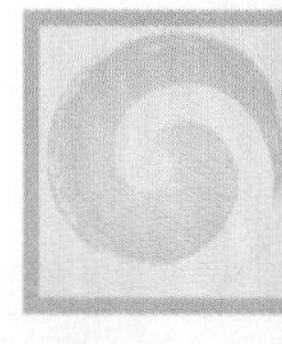
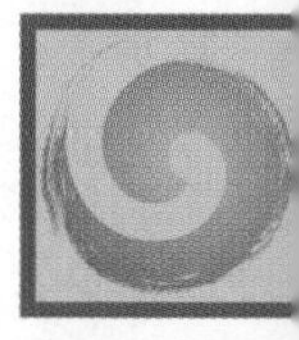
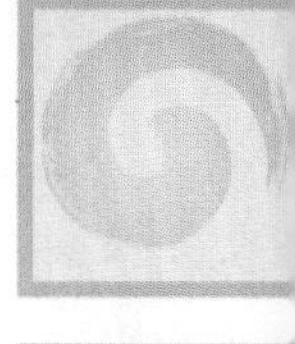
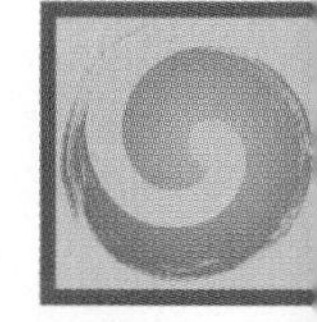
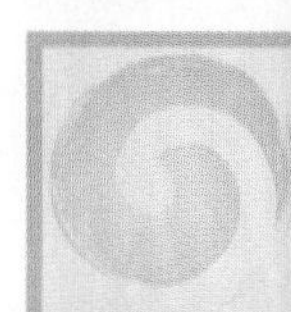

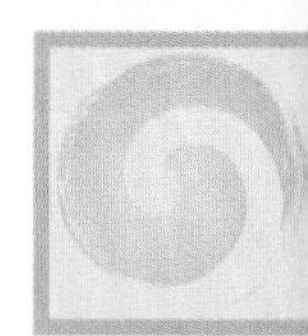
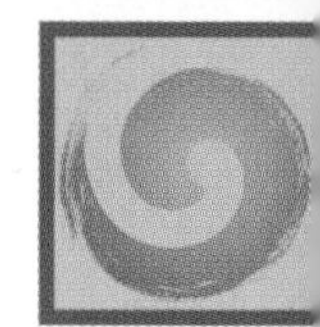
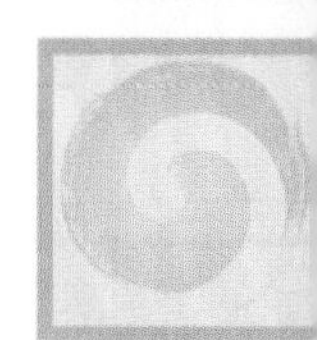
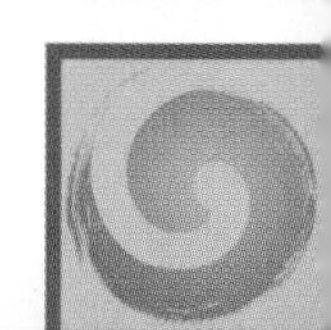

# TEMA 3 De compras

## De tienda en tienda

### Carlos llama por teléfono a la pastelería

*Carlos calls the pastry shop to place an order....*

EMPLEADO: Pastelería Ilusión, a sus órdenes.
CARLOS: Disculpe, deseo comprar un pastel.
EMPLEADO: Claro, ¿para cuántas personas?
CARLOS: Para treinta personas.
EMPLEADO: ¿De vainilla o de chocolate?
CARLOS: De chocolate.
EMPLEADO: ¿Para cuándo lo quiere?
CARLOS: Para el sábado por la mañana.
EMPLEADO: Muy bien. Son cincuenta dólares.
CARLOS: Solamente tengo treinta dólares. ¿Me lo puede dejar más barato?
EMPLEADO: Lo siento, señor. Nuestros precios son fijos, pero hay pasteles más baratos en el supermercado que está cerca del centro comercial.
CARLOS: ¿Tienen pastelería?
EMPLEADO: Sí, la sección de pastelería está cerca de la fruta, al lado del teléfono público.
CARLOS: Gracias.

**A. ¿Comprende Ud.?** Answer the following questions based on the dialog.

1. ¿Por qué llama Carlos a la pastelería?
2. ¿Para cuándo necesita Carlos el pastel?
3. ¿Por qué no compra Carlos el pastel en la pastelería?
4. ¿Cuántas personas hay en la fiesta de Carlos?
5. ¿Qué tipo de pastel busca Carlos?
6. ¿Dónde hay pasteles más baratos?

**Answers for A.** 1) *Para comprar un pastel.* 2) *Para el sábado.* 3) *Porque es muy caro.* 4) *Treinta.* 5) *De chocolate.* 6) *En el supermercado.*

**B. De compras.** Match the store with the items to be purchased.

| | |
|---|---|
| 1. piña | a. pastelería |
| 2. bistec | b. carnicería |
| 3. pastel | c. tortillería |
| 4. pan | d. panadería |
| 5. tortillas de maíz | e. frutería |

**C. No hay supermercado.** One of you has always lived in the United States, in a big city, where you shop at the **supermercado**; you are visiting a friend who is from a small town in Colombia, where shopping is done at small specialty stores. Role-play a situation where the person from Colombia explains to the other where to go to buy different items.

MODELO: E1: *¿Dónde compras el bistec?*
E2: *Yo compro el bistec en la carnicería.*

**Suggestion for C.** Present other *-ería* words, such as *lechería, cervecería, peluquería*. You may also mention that the person associated is usually an *-ero/a* word, as in *zapatero, peluquera*.

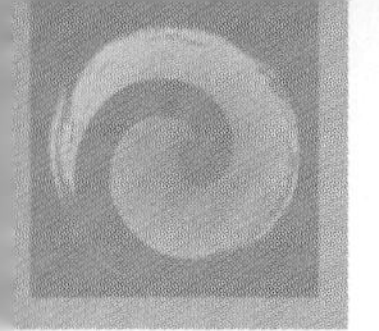

# La comida

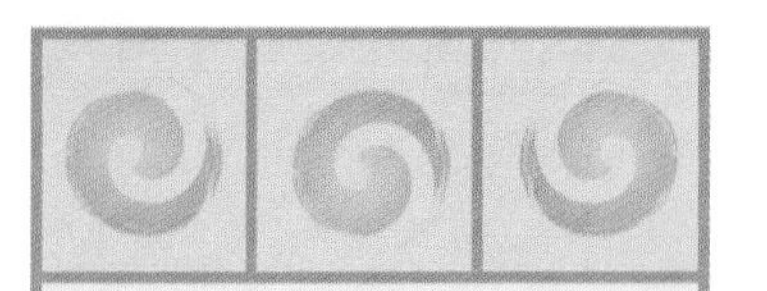

**¡ojo!**

Vocabulary for food varies from one Spanish-speaking country to another. In Spain, a **tortilla** is made of eggs (*omelet*), and potatoes are **patatas**. Depending on where you are, bananas might be **plátanos** or **guineos**. The best advice is to ask how something is said locally. The **ticos** (Costa Ricans), for example, call strawberries **frutillas**, not **fresas**.

**Variation.** Introduce *kilos* as the weight measurement in Hispanic countries, explaining that a *kilo* is equivalent to 2.2 pounds. Have students read the dialog again, correcting prices and weights to correspond to these measurements. Ask several students how much they weigh in pounds and how much that would be in *kilos*. Be careful to choose students of average/normal weight.

## ¿No hay nada más barato?

*Mary is shopping at the fish shop....*

MARY: Señor, ¿puede decirme cuánto cuesta la libra de camarones?
EMPLEADO: Con mucho gusto. Diez dólares la libra.
MARY: ¡Qué caros! ¿No me los puede dejar más baratos?
EMPLEADO: Lo siento, no puedo.
MARY: Entonces, ¿no tiene algo más barato?
EMPLEADO: Sí, tenemos salmón. Cuesta solamente cuatro dólares con cincuenta centavos la libra.
MARY: Necesito quince libras, ¿no hay descuento por esa cantidad?
EMPLEADO: Bueno, por quince libras le voy a hacer el diez por ciento de descuento.

**A. ¿Comprende Ud.?** Answer these questions with information from the dialog.

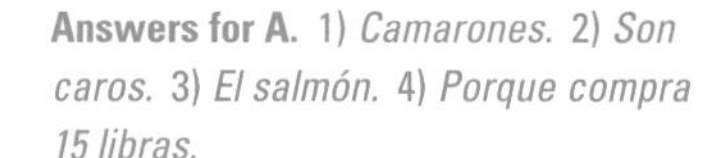
**Answers for A.** 1) *Camarones.* 2) *Son caros.* 3) *El salmón.* 4) *Porque compra 15 libras.*

1. ¿Qué tipo de comida busca Ana?
2. ¿Qué problema hay con el precio?
3. ¿Qué es más barato que los camarones?
4. ¿Por qué hay un descuento en la compra de Ana?

**B. A comer.** Plan a shopping list for your weekend picnic with a classmate. Then decide who will bring each item and the quantity needed.

MODELO: E1: *Necesitamos tres papas y dos cebollas.*
E2: *Yo compro las papas.*

**C. ¿Alguien o nadie? ¿Siempre o nunca?** Prepare a list of food items. In groups of four, ask if someone (**alguien**) eats these items. If the answer is nobody, write **nadie** next to that item. Then inquire whether it is eaten always (**siempre**) or never (**nunca**).

MODELO: E1: *¿Alguien come pescado?*
E2: *Yo nunca como pescado.*
E3: *Yo siempre como pescado.*
E4: *Nadie en mi familia come pescado.*

**D. Una cena elegante.** You and a friend are on the phone planning an elegant dinner party. You have a budget of $100. Decide what you need to buy, which stores you will shop at to buy everything, and who will be responsible for doing it. Don't forget to tell how much you are spending on each item.

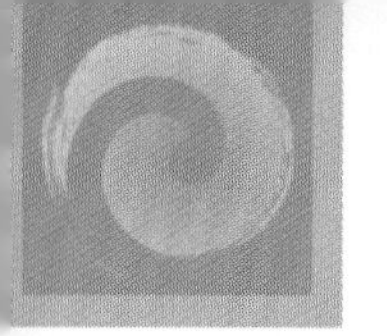

# Preposiciones de lugar
## (*Prepositions of location*)

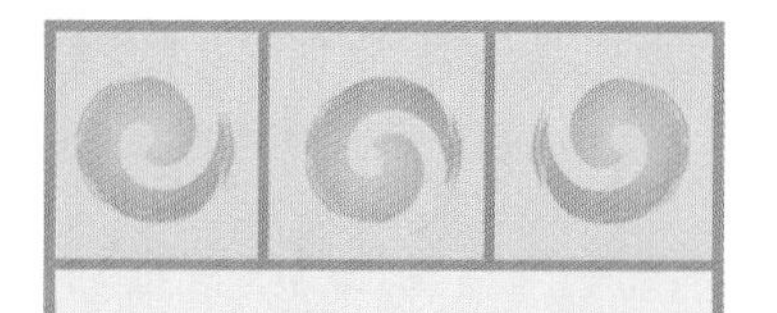

**Para averiguar**

1. What happens to **de** when it is followed by the masculine definite article **el**?
2. Which of the two *to be* verbs in Spanish, **ser** or **estar**, is used with prepositions of place?

- The following prepositions indicate where something is in relation to something else:

| | |
|---|---|
| **con** | *with* |
| **en** | *in/on* |
| **entre** | *between/among* |
| **cerca de** | *close to* |
| **lejos de** | *far from* |
| **al lado de** | *next to* |
| **debajo de** | *under* |
| **delante de** | *ahead of* |
| **enfrente de** | *across from, in front of* |
| **dentro de** | *inside of* |
| **detrás de** | *behind* |
| **encima de** | *on top of* |
| **alrededor de** | *around* |

- When the definite article **el** (*the*) follows the preposition **de**, they contract to form **del**. **De** does not contract with **la**, **los**, or **las**.

| | |
|---|---|
| Mi casa está cerca **del** centro comercial. | *My house is near the mall.* |
| Nuestro apartamento está lejos **de la** casa. | *Our apartment is far from the house.* |
| El televisor está encima **de la** mesa. | *The television is on top of the table.* |
| La casa **del** perro está al lado de mi casa. | *The dog's house is next to my house.* |
| La sala está cerca **del** dormitorio. | *The den is near the bedroom.* |

- Prepositions of placement use the verb **estar** to indicate location.

| | |
|---|---|
| El libro **está dentro de** la mochila. | *The book is inside the backpack.* |
| El televisor **está encima de** la mesa. | *The television is on top of the table.* |
| La casa del perro **está al lado de** mi casa. | *The dog's house is next to my house.* |
| La sala **está cerca del** dormitorio. | *The den is near the bedroom.* |

## A lo personal

**A. ¿Dónde están?** Tell where the following are.

MODELO: Mi casa/apartamento — la universidad.
*Mi casa **está cerca de** la universidad.*

1. mi centro comercial favorito — mi casa/apartamento
2. mi casa — mi jardín
3. la clase de español — la cafetería
4. el escritorio del/de la profesor/a — los pupitres de los estudiantes
5. el primer piso — el segundo piso
6. la Universidad de California — la Universidad de Nueva York
7. los libros — la mochila
8. la biblioteca — los libros
9. los estudiantes — la universidad
10. las tiendas — el centro comercial

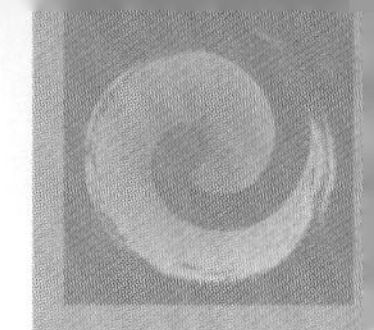

**B. ¿Cuál es su relación?** Describe the location of these items in relation to the others.

MODELO: librería — almacén
*La librería está al lado del almacén.*

1. restaurante — tienda de ropa elegante para damas
2. el coche rojo — la joyería
3. la librería escolar — la zapatería
4. los niños — el coche verde
5. la carnicería — la pescadería
6. el coche verde — el almacén
7. el dinero — el coche rojo
8. la zapatería — la carnicería

**C. ¿Dónde?** Use elements from the columns below to explain the location of the items in the first column in relation to those in the third column, to describe where different things are at in your house.

| | | |
|---|---|---|
| el televisor | debajo de | el estante |
| el estéreo | encima de | la puerta |
| los libros | cerca de | las ventanas |
| la computadora | detrás de | el escritorio |
| las plantas | lejos de | el armario |
| la mesa | enfrente de | el dormitorio |
| las sillas | al lado de | la sala |

**D. Tu ciudad.** Work with a classmate to draw a map of a commercial street that you both know in your area. Label the stores and then take turns describing the locations of the shops.

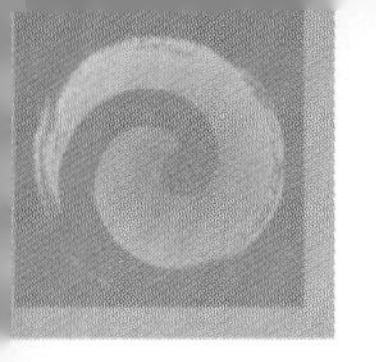

# Expresiones afirmativas y negativas
## (*Affirmative and negative expressions*)

**Para averiguar**

1. What is the antonym of **algo**, **alguien**, **alguno**, **también**, and **siempre**?
2. When a negative expression follows the verb, what must precede the verb?
3. What happens to **alguno** and **ninguno** before singular, masculine nouns?
4. What usually happens to the plural ending of **algunos/as** when they are put into the negative?

- Unlike English, Spanish has double negatives. When negative expressions are placed after the verb, **no** must be placed immediately before the verb. **No** is *not* required when a negative precedes the verb.

| Afirmativas | | Negativas | |
|---|---|---|---|
| **algo** | *something* | **nada** | *nothing* |
| **alguien** | *someone* | **nadie** | *nobody* |
| **alguno/a/os/as** | *some/any* | **ninguno/a** | *none, not one* |
| **también** | *also* | **tampoco** | *neither* |
| **siempre** | *always* | **nunca** | *never* |
| **y...o** | *and...or* | **ni...ni** | *neither...nor* |
| **a veces** | *sometimes* | | |

—¿Desea Ud. comprar **algo**? — *Do you want to buy something?*
—**No** deseo comprar **nada,** gracias. — *I don't want to buy anything, thank you.*

—¿Desea Ud. mirar **algo**? — *Do you want to look at something?*
—**No** deseo mirar **nada, tampoco.** — *I don't want to look at anything either.*

—¿Con quién hablas? — *With whom are you speaking?*
—**No** hablo con **nadie**. — *I'm not talking with anybody.*
—Entonces, ¿quién habla? — *Who's talking then?*
—**Nadie** habla. Es la televisión. — *No one is talking. It's the TV.*

- **Alguno** and **ninguno** must agree in number and gender with the noun they describe. They become **algún** and **ningún** before masculine singular nouns. **Ninguno/a** is rarely used in the plural.

**Algunos** estudiantes están en la cafetería. — *Some students are at the cafeteria.*
**No** hay **ningún** estudiante en la clase. — *There aren't any students in class.*
**No** tengo **ninguna** idea. — *I don't have any idea.*

## A lo personal

**A. La clienta vieja.** Oh no, she's back! Doña Gloria has shopped in Don Ramón's market for years. How would he respond to her complaints?

MODELO: —*Nunca* hay carne a buen precio.
—*Siempre hay carne a buen precio.*

1. *Nunca* hay *nadie* para llevar las compras al carro.
2. Los precios *siempre* son altos.
3. *No* hay *ninguna* fruta tropical. (¡OJO!)
4. Hay *algunos* insectos en la fruta.
5. *También* el pan está viejo.
6. *Alguien* necesita abrir otro mercado más moderno.

**B. Diálogo.** Complete the following conversation between Ana María (A) and Roberto (R) with logical affirmative or negative expressions in the correct form.

A: Yo necesito ________ cosas del supermercado. ¿Tú necesitas ________?
R: No necesito ________, gracias. Pero, deseo comer algo especial. No sé qué…
A: Puedo comprar ________ fresas o bananas.
R: No, no me gustan ________ las fresas ________ las bananas. Deseo ________ dulce (*sweet*).
A: Tal vez un pastel.
R: No, ________ me gustan los pasteles. Tienen muchas calorías.
A: ¡Eres imposible! ¡No hay ________ como tú! Entonces, no te compro ________.

**C. Contradicciones.** Ricardo always contradicts Alicia. How would he respond to her statements?

MODELO: *Siempre* compras ropa fea.
*Nunca compro ropa fea.*

1. No tengo *nada* elegante que llevar a la fiesta.
2. *Nunca* estoy en las tiendas.
3. Necesito *algunas* blusas.
4. *A veces* compro *algo* para Ricardo.
5. *Nunca* uso tu ropa.
6. *Alguien* desea botas de piel (*leather*).
7. *Siempre* tienes *algunas* manchas (*stains*) en las camisas.
8. *Tampoco* tienes zapatos elegantes.

**D. Busca un regalo.** Complete the following conversation between Alfonso and Javier with logical affirmative or negative expressions in the correct form.

A: ¿Buscas algo especial en las tiendas?
J: Sí, busco ________ regalos para tu hermana, Liliana. Mañana es su cumpleaños.
A: Eso es difícil. Liliana ya tiene de todo. No necesita ________.
J: Entonces buscamos ________ cómico. ¿Le gustan los deportes?
A: ¡No! No le gusta ________ deporte, ¡ ________ para mirar ________ para practicar!
J: Pues, compramos dos entradas para el partido de fútbol del domingo. Ella puede invitar a ________.
A: Ella no tiene ________ amiga interesada en el fútbol.
J: ¡Por eso! Ella no desea ir, ni sus amigas, ________. Pero tú deseas ir, y yo ________.
A: ¡Ay, Javier! No hay ________ como tú!

**E. En mi familia.** Change the italicized words to describe what you, your friends, and your family do.

1. Yo *siempre* compro *flores en la floristería.*
2. *Algunos amigos* desean comprar pizza. (¡OJO!)
3. *Todos los días* mi mamá prepara *pan fresco.*
4. *Nunca* comemos en *la cafetería de la universidad.*
5. Mis padres preparan *algo* especial *los domingos.*
6. *Nunca* hay *nada* de comer en *mi refrigerador.*
7. *Siempre* hay *cerveza y champán* en mi refrigerador *también.*

# TEMA 4 La ropa

## La moda personal

| *Colores* |
|---|
| *rojo* |
| *azul* |
| *verde* |
| *amarillo* |
| *blanco* |
| *negro* |

**Note.** Point out to students that purse is also translated as *bolsa* in some Spanish-speeaking areas.

| *Más colores* |
|---|
| *rosa/rosado* |
| *morado/violeta* |
| *marrón/café* |
| *azul claro* |
| *azul marino* |
| *gris* |
| *anaranjado* |
| *granate* |

### Isabel compra un vestido de fiesta

ISABEL: Perdone, ¿tiene vestidos de fiesta de color rojo?
VENDEDORA: ¿De qué talla?
ISABEL: La talla ocho, por favor.
VENDEDORA: ¿Le gustan los vestidos cortos o largos?
ISABEL: Me gustan los cortos.
VENDEDORA: ¿Le gusta este vestido? Es muy bonito y además está rebajado al cincuenta por ciento.
ISABEL: ¡Sí, me gusta mucho! Aquí tiene mi tarjeta de crédito.
VENDEDORA: Haga el favor de firmar aquí. Gracias, aquí tiene el recibo.

**A. ¿Qué compra Isabel?** Answer the following questions based on the dialog.

1. ¿De qué color es el vestido que desea ver Isabel?
2. ¿Qué talla necesita Isabel?
3. ¿Desea un vestido largo o corto?
4. ¿Cuánto descuento tiene el vestido que compra Isabel?

**Answers for A.** 1) *Rojo.* 2) *Talla 8.* 3) *Corto.* 4) *El 50%.*

**B. Comprando ropa.** With a classmate create a dialog in which one of you is the salesperson and the other is shopping for a particular clothing item. Model your conversation after the dialog at the beginning of this section.

**C. ¿Cuál es?** Match a clothing item from the list with the appropriate sentence.

| | |
|---|---|
| 1. En diciembre en Nueva York se necesita __________. | a. una sudadera |
| 2. En julio en Acapulco se necesita __________. | b. un traje de baño |
| 3. Por las mañanas para correr, uso __________. | c. un bolso |
| 4. De mi dormitorio al baño, uso __________. | d. un abrigo |
| 5. El hombre de negocios usa __________ en la oficina. | e. una bata |
| 6. Tengo mi dinero en __________. | f. un traje |

**D. ¿Le gusta?** As a salesperson in a store working on commision, you are eager to sell as much as possible to your customer. Show your customer various items, always asking **¿Le gusta(n)?** A classmate, as the customer, will respond with **(No) me gusta(n)**. A third student will be the customer's friend, also asked his/her opinion with **¿Te gusta(n)?**

MODELO: E1: Señor(ita), ¿le gusta la camisa/falda?
E2: *Me gusta el color. ¿Te gusta, ______?*
E3: *Sí, es muy bonita.*

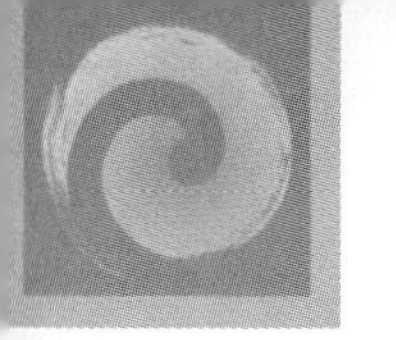

# ABC Problemas con las compras

Estos pantalones me quedan estrechos.

Esta blusa me queda ancha.

## Isabel cambia el vestido rojo

*Isabel exchanges her dress after she finds a stain on it....*

ISABEL: Señorita, deseo cambiar este vestido, por favor.
VENDEDORA: ¿Por qué?
ISABEL: Porque tiene una mancha en la falda. Mire, aquí junto al botón.
VENDEDORA: Es verdad. Hay otro vestido igual, pero es azul.
ISABEL: Muy bien, entonces me llevo el azul.
VENDEDORA: ¿Tiene su recibo y su tarjeta de crédito?
ISABEL: Sí, aquí tiene.
VENDEDORA: Gracias. Necesita firmar aquí, por favor. Aquí tiene el recibo.

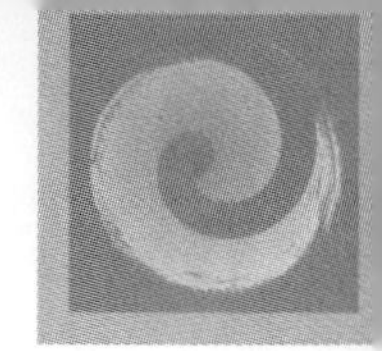

**A. ¿Comprende Ud.?** Answer the following questions based on the dialog.

1. ¿Dónde está Isabel?
2. ¿Qué problema hay con el vestido?
3. ¿Por qué no compra otro vestido rojo?
4. ¿Qué documentos necesita para cambiar el vestido?

**Answers for A.** 1) *En el centro comercial.* 2) *Tiene una mancha.* 3) *Porque no hay.* 4) *La tarjeta de crédito y el recibo.*

**B. Mala suerte.** You have purchased a clothing item and discovered it has a problem (size, color, fit) or that you simply don't like it. Return it to the store for an exchange. A classmate will be the salesclerk accepting your exchange and asking you for your receipt and the reason for it.

MODELO: E1: *Señor, necesito cambiar estas gafas de sol.*
E2: *¿Tienen algún problema?*

**C. El/La millonario/a.** You've just won the lottery! A shopping spree is in order for a new wardrobe. Prepare your list, including sizes, colors, and quantities desired. In groups of four, compare your lists and decide which item(s) are the most popular.

**D. Ocho días de vacaciones.** You've just graduated from college and are heading with a friend to the beach house of his/her parents for a week. In order to pack the car with food, clothing, and reading material, you need to get organized. Plan with a classmate each item to be taken, whether you have it or will need to buy it for the trip, and whose responsibility it is.

MODELO: E1: *Yo tengo un sombrero y una novela romántica.*
E2: *Yo necesito comprar un libro y un traje de baño.*

**Suggestion for D.** Point out that it is common in Spanish to refer to one week as *ocho días* and two weeks as *quince días.* After all, if you count from Sunday to Sunday you end up with eight!

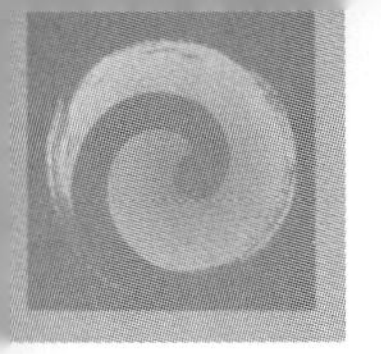

# Me/te/le gusta(n)
## (*Expressing likes and dislikes:* gustar)

- Although the most convenient English translations of **me gusta** and **te gusta** are *I like* and *you like,* they literally mean (it) *is pleasing to me* and (it) *is pleasing to you.*

- **Me/te/le gusta** may be followed by a verb or a noun.

| | |
|---|---|
| —¿**Te gusta comprar** ropa? | *Do you like to buy clothes?* |
| —Sí, **me gusta comprar** ropa. | *Yes, I like to buy clothes.* |
| —No, no **me gusta comprar** ropa. | *No, I don't like to buy clothes.* |
| —¿**Te gusta la ropa** cara? | *Do you like expensive clothes?* |
| —Sí, **me gusta la ropa** cara. | *Yes, I like expensive clothes.* |

- If the noun following the verb is plural, or if the verb is followed by a series of items (even if these are singular), use **gustan**. However, if the verb is followed by a series of infinitives, use **gusta**.

| | |
|---|---|
| Me gust**a el vestido** rojo. | *I like the red dress.* |
| Me gust**an los zapatos** elegantes. | *I like elegant shoes.* |
| Me gust**an el fútbol**, **el tenis** y **la natación**. | *I like soccer, tennis, and swimming.* |
| Me gust**a jugar**, **estudiar** y **bailar**. | *I like to play, to study, and to dance.* |

- To tell/ask the name of the person who is pleased or displeased by something, use **a** before the name.

| | |
|---|---|
| —¿**A María** le gusta el centro comercial? | *Does María like the mall?* |
| —No, **a ella** le gustan las tiendas pequeñas. | *No, she likes small stores.* |

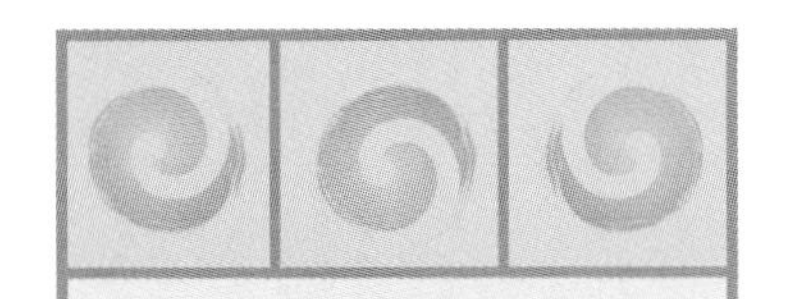

### Para averiguar

1. What does **me gusta** mean in English? What is the literal meaning?
2. How do you say *you like* (familiar)?
3. How do you say *you like* (formal), *he likes,* or *she likes*?
4. If the noun following the verb is plural, what form of the verb is used?

## A lo personal

**A. ¿Te gusta(n)...?** Determine which of the following subjects matches the verb and ask a classmate about his/her likes and dislikes.

MODELO: ¿Te gust**a** (la música latina/las canciones en español)?
E1: *¿Te gust**a la** música latina?*
E2: *Sí, me gust**a la** música latina.*

¿Te gust**an** (el cine/los programas de televisión)?
E1: *¿Te gust**an los** programas de televisión?*
E2: *No, no me gust**an los** programas de televisión.*

1. ¿Te gustan (la ropa deportiva/los trajes formales)?
2. ¿Te gusta (el invierno/los días del verano)?
3. ¿Te gustan (la tarjeta de crédito/los precios rebajados)?
4. ¿Te gustan (la minifalda/las sandalias)?
5. ¿Te gusta (el color amarillo/las rayas (*stripes*) rojas)?

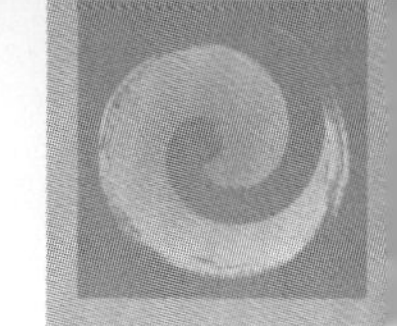

**B. Entrevista.** Find out the preferences of a classmate through the following questions. Take notes, and report his/her answers to the class.

MODELO: E1: *Francisco, ¿qué te gusta más, comer en casa o en restaurantes?*
E2: *Me gusta más comer en casa.*
E1: *(A Francisco) le gusta más comer en casa.*

¿Qué te gusta más…

1. …la comida mexicana o la comida italiana?
2. …la carne o el pescado?
3. …el pan o los pasteles?
4. …el peperoni o las anchoas en la pizza?
5. …un centro comercial grande o las tiendas pequeñas?
6. …el dinero o las tarjetas de crédito?
7. …las rebajas o el precio original?

**C. ¿Qué te gusta hacer?** What do you like to do in the following situations?

MODELO: ¿Qué te gusta hacer cuando estás aburrido?
*Cuando estoy aburrido me gusta mirar la televisión.*

¿Qué te gusta hacer cuando…

1. …estás triste?
2. …hay un examen de español?
3. …tu amigo celebra su cumpleaños?
4. …no hay comida en casa?
5. …hay zapatos rebajados, pero no tienes dinero?
6. …hay una fiesta y no te gusta tu ropa?
7. …deseas demostrar tu amor a una persona especial?

**D. Firma aquí.** Walk around your classroom to find out some of your classmates' likes and dislikes. As you find people to fit each category, have them sign their name in the appropriate space. Then, share your findings with the rest of the class.

Alguien a quien le gusta…

1. …estudiar español los viernes por la noche
   ________________________________
2. …comer comida mexicana todos los días
   ________________________________
3. …comprar ropa cara en el centro comercial
   ________________________________
4. …mirar el programa ER en la televisión
   ________________________________
5. …escuchar música de Ricky Martin
   ________________________________
6. …bailar salsa en un club los fines de semana
   ________________________________

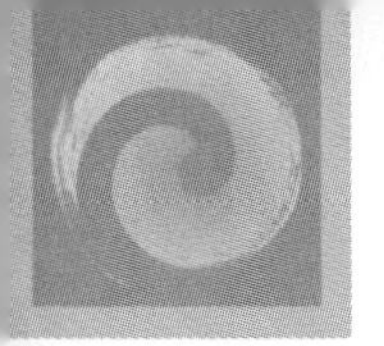

# Pronombres y adjetivos demostrativos
## (*Demonstrative pronouns and adjectives*)

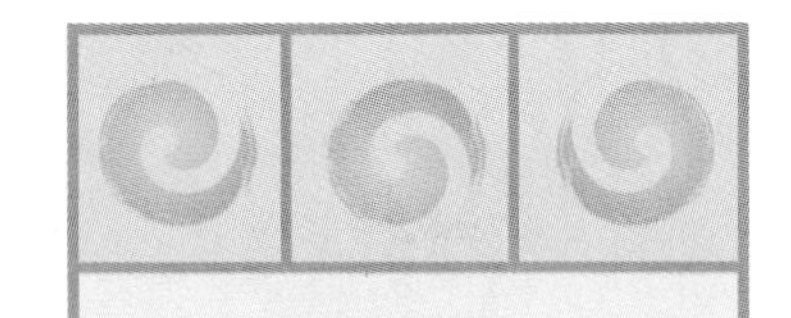

### Para averiguar

1. How do you say *this* or *that* in Spanish? What is the difference between **ese** and **aquel**?
2. How do you say *this one* instead of *this hat*?
3. What is unusual about the masculine singular endings of *this* and *that*?

**Suggestion.** Bring three shirts, three ties, etc. to class. Keep one of each yourself and give the others to different students. Use *este/ese/aquel* to ask students if they prefer the one they have, the one you have, or the one that the other student has. (*¿Prefiere Ud. esta camisa que tengo yo, esa camisa que tiene Ud. o aquella camisa que tiene…?*)

- Use the demonstrative adjectives to say *this* or *that*. **Ese/esa** and **aquel/aquella** may both be used to say *that* but **aquel** is generally used to describe something at a greater distance.

- ¡OJO! None of the masculine singular forms of the demonstrative adjectives end in **-o**. The masculine singular forms of *this* and *that* end in **-e** rather than **-o**.

| este | (*this*) | ese | (*that*) | aquel | (*that—over there*) |
|---|---|---|---|---|---|
| **este** libro | *this book* | **ese** libro | *that book* | **aquel** libro | *that book* |
| **esta** falda | *this skirt* | **esa** falda | *that skirt* | **aquella** falda | *that skirt* |
| **estos** libros | *these books* | **esos** libros | *those books* | **aquellos** libros | *those books* |
| **estas** faldas | *these skirts* | **esas** faldas | *those skirts* | **aquellas** faldas | *those skirts* |

¿Te gustan **estos** pantalones? — *Do you like these pants?*
**Ese** vestido va bien con esos zapatos. — *That dress looks good with those shoes.*
¿Puedo probarme **aquel** traje? — *May I try on that suit (over there)?*

- The demonstrative pronouns look just like the adjectives, except that they have written accents and the noun is omitted.

—¿Te gustan **estos** zapatos? — *Do you like these shoes?*
—No, prefiero **éstos**. — *No, I prefer these.*

—**Esa** corbata es muy bonita. — *That tie is pretty.*
—A mí me gusta **ésa**. — *I like that one.*

—¿Puedo probarme **aquel** sombrero? — *May I try on that hat (over there)?*
—¿Por qué? ¿No te gusta **éste**? — *Why? Don't you like this one?*

- To say *this* or *that* referring to a general idea or situation rather than to a specific noun, or when referring to a noun that has not yet been identified, use the neuter form of the demonstratives: **esto, eso,** and **aquello**.

**Eso** es imposible. — *That is impossible.*
**Esto** es muy importante — *This is very important.*
¿Qué es **aquello**? — *What is that (over there)?*

## A lo personal

**A. Mis cosas.** Describe three pieces of clothing or other personal items you have with you using **este/a/os/as**.

MODELO: *Esta camisa es roja.*
*Éstos son mis zapatos nuevos.*
*Este libro es nuevo.*

**B. De compras.** You are shopping with a friend. The items that you have found are just the opposite of the ones that your friend is holding. Describe your friend's items using the correct form of the demonstrative adjective.

**Follow up for B.** Have students use *ese/a/os/as* to compliment each other's clothes. (*Me gustan esos zapatos, Tracey.*)

MODELO: Este vestido es muy largo.
*Ese vestido es muy corto.*

1. Estos zapatos son muy grandes.
2. Esta camisa es muy formal.
3. Estas medias son baratas.
4. Esta falda es muy larga.
5. Este abrigo es muy feo.
6. Este cinturón es demasiado (*too*) corto.
7. Estos suéteres son muy caros.
8. Estas botas son de buena calidad.

**C. Mis lugares favoritos.** React to your classmate's preferences.

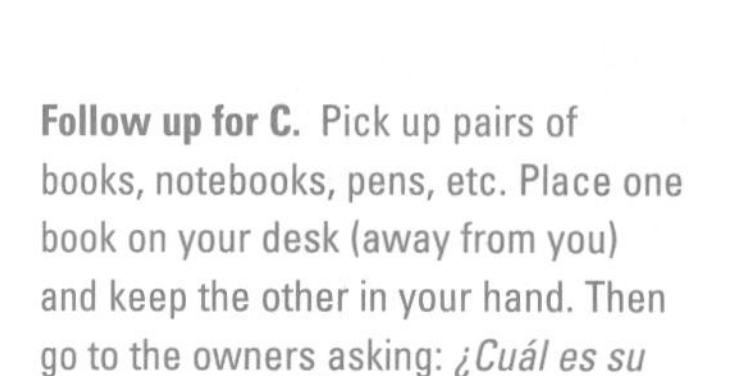

**Follow up for C.** Pick up pairs of books, notebooks, pens, etc. Place one book on your desk (away from you) and keep the other in your hand. Then go to the owners asking: *¿Cuál es su libro, éste o ése?*

MODELO: su tienda favorita
E1: *¿Cuál es tu tienda favorita?*
E2: *Mi tienda favorita es Macy's.*
E1: *Esa tienda me gusta a mí también. Tiene ropa bonita.* o
*Esa tienda no me gusta. Tiene precios muy altos.* o
*No conozco esa tienda.*

1. su restaurante favorito
2. su película favorita
3. su color favorito
4. su actriz favorita
5. su clase favorita
6. su programa de televisión favorito
7. su canción favorita
8. su actor favorito

**D. Entrevista.** Complete the following questions with the correct form of the demonstrative adjective or pronoun **(este/a)(éste/a)**. Then use them to interview a classmate.

1. ¿Qué estudias ________ noche?
2. ¿Hay una fiesta _____ fin de semana?
3. ¿Tienes planes para ______ verano?
4. ¿________ año deseas viajar a México?
5. ¿Tienes otra clase de español después de ______?
6. ¿Buscas otro profesor de literatura o te gusta ________?
7. ¿Necesitas una mochila nueva o está bien _________?
8. ¿Prefieres hacer otro ejercicio o te gusta ________?

**E. ¿Qué opinas?** What is your opinion of these possibilities?

MODELO: Los hombres llevan faldas.
*Eso es posible.*

verdad terrible ridículo posible imposible estupendo me gusta probable

1. No tenemos aire acondicionado en las casas, la ropa tiene aire acondicionado.
2. Los hombres y las mujeres llevan la misma (*same*) ropa.
3. Nunca puedes llevar vaqueros (*blue jeans*).
4. Es importante llevar ropa formal a la clase de español.

# Vocabulario

## TEMA 3
### De compras

**Sustantivos**

| | |
|---|---|
| **la banana** | *banana* |
| **el bistec** | *steak* |
| **el camarón** | *shrimp* |
| **la carnicería** | *butcher shop* |
| **la cantidad** | *quantity* |
| **la cebolla** | *onion* |
| **el cereal** | *cereal* |
| **el descuento** | *discount* |
| **la frutería** | *fruit stand* |
| **el huevo** | *egg* |
| **la leche** | *milk* |
| **la lechuga** | *lettuce* |
| **la libra** | *pound* |
| **la mantequilla** | *butter* |
| **la naranja** | *orange* |
| **el pan** | *bread* |
| **la panadería** | *bakery* |
| **la papa** | *potato* |
| **el pastel** | *cake* |
| **la pastelería** | *bakery (pastries)* |
| **la pescadería** | *fish market* |
| **el pescado** | *fish* |
| **la piña** | *pineapple* |
| **el pollo** | *chicken* |
| **el precio** | *price* |
| **el queso** | *cheese* |
| **el refresco** | *soda* |
| **el salmón** | *salmon* |
| **el supermercado** | *supermarket* |
| **el tomate** | *tomato* |
| **la tortillería** | *tortilla bakery* |
| **la uva** | *grape* |
| **la zanahoria** | *carrot* |

**Verbos**

| | |
|---|---|
| **decir (i)** | *to say, tell* |
| **dejar** | *to let* |
| **vender** | *to sell* |

**Adjetivos**

| | |
|---|---|
| **caro/a** | *expensive* |
| **fijo/a** | *fixed, set* |
| **fresco/a** | *fresh* |

**Otras expresiones**

| | |
|---|---|
| **claro** | *sure* |
| **por ciento** | *percent* |

## TEMA 4
### La ropa

**Sustantivos**

| | |
|---|---|
| **el abrigo** | *overcoat* |
| **la bata** | *robe* |
| **el bolso** | *purse* |
| **el botón** | *button* |
| **la caja** | *cashier* |
| **los calzoncillos** | *men's undershorts* |
| **el camisón** | *nightgown* |
| **la falda** | *skirt* |
| **las gafas (de sol)** | *(sun) glasses* |
| **el impuesto** | *tax* |
| **la mancha** | *stain* |
| **el paraguas** | *umbrella* |
| **el problema** | *problem* |
| **la raya** | *stripe* |
| **el sombrero** | *hat* |
| **el sostén** | *bra* |
| **la sudadera** | *sweatshirt* |
| **el suéter** | *sweater* |
| **la talla** | *size* |
| **los vaqueros** | *blue jeans* |
| **el vestido** | *dress* |

**Verbos**

| | |
|---|---|
| **cambiar** | *to change, exchange* |
| **conducir (zc)** | *to drive* |
| **devolver (ue)** | *to return (something)* |
| **necesitar** | *to need* |
| **perdonar** | *to forgive* |

**Adjetivos**

| | |
|---|---|
| **corto/a** | *short (length)* |
| **igual** | *equal* |
| **largo/a** | *long* |
| **mediano/a** | *medium* |
| **otro/a** | *other* |
| **rebajado/a** | *reduced* |

**Otras expresiones**

| | |
|---|---|
| **además** | *besides* |
| **entonces** | *then, next* |
| **haga el favor** | *please* |
| **mismo/a** | *same* |
| **nada** | *nothing* |

# Reunión B

**A escuchar.** **Ana y José.** Listen to the selection and then complete the following exercise by writing **Cierto (C)** or **Falso (F)** according to the information you hear.

1. _____ Ana busca un suéter para su hija.
2. _____ A José le gusta el suéter azul con rayas rojas.
3. _____ El precio de ese suéter es de ochenta y nueve dólares con noventa y nueve centavos.
4. _____ Hay un descuento en el suéter azul.
5. _____ Ana va a pagar con su tarjeta de crédito.

**Tapescript for A escuchar. Ana y José.**
ANA: Señor, necesito un suéter azul marino o negro de talla mediana para mi hijo.
VENDEDOR: Tengo estos tres modelos. ¿Cuál le gusta?
JOSÉ: No me gusta ninguno. Quiero este suéter azul claro con rayas rojas.
ANA: Es muy caro. Cuesta ochenta y nueve dólares con noventa y nueve centavos.
VENDEDOR: Aquel suéter que le gusta al niño está rebajado un treinta y tres por ciento.
ANA: Entonces lo compro. Voy a pagar con un cheque. ¿Cuánto es?
VENDEDOR: Sesenta y tres dólares, más diez por ciento de impuestos, son sesenta y nueve dólares con treinta centavos. Por favor, escriba su teléfono en el cheque. También necesito su licencia de conducir.
ANA: Aquí tiene el cheque y mi licencia de conducir.
VENDEDOR: Gracias, aquí tiene su recibo.

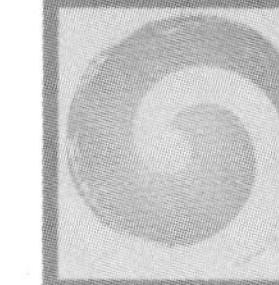

**A conversar.** A classmate and you have decided to join **Club de Música Hispana.** Each of you will prepare a list of the 11 selections you prefer. Then, compare your lists and decide which 11 you jointly will order.

## ¿Lo sabía?

Look at the following ad promoting popular Latin music. Do you recognize any artists? Do you find any differences between this ad and those you usually see promoting music in the U.S.?

**A buscar.** Select one Latin artist from the article and look for more information on him/her on the Internet or in magazines. You may wish to go to a local music store to see which Latin performers it carries. Then, present your findings to the rest of the class. You may even bring a sample of the artist's music if you'd like.

**Answers for A escuchar.** 1) *F.* 2) *C.* 3) *C.* 4) *C.* 5) *F.*

# ¡TRATO HECHO!

## Rincón profesional: De compras en la red

¿Qué desea Ud.? ¡El Internet está listo para servir!

¡Pobre de mí! Necesito otra botella de mi perfume favorito, pero es español y no puedo comprarlo aquí. Tengo que usar otro perfume o tengo que ir a España.

¿Qué puedo hacer?

Pues, no se preocupe Ud. ¡Ponga su computadora a trabajar, haga una búsqueda con un "buscador internacional" o un "motor de búsqueda" y vaya de compras por la red en París, en Madrid, en Moscú o en Lima! Todo lo que Ud. necesita, lo puede encontrar en el Internet.

El fenómeno de compras por Internet revoluciona el concepto de ir de compras. En Argentina, por ejemplo, en un año el número de productos vendidos "en línea" subió de 5.000 a 50.000. ¡En un año! Los consumidores y vendedores con medio mundo de distancia pueden realizar sus transacciones con un simple "click click", y unas cartas electrónicas. Entonces…¡mágicamente!, llega el producto a su casa u oficina—tal vez en menos de veinticuatro horas. En uno de los motores de búsqueda, la palabra "perfume" aparece en más de 26.000 sitios de la red, todos éstos relacionados con la venta de perfume. ¡Imagínese! ¡26.000 en 20 segundos!

**¿Comprende Ud.?**

1. How has shopping changed?
2. If I can't find my favorite products locally, what can I do?
3. How can I find products on the net?
4. How many matches were there for the search for perfume?

**A escuchar.** **Ventas en TV.** Listen to the following conversation between Marco and Jorge and then answer the questions below.

**¿Comprende Ud.?**

1. ¿Dónde trabajan Marco y Jorge?
2. ¿Hoy venden vestidos de mujer?
3. ¿Cuántos colores de pantalones tienen?
4. ¿Cuánto cuestan?
5. ¿Jorge rebaja el precio?
6. ¿Los clientes pueden pagar en efectivo?

**Tapescript for A escuchar. Ventas en TV.**
*Marco and Jorge are working at the Home Shopping TV channel. In this program, they are selling children's pants.*
MARCO: Jorge, mira estos pantalones para niño.
JORGE: Sí, me gustan mucho. Atención, televidentes, los pantalones son de muy buena calidad y los tenemos en siete colores.
MARCO: Jorge, seguro que estos pantalones son muy caros. Seguro que cuestan cincuenta dólares cada uno.
JORGE: No, no cuestan cincuenta, ni cuarenta, ni treinta. Es increíble, pero solamente cuestan veintiocho dólares.
MARCO: ¿Cómo? ¡No es posible! Son muy baratos.
JORGE: Pero eso no es todo. Como necesitamos vender cinco mil pantalones hoy mismo, vamos a rebajar el precio a diecinueve dólares.
MARCO: Ay, Jorge, así no ganamos dinero. Bueno, no importa, nuestros clientes son muy importantes.
JORGE: Claro, pero hay que llamar ahora mismo. Nuestros teléfonos están en la pantalla de su televisión. Solamente necesita su tarjeta de crédito.

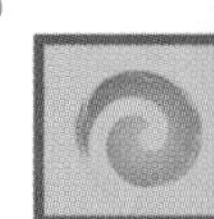

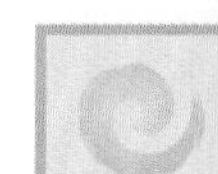

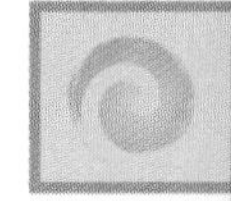

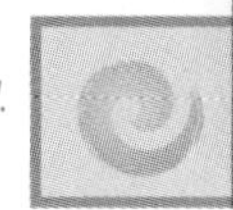

**Answers for A escuchar.**
1) *En el Home Shopping Channel.* 2) *No.* 3) *Siete.* 4) *$28.* 5) *Sí.* 6) *No.*

**Comprando libros.** You would like to buy some books from a catalog. Student 1 will be the buyer and student 2 the operator taking orders by phone. The operator should politely greet the caller and ask for specific details regarding the customer's order.

**Anuncios en la red.** You are part of a marketing team looking to break into the booming Spanish-speaking market. Choose a product or a store that you would like to market in Spain, South America, or in the U.S., and design a web page for that product. Don't forget to tell the pertinent benefits, features, styles, and prices.

## A leer

> Before reading this passage, you might want to quickly review the chapter vocabulary—especially the meanings of verbs. Then, skim each paragraph and let your eye catch familiar words. Next, look at the words near the familiar words. If you recognize **económico** in the first sentence, focus on **de lujo**. While the meaning may not be obvious at first, stay there a moment and think about it: what automobile marketing concept is linked with *economy class car*? Can you see the connection between the Spanish word **de lujo** and one in English?

**Antes de leer.** You and one of your classmates are writing an article to try to increase the consumer market using the Internet to buy/sell/trade cars. What points would you stress in your article? What would be the main advantages that you would like to present? Make a list of as many as possible and then see if the writers of the article that follows share your ideas.

*Buying a car through the Internet is becoming more and more popular. People save money because they know the list price and how much the optional equipment costs.*

Foto del interior de una de las oficinas de la empresa Yahoo.

¿Necesita comprar un coche? ¿Nuevo o usado? ¿Económico o de lujo? ¿Tiene poco o mucho dinero? En el Internet hay todo lo que Ud. quiere. Es un mercado de coches muy importante. Cada día más personas usan el Internet para comprar un coche. Es muy fácil. En la pantalla aparece un cuestionario. Allí escribe sus datos personales. Después, llena la información sobre el coche que le gusta: la marca, el modelo, el año, el color y los accesorios que desea. El Internet da el precio básico o de lista y el costo de las cosas opcionales.

¿No tiene dinero? No importa, el Internet ofrece préstamos para comprar el coche de sus sueños y para pagar el seguro. ¿Tardan mucho tiempo? No, el Internet manda en segundos la información a la agencia de coches y ellos contestan por correo electrónico o llaman por teléfono.

¿Necesita vender su coche viejo? ¡No hay problema! El Internet también tiene los precios de coches usados. Además, tiene una sección de anuncios clasificados. ¡Ahora es muy fácil comprar o vender un coche desde su propia casa!

**¿Cierto (C) o Falso (F)?** Without looking back at the article, mark the statements based on what you remember. Then, you may go back and check for accuracy.

1. _____ Solamente puede comprar un coche en una agencia.
2. _____ El Internet sólo vende coches de lujo.
3. _____ Tiene que llenar un cuestionario con sus datos personales.
4. _____ Si desea, puede ordenar diferentes accesorios para su coche.
5. _____ El Internet manda la información en tres días.
6. _____ Puede vender su coche en el Internet.
7. _____ Con un préstamo paga el coche y el seguro.

## A escribir

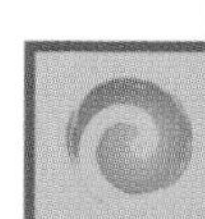

Enter the Internet and locate a car dealer offering on-line services in Spanish. Then, write an order to buy the car of your dreams. Don't forget to enter your personal data and all the necessary information about the car you want. Bring your order to class and share it with your classmates. Make sure you don't send the order to the dealer unless you are seriously planning to buy a new car.

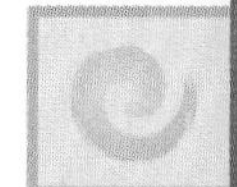

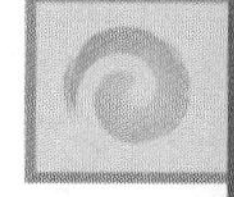

# 3 En familia

LECCIÓN TRES

CHECK OUT THE *¡TRATO HECHO!* WEBSITE AND CD-ROM FOR ACTIVITIES, GAMES, SELF-TESTS, AND MUCH MORE!

TEMA 1

## La familia

- Entre nosotros
- Los estudiantes y sus familias
- Adjetivos posesivos
- Los números de 100 en adelante, fechas

TEMA 2

## La casa

- Cosas de casa
- Mi dormitorio
- Los verbos regulares: *-er* e *-ir*
- Más práctica con verbos en *-er*, *-ir*

TEMA 3

## Los quehaceres domésticos

- Hay que limpiar
- ¿Qué pasa?
- Los comparativos
- Los superlativos

TEMA 4

## La guardería infantil

- De visita en la guardería
- Fabiola y Elvira en la guardería
- Los verbos *tener* y *venir*
- Los verbos irregulares en *-er* e *-ir*

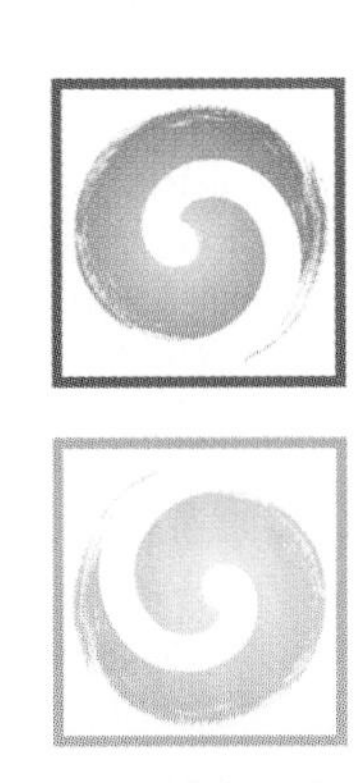

# ¡TRATO HECHO!

- Rincón profesional: Decoradores de interiores
- A escuchar
- A leer
- A escribir

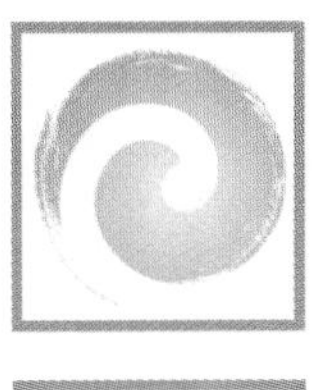

# TEMA 1 La familia

## Entre nosotros

**Expansion.** Mention the importance of the godparent/godchild relationship in Hispanic culture, citing examples such as baptism, *quinceañera* parties, wedding involvement, and responsibilities to participate in birthdays, saint's days, etc. Introduce vocabulary such as *padrino, madrina, el/la ahijado/a*. You may also choose to expand family vocabulary by including *bisabuelo/a*.

Esta foto es de tres generaciones: un niño, sus padres y sus abuelos.

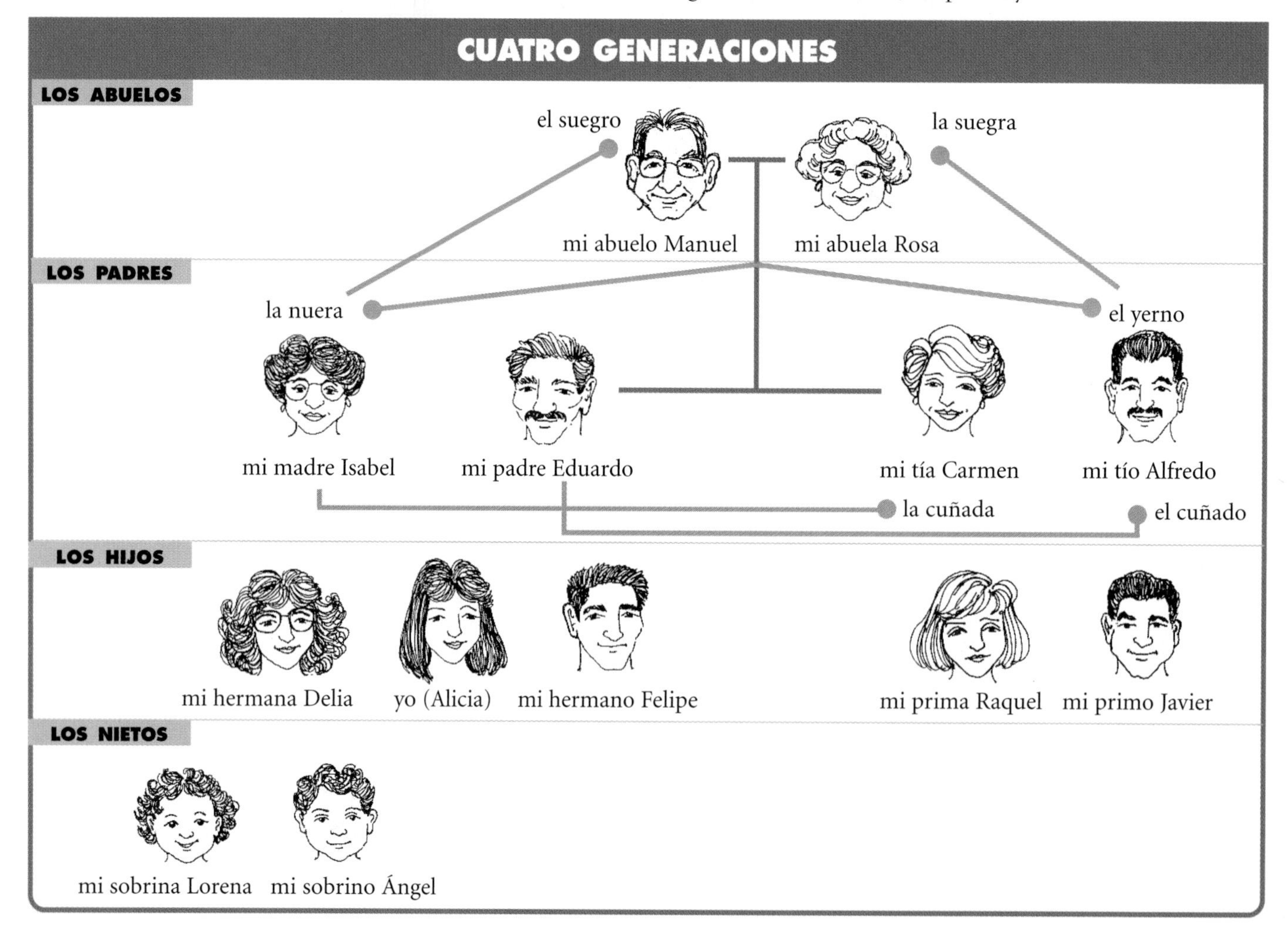

## En la clase del profesor Yuja-Fournier

*In Prof. Yuja's class, students talk about their families....*

PROF. YUJA-FOURNIER: En esta foto de mi familia están mis padres, Nicolás y Elena, mi esposa Gloria y mis dos hijos, Elenita y Beto.

CARLOS: ¿De dónde son sus padres?

PROF. YUJA-FOURNIER: Son de México. Mi padre es descendiente de maya-quichés y de españoles y mi madre de franceses. Carlos, tus abuelos son de Colombia, ¿verdad?

CARLOS: Sí, todos los demás somos de los Estados Unidos. Mis padres, mi hermana Ángela, mi tío Enrique, su esposa Clara y mis primos Silvia y Enriquito viven en Nueva York. Solamente yo vivo en California.

PROF. YUJA-FOURNIER: Isabel, ¿de dónde es tu familia?

ISABEL: Nosotros somos de Perú, pero mi abuelo paterno es descendiente de japoneses.

PROF. YUJA-FOURNIER: Isabel, ¿a qué se dedican tus padres?

ISABEL: Tienen un restaurante de comida típica peruana. Mi hermano Ernesto y mi abuela materna trabajan con ellos.

**A. ¿Comprende Ud.?** Answer the following questions based on the dialog.

1. ¿De dónde es el apellido Fournier?
2. ¿Está casado el profesor?
3. ¿Dónde viven los padres de Carlos?
4. ¿Cuál es la profesión de los padres de Isabel?

**Answers for A.** 1) *Francia.* 2) *Sí.* 3) *En Nueva York.* 4) *Tienen un restaurante.*

**B. La familia de Alicia.** Use the family tree to complete Alicia's description of her family.

Mis _________, Manuel y Rosa, son los padres de mi padre y los _________ de mi madre. Los padres de mi madre están muertos. Mi padre se llama _________ y mi madre Isabel. La nuera de mis abuelos es mi madre _________ y _________es su yerno. Mi padre tiene una hermana, mi _________ Carmen, la _________ de mi madre. Tengo dos ___________. Son hijos de mi tío Alfredo y su esposa Carmen. También tengo dos __________. Son hijos de mi hermana Delia. Mi sobrino se llama _________ y mi sobrina se llama _________ .

**C. ¿Quién es?** Fill in the correct family word according to the description.

1. La madre de mi madre es mi _____.
2. El hijo de mi hermano es mi _____.
3. La esposa de mi hermano es mi _____.
4. Los hijos de mis tíos son mis _____.
5. Para mis abuelos, yo soy su _____.
6. Los padres de mi esposo son mis _____.

**D. Tres generaciones.** Take five minutes to sketch your family tree and describe important members of your family to the group. If you would rather describe someone else's family, feel free to do so.

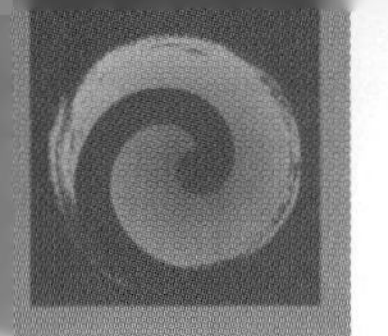

# Los estudiantes y sus familias

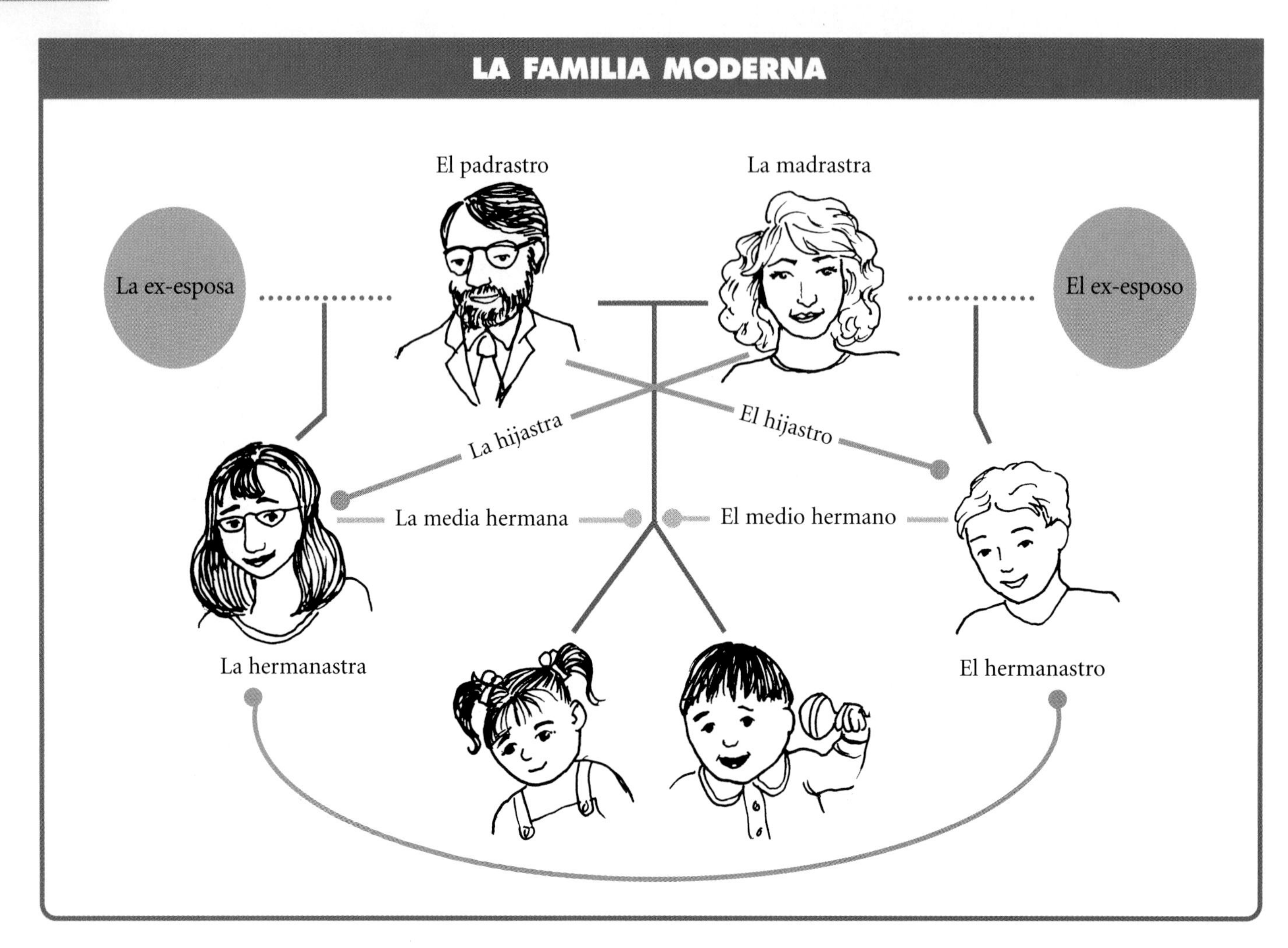


Suggestion. Welcome discussion of "modern" or alternative family groupings, so that students feel free to discuss their own families. Always allow them to fabricate a family or use the family of a friend as an example.

## Hablando de la familia

*Ana and Mary get to know each other....*

MARY: ¿José es tu hijo? Estás muy joven.
ANA: Bueno, es que José es mi primo, pero voy a adoptarlo. Sus padres, mis tíos Raúl y Estela, ya están muertos.
MARY: Lo siento. ¿Con quién vives?
ANA: Mi hermana Lucero y yo vivimos juntas en la casa de mis padres. Nosotras somos estadounidenses, pero nuestros padres son de Costa Rica. Ellos viven allí desde hace cuatro años.
MARY: ¿Y quién maneja el negocio de tus padres?
ANA: Lucero y yo trabajamos en la agencia de viajes de nuestros padres. Mary, ¿tú eres casada?
MARY: No, soy soltera, pero soy novia de Carlos.Vivo con mis padres, soy hija única. Mis abuelos son de Inglaterra, pero mis padres y yo somos norteamericanos. Ana, ¿tú tienes novio?
ANA: No, solamente amigos.

**A. Para terminar.** Answer the following questions based on the dialog.

1. ¿Por qué no vive José con sus padres?
2. ¿Con quién vive Ana?
3. ¿Cuántos hermanos/as tiene Mary?
4. ¿Cómo se llama el novio de Mary?

**Answers for A.** 1) *Sus padres están muertos.* 2) *Con Lucero.* 3) *Ninguno.* 4) *Carlos.*

**B. Mi familia.** With a classmate, describe four of your family members, including what they are like, what they like, and what they always/never do.

MODELO: *Mi hermanastro Javier es activo. Le gusta bailar. ¡Nunca estudia!*

**C. Familias famosas.** You are discussing famous people with a classmate. Can you answer these questions?

1. ¿Cómo se llama la esposa de Bill Clinton?
2. ¿Quién es el esposo de Melanie Griffith?
3. ¿Cómo se llama la hija de Madonna?
4. ¿Quién es el hijo de Julio Iglesias?
5. ¿Cómo se llaman los hermanos de Stephen Baldwin?

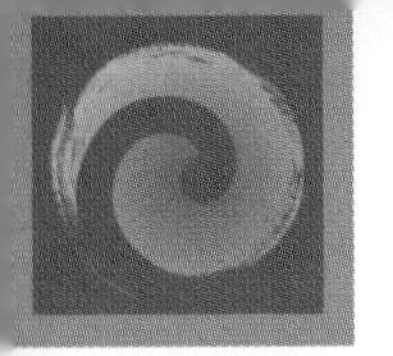

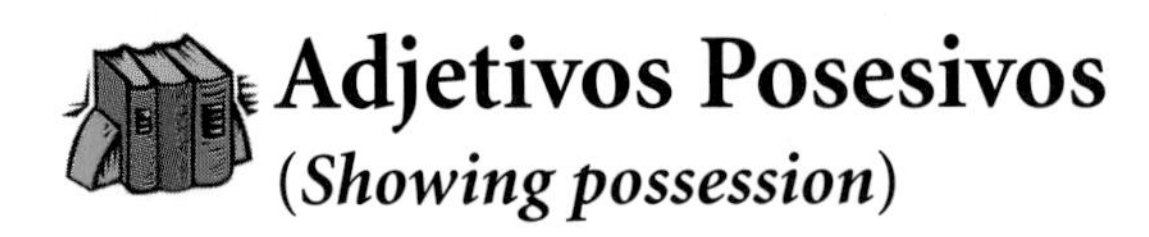

# Adjetivos Posesivos
## (*Showing possession*)

**Para averiguar**

1. What can **su(s)** mean? How can you reword a sentence to avoid the ambiguity that **su(s)** can bring?
2. What do you use in Spanish instead of an *'s* to show possession?

- Possessive adjectives are useful when talking about family and belongings.

**Los adjetivos posesivos**

| singular | | | plural | | |
|---|---|---|---|---|---|
| yo | **mi(s)** | *my* | nosotros/as | **nuestro/a/os/as** | *our* |
| tú | **tu(s)** | *your* | vosotros/as | **vuestro/a/os/as** | *your* |
| él | **su(s)** | *his/its* | ellos | **su(s)** | *their* |
| ella | **su(s)** | *her/its* | ellas | **su(s)** | *their* |
| usted | **su(s)** | *your* | ustedes | **su(s)** | *your* |

- Possessive adjectives agree in number with the noun that follows them. Only **nuestro/a** and **vuestro/a** have additional forms for masculine or feminine nouns.

| | |
|---|---|
| **Nuestra** familia es grande. | *Our family is big.* |
| **Mi** casa es vieja. | *My house is old.* |
| **Mis** libros son nuevos. | *My books are new.* |
| **Nuestros** libros son interesantes. | *Our books are interesting.* |

- Since **su(s)** can mean *his, her, its, your,* or *their,* it is often rephrased using **de** + **él**, **ella**, **usted**, **ellos**, **ellas**, or **ustedes** for clarity. Note that **de** + **él** (accented—meaning *he*) does not contract the way that **de** + **el** (unaccented—meaning *the*) contracts to **del**.

| | | |
|---|---|---|
| sus amigos | los amigos **de él** | *his friends* |
| | los amigos **de ella** | *her friends* |
| | los amigos **de usted/es** | *your friends* |
| | los amigos **de ellos/ellas** | *their friends* |

| | |
|---|---|
| Prefiero a los amigos **de él**. | *I prefer his friends.* |
| No me gustan los amigos **de ella.** | *I don't like her friends.* |

- Use the *definite article* + *noun* + **de** instead of *'s* to show possession in Spanish.

| | |
|---|---|
| la casa **de** Ramón | *Ramon's house* |
| las preguntas **de** los estudiantes | *the students' questions* |

## A lo personal

**A. Posesión.** Give the appropriate form of the possessive adjectives **mi(s)**, **tu(s)**, **su(s)**, **nuestro/a/os/as**. When you are finished, check your answers with a classmate.

MODELO: *Yo* tengo tres hermanas en Los Ángeles. ____ hermanas están en Los Ángeles.
*__Mis__ hermanas están en Los Ángeles.*

1. *Tenemos* una casa vieja. ________ casa es vieja.
2. *Ustedes* tienen una familia pequeña. ________ familia es pequeña.
3. *Usted* tiene tres perros grandes. ________ perros son grandes.

4. *Yo* tengo una hija alta. ________ hija es alta.
5. *Tú* tienes gatos cómicos. ________ gatos son cómicos.
6. *Ellos* tienen un coche nuevo. ________ coche es nuevo.
7. *Nosotros* tenemos una profesora excelente. ________ profesora es excelente.
8. *Ella* tiene a dos hijos en Cali. ________ hijos están en Cali.
9. *Ellos* tienen a un hijo en México. ________ hijo está en México.
10. *Él* tiene amigos simpáticos. ________ amigos son simpáticos.

**B. ¿Quién?** To what celebrities might these statements refer?

MODELO: Su casa es muy grande.
*La casa del presidente es muy grande.*

1. Sus zapatos son muy grandes.
2. Su hijo es cantante (*singer*).
3. Sus padres son de España.
4. Sus libros son muy populares.
5. Su esposo es muy guapo.
6. Su música es romántica.
7. Su programa de televisión es cómico.
8. Sus tacos son famosos.
9. Su perro es un héroe.
10. Sus películas son tontas (*silly*).

**C. ¿De dónde…?** Tell what language these friends speak.

MODELO: *Soy* de México. ________ idioma es el ________.
***Mi** idioma es el **español**.*

1. *Eres* de Brasil. ________ idioma es el ________________.
2. *Somos* de Francia. ________ lengua es el ______________.
3. Ud. *es* de Colombia. ________ idioma es el ___________.
4. Ellos *son* de Inglaterra. ________ idioma es el _________.
5. Él *es* de Suiza. _______ lenguas son el ________ y el ________.

**D. La casa de mis padres.** This young woman's boyfriend is going to visit her parents for the first time. Complete the conversation using **mi(s)**, **tu(s)**, or **su(s)**.

ELLA: ¿Vienes conmigo a la casa de ________ padres este fin de semana?
ÉL: Sí. ¿Dónde está ________ casa?
ELLA: No está lejos de aquí.
ÉL: ¿Y cómo son ________ padres?
ELLA: ________ padre es alto y tiene barba. Es muy simpático. Le gusta hablar mucho. ________ madre es alta y rubia. No habla mucho. Es muy seria.
ÉL: ¿Cuántos años tienen?
ELLA: ________ padre tiene cincuenta años y ________ madre cuarenta y nueve.
ÉL: ¿ ________ hermanos viven con ________ padres?
ELLA: No. Todos ya son grandes y tienen ________ propias familias.

**E. Entrevista.** Interview a classmate using the following questions.

1. ¿Cuántas personas hay en tu familia? ¿Dónde viven los miembros de tu familia?
2. ¿Cómo se llama tu mejor amigo/a? ¿Cómo es?
3. ¿Eres casado/a? ¿Cómo es el/la esposo/a perfecto/a?

**F. Una visita.** A new friend is going to spend the weekend with your family. With a classmate, prepare a conversation in which you explain:

- where your family lives
- what your house is like
- what your house is near
- who the members of the family are
- how old each family member is
- what your family members are like

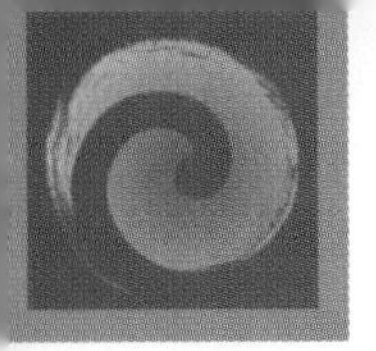

# Los números de 100 en adelante, fechas (*Numbers and dates*)

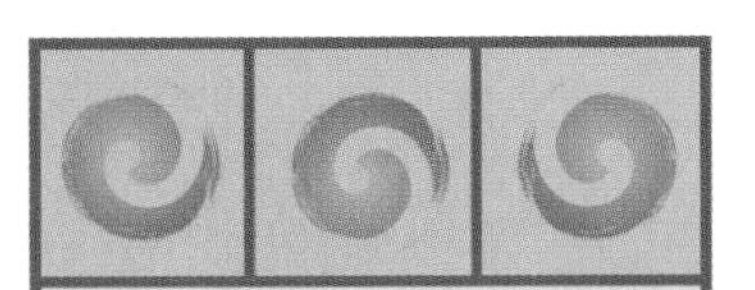

## Para averiguar

1. In which of the following numbers would you translate the word one: *one hundred, one thousand, one million*?
2. How do you express *years* in Spanish when referring to the date?

- Use the following numbers to count from 100 to 999.

| | | | |
|---|---|---|---|
| 100 | **cien** | 500 | **quinientos** |
| 101 | **ciento uno** | 600 | **seiscientos** |
| 102 | **ciento dos…** | 700 | **setecientos** |
| 200 | **doscientos** | 800 | **ochocientos** |
| 300 | **trescientos** | 900 | **novecientos** |
| 400 | **cuatrocientos** | 999 | **novecientos noventa y nueve** |

- Use **cien** to say *one hundred* exactly, but use **ciento** in 101 to 199. Never use the word **un** before **cien** or **ciento**. Although **cien** is used before both masculine and feminine nouns, multiples of one hundred (for example, 200, 300, etc.) agree in gender with the nouns they modify.

trescient**os** pesos — doscient**as** págin**as**
quinient**os** años — setecient**as** cuatro peset**as**

- Spanish uses a period (.) to designate numbers in the thousands, and a comma (,) to designate decimal points.

Spanish **1.543** (English **1,543**) — Mil quinientos cuarenta y tres
Spanish **3,25** (English **3.25**) — Tres con veinticinco

- The word for *thousand* is **mil. Mil** is not pluralized, nor is **un** used before it.

1.543 — **mil** quinientos cuarenta y tres
2.001 — dos **mil** uno
5.187 — cinco **mil** ciento ochenta y siete

- Note that years are expressed using **mil**, not hundreds, when indicating the date.

1492 — mil cuatrocientos noventa y dos
1998 — mil novecientos noventa y ocho

- When counting in the millions, say **un millón, dos millones, tres millones**…. Use **de** before a noun that directly follows **millón/millones**. If another number is between the word **millón/millones** and the noun, **de** is not needed.

un millón **de** dólares — un millón doscientos mil dólares
dos millones **de** pesetas — dos millones novecientas pesetas

## ¡ojo!

**La fecha**

Sunday is first day of the week on English calendars, Monday on Spanish ones.

- To express the date, use the ordinal number **primero** for the first of the month, but use the cardinal numbers **dos, tres, cuatro**… for the other days. When saying you are going to do something *on a certain date*, do not translate the word *on*. The names of the months are not capitalized in Spanish.

| | | | |
|---|---|---|---|
| **enero** | **abril** | **julio** | **octubre** |
| **febrero** | **mayo** | **agosto** | **noviembre** |
| **marzo** | **junio** | **septiembre** | **diciembre** |

No hay clase el **primero** de diciembre. — *There is no class on December 1st.*
Mi cumpleaños es el **catorce** de agosto. — *My birthday is (on) August fourteenth.*

- When writing dates with numbers in Spanish, write the day first, then the month.

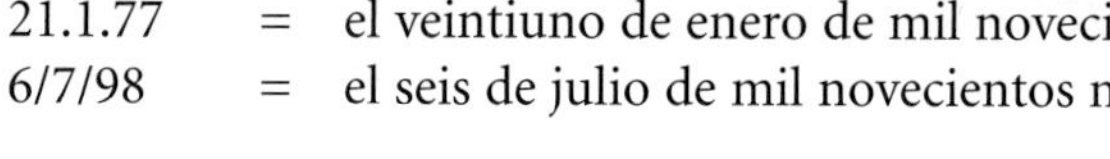

| | | |
|---|---|---|
| 4–10–96 | = | el cuatro de octubre de mil novecientos noventa y seis |
| 21.1.77 | = | el veintiuno de enero de mil novecientos setenta y siete |
| 6/7/98 | = | el seis de julio de mil novecientos noventa y ocho |

## A lo personal

**A. Números.** Read the following numbers in Spanish.

| | | | |
|---|---|---|---|
| 1. 101 | 2. 415 | 3. 539 | 4. 764 |
| 5. 1.385 | 6. 50.199 | 7. 100.079 | 8. 1.253.941 |

**B. Fechas importantes.** Can you fill in the missing information in the following dates? If you do not know, guess.

1. la Declaración de la Independencia de los Estados Unidos: el 4 de julio de ________
2. el comienzo de la Independencia Mexicana: el 16 de ________ de 1810
3. el bombardeo de Pearl Harbor: el 7 de diciembre de ________
4. la bomba atómica en Hiroshima: el 6 de agosto de ________
5. el asesinato del presidente Kennedy: el 22 de ________ de 1963
6. la primera persona en la luna: el 20 de julio de ________

**Answers for B.** 1) *el 4 de julio de 1776.* 2) *el 16 de septiembre de 1810.* 3) *el 7 de diciembre de 1941.* 4) *el 6 de agosto de 1945.* 5) *el 22 de noviembre de 1963.* 6) *el 20 de julio de 1969.*

**C. Los signos del zodíaco.** Here are the dates of birth of some famous people. Say when they were born and give their sign.

MODELO: Antonio Banderas (10/8/60)
*Antonio Banderas nació el 10 de agosto de 1960. Su horóscopo es Leo.*

1. Gloria Estefan (9/1/57)
2. Andy García (12/4/56)
3. Jennifer López (24/7/70)
4. Plácido Domingo (21/1/41)
5. Cameron Díaz (30/8/72)
6. Salma Hayek (2/9/68)
7. Luis Miguel (19/4/70)
8. Ricky Martin (24/12/71)

**ARIES**
(21 de marzo / 19 de abril)

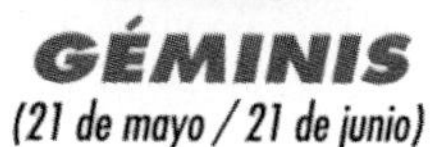

**CÁNCER**
(22 de junio / 22 de julio)

**LEO**
(23 de julio / 22 de agosto)

**VIRGO**
(23 de agosto / 21 de septiembre)

**LIBRA**
(22 de septiembre / 22 de octubre)

**ESCORPIÓN**
(23 de octubre / 21 de noviembre)

**SAGITARIO**
(22 de noviembre / 21 de diciembre)

**CAPRICORNIO**
(22 de diciembre / 19 de enero)

**ACUARIO**
(20 de enero / 19 de febrero)

**PISCIS**
(20 de febrero / 20 de marzo)

# TEMA 2 La casa

## Cosas de casa

**¡ojo!**

The word for bedroom has several equivalents in Spanish, depending on the region. Some of them are: **habitación**, **alcoba**, **dormitorio**, **cuarto**, and **recámara**.

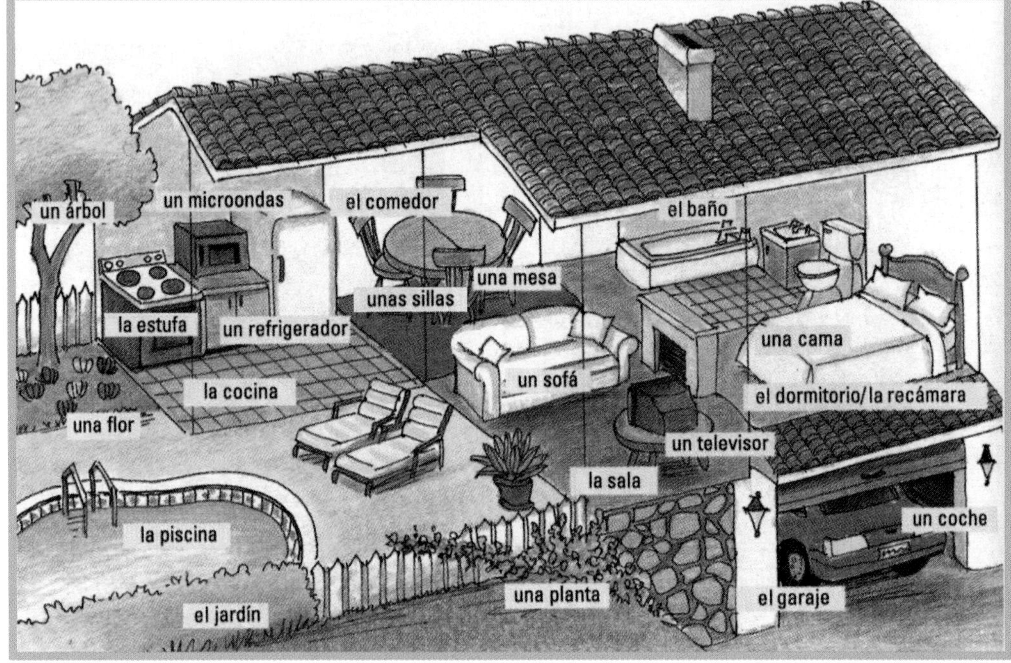


**Expansion.** Mention that vocabulary for the house may have regional variations, e.g., *piscina=alberca, refrigerador=frigorífico, alfombra=tapete, alcoba=dormitorio=recámara=cuarto=habitación.*

### Mi casa es…

*Lázaro asks his students about their homes….*

LÁZARO: ¿Dónde viven ustedes?
RAÚL: Yo vivo con mis padres y mi hermano Miguel. Alquilamos un apartamento en el tercer piso. Desde el balcón veo la piscina.
FABIOLA: Mis padres, mi hermana Elvira y yo vivimos en nuestra propia casa. Es pequeña, de un piso con un garaje para dos coches. Hay dos dormitorios, un baño, cocina, sala y comedor.
JEANNE: Mis padres están divorciados. Yo vivo con mi mamá en un condominio de dos pisos. En el patio hay una mesa con sillas; allí leo mis libros favoritos.
LÁZARO: Jeanne, ¿tú entiendes el español, verdad?
JEANNE: Sí, señor Frankel. Yo aprendo español con mi amigo Raúl.
LÁZARO: ¡Qué bien! Gracias, Raúl. José, ¿tú vives con tus tíos?
JOSÉ: No, ellos están en Costa Rica. Yo vivo en su casa con mis primas Lucero y Ana. La casa es muy grande, con cuatro dormitorios y un jardín grande con piscina.

**Answers for A.** 1) *Con sus padres y su hermano.* 2) *Porque están divorciados.* 3) *No.* 4) *Raúl.*

**A. ¿Comprende Ud.?** Answer the questions based on the dialog.

1. ¿Con quién vive Raúl?
2. ¿Por qué no viven juntos (*together*) el padre y la madre de Jeanne?
3. ¿Fabiola es hija única?
4. ¿Quién practica español con Jeanne?

**B. Yo prefiero...** Read the following ads for apartments to rent/buy. Discuss with your classmate which you prefer and why.

**COMPRE/ALQUILE**
Apartamento con 3 habitaciones, 2 baños, estudio, piscina, seguridad. Disponible en agosto.
Tel. 233-0940 (24h)

**URBANIZACIÓN "LA DUQUESA"**
Precioso apartamento, 3 habitaciones, 2 baños, estudio, seguridad, balcón, preciosa vista ciudad, excelentes condiciones. Buenos precios y localidad conveniente. Tel: 778-0998 (horas de trabajo)

**APARTAMENTO FRENTE AL MAR EN SANTA LUCRECIA.**
Torres altas de Golf, apt. 34. 6 habitaciones, 2 baños, cuarto de empleada, cuarto de huéspedes, 300 metros cuadrados. Incluye aire acondicionado, lavadora, secadora, calentador, etc. Tel: 454-5932 (noches)

Suggestion for B. Contrast square feet with square meters, providing the rough comparison that 1 square meter is a little less than 10 square feet. Ask students to discuss the size of their house/apartment in meters.

**C. Donde vivo yo.** After looking at the floor plan below for the Arias's house, draw the floor plan of your house and compare it with a classmate's. Make sure to label each area appropriately.

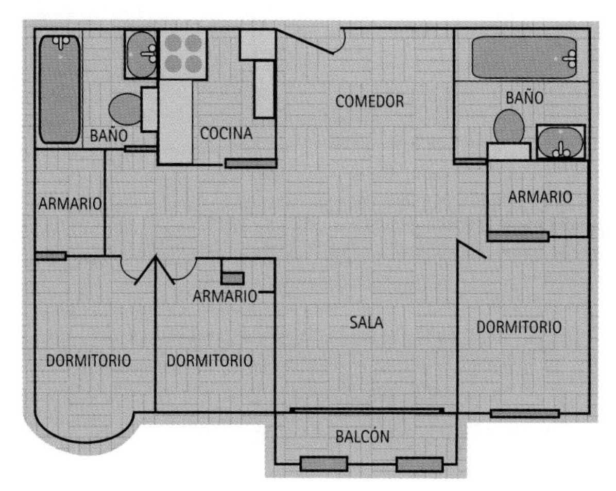


**D. Apartamentos nuevos.** Read the ad (**anuncio**) for apartments in Mexico. Then answer the questions.

1. No usan la palabra **apartamento**. ¿Qué palabra usan?
2. ¿Qué tipo de cuartos tienen los apartamentos?
3. ¿Cuántas recámaras (dormitorios) hay? ¿Cuántos baños?
4. ¿En qué calle está el Residencial Santa Fé?
5. ¿Está cerca de la Universidad Iberoamericana?

Suggestion for D. This ad cites the price in Mexican new pesos. The exchange rate at printing is 10 pesos to the dollar. What is the price of the apartment? Ask students to check today's exchange rate on the Internet or in the newspaper.

60% Vendido

**Residencial Santa Fé**

NORTE
BOSQUES DE LAS LOMAS
U. IBEROAMERICANA
VASCO DE QUIROGA
RESIDENCIAL SANTA FE
SUR

**Departamentos**
**Desde N$ 44,800.00**
- Superficie 110 m²
- 3 recámaras
- 2 baños
- Sala – comedor amplio
- Cuarto de servicio integrado
- Estacionamiento
- 20% de enganche diferido en 12 meses
- Reserve con N$ 15,000.00

**Preventa**

**UBICA** Vasco de Quiroga No. 1805, Santa Fé
Tel. 557-7759 557-7023

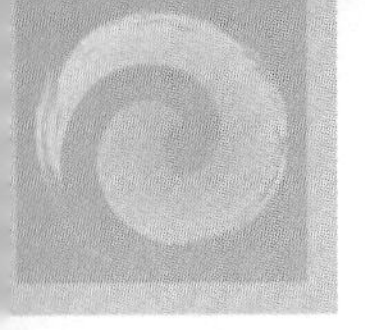

# Mi dormitorio

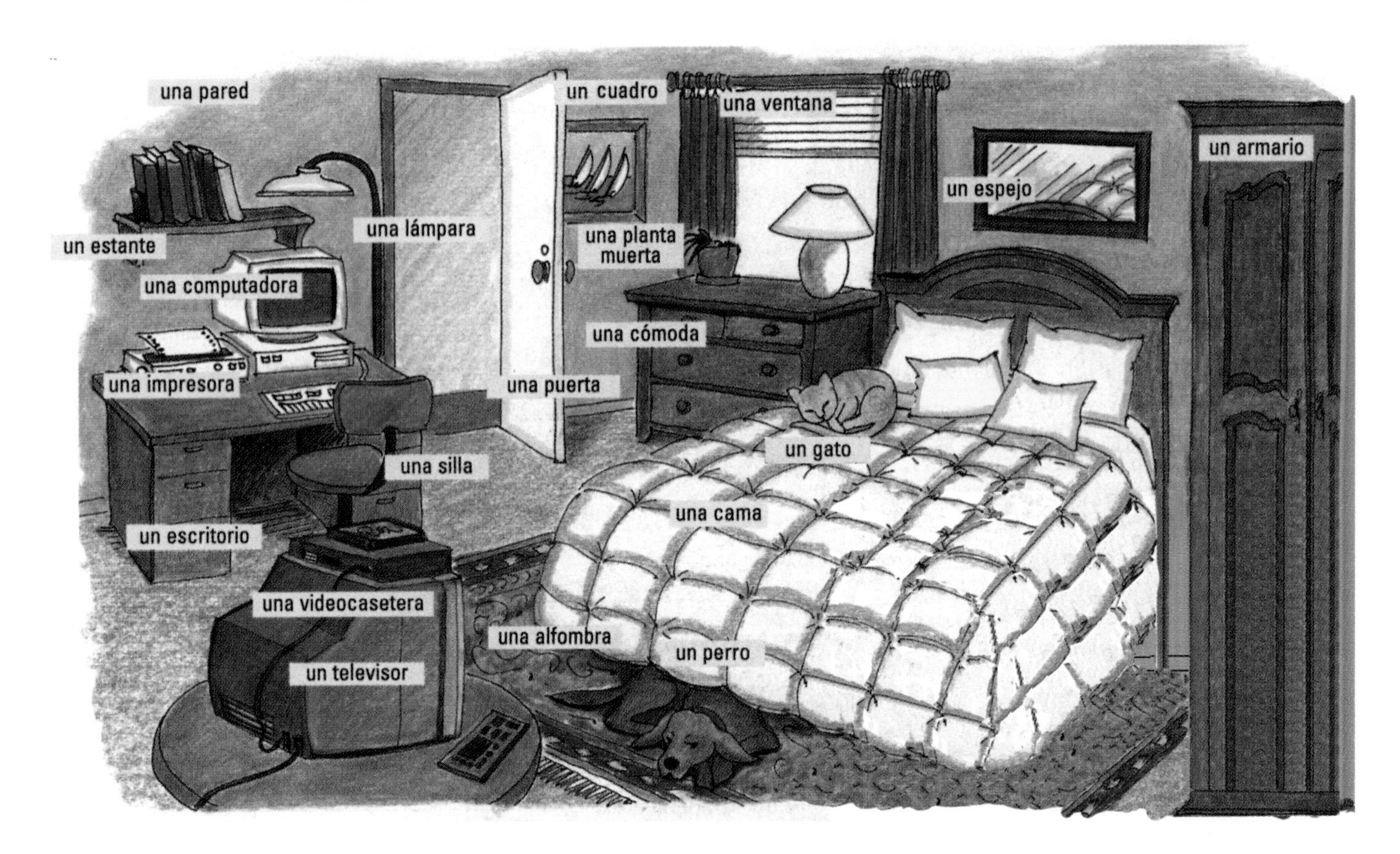


## Mi lugar favorito en mi casa

*Lázaro's students talk about their favorite places at home....*

LÁZARO: Mi lugar favorito en mi casa es el jardín. Hay una parrilla para asar carne y en el verano invito a mis amigos a comer. ¿Cuál es su lugar favorito en su casa?

RAÚL: Me gusta mi dormitorio. Hay dos camas, dos escritorios, dos sillas, un armario grande y una alfombra. Allí recibo a mis amigos cuando acabo la tarea.

FABIOLA: A mí me gusta el estudio porque allí están la computadora y la impresora. Todos los días escribo a mis amigos por correo electrónico.

JEANNE: A mí me gusta la cocina porque estoy cerca de mi familia. Todas las tardes después de las clases, bebo un vaso de leche y charlo con mi mamá.

LÁZARO: Gracias, Jeanne. ¿Cuál es tu lugar favorito en tu casa, José?

JOSÉ: Creo que la sala es mi lugar favorito. Los sillones son muy cómodos. En las paredes, hay fotos de mi familia. Cuando estoy allí, puedo recordar a mis padres.

LÁZARO: ¿A quién le gusta ver la televisión?

TODOS: ¡A mí, a mí!

**Answers for A.** 1) *Asar carne en la parrilla.* 2) *Beber leche y charlar con su mamá.* 3) *Porque hay fotos de su familia.* 4) *A todos.*

**A. ¿Comprende Ud.?** Answer the questions based on the dialog.

1. ¿Qué le gusta hacer a Lázaro en el verano?
2. ¿Qué le gusta hacer a Jeanne después de clase?
3. ¿Por qué prefiere José la sala?
4. ¿A cuántos estudiantes les gusta mirar la televisión?

**B. ¿En qué tienda?** Discuss with your classmate what each of these businesses offers for your house. Also mention the telephone number and address. List all household items you can that might be found in that store.

**C. Así es mi dormitorio.** Discuss with a classmate just what is in your bedroom. Include as many items as possible. Draw a sketch to help with your description.

**D. ¿Adónde vamos?** You are moving to a new house. Fill out the change of address form for the post office.

**Variation for D.** Brainstorm what needs to be done when you move: who needs to be notified, etc. Prepare a list on the board. Example: *Preparar todo lo necesario para el viaje, como reservas en la línea aérea, hotel y automóvil de alquiler.* Use this activity to reinforce numbers and dates previously introduced.

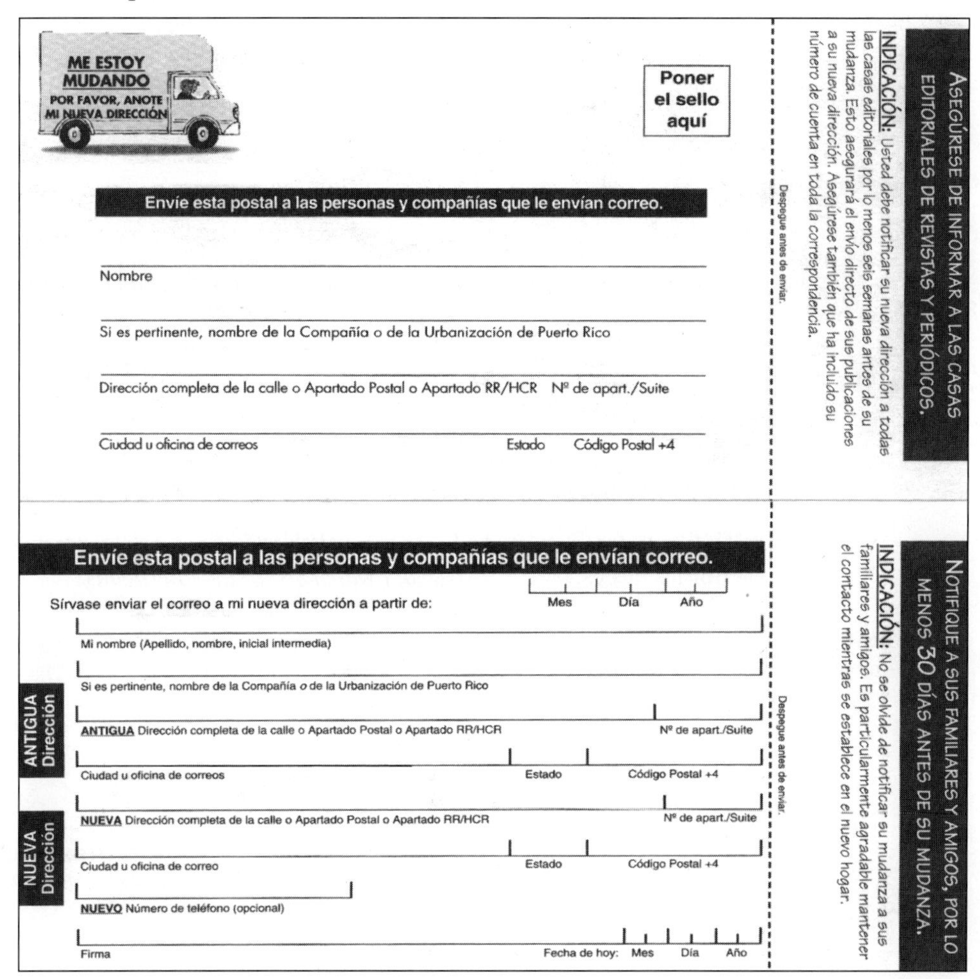

ME ESTOY MUDANDO
POR FAVOR, ANOTE MI NUEVA DIRECCIÓN

Poner el sello aquí

**Envíe esta postal a las personas y compañías que le envían correo.**

Nombre

Si es pertinente, nombre de la Compañía o de la Urbanización de Puerto Rico

Dirección completa de la calle o Apartado Postal o Apartado RR/HCR  Nº de apart./Suite

Ciudad u oficina de correos  Estado  Código Postal +4

ASEGÚRESE DE INFORMAR A LAS CASAS EDITORIALES DE REVISTAS Y PERIÓDICOS.

INDICACIÓN: Usted debe notificar su nueva dirección a todas las casas editoriales por lo menos seis semanas antes de su mudanza. Esto asegurará el envío directo de sus publicaciones a su nueva dirección. Asegúrese también que ha incluido su número de cuenta en toda la correspondencia.

Despegue antes de enviar.

**Envíe esta postal a las personas y compañías que le envían correo.**

Sírvase enviar el correo a mi nueva dirección a partir de: Mes Día Año

Mi nombre (Apellido, nombre, inicial intermedia)

Si es pertinente, nombre de la Compañía o de la Urbanización de Puerto Rico

ANTIGUA Dirección

ANTIGUA Dirección completa de la calle o Apartado Postal o Apartado RR/HCR  Nº de apart./Suite

Ciudad u oficina de correos  Estado  Código Postal +4

NUEVA Dirección

NUEVA Dirección completa de la calle o Apartado Postal o Apartado RR/HCR  Nº de apart./Suite

Ciudad u oficina de correo  Estado  Código Postal +4

NUEVO Número de teléfono (opcional)

Firma  Fecha de hoy: Mes Día Año

Despegue antes de enviar.

NOTIFIQUE A SUS FAMILIARES Y AMIGOS, POR LO MENOS 30 DÍAS ANTES DE SU MUDANZA.

INDICACIÓN: No se olvide de notificar su mudanza a sus familiares y amigos. Es particularmente agradable mantener el contacto mientras se establece en el nuevo hogar.

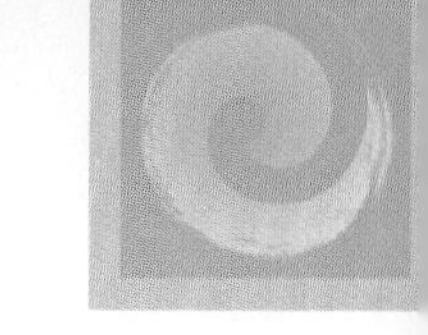

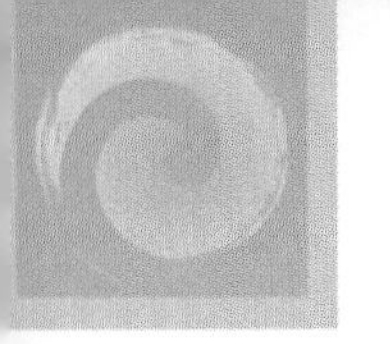

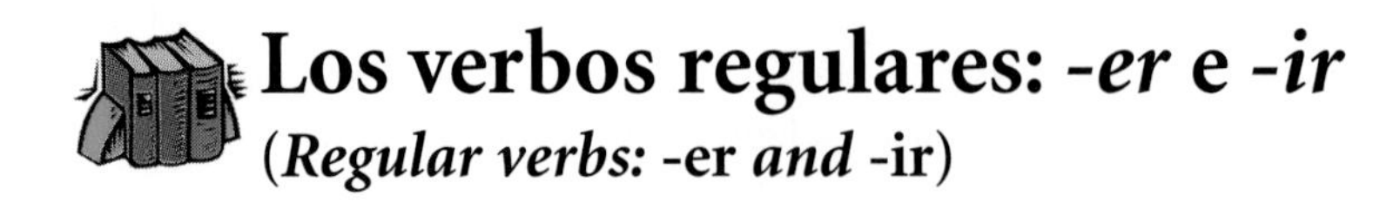

# Los verbos regulares: *-er* e *-ir* (*Regular verbs:* -er *and* -ir)

Verbs ending in **-er** and **-ir** are conjugated alike except for two forms. Which ones?

- Like **-ar** verbs, many **-er** and **-ir** verbs follow similar patterns. Most **-er** and **-ir** verbs are conjugated alike, except in the **nosotros** and **vosotros** forms.

| **comer** (*to eat*) | | **vivir** (*to live*) | |
|---|---|---|---|
| yo | com**o** | yo | viv**o** |
| tú | com**es** | tú | viv**es** |
| él, ella, usted | com**e** | él, ella, usted | viv**e** |
| nosotros/as | com**emos** | nosotros/as | viv**imos** |
| vosotros/as | com**éis** | vosotros/as | viv**ís** |
| ellos, ellas, ustedes | com**en** | ellos, ellas, ustedes | viv**en** |

- The following **-er** and **-ir** verbs are conjugated like **comer** and **vivir**.

| | | | |
|---|---|---|---|
| **aprender (a)** | *to learn* | **vender** | *to sell* |
| **beber** | *to drink* | **abrir** | *to open* |
| **comprender** | *to understand* | **asistir (a)** | *to attend* |
| **correr** | *to run* | **decidir** | *to decide* |
| **creer** | *to believe* | **escribir** | *to write* |
| **deber** | *to owe; should, ought to* | **insistir (en)** | *to insist (on)* |
| **leer** | *to read* | **recibir** | *to receive* |

- Note the use of prepositions after **aprender**, **asistir**, and **insistir** in the following examples.

**Aprendemos a** hablar, **a** escribir y **a** leer. — *We learn to speak, to write, and to read.*
**Asisto a** clase todos los días. — *I attend class every day.*
**Insisto en** comprender todo. — *I insist on understanding everything.*

- **Ver** uses the same endings as regular **-er** verbs, but keeps the **e** in the **yo** form.

**veo, ves, ve, vemos, veis, ven.**

—¿**Ves** la televisión por las mañanas? — *Do you watch television in the mornings?*
—No, **veo** la tele por las tardes. — *No, I watch TV in the afternoons.*

—¿**Ven** a Carlos desde aquí? — *Do you see Carlos from here?*
—Sí, **vemos** a Carlos y a Mary. — *Yes, we see Carlos and Mary.*

## A lo personal

**A. ¿Qué leen?** Which magazine do these people probably read?

MODELO: A mi abuelo le gusta hacer viajes. (Él)...
*Lee GeoMundo.*

1. A mis hermanos les gusta estudiar las ciencias. (Ellos)...
2. Nosotros trabajamos en un hospital. (Nosotros)...
3. A mi sobrino le gusta mucho el fútbol. (Él)...
4. ¿Te gusta ver telenovelas? ¿(Tú)...?
5. ¿Ustedes tienen una casa nueva? ¿(Ustedes)...?

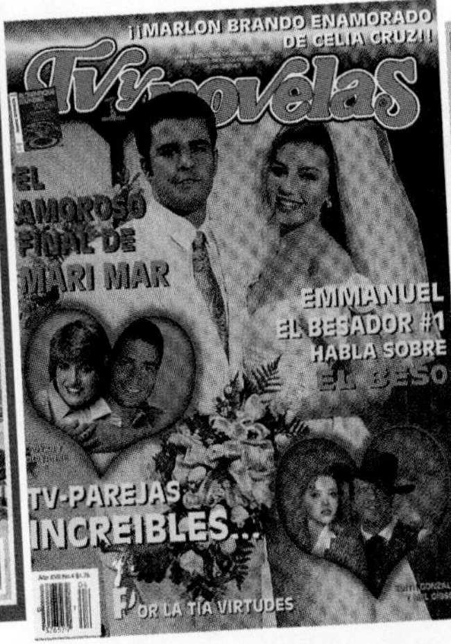

**B. Una familia de diplomáticos.** Name the countries in which family members presently live.

MODELO: *Nuestros abuelos viven en Venezuela.*

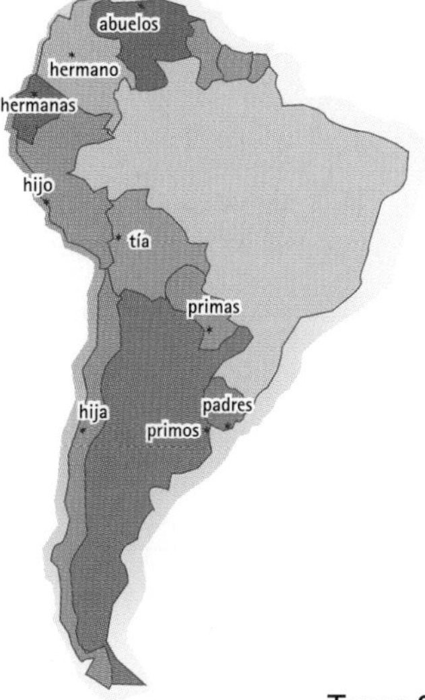

## Más práctica con verbos en *-er* e *-ir*
### (*More practice with* -er *and* -ir *verbs*)

**A. ¿Quién?** Who in your class does these things? If no one does, use **nadie**.

MODELO: beber café
*El profesor bebe café.* o
*Muchos estudiantes beben café.* o
*Nadie bebe café.*

1. leer bien el español
2. asistir a clase siempre
3. comer en clase
4. deber estudiar esta noche
5. comprender todo en clase
6. escribir mucho en la pizarra
7. aprender mucho
8. insistir en hablar español

**B. ¿Qué hacen?** Say what you and your friends do in each place listed in the third column. Form logical sentences.

| | | |
|---|---|---|
| Yo | recibir ayuda | en el parque |
| El/La profesor/a | comer | en el gimnasio |
| Nosotros | abrir las ventanas | en un cine |
| Los estudiantes | beber | en clase |
| Mi amigo Iván | aprender mucho | en casa |
| Mi amiga María | leer libros/el periódico | en la biblioteca |
| Ellos | escribir composiciones | en la librería |
| | hacer tareas | en un bar |
| | correr | en una discoteca |
| | deber escuchar bien | en la iglesia |
| | insistir en hablar español | en la universidad |
| | asistir a clases | |
| | vender libros | |
| | comprender mucho/poco | |

**C. ¿Qué hacemos en…?** On a separate sheet of paper write the following headings: **la cafetería**, **la clase**, and **el centro comercial**. Then, brainstorm with a classmate to write as many activity verbs as possible for each one.

MODELO:

| la cafetería | la clase | el centro comercial |
|---|---|---|
| *almorzar* | *escribir* | *vender* |

**D. Y ahora…** Use your list of verbs from Activity C to form sentences telling what people do in each place.

MODELO: *Nosotros almorzamos con amigos en la cafetería.*
*Los estudiantes escriben composiciones en la clase.*
*Ellos venden ropa en el centro comercial.*

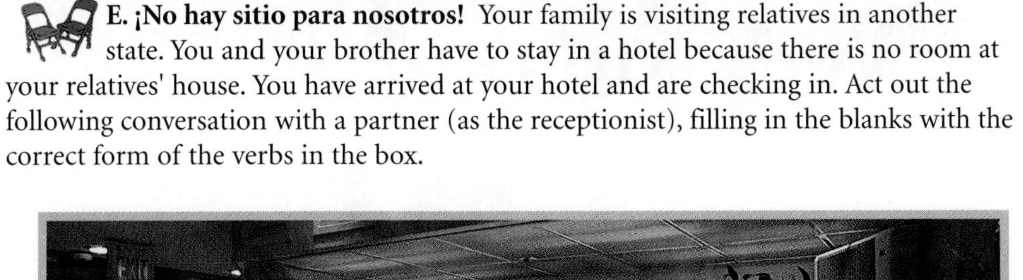

**E. ¡No hay sitio para nosotros!** Your family is visiting relatives in another state. You and your brother have to stay in a hotel because there is no room at your relatives' house. You have arrived at your hotel and are checking in. Act out the following conversation with a partner (as the receptionist), filling in the blanks with the correct form of the verbs in the box.

| tener | necesitar | saber | creer | vender | beber | abrir | insistir | ser | escribir |
|---|---|---|---|---|---|---|---|---|---|

RECEPCIONISTA: Hola, buenas tardes. ¿En qué puedo ayudarles?

UD: Hola, buenas tardes. ¿ _____________ usted habitaciones libres?

RECEPCIONISTA: ¿ _____________ para esta noche o para mañana?

UD: Para esta noche. Nosotros _____________ pasar la noche aquí porque no hay bastantes (*enough*) habitaciones en la casa de mis familiares.

RECEPCIONISTA: Ah, ya veo… Pues ustedes _____________ suerte. Sí _____________ habitaciones libres para esta noche.

UD: ¡Qué bien! Señor, ¿ _____________ si hay algún buen restaurante cerca de aquí?

RECEPCIONISTA: Sí, hay varios restaurantes en el hotel. Yo _____________ que el restaurante italiano en el segundo piso del hotel está abierto.

UD: ¿ _____________ ustedes bebidas dentro del hotel?

RECEPCIONISTA: No, no _____________ bebidas. Pero nosotros siempre _____________ en el bar de enfrente, ése de las luces de neón. Los meseros son muy simpáticos y ellos siempre _____________ en beber con nosotros.

UD: ¡Qué simpáticos! ¿ _____________ Ud. a qué hora _____________ el bar?

RECEPCIONISTA: No estoy seguro, pero _____________ que a las ocho de la noche.

UD: Perfecto, entonces tengo tiempo para _____________ una tarjeta postal para mi amigo Pedro, antes de ir al bar.

RECEPCIONISTA: Muy bien, aquí tienen su llave. Si necesitan algo, el número de la recepción es el 346 desde su habitación.

UD: Muchas gracias por todo. ¡Hasta luego!

RECEPCIONISTA: ¡Hasta luego! ¡Que se diviertan esta noche!

# Vocabulario

## TEMA 1

### La familia

**Sustantivos**

| | |
|---|---|
| **el/la abuelo/a** | *grandfather, grandmother* |
| **el año** | *year* |
| **el antepasado** | *ancestor* |
| **la carrera** | *career (university studies)* |
| **la casa** | *house* |
| **la ciudad** | *city* |
| **la comida** | *food* |
| **el/la cuñado/a** | *brother/sister-in-law* |
| **el/la descendiente** | *descendant* |
| **el/la esposo/a** | *husband, wife* |
| **los Estados Unidos** | *United States* |
| **la foto(grafía)** | *photo(graph)* |
| **el/la hermano/a** | *brother, sister* |
| **el/la hermanastro/a** | *stepbrother/sister* |
| **el/la hijastro/a** | *stepson/daughter* |
| **el/la/hijo/a** | *son/daughter* |
| **la madrastra** | *stepmother* |
| **la madre/mamá** | *mother/mom* |
| **el/la medio hermano/a** | *half brother/sister* |
| **la nuera** | *daughter-in-law* |
| **el origen** | *origin* |
| **el padrastro** | *stepfather* |
| **el padre/papá** | *father/dad* |
| **el/la primo/a** | *cousin* |
| **el/la suegro/a** | *father/mother-in-law* |
| **el/la tío/a** | *uncle, aunt* |
| **el yerno** | *son-in-law* |

**Verbos**

| | |
|---|---|
| **adoptar** | *to adopt* |
| **casarse (con)** | *to get married (to)* |
| **dedicarse (a)** | *to work at, dedicate oneself to* |
| **descender** | *to descend* |
| **enseñar** | *to teach* |
| **manejar** | *to operate* |
| **vivir** | *to live* |

**Adjetivos**

| | |
|---|---|
| **americano/a** | *American* |
| **casado/a** | *married* |
| **materno/a** | *maternal* |
| **muerto/a** | *dead* |
| **privado/a** | *private* |
| **soltero/a** | *single* |
| **típico/a** | *typical* |

**Otras expresiones**

| | |
|---|---|
| **ya** | *already* |
| **afuera** | *outside* |

## TEMA 2

### La casa

**Sustantivos**

| | |
|---|---|
| **la alfombra** | *carpet* |
| **el armario** | *cupboard, closet* |
| **el automóvil** | *automobile* |
| **el balcón** | *balcony* |
| **la cama** | *bed* |
| **la cocina** | *kitchen* |
| **el comedor** | *dining room* |
| **la cómoda** | *dresser* |
| **el correo electrónico** | *e-mail* |
| **el cuadro** | *the painting* |
| **el dormitorio** | *bedroom* |
| **el espejo** | *mirror* |
| **el estudio** | *study* |
| **la estufa** | *stove* |
| **la flor** | *flower* |
| **el garaje** | *garage* |
| **el gas** | *gas (natural)* |
| **el gato** | *cat* |
| **el horno (microondas)** | *oven (microwave)* |
| **la impresora** | *printer* |
| **el jardín** | *garden* |
| **la pared** | *wall* |
| **la parrilla** | *grill, barbecue* |
| **la parte** | *part* |
| **el perro** | *dog* |
| **la piscina** | *swimming pool* |
| **la pulgada** | *inch* |
| **el refrigerador, la nevera** | *refrigerator* |
| **la sala** | *living room* |
| **el sillón** | *armchair* |
| **el sofá** | *couch* |
| **el/la vecino/a** | *neighbor* |

**Verbos**

| | |
|---|---|
| **alquilar** | *to rent* |
| **cocinar** | *to cook* |
| **comer** | *to eat* |
| **compartir** | *to share* |
| **comprender** | *to understand* |
| **correr** | *to run* |
| **leer** | *to read* |
| **recordar (ue)** | *to remember* |
| **salir (g)** | *to leave, go out* |
| **ver** | *to see* |
| **visitar** | *to visit* |

**Adjetivos**

| | |
|---|---|
| **cómodo/a** | *comfortable* |
| **propio/a** | *own* |

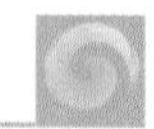

# Reunión A

**A escuchar. Se alquila una casa.** Indicate who says the following lines, either **Ana (A)** or **la Sra. Peralta (P).**

1. ______ ¿Ud. alquila una casa?
2. ______ Tiene tres dormitorios, dos baños y medio, sala, comedor y garaje.
3. ______ ¿De qué color es la alfombra?
4. ______ ¡Es mucho dinero!
5. ______ La casa está desocupada.
6. ______ ¿Puede venir mañana sábado?

**Tapescript for A escuchar. Se alquila una casa.**
SRA. PERALTA: Buenos días, soy la Sra. Peralta. ¿Ud. alquila una casa?
ANA: Sí, es una casa de un piso, con tres dormitorios, dos baños y medio, sala, comedor formal, cocina y garaje para dos automóviles.
SRA. PERALTA: ¿De qué color es la alfombra?
ANA: Es de color crema. En los baños y la cocina hay mosaicos; creo que son rosa y café.
SRA. PERALTA: En el periódico dice que el alquiler es de mil dólares al mes y debo dar novecientos dólares de depósito. ¡Es mucho dinero!
ANA: Sí, pero la casa es muy bonita. También necesita rellenar una solicitud y pagar quince dólares por un informe sobre su crédito.
SRA. PERALTA: ¿Cuándo puedo ver la casa?
ANA: Ahora está desocupada. Puede venir mañana sábado, de diez de la mañana a tres de la tarde.

**Answers for A escuchar.**
1) *La Sra. Peralta.* 2) *Ana.* 3) *La Sra. Peralta.* 4) *La Sra. Peralta.* 5) *Ana.* 6) *Ana.*

**A conversar.** With two classmates discuss your homes, mentioning the number of rooms, your favorite spot, the size of the kitchen, whether there is a pool or not, if there is a garden, and any additional information that makes your house or apartment special.

## ¿Lo sabía?

Check out the advertisement on remodeling your home. What does *Palacio* offer that you would like to do in your home? Why would you do business with this company? Why not?

¿Cómo la ves? Encantadora, ¿verdad? Tu casa también puede serlo con la Renovación PALACIO. Un sistema revolucionario para cambiar las puertas, las ventanas, poner escaleras, instalar cocinas, colocar parquets, etc. De la forma más fácil, rápida y económica. Con la garantía de un fabricante líder, capaz de ofrecer buenos precios, presupuestos inamovibles y con una fuerza imparable de profesionales con mucho empuje. Esto es PALACIO. Una gran exposición, un stock permanente y un servicio completo a tu medida. Todo en uno. Descubre los encantos que puede tener tu casa. En nuestra guía práctica o en uno de nuestros centros. Estarás encantado con PALACIO. La renovación total de puertas adentro.

**La revolución PALACIO ha llegado a esta casa.**

**PALACIO**
Pista de Ademuz, La Cañada
(Centro comercial)
(96) 138-3446

**A buscar.** Search the Internet for articles (in Spanish) on remodeling a house. Make a list of five helpful tips or ideas that you found in these articles and share them with the rest of the class.

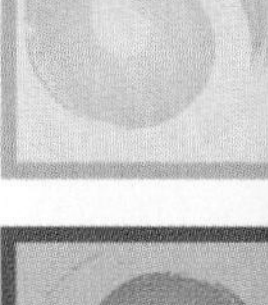
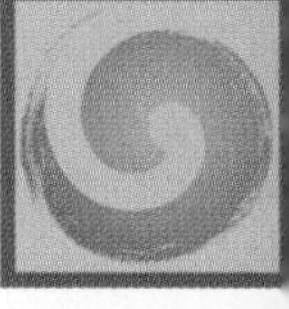

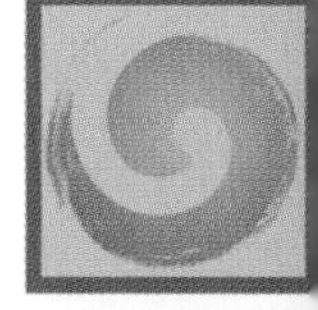
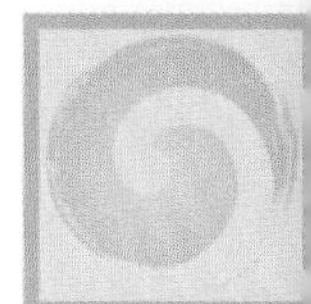
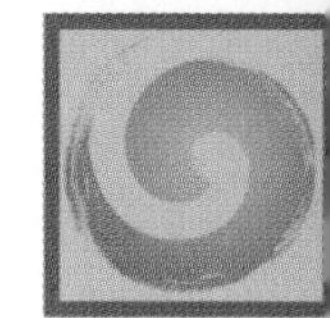
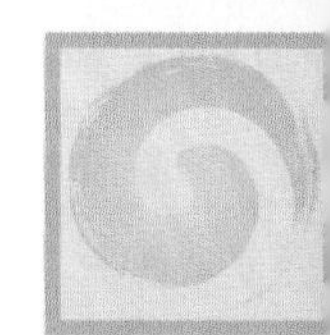

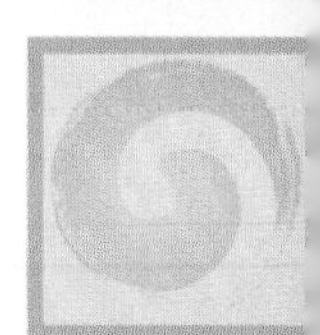

# TEMA 3 Los quehaceres domésticos

## Hay que limpiar

Lucero hace la cama, limpia el piso y barre el patio.

José lava los platos y quita el polvo.

Ana seca los platos y aspira la alfombra.

### ¿Qué haces en casa?

*Ana, José, and Lucero are trying to divide household chores among themselves....*

ANA: Hay que limpiar muy bien la casa. Primero, vamos a hacer nuestras camas. José, tú aspiras toda la casa.

JOSÉ: Aspirar es aburridísimo. Es más divertido sacudir que aspirar.

ANA: Bueno, creo que tú sacudes mejor que yo. Entonces yo aspiro, pero Lucero y tú limpian sus dormitorios. Tu dormitorio está tan desorganizado como el de Lucero.

JOSÉ: Es que tengo muchísimas cosas y no tengo tanto espacio como tú en el armario.

ANA: Es verdad, yo tengo menos cosas que tú. Puedes poner algunas cosas en mi dormitorio.

LUCERO: También hay que barrer el patio, lavar los baños y la cocina.

ANA: El patio no está sucio y además no hay tiempo para barrerlo. Hay tres baños, todos podemos limpiar uno.

LUCERO: ¿Quién limpia la cocina?

JOSÉ: Yo limpio la mesa y lavo los platos. Ana seca los platos y los guarda en la alacena y tú limpias el piso.

**A. ¿Comprende Ud.?** Answer the questions based on the dialog.

1. ¿A quién no le gusta aspirar?
2. ¿Quiénes tienen el dormitorio desorganizado?
3. ¿Cuántos baños limpia cada (*each*) persona?
4. ¿Qué dormitorio tiene más espacio?

**Answers for A.** 1) *A José.* 2) *José y Lucero.* 3) *Uno.* 4) *El de Ana.*

**B. ¿Y en su casa?** Make a list of household chores and discuss with your classmate whose responsibility each one is in your house.

**Warm-up for B.** Model what chores you do in your house, writing on the board, e.g., *Yo lavo los platos, quito el polvo de los muebles y barro el patio.* Ask students to describe what they do.

**C. Mis responsabilidades en casa.** Pick two rooms of your house and say what you do there. You may include activities or chores. Compare your activities/chores with other students in groups of four.

MODELO: *En la cocina yo lavo y seco los platos. En mi dormitorio miro la televisión y estudio.*

**D. ¡Muebles nuevos!** You've been working overtime and expect a big paycheck. You'd like to buy some new furniture for your apartment. Select items from the ad or include additional items and prepare a shopping list, including price. Compare your list with a classmate's, including which items are more or less expensive, better for your house or his/hers.

**Expansion for D.** Bring in additional furniture ads from magazines and newspapers. Encourage students to look for items they really would want to purchase for their home/apartment.

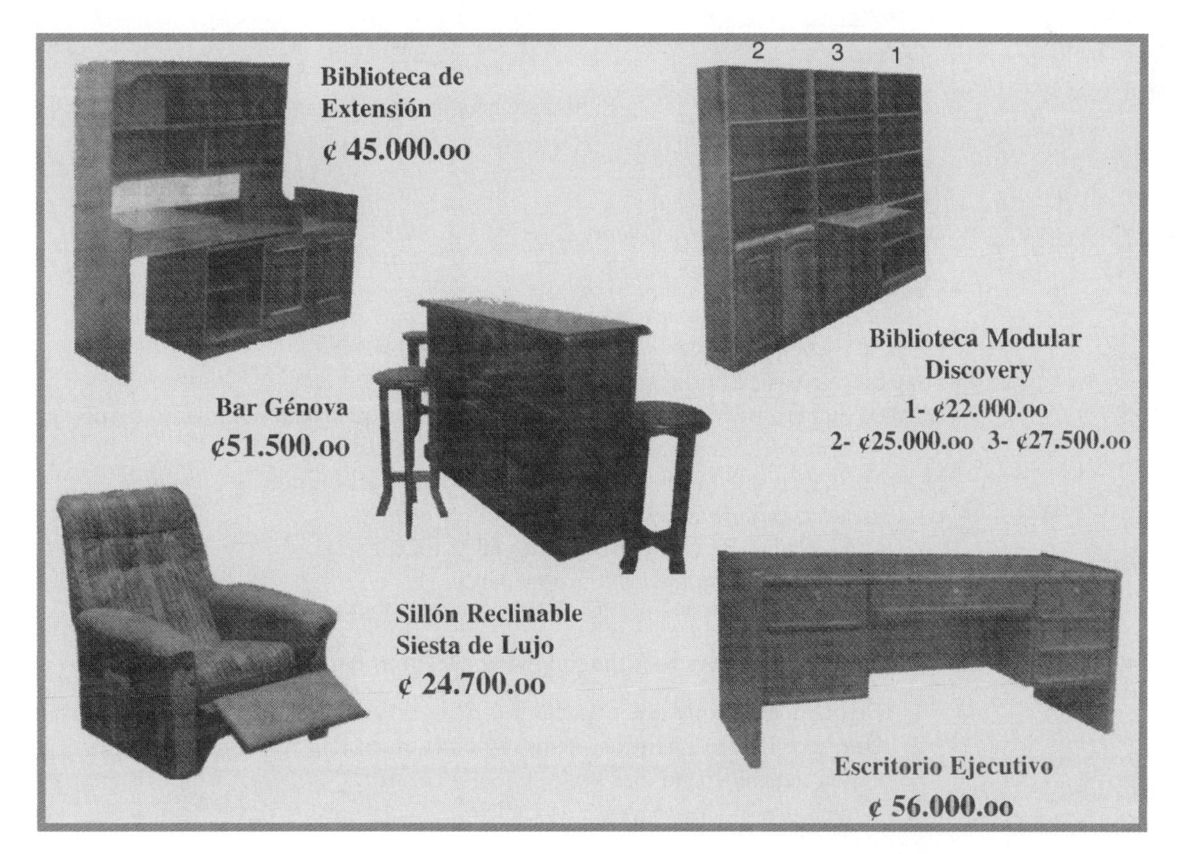

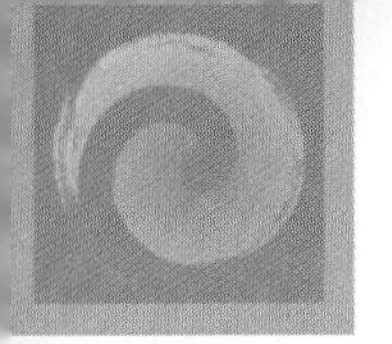

# ¿Qué pasa?

Ella mira la televisión.

Él come.

Él estudia.

Ella lee un libro.

Ella trabaja.

Ella juega al tenis.

Él no hace nada en especial.

Ella duerme.

## ¿Qué haces?

*Lázaro talks to Isabel on the phone....*

LÁZARO: Hola, Isabel, ¿qué haces?
ISABEL: Lavo y plancho la ropa. ¿Y tú, Lázaro?
LÁZARO: Escucho música.
ISABEL: ¿No vas a limpiar tu apartamento?
LÁZARO: Sí, pero puedo escuchar música y hacer los quehaceres al mismo tiempo. Hoy limpio el refrigerador y el horno. ¡Están sucísimos!
ISABEL: Sí, creo que tu refrigerador es el más sucio del mundo.
LÁZARO: Gracias, pero no está tan sucio como tu coche.
ISABEL: Es verdad. Te invito esta tarde a lavar mi coche.
LÁZARO: Bueno, estoy allí a las tres de la tarde.

**Answers for A.** 1) *De Isabel.* 2) *Los quehaceres.* 3) *Isabel.* 4) *A las tres.*

**A. ¿Comprende Ud.?** Answer the following questions based on the dialog.

1. ¿De quién es la ropa que plancha Isabel?
2. ¿Qué hace Lázaro mientras (*while*) escucha música?
3. ¿Quién tiene el coche más sucio, Isabel o Lázaro?
4. ¿A qué hora va Lázaro a casa de Isabel?

**B. En el centro estudiantil.** First say if anyone is or is not doing these things based on the illustration below. Then say if anyone in your class is doing these things.

MODELO: ¿Alguien come?
*Sí, el estudiante con bigote come.* o
*Nadie en mi clase come.*

¿Alguien…

1. …lee?
2. …duerme?
3. …bebe?
4. …hace ejercicio?
5. …usa una computadora?
6. …escucha música?
7. …abre una ventana?
8. …escribe algo?

**C. ¿Quién es la mejor/peor persona?** We all have chores to do around the house, and some of us do certain ones better. For each responsibility, tell your classmate who does that job best (or worst!) and find out who does that same job best in his/her home.

MODELO: *Mi madre es la mejor persona para limpiar el baño.*

1. lavar la ropa
2. planchar la ropa
3. limpiar el refrigerador
4. barrer el patio
5. hacer la cama
6. lavar y secar los platos

SU ASPIRADORA DEBE HACER EL TRABAJO PESADO, NO USTED.

Las características innovadoras de Kenmore hacen de sus electrodomésticos los preferidos de América. Y ahora, con estos precios especiales, es más fácil que nunca tener un electrodoméstico Kenmore en su hogar.

**199.99 Aspiradora Kenmore de 12 amperios.** Cuenta con filtro de aire triple, manguera giratoria y suplementos para facilitar la limpieza general.

**99.99 Aspiradora vertical Kenmore de 11.0 amperios** Cuenta con motor de sistema "Powerpath" y ajuste para diferentes grosores de alfombra. Además, suplementos para limpieza general.

**D. Un apartamento desordenado.** Your apartment is a disaster and your parents are coming for dinner. Your old vacuum cleaner doesn't work and you must vacuum the carpeting before they arrive! Discuss with your roommate which one to buy from the ad, indicating price and why you prefer one over another.

**Variation for D.** What other appliances are needed? Have students mention items that they really need, mentioning price and at what store they would purchase the item. Ads could be brought in to show price and source of merchandise.

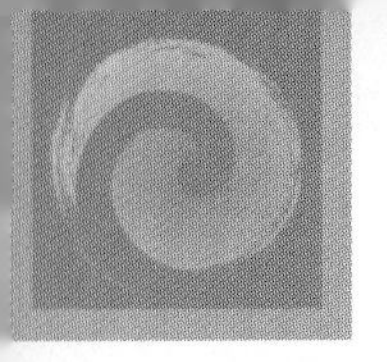

# Los comparativos
## (*Comparisons*)

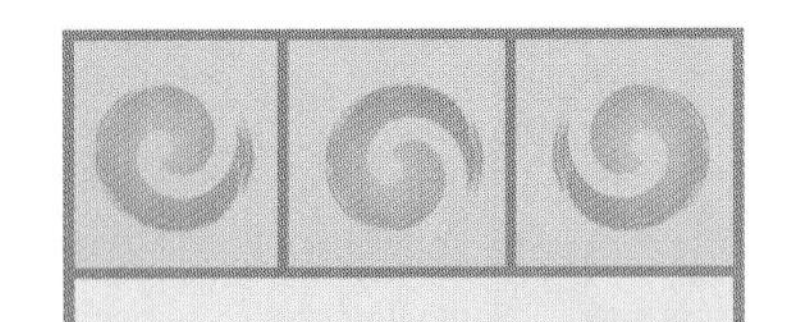

### Para averiguar

1. How do you say *more... than, less... than,* and *as... as* in Spanish?
2. Do you use **tan** or **tanto/a/os/as** before adjectives and adverbs? Which do you use before nouns?
3. Which four adjectives have irregular comparatives?

- To compare people, things or actions, use the following expressions with an adjective or an adverb: **más... que, menos... que,** or **tan... como.**

| | |
|---|---|
| Fabiola es **más alta que** Elvira. | *Fabiola is taller than Elvira.* |
| Elvira es **menos alta que** Fabiola. | *Elvira is less tall than Fabiola.* |
| Elvira es **tan bonita como** Fabiola. | *Elvira is as pretty as Fabiola.* |
| Elvira se levanta **más temprano que** Fabiola. | *Elvira gets up earlier than Fabiola.* |
| Me acuesto **menos tarde que** antes. | *I go to bed less late than before.* |
| Salgo **tan frecuentemente como** ustedes. | *I go out as often as you.* |

- To say *better, worse, older,* or *younger*, use the following irregular comparatives.

| | |
|---|---|
| Esta guardería es **mejor que** aquélla. | *This day care is better than that one.* |
| Un refrigerio de dulces es **peor que** uno de frutas. | *A snack of candy is worse than a snack of fruit.* |
| Tengo un hermano **mayor** y una hermana **menor.** | *I have one older brother and one younger sister.* |

- **Más... que** and **menos... que** can also be used with a noun to say *how much.* With nouns, use **tanto/a/os/as... como** rather than **tan... como.**

| | |
|---|---|
| Mi esposo toma **más jugo que** yo. | *My husband drinks more juice than I do.* |
| Fabio duerme **menos horas que** antes. | *Fabio sleeps less hours than before.* |
| Dormimos **tantas horas como** trabajamos. | *We sleep as many hours as we work.* |

- **Más, menos,** and **tanto** may all be used with verbs.

| | |
|---|---|
| Comprendo **más** ahora. | *I understand more now.* |
| Necesitas comer **menos.** | *You need to eat less.* |
| ¡No debes hablar **tanto**! | *You shouldn't talk so much!* |

## A lo personal

**A. Los intereses.** Compare the following things in terms of your interest.

MODELO: el cine/el teatro
*Para mí, el cine es más interesante que el teatro.* o
*Para mí, el cine es tan interesante como el teatro.* o
*Para mí, el cine es menos interesante que el teatro.*

1. el cine/la televisión
2. la literatura/la música
3. la psicología/la química
4. los documentales/las películas de ciencia ficción
5. la música clásica/la música rock
6. los museos/la playa
7. el arte moderno/el arte medieval
8. Europa/América del Sur

**B. Las madres de hoy.** Mothers today have different demands than mothers thirty years ago. Compare these activities of mothers then and now. Begin with **Las madres ahora...** and use **más... que** or **menos... que.**

MODELO: comprar comida rápida
*Las madres ahora compran más comida rápida que las madres de antes.*

1. trabajar fuera de casa
2. preparar comida fresca
3. trabajar en el jardín
4. depender de guarderías
5. tener estrés

**C. La ciudad o el campo.** Compare your impressions of life in the big city to life in a small country town.

MODELO: problemas
*Hay más problemas en la ciudad que en el campo.* o
*Hay tantos problemas en la ciudad como en el campo.* o
*Hay menos problemas en la ciudad que en el campo.*

1. delincuencia
2. contaminación
3. violencia doméstica
4. estrés
5. drogas
6. estudiantes universitarios
7. tolerancia
8. desempleo
9. tiempo libre
10. tecnología

**D. Compañeros de cuarto.** Who does more chores? Compare yourself to your roommate, spouse, or parents.

MODELO: lavar la ropa
*Lavo más ropa que mi compañero de cuarto.* o
*Lavo menos ropa que mi compañero de cuarto.* o
*Lavo tanta ropa como mi compañero de cuarto.*

1. lavar platos
2. comprar comida
3. sacar la basura
4. planchar la ropa
5. quitar el polvo
6. hacer trabajo en casa

**E. Después de graduarme.** How do you expect your life to change after graduation? Write at least five sentences comparing your life now and your life in the future. Use **Voy a** + *infinitive* to talk about the future.

dinero problemas tiempo libre estrés trabajo aburrido/a responsabilidades contento/a

MODELO: Voy a ser... *más independiente después de graduarme.*

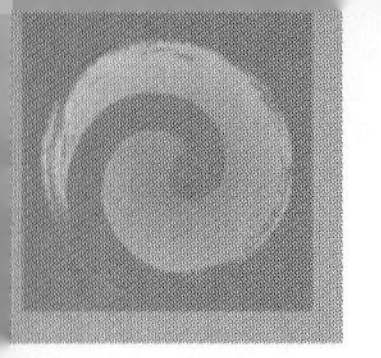

# Los superlativos
## (*Superlatives*)

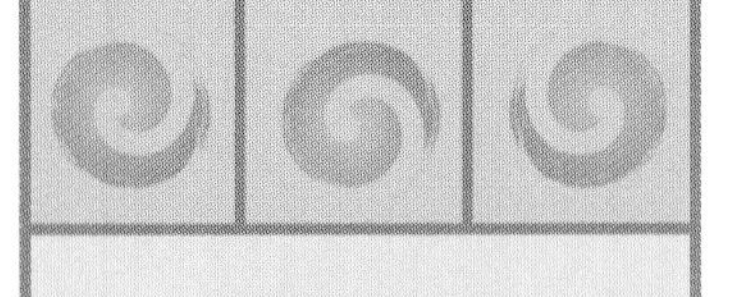

### Para averiguar

1. What is the superlative and how do you express it in Spanish?
2. In phrases such as *the biggest in the world*, how do you translate the word *in*?

- The superlative is used to describe someone or something as *the most/least + adjective.*

Es **el** estudiante **más inteligente de** la clase pero es **el menos estudioso.**
*He is the most intelligent student in the class, but he is the least studious.*

- The superlative is expressed by using a definite article with the comparative.

| | |
|---|---|
| Mi hermana es **más alta.** | *My sister is taller.* |
| Mi hermana es **la más alta.** | *My sister is the tallest.* |
| Uds. son **mejores.** | *You are better.* |
| Uds. son **los mejores.** | *You are the best.* |

- If a noun accompanies the adjective, the article is placed before it. Note that where English uses *in* after the superlative to express which group is being compared, Spanish uses **de.**

| | |
|---|---|
| Mi hermana es **la** más alta **de** mi familia. | *My sister is the tallest in my family.* |
| México es **la** ciudad más grande **del** mundo. | *Mexico City is the largest city in the world.* |

- Remember that those adjectives and adverbs that have irregular forms in the comparative use the same forms in the superlative.

| | |
|---|---|
| María es **la mejor** estudiante. | *Maria is the best student.* |
| Andrés es **el peor** profesor. | *Andres is the worst professor.* |
| Arturo es **el menor.** | *Arturo is the youngest.* |
| Ramona es **la mayor.** | *Ramona is the oldest.* |

## A lo personal

**A. Opiniones.** Name the person or thing you feel fits each category. Your classmates will say whether or not they agree.

MODELO: el actor más guapo
E1: *Antonio Banderas es el más guapo.*
E2: *Yo también creo que es el más guapo.*
E3: *No es el más guapo. El más guapo es Brad Pitt.*

1. el actor más guapo
2. la actriz más bonita
3. el curso más difícil de la universidad
4. la ciudad más bonita de nuestro estado
5. el programa de televisión más tonto
6. la canción más bonita del año
7. la película más interesante de este año
8. la película menos interesante de este año
9. la mejor clase de la universidad
10. el mejor profesor de matemáticas

**B. Lo mejor y lo peor.** On a sheet of paper, write the names of the following people and places. Two students will then tell what they wrote and a third student will decide who is right.

MODELO: el peor restaurante de la ciudad
E1: Mama's *es el peor restaurante de la ciudad.*
E2: La Olla Podrida *es el peor restaurante de la ciudad.*
E3: *Jaime tiene razón.* Mama's *es peor que* La Olla Podrida.

1. el mejor restaurante de la ciudad
2. el lugar más divertido de los Estados Unidos
3. el lugar más aburrido de los Estados Unidos
4. el mejor jugador de baloncesto
5. la mejor jugadora profesional de tenis
6. el mejor centro comercial de su ciudad

**C. ¡Es lo máximo!** Write a superlative statement about each of the following.

MODELO: el perro
*El perro es el mejor amigo del hombre.*

1. Bill Gates
2. La Madre Teresa
3. Michael Jordan
4. Su profesor/a de español (¡Cuidado!)
5. Frankenstein
6. Disneylandia
7. Elvis Presley
8. Las hamburguesas de McDonald's
9. Oprah Winfrey
10. Los rascacielos (*skyscrapers*) de Nueva York.

**D. La pareja de mis sueños.** After dating many people, you have finally found the perfect one for you. Make a list of ten reasons why he or she is the best of all.

MODELO: *Él es el más romántico de todos.*
*Ella es la más fascinante de todas.*

**E. Nuestras familias.** With a classmate, take turns answering the following questions about several members of your respective families.

1. ¿Quién es el/la más inteligente de tu familia?
2. ¿Quién es el mayor de todos tus hermanos?
3. ¿Quién es la persona más activa en tu casa?
4. ¿Quién es el menor de todos tus hermanos?
5. ¿Quién es la persona más atractiva de tu familia?
6. ¿Quién es la persona menos trabajadora de tu familia?
7. ¿Quién es el/la mejor estudiante de tu clase?
8. ¿Quién es el/la peor cocinero/a (*cook*) de tu familia?
9. ¿Quién es la persona más interesante de tu familia?
10. ¿Quién es tu persona favorita de tu casa?

# TEMA 4 La guardería infantil

## De visita en la guardería

### ¿Cómo es la guardería?

*Mrs. Reyes is checking out the local day care....*

SRA. REYES: Buenos días, señor. Soy la señora Reyes y deseo información acerca de la guardería.

EMPLEADO: Cobramos cien dólares a la semana por niño. Puede dejarlos desde las siete de la mañana y recogerlos hasta las seis de la tarde. Después de las seis de la tarde, cobramos diez dólares por hora.

SRA. REYES: ¿Dónde pueden hacer la tarea?

EMPLEADO: Tenemos un cuarto con pupitres y pizarras para hacer la tarea. Una maestra viene de tres a seis de la tarde. También tenemos un cuarto con camas para la hora de la siesta.

SRA. REYES: ¿Qué pasa si un niño tiene un accidente?

EMPLEADO: Hay una sección de enfermería. Tiene que firmar un papel para autorizar tratamiento médico en caso de alguna emergencia. Y, ¿cómo se llaman sus niñas?

SRA. REYES: La mayor se llama Fabiola y tiene ocho años. La menor se llama Elvira y tiene cuatro años.

EMPLEADO: ¿Las dos van a la escuela?

SRA. REYES: Solamente Fabiola. Sale a las tres de la tarde.

**A. ¿Comprende Ud.?** Answer the following questions based on the dialog.

1. ¿Qué desea la señora Reyes?
2. ¿Dónde hacen los niños su tarea?
3. ¿Qué hacen si un niño tiene un accidente?
4. ¿Cuánto cobra la guardería infantil por niño?

**Answers for A.** 1) *Información.* 2) *En un cuarto con pupitres.* 3) *Ir a la enfermería.* 4) *100 dólares.*

**B. Buscando niñero/a.** Read the following ads for a babysitter to come to your house to take care of your younger sister while your parents are at work and you are at school. Hopefully, this person can also help with the housekeeping. After calling each ad, you're disappointed and decide to write your own ad. Compare your requirements with those of other students in groups of three.

**Suggestion for B.** Day care is a great need for working parents. Encourage students to look for ads in English/Spanish in the local newspapers that might serve as models for their ad project.

## EMPLEO

### Niñera

Se ofrece niñera para cuidado de niños.
Referencias. Sin experiencia. No hace limpieza.
Se pide seguro médico y comidas.
Llamar al 404-9302.

### Doméstica/Niños

Señora de ochenta y ocho años se ofrece para cuidar niños. No cuida a adolescentes. Sin transporte. Mucha experiencia. Requiere acceso para silla de ruedas. Llamar al 893-3849 de ocho a nueve de la mañana para más información.

### Chica para limpieza y niños

Experiencia en limpieza doméstica.
Referencias. Cuida niños. Cocina. Limpia.
Fuma. Necesita transporte privado
y habitación privada.
Interesados llamar al 402-2821(sólo noches)

**C. La entrevista.** You've received three calls from people interested in the babysitting job you advertised. Now you must interview each one to find the perfect candidate. Discuss with a classmate what questions you need to ask and then interview two other classmates and decide which one to hire.

MODELO: *¿Ud. puede conducir?*

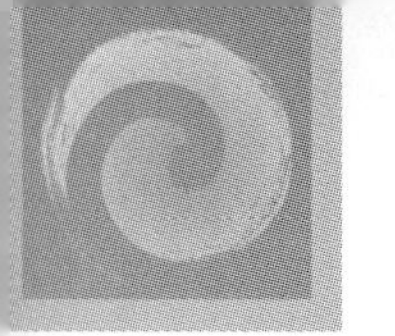

# ABC Fabiola y Elvira en la guardería

## El primer día de Fabiola y Elvira en la guardería infantil

*It is the first day of school for Mrs. Reyes's daughters….*

SRA. REYES: ¿Dónde ponen sus cosas las niñas?
NIÑERA: Aquí están los armarios; cada niño tiene un lugar especial.
SRA. REYES: Las dos niñas traen sus loncheras. Hoy Fabiola almuerza en la guardería porque no tiene clases.
NIÑERA: Aquí almorzamos a las doce y media todos los días. Hay un refrigerio a las tres y media de la tarde. Pueden beber jugos de frutas, agua y leche.
SRA. REYES: Fabiola ya no duerme siesta, pero Elvira duerme a la una de la tarde. Trae su cobija y su almohada porque no puede dormir sin ellas.
NIÑERA: Fabiola y Elvira, vamos a salir al patio a jugar con los niños.
SRA. REYES: Elvira tiene miedo de estar en la guardería. Si tiene problemas, Fabiola puede ayudar. Ella quiere mucho a su hermana y es muy responsable.
NIÑERA: ¿Oyen cómo cantan los niños en el patio?

**A. ¿Comprende Ud.?** Answer the questions based on the dialog.

1. ¿A qué hora es el almuerzo en la guardería?
2. ¿Duermen siesta todos los niños?
3. ¿Adónde salen los niños a jugar?
4. ¿Quién es mayor, Fabiola o Elvira?

**Answers for A.**
1) *A las doce y media.*
2) *No.* 3) *Al patio.* 4) *Fabiola.*

**B. El primer día en la guardería.** You have to drop your little brother off on his first day at day care. You want to be sure that he has everything he needs so he won't be scared. Prepare a list and then compare with a classmate what items are necessary.

MODELO: *Mi hermanito necesita:*
*su mochila*
*su cobija y almohada*
*su lonchera con jugo y el almuerzo*

**C. ¿De qué hablan?** Look at the cover from the magazine **Ser padres**. Think about what might be discussed in each article, coming up with two possible items to share with a classmate.

MODELO: El artículo sobre Disciplina Positiva
1. *Dar un dulce por ser bueno/a.*
2. *Ideas para los padres.*

**Expansion.** Discuss how important baptism is, perhaps encouraging students to share personal family histories, especially if you have Hispanic students in class who might bring photos and invitations to class.

**D. El valor de trabajar con niños.** With a classmate, prepare a list of reasons why parents often both work, if there is a two-parent family. Now, in groups of six, with three students opposing both parents working, and three defending why both parents need to work, state your reasons for each belief. Take turns between each side!

MODELO: Grupo A: *Es necesario tener suficiente dinero para comprar una casa.*
Grupo B: *¡Pero el niño necesita a sus padres en casa con él!*

**Variation for D.** The topic of working parents is one that could expand into a class debate on the value/need for both parents to work, potential damage to the child, problems encountered in finding adequate day care, its expense, etc. As time allows, students could look for articles on this topic and have a class discussion.

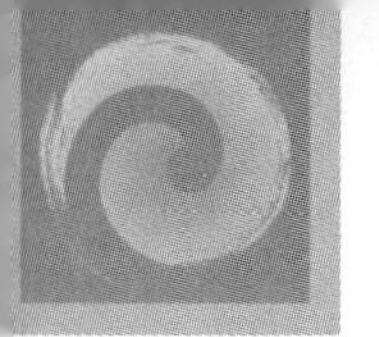

# Los verbos *tener* y *venir*

## (Tener/venir, *and expressions with* tener)

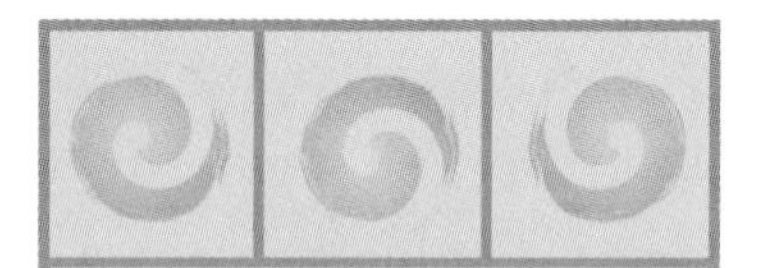

**Para averiguar**

1. **Tener** and **venir** are conjugated alike except for two forms. Which ones?
2. How do you tell your age in Spanish? How do you tell what you have to do?

- The verb **tener** (*to have*) is useful when describing your family and possessions.

| | |
|---|---|
| —¿**Tienes** un cuarto en una residencia? | *Do you have a room in a dorm?* |
| —**Tengo** un apartamento. | *I have an apartment.* |

| **tener** (*to have*) | | | |
|---|---|---|---|
| yo | **tengo** | nosotros/as | **tenemos** |
| tú | **tienes** | vosotros/as | **tenéis** |
| él, ella, usted | **tiene** | ellos, ellas, ustedes | **tienen** |

- **Tener** generally means *to have*. It is also used in these idiomatic expressions.

| | |
|---|---|
| **tener... años** | *to be... years old* |
| **tener calor** | *to be hot* |
| **tener frío** | *to be cold* |
| **tener ganas de...** | *to feel like...* |
| **tener hambre** | *to be hungry* |
| **tener miedo** | *to be afraid* |
| **tener prisa** | *to be in a hurry* |
| **tener razón** | *to be right* |
| **tener sed** | *to be thirsty* |
| **tener sueño** | *to be sleepy* |

- Use **tener que** + an *infinitive* to say that someone has to do something.

| | |
|---|---|
| —**Tengo** sed. ¿**Tienes** ganas de tomar algo? | —*I'm thirsty. Do you feel like drinking something?* |
| —No **tenemos** tiempo. | —*We don't have time.* |
| —**Tienes** razón. **Tenemos que** regresar al trabajo. | —*You're right. We have to go back to work.* |

- *Venir* (*to come*) is conjugated like **tener** except for the ending of the **nosotros** and **vosotros** forms.

| | |
|---|---|
| —¿**Vienen** las niñas aquí con frecuencia? | *Do the girls come here often?* |
| —Sí, **vienen** casi todos los días. | *Yes, they come almost every day.* |

| **venir** (*to come*) | | | |
|---|---|---|---|
| yo | **vengo** | nosotros/as | **venimos** |
| tú | **vienes** | vosotros/as | **venís** |
| él, ella, usted | **viene** | ellos, ellas, ustedes | **vienen** |

## A lo personal

**A. ¿Tener o venir?** Complete one question from each group with the correct form of **tener** and the other with the correct form of **venir**. Then use the questions to interview someone in your class.

MODELO: ¿ ________ (tú) un compañero/a de cuarto? ¿ ________ (Uds.) juntos/as a la universidad?
*¿Tienes un compañero/a de cuarto? ¿Vienen Uds. juntos/as a la universidad?*

1. ¿Qué días ________ (tú) clases? ¿ ________ (tú) a la universidad los fines de semana?
2. ¿ ________ (nosotros) un examen la próxima semana? Los días de exámenes, ¿ ________ (tú) a la universidad temprano para estudiar?
3. ¿ ________ (nosotros) un buen gimnasio en la universidad? ¿ ________ muchos estudiantes a la universidad para hacer ejercicio?
4. ¿ ________ nuestra universidad una biblioteca grande? ¿ ________ (tú) a la biblioteca los fines de semana?

**B. ¿Qué tienen?** Complete each sentence with a form of **tener** and logical items.

MODELO: En mi mochila, (yo)...
*En mi mochila tengo tres libros, un lápiz, dos cuadernos y una calculadora.* o
*No tengo mochila.*

1. En su oficina, el profesor...
2. En su cuarto, los estudiantes típicos...
3. En el salón de clase, nosotros...
4. En la sala, una familia típica...
5. En la guardería, ellos...
6. En mi escritorio, yo...

**C. ¿Cómo son?** Describe the following celebrities and give the age of each one.

MODELO: Connie Chung (20/8/46)
*Tiene el pelo negro y los ojos negros. Tiene ________ años.*

1. Madonna (16/8/58)
2. Jennifer López (24/7/70)
3. Antonio Banderas (10/8/60)
4. Cameron Díaz (30/8/72)
5. Gloria Estefan (1/9/57)
6. Salma Hayek (2/9/68)

**D. Expresiones.** Complete the following sentences with the appropriate **tener** expression.

| tener hambre | tener frío | tener prisa | tener sueño | tener calor | tener sed |
|---|---|---|---|---|---|

1. Estamos cansados. Todos...
2. ¿Quieres un sándwich? ¿(Tú)...?
3. ¡Cierren las ventanas, por favor! Mis hijos...
4. ¡Abran las ventanas, por favor! (Nosotros)...
5. ¡Más rápido! (Yo)...
6. ¿Quiere Ud. tomar una Coca-Cola? ¿(Ud.)...?

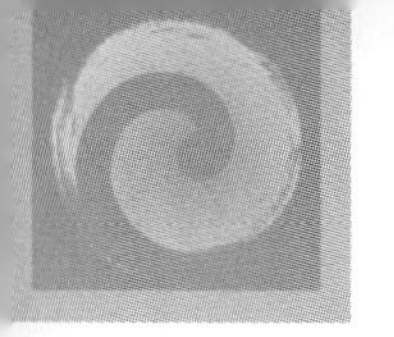

# Los verbos irregulares: *-er* e *-ir*
## (*Irregular verbs*: -er *and* -ir)

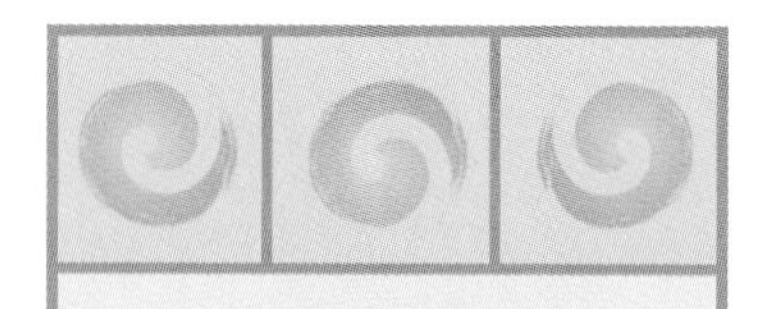

**Para averiguar**

1. Which five verbs are conjugated like **-er** and **-ir** verbs in the present indicative in all forms except the **yo** form? What is the **yo** form of each of these verbs?
2. What are the last three letters of the **yo** form of verbs that end in **-cer**, **-cir**?

- In the present indicative, the following verbs are conjugated like **-er** or **-ir** verbs except for the **yo** form.

| | |
|---|---|
| **hacer** (*to make, to do*) | **hago**, haces, hace, hacemos, hacéis, hacen |
| **poner** (*to put, to place*) | **pongo**, pones, pone, ponemos, ponéis, ponen |
| **saber** (*to know*) | **sé**, sabes, sabe, sabemos, sabéis, saben |
| **salir** (*to go out, to leave*) | **salgo**, sales, sale, salimos, salís, salen |
| **traer** (*to bring*) | **traigo**, traes, trae, traemos, traéis, traen |

- The verb **oír** (*to hear*) follows a slightly different pattern.

**oigo**, **oyes**, **oye**, **oímos**, **oís**, **oyen**

- With verbs ending in **-cer** and **-cir**, the letter **z** is inserted before the **c** in the **yo** form.

| | |
|---|---|
| **parecer** (*to seem, to appear*) | **parezco**, pareces, parece, parecemos, parecéis, parecen |
| **conocer** (*to be familiar with, to know people*) | **conozco**, conoces, conoce, conocemos, conocéis, conocen |
| **traducir** (*to translate*) | **traduzco**, traduces, traduce, traducimos, traducís, traducen |
| **conducir** (*to drive*) | **conduzco**, conduces, conduce, conducimos, conducís, conducen |

- The English translation of both **saber** and **conocer** is *to know*. You will study these verbs in Lección 5, but for now keep in mind the following information.

  Use **conocer** to say that someone is personally familiar with a person or place.

| | |
|---|---|
| Yo **conozco** un buen restaurante. | *I know a good restaurant.* |
| Yo **conozco a** tu hermano. | *I know your brother.* |

  Use **saber** to say that someone knows information or facts, or how to do something.

| | |
|---|---|
| Yo **sé** su número de teléfono. | *I know his phone number.* |
| Yo **sé** hablar español. | *I know how to speak Spanish.* |

## A lo personal

**A. ¿Con qué frecuencia?** How often do you do the following in class? Use **siempre**, **a veces**, or **nunca** in your responses.

MODELO: salir de clase temprano
*Nunca salgo de clase temprano.*

1. oír palabras nuevas
2. saber las respuestas
3. poner algo debajo de su silla
4. hacer preguntas
5. traer su libro a clase
6. traer un diccionario a clase
7. salir de la clase
8. oír a estudiantes en el pasillo

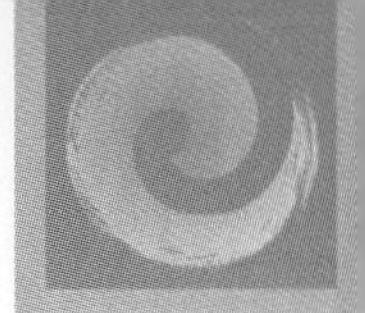

**B. ¿En tu familia?** Ask a classmate if the indicated member of his/her family does the activity in parentheses.

MODELO: tus hermanos (hacer la cama)
E1: *¿Hacen tus hermanos la cama todos los días?*
E2: *Mis hermanos nunca hacen la cama.*

1. tus padres (escribir muchos cheques)
2. tu madre (conocer a todos los vecinos)
3. tu padre (ver la televisión todos los días)
4. tus abuelos (hacer la comida en casa)
5. tú (saber limpiar la casa)
6. tú (hacer la cama)
7. tú (quitar el polvo)
8. tú (salir con los amigos antes de limpiar la casa)
9. tu hermano/a (saber hablar español)
10. tu padre (traer regalos a casa)

**C. Entrevista.** Interview a classmate using the following questions.

1. ¿Conoces a mucha gente aquí? ¿Conoces a otros profesores de español?
2. ¿Sales los fines de semana? ¿Con quién sales generalmente?
3. ¿Haces ejercicio todos los días? ¿Corres a veces?
4. ¿Escribes muchas cartas o llamas más por teléfono?
5. ¿Lees el periódico? ¿Crees todo lo que (*that*) lees en el periódico? ¿Qué revistas lees con más frecuencia? ¿A veces lees revistas o periódicos en español?
6. En tu opinión, ¿quién escribe libros interesantes? ¿Lees todos sus libros? ¿Por qué son interesantes?

**D. La fiesta.** You and your roommate are having a party tonight. The house is a mess; you have no food or drinks yet. Divide up this list of chores and tell which of you will do it.

MODELO: llamar a los invitados
E1: *Yo llamo a los invitados.*
traer la música
E1: *Tú traes la música.*

1. hacer el pastel
2. comprar los refrescos
3. poner la ropa en el armario
4. poner los platos en el lavaplatos
5. salir de las clases temprano para limpiar
6. limpiar la sala
7. traer la comida
8. poner las decoraciones
9. hacer las camas
10. poner las alfombras en el garaje
11. oír los mensajes
12. conducir al supermercado
13. traer las bebidas (*drinks*)
14. salir a comprar

# Vocabulario

## TEMA 3
### Los quehaceres domésticos

**Sustantivos**

| | |
|---|---|
| **la alacena** | *cupboard* |
| **la aspiradora** | *vacuum cleaner* |
| **el espacio** | *space* |
| **el mundo** | *world* |
| **el plato** | *dish, plate* |
| **el polvo** | *dust* |
| **el quehacer** | *chore* |
| **el/la trabajador/a** | *worker* |

**Verbos**

| | |
|---|---|
| **aspirar** | *to vacuum* |
| **barrer** | *to sweep* |
| **guardar** | *to keep, put away* |
| **hacer** (g) | *to do, make* |
| **lavar** | *to wash* |
| **limpiar** | *to clean* |
| **oír** | *to hear* |
| **planchar** | *to iron* |
| **poner** (g) | *to put, place* |
| **quitar el polvo** | *to dust* |
| **sacudir** | *to shake* |
| **traer** (g) (i) | *to bring* |
| **tener** (g) | *to have* |
| **venir** (g) (ie) | *to come* |

**Adjetivos**

| | |
|---|---|
| **alguno/a** | *some* |
| **desordenado/a** | *messy* |
| **desorganizado/a** | *disorganized* |
| **divertido/a** | *fun, enjoyable* |
| **doméstico/a** | *household* |

**Otras expresiones**

| | |
|---|---|
| **acá** | *here* |
| **al mismo tiempo** | *at the same time* |
| **del frente** | *out in front* |
| **me parece bien** | *sounds good to me* |
| **mejor** | *better* |
| **peor** | *worse* |

## TEMA 4
### La guardería infantil

**Sustantivos**

| | |
|---|---|
| **el accidente** | *accident* |
| **la almohada** | *pillow* |
| **la cobija** | *blanket* |
| **el/la empleado/a** | *employee* |
| **la enfermería** | *infirmary, sick bay* |
| **el/la enfermero/a** | *nurse* |
| **la guardería** | *childcare* |
| **el juego** | *game* |
| **el jugo** | *juice* |
| **la lonchera** | *lunch box* |
| **el refrigerio** | *snack* |
| **la siesta** | *nap* |
| **el tratamiento** | *treatment* |

**Verbos**

| | |
|---|---|
| **almorzar** (ue) | *to have lunch* |
| **autorizar** | *to authorize* |
| **beber** | *to drink* |
| **cobrar** | *to charge* |
| **enseñar** | *to show, teach* |
| **poder**(ue) | *to be able, can* |

**Adjetivos**

| | |
|---|---|
| **infantil** | *related to children* |
| **principal** | *main* |
| **responsable** | *responsible* |

**Otras expresiones**

| | |
|---|---|
| **acerca de** | *about, concerning* |
| **normalmente** | *usually* |
| **personalmente** | *personally* |
| **por adelantado** | *in advance* |

**¡OJO! Expressions with *tener* should also be studied.**

# Reunión B

**A escuchar. Ana habla con la asistente social.** Complete the sentences with the information you hear.

1. De nacionalidad Ana y José son _______________.
2. Ana nació el catorce de septiembre de _______________.
3. José nació el tres de _______________ de mil novecientos noventa.
4. Ana es _________________.
5. Ana gana aproximadamente ____________mil dólares anualmente.
6. El alquiler de la casa es ____________ dólares mensuales.

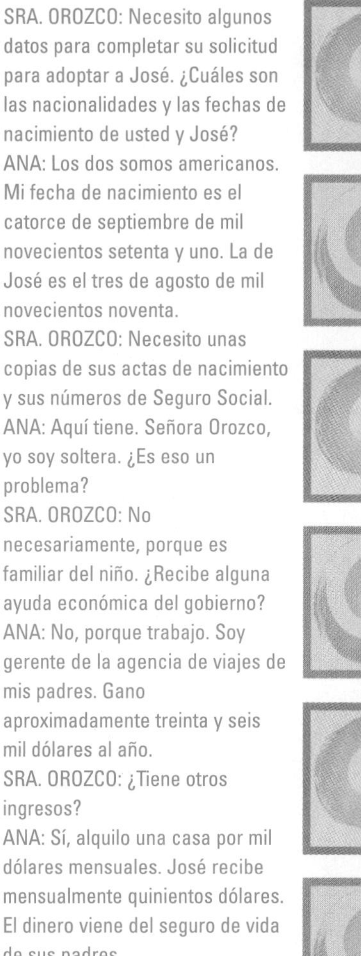

**Tapescript for A escuchar.**
**Ana habla con la asistente social.**
SRA. OROZCO: Necesito algunos datos para completar su solicitud para adoptar a José. ¿Cuáles son las nacionalidades y las fechas de nacimiento de usted y José?
ANA: Los dos somos americanos. Mi fecha de nacimiento es el catorce de septiembre de mil novecientos setenta y uno. La de José es el tres de agosto de mil novecientos noventa.
SRA. OROZCO: Necesito unas copias de sus actas de nacimiento y sus números de Seguro Social.
ANA: Aquí tiene. Señora Orozco, yo soy soltera. ¿Es eso un problema?
SRA. OROZCO: No necesariamente, porque es familiar del niño. ¿Recibe alguna ayuda económica del gobierno?
ANA: No, porque trabajo. Soy gerente de la agencia de viajes de mis padres. Gano aproximadamente treinta y seis mil dólares al año.
SRA. OROZCO: ¿Tiene otros ingresos?
ANA: Sí, alquilo una casa por mil dólares mensuales. José recibe mensualmente quinientos dólares. El dinero viene del seguro de vida de sus padres.
SRA. OROZCO: Está bien. Necesitamos estudiar su solicitud. Yo la llamo lo más pronto posible.

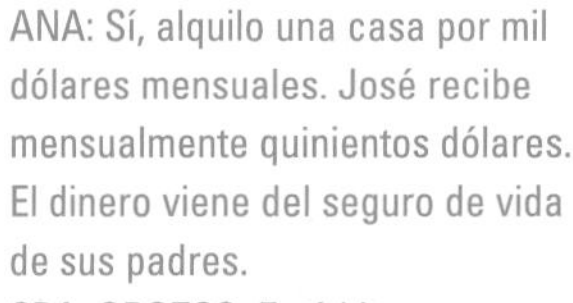

**Answers for A escuchar.**
1) *Americanos.* 2) *Mil novecientos setenta y uno.* 3) *Agosto.* 4) *Soltera.* 5) *Treinta y seis.* 6) *Mil.*

**A conversar.** You are planning to move in with your best friend. Discuss how much rent you can afford, the size and location of the house/apartment you're looking for, the necessary amenities such as number of baths, large or small kitchen, view, pets allowed, etc.

**¿Lo sabía?** Look at the brochure on child care for low-income families. Is it easy to obtain assistance? What are some of the problems in getting help? How old are the children eligible for this program? Must the parent(s) work to qualify?

**Programas de ayuda para el cuidado de niños para familias con ingresos bajos**

¿Tiene Ud. bajos ingresos?
¿Está Ud. a riesgo de depender del estado?

**Servicios para todas las edades:**
Desde recién nacidos hasta los doce años, o hasta los diecisiete años, si hay incapacidad física o mental para cuidarse por sí mismos.

**Elegibilidad y cuotas:**
Son elegibles las familias con bajos ingresos a riesgo de dependencia del estado que necesitan del cuidado de niños para poder trabajar. Se da prioridad a las madres adolescentes y a todos aquellos que estén trabajando.

**Servicios:**
Los padres seleccionan el lugar deseado para el cuidado de sus niños.

**Entrenamiento de trabajo:**
Los participantes del entrenamiento de trabajo pueden cualificar para obtener asistencia en el cuidado de sus niños mientras están inscritos en el programa. Los pagos del cuidado de niños mientras los padres están en el entrenamiento de trabajo están reducidos.

**Los padres seleccionan el centro contratado con la Fuerza de Trabajo al que quieren asistir. Llame al (303) 834-2034 para obtener más información.**

**A buscar.** Imagine that you'll be moving soon to the Spanish-speaking country of your choice. Search the Internet and try to find an apartment in that country that meets all of your specifications. Once you make a decision, present your findings to a group of your classmates and compare your choices.

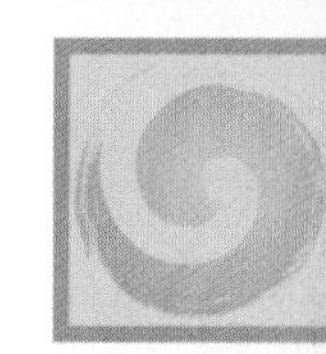

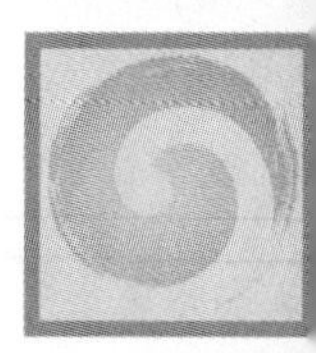



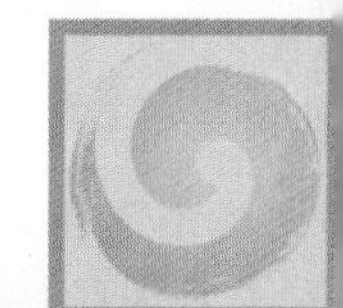

# ¡TRATO HECHO!

## Rincón profesional: Decoradores de interiores

*¡El hada madrina de su casa! Interiores por Kira*

Si su casa necesita un tratamiento de belleza, transfórmela con la varita mágica de Kira, el hada madrina de las casas.
Kira mira sus muebles y objetos con una visión creativa. Con el uso de los colores perfectos y de la luz, los espacios viejos se transforman en espacios maravillosos, modernos, alegres y elegantes. ¿Cuál es el sueño de su familia? Kira lo puede hacer realidad en:

- los dormitorios: con colores serenos, luces suaves, camas grandes y cómodas y armarios amplios.
- la cocina: con colores alegres, electrodomésticos modernos y eficientes y espacios que llaman cariñosamente a la familia.

- el comedor: con mesas, sillas y armarios que demuestran elegancia y funcionalidad.
- la sala: con colores y muebles que anuncian al mundo el estilo de vida y la personalidad de Ud. y su familia. Muebles modernos o tradicionales. Sala elegante o informal. Sillones o sofás. Arte para las paredes—lo que Ud. quiera.

• los baños: lujosos, grandes, con bañeras de todas las formas—¡hasta en forma de corazón!
• jardines, salas de recreo, *master suites,* lo que sueñe Ud.

Kira, el hada madrina de las casas tiene la magia—¡Ud. sólo necesita el sueño!

**¿Comprende Ud.?**

1. Who is the Fairy Godmother of interior design?
2. What does she transform?
3. Name three ways that the Fairy Godmother transforms houses.
4. How is a house different after Kira's visit?

**A escuchar.** **Una casa fabulosa.** Listen as Guillermo and Lidia talk about a friend's house and answer the questions based on their dialog.

**¿Comprende Ud.?**

1. ______ ¿De quién es la casa bonita?
2. ______ ¿Cuántas habitaciones hay en la casa?
3. ______ ¿Tienen baño todas las habitaciones?
4. ______ ¿Cuántos metros mide la cocina?

**Tapescript for A escuchar. Una casa fabulosa.**
LIDIA: Esta tarde voy a visitar la casa de los Montoya. Mi hermano dice que es la casa más bonita de la ciudad.
GUILLERMO: Sí, yo conozco la casa y me gusta muchísimo. Tiene siete dormitorios y todos tienen baño completo. Además, en la planta baja hay tres baños más.
LIDIA: Debe ser una casa grandísima.
GUILLERMO: Sí, tiene ascensor y el garaje es más grande que mi apartamento.
LIDIA: ¿Cómo es la cocina?
GUILLERMO: La cocina mide 60 metros cuadrados. Tiene cuatro hornos, dos lavaplatos y tres fregaderos. En el comedor hay espacio para 40 personas.
LIDIA: Claro, a los Montoya les gusta hacer fiestas.
GUILLERMO: Después de comer, los invitados pueden pasar al salón de baile.

**Answers for A escuchar.**
1) *De los Montoya.* 2) *Siete dormitorios.* 3) *Sí.* 4) *Mide 60 metros cuadrados.*

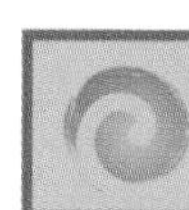
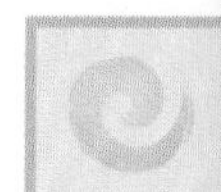

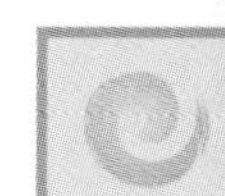

**En mi casa.** Ask another student to draw the floor plan of your home in the space provided below. You need to describe each room and its location in reference to the rest of the house. Don't look at your partner's drawing until he/she finishes. Let's see how close his/her drawing is to the real one.

**Vamos a diseñar.** Congratulations on your decision to design and furnish your new home. Each member of the family will design and furnish his/her own room and bath; all of you will design the kitchen, living room, dining room, and back yard. The members of the family are mother and father, sister, brother, grandpa and grandma, and of course, the family pet. Make sure that all the people in your group agree on colors and type of furniture to be used in shared rooms.

## A leer

As you skim this information on color and interior design, focus on how much you are able to understand without consulting the dictionary. Can you make sense of it without looking up a single English word? Let your imagination fill in the blanks. If you make a mistake, don't worry about it. This is a new skill. And, practice really does make perfect!

**Antes de leer.** With a partner write down a list of colors. Then, next to each color, write a couple of adjectives to indicate what emotions, feelings, or reactions you associate with it. When you finish, compare your perceptions with the information presented below.

*Color is one of the most important elements in interior design. It makes the house look larger or smaller, darker or lighter, and it may influence people's mood. Color is also the cheapest way to redecorate a room.*

El color es un elemento muy importante en la decoración de su casa. Es importante escoger solamente tres colores: uno claro, otro mediano y otro más oscuro. El color claro es para las paredes y los pisos, el mediano para las cortinas y los muebles más grandes y el más oscuro para los muebles pequeños y accesorios.

Una combinación de colores similares, como el verde y el azul, o el rosa y el salmón, crean un ambiente de relajación. Para crear una habitación estimulante y llena de vida puede usar colores que contrastan, como el rojo y el verde. Hay personas que prefieren un sólo color, neutro, en diferentes tonos. Esto crea un ambiente para calmar los nervios.

Hay que recordar también que una habitación de color negro parece más oscura y más pequeña; los colores claros hacen ver la habitación más grande. La casa parece más alta si el techo tiene un color más claro que las paredes.

Usted puede usar el color para crear un ambiente especial en su casa y para reflejar sus gustos personales. ¡Mucha suerte!

**¿Cierto (C) o Falso (F)?** Para decorar su casa:

1. _____ Es mejor seleccionar cinco colores.
2. _____ Las paredes y los pisos deben ser de colores claros.
3. _____ El color más oscuro es para los techos.
4. _____ Hay que usar verde y azul para un ambiente estimulante y vivo.
5. _____ El color negro hace ver más grande una habitación.

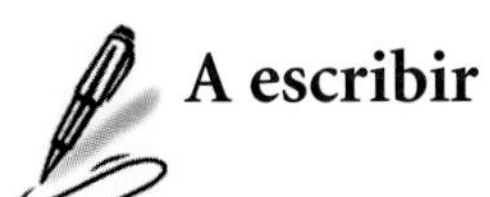

## A escribir

In two paragraphs describe the color scheme in your own home. Do those colors have an effect on your moods? Pay attention to your mood when in different color rooms and explain how and when those colors affect you.

# 4 ¡Que se diviertan!

LECCIÓN CUATRO

CHECK OUT THE *¡TRATO HECHO!* WEBSITE AND CD-ROM FOR ACTIVITIES, GAMES, SELF-TESTS, AND MUCH MORE!

TEMA 1

## Las diversiones

- ¿Qué tiempo hace?
- ¿Adónde van?
- El verbo *ir*
- El futuro inmediato y el pasado reciente

TEMA 2

## El tiempo libre

- ¿Qué quieren hacer?
- ¿Quieren tomar algo?
- Los verbos con cambios en la raíz
- Más cambios en la raíz

TEMA 3

## La rutina diaria

- ¿Qué haces todos los días?
- ¿Cómo son sus relaciones?
- Los verbos reflexivos
- Más sobre los reflexivos

TEMA 4

## Los deportes

- Mi actividad favorita
- ¿A qué juegas tú?
- Posición de adjetivos
- El presente progresivo

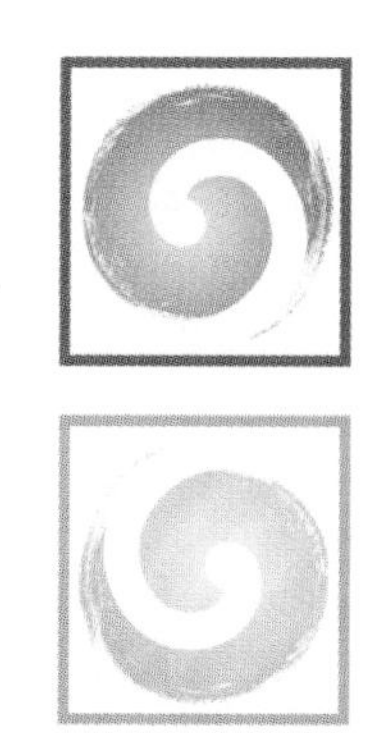

# ¡TRATO HECHO!

- Rincón profesional: El espectáculo
- A escuchar
- El buzón de Doña Rosa
- A leer
- A escribir

# TEMA 1 Las diversiones

## ¿Qué tiempo hace?

Suggestion. Mention that seasons are reversed south of the equator. Ask students to name the months of winter and summer in the southern countries of South America.

En el verano...
...hace (mucho) calor.
...hace sol.
...el cielo está despejado.

En el otoño...
...hace viento.
...hace fresco.

En el invierno...
...nieva.
...el cielo está nublado.
...hace frío.

En la primavera...
...hace buen tiempo.
...llueve.

Suggestion. Explain the conversion from Fahrenheit to Celsius. Subtract 32, and multiply by 5/9. For example, 86F – 32 = 54. 54 × 5 – 270. 270/9 = 30C. To convert to Fahrenheit from Celsius, multiply by 1.8 and add 32. For example, 10C × 1.8 – 18. 18 + 32 = 50F.

### Visitando a los amigos

*Isabel and Mary are visiting the apartment of Lázaro and Carlos....*

LÁZARO: ¡Qué frío hace! La temperatura es de tres grados centígrados bajo cero y la calefacción de nuestro apartamento no funciona.

CARLOS: El técnico viene mañana por la mañana. Es importante arreglar la calefacción porque hace mucho frío y a Lázaro sólo le gusta el calor.

LÁZARO: Mi mamá acaba de hablar por teléfono con mi abuelo en Argentina y dice que allí es verano. El cielo está despejado y hace mucho calor.

ISABEL: En Bogotá llueve mucho. Allí casi siempre está nublado y el clima es húmedo. También hace frío porque la ciudad está alta en las montañas.

LÁZARO: ¡Tengo mucho frío! ¿Por qué no vamos al cine del centro comercial? Allí hace calor.

ISABEL: Sí, vamos. Carlos y Mary, ¿por qué no van con nosotros?

MARY: Sí, claro. Carlos, ¿tú puedes ir al cine?

CARLOS: Con mucho gusto.

**A. ¿Comprende Ud.?** Answer the following questions based on the dialog.

1. ¿Por qué va a venir el técnico?
2. ¿Es invierno en Argentina?
3. ¿Por qué no hace frío en el cine?
4. ¿A quién no le gusta el frío?

**Answers for A.** 1) *Porque la calefacción no funciona.* 2) *No.* 3) *Hay calefacción.* 4) *A Lázaro.*

**B. ¿Qué tiempo hace?** Provide a description for the weather based on the drawings.

MODELO: *El cielo está nublado.*

1 
2 
3 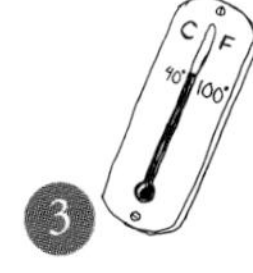
4 
5 
6 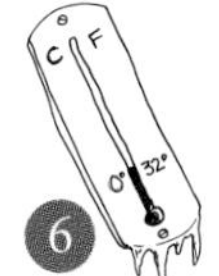

**Answers for B.** 1) *Hace sol.* 2) *Nieva.* 3) *Hace (mucho) calor.* 4) *Llueve.* 5) *Hace viento.* 6) *Hace (mucho) frío.*

**C. Las estaciones y el tiempo.** List the seasons, what the weather is like during each one in your part of the country, and some possible activities to do during that time. Compare your list with your classmate's.

**D. ¿Qué le gusta hacer?** Answer the following questions, then ask your classmate. ¡OJO! Remember to use **tú** forms when asking your classmate.

1. ¿Le gusta ir al parque cuando nieva?
2. ¿Le gusta ir a la playa cuando llueve? ¿Al cine?
3. ¿Estudia en la biblioteca cuando hace buen tiempo? ¿Qué hace?
4. ¿Qué hace cuando hace mucho frío?
5. ¿Cuál es su actividad favorita cuando hace calor?
6. Cuando hace fresco, ¿qué hace?

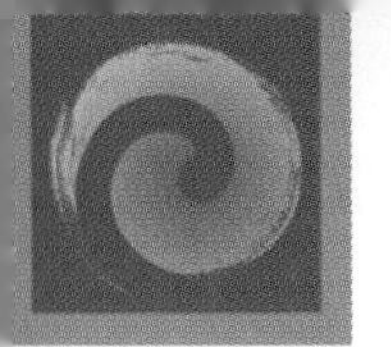

# ABC ¿Adónde van?

## ¿Vienes conmigo?

*After finishing their classes, Ana invites Isabel to exercise with her....*

ANA: Mary y yo vamos a salir a correr esta tarde. ¿Por qué no vienes con nosotras?

ISABEL: No puedo ir. Acabo de hacer planes con mi familia y vamos a pasar unos días en las montañas. Salimos en dos horas.

ANA: ¿Va a ir Lázaro?

ISABEL: Sí, también va su familia. Va a pedir mi mano.

ANA: ¿De verdad? ¡Felicidades! ¿Cuándo es la boda?

ISABEL: No sé. Vamos a fijar la fecha este fin de semana. ¿Por qué no vienes con nosotros? Hay nieve y vamos a esquiar.

ANA: No, gracias. Hace frío y no me gustan los deportes de invierno. Me gusta nadar cuando hace buen tiempo y cuando hace frío, salgo a correr.

ISABEL: El informe del tiempo dice que va a llover esta tarde.

ANA: ¡Qué lástima! Entonces tengo que ir al gimnasio.

**Answers for A.** 1) *A correr.* 2) *En dos horas.* 3) *La mano de Isabel.* 4) *Esquiar.*

**A. ¿Comprende Ud.?** Answer the following questions based on the dialog.

1. ¿Adónde van Ana y Mary?
2. ¿Cuándo va Isabel a las montañas?
3. ¿Qué va a pedir Lázaro a la familia de Isabel?
4. ¿Qué van a hacer Isabel y Lázaro en las montañas?

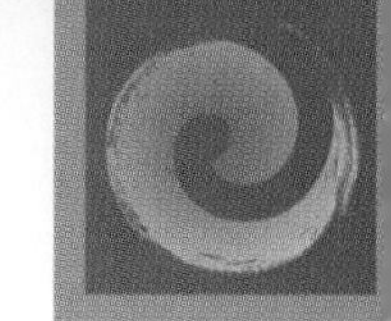

**B. ¿Antes o después?** Based on what these people say, decide if they have just done the activity mentioned (**acabo de/ acaba de/ acabamos de/ acaban de**) or will do it shortly (**voy a/ va a/ vamos a/ van a**).

New words: *mudarme, jubilarse*

MODELO: Estamos nerviosos. (Vamos a/Acabamos de) tener un examen.
*Vamos a tener un examen.*

1. Mi hermana sale del hospital. (Va a/Acaba de) tener un bebé.
2. Mi esposa está embarazada. (Va a/Acaba de) tener un bebé.
3. Tengo mucha hambre. (Voy a/Acabo de) almorzar.
4. Ya no vivo con mis padres. (Voy a/Acabo de) mudarme.
5. Todavía estudio en la universidad. (Voy a/Acabo de) graduarme este año.
6. Mis padres no trabajan ahora. (Van a/Acaban de) jubilarse.
7. Regresamos del centro comercial. (Vamos a/Acabamos de) comprar una alfombra.
8. Mis padres no están aquí. (Van a/Acaban de) irse.
9. Estamos muy cansados. (Vamos a/Acabamos de) correr 10 kilómetros.
10. No tengo esposa. (Vamos a/Acabamos de) divorciarnos.

**C. ¿Qué acaba de hacer?** Ask your classmate several questions regarding what he/she may have just done.

MODELO: E1: *¿Acabas de...terminar tu tarea de español?*
E2: *No, acabo de...terminar mi tarea de inglés.*

**D. De vacaciones.** You are planning a vacation. Explain to a classmate why you want to visit the following places.

**Suggestion for D.** Show photos of the places listed, if available, or ask students to search the Internet or library.

MODELO: a España
E1: *¿Por qué no vamos a España?*
E2: *¿Para qué?*
E1: *Para correr con los toros.*

1. a Puerto Rico
2. a Perú
3. a Argentina
4. a México
5. a Panamá
6. a Chile

- esquiar en los Andes
- visitar el viejo San Juan e ir a la playa
- visitar Machu Picchu, la ciudad sagrada de los incas
- ver las pirámides
- ver el canal
- hacer un viaje a Tierra del Fuego y a la Antártida argentina

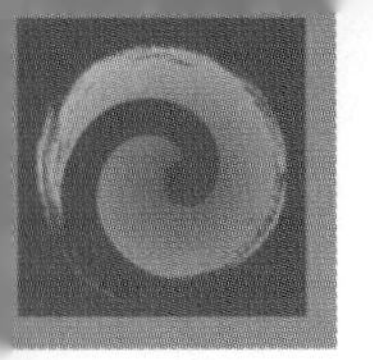

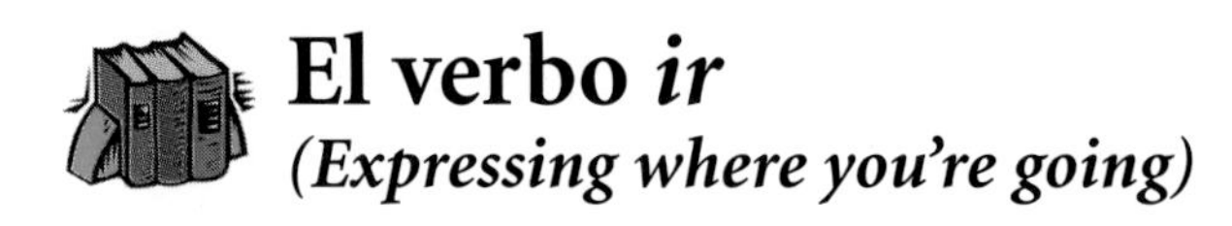

# El verbo *ir*
## *(Expressing where you're going)*

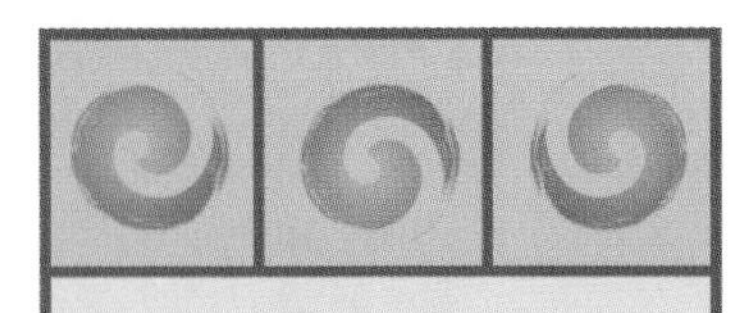

**Para averiguar**

1. You use **dónde** to ask where something is located. What question word do you use to ask where someone is going?
2. What happens to the preposition **a** when it is followed by the definite article **el**?
3. What does **para** mean when it is followed by an infinitive?

| ir *(to go)* | | | |
|---|---|---|---|
| yo | **voy** | nosotros/as | **vamos** |
| tú | **vas** | vosotros/as | **vais** |
| él,ella, Ud. | **va** | ellos, ellas, ustedes | **van** |

—¿**Vas** al trabajo todos los días? — *—Do you go to work every day?*
—No, sólo **voy** los lunes. — *—No, I only go on Mondays.*

- Use **adónde** to ask where someone is going. To answer, use the preposition **a** *(to)*, which contracts with the definite article **el** to form **al**.

  —¿**Adónde** van Uds.? — *—Where are you going?*
  —Vamos **a** clase y **al** cine. — *—We're going to class and to the movies.*

- To explain for what purpose you are going somewhere, use **para** *(for, in order to)* with an infinitive.

  —Voy a Los Ángeles este fin de semana. — *—I'm going to L.A. this weekend.*
  —¿Sí? ¿**Para** qué? — *—Really? What for?*
  —**Para asistir** a un concierto. — *—To attend a concert.*

## A lo personal

**A. ¿Adónde van?** Use the correct form of the verb **ir** and an appropriate place to complete these sentences.

1. Para divertirnos, mis amigos y yo…
2. Para comprar comida, mi madre…
3. Para pasar una noche romántica, los jóvenes…
4. Para descansar, yo…
5. Para hacer ejercicio, muchos estudiantes…
6. Para celebrar mi cumpleaños, yo…
7. Para pasar una tarde tranquila, mi padre…
8. Para comprar ropa, yo…

Now ask your classmates and instructor where they go to do these same things.

MODELO: A otro/a estudiante:
*—¿Adónde vas para divertirte?*
*—Voy a muchas fiestas.*
A su profesor/a:
*—¿Adónde va Ud. para divertirse?*
*—Voy a muchos conciertos.*

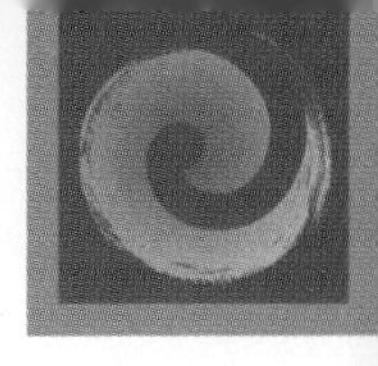

**B. ¿Adónde van todos?** Alicia is explaining where everyone is going today and for what purpose. What does she say?

MODELO: Ramón y yo…
*Ramón y yo vamos a un café para almorzar.*

**Note.** Write the words *estadio* and *lago* on the board to facilitate task for students.

1. Adela

2. los padres de Ramón

3. Martín

4. mis sobrinos

5. el perro

**C. Capitales.** In January, the following people are going to different Latin American cities. Which countries will they visit? Tell whether you think it is hot or cold there. ¡OJO! Refer to the maps inside the cover of the book for more hints.

**Note.** Point out to students that Portuguese, and not Spanish, is spoken in Brazil.

MODELO: yo/Caracas.
*Yo voy a Caracas. Voy a Venezuela.*
*Hace calor en enero.*

1. nosotros/Buenos Aires
2. ellos/Lima
3. tú/Bogotá
4. ustedes/Asunción
5. ella/Santiago
6. él/Montevideo

Venezuela
Colombia
Ecuador
Perú
Brasil
Bolivia
Paraguay
Chile
Uruguay
Argentina

**D. Fantasía.** Money is never a problem for you! Tell where you go first in each of the following situations.

1. Ud. gana catorce millones de dólares en la lotería.
2. Hay una fiesta de gala muy importante y Ud. necesita ropa nueva.
3. Ud. está muy aburrido/a en casa el sábado.
4. En su ciudad está haciendo mucho, mucho frío.

Now, interview three classmates that you don't know very well and compare their fantasy answers with your own.

**E. Una conversación.** With a classmate, prepare a conversation in which you talk about where you are going after your Spanish class today and what your purpose is for going there.

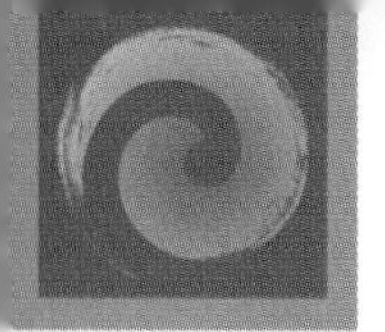

# El futuro inmediato y el pasado reciente
## *(Immediate future and recent past)*

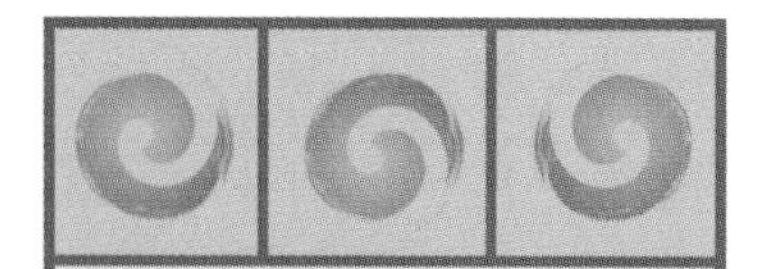

**Para averiguar**

1. What structure do you use to say you are *going to do* something? What structure do you use to say *you have just done* something?
2. The following expressions refer to the past. What are the corresponding expressions that refer to the future? **hace una hora, ayer por la tarde, anoche, anteayer, la semana pasada.**

- To say what you are going to do, use the structure **ir a** + *infinitive.*

| | |
|---|---|
| —¿**Vas a** comer en el restaurante? | *Are you going to eat at the restaurant?* |
| —Sí, **voy a** comer con mi novia. | *Yes, I'm going to eat with my girlfriend.* |
| —¿Qué **van a** hacer después? | *What are you going to do afterwards?* |
| —**Vamos a ir a** bailar al club. | *We're going to dance at the club.* |

- To say what you have just done, use **acabar de** + *infinitive.*

| | |
|---|---|
| —**Acabo de** recibir una carta de mis padres. | *I have just received a letter from my parents.* |
| —**Acaban de** llegar de México. | *They have just arrived from Mexico.* |

- The following adverbs of time are useful to talk about when you are going to do something or when you did something.

| En el futuro | |
|---|---|
| **en una hora** | *in an hour* |
| **esta mañana** | *this morning* |
| **esta tarde** | *this afternoon* |
| **mañana** | *tomorrow* |
| **mañana por la mañana** | *tomorrow morning* |
| **mañana por la tarde** | *tomorrow afternoon* |
| **mañana por la noche** | *tomorrow night* |
| **pasado mañana** | *the day after tomorrow* |
| **en tres días** | *in three days* |
| **este fin de semana** | *this weekend* |
| **la semana próxima** | *next week* |
| **En el pasado** | |
| **hace una hora** | *an hour ago* |
| **ayer** | *yesterday* |
| **ayer por la mañana** | *yesterday morning* |
| **ayer por la tarde** | *yesterday afternoon* |
| **anoche** | *last night* |
| **anteayer** | *the day before yesterday* |
| **hace tres días** | *three days ago* |
| **la semana pasada** | *last week* |
| **el fin de semana pasado** | *last weekend* |

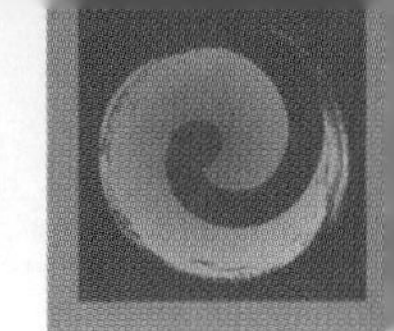

## A lo personal

**A. El horario.** Your nosy friend calls you at five o'clock on your cellular phone and wants to know exactly what you're doing. According to the following agenda, tell your friend whether you have finished doing the activity or you are going to do it.

MODELO: —¿Vas a almorzar? —*Acabo de almorzar.*
—¿Vas a cenar? —*Voy a cenar a las siete.*

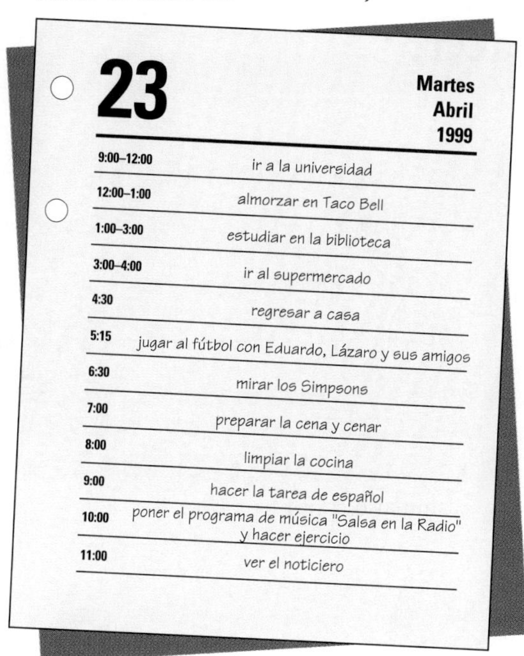

**23** Martes Abril 1999

| | |
|---|---|
| 9:00–12:00 | ir a la universidad |
| 12:00–1:00 | almorzar en Taco Bell |
| 1:00–3:00 | estudiar en la biblioteca |
| 3:00–4:00 | ir al supermercado |
| 4:30 | regresar a casa |
| 5:15 | jugar al fútbol con Eduardo, Lázaro y sus amigos |
| 6:30 | mirar los Simpsons |
| 7:00 | preparar la cena y cenar |
| 8:00 | limpiar la cocina |
| 9:00 | hacer la tarea de español |
| 10:00 | poner el programa de música "Salsa en la Radio" y hacer ejercicio |
| 11:00 | ver el noticiero |

1. ¿Vas a limpiar la cocina?
2. ¿Vas a comprar la comida?
3. ¿Vas a mirar los Simpsons?
4. ¿Vas a escuchar la radio?
5. ¿Vas a estudiar en la biblioteca?
6. ¿Vas a jugar al fútbol?
7. ¿Vas a preparar la cena?
8. ¿Vas a hacer la tarea?
9. ¿Vas a hacer ejercicio?
10. ¿Vas a ver el noticiero?

**B. ¿Qué van a hacer?** Complete the following statements logically.

MODELO: Mi mejor amigo/a acaba de casarse. Ahora...
*Ahora va a hacer un viaje con su esposo/a.*

1. Acabo de graduarme. Ahora...
2. Mis padres acaban de jubilarse. Ahora...
3. Mi mejor amigo/a acaba de perder su trabajo. Ahora...
4. Mi hermano acaba de comprar una casa. Ahora...
5. Mi compañero/a de cuarto acaba de regresar a casa después de clase. Ahora...
6. Acabamos de empezar la clase hoy. Ahora...
7. Acabo de ganar diez millones de dólares en la lotería. Ahora...
8. Nosotros acabamos de hacer el examen final de la clase de español. Ahora...

**C. Entrevista.** Ask a classmate the following questions, then share your findings with the rest of the class.

1. ¿Acabas de comer? ¿Dónde?
2. ¿Qué vas a hacer esta noche? ¿Vas a estudiar mucho? ¿Qué vas a estudiar?
3. ¿Qué vas a hacer durante las vacaciones del verano? ¿Vas a trabajar? ¿Vas a tomar clases? ¿Vas a viajar?
4. ¿Tienes hijos? ¿Vas a tener hijos en el futuro?
5. ¿Acabas de decir la verdad o de mentir?

# ABC ¿Qué quieren hacer?

En mi tiempo libre quiero...

## ¿Qué hacemos esta noche?

*The four friends talk in Lázaro's apartment....*

CARLOS: ¿Qué van a hacer Isabel y tú esta noche?
LÁZARO: No tenemos ningún plan.
CARLOS: ¿Por qué no van a la discoteca con nosotros? Queremos celebrar su compromiso matrimonial.
LÁZARO: Gracias, pero no me gustan las discotecas. Siempre hay mucho ruido.
ISABEL: Estoy de acuerdo con Lázaro. Yo también prefiero un lugar más tranquilo. Vamos a bailar a otro lado.
MARY: Hay un restaurante-bar donde bailan salsa los viernes por la noche. Una pareja de bailarines enseña a bailar de las siete y media a las ocho de la noche.
CARLOS: ¡Qué buen plan! Todos podemos aprender a bailar. Mary y yo los recogemos a las seis y media de la tarde.
ISABEL: A las seis y media no puedo. Prefiero ir a las siete.
MARY: ¡Perfecto! Nos vemos a las siete.

**Suggestion.** Mention the popularity of dancing in Hispanic countries. Introduce other rhythms, such as *cumbia, merengue.* Play music samples, if available. Ask students if they have such music at home.

**A. ¿Comprende Ud.?** Answer the questions based on the dialog.

1. ¿Qué están celebrando los amigos?
2. ¿Por qué no le gustan las discotecas a Lázaro?
3. ¿Por qué tienen que llegar al restaurante antes de las siete y media?
4. ¿Quién va a conducir?

**Answers for A.** 1) *El compromiso de Lázaro e Isabel.* 2) *Porque hay mucho ruido.* 3) *Porque la clase es a las siete y media.* 4) *Carlos o Mary.*

**B. ¿Para qué?** When you go to the following places, what is it that you want (**Quiero...**), prefer (**Prefiero...**), or are able (**Puedo...**) to do? Share your responses with a classmate.

MODELO: a la clase de español (aprender, dormir, divertirse)
*Prefiero ir a la clase de español para aprender.*

1. al gimnasio (tomar café, levantar pesas, ir de compras, hablar con amigos)
2. a un club (bailar, divertirse, conocer a muchachos/as, practicar español)
3. al parque (caminar, descansar, trabajar, correr, estudiar)
4. a una fiesta (mirar la televisión, estar con amigos, comer, hacer ejercicio)
5. a la playa (jugar al vólibol, trabajar, tomar el sol, nadar, descansar)
6. al centro comercial (comprar ropa, mirar a la gente, ir al cine, practicar esquí)

**C. Entrevista.** Interview a classmate about his/her favorite activities.

1. ¿Qué vas a ver en la televisión esta noche?
2. ¿Vas a ir a las montañas este fin de semana?
3. ¿Acabas de hacer ejercicio? ¿Dónde?
4. ¿Qué vas a hacer este fin de semana?
5. ¿Vas a una discoteca para bailar salsa?

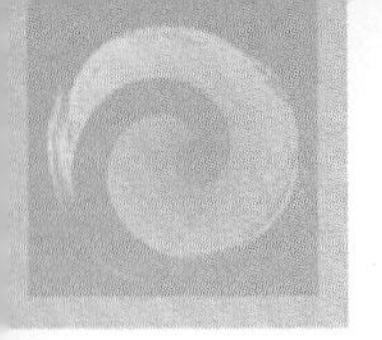

# ¿Quieren tomar algo?

una cerveza mexicana

una copa de vino (tinto/blanco)

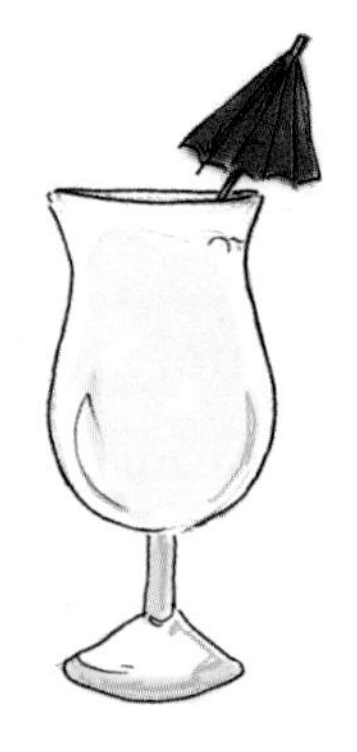

una piña colada

una limonada con hielo

## ¿Qué van a tomar?

*Carlos, Mary, Lázaro, and Isabel celebrate at the restaurante-bar....*

MESERO: Buenas noches. ¡Bienvenidos a la noche salsera! ¿Qué desean tomar?
ISABEL: Por favor, un vino blanco frío.
MARY: Para mí una piña colada helada, por favor.
LÁZARO: Yo quiero una cerveza bien fría.
MESERO: ¿Prefiere cerveza importada o nacional?
LÁZARO: Prefiero importada. Quiero una cerveza mexicana.
CARLOS: Yo sólo quiero una limonada sin hielo. No quiero alcohol porque voy a conducir.
MESERO: Muy bien. Vuelvo en un momento.

*Más tarde...*

CARLOS Y MARY: ¡Un brindis por los futuros esposos!

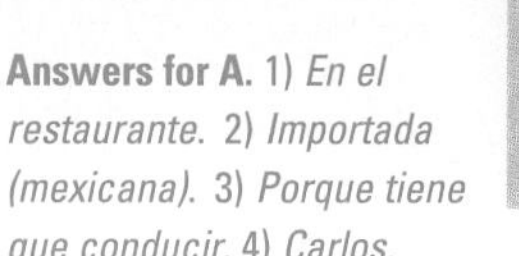

**A. Para comprender.** Answer the following questions based on the dialog.

1. ¿Dónde están los cuatro amigos?
2. ¿Qué tipo de cerveza le gusta a Lázaro?
3. ¿Por qué no quiere Carlos beber alcohol?
4. ¿Quién es la única (*only*) persona que no toma una bebida fría?

**Answers for A.** 1) *En el restaurante.* 2) *Importada (mexicana).* 3) *Porque tiene que conducir.* 4) *Carlos.*

**B. Preferencias.** Change the italicized words to say what you prefer to drink in these situations. Compare your choices with a classmate's.

1. Por la mañana, tomo *jugo de melón.*
2. Después de un partido de tenis o de básquetbol, me gusta tomar *leche.*
3. En un bar, prefiero tomar *agua.*
4. Con el almuerzo, tomo *vino* por lo general.
5. Cuando tengo mucha sed tomo *café* .
6. Casi nunca tomo *cerveza.*

**C. ¿Qué hago yo?** Complete the following sentences with your personal choices. In pairs, compare your selections.

Mi restaurante favorito

1. Almuerzo con frecuencia en el restaurante ____________.
2. Sirven comida ____________.
3. Para beber, yo pido ____________.
4. Empiezan a servir el almuerzo a las ____________.
5. Cierran a las ____________.

Este fin de semana

1. Pienso ir a ____________.
2. Quiero visitar a mis amigos de la secundaria en ____________.
3. Voy a dormir hasta las ____________.
4. Tengo que ____________ mucho el domingo.
5. Vuelvo a casa por la noche ____________.

Los deportes

1. Practico ____________.
2. Normalmente, juego por la ____________.
3. Juego con mis ____________.
4. Nunca pierdo; casi siempre ____________.
5. A veces pierdo la ____________.

**D. En el café.** You are traveling with a friend in Mexico and decide to stop for a drink at a café. Role-play the scene with two classmates, one of whom will play the waiter or waitress. Ask for a table, inquire about the price of different drinks, agree on something to order, and comment on the restaurant. Is it more or less expensive than a similar café in the United States? What other differences do you think you may encounter?

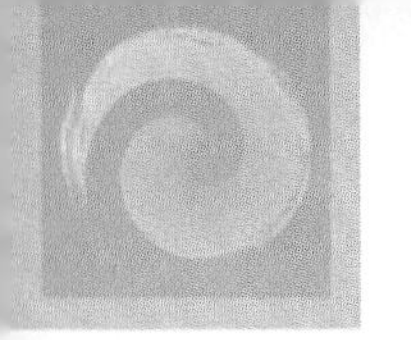

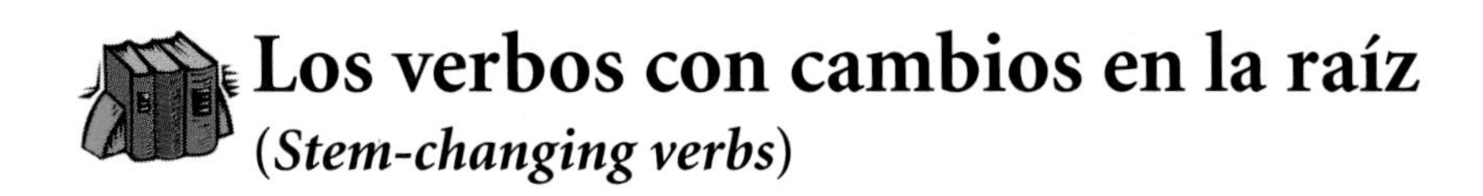

# Los verbos con cambios en la raíz
## (*Stem-changing verbs*)

Para averiguar

In stem-changing verbs, **e** becomes **ie** or **i** and **o** becomes **ue** in all forms except two. Which are they?

- Some **-ar, -er,** and **-ir** verbs have vowel changes in the stem when they are conjugated. The stressed **e** will become **ie** or **i,** and the stressed **o** will become **ue** in all forms except **nosotros** and **vosotros**.

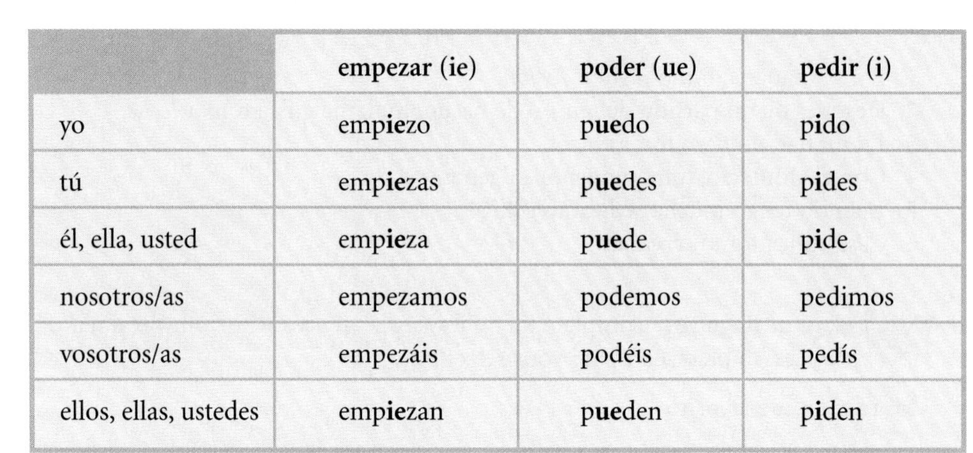

| | empezar (ie) | poder (ue) | pedir (i) |
|---|---|---|---|
| yo | emp**ie**zo | p**ue**do | p**i**do |
| tú | emp**ie**zas | p**ue**des | p**i**des |
| él, ella, usted | emp**ie**za | p**ue**de | p**i**de |
| nosotros/as | empezamos | podemos | pedimos |
| vosotros/as | empezáis | podéis | pedís |
| ellos, ellas, ustedes | emp**ie**zan | p**ue**den | p**i**den |

- Other verbs that have stem changes are:

| **e → ie** | | **o → ue** | | **e → i** | |
|---|---|---|---|---|---|
| **cerrar** | *to close* | **almorzar** | *to eat lunch* | **decir** | *to say, to tell* |
| **entender** | *to understand* | **dormir** | *to sleep* | **repetir** | *to repeat* |
| **mentir** | *to lie* | **encontrar** | *to find, to meet* | **servir** | *to serve* |
| **pensar** | *to think, to plan* | **volver** | *to return* | **seguir** | *to follow* |
| **perder** | *to lose* | **poder** | *can, to be able to* | **pedir** | *to ask for* |
| **preferir** | *to prefer* | **acostar(se)** | *to go to bed* | **medir** | *to measure* |
| **querer** | *to want* | **costar** | *to cost* | **elegir** | *to elect* |

- **Jugar** is the only stem-changing verb in which **u** changes to **ue**.

**juego**, j**ue**gas, j**ue**ga, jugamos, jugáis, j**ue**gan

## A lo personal

**A. ¡Yo también!** Two friends are talking about their daily activities. Do you do the same things?

MODELO: Dormimos hasta las nueve todos los días.
*Yo duermo hasta las siete o las ocho.*

1. Almorzamos en McDonald's por lo general.
2. Jugamos al tenis todos los días.
3. Volvemos a casa a las tres de la tarde.
4. Empezamos nuestras tareas entre las cuatro y las cuatro y media de la tarde.

5. Preferimos cenar *(to eat dinner)* a las ocho o las nueve.
6. Pedimos una pizza dos o tres veces a la semana.
7. Dormimos siete u ocho horas todas las noches.
8. Repetimos las mismas actividades todos los días.

**B. En mi familia.** Who in your family does the following activities? Check the appropriate column, then compare your answers with your classmate's.

MODELO: perder la paciencia con frecuencia
*Mi padre pierde la paciencia con frecuencia.*

| | PAPÁ | MAMÁ | MI HERMANO/A | YO | ? |
|---|---|---|---|---|---|
| 1. pedir ravioles en un restaurante italiano | | | | | |
| 2. dormir mucho | | | | | |
| 3. entender los problemas de otros | | | | | |
| 4. servir la cena | | | | | |
| 5. jugar al tenis | | | | | |
| 6. volver tarde a casa | | | | | |
| 7. perder cosas con frecuencia | | | | | |
| 8. repetir siempre las mismas cosas | | | | | |
| 9. pensar mucho en sus problemas | | | | | |
| 10. mentir a veces | | | | | |

**C. Una invitación.** Complete the conversation with the correct form of the verbs below.

empezar    pensar    querer    tener    jugar    preferir

—Felipe, ¿________ mirar el partido de fútbol con nosotros el sábado?
—¿Qué equipos ________?
—Los equipos nacionales de Italia y Brasil.
—¿A qué hora ________ el partido?
—A la una de la tarde.
—Sí, me gustaría mucho ver ese partido. El equipo de Italia es mi favorito. Y tú, ¿qué equipo ________?
—No ________ preferencia pero todos ________ que el equipo de Italia es muy bueno.

**D. Una conversación.** With another student, prepare a conversation in which you invite a friend to go to a concert, a soccer or basketball game, or to see a movie. Be sure to talk about the time the activity will start and if you will do something afterwards.

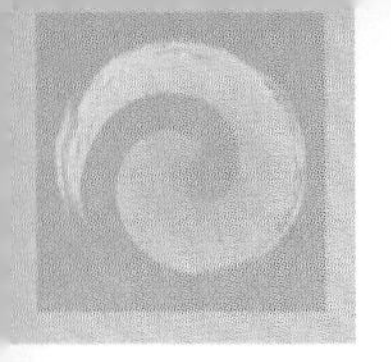

## Más cambios en la raíz
### (*More stem changes*)

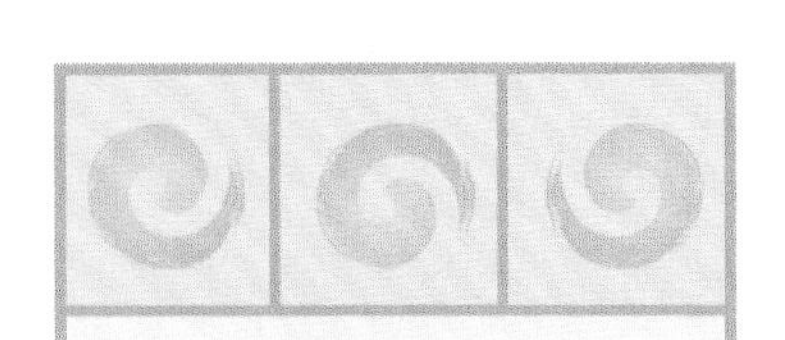

**Para averiguar**

1. What are some stem-changing verbs with an irregular **yo** form?
2. What are some stem-changing verbs that can be used with an infinitive?

- **Decir** is conjugated like **pedir**, but the **yo** form is irregular.

  **digo**, dices, dice, decimos, decís, dicen

- The **u** in **seguir** is dropped in the **yo** form.

  **sigo**, sigues, sigue, seguimos, seguís, siguen

- **Pensar** + *infinitive* is used to express future plans.

| | |
|---|---|
| **Pienso comprar** un coche. | *I plan on buying a car.* |
| ¿**Piensas dar** una fiesta? | *Do you plan on giving a party?* |

- Other stem-changing verbs that may be used with an infinitive include **poder**, **querer**, and **preferir,** among others.

| | |
|---|---|
| **Puedo ir** a clase mañana. | *I can go to class tomorrow.* |
| **Quiero comer** en casa. | *I want to eat at home.* |
| **Prefiero volver** temprano. | *I prefer to return early.* |

### A lo personal

**A. ¿Qué piensan hacer?** Guess what the following people plan to do based on the information given. Complete each statement with the correct form of **pensar** and the appropriate verb.

dormir    decir    repetir    servir    pedir

MODELO: Hay una fiesta a las ocho.
*Pensamos salir a las siete.*

1. Elena tiene una jarra (*pitcher*) en la mano. Ella ______ ______ la sangría.
2. Jorge y Pablo están muy cansados. Ellos ______ ______.
3. Nosotros estamos en un restaurante italiano. Nosotros ______ ______ pasta.
4. Tú eres testigo (*witness*) en un juicio. Tú ______ ______ la verdad.
5. Los estudiantes no entienden bien. La profesora ______ ______ la pregunta.

**B. ¿Por qué hacen eso?** Choose the logical reason why these people do what they do.

tener sueño    tener calor    tener prisa    tener sed    tener frío
tener ganas de hacer un viaje    tener hambre

MODELO: ¿Por qué duermen los niños?
*Duermen porque tienen sueño.*

1. ¿Por qué almuerzas tan temprano?
2. ¿Por qué corremos?
3. ¿Por qué piden ellas algo para tomar?
4. ¿Por qué cierran ellas la ventana?
5. ¿Por qué piensas en las vacaciones?
6. ¿Por qué pides más hielo?

**C. Entrevista.** Interview a classmate, using the following questions. Then switch roles.

1. ¿Prefieres nadar en una piscina o en un lago? ¿Hay una piscina en tu apartamento? ¿A qué hora cierran la piscina? ¿Duermes al lado de la piscina a veces?
2. Para ti, ¿es importante almorzar todos los días? Dicen que el desayuno y el almuerzo son las comidas más importantes. ¿Cuál es la comida más importante para ti? ¿A qué hora tienes hambre por la mañana? ¿Prefieres seguir la misma rutina todos los días? ¿Duermes las mismas horas todos los días?
3. ¿Piensas mucho en tus amigos de la escuela secundaria? ¿Encuentras la universidad más interesante que la escuela secundaria? ¿más difícil?
4. ¿En qué piensas en este momento? ¿Por qué? ¿Piensas mucho en tus problemas?

**D. Lázaro.** In writing, narrate Lázaro's dream of his proposal to Isabel based on the pictures. Feel free to add any additional details you'd like.

1. (dormir)

2. (empezar) a soñar

3. (soñar) que está en un restaurante elegante

4. el mesero (servir) la ensalada

5. encima de la ensalada ella (encontrar) un diamante

6. Lázaro (pedir) la mano de Isabel en matrimonio

7. ella (decir) "sí"

8. después de un beso, ¡ay! tan romántico, él (seguir) su sueño y ella (volver) a su comida

# Vocabulario

## TEMA 1
### Las diversiones

**Sustantivos**

| | |
|---|---|
| **la boda** | *wedding* |
| **la calefacción** | *heating* |
| **el calor** | *heat* |
| **las cartas** | *playing cards* |
| **el centígrado** | *centigrade* |
| **el cielo** | *sky* |
| **el clima** | *climate* |
| **la costa** | *coast* |
| **el ejercicio aeróbico** | *aerobic exercise* |
| **el esquí acuático** | *water skiing* |
| **el gimnasio** | *gymnasium* |
| **el grado** | *degree (temperature)* |
| **el invierno** | *winter* |
| **la montaña** | *mountain* |
| **el noticiero** | *news program* |
| **el otoño** | *fall* |
| **la primavera** | *spring* |
| **el sol** | *sun* |
| **la temperatura** | *temperature* |
| **el tiempo** | *weather* |
| **el verano** | *summer* |
| **el viento** | *wind* |

**Verbos**

| | |
|---|---|
| **arreglar** | *to repair, arrange* |
| **divertirse (ie)** | *to enjoy oneself; have a good time* |
| **esquiar** | *to ski* |
| **felicitar** | *to congratulate* |
| **fijar** | *to set (date)* |
| **funcionar** | *to function, work* |
| **llover (ue)** | *to rain* |
| **mentir(ie)** | *to lie* |
| **nadar** | *to swim* |
| **nevar (ie)** | *to snow* |
| **pedir (i)** | *to order, ask for* |
| **pintar** | *to paint* |

**Adjetivos**

| | |
|---|---|
| **despejado/a** | *clear* |
| **fresco/a** | *cool* |
| **húmedo/a** | *humid* |
| **nublado/a** | *cloudy* |

## TEMA 2
### El tiempo libre

**Sustantivos**

| | |
|---|---|
| **el bailarín, la bailarina** | *dancer* |
| **el brindis** | *toast* |
| **la cerveza** | *beer* |
| **la copa** | *wine glass* |
| **el compromiso** | *engagement* |
| **la felicidad** | *happiness* |
| **el hielo** | *ice* |
| **la mano** | *hand* |
| **la pareja** | *couple, pair* |
| **las pesas** | *free weights* |
| **el ruido** | *noise* |
| **la salud** | *health* |

**Verbos**

| | |
|---|---|
| **celebrar** | *to celebrate* |
| **costar (ue)** | *to cost* |
| **levantar** | *to lift* |
| **manejar** | *to drive* |
| **medir (i)** | *to measure* |
| **pedir (i)** | *to ask for* |
| **pensar (ie)** | *to think, plan on* |
| **poder (ue)** | *can, to be able to* |
| **preferir (ie)** | *to prefer* |
| **querer (ie)** | *to want* |
| **soñar (ue)** | *to dream* |
| **volver (ue)** | *to return* |

**Adjetivos**

| | |
|---|---|
| **blanco/a** | *white (wine)* |
| **helado/a** | *iced* |
| **tinto** | *red (wine)* |

**Otras expresiones**

| | |
|---|---|
| **estar de acuerdo** | *to agree* |
| **ningún/o/a** | *none* |
| **¡Salud!** | *Cheers!* |
| **sin** | *without* |

# Reunión A

**A escuchar. El trabajo del sábado.** Ana and Lucero need extra help for the travel agency on Saturday. Listen to their conversation, then say whether the statement refers to **Ana (A), Lucero (L), or José (J).**

1. _____ Tiene que estudiar este fin de semana.
2. _____ Puede trabajar sola el sábado.
3. _____ Si trabaja, no puede ver el campeonato de fútbol.
4. _____ Va a decir, "Agencia de viajes Castro, ¿en qué puedo servirle?"
5. _____ Vuelve después del almuerzo.
6. _____ Va a estudiar en la agencia.

**A conversar.** Describe a vacation you're planning to a classmate. He/she will ask questions to determine where you're going, with whom, for how long, and what activities you're going to enjoy.

**¿Lo sabía?**

Chayanne llega a la pantalla (*screen*) grande. La película *Dance with Me* es algo nuevo en la vida del cantante puertorriqueño Chayanne. Es su debut como actor cinematográfico. Los actores principales son Vanessa Williams, Kris Kristofferson y Joan Plowright. El popular cantante demuestra su talento extraordinario para la danza, especialmente la salsa. En sus conciertos, canta y baila solamente música pop. Pero de niño, aprende los pasos de salsa de su madre y su hermana. Su madre es su maestra. Su padre es serio, disciplinado y trabajador. Chayanne es un hombre de familia: "Soy muy egoísta en todo lo que se refiere a mis relaciones familiares". En relación a su propio hijo, Chayanne quiere protegerlo de toda publicidad.

**¿Comprende Ud.?** Answer the questions based on the article above.

1. ¿Qué pasa en la vida de Chayanne?
2. ¿Quién es su maestra?
3. ¿Qué tipo de música canta y baila en sus conciertos?
4. ¿Qué quiere él para su familia?

**A buscar.** Search the Internet or magazines for who's "hot" in the Latin music scene. Share your findings with the class. If possible, bring in articles or photos to share with others. If you have a collection of popular music from Hispanic artists, bring it to class so that other students may hear it.

**Tapescript for A escuchar. El trabajo del sábado.**

ANA: La semana próxima tengo exámenes y tengo que estudiar este fin de semana.
LUCERO: Si quieres, Ana, yo trabajo sola el sábado en la agencia de viajes.
ANA: No, gracias. Los sábados hay mucho trabajo. ¿Por qué no empiezas a trabajar a las nueve de la mañana y yo empiezo a la hora del almuerzo?
LUCERO: Está bien. Almuerzo al mediodía, más o menos.
ANA: José, ¿me haces un favor?
JOSÉ: Sí, claro.
ANA: ¿Puedes contestar las llamadas de teléfono en la agencia el sábado? Solamente hasta la una de la tarde. Tú entiendes inglés y español.
JOSÉ: Pero . . . ¡me pierdo el campeonato de fútbol!
LUCERO: Siempre lo repiten por la noche.
JOSÉ: Está bien. ¿Qué tengo que decir?
ANA: Solamente dices: "Agencia de viajes Castro, ¿en qué puedo servirle?"
LUCERO: Después tomas su nombre, número de teléfono y le dices que llamamos lo más pronto posible.
JOSÉ: ¿Eso es todo? Es muy fácil.
LUCERO: Gracias, José. Yo vuelvo después del almuerzo y entonces puedes volver a casa.
JOSÉ: ¿A qué hora cierran la agencia los sábados?
ANA: Cerramos a las seis de la tarde.
JOSÉ: Si quieren, yo sigo contestando las llamadas hasta las seis para que puedas estudiar.
ANA: Gracias, José. Yo voy a estar estudiando en la agencia de viajes.
LUCERO: Yo te ayudo a cerrar el negocio por la tarde.
ANA: Gracias, Lucero.

**Answers for A escuchar.** 1) *Ana.* 2) *Lucero.* 3) *José.* 4) *José.* 5) *Lucero.* 6) *Ana.*

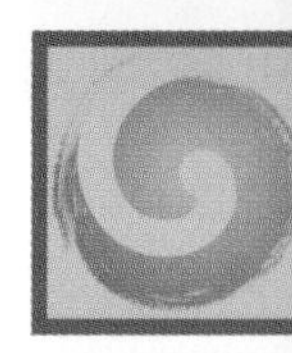
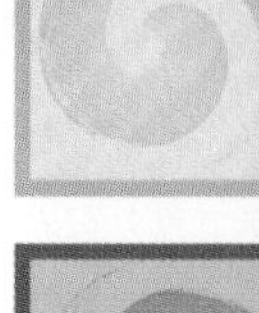

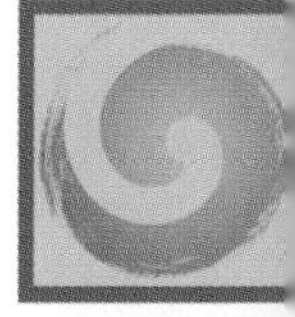
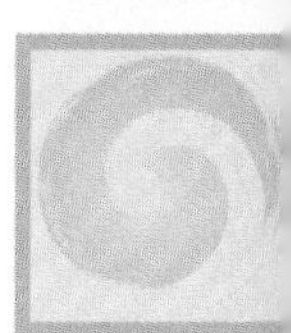
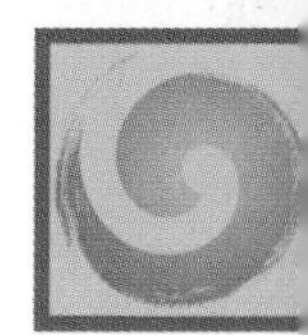
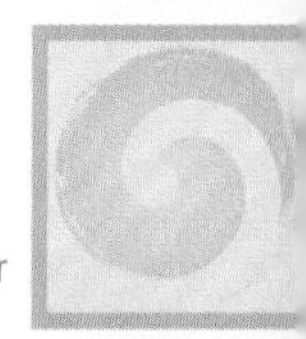
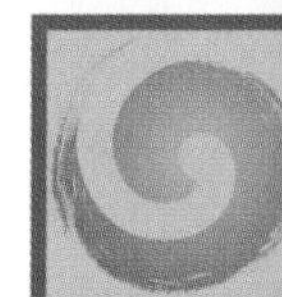
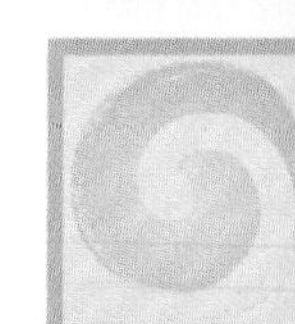

## ¿Qué haces todos los días?

**Expansion.** Model each verb shown by referring to yourself and acting out the action, e.g., *Me despierto a las seis. Me levanto a las seis y diez. Me lavo los dientes. . . .*

### ¿A qué hora te levantas?

*In Professor Yuja's class, students talk about their daily routine. . . .*

PROF. YUJA: ¿Cuál es su rutina diaria?
ISABEL: Yo me levanto a las siete, me baño, me seco, me visto, me peino, me maquillo, desayuno y me lavo los dientes. Salgo para la universidad a las ocho y media de la mañana.
CARLOS: Yo me levanto a las cinco porque preparo mi desayuno todos los días. Me baño por las noches. Por las mañanas me afeito, me visto, me peino y salgo para la universidad a las ocho.
MARY: Yo nunca tengo hambre por las mañanas. Sólo tomo un vaso de agua. Me baño por la mañana pero me lavo el pelo por la noche.
ISABEL: ¿Te acuestas con el pelo mojado?
MARY: No, antes de acostarme me seco el pelo con el secador.
ANA: Lucero y yo nos levantamos a las seis para preparar el desayuno. Yo me arreglo y salgo a dejar a José en la escuela. Después voy a la universidad.
PROF. YUJA: ¿No bañas a tu hijo?
ANA: No, José ya tiene ocho años. Él se baña solo.

**Answers for A.** 1) *Carlos.* 2) *Mary.* 3) *Ana.* 4) *Carlos.*

**A. ¿Comprende Ud.?** Answer the following questions based on the dialog.

1. ¿Quién se levanta más temprano (*early*)?
2. ¿Quién no toma desayuno por la mañana?
3. ¿Quién lleva a José a clase?
4. ¿Quién se afeita por la mañana?

**B. ¿En qué orden?** Match each activity of a typical day with the logical hour given below.

Me levanto...
Antes de salir, me baño y me visto...
Me voy para la universidad...
Almuerzo...
Vuelvo a casa...
Preparo la cena...
Veo un poco de televisión...
Me acuesto...
Me duermo...

MODELO: Me despierto a las siete. 

1. 
2. 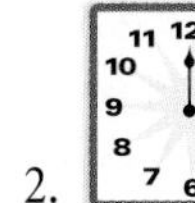 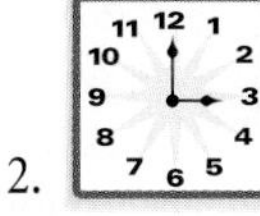
3. 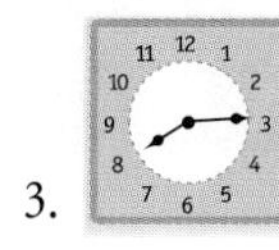
4. 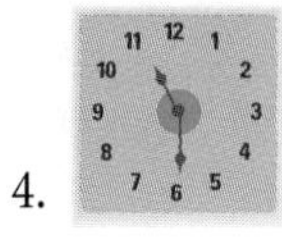
5. 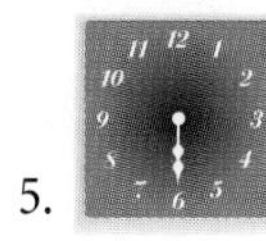
6. 
7. 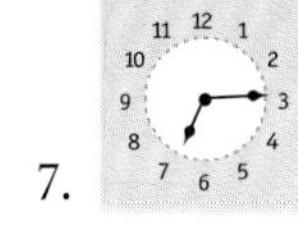
8. 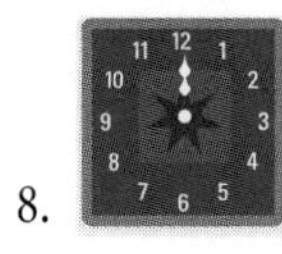
9. 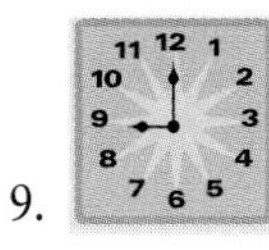

 Now, go back and say at what time you do each of the activities, and ask a classmate when he/she does them.

**C. ¿Qué hacen?** Complete Ana's description of a typical Sunday with the correct form of the appropriate verb.

| | | | | |
|---|---|---|---|---|
| me duermo | se viste | nos levantamos | despertamos | |
| se acuestan | acostamos | me visto | vamos | me baño |

1. Lucero y yo __________________ a las ocho.
2. Nosotras __________________ a José a las ocho y cuarto.
3. Yo __________________primero y luego __________________.
4. José __________________solo.
5. Todos __________________a la iglesia (*church*) a las nueve.
6. Por la noche, Lucero y yo __________________a José.
7. Las dos __________________ a las diez.
8. Yo no __________________fácilmente.

**D. ¿Y Ud.?** Change the italicized words to describe your emotions and worries. Then ask a classmate about his/her reactions in the same situations.

MODELO: *Yo me divierto cuando voy a bailar, y tú, ¿cómo te diviertes?*

1. Me divierto cuando *salgo a bailar.*
2. No me divierto cuando *miro un partido de fútbol con mi novio/a.*
3. Me enojo con frecuencia con *mi compañero/a de cuarto.*
4. Me enojo cuando *no comprendo la tarea.*
5. Me preocupo a veces por *mi trabajo.*
6. Nunca me preocupo por *mi familia.*
7. Me pongo de mal humor cuando *mis amigos hablan de política.*
8. Me pongo de buen humor cuando *termino un examen.*

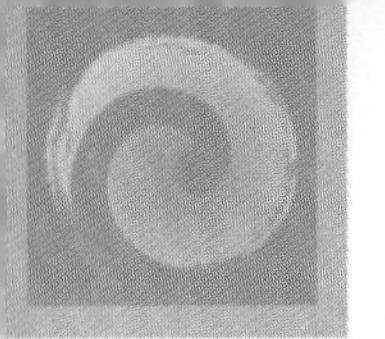

# ABC ¿Cómo son sus relaciones?

**Suggestion.** Model reciprocal use of reflexives by talking about you and your spouse, child, friend, e.g., *Mi esposo y yo nos hablamos mucho. Nos abrazamos a menudo. No nos peleamos mucho.*

Nos vemos todos los días.
Nos lo contamos todo.
Nos abrazamos (*hug*).
Nos llamamos a menudo.
Nos llevamos bien.
Raramente nos peleamos (*fight*).

## ¡Nos vemos mañana!

*Ana, Mary, and Isabel chat after Spanish class. . . .*

ANA: Mañana es sábado y no hay clases. ¿Por qué no nos vemos por la noche?
MARY: No puedo. Carlos y yo vamos a una fiesta.
ANA: Carlos y tú se llevan muy bien, ¿verdad?
MARY: Sí, nos comprendemos bastante (*quite*) bien.
ISABEL: Yo no tengo planes para el sábado. Lázaro y yo nos peleamos. No nos hablamos desde ayer.
MARY: Lo siento. Ustedes nunca se pelean. ¿Se sienten mal?
ISABEL: Sí, creo que no nos conocemos bien todavía.
ANA: Bueno, podemos encontrarnos en el parque y correr un rato. Después podemos ayudarnos con nuestra tarea de español.
ISABEL: ¿Por qué no me llamas por teléfono mañana por la mañana para decidir?
ANA: Bien. Mañana hablamos.

**A. ¿Comprende Ud.?** Answer the following questions based on the dialog.

1. ¿Qué día es hoy en el diálogo?
2. ¿Qué problema tiene Isabel?
3. ¿Adónde va Mary el sábado por la noche?
4. ¿Quiénes tienen tarea de español?

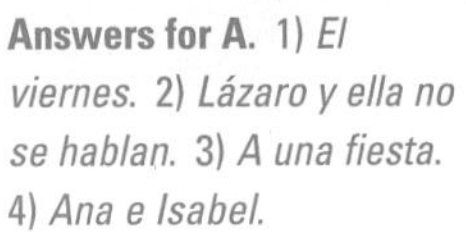

**Answers for A.** 1) *El viernes.* 2) *Lázaro y ella no se hablan.* 3) *A una fiesta.* 4) *Ana e Isabel.*

**B. ¿Se llevan bien?** Isabel made the following statements about her relationship with Lázaro. Discuss with your classmate whether or not they get along.

MODELO: Nos abrazamos mucho.
E1: *Se llevan mal.*
E2: *No se llevan bien.*

1. Nos llamamos por teléfono a menudo.
2. Nos peleamos todas las noches.
3. Siempre nos ayudamos con nuestros problemas.
4. A veces nos decimos cosas feas.
5. A veces no nos hablamos por muchas horas.
6. Si no nos vemos todos los días, nos ponemos tristes.
7. Nos comprendemos muy bien.
8. Nos decimos nuestros secretos.

**C. Los novios.** Complete the following paragraph with the correct verb.

| | | | |
|---|---|---|---|
| nos decimos | nos llevamos | nos encontramos | nos conocemos |
| nos vemos | nos llamamos | nos abrazamos | nos besamos |

Hace tres años que mi novia y yo ______________. ______________ en un restaurante casi todos los días para almorzar. Los días que no ______________, ______________ por teléfono. A veces nos enojamos (*get angry*) y nos peleamos, pero por lo general ______________ bien. Después de pelearnos, siempre ______________, ______________ y ______________ que nos queremos mucho.

**D. ¿Se separan?** Make a list of behaviors/activities that help or hurt a relationship. In groups of four, compare your lists.

MODELO: Ayuda: *Hablar de los problemas*
No ayuda: *No llamar el día de su cumpleaños*

| Ayuda | No ayuda |
|---|---|
| | |

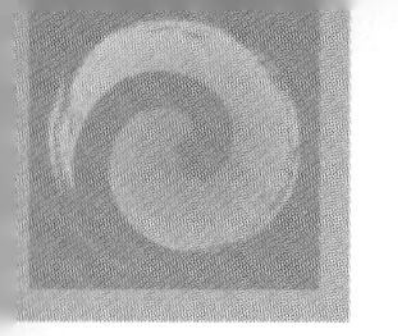

# Los verbos reflexivos
## (*Reflexive verbs*)

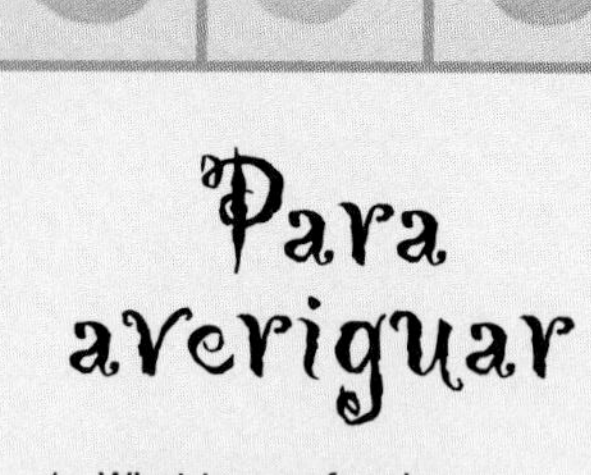

**Para averiguar**

1. What types of verbs are generally reflexive in Spanish?
2. What are the reflexive pronouns?

- Reflexive verbs describe actions that people do to or for themselves.

NON-REFLEXIVE

Adela baña al perro.

REFLEXIVE

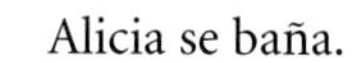

Alicia se baña.

- Reflexive verbs are often used to describe changes in state of mind.

Lázaro **se enoja** y **se calma** rápidamente. *Lazaro gets mad and calms down fast.*

- Reflexive verbs are preceded by reflexive pronouns. The pronoun **se** attached to the infinitive indicates that the verb is reflexive (bañar**se**). **Se** is also modified to reflect the same person as the subject.

| **lavarse** *(to wash oneself)* | | | |
|---|---|---|---|
| yo | **me** lavo | nosotros/as | **nos** lavamos |
| tú | **te** lavas | vosotros/as | **os** laváis |
| él, ella, Ud. | **se** lava | ellos, ellas, Uds. | **se** lavan |

- Other reflexive verbs are:

| | | | |
|---|---|---|---|
| **acostarse (ue)** | *to go to bed* | **irse** | *to go away* |
| **bañarse** | *to bathe* | **llamarse** | *to be named, called* |
| **calmarse** | *to calm down* | **levantarse** | *to get up* |
| **casarse (con)** | *to get married (to)* | **llevarse bien** | *to get along* |
| **despertarse (ie)** | *to wake up* | **ponerse (+ *adj.*)** | *to become* |
| **divertirse (ie)** | *to have fun* | **preocuparse** | *to worry* |
| **divorciarse** | *to get divorced* | **quedarse** | *to stay* |
| **dormirse (ue)** | *to fall asleep* | **sentarse (ie)** | *to sit* |
| **encontrarse (ue)** | *to meet* | **sentirse (ie)** | *to feel* |
| **enojarse** | *to get angry* | **vestirse (i)** | *to get dressed* |

## A lo personal

**A. Antónimos.** Using a verb from the list on page 152, say the opposite of the statements given.

MODELO: No me acuesto,...
*No me acuesto, me levanto.*

1. Mis padres no se despiertan,...
2. A veces me enojo, pero después...
3. No me voy, al contrario...
4. ¿Te levantas o...?

**B. ¿Qué hacen?** Complete the sentences logically with the correct form of the appropriate verb to say what Adela and her husband do on Saturdays. ¡OJO! Not all their activities are expressed with reflexive verbs.

| despertar(se) | vestir(se) | lavar(se) | abrazar(se) | levantar(se) |
|---|---|---|---|---|

1. Mi esposo y yo _______.
2. Después, yo _______ a nuestros hijos.
3. Primero yo _______.
4. Después, _______ a mi hijo.
5. Martín y mi hijo _______ el coche.
6. Después, _______ las manos.
7. Antes de acostarnos, Martín y yo _______ a nuestros hijos.
8. Antes de acostarnos, _______ nosotros también.

**C. El extraterrestre.** An extraterrestrial has moved in with you but he does not quite understand how things are done on Earth. Tell him what humans normally do.

MODELO: ¿Me acuesto en el refrigerador?
*Nosotros nos acostamos en la cama.*

1. ¿Me levanto durante la noche?
2. ¿Me acuesto durante el día?
3. ¿Me visto y después me baño?
4. ¿Me baño en la cocina?
5. ¿Me lavo el pelo en la piscina?
6. ¿Me visto en el autobús?

**D. Entrevista.** Interview a classmate using the following questions.

1. ¿A qué hora te acuestas por lo general? ¿Y a qué hora te levantas? ¿Te duermes fácilmente? ¿Te despiertas fácilmente? ¿Necesitas café para despertarte?
2. ¿Te enojas con frecuencia? ¿Cuándo te pones de mal humor? ¿Con quién te enojas de vez en cuando? ¿Te llevas bien con tus vecinos (*neighbors*)? ¿Y con tu compañero/a de cuarto?
3. ¿Te pones nervioso/a fácilmente? ¿Cuándo te pones nervioso/a? ¿Te pones incómodo/a con la gente (*people*) que no es como tú? ¿Qué haces para calmarte?

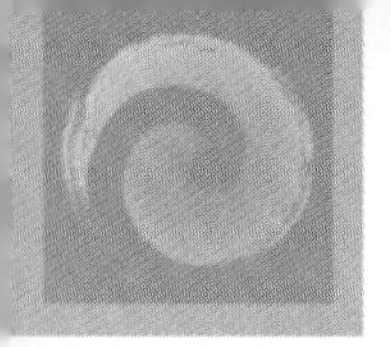

# Más sobre los reflexivos
## (*More about reflexives*)

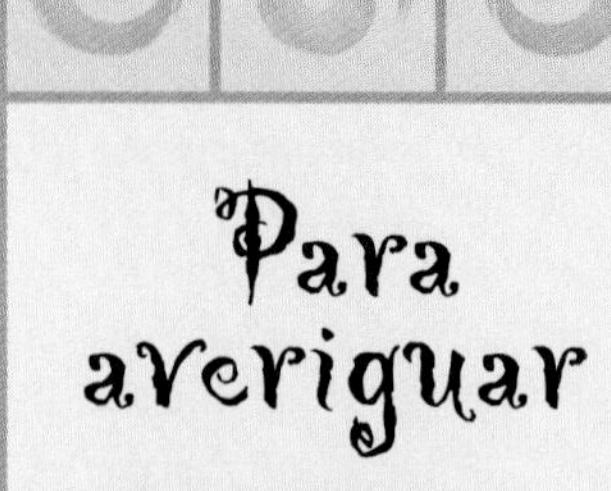

**Para averiguar**

1. Where are the reflexive pronouns placed when a conjugated verb is followed by an infinitive?
2. What is a reciprocal verb?

- When a conjugated verb is followed by a reflexive verb in the infinitive, the reflexive pronoun can be attached to the end of the infinitive or placed before the conjugated verb. The pronoun must correspond to the subject of the conjugated verb.

| | |
|---|---|
| Quiero divertir**me**. | *I want to have fun (enjoy myself).* |
| **Me** quiero divertir. | *I want to have fun (enjoy myself).* |
| Podemos levantar**nos** tarde. | *We can get up late (ourselves).* |
| **Nos** podemos levantar tarde. | *We can get up late (ourselves).* |

- Reciprocal verbs are conjugated in the same way as reflexive verbs. Whereas reflexive verbs indicate that someone is doing something to oneself, reciprocal verbs indicate that two or more people are doing something to each other. Many verbs can be made reciprocal by simply adding the reflexive/reciprocal pronouns.

| | |
|---|---|
| Mis padres nunca **se** hablan. | *My parents never talk to each other.* |
| **Nos** vemos con frecuencia. | *We see each other frequently.* |
| Mi novia y yo **nos** queremos mucho. | *My girlfriend and I love each other a lot.* |
| El perro y el gato no **se** llevan bien. | *The dog and the cat don't get along well.* |

## A lo personal

**A. ¿Quiénes son?** Which of your acquaintances or which celebrities might the following statements describe?

MODELO: No se llevan bien.
*Mi novio y mi compañera de cuarto no se llevan bien.* o
*El presidente y el Congreso no se llevan bien.*

1. Se llevan muy bien.
2. Se quieren mucho.
3. Nunca se hablan.
4. Se enojan con frecuencia.
5. Se ven todos los días.
6. Se divorcian.

**B. Mis amigos y yo.** Form complete sentences to describe yourself and the others mentioned.

MODELO: (yo) poder/levantarse tarde/todos los días
*Puedo levantarme tarde todos los días.* o
*No puedo levantarme tarde todos los días.*

1. mis hermanos/preferir/quedarse en casa/los fines de semana
2. mis amigos y yo/querer/divertirse/con frecuencia
3. (yo)/tener que/levantarse temprano/los sábados
4. (tú)/preferir/bañarse/por la mañana
5. mi mejor amigo(a)/preferir/vestirse con vaqueros
6. (nosotros)/poder/calmarse/antes de los exámenes
7. mi madre/poder/dormirse/después de tomar café
8. (yo)/necesitar/acostarse/más temprano
9. mis primos/pelearse/todos los días

**C. Somos diferentes.** You and your roommate are very different in a number of ways. Respond to these statements by your roommate saying you like to do the opposite or something else.

1. Me gusta levantarme muy tarde.
2. Me gusta acostarme temprano.
3. Me baño por la noche.
4. En mi tiempo libre me gusta dormir.

**D. Una pareja feliz.** Use the verbs below to recount the courtship of Pablo and Felicia. Working with a partner, add as many details as you can.

MODELO: *Pablo y Felicia se ven por primera vez en un café. Él mira a Felicia y ella se sienta en la mesa de al lado....*

verse por primera vez
mirarse a los ojos
levantarse
presentarse
hablarse por horas
no poder separarse

pedirse los números de teléfono
empezar a llamarse
encontrarse después del trabajo
abrazarse con pasión
quererse
casarse

**E. En México.** You are in Mexico on a study-abroad program for the summer and you are just getting to know your roommate. Role-play a scene with a classmate where you discuss the following:

- what time you like to get up
- what time you usually go to bed
- whether you usually bathe in the morning or evening
- whether or not you like to stay home
- what you like to do in your free time

# TEMA 4 Los deportes

## ABC Mi actividad favorita

### La escuela California gana el Trofeo Americano

*California School plays Louisiana in the American Soccer Cup Championship....*

LOCUTOR: Estamos en el Campeonato Nacional Mixto Infantil de Fútbol en la ciudad de Washington. La Agencia de Viajes Castro y Radio K-USA patrocinan esta transmisión.

LUCERO: ¡Ay, Ana! Estoy muy nerviosa. Ésta es la segunda parte y el partido está empatado dos a dos.

ANA: Eres muy pesimista. Yo sé que nosotros tenemos el mejor equipo de la liga infantil.

LOCUTOR: Lázaro Frankel, el entrenador del equipo California, pide tiempo muerto para hablar con los jugadores José Galván y Fabiola Reyes. Los aficionados protestan.

LÁZARO: Yo sé que pueden meter otro gol. Ustedes son muy fuertes. José, tú eres un buen pateador y tú, Fabiola, eres muy rápida.

LOCUTOR: Galván y Reyes vuelven al terreno de juego. Estos muchachos son unos jugadores excelentes. Son rápidos y manejan muy bien la pelota.

LÁZARO: ¡Adelante, muchachos, solamente faltan cinco minutos para el final del partido!

LOCUTOR: ¡Cuidado! Reyes aparece por el lado derecho y manda la pelota al centro. Galván patea muy fuerte la pelota y el guardameta no puede hacer nada. ¡Gooooooooooool! ¡Qué buen gol! Son los nuevos campeones nacionales.

**Answers for A.** 1) *Sí.* 2) *Sí.* 3) *No.* 4) *Sí.* 5) *Sí.* 6) *No.*

**A. ¿Así es?** Mark the following statements with **Sí** or **No** based on the dialog.

1. _____ Estamos en un campeonato de fútbol.
2. _____ Dos empresas importantes patrocinan el evento.
3. _____ Los equipos están empatados tres a tres.
4. _____ José y Fabiola son buenos jugadores.
5. _____ El partido se termina en unos minutos.
6. _____ La Escuela California pierde el campeonato.

el tenis

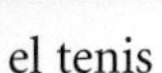

el fútbol

el fútbol americano

el básquetbol, baloncesto

el ciclismo

el boxeo

el béisbol

**Expansion.** Bring articles from newspapers, magazines or the Internet featuring Hispanic sports and star athletes. Ask students to do the research if you don't have articles on hand.

**B. ¿Cuál es su deporte?** Match the star athlete with the sport he/she plays.

1. Arantxa Sánchez Vicario
2. Michael Jordan
3. Miguel Induráin
4. Sammy Sosa
5. Oscar de la Hoya
6. Terrell Davis
7. Diego Maradona

a. el básquetbol
b. el ciclismo
c. el béisbol
d. el fútbol americano
e. el boxeo
f. el fútbol
g. el tenis

**Answers for B.** 1) *G.* 2) *A.* 3) *B.* 4) *C.* 5) *E.* 6) *D.* 7) *F.*

**C. Mi deporte favorito.** Discuss with a classmate your favorite sport to participate in and/or watch. When do you practice this activity? With whom? Where? Who are the best teams/players? Do you go to the games or watch them on television?

MODELO: *Mi deporte favorito es el tenis. Juego con mis amigos en una cancha en el parque. Mi tenista favorito es el español, Carlos Moya. ¿Y cuál es tu deporte favorito?*

GIMNASIO CONTRY
- Pesas
- Gimnasia aeróbica
- Baños de vapor

Tels.: 57-97-96
AVE. REVOLUCIÓN 3633 SUR
COL. COUNTRY MTY., N.L.

**D. ¿Quién soy yo?** You are about to become the top athlete in your sport, earning a salary of many millions. Several of your classmates will ask you questions to attempt to determine your identity. You may only answer **Sí** or **No**. If they do not guess your identity in seven questions, you win!

MODELO: E1: *¿Eres un hombre?*
E2: *Sí.*
E3: *¿Juegas en un equipo profesional?*
E2: *Sí.*

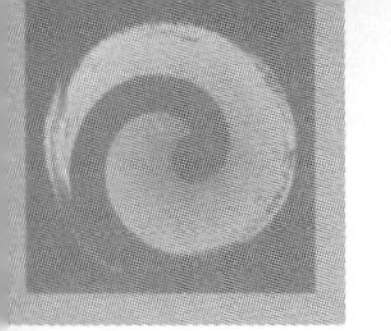

# ABC ¿A qué juegas tú?

## ¿Juegas al tenis?

*Lázaro and Carlos play tennis at the university....*

LÁZARO: Carlos, gracias por practicar conmigo.
CARLOS: Me gusta mucho el tenis. ¿Estás tomando clases?
LÁZARO: Sí, vengo a la universidad todos los viernes por la tarde.
CARLOS: ¿Por qué estás aprendiendo a jugar al tenis?
LÁZARO: Porque Isabel quiere jugar conmigo y ella es campeona de tenis.
CARLOS: Sí, hoy está participando en un torneo de tenis con el equipo de la universidad.
LÁZARO: Tú eres un buen jugador. ¿Por qué no participas en el torneo?
CARLOS: No tengo tiempo. Estoy trabajando y estudiando este semestre, pero juego todos los fines de semana.

**Answers for A.** 1) *Al tenis.* 2) *Carlos.* 3) *Isabel.* 4) *Para jugar con Isabel.*

**A. ¿Comprende Ud.?** Answer the following with information from the dialog.

1. ¿A qué deporte juegan Carlos y Lázaro?
2. ¿Quién es mejor jugador, Lázaro o Carlos?
3. ¿Quién va a jugar en el torneo universitario?
4. ¿Por qué quiere aprender Lázaro a jugar?

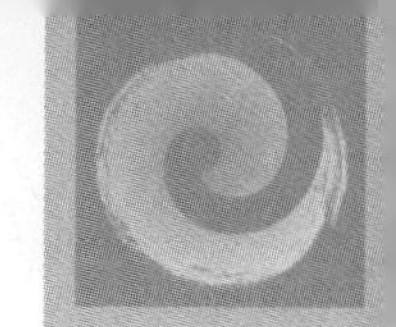

**B. Los deportes más populares.** List two sports that are very popular and describe where they are played, what type of weather is necessary, the benefits of each sport, and at least one famous player of each. Compare your list with your classmate's, inquiring whether he/she participates in any of the sports listed.

**C. Panorama deportivo.** After reading the following contents of a sports magazine, decide which article you would choose to read first, what page it is on, and share that information with a classmate. Mention words that are cognates which help you to understand the descriptions. Could you update the information contained in any of the articles with today's news?

# CONTENIDO

**3**
**Miami fuera de la liga de fútbol profesional**

**12 BEISBOL**
**Silencio en las alturas**
Ocho latinos sacan 40 o más jonrones en la temporada de este año.

**20 FÚTBOL**
**Lluvia de países internacionales**
Brasil, Argentina, Uruguay, Colombia y Paraguay están a la cabeza de los países suramericanos exportadores de jugadores al balompié europeo.

**23**
**Francia gana la Copa Mundial**
La historia de los títulos mundiales ganados por Francia.

**31**
**Copa libertadores**

**32 CICLISMO**
**Marlon Pérez campeón de la humildad**
El pedalista antioqueño obtuvo el Campeonato Mundial de ciclismo.

**36 BALONCESTO**
Estados Unidos repitió título mundial

**42 BOXEO**
**Oscar de la Hoya—campeón popular**

**44 TENIS**
**Arantxa Sánchez Vicario gana en Francia**
Figura del tenis en el campeonato de Virginia

**Nuestra Portada** *Sammy Sosa* *El rey del jonrón*

**D. Entrevista.** As a cub reporter, you can't believe your luck. You've been given the chance to interview the number one soccer player in the world! Prepare questions you really would want to ask the star, and have your classmate answer them as if he/she were the champion.

MODELO: E1: *¿Usted es de Brasil?*
E2: *Sí, mi familia vive en Río de Janeiro.*

**Variation for D.** Have information available about some current soccer stars. You may also allow students to select a different sport, especially one currently in the news, such as the World Series or the Super Bowl.

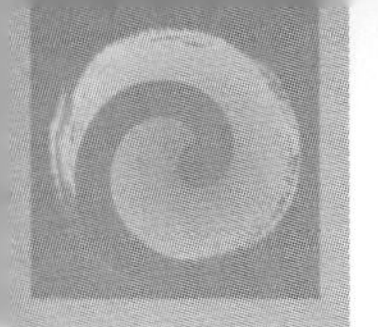

# Posición de adjetivos
## (*Adjective placement*)

- You have already seen that most adjectives of description are placed after the noun, and match the noun in gender and number.

| | |
|---|---|
| un libro **aburrido** | *a boring book* |
| unas chaquetas **rojas** | *some red jackets* |

- A few descriptive adjectives may be placed before the noun they modify, but may change form or meaning in that position. When placed before the noun, the adjective **grande** changes meaning from *big* to *great.* If the noun is singular, both the masculine and feminine forms change to **gran**. When the noun is plural, use the regular form **grandes**.

| | |
|---|---|
| Plácido Domingo es **un gran** cantante. | *Plácido Domingo is a great singer.* |
| Gloria Estefan es **una gran** cantante. | *Gloria Estefan is a great singer.* |
| Gloria Estefan and Plácido Domingo son **grandes** cantantes. | *Gloria Estefan and Plácido Domingo are great singers.* |

- **Bueno** and **malo** change form by dropping the **-o** if placed before a masculine singular noun. If placed before a feminine noun, however, the regular feminine form is used.

| | |
|---|---|
| Hace **buen** tiempo | *The weather is good.* |
| Hace **mal** tiempo | *The weather is bad.* |
| Es una buen**a** idea. | *It's a good idea.* |
| Es una mal**a** idea. | *It's a bad idea.* |

**Ordinal Numbers**

- Ordinal numbers put things in special sequence or order. In Spanish, they are adjectives and will agree in number and gender with the noun they modify. They are:

| | | | |
|---|---|---|---|
| **primero/a/os/as*** | *first* | **sexto/a/os/as** | *sixth* |
| **segundo/a/os/as** | *second* | **séptimo/a/os/as** | *seventh* |
| **tercero/a/os/as*** | *third* | **octavo/a/os/as** | *eighth* |
| **cuarto/a/os/as** | *fourth* | **noveno/a/os/as** | *ninth* |
| **quinto/a/os/as** | *fifth* | **décimo/a/os/as** | *tenth* |

| | |
|---|---|
| la **segunda** silla | *the second chair* |
| el **cuarto** examen | *the fourth exam* |
| las **primeras** noticias | *the first news* |
| los **quintos** participantes | *the fifth contestants* |

*The ordinal numbers **primero** and **tercero** are the only two that drop the **-o** before masculine, singular nouns.

| | |
|---|---|
| el **primer** ejercicio | *the first exercise* |
| el **tercer** libro | *the third book* |

## A lo personal

**A. ¿Buena noticia o mala noticia?** Say whether each of the following statements is good news or bad news.

MODELO: Recibe una "F" en el examen de matemáticas.
*Es una mala noticia.*

1. Ud. tiene el boleto que gana la lotería.
2. Su equipo favorito de fútbol pierde el campeonato.
3. Sus padres vienen de visita.
4. No hay clase de español hoy. (¡Ojo con su respuesta!)
5. Su perro se acaba de comer la tarea de español.
6. Su novio/a no está enojado/a con usted.

**B. ¿Quiénes son?** Each of these people is famous for a "first." What "first" do you associate with them?

MODELO: "Sox" el gato
*El primer gato.*

1. George Washington
2. Adán y Eva
3. Neil Armstrong
4. Wilbur and Orville Wright
5. Alexander Graham Bell
6. Jackie Robinson

**C. Los grandes...** Name a famous person that exemplifies the following statements. When you are finished, work with a classmate and compare answers.

MODELO: una gran señora
*Jacqueline Kennedy es una gran señora.*
una señora grande
*Roseanne es una señora grande.*

1. una gran actriz
2. una actriz grande
3. un gran actor
4. un actor grande
5. un gran deportista
6. un deportista grande
7. una gran deportista
8. una deportista grande

**D. Entrevista.** Ask a classmate these questions. The answer will always use the following number in sequence.

MODELO: ¿Lees el tercer capítulo?
*No, leo el cuarto capítulo.*

1. ¿Tienes la primera tarea de la clase de español de este semestre?
2. ¿Te gusta la octava sinfonía de Beethoven?
3. ¿Tienes un apartamento en el segundo piso del edificio?
4. ¿Es la sexta vez que vas a un partido de fútbol?
5. ¿Eres el primer miembro de tu familia que asiste a la universidad?
6. ¿El jueves es el tercer día de la semana?

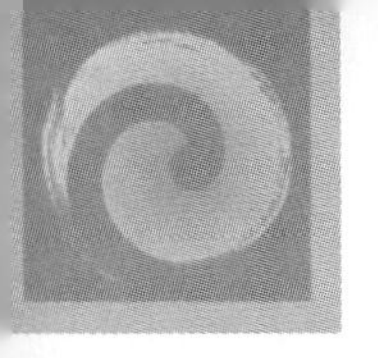

# El presente progresivo
## (*The present progressive tense*)

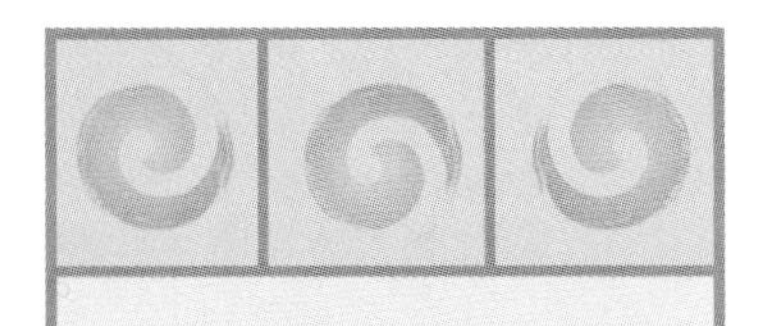

**Para averiguar**

1. What is a present participle? Give an example of one.
2. How are the present progressive forms for **-er** and for **-ir** verbs different from **-ar** verbs in Spanish?
3. Do any verbs have irregular present participles? Name two of them.

- To tell what someone is in the process of doing at a particular moment, use the present progressive.

- The present progressive is composed of a conjugated form of the verb **estar** followed by the present participle. To form the present participle of most verbs, drop the **-ar**, **-er**, or **-ir** ending of the infinitive and add **-ando** to **-ar** verbs, and **-iendo** to **-er** and **-ir** verbs.

| | | |
|---|---|---|
| **hablar** | ¿Quién **está hablando**? | *Who **is talking**?* |
| **comer** | **Estamos comiendo.** | *We **are eating**.* |
| **escribir** | ¿Qué **estás escribiendo**? | *What **are you writing**?* |

- **Leer** and **dormir** have irregular present participles.

| | | |
|---|---|---|
| **leer** | Estoy le**y**endo. | *I am reading.* |
| **dormir** | Están d**u**rmiendo. | *They are sleeping.* |

- In Spanish the present progressive is rarely used with verbs that indicate *coming* and *going*. The present is used instead.

**Voy a salir** con mis amigos. — *I am going out with my friends.*
**Vienen** ahora. — *They're coming now.*

- Do not use the present progressive to express future actions as you do in English, use the immediate future **ir a** + *infinitive* instead.

**Voy a trabajar** este fin de semana. — *I am working this weekend.*

- The present participle of stem-changing **-ar** and **-er** verbs is formed regularly, with no stem changes.

**almorzar** — Los niños están **almorzando**.
**perder** — Estamos **perdiendo**.

- Stem-changing **-ir** verbs have the following changes in the present participle.

**dormir** — o → u — Todos están d**u**rmiendo.
**seguir** — e → i — Alguien está s**i**guiendo nuestro coche.

- With the present progressive (**estar** + **-ndo**), the reflexive pronoun can either be placed before the conjugated form of **estar** or attached to the end of the present participle. In the latter case, a written accent is added to the stressed vowel of the present participle.

**Me** estoy divirtiendo. — Estoy diverti**é**ndo**me**.
**Se** está acostando. — Está acost**á**ndo**se**.

## A lo personal

**A. ¿Qué hacen?** Complete each sentence with the present participle of one of the verbs below to see what Ramón says everyone is doing.

jugar hacer hablar correr dormir preparar trabajar visitar

MODELO: *Alicia está durmiendo en la cama.*

1. Yo estoy ________ el desayuno para todos.
2. Mi hermana está ________ con una amiga por teléfono.
3. Sus hijos están ________ al fútbol en el patio.
4. Su esposo Martín está ________ ejercicio en el garaje.
5. Mis padres no están en Monterrey. Están ________ a mis primos en Puebla.
6. Los vecinos están ________ en su jardín.
7. El perro está ________ tras un gato.

**B. ¿Qué están haciendo?** Follow the model and supply an appropriate verb to form logical sentences using the correct form of the present progressive.

**Note.** Point out that the idiomatic expression for "to take a nap" is *dormir la siesta.*

MODELO: Mi hermana/una carta
*Mi hermana está escribiendo una carta.*

1. Mis padres/un libro
2. Mi abuela/por teléfono
3. Yo/una Coca-Cola
4. Mi hermana/la siesta
5. Yo/en la oficina
6. Tú/en el restaurante

**C. Una llamada telefónica.** A friend calls to ask you what you are doing. Answer using the cues provided and ask the time at which your friend does that activity. Respond logically. Then switch roles.

MODELO: leer el periódico
E1: *¿Qué estás haciendo?*
E2: *Estoy leyendo el periódico.*
E1: *¿A qué hora lees el periódico?*
E2: *A las nueve de la mañana.*

1. hacer la tarea de español
2. descansar
3. mirar mi programa favorito
4. poner la mesa para la cena
5. preparar el desayuno
6. hacer ejercicio
7. limpiar la casa
8. tomar un café

**D. ¿Qué están haciendo ahora?** Write a statement about what each numbered person or group is doing.

# Vocabulario

## TEMA 3

### La rutina diaria

| Sustantivos | |
|---|---|
| **la cara** | *face* |
| **el cuerpo** | *body* |
| **el diente** | *tooth* |
| **el pelo** | *hair* |
| **la rutina** | *routine* |

| Verbos | |
|---|---|
| **abrazarse** | *to hug one another* |
| **acostarse (ue)** | *to go to bed* |
| **afeitarse** | *to shave oneself* |
| **ayudarse** | *to help each other* |
| **bañarse** | *to bathe oneself* |
| **comprenderse** | *to understand each other* |
| **despertarse (ie)** | *to wake up oneself* |
| **divorciarse** | *to divorce* |
| **dormirse (ue)** | *to fall asleep* |
| **encontrarse (ue)** | *to meet, bump into* |
| **lavarse** | *to get washed* |
| **levantarse** | *to get oneself up* |
| **maquillarse** | *to put on make-up* |
| **peinarse** | *to comb one's hair* |
| **pelearse** | *to fight* |
| **preocuparse** | *to worry* |
| **secarse** | *to dry off* |
| **sentirse (ie)** | *to feel* |
| **vestirse (i)** | *to get dressed* |

| Otras expresiones | |
|---|---|
| **a menudo** | *often* |
| **diario/a** | *daily* |
| **llevarse bien** | *to get along with* |
| **llevarse mal** | *to not get along with* |
| **un rato** | *a while* |

## TEMA 4

### Los deportes

| Sustantivos | |
|---|---|
| **el/la aficionado/a** | *fan* |
| **el/la campeón/ona** | *champion* |
| **el campeonato** | *championship* |
| **el/la entrenador/a** | *coach* |
| **el fútbol** | *soccer* |
| **la gimnasia** | *gymnastics* |
| **el gol** | *goal* |
| **el guardameta/ el portero** | *goalie* |
| **el hockey sobre hielo** | *ice hockey* |
| **el/la jugador/a** | *player* |
| **la liga** | *league* |
| **la llamada** | *call* |
| **el/la locutor/a** | *announcer* |
| **la lucha libre** | *wrestling* |
| **la meta/la portería** | *goal (post)* |
| **la natación** | *swimming* |
| **el partido** | *game, match* |
| **el/la pateador/a** | *kicker* |
| **la pelota** | *ball* |
| **el punto** | *point* |
| **la transmisión** | *broadcast* |
| **el trofeo** | *trophy* |

| Verbos | |
|---|---|
| **enojarse** | *to get angry* |
| **parar** | *to stop* |
| **patear** | *to kick* |
| **patrocinar** | *to sponsor* |

| Adjetivos | |
|---|---|
| **emocionante** | *exciting* |
| **empatado/a** | *tied* |
| **lento/a** | *slow* |
| **mixto/a** | *mixed* |
| **peligroso/a** | *dangerous* |

| Otras expresiones | |
|---|---|
| **¡Adelante!** | *Forward, go on!* |

# Reunión B

## A escuchar. **Isabel y Lázaro se van a casar.**

Ana and Lucero are discussing the engagement of Isabel and Lázaro. Listen to their conversation, then say whether each of the statements that follow is **Cierto** (C) or **Falso** (F).

1. _____ Ana está contenta porque Isabel y Lázaro se van a casar.
2. _____ Isabel y Lázaro siempre se están contando sus secretos.
3. _____ Los novios siempre están abrazándose y besándose.
4. _____ Se van a casar en julio.
5. _____ Lucero está buscando un viaje para su luna de miel.
6. _____ Lucero cree que Isabel y Lázaro se llevan muy bien.

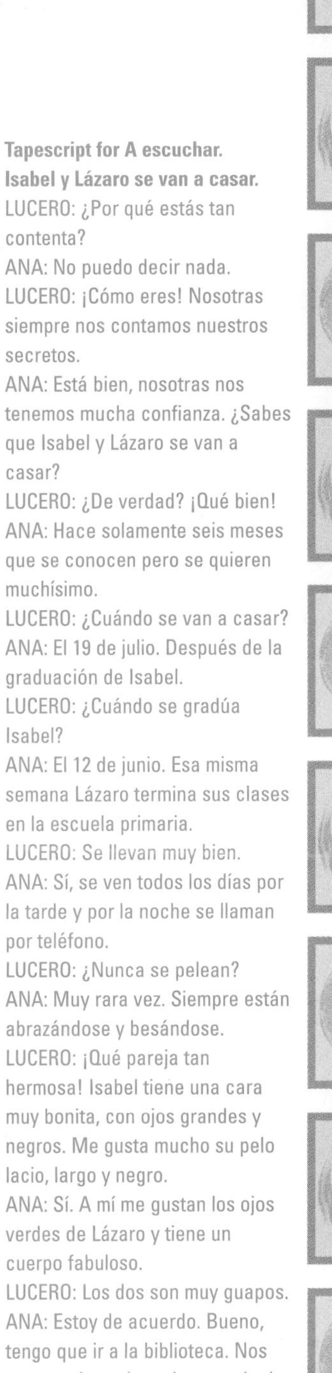

**Tapescript for A escuchar. Isabel y Lázaro se van a casar.**
LUCERO: ¿Por qué estás tan contenta?
ANA: No puedo decir nada.
LUCERO: ¡Cómo eres! Nosotras siempre nos contamos nuestros secretos.
ANA: Está bien, nosotras nos tenemos mucha confianza. ¿Sabes que Isabel y Lázaro se van a casar?
LUCERO: ¿De verdad? ¡Qué bien!
ANA: Hace solamente seis meses que se conocen pero se quieren muchísimo.
LUCERO: ¿Cuándo se van a casar?
ANA: El 19 de julio. Después de la graduación de Isabel.
LUCERO: ¿Cuándo se gradúa Isabel?
ANA: El 12 de junio. Esa misma semana Lázaro termina sus clases en la escuela primaria.
LUCERO: Se llevan muy bien.
ANA: Sí, se ven todos los días por la tarde y por la noche se llaman por teléfono.
LUCERO: ¿Nunca se pelean?
ANA: Muy rara vez. Siempre están abrazándose y besándose.
LUCERO: ¡Qué pareja tan hermosa! Isabel tiene una cara muy bonita, con ojos grandes y negros. Me gusta mucho su pelo lacio, largo y negro.
ANA: Sí. A mí me gustan los ojos verdes de Lázaro y tiene un cuerpo fabuloso.
LUCERO: Los dos son muy guapos.
ANA: Estoy de acuerdo. Bueno, tengo que ir a la biblioteca. Nos vemos a la tarde en la agencia de viajes.
LUCERO: Sí, hasta pronto.

**Answers for A escuchar.** 1) *C.* 2) *F.* 3) *C.* 4) *C.* 5) *F.* 6) *C.*

## A conversar.

Interview an athlete from your college team about his/her daily routine. You may interview a classmate if you wish.

MODELO: E1: *¿A qué hora te levantas?*
E2: *Me levanto a las seis de la mañana.*

## ¿Lo sabía?

**Sammy Sosa, el rey del jonrón.** Sammy Sosa, dominicano, es el rey del jonrón con 66 a su favor, cinco más de los 61 conseguidos por Roger Maris y solamente cuatro menos de los setenta de Mark McGwire. Es el jugador hispano de béisbol de quien más se habla hoy. Su equipo se llama Chicago Cubs. Tiene veintinueve años y su mujer, Sonia, está muy orgullosa (*proud*) de él. Él es padre de cuatro hijos: Keysha, de cinco años, Kenia, de cuatro, Sammy Jr., de casi dos y el bebé, Michael, de un año. De niño, en la República Dominicana, trabajó de limpiabotas (*shoeshine boy*). Ahora, en realidad vive un sueño, con una casa fabulosa, una familia perfecta y una carrera estupenda.

**¿Comprende Ud.?** Answer the following questions based on the article above.

1. ¿De dónde es Sammy Sosa?
2. ¿Cuántos jonrones tiene en la temporada del 98?
3. ¿Cómo se llama su equipo?
4. ¿Cómo se llama su esposa?
5. ¿Cuántos años tienen sus hijos?

## A buscar.

The world of sports changes daily, so yesterday's champions may not still be today's. Look on the Internet or in newspapers and magazines for information on the champions of today. Then use that information to fill in the blanks below. Compare your answers with those of a classmate.

1. la persona más rápida del mundo hoy ____________________
2. el mejor jugador de tenis este año ____________________
3. un boxeador excelente del momento ____________________
4. un hombre fuerte de la lucha libre ____________________
5. una mujer talentosa en la gimnasia ____________________
6. el futbolista hispano que gana más ____________________

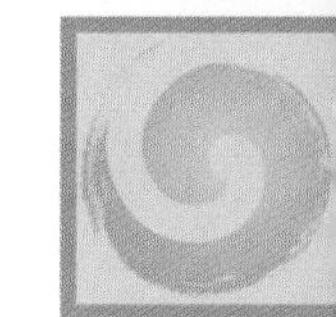

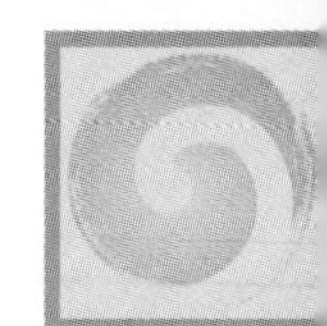

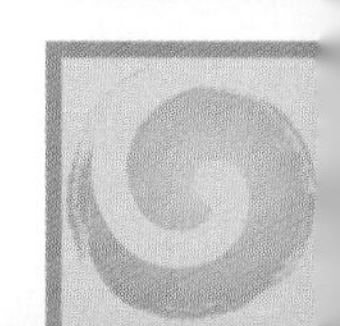

# ¡TRATO HECHO!

## Rincón profesional: El espectáculo

*¡Quiero ser estrella...pero no puedo cantar!*

Millones de nosotros soñamos con ser una estrella internacional de cine, de la música rock, de baloncesto o de béisbol. Pero son muy pocos los que alcanzan el gran éxito de Sammy Sosa, Antonio Banderas, Gloria Estefan o Ricky Martin.

Sin embargo, si Ud. sueña con una vida iluminada por la fama internacional, pero no cuenta con el talento necesario, hay otras maneras de vivir la energía y emoción de estas profesiones. Si Ud. no es el centro de atención, puede llegar a ser operador/a de luz en los teatros, en los estudios de televisión o en los estadios deportivos.

Por cada individuo que alcanza la fama local, regional o internacional, hay todo un equipo de profesionales expertos con una variedad enorme de talentos que contribuyen al éxito de la estrella. Su cantante favorito no existe sin los ingenieros de sonido. No hay conciertos ni teatro en vivo sin los artistas, carpinteros, cargadores de escenarios y los técnicos de luz y sonido. No hay partidos de fútbol o béisbol si no hay entrenadores, terapeutas físicos y vendedores de boletos, hasta incluso vendedores de hamburguesas y cerveza. Para cada función hay empleos para agentes de publicidad, de viajes, cocineros, camareros, locutores, etc. ¡Imagínese a su actriz favorita sin sus estilistas de pelo y vestuario!

Tal vez Ud. no pueda ser una estrella famosa, pero puede participar en el mundo del "glamour" al servicio de la industria de las diversiones. Y piense cómo pueden crecer las oportunidades si Ud. entra en el mundo de diversiones bilingüe.

**¿Comprende Ud?** Answer the following questions based on the reading.

1. If you can't be in the spotlight, what might you be able to do?
2. Name several other occupations "behind the scenes" that are necessary for the entertainment industry.
3. Do you have a career interest that might be needed in the entertainment industry?
4. Would the ability to speak Spanish be helpful? Why?

**Tapescript for A escuchar. El concierto.**
GLORIA: Avelina, ¿vas a ir al concierto de música hispana el martes?
AVELINA: No sé. Me gusta mucho la música hispana, pero tengo que estudiar para un examen de historia.
GLORIA: Van a asistir más de tres mil personas y van a participar Tito Puente, Celia Cruz, Carlos Santana y la Sonora Dinamita.
AVELINA: Yo no puedo ir ese día.
GLORIA: Hay otro concierto el sábado 15 de mayo a las ocho de la noche. Puedo cambiar mis boletos para ese día.
AVELINA: ¿Cuánto cuestan los boletos?
GLORIA: En la sección de orquesta cuestan 45 dólares y los demás 35. Puedes comprar los boletos en la taquilla o por teléfono con tu tarjeta de crédito en la agencia Boletrones.
AVELINA: Está bien, vamos al concierto del 15 de mayo.

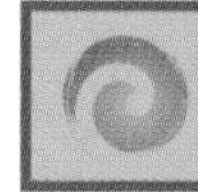

**A escuchar. El concierto.** Avelina is going to attend a Spanish music concert at the Teatro Nacional and now she's talking with a friend on the telephone.

**¿Comprende Ud.?** Answer the following questions based on the dialog.

1. ¿Adónde va a ir Gloria?
2. ¿Qué artistas van a participar en el concierto?
3. ¿Cuándo es el segundo concierto?
4. ¿Cuánto cuestan los boletos?
5. ¿A qué concierto deciden ir Gloria y Avelina?

**Answers for A escuchar.**
1) *A un concierto.* 2) *Tito Puente, Celia Cruz, Carlos Santana y Sonora Dinamita.* 3) *El sábado 15 de mayo.* 4) *45 y 35 dólares.* 5) *Al del 15 de mayo.*

## El buzón de Doña Rosa

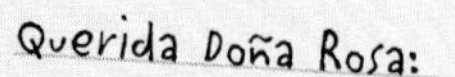

Querida Doña Rosa:

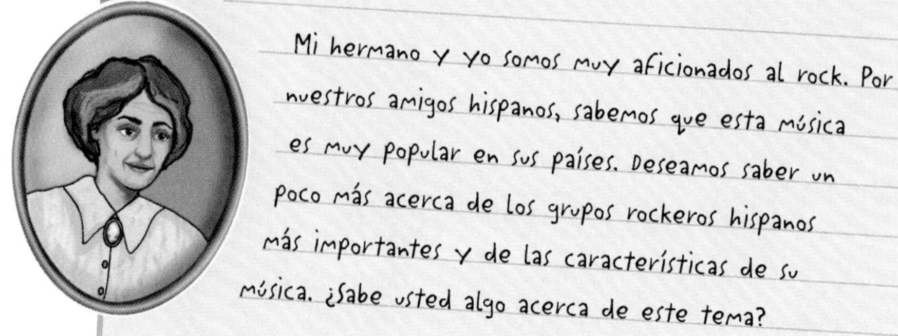

Mi hermano y yo somos muy aficionados al rock. Por nuestros amigos hispanos, sabemos que esta música es muy popular en sus países. Deseamos saber un poco más acerca de los grupos rockeros hispanos más importantes y de las características de su música. ¿Sabe usted algo acerca de este tema?

Dos rockeros de corazón

**What does Doña Rosa say?** Do you ever listen to Spanish music on the radio? Do you know any famous Spanish groups? With a partner, write an answer to the letter from *Dos rockeros de corazón.*

### El rock hispano

El rock en español puede incorporar música de diferentes géneros. Muchas veces combina algunos elementos románticos característicos de la música hispanoamericana en general, como los sentimientos amorosos. Otras veces combina elementos de protesta social. Entre los grupos rockeros más importantes tenemos: en México, "Maná" y "Café Tacuba"; en Colombia, "Aterciopelado"; en Argentina, "Los Fabulosos Cadillacs"; en los Estados Unidos, "Yeska", que combina el rock con la música tropical y el grupo multicultural "King Changó".

**Un concierto para beneficiencia.** Your committee wants to raise money for the victims of a terrible natural disaster in Central America. Plan an event to include famous Latino and U.S. stars from the entertainment and sports fields. You will need to think about ticket sales, booking agents, publicity, housing, and food for the stars and many other details. Write a plan for the event.

## A leer

As you skim this paragraph on the response of the entertainment industry to the growing Hispanic audience, pay attention to the numbers and statistics. Each of these numbers is there to support an important point that the article is making. Take note! Also note the nouns **ventas** and **asistentes**, and the adjectives **conocidas** and **relacionados**. Can you recognize any of the new verbs?

**Antes de leer.** Before you read this article, brainstorm for possible reasons that would explain why Hispanics attend movies more frequently than any other group in the U.S. Then, compare your list with the results presented in the reading below.

*In 1990, Hispanics in the United States spent about 640 million dollars on entertainment. A large part of that money was spent at movie theaters and the amount is growing.*

La reportera Amy Wallace escribe que los latinos componen el 10.7 por ciento de la población, pero van al cine más que cualquier otro grupo[1]. Hay dos razones muy importantes: la primera es que la población latina es muy joven y la mayoría de los asistentes al cine tienen entre 12 y 34 años. La segunda razón es que casi todos los latinos viven en ciudades grandes, donde hay más cines. En Los Ángeles, el 45% del público es latino y según el reporte de Nielsen, el 47% de ellos va al cine una vez al mes. El público latino está creciendo cada año: las ventas de boletos aumentaron en un 22% entre 1996 y 1997.

Los productores de cine ahora contratan a más estrellas hispanas en películas e invierten más dinero en temas relacionados con este grupo para vender más.

**¿Comprende Ud?** Answer the following questions based on the reading.

1. Why do Hispanics go to movies more often than other groups?
2. How often does the average Hispanic person go to see a movie?
3. Why is this information relevant to movie producers?
4. What other activities do you think are favored by Hispanics in their free time?

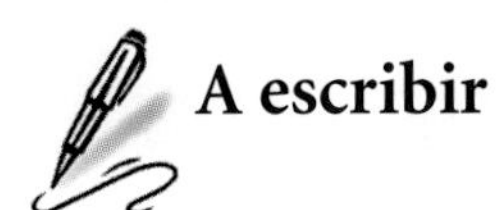

## A escribir

In Spanish, describe with as much detail as possible your favorite Hispanic actress/actor. Make sure to mention the reasons why he/she has your vote, what movies or plays he/she has been a part of, and any other information that you may consider relevant when talking about this celebrity.

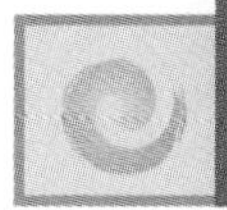

# 5 ¡A trabajar!

LECCIÓN CINCO

CHECK OUT THE *¡TRATO HECHO!* WEBSITE AND CD-ROM FOR ACTIVITIES, GAMES, SELF-TESTS, AND MUCH MORE!

TEMA 1

## La oficina

- ¿Qué sabe hacer?
- Un empleo para Ud.
- *Saber* y *conocer*
- *Por* y *para*

TEMA 2

## Una solicitud de empleo

- Buscando trabajo
- Una llamada
- Introducción al pretérito
- Los pronombres preposicionales

TEMA 3

## Una entrevista con el jefe

- El currículum vitae
- Las profesiones y los oficios
- Verbos irregulares en el pretérito
- Más verbos irregulares en el pretérito

TEMA 4

## El primer día de trabajo

- ¿Hay beneficios?
- La experiencia laboral
- Verbos en el pretérito con cambios en la raíz
- Más práctica con el pretérito

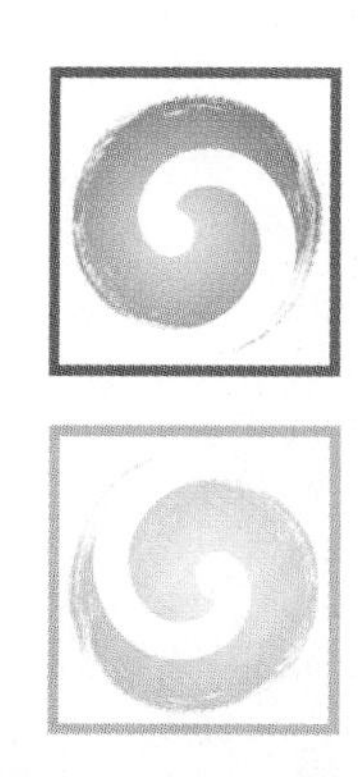

# ¡TRATO HECHO!

- Rincón profesional: Buscando trabajo en el Internet
- A escuchar
- A leer
- A escribir

# TEMA 1 La oficina

## ¿Qué sabe hacer?

Agencia de Viajes Castro
4667 Loma Vista Rd.
Ventura, CA 93003

30 de junio del 2000

Sr. Ángel Díez
Avda. Barañáin, 11
31011 Pamplona (Navarra) España

Estimado Señor Díez:

Acabo de recibir su cheque con fecha del 25 de junio por la cantidad de 200 dólares. Adjunto le envío su pasaje de ida y vuelta Madrid-Los Ángeles con Iberia, con fecha de salida del 4 de agosto. Sírvase mandarme el balance de 500 dólares cuanto antes, para que esté en mi poder por lo menos quince días antes de la fecha de salida. Cuando Ud. desee fijar la fecha de regreso debe llamar con una semana de anticipación a la oficina de Iberia, cuyo teléfono es el 9-48-32-07.

Adjunto también le envío un folleto en el cual aparecen las últimas cotizaciones de la moneda internacional, así como direcciones de lugares donde Ud. puede efectuar cambio de moneda.

Le deseo un viaje feliz y espero poder seguir sirviéndole en el futuro.

Atentamente,

*Lucero Castro*

### Echando una mano

*José is helping out at the travel agency….*

JOSÉ: Ana, me gusta venir contigo a la agencia de viajes porque aprendo muchas cosas. Ya sé contestar el teléfono, usar la computadora, sacar fotocopias y archivar papeles. Además sé hablar dos lenguas.

ANA: ¿Puedes sacar unas fotocopias, por favor? ¿Sabes usar esta fotocopiadora?

JOSÉ: Sí, es igual que la fotocopiadora de la escuela. ¿Cuántas copias quieres?

ANA: De este documento necesito cinco copias, por un lado solamente. De este folleto necesito cinco copias por los dos lados. Después, ¿puedes poner una copia del folleto en cada sobre? Aquí tienes unos sobres.

*Unos minutos más tarde…*

JOSÉ: Ya están listos. ¿Cierro los sobres y les pongo una estampilla?

ANA: Sí, por favor. Las direcciones de los destinatarios están en la computadora. Ya estoy haciendo unas etiquetas. ¿Puedes pegar las etiquetas en los sobres, por favor?

JOSÉ: Claro. Oye Ana, ¿qué hacen Lucero y tú en el negocio?

ANA: Lucero lleva la contabilidad: los ingresos y las salidas. Yo hago la declaración anual de impuestos. Las dos contestamos las llamadas telefónicas y atendemos a los clientes que llegan a la agencia de viajes.

JOSÉ: ¡Qué negocio tan interesante! ¿Puedo venir contigo todos los sábados?

ANA: Claro, puedes venir conmigo todos los días.

**A. ¿Comprende Ud.?** Answer the following questions based on the dialog.

1. ¿Cuántos idiomas habla José?
2. ¿Quién contesta el teléfono normalmente?
3. ¿Está abierta la agencia durante el fin de semana?
4. ¿Cuántas personas trabajan en la agencia?

**Answers for A.** 1) *Dos.* 2) *Ana y Lucero.* 3) *Sí, el sábado.* 4) *Dos.*

**B. ¿Qué sabe Ud.?** You are applying for a job with Kinko's, a company specializing in copying, computer use, and mailing. They have several entry-level positions available and want to know what skills you have. Answer the following questions, then talk with a classmate about what type of position each of you might be qualified to fill.

1. ¿Sabe contestar el teléfono?
2. ¿Conoce Ud. a alguien aquí?
3. ¿Sabe Ud. usar una computadora?
4. ¿Conoce Ud. bastante bien esta ciudad?
5. ¿Sabe manejar una imprenta? (*printing press*)
6. ¿Qué más sabe Ud. relacionado con este puesto?

**C. Mi oficina.** Now you're the owner of a small business, one about the size of Ana and Lucero's travel agency. You can't keep up with the work and need to hire an office assistant to serve as receptionist, secretary, and accountant (**contador/a**). Prepare a list of questions to ask potential candidates about which office skills they have. Compare your list with a classmate and then role-play an interview.

**D. Sea fanfarrón/fanfarrona.** Be honest. You really don't know how to do everything they asked for in the job description, but you're desperate. Prepare an outline of your MANY talents, from knowing how to type (**escribir a máquina**) to speaking several languages to preparing excellent coffee drinks to... Submit your brag sheet to an interviewing panel (three classmates), and be prepared to answer their questions, acting as if you really can do all those things.

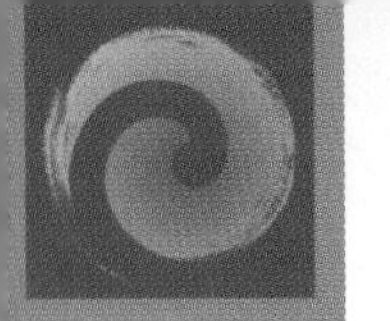

# ABC Un empleo para Ud.

## En la clase del profesor Yuja

*Prof. Yuja has a contact for a job opportunity for one of his students....*

ISABEL: Profesor Yuja, hay un mensaje para usted sobre el escritorio.

PROF. YUJA: ¿Para mí? Gracias, es de una compañía multinacional muy importante. Se llama Empresas Universales. Tienen una vacante en el departamento de ventas.

ISABEL: Yo conozco muy bien esa compañía. Sé que exporta computadoras. ¿Tienen requisitos?

PROF. YUJA: Sí, se necesita un grado en administración de empresas, ser bilingüe, saber bastante de computadoras y estar dispuesto a viajar por dos años.

ISABEL: Yo no quiero viajar por ahora porque me comprometí con mi novio hace un mes. Nos vamos a casar muy pronto.

CARLOS: A mí sí me interesa y cumplo con todos los requisitos. ¿Piden experiencia?

PROF. YUJA: La experiencia no es absolutamente necesaria. El mensaje dice que puedes comunicarte con ellos por fax o por correo electrónico. Tienes que dirigir el mensaje a la jefa de personal, la señora Aurora Benítez.

CARLOS: Profesor Yuja, ¿puedo enviar mi solicitud por medio de su computadora?

PROF. YUJA: Claro, nuestras computadoras son compatibles y tú conoces el programa que tengo. Yo voy a estar en mi oficina de las tres a las seis de la tarde.

CARLOS: Muchas gracias. Yo traigo un disquete para copiar la información directamente de su computadora.

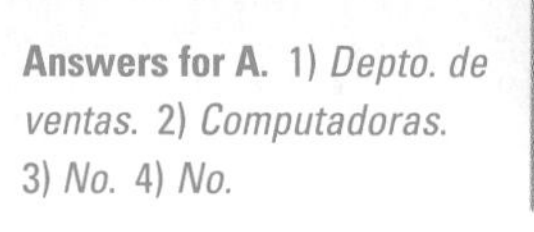

**A. ¿Comprende Ud.?** Answer the following questions based on the dialog.

1. ¿En qué departamento ofrecen trabajo en la empresa?
2. ¿Qué tipo de material vende la empresa?
3. ¿Es necesario solicitar el trabajo en persona?
4. ¿Es necesario tener experiencia?

**Answers for A.** 1) *Depto. de ventas.* 2) *Computadoras.* 3) *No.* 4) *No.*

**B. Un empleo para Ud.** As you can see from the cartoon above, there are many different types of jobs. You haven't been too successful at landing one so far, so your counselor at the employment agency has suggested that you organize your thoughts. Select four possible jobs you think you qualify for, list the qualifications for each, how much money you need to earn, and what experience you have that qualifies you for each one.

**C. El trabajo para mí.** You've given your list to your counselor (a classmate). He/she will evaluate your possibilities, select which one you're best qualified for, ask you a few questions, and provide you with a job description for a position that is open currently. (You have to return the favor by evaluating his/her possibilities too.) Then, each of you must write the description of the available position.

**D. El/la empleado/a ideal para nosotros.** You've made the cut and been granted an interview. The problem is that there are two candidates, both with good qualifications. In groups of four, alternating roles of employer and applicant, ask questions based on the candidates' lists of qualifications and the job descriptions written in the previous activity. *¡A ver quién gana!*

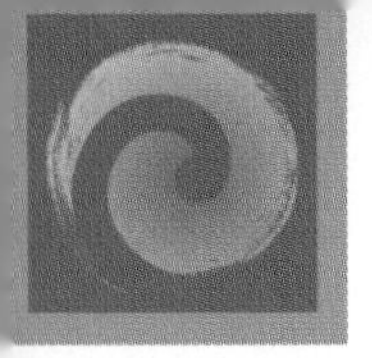

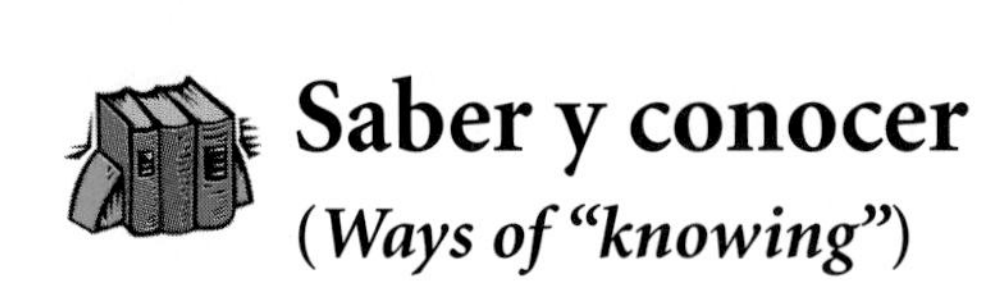

# Saber y conocer
## (*Ways of "knowing"*)

- The English meaning of both **saber** and **conocer** is *to know* as you learned in Lección 3. Remember to use **conocer** to say that someone is personally familiar with a person or place and to use **saber** to say that someone knows information or facts or "how to" do something.

| | |
|---|---|
| Yo **conozco** a Antonio Banderas. | *I know Antonio Banderas (personally).* |
| Yo **sé** cocinar. | *I know how to cook.* |

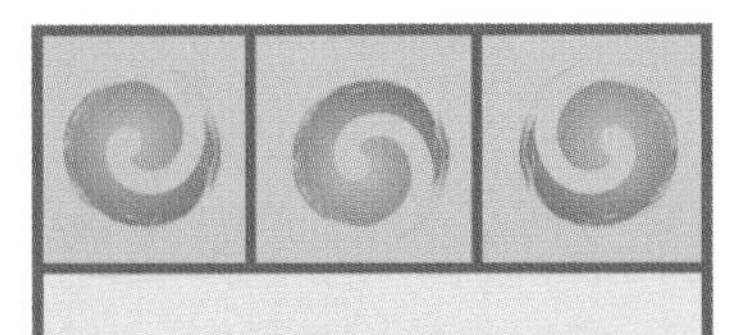

### Para averiguar

1. What is the **yo** form of **saber**?
2. Would you use **saber** or **conocer** to ask if someone knows a friend of yours?
3. Tell the **yo** form of **conocer**.

## A lo personal

**A. ¿Conoce usted... ?** Tell whether or not you know people or places that fit the descriptions in the following sentences.

MODELO: ¿Conoce Ud. a una persona famosa?
*Sí, conozco a Gloria Estefan.*

¿Conoce Ud...

1. ...un buen restaurante mexicano?
2. ...a un millonario?
3. ...a una buena secretaria bilingüe?
4. ...un hotel excelente en Nueva York?
5. ...al presidente de los Estados Unidos?
6. ...a un/a profesor/a de español excelente?
7. ...a un deportista famoso?
8. ...a todos los profesores de la universidad?
9. ...un centro comercial en su ciudad?
10. ...a una estudiante inteligente?

**B. ¿Sabe usted... ?** Tell whether or not you know how to do the following activities.

MODELO: ¿Sabe usted usar la fotocopiadora?
*Sí, sé usar la fotocopiadora.*

¿Sabe usted...

1. ...cómo contestan el teléfono en México?
2. ...hablar japonés?
3. ...hacer la declaración de impuestos?
4. ...administrar un negocio grande?
5. ...navegar la red (*Internet*)?
6. ...pegar etiquetas en los sobres?
7. ...escribir cartas de negocios?
8. ...escribir a máquina?
9. ...cocinar comida española?
10. ...hablar español bien?

**C. ¿Saber o conocer?** Complete these questions with the **tú** form of **saber** or **conocer** and ask a classmate to respond.

MODELO: __________ el nombre del primer presidente de los Estados Unidos?
E1: *¿**Sabes** el nombre del primer presidente de los Estados Unidos?*
E2: *Sí, yo **sé** su nombre. Es Jorge Washington.*

1. ¿__________ a todos los estudiantes de la clase?
2. ¿__________ cómo se llaman todos los estudiantes?
3. ¿__________ cuál es la tarea para mañana?
4. ¿__________ las horas de oficina de nuestro/a profesor/a?
5. ¿__________ en qué edificio está su oficina?
6. ¿__________ un buen restaurante italiano en esta ciudad?
7. ¿__________ dónde está mi casa?
8. ¿__________ mi casa?

**D. Alguien que sabe.** Ana's business needs people who know how to do the following things. Tell if you know how to do them. If not, ask classmates if they know someone who can.

MODELO: hacer las cuentas
E1: *Yo sé hacer las cuentas.* o *No sé hacer las cuentas. Mariam, ¿conoces a alguien?*
E2: *No conozco a nadie.* o *Mi hermana sabe hacer las cuentas.*

1. sacar fotocopias
2. operar la computadora
3. hacer la publicidad
4. manejar un autobús
5. contestar el teléfono en varios idiomas
6. navegar la red
7. preparar la declaración de impuestos
8. escribir a máquina

**E. Entre todos.** Move around the classroom and find at least one person that **sabe** or **conoce** each of the following items. Then, write the name of the person next to the corresponding item.

MODELO: bailar la rumba
*Tom sabe bailar la rumba.*

1. España __________
2. un actor famoso __________
3. jugar al tenis __________
4. hablar francés __________
5. Puerto Rico __________
6. el número de teléfono de su profesor __________
7. un restaurante cubano __________
8. un cantante hispano __________
9. Ecuador __________
10. las respuestas a todas las preguntas __________

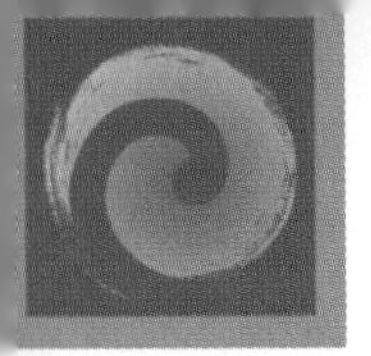

# Por y para
## (Por *and* para *contrasted*)

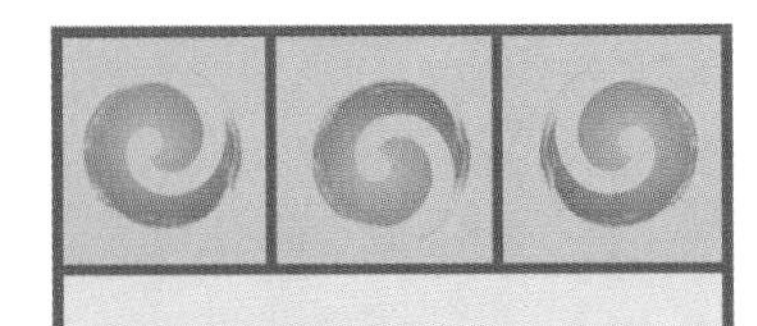

**Para averiguar**

1. Do you use **por** or **para** to indicate movement through time and space? Which one do you use to describe a destination or a point in time?
2. What does **para** mean when it is followed by an infinitive?
3. Do you use **por** or **para** to express means? an exchange? to say for whom something is intended?

**Note.** Point out that in some countries, the preposition *a* is placed before *por* when seeking a person or object.

- The prepositions **por** and **para** are often confused because they can both mean *for* in English.

**Use por:**

- to state during or for what period of time *(during, for)*
  Quiero reservar una habitación **por** tres noches.
  Vamos a llegar el 15 de junio **por** la tarde.
- to indicate movement or location in space *(through, along, past, around)*
  Vamos **por** esta calle y pasamos **por** esta casa.
  ¿Por qué está mirando **por** la ventana?
  ¿Hay un banco **por** acá?
- to express the motive of an action *(on account of, because of, for)*
  Lo hice **por** mi familia.
  Estoy muy contento **por** ellos.
- to express an exchange *(in exchange for)*
  Gracias **por** venir.
  Pago doscientos dólares **por** un televisor.
- to express means *(by, by way of, via)*
  Hago las reservaciones **por** teléfono.
  No me gusta viajar **por** avión.
- to express a person or object sought *(for, to "go for")*
  Vamos a Nogales (a) **por** el pan que nos gusta.
  Vamos (a) **por** el carro mañana.
  Pasamos (a) **por** Glenn a las ocho.

**Use para:**

- to indicate a point in time or a deadline *(for, by)*
  Necesitamos reservaciones **para** mañana.
  Debemos llegar **para** las seis.
- to name a destination *(for)*
  Salimos mañana **para** Barcelona.
  Papá fue **para** el banco.
- to express a recipient or person(s) intended *(for)*
  Compré estos regalos **para** mi tía.
  Necesito una mesa **para** dos.
- to indicate "by the standards of" a certain situation or individual *(for)*
  Ella es muy inteligente **para** una niña de cinco años.
  Él habla bien **para** un extranjero.
- to indicate "from the perspective of" a certain individual
  **Para** papá es difícil leer sin los anteojos.
  **Para** mí las matemáticas son imposibles.
- to express purpose, goal or intent *(to, in order to)*
  Regreso al hotel **para** descansar.
  **Para** llegar al mediodía, tenemos que salir temprano.

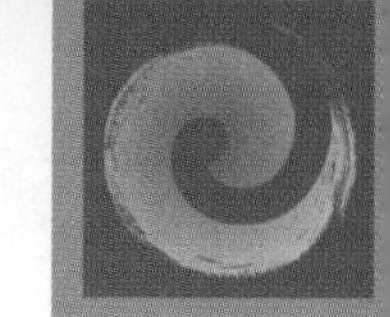

- **Por** is also used in these idiomatic expressions:

| | | | |
|---|---|---|---|
| **por eso** | *therefore* | **por lo general** | *in general* |
| **por cierto** | *by the way* | **por lo menos** | *at least* |
| **por favor** | *please* | **por primera vez** | *for the first time* |
| **por fin** | *finally* | **por supuesto** | *of course* |

## A lo personal

**A. ¿Por or para?** For each item listed below, say what Ana and Lucero use it for and indicate how much you think they pay for it.

MODELO: el mapa
*Ana y Lucero usan el mapa para encontrar los destinos de sus clientes en la agencia.*
*Ana y Lucero pagan 30 dólares por el mapa.*

1. la fotocopiadora
2. la calculadora
3. una docena de bolígrafos
4. el servicio de Internet
5. los folletos de publicidad
6. los boletos de avión

**B. En la recepción.** You are working with a client of Ana's travel agency. Complete the following conversation with **por** or **para**.

—Buenas tardes. Necesitamos una habitación ________ tres noches.
—¿ ________ cuántas personas?
—Sólo ________ nosotros dos.
—Bueno, tenemos una habitación doble ________ 16.000 pesetas la noche.
—¿Podemos hacer la reservación ahora?
— ________ supuesto. ¿____________ qué fecha necesita la reservación?

**Follow up for B.** Complete the following sentences and explain why *por* or *para* is used in each one.

1. *Me gusta salir para . . .*
2. *Prefiero viajar por . . .*
3. *Cuando viajo, me preocupo por . . .*
4. *De viaje, siempre compro algo para . . .*
5. *Este verano voy a estar de vacaciones por . . .*
6. *Me gusta dar un paseo por . . .*
7. *Para ir de mi casa al aeropuerto, tengo que pasar por . . .*
8. *Se puede comprar un boleto para Madrid por . . .*
9. *Para conseguir un pasaporte, uno tiene que esperar por . . .*
10. *Estamos en clase por . . .*
11. *El español es muy fácil para . . .*
12. *Quiero aprender el español para . . .*

**C. Clientes de la Agencia.** One of Ana and Lucero's clients is taking her family on a vacation to Port Aventura. Help Ana answer the following questions.

1. ¿Por qué autopista se puede llegar a Port Aventura?
2. ¿Por cuántos meses está abierto cada año?
3. ¿Cuánto cuesta la entrada para los adultos? ¿Para los niños?
4. ¿Qué servicios hay para familias con hijos pequeños? ¿Para familias con animales?
5. Si la familia aparca allí ¿cuánto paga por estacionar un coche? ¿Cuánto paga por una moto?
6. ¿Cuántos locales hay para comer? ¿Hay algo para una persona que esté a dieta?

## Guía práctica de Port Aventura

**Dónde está:** en Valseca-Salou, a 113 km. de Barcelona
**Cómo llegar:** Autopista A-7
**Principales atractivos:** atracciones-el Dragón Khan es la estrella-espectáculos, áreas temáticas - Polinesia, México, China, Mediterráneo y Far West, artesanía popular, restaurantes y souvenirs.
**Calendario:** desde el 1 de abril al último domingo de octubre
**Precio entradas:** *Adultos:* 1er día: 3.800, 2do día : 1.400; pase de 2 días: 5.200; pase temporada: 9.500. *Niños (de 4 a 12 años) y mayores de 65 años:* 1er día: 3.000; 2º día 1.200; pase de 2 días: 4,200; pase temporada: 7.500. *Niños menores de 4 años acompañados:* gratis.
**Aparcamiento:** cabida para 5.500 turismos y 230 autocares. Precios : moto: 120 día; coche: 400 día; furgoneta: 800 día.
**Sevicios:** alquiler sillita niño: 300; silla de ruedas: 500-1.000; consigna: 200. Guardería para gatos y perros con certificado de vacunación. Lavabos con instalaciones para cambiar bebés.
**Comida:** 28 locales (12 restaurantes de especialidades); precios desde 850 a 4.000; menú infantil 650, posibilidad de menús bajos en calorías o sin sal; precio de refresco o helado: 150.
**Seguridad y sanidad:** equipo médico, ambulancias y helipuerto.
**Recuerdos:** desde un pin (200 ptas.) a un amate mexicano (14.000 ptas.). Pero la mayoría (camisetas, collares, chaleco, etc.), entre las 700 y las 2.500 ptas.

# TEMA 2 Una solicitud de empleo

## Buscando trabajo

### Una llamada telefónica.

*Carlos receives a phone call from Empresas Universales....*

CARLOS: ¿Aló?

DRA. BENÍTEZ: Buenas tardes. Soy la doctora Aurora Benítez, jefa de personal de Empresas Universales. Busco al señor Carlos Montoya.

CARLOS: Yo soy Carlos Montoya.

DRA. BENÍTEZ: Señor Montoya, recibí su solicitud y su currículum vitae para el puesto de ventas. Empecé a hacer entrevistas esta semana y deseo hacer una cita con Ud. ¿Cuándo puede venir?

CARLOS: ¿Cuándo es más conveniente para usted?

DRA. BENÍTEZ: Nuestras oficinas están abiertas de las ocho de la mañana a las cinco de la tarde, pero organicé mi horario para tener libre la tarde del martes 30 de mayo, a las tres de la tarde. ¿Puede venir en esa fecha?

CARLOS: ¡Perfecto!

DRA. BENÍTEZ: Entonces quedamos en eso. Yo me comunico con usted por teléfono el martes por la mañana para confirmar nuestra cita. Por cierto, señor Montoya, busqué su diploma de administración de empresas, pero no lo encontré. ¿Ya se graduó?

CARLOS: No, pero ya terminé las clases. Mis exámenes finales empezaron esta semana. Hace cinco minutos que llegué de mi primer examen.

DRA. BENÍTEZ: ¡Mucha suerte! Bueno, hablamos el martes.

CARLOS: Gracias, espero su llamada.

**Answers for A.** 1) *Jefa de personal.* 2) *El martes, 30 de mayo.* 3) *Administración de empresas.* 4) *El martes.*

**A. ¿Comprende Ud.?** Answer the following questions based on the dialog.

1. ¿Qué trabajo tiene la Dra. Benítez?
2. ¿Para cuándo es la cita de Carlos?
3. ¿Qué estudia Carlos?
4. ¿Cuándo va a llamar la Dra. Benítez a Carlos?

Empresa necesita
**SECRETARIA EJECUTIVA**

· Totalmente bilingüe
· Buena experiencia y referencias
· Salario de acuerdo a capacidad personal
Remitan su C.V. a la atención del
Jefe de Personal, Avda. Constitución 46,
46023 Valencia.

**GUIA TURÍSTICO**
Empresa en expansión
requiere contratar guía:

- Excelente presencia y educación
- Dominio del inglés y del español, escrito y hablado
- Experiencia en labores similares

Interesados llamen a la Oficina de
Recursos Humanos, al
(91)839-2930 (horas de oficina).

**IDEAS Y MODA**
**Solicita:**
**GERENTE FINANCIERO ADMINISTRATIVO**
Los requisitos incluyen:
· Diploma en administración de empresas
· Título en contabilidad
· Experiencia de diez años como mínimo
Interesados sírvanse llamar al
(93)382-3914 para concertar
una entrevista (horas de
oficina, lunes a viernes).

**Note.** Point out that in Spain the zip code in addresses is placed before the name of the city.

**B. Anuncios clasificados.** The ads above list three different positions. Answer the following questions based on information from the ads.

1. ¿Cuáles son los tres trabajos?
2. ¿Cuántas lenguas necesita saber hablar la secretaria?
3. Para la posición de guía turístico, ¿es necesario tener experiencia?
4. Si uno tiene interés en uno de esos puestos, ¿qué debe hacer?
5. ¿Cuáles son los requisitos para ser gerente administrativo financiero?

**C. Una solicitud.** You're ready for your first really important job. You want to make a good impression, so it's important that your application be filled out correctly and completely. Fill out the application, then trade with a classmate to evaluate what each of you has done.

**Pre-solicitud de Empleo**

**I. CONFIDENCIAL**
Fecha: ____________
Puesto Solicitado: ____________
Sueldo Deseado: ____________

**II. DATOS PERSONALES**
Nombre(s) y Apellido(s) ____________
Dirección: ____________
Calle: ____________
C.P.: ____________
Ciudad: ____________ País: ____________

Teléfono(s): Casa ____________ Oficina: ____________
Dirección Electrónica: ____________
Fecha de nacimiento: Día ________ Mes ________ Año ________
Sexo: ________ Estado Civil: ____________

**III. ESCOLARIDAD**
Nivel de escolaridad:
○ Bachillerato ○ Licenciatura ○ Maestría ○ Doctorado
Carrera: ____________ Escuela: ____________
Areas de mayor interés: ____________

**IV. EXPERIENCIA**
Empresa: ____________
Dirección: ____________
Puesto: ____________
Funciones desempeñadas: ____________

**V. OTROS**
Idiomas: ____________
Manejo de paquetería (sistemas y equipo de cómputo): ____________

**Note.** Point out that in many Spanish-speaking countries *bachillerato* is the equivalent of High School and *licenciatura* is a slightly higher degree than a bachelor's degree in the U.S.

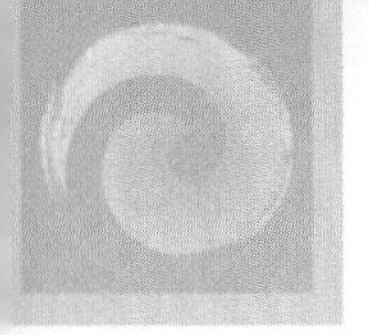

# ABC Una llamada

## Tengo un mensaje para ti.

*Mary calls Lucero's travel agency....*

LUCERO: Buenos días, Agencia de viajes Castro. ¿En qué puedo servirle?
MARY: Buenos días. Por favor, ¿puede comunicarme con la señorita Ana Castro?
LUCERO: La señorita Castro no está en la oficina en este momento. ¿De parte de quién?
MARY: Soy Mary Lancaster, una compañera de la universidad. ¿No sabe a qué hora regresa?
LUCERO: Salió a almorzar. Regresa como a las dos de la tarde. ¿Quiere dejarle algún mensaje?
MARY: Sí, por favor, Isabel y yo vamos a reunirnos a las seis para hacer nuestro proyecto para la clase de español. Si Ana quiere trabajar con nosotras, nos puede llamar a mí o a Isabel. Ella tiene nuestros números de teléfono.
LUCERO: Yo le doy a ella el mensaje lo más pronto posible. ¡Un momento! En este momento está llegando Ana. ¿Quiere hablar con ella?
MARY: ¡Claro! Muchas gracias.
LUCERO: Ana, esta llamada es para ti.
ANA: ¿Para mí?
LUCERO: Sí, es Mary.
ANA: Gracias, Lucero.

**Answers for A.** 1) *Con Ana.* 2) *Lucero.* 3) *A las seis.* 4) *Almorzando.*

**A. ¿Comprende Ud.?** Answer the following questions based on the dialog.

1. ¿Con quién quiere hablar Mary?
2. ¿Quién contesta el teléfono?
3. ¿Cuándo es la reunión para el proyecto de español?
4. ¿Dónde está Ana?

**B. Una carta inicial.** You've seen a job advertised that you're interested in. Write a brief cover letter stating that you're sending your resumé along with letters of recommendation. Use the letter below as a model but use your own words to write your cover letter.

Calle Mariposa, 23
San Antonio, Texas 21354
2 de septiembre del 2000

Gerente de Ventas
Almacén La Joya
4000 Avenida de los Árboles
San Antonio, Texas 21356

Estimado señor:

En respuesta a su anuncio del día 28 de agosto que apareció en La Opinión, solicito el puesto de dependiente en su almacén. Adjunto le envío mi currículum vitae y dos cartas de recomendación.
Le agradezco su atención a esta carta.

Atentamente,

*María del Mar de León*

**C. Una carta de recomendación.** A friend has asked for a letter of recommendation to accompany his job application. Discuss with him/her (a classmate) what information you should include in such a letter, then write it.

**D. ¿Firmar o no?** You've been offered a position, but are unsure of whether to sign the contract or not. Discuss with two other classmates what you should expect regarding salary, schedule, benefits such as insurance and retirement, and vacation.

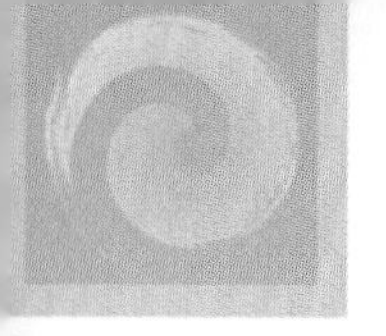

# Introducción al pretérito
## (*Introducing the simple past tense*)

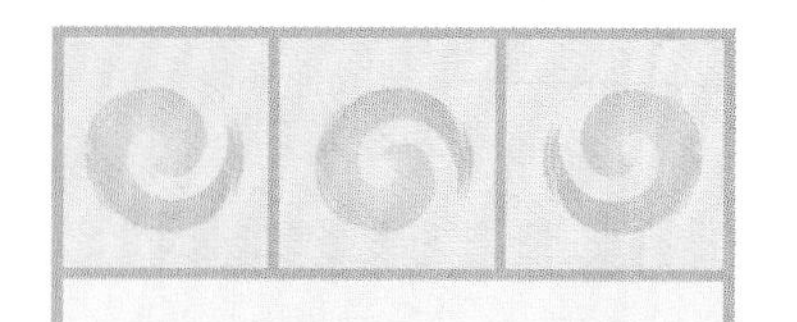

### Para averiguar

1. What verb tense do you use to tell what someone did or what happened at some moment in the past?
2. Which preterite forms look like the present tense?
3. What spelling changes occur in the preterite **yo** forms of verbs ending in **-car**, **-gar**, and **-zar**?

**Warm-up.** Have students say whether the verb is in the present or the past.

1. *yo (compro, compré, hablé, bailo, me levanté, me despierto, me desperté, comí, como, leí, viví, vivo, salgo, salí, voy, fui, hice, hago, doy, di)*
2. *tú (hablaste, hablas, leíste, lees, vas, fuiste, saliste, hiciste, haces)*
3. *él (baila, bailó, salió, sale, dio, da, hace, hizo, fue, es, mira, miró)*
4. *ellos (salieron, salen, fueron, van, hacen, hicieron, abrieron, se levantaron, se levantan, dan, dieron)*

- To say what you did at some point in the past, use the preterite. Here are the forms of the preterite of regular **-ar**, **-er**, and **-ir** verbs. Note that the **nosotros** form of **-ar** and **-ir** verbs looks the same as the present tense. Context will clarify the meaning. The **nosotros** form of **-er** verbs has an **i** instead of the **e** in the ending of the preterite.

| | comprar | comer | abrir |
|---|---|---|---|
| yo | compr**é** | com**í** | abr**í** |
| tú | compr**aste** | com**iste** | abr**iste** |
| él, ella, Ud. | compr**ó** | com**ió** | abr**ió** |
| nosotros/as | compr**amos** | com**imos** | abr**imos** |
| vosotros/as | compr**asteis** | com**isteis** | abr**isteis** |
| ellos, ellas, ustedes | compr**aron** | com**ieron** | abr**ieron** |

—¿Ya **comiste**?
—Sí, **comí** en casa antes de salir.

*—Did you already eat?*
*—Yes, I ate at home before leaving.*

—¿**Compraste** algo?
—**Compré** un disco para la computadora.

*—Did you buy anything?*
*—I bought a disk for the computer.*

—¿**Escribiste** el precio?
—Sí, lo **escribí** en el libro.

*—Did you write down the price?*
*—Yes, I wrote it down in the book.*

### CAMBIOS ORTOGRÁFICOS

- In the preterite, **-ar** verbs ending in **-car**, **-gar**, and **-zar** have the following spelling changes in the **yo** form.

**buscar** → **busqué**, buscaste, buscó, buscamos, buscasteis, buscaron

**pagar** → **pagué**, pagaste, pagó, pagamos, pagasteis, pagaron

**empezar** → **empecé**, empezaste, empezó, empezamos, empezasteis, empezaron

—¿**Pagaste** las cuentas?
—Sí, **pagué** las cuentas ayer.

*Did you pay the bills?*
*Yes, I paid the bills yesterday.*

—¿**Empezaste** la tarea?
—Sí, la **empecé** hace una hora.

*Did you start your homework?*
*Yes, I started it an hour ago.*

—¿**Buscaste** la información?
—Sí, **busqué** la información en el Internet.

*Did you look for the information?*
*Yes, I looked for the information on the Internet.*

- When used in the preterite, verbs with infinitives ending in **-eer** (**creer, leer, proveer**) have a spelling change in the third person, singular and plural. A general spelling rule states that an unaccented **i** will change to **y** when between two vowels.

  **leer** leí, leíste, leyó, leímos, leísteis, leyeron

## A lo personal

**A. ¿Cuántas veces?** Say how many times you did the following things last week.

| nunca | una vez | dos veces | más de dos veces |
|---|---|---|---|

1. Escribí un informe.
2. Hablé con mis padres.
3. Lavé la ropa.
4. Compré ropa nueva.
5. Comí en un restaurante.
6. Trabajé.
7. Navegué el Internet.
8. Empecé un libro nuevo.

**B. Ayer.** Here is what Juan did. Say whether or not you did the same.

MODELO: Jugó al tenis ayer por la tarde.
*Yo también jugué al tenis ayer por la tarde.* o *Yo no jugué al tenis ayer.*

1. Jugó al baloncesto el fin de semana pasado.
2. Anoche empezó a estudiar muy tarde.
3. Anoche practicó su pronunciación de español con los casetes.
4. Dedicó mucho tiempo al español el fin de semana pasado.
5. Ayer almorzó en casa.
6. La última vez que compró zapatos buscó por mucho tiempo antes de decidirse.
7. Pagó más de cien dólares la última vez que compró un boleto de avión.
8. Navegó la red esta mañana antes de salir de casa.

**C. La última vez.** Ask a classmate when he/she last did the following things.

| ayer | en mayo | anoche | anteayer | la semana pasada |
|---|---|---|---|---|
| hace mucho tiempo | | el mes pasado | hace tres días | |

MODELO: hablar por teléfono
E1: *¿Cuándo hablaste por teléfono por última vez?*
E2: *Hablé por teléfono esta mañana.*

comer pizza
E1: *¿Cuándo comiste pizza por última vez?*
E2: *Comí pizza anoche.*

1. bailar
2. estudiar todo el día
3. levantarse temprano
4. tomar una Coca-Cola
5. salir con amigos
6. asistir a un concierto
7. comer una hamburguesa
8. leer un libro interesante
9. investigar algo en la biblioteca
10. buscar un empleo

# Los pronombres preposicionales
## (*Using pronouns after a preposition*)

**Para averiguar**

1. Which two prepositional pronouns are different from the subject pronouns?
2. How do you say *with me? with you* (singular, familiar)? *with him?*

- Use the following pronouns as objects of a preposition. Note that the prepositional pronouns are the same as the subject pronouns, except for **mí** and **ti**. **Mí** has a written accent to distinguish it from the possessive adjective **mi** (*my*).

| Prepositional pronouns | | | |
|---|---|---|---|
| Singular | | Plural | |
| **mí** | *me* | **nosotros/as** | *us* |
| **ti** | *you* | **vosotros/as** | *you* |
| **él** | *him* | **ellos** | *them* |
| **ella** | *her* | **ellas** | *them* |
| **usted** | *you* | **ustedes** | *you* |

—¿Hay alguien detrás **de ti**? — *Is there someone behind you?*
—Mi esposo está detrás **de mí** pero no hay nadie detrás **de él**. — *My husband is behind me, but there is nobody behind him.*

- Review the following prepositions and prepositional phrases.

| | | | |
|---|---|---|---|
| **a** | *to, at* | **después de** | *after* |
| **acerca de** | *about* | **en** | *in, at, on* |
| **antes de** | *before (time/space)* | **hasta** | *until* |
| **ante** | *before (in the presence of)* | **para** | *for, in order to* |
| **a la derecha de** | *to the right of* | **por** | *for, through, by, because of* |
| **a la izquierda de** | *to the left of* | **sin** | *without* |
| **con** | *with* | **sobre** | *over, about* |
| **de, desde** | *from* | **tras** | *behind* |

- Use **conmigo** and **contigo** to say *with me* and *with you* (singular, familiar). Otherwise, use regular prepositional pronouns after **con**.

—Yo voy a la tienda y papá va al banco. — *I go to the store and Dad goes to the bank.*
—¿Prefieres ir **conmigo** o **con él**? — *Do you prefer to go with me or with him?*
—Prefiero ir **contigo**. — *I prefer to go with you.*
—Entonces Papá va al banco **con ella**. — *Then Dad goes to the bank with her.*

## A lo personal

**A. Para mí.** You and a friend are starting new jobs. You will work in a travel agency, your friend will work in a restaurant. For which of you are the following statements true?

MODELO: Es importante tener mucha experiencia.
*Para mí es importante, pero para él/ella no es muy importante.* o
*Para nosotros/as dos no es importante.*

1. Es importante tener paciencia.
2. Es interesante probar comida exótica.
3. Es aburrido hacer cuentas.
4. Es difícil ir de vacaciones cada año.
5. Es fácil usar la computadora.
6. Es divertido hablar con los clientes.
7. Es necesario conocer otros idiomas.
8. Es bueno trabajar por las noches.

**B. Regalos.** As part of your travel agency duties, you took a trip around the world. A classmate will ask what you brought for the following people. Answer using a prepositional pronoun.

MODELO: para tu hermana
E1: *¿Qué compraste para tu hermana?*
E2: *Compré una chaqueta de cuero en Argentina para ella.* o
*No compré nada para ella.*

| | |
|---|---|
| una botella de vino en Francia | una pulsera de plata en México |
| un libro de arte en el museo del Prado | una blusa de seda en Japón |
| una chaqueta de cuero en Argentina | chocolate en Bélgica |
| unas tarjetas postales | nada |

1. para tu mejor amigo/a
2. para el/la profesor/a de español
3. para los estudiantes de la clase de español
4. para tu madre
5. para tu padre
6. para ti
7 para tu novio/a
8. para tu compañero/a de cuarto

**C. Entrevista.** Interview a classmate using the following questions. Use a prepositional pronoun in your answers where appropriate.

1. ¿Te gusta trabajar con los otros estudiantes en la clase? ¿Cuándo fue la última vez que trabajaste con ellos?
2. ¿Hablaste mucho con tus compañeros hoy? ¿Sobre qué hablaste con ellos? ¿Perdiste la paciencia con los otros estudiantes?
3. ¿Llevaste muchos libros contigo hoy para tus clases? ¿Prefieres llevar los libros contigo o dejar los libros en casa?
4. Para ti, ¿es importante estar bien preparado/a para las clases?

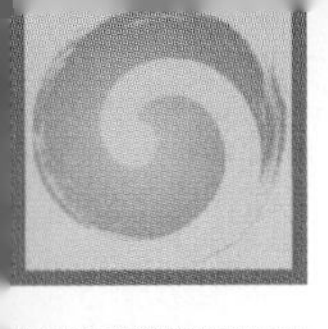

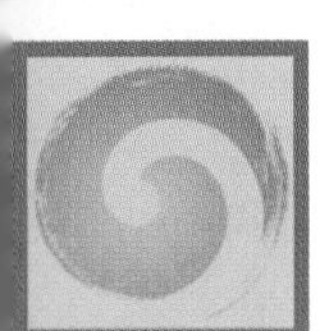

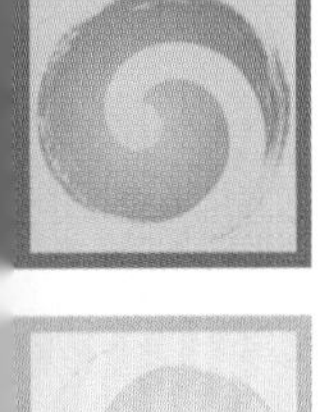
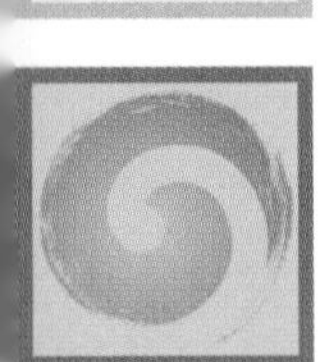

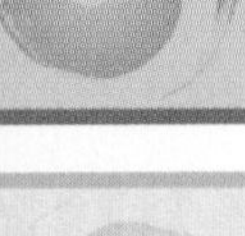

# Vocabulario

## TEMA 1

### La oficina

**Sustantivos**

| | |
|---|---|
| **la compañía** | *company* |
| **el/la cliente/a** | *client* |
| **el destinatario** | *addressee, payee* |
| **el disquete** | *diskette* |
| **la docena** | *dozen* |
| **el documento** | *document* |
| **la estampilla, el sello** | *stamp* |
| **la etiqueta** | *label* |
| **el folleto** | *brochure, pamphlet* |
| **la fotocopia** | *photocopy* |
| **la fotocopiadora** | *copying machine* |
| **el ingreso** | *income* |
| **el/la jefe/a** | *boss* |
| **el mensaje** | *message* |
| **el negocio** | *business* |
| **el presupuesto** | *budget* |
| **el programa** | *program* |
| **la publicidad** | *advertising* |
| **el puesto** | *job, position* |
| **el requisito** | *requirement* |
| **la salida** | *exit* |
| **el sobre** | *envelope* |
| **la solicitud** | *application* |
| **la vacante** | *vacancy* |
| **la venta** | *sale* |

**Verbos**

| | |
|---|---|
| **aconsejar** | *to advise* |
| **aprender** | *to learn* |
| **archivar** | *to file* |
| **atender (ie) + a** | *to pay attention to, assist* |
| **comprometerse** | *to become engaged* |
| **conocer (a)** | *to know, be acquainted with* |
| **contestar** | *to answer* |
| **dirigir** | *to manage, run* |
| **enviar** | *to send* |
| **exportar** | *to export* |
| **llenar** | *to fill* |
| **pegar** | *to stick* |
| **sacar** | *to get, take out* |

**Adjetivos**

| | |
|---|---|
| **disponible** | *available* |
| **dispuesto/a** | *ready* |

## TEMA 2

### Una solicitud de empleo

**Sustantivos**

| | |
|---|---|
| **la cita** | *date, appointment* |
| **el currículum vitae** | *resumé* |
| **los días hábiles** | *workdays* |
| **el/la doctor/a** | *doctor* |
| **el empleo** | *job, employment* |
| **la entrevista** | *interview* |
| **la suerte** | *luck* |
| **el título** | *degree, title* |

**Verbos**

| | |
|---|---|
| **comunicarse** | *to be in touch with* |
| **confirmar** | *to confirm* |
| **dejar** | *to leave (behind)* |
| **empezar (ie)** | *to begin* |
| **esperar** | *to wait (for), hope* |
| **graduarse** | *to graduate* |
| **juntarse** | *to get together* |
| **llegar** | *to arrive* |
| **organizar** | *to organize* |
| **quedar (en)** | *to agree* |
| **terminar** | *to finish* |

**Adjetivos**

| | |
|---|---|
| **final** | *final, end* |
| **libre** | *free* |

**Otras expresiones**

| | |
|---|---|
| **conmigo** | *with me* |
| **contigo** | *with you* |
| **por cierto** | *by the way* |
| **por eso** | *therefore* |
| **por fin** | *finally* |
| **por lo menos** | *at least* |
| **por medio de** | *by means of* |
| **¿De parte de quién?** | *Who's calling?* |
| **en este momento** | *right now* |
| **lo más pronto posible** | *as soon as possible* |

# Reunión A

**A escuchar. La entrevista.** Dr. Benítez and Carlos are discussing his new position. Listen to their conversation, then say whether each of the statements that follows is **Cierto (C)** or **Falso (F)**.

1. _____ Empresas Universales exporta computadoras.
2. _____ Se fundó la compañía hace diez años.
3. _____ Hay sucursales en dos países hispanoamericanos.
4. _____ Carlos va a recibir un sueldo de $40.000 al año para empezar.
5. _____ Hay seguro de salud, de vida y un plan de jubilación.
6. _____ Carlos tiene que ir a Ecuador y a Paraguay por seis meses.

**A conversar.** Your boss (your classmate) wants to implement a company program to help promote minorities at work. You disagree with his/her idea. Role-play the situation while each one of you comes up with three reasons to support your view.

**¿Lo sabía?**

**Buscando personal multicultural**

La población hispana es la de más crecimiento (*growth*) en los EE.UU. en cuanto a su poder económico. En este momento hay 25 millones de hispanos; para el año 2010, serán el grupo minoritario más grande de la nación, con un trillón de dólares para gastar en sus compras. En el 2050, uno de cada cinco americanos será de ascendencia hispana. Al tener familias más grandes y más jóvenes, los hispanos compran más productos como comida, ropa y maquillaje que otros grupos. Las empresas se dan cuenta (*realize*) de las ventajas de tener a los hispanos como clientes y como empleados. Muchas compañías como Compaq y General Motors tienen programas para promover al personal hispano a posiciones a todos los niveles, incluso miembros de la junta directiva.

**¿Comprende Ud.?** Answer the following questions based on the article.

1. ¿Cuántos hispanos hay ahora en los EE. UU.?
2. Para el año 2010, ¿qué va a pasar?
3. ¿Cuál será el porcentaje de personas de ascendencia hispana en el año 2050?
4. ¿Por qué compran más productos las familias hispanas?

**A buscar.** There are many organizations promoting Hispanic opportunities in business, including the U.S. Hispanic Chamber of Commerce and magazines such as *Hispanic, Hispanic Business* and *Latina Style*. Search the Internet for information or bring in copies of periodicals highlighting employment opportunities for Hispanics, either in the United States or abroad. Share your findings with the class.

**Tapescript for A escuchar. La entrevista.**

DRA. BENÍTEZ: Buenos días, señor Montoya. Siéntese por favor.
CARLOS: Buenos días, señora . . ., perdón, doctora Benítez. Mucho gusto en conocerla.
DRA. BENÍTEZ: Igualmente. Nosotros exportamos computadoras. Le mandé un folleto con la historia de la empresa.
CARLOS: Sí, claro. Me enteré de que se fundó hace quince años y de que tiene sucursales en 10 países hispanoamericanos. El año pasado exportó varios miles de millones de dólares en computadoras. ¡Me impresionó mucho la organización de la compañía!
DRA. BENÍTEZ: ¡Excelente! Empresas Universales ofrece un sueldo de 40.000 dólares al año para empezar. Después del entrenamiento le aumentamos el sueldo a 60.000 dólares más el diez por ciento de comisión sobre las ventas.

CARLOS: ¿Qué beneficios ofrece?
DRA. BENÍTEZ: Seguro de salud y un plan de jubilación.

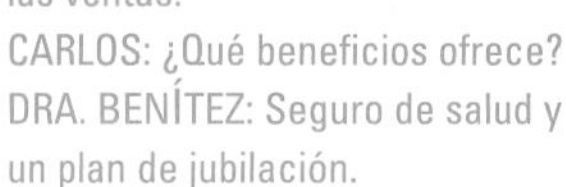

CARLOS: ¿En qué consiste el plan de jubilación?
DRA. BENÍTEZ: Es muy bueno. Usted contribuye con el ocho por ciento de su sueldo. Nosotros ponemos una cantidad igual.

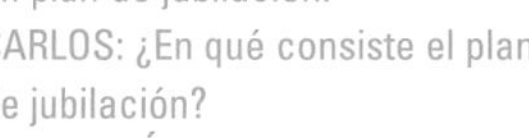

CARLOS: Me parece muy bien.
DRA. BENÍTEZ: También ofrecemos seguro de vida porque tiene que viajar mucho. Tiene que ir a Perú por seis meses y después a Colombia por otros seis meses para su entrenamiento. ¿Qué piensa de esto?

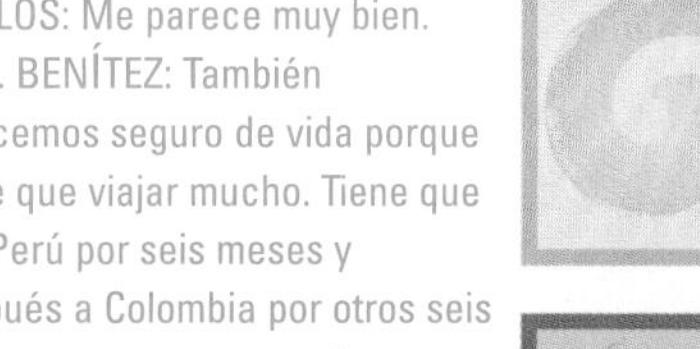

CARLOS: Me parece muy emocionante.
DRA. BENÍTEZ: Bueno, llamé al señor Habib. Él es el gerente de ventas del mercado hispanoamericano. Quiere hacerle unas preguntas.

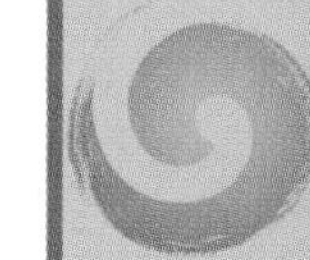

**Answers for A escuchar.**
1) *C.* 2) *F.* 3) *F.* 4) *C.* 5) *C.* 6) *F.*

# TEMA 3 Una entrevista con el jefe

## El currículum vitae

### ¿Cuándo se graduó usted?

*Carlos goes to his first job interview....*

SR. HABIB: Buenos días, señor Montoya, ¿pudo encontrar fácilmente nuestras oficinas?

CARLOS: Buenos días, señor Habib. Sí, gracias, vine muy temprano para buscar la dirección con calma.

SR. HABIB: Leí su solicitud y vi que se gradúa muy pronto. ¿Dónde asistió a la escuela secundaria?

CARLOS: En Hayward, California. Viví allí por dieciocho años. Después me mudé a Los Ángeles para asistir a la universidad.

SR. HABIB: ¿Trabajó alguna vez?

CARLOS: Trabajé por tres años en una pizzería. Ahora trabajo en la biblioteca de la universidad, en el departamento de compras.

SR. HABIB: Supe que se especializó en el mercado hispanoamericano. ¿Qué otra cosa puede ofrecer a Empresas Universales?

CARLOS: Soy bilingüe: domino el inglés y el español. Soy muy activo y me gusta mucho la gente.

SR. HABIB: ¿Dónde aprendió a hablar español?

CARLOS: Mis padres son colombianos y siempre me hablaron en español. Después tomé muchos cursos de español porque siempre quise viajar a Colombia.

SR. HABIB: Empezamos a hacer entrevistas esta semana y vamos a tomar una decisión en un par de semanas. Nosotros nos comunicamos con usted. Gracias por venir.

**A. ¿Comprende Ud.?** Answer the following questions based on the dialog.

1. ¿Dónde estudió Carlos antes de ir a la universidad?
2. ¿Qué especialización tiene Carlos?
3. ¿De dónde son los padres de Carlos?
4. ¿Adónde quiere viajar Carlos?

**Answers for A.** 1) *En Hayward.* 2) *Mercado hispanoamericano.* 3) *De Colombia.* 4) *A Colombia.*

**B. El currículum de la Dra. Cambianica.** Answer the following questions based on the resumé.

1. ¿Cuál es el título más avanzado de la Dra. Cambianica?
2. ¿Dónde recibió ese título?
3. ¿Cuál era (*was*) su posición de 1991 a 1995?
4. ¿Cuál es su especialidad en cuanto a seminarios?
5. ¿Cuál era su puesto en el III Congreso Mundial de Educación de Moscú en julio de 1998?
6. ¿Puede nombrar su trabajo hoy?

**Currículum Vitae**
**Dra. Carmen Cambianica**
**Directora General de Cultura y Educación**

**TÍTULOS:**
- ° Maestra Normal Nacional
- ° Abogada: Universidad Nacional de Buenos Aires. Recibida con medalla de oro.
- ° Licenciada en Derecho administrativo y Ciencias de la administración.

**CARGOS DESEMPEÑADOS EN LA CARRERA DOCENTE:**
- ° Jefa de trabajos prácticos en la Facultad de Derecho de la Universidad Nacional de Buenos Aires.
- ° Auxiliar interina en la Cátedra de Derecho Administrativo de la Universidad de Buenos Aires.
- ° Miembro Fundador de la Asociación Argentina de Derecho Administrativo.
- ° Autora de numerosas publicaciones en la materia de Derecho Administrativo.

**DESEMPEÑO INSTITUCIONAL:**
- ° Directora de asuntos legales en la municipalidad de San Buenaventura
- ° Secretaria de gobierno en la municipalidad de Sierra Madre
- ° Senadora provincial de 1991 a 1995.
- ° Asesora Honoraria del Consejo Provincial de la Mujer.
- ° Senadora Provincial reelecta de 1996 a 1998.
- ° Directora General de Escuelas y Cultura de la Provincia de Buenos Aires.

**SEMINARIOS Y CURSOS:**
- ° Seminarios y cursos realizados sobre la especialidad de "Derecho Administrativo".

**ASISTENCIA A CONFERENCIAS Y CONGRESOS:**
- ° Directora general de escuelas y cultura de la provincia de Buenos Aires ante la XXVII Reunión de la Conferencia General de la UNESCO - ROMA Octubre de 1996.
- ° Directora general de escuelas y cultura de la provincia de Buenos Aires ante el III Congreso Mundial de Educación - MOSCÚ Julio de 1998.

**C. ¿Tiene Ud. un C. V.?** Have you prepared a resumé in Spanish? If so, bring it to class. If not, sit with a classmate and prepare a rough draft of what you need. Compare what you have or plan to write with the resumé for Activity B.

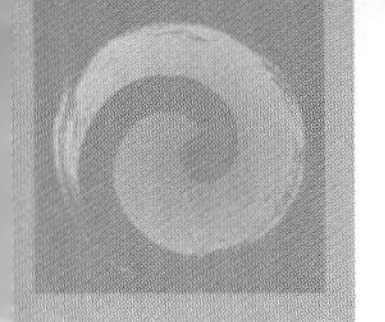

# ABC Las profesiones y los oficios

el/la plomero/a

el/la mecánico

el/la bombero/a

el/la peluquero/a

el policía/la mujer policía

el/la locutor/a

## ¿Qué tal te fue?

*Carlos tells Isabel about his interview....*

ISABEL: Hola, Carlos. ¿Qué tal te fue en la entrevista?

CARLOS: No sé. Me puse muy nervioso. Tuve dos entrevistas. Primero me recibió la jefa de personal y se portó muy amable conmigo. Pienso que le caí bien.

ISABEL: ¿Cómo sabes que le caíste bien?

CARLOS: Porque hablamos por mucho tiempo y estuvo muy amable conmigo. Además me dio folletos e información de Empresas Universales. Después trajo al señor Habib, el gerente de ventas del mercado hispanoamericano.

ISABEL: ¿Cómo te fue con el señor Habib?

CARLOS: Pues, estuvo muy serio conmigo. Leyó mi currículum con mucho cuidado y me hizo muchas preguntas.

ISABEL: ¿Y en qué quedaron? ¿Te dieron esperanzas?

CARLOS: Me van a llamar en un par de semanas. El señor Habib me dijo que tienen diez candidatos para ese puesto.

ISABEL: ¡Te deseo mucha suerte!

CARLOS: Gracias, adiós. Saluda a Lázaro, por favor.

ISABEL: Con mucho gusto. Hasta pronto.

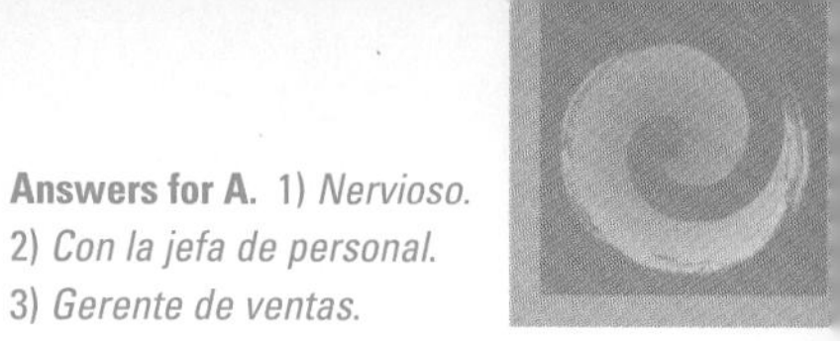

**A. ¿Comprende Ud.?** Answer the following questions based on the dialog.

1. ¿Cómo estuvo Carlos en la entrevista?
2. ¿Con quién tuvo la primera entrevista?
3. ¿Cuál es el puesto del Sr. Habib?
4. ¿Cuántos candidatos hay para el puesto?

**Answers for A.** 1) *Nervioso.* 2) *Con la jefa de personal.* 3) *Gerente de ventas.* 4) *Diez.*

**B. ¿Quién ganó más?** You have relatives who've been mechanics, hair stylists, police officers, radio announcers, plumbers and firemen. Fill in the chart with probable salary statistics for each.

| | Sueldo anual |
|---|---|
| Mecánico | |
| Peluquero/a | |
| Policía | |
| Locutor/a | |
| Plomero/a | |
| Bombero/a | |

**C. Requisitos del trabajo.** Prepare a list of job requirements for the trades and professions pictured below. Include probable annual salaries, experience necessary, required education, and desirable personality traits. Then decide which most appeals to you. Compare your notes with those of a classmate.

**Expansion for C.** Ask students who can identify the singer pictured among these three professions. (It is Selena, a well-known Tex-Mex singer whose tragic death increased the popularity of her music and of the Tex-Mex sound in the U.S. and in other countries.)

**D. ¡No conseguí el trabajo!** You recently interviewed for a position in one of the career areas listed at the beginning of the section, but you didn't get the job. Select a career, then discuss your application process from submission of paperwork to actual interview. Try to figure out why you weren't hired. Share your experience with a classmate.

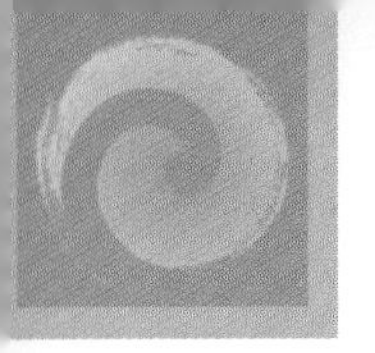

# Verbos irregulares en el pretérito
## (*Irregular preterite forms*)

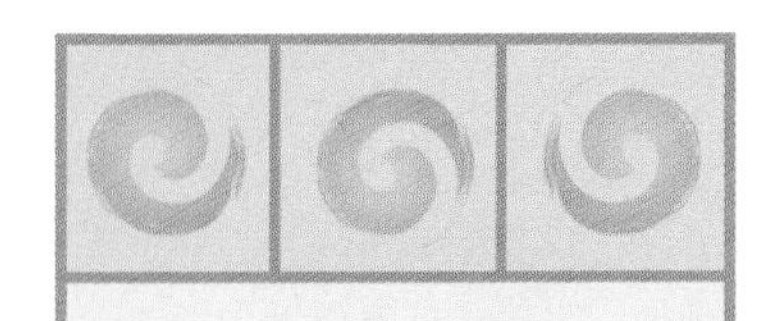

**Para averiguar**

1. What are two ways that "strong" preterites are irregular?
2. What is the additional spelling change in the verb **hacer** in the **Ud., él, ella** forms?
3. Give the preterite stem for the following verbs: **saber**, **venir**, **querer**, **poder**, **poner**.
4. What are the endings for all of these preterites?

- The following verbs are sometimes called "strong" preterites because they are irregular both in the stem and in the endings. All of these verbs use the same endings (**-e**, **-iste**, **-o**, **-imos**, **-isteis**, **-ieron**).

| Infinitive | | Stem |
|---|---|---|
| **venir** — vin- | → | vin**e**, vin**iste**, vin**o**, vin**imos**, vin**isteis**, vin**ieron** |
| **saber** — sup- | → | sup**e**, sup**iste**, sup**o**, sup**imos**, sup**isteis**, sup**ieron** |
| **poner** — pus- | → | pus**e**, pus**iste**, pus**o**, pus**imos**, pus**isteis**, pus**ieron** |
| **poder** — pud- | → | pud**e**, pud**iste**, pud**o**, pud**imos**, pud**isteis**, pud**ieron** |
| **querer** — quis- | → | quis**e**, quis**iste**, quis**o**, quis**imos**, quis**isteis**, quis**ieron** |
| **hacer** — hic- | → | hic**e**, hic**iste**, hi**zo**, hic**imos**, hic**isteis**, hic**ieron** |

Yo no **supe** del examen hasta hoy. — *I didn't find out about the exam until today.*

¿Cuándo **pusiste** el mensaje aquí? — *When did you put the message here?*

No **pudo** ir a la fiesta. — *He couldn't (wasn't able to) go to the party.*

Nosotros **vinimos** a ayudarte. — *We came to help you.*

**Quisieron** encontrar un buen empleo. — *They made an effort to find a good job.*

¿Qué **hicieron** ustedes en la oficina? — *What did you do at the office?*

- In the **Ud.**, **él**, and **ella** forms of **hacer,** the **-c** changes to **-z** to preserve the original soft sound.

Yo hi**c**e fotocopias y ella hi**z**o su tarea. — *I made copies and she did her homework.*

- Sometimes the verbs **conocer**, **saber**, **querer** and **poder** have particular meanings when used in the preterite. You will practice these verbs in **Lección 7**, but for now, keep the following in mind when using these verbs:

| | | In the Preterite | | |
|---|---|---|---|---|
| **conocer** | → | **conocí** | → | implies that you met someone |
| **saber** | → | **supe** | → | implies that you found out about something |
| **querer** | → | **quise** | → | implies that you tried/wanted to do something |
| **poder** | → | **pude** | → | implies that you managed to do something |

## A lo personal

**A. La semana pasada.** Indicate how often you and others did the following in your Spanish class last week.

| nunca | una vez | dos veces | más de dos veces |
|---|---|---|---|

1. No hice la tarea.
2. El/la profesor/a no vino a clase.
3. Hice una pregunta.
4. No pude contestar en clase.
5. Me puse nervioso/a en clase.
6. No quise venir a clase.
7. Hicimos algo divertido.
8. Supimos los resultados de una prueba.
9. Sus compañeros hicieron la tarea.
10. Su amigo no pudo asistir a clase.

**B. ¿Qué sucedió?** Ask a classmate what happened the last time he/she did the following things.

1. La última vez que no pudiste venir a clase...

   a. ¿llamaste al/a la profesor/a para saber qué hacer para la siguiente clase?
   b. ¿llamaste a otro/a estudiante para saber qué hacer para la siguiente clase?
   c. ¿no hiciste nada para prepararte para la siguiente clase?

2. Cuando supiste la nota de tu último examen de español...

   a. ¿te gustó la nota?
   b. ¿te enojaste?
   c. ¿no tuviste ninguna reacción?

3. La última vez que no pudiste comprender algo en clase...

   a. ¿te pusiste nervioso/a y no hiciste nada?
   b. ¿hiciste una pregunta?
   c. ¿buscaste la explicación en el libro?

4. La última vez que tuviste un examen muy importante...

   a. ¿estudiaste toda la noche anterior?
   b. ¿saliste con amigos toda la noche anterior?
   c. ¿no pudiste dormir en toda la noche anterior?

5. La última vez que quisiste dormir una siesta por la tarde...

   a. ¿pudiste dormir?
   b. ¿llamó alguien?
   c. ¿hicieron tus hijos, tus vecinos o tu compañero/a de cuarto demasiado ruido?

6. La última vez que viniste a la universidad...

   a. ¿pusiste todos tus libros en la mochila?
   b. ¿viniste solo/a o con amigos/as?
   c. ¿supiste qué hacer en todas las clases?

**C. Entrevista.** Ask a classmate the following questions.

1. ¿Quién fue tu mejor profesor/a el año pasado?
2. ¿Cuál fue tu mejor clase el año pasado?
3. ¿Qué hiciste para prepararte para la clase de español hoy?
4. ¿A qué hora viniste al campus hoy?
5. ¿Dónde pusiste la mochila en la clase?
6. ¿Qué hiciste anoche?

# Más verbos irregulares en el pretérito
## (*More irregular preterite forms*)

### Para averiguar

1. What two irregular verbs are identical in the preterite?
2. Which **-ar** verb uses the regular **-er/-ir** endings in the preterite tense?
3. Which person loses the **i** after **j** spelling changes?

- **Dar** is the only **-ar** verb to use the regular preterite endings of **-er/-ir** verbs.

| | |
|---|---|
| **dar** | di, diste, dio, dimos, disteis, dieron |

| | |
|---|---|
| El profesor **dio** un examen ayer. | *The professor gave an exam yesterday.* |
| Los estudiantes **dieron** una fiesta. | *The students gave a party.* |

- **Ir** and **ser** have identical conjugations in the preterite tense.

| | |
|---|---|
| **ir/ser** | fui, fuiste, fue, fuimos, fuisteis, fueron |

| | |
|---|---|
| El profesor **fue** a México. | *The teacher went to Mexico.* |
| ¿Quién **fue** esa persona? | *Who was that person?* |
| —Mis amigos **fueron** a un concierto. | *My friends went to a concert.* |
| —¿Tú no **fuiste** con ellos? | *Didn't you go with them?* |

- **Tener** and **estar** have spelling changes in the stem and use the "strong" preterite endings:

| | |
|---|---|
| **tener** | tuve, tuviste, tuvo, tuvimos, tuvisteis, tuvieron |
| **estar** | estuve, estuviste, estuvo, estuvimos, estuvisteis, estuvieron |

| | |
|---|---|
| —¿**Tuvieron** un niño? | *Did they have a boy?* |
| —No, ella **tuvo** una niña. | *No, she had a girl.* |
| —¿Cuánto tiempo **estuvieron** en Perú? | *How long were you in Peru?* |
| —**Estuvimos** allí por una semana. | *We were there for a week.* |

- Verbs ending in **-cir: decir**, **traducir** have a stem change to **j. Traer** also has a stem change to **j**. After the **j**, omit the **i** in the third person plural "strong" preterite endings.

| | |
|---|---|
| **decir** | dije, dijiste, dijo, dijimos, dijisteis, dijeron |
| **traducir** | traduje, tradujiste, tradujo, tradujimos, tradujisteis, tradujeron |
| **traer** | traje, trajiste, trajo, trajimos, trajisteis, trajeron |

| | |
|---|---|
| —Yo no **dije** nada. | *I didn't say anything.* |
| —Pues ella **dijo** muchas cosas. | *She said many things.* |
| —¿**Trajiste** ropa para la entrevista? | *Did you bring clothes for the interview?* |
| —Sí, **traje** ropa nueva. | *Yes, I brought new clothes.* |
| —¿**Tradujiste** los documentos? | *Did you translate the documents?* |
| —Sí, los **traduje** ayer. | *Yes, I translated them yesterday.* |

## A lo personal

**A. ¿Qué hicieron?** Say whether or not the following people were at the university yesterday.

MODELO: Mis profesores...
*Mis profesores estuvieron en la universidad ayer.*

1. Yo...
2. Mi mejor amigo/a...
3. Todos nosotros en la clase de español...
4. Todas las secretarias...
5. El presidente de la universidad...
6. Gloria Estefan...

**B. ¿Quién?** Name classmates who brought the following things to class today.

MODELO: una mochila azul
*Ana, David y yo trajimos una mochila azul.* o *Nadie trajo una mochila azul.*

1. una mochila verde
2. el libro de español
3. un bolígrafo rojo
4. un cuaderno amarillo
5. un paraguas (*umbrella*)
6. una calculadora
7. una bolsa negra de cuero
8. algo de comer
9. una Coca-Cola
10. un millón de dólares

**C. El fin de semana.** Ask a classmate if he/she did the following things last weekend.

MODELO: tener que trabajar
E1: *¿Tuviste que trabajar el fin de semana pasado?*
E2: *Sí, tuve que trabajar.* o *No, no tuve que trabajar.*

1. traer cerveza a casa
2. ir a una fiesta
3. tener que estudiar mucho
4. ir de compras
5. traducir la lectura del libro de español
6. decir la verdad
7. estar en casa todo el día
8. dar una fiesta

**D. Ayer.** Prepare a role-play with a classmate in which you talk about what you did yesterday. Discuss:

- whether or not you had to work
- whether or not you came to campus
- how much time you were at work or on campus
- what time you went home
- what you did last night

## ¿Hay beneficios?

### Una buena noticia

*Dr. Benítez calls to tell Carlos about the job he applied for…*

DRA. BENÍTEZ: Aló, ¿con quién hablo?
CONTESTADORA AUTOMÁTICA: "Gracias por llamar…"
DRA. BENÍTEZ: Buenos días, ¿puedo hablar con el licenciado Montoya?
CONTESTADORA AUTOMÁTICA: " … Lázaro y Carlos o no están en casa o no pueden contestar el teléfono en este momento. Al terminar la música, por favor deje su nombre, su número de teléfono y la hora en que hizo la llamada. Nosotros devolvemos su llamada lo más pronto posible."
DRA. BENÍTEZ: Este mensaje es para el licenciado Montoya. Son las diez de la mañana. Soy la doctora Benítez de Empresas Universales. Preferí darle la buena noticia inmediatamente: el señor Habib leyó las 10 solicitudes y decidió que usted es la mejor persona para el puesto de vendedor. ¡Felicidades! Voy a estar en mi oficina todo el día. Usted ya sabe mi teléfono. ¡Adiós!

**Answers for A.** 1) *Lázaro.* 2) *A las diez.* 3) *El de vendedor.* 4) *En su oficina.*

**A. ¿Comprende Ud.?** Answer the following questions based on the dialog.

1. ¿Quién es el compañero de cuarto de Carlos?
2. ¿A qué hora llamó la Dra. Benítez?
3. ¿Qué trabajo consiguió Carlos?
4. ¿Dónde va a estar la Dra. Benítez hoy?

**B. Un mensaje para el/la nuevo/a empleado/a.** You've called to give the good news to a job applicant that he/she has been hired and he/she needs to start in two weeks. He/She isn't at home, but there is an answering machine. "Record" your message, then compare it with a classmate's.

**C. ¡Estoy nervioso/a!** Tomorrow is the first day of your new job. You're so nervous that unless you make a list of everything to remember for tomorrow, you're sure to forget something. Prepare your schedule from getting up, getting dressed, eating breakfast, packing lunch, taking the dog out for a walk, remembering to take along copies of your paperwork, etc. to returning home at night after the BIG DAY! List at least eight things you must remember. Compare your list with that of a classmate.

**D. Soy el/la jefe/a.** Now you're the boss, with a different set of priorities. What did you expect from your new employee on his/her first day? Using the past tense, cite three things your new employee did well and three that concerned you on his/her first day. Compare your notes with another manager, seeing if your perceptions agree with his/hers.

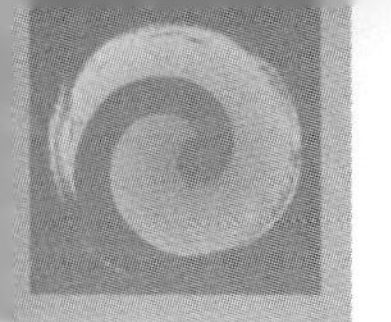

# La experiencia laboral

el estado
(abogado/a, empleado/a,
programador/a de
computadoras)

una empresa grande
(jefe/a de personal,
secretario/a, hombre/mujer
de negocios, contable)

un hospital
(enfermero/a, médico/a,
psiquiatra)

un restaurante
(mesero/a, cocinero/a)

una tienda
(dependiente/a, director/a
de publicidad, cajero/a)

una escuela
(maestro/a, director/a)

una fábrica
(obrero/a, ingeniero/a)

un teatro
(actor, actriz, cantante,
músico)

## ¿Qué experiencia tienes?

*Carlos meets his new boss….*

DRA. MUÑOZ: Buenos días, señor Montoya. Soy la doctora Muñoz. Yo voy a ser su jefa aquí en la casa matriz.

CARLOS: Mucho gusto.

DRA. MUÑOZ: Igualmente. Señor Montoya, pedí su expediente y leí que es bilingüe. ¡Me alegro!

CARLOS: Sí, yo nací aquí, pero mis padres nacieron en Bogotá y vinieron a los Estados Unidos hace treinta años. ¿Usted es colombiana?

DRA. MUÑOZ: Sí, soy de Bucaramanga. Pero me puedes hablar de tú. Me llamo Alejandra. ¿Estuviste alguna vez en Colombia?

CARLOS: No, pero voy a estar allí por seis meses. Firmé un contrato temporal por un año y medio. Voy a estar aquí por seis meses para mi entrenamiento. Después voy a ir a Colombia por seis meses y a Perú por otros seis.

DRA. MUÑOZ: Sí, ya me encargué de los detalles. Primero voy a mostrarte las instalaciones. Mi oficina está en el tercer piso y mi extensión es 282.

CARLOS: Gracias, Alejandra. Creo que vamos a llevarnos muy bien.

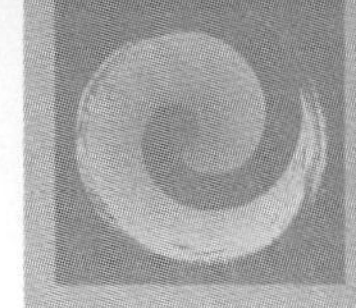

**A. ¿Comprende Ud.?** Answer the following questions based on the dialog.

1. ¿Cuándo vinieron a Estados Unidos los padres de Carlos?
2. ¿De qué ciudad es la Dra. Muñoz?
3. ¿Cuánto tiempo va a estar Carlos en entrenamiento?
4. ¿Dónde está la oficina de la Dra. Muñoz?

**Answers for A.** 1) *Hace 30 años.* 2) *Bucaramanga.* 3) *Por seis meses.* 4) *En el tercer piso.*

**B. ¿Qué aprendió Ud. de joven?** While you were in college, you worked at each of the following jobs. For each, list at least two advantages (**ventajas**) and two disadvantages (**desventajas**). Compare your thoughts with a classmate, saying if you really worked at that job and, if so, whether or not you liked it. If not, pretend, including how much you earned, how long you worked there, etc.

1. cajero/a
2. mesero/a
3. secretario/a
4. obrero/a
5. dependiente/a

**C. ¿Qué hicieron?** Marisol is talking about the jobs her family members held before retiring. Identify the job and then in groups of two discuss the probable salaries earned, and the necessary preparation for each position.

MODELO: Mi abuelo tocó el saxofón con una orquesta.
*Fue músico. Estudió música. Ganó 28,000.00 dólares al año.*

1. Mi madre trabajó en una tienda.
2. Mi padre enseñó en una escuela.
3. Mi tía trabajó para el estado.
4. Mi tío trabajó para una empresa grande.
5. Mi abuelo trabajó en un hospital.
6. Mi abuela trabajó en un restaurante.

**D. ¿Oíste las noticias?** You've just finished your first day on the job. Now you're going out to celebrate with a friend. Role-play by having a classmate ask you what you wore, what is the title of your new position, what duties you were given, whom you met, what you have to know or learn to keep your job, who your boss is, and more.

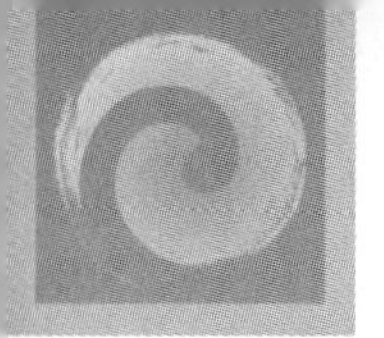

# Verbos en el pretérito con cambios en la ra
## (*Stem-changing forms in the preterite tense*)

**Para averiguar**

1. While **-ar**, **-er**, and **-ir** verbs all have stem changes in the present tense, which is the only group that has stem changes in the preterite?
2. Tell which persons have stem changes in **-ir** preterite conjugations.
3. What happens to an **-o** in **-ir** preterite stem changing verbs?
4. What happens to an **-e** in **-ir** preterite stem changing verbs?

**Clarification.** Note that activity topics in this section will vary to allow students to practice the preterite in a variety of contexts.

- The **-ar** and **-er** stem-changing verbs form the preterite like non-stem changing verbs:

| | |
|---|---|
| **pensar** | pensé, pensaste, pensó, pensamos, pensasteis, pensaron |
| **entender** | entendí, entendiste, entendió, entendimos, entendisteis, entendieron |

| | |
|---|---|
| —Yo **pensé** en ti ayer. | *I thought about you yesterday.* |
| —Ellos **pensaron** en mí también. | *They also thought about me.* |
| —No **entendí** nada. | *I didn't understand anything.* |
| —Él **entendió** un poco. | *He understood a little.* |

- Only **-ir** verbs have stem changes in the preterite tense. In stem-changing **-ir** verbs, **e** becomes **i**, and **o** becomes **u** in the third-person (**él, ella, usted, ellos, ellas, ustedes**) preterite forms.

| | |
|---|---|
| **pedir** | pedí, pediste, p**i**dió, pedimos, pedisteis, p**i**dieron |
| **dormir** | dormí, dormiste, d**u**rmió, dormimos, dormisteis, d**u**rmieron |

| | |
|---|---|
| —Yo **pedí** un bistec. | *I ordered a steak.* |
| —Ella **pidió** sopa. | *She ordered soup.* |
| —Yo **dormí** dos horas. | *I slept two hours.* |
| —Ellos **durmieron** tres horas. | *They slept three hours.* |

- Other **-ir** stem changing verbs that follow this pattern are:

**servir, repetir, seguir, preferir, morir**

## A lo personal

**A. En el restaurante.** Yesterday, Carlos and Lázaro went to an expensive restaurant to celebrate Carlos' new job. Say whether Carlos and Lázaro or the waiter did the following.

MODELO: traer la comida
*El mesero trajo la comida.*

1. seguir al maitre (*maitre d'*) a la mesa
2. pedir el menú
3. servir la comida
4. preferir la ensalada a la sopa
5. repetir la orden para estar seguro
6. pagar la cuenta (*bill*)
7. recibir una propina (*tip*)
8. repetir el especial del día
9. preparar el postre (*dessert*) cerca de la mesa
10. pedir otro café

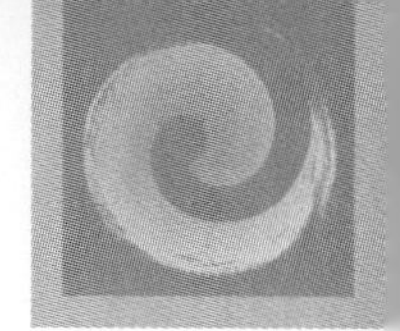

**B. Acerca de los Estados Unidos.** Working with a classmate, answer these questions about the history of the United States.

1. ¿Quién escribió la Declaración de la Independencia de los Estados Unidos? ¿En qué año escribió este documento? ¿Para qué sirvió? ¿Cuál es el nombre de una de las personas que firmó la Declaración de la Independencia?
2. ¿Quién fue el primer presidente de los Estados Unidos? ¿En qué guerra sirvió como general? ¿Qué río famoso cruzó durante la guerra? ¿Con quién se casó?
3. ¿Quién fue presidente de los Estados Unidos durante la Guerra Civil? ¿En qué año empezó la guerra? ¿Cuándo terminó? ¿Quién fue el general más importante de esta guerra?
4. ¿Qué presidente murió en Dallas en 1963? ¿Qué presidente fue un actor popular antes de ser presidente? ¿Quién ganó las últimas elecciones presidenciales?

**C. El día de los enamorados.** Complete the letter by using the correct preterite forms of the verbs in parentheses.

Querido Memo:

Ayer Ernesto y yo (ir) ________ (1) de compras al centro comercial de Guadalupe. (Estar) ________ (2) en tres tiendas. (Poder) ________ (3) ver muchas blusas. Yo (tener) ________ (4) mucho cuidado cuando (hacer) ________ (5) la selección de la blusa, porque no (poder) ________ (6) conseguir mucho dinero para la ocasión. En la Tienda París el dependiente (traer) ________ (7) una blusa de seda muy bonita y a buen precio. Cuando yo (ver) ________ (8) la blusa, ahí mismo decidí comprarla. Pedí un descuento y él me lo (dar) ________ (9).

Después yo (ir) ________ (10) a casa de Conchita y le (dar) ________ (11) la blusa para el Día de los Enamorados. (Ser) ________ (12) un momento muy romántico. Ella me (besar) ________(13) y (decir) ________ (14): "Gracias, Ignacio. Te quiero." Después, ella lo (15) ______(repetir) varias veces.

Después Conchita y yo (ir) ________ (16) a comer a un restaurante italiano. Invitamos a sus padres, pero ellos no (querer) ________ (17) ir. (18) ________ (preferir) quedarse en casa. Nosotros no (saber) ________ (19) por qué, pero (ser) ________ (20) mejor. Cuando Conchita y yo (estar) ________ (21) solos en el restaurante, yo (22) ________ (pedir) champán y cuando el mesero nos (23) __________ (servir), ella y yo (24) ________ (hacer) planes para nuestra boda. Te vamos a invitar, por supuesto. Te dejo porque tengo que estudiar.

Un fuerte abrazo,

*Nacho*

# Más práctica con el pretérito (*More practice with the preterite*)

## A lo personal

**A. ¿Qué leyeron?** Here is part of the *Table of Contents* from ***Clara*** magazine. What did the following people read about if they read the article on the indicated page?

MODELO: mi novio/a (110)
*Mi novio/a leyó la sección sobre música en la página 110.*

1. mi abuelo (118)
2. nosotros (112)
3. los estudiantes (111)
4. yo (120)
5. mi amiga que es actriz (114)
6. mi compañera de cuarto (42)
7. mi amigo y yo (26)

**Sumario**

| MODA | |
|---|---|
| Moda tendencias | 2 |
| Moda tallas grandes | 4 |
| Moda premamá | 6 |
| Complementos: | |
| Los accesorios primaverales | 8 |
| **BELLEZA** | |
| Consejos de tres famosos estilistas | 10 |
| Vencer la celulitis | 16 |
| Novedades de belleza | 18 |
| En forma: | |
| Equitación | 20 |
| Ponte en forma | 21 |
| **SALUD** | |
| La alergia | 26 |
| Vida cotidiana | |
| ¿Qué es la patria potestad? | 36 |
| Dinero: | |
| Preparémonos para un nuevo México | 39 |
| Profesiones: | |
| Una profesión para mentes creativas | 42 |
| **HIJOS** | |
| La rivalidad entre hermanos | 45 |
| Psicología | |
| Ideas que torturan | 58 |
| **COCINA** | |
| Menú de temporada: | |
| Comienzo de primavera | 66 |
| La carne molida | 72 |
| Fichas | 73 |
| **CASA** | |
| Decoración: | |
| Cada cosa en su sitio | 92 |
| Recupera espacios perdidos | 96 |
| Animales: | |
| Alimento para perros | 97 |
| Plantas: | |
| Las prímulas | 100 |
| Perejil, alimento excepcional | 101 |
| Agenda de cuidados | 101 |
| **TIEMPO LIBRE** | |
| Música | 110 |
| Libros | 111 |
| Arte | 112 |
| Cine | 113 |
| Espectáculos | 114 |
| **PUNTOS DE VISTA** | |
| Marcos Llunas | 116 |
| Astrología | 118 |
| **VIAJES** | |
| Nueva York | 120 |
| Fin de semana | 126 |
| Paquetes | 127 |

**B. ¿Quién?** Name a person or persons who did each of the following things.

MODELO: Fue presidente de los Estados Unidos durante los años setenta.
*Richard Nixon, Gerald Ford y Jimmy Carter fueron presidentes de los Estados Unidos durante los años setenta.*

1. quiso ser presidente
2. dijo algo tonto recientemente
3. hizo una película popular
4. no estuvo en clase la última vez
5. tuvo un gran éxito
6. repitió sus errores
7. leyó el Gettysburg Address

**C. ¿Qué hiciste ayer?** Supply the missing verb forms in the following dialog.

PATRICIO: ¡Hola Hernán! ¿Qué tal? Ayer (tú) no (1)________ (ir) a clase. ¿Qué (2)________ (pasar)?

HERNÁN: Cuando (3)________ (despertarse), (4)________ (decidir) dar un paseo por el parque con Óscar.

PATRICIO: ¿Óscar no (5)________ (ir) a clase tampoco?

HERNÁN: No, nosotros (6)________ (pasar) el día en el parque. Él (7)________ (leer) un libro, y yo (8)________ (jugar) al frisbee con Marisol. Ella (9)________ (llevar) unos bocadillos y todos (10)________ (hacer) un picnic.

PATRICIO: Yo también (11) ________ (pensar) faltar a clase, pero ayer (12)________ (ser) el examen de química.

HERNÁN: A mí no me gusta la química. Yo siempre (13)________ (preferir) la biología.

PATRICIO: ¿Qué (14)________ (hacer) ustedes después de jugar en el parque?

HERNÁN: (15)________ (ir) al cine para ver una película nueva. (16) ________ (ser) una película de terror y Óscar (17)________ (tener) mucho miedo.

PATRICIO: Yo (18) ________ (comer) con Alejandra y después nosotros (19)________ (salir) a bailar. En la discoteca (20)________ (encontrarse) con muchos amigos y cuando (21) ________ (terminar) la noche, todos (22)________ (desayunar) juntos. (23)________ (ser) muy divertido.

HERNÁN: ¡Qué bien! Esta noche vamos a hacer una fiesta, ¿quieres venir?

PATRICIO: ¡Sí! (24)________ (hablar) con Alejandra esta mañana y ella quiere salir esta noche también. ¿Puede venir ella a la fiesta?

HERNÁN: ¡Claro! Creo que Óscar ya (25)________ (invitar) a Alejandra. Sé que ellos (26)________ (hablar) esta mañana también.

PATRICIO: De acuerdo. Nos vemos esta noche, ¡hasta luego!

**D. Entrevista.** Ask your partner the following questions and then switch roles.

1. ¿Estuviste en casa todo el día ayer? ¿Qué hiciste? ¿Leíste el periódico? ¿Creíste todo lo que leíste? ¿Qué más hiciste?
2. ¿Cuándo tuviste una fiesta por última vez? ¿Cuántas personas fueron? ¿Hasta qué hora estuvieron allí? ¿Llevaron los invitados algo para tomar o comer? ¿Qué hicieron en la fiesta?
3. ¿Cuándo comiste en un restaurante por última vez? ¿Con quién comiste? ¿Adónde fueron? ¿Trajo el mesero la comida en seguida o tuvieron que esperar un poco? ¿Pudiste comerte todo o te llevaste un poco de comida a casa?

**E. El rey.** Elvis has been spotted in this city. As the best detective agency in town, you were contracted to follow him all day yesterday and to write a report on all of his actions.

MODELO: *Se despertó a la medianoche y…*

# Vocabulario

## TEMA 3

### Una entrevista con el jefe

**Sustantivos**

| | |
|---|---|
| **el/la bombero** | *firefighter* |
| **el/la candidato/a** | *candidate* |
| **el curso** | *course* |
| **los folletos** | *pamphlets* |
| **la gente** | *people* |
| **el/la gerente** | *manager* |
| **el/la locutor/a** | *announcer* |
| **el/la mecánico** | *mechanic* |
| **el pasatiempo** | *pastime* |
| **el/la peluquero/a** | *hairstylist* |
| **el/la plomero/a** | *plumber* |
| **el policía/la mujer policía** | *police officer* |

**Verbos**

| | |
|---|---|
| **dar** | *to give* |
| **dominar** | *to have a good command of* |
| **especializarse (en)** | *to specialize in* |
| **mudarse** | *to move* |
| **pensar (ie)** | *to think, plan* |
| **portarse** | *to behave* |

**Adjetivos**

| | |
|---|---|
| **amable** | *kind* |
| **bilingüe** | *bilingual* |

**Otras expresiones**

| | |
|---|---|
| **allí** | *there* |
| **caer bien/mal** | *to make a good/bad impression* |
| **con cuidado** | *carefully* |
| **después** | *afterwards* |
| **tomar una decisión** | *to make a decision* |
| **un par (de)** | *a couple (of)* |

## TEMA 4

### El primer día de trabajo

**Sustantivos**

| | |
|---|---|
| **el/la abogado/a** | *attorney, lawyer* |
| **el actor** | *actor* |
| **la actriz** | *actress* |
| **el/la cajero/a** | *cashier* |
| **el/la cantante** | *singer* |
| **la casa matriz** | *home office* |
| **el/la cocinero/a** | *cook* |
| **el/la contador/a, contable** | *accountant* |
| **el contrato** | *contract* |
| **el/la dependiente/a** | *salesclerk* |
| **el/la director/a** | *director* |
| **el estado** | *state* |
| **el expediente** | *file, dossier* |
| **la experiencia** | *experience* |
| **la fábrica** | *factory* |
| **el hombre/la mujer de negocios** | *businessman/woman* |
| **el/la ingeniero/a** | *engineer* |
| **el/la licenciado/a** | *graduate (bachelor's)* |
| **el/la médico/a** | *doctor* |
| **el/la mesero/a** | *waiter, waitress* |
| **el/la músico** | *musician* |
| **las noticias** | *news* |
| **el/la obrero/a** | *worker* |
| **el/la programador/a** | *programmer* |
| **el/la psiquiatra** | *psychiatrist* |
| **la publicidad** | *advertising* |
| **el/la secretario/a** | *secretary* |
| **el teatro** | *theater* |

**Verbos**

| | |
|---|---|
| **encargarse (de)** | *to take charge of* |
| **nacer** | *to be born* |

**Adjetivos**

| | |
|---|---|
| **asegurado/a** | *insured* |
| **temporal** | *temporary* |

**Otras expresiones**

| | |
|---|---|
| **ambos/as** | *both* |
| **felicidades** | *congratulations* |

# Reunión B

**A escuchar.** **¿Qué hiciste esta mañana?** Carlos is asking Professor Yuja about his exam results and telling him about his first day on the job. Listen to the conversation and complete the sentences based on what you hear.

1. Carlos sacó una _______________ en el examen.
2. La jefa de Carlos es la doctora _______________.
3. Carlos tuvo que aprender los _______________ de los componentes de las computadoras.
4. La doctora Muñoz llegó hace varios años de _______________.
5. Carlos recibe un buen sueldo y además una _______________.
6. Pueden despedir a Carlos _______________ del entrenamiento.

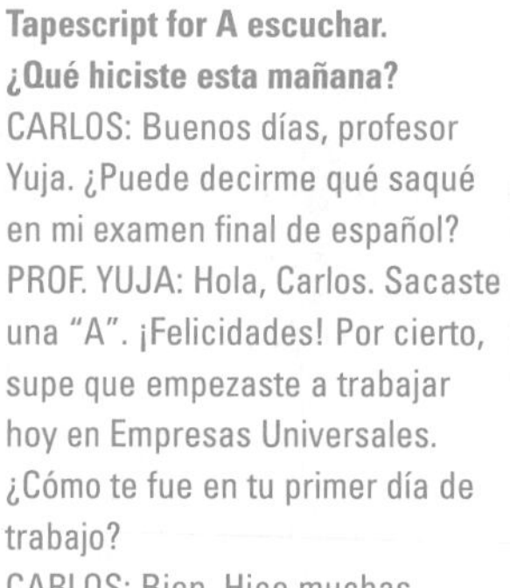

**Tapescript for A escuchar. ¿Qué hiciste esta mañana?**
CARLOS: Buenos días, profesor Yuja. ¿Puede decirme qué saqué en mi examen final de español?
PROF. YUJA: Hola, Carlos. Sacaste una "A". ¡Felicidades! Por cierto, supe que empezaste a trabajar hoy en Empresas Universales. ¿Cómo te fue en tu primer día de trabajo?
CARLOS: Bien. Hice muchas cosas. Mi jefa, la doctora Muñoz me llevó a recorrer las instalaciones y me dio una oficina. Además, me enseñó los tipos de computadoras que venden. Tuve que aprender los nombres de todos los componentes en inglés y español.
PROF. YUJA: ¡Qué interesante! ¿Cómo es la doctora Muñoz?
CARLOS: Es joven y muy amable. Llegó hace varios años de Colombia.
PROF. YUJA: Creo que yo la conocí hace varios años. Estudió ingeniería electrónica en esta universidad. ¿Cómo son los sueldos?
CARLOS: Muy buenos. Además pagan comisión.
PROF. YUJA: ¡Vas a ganar más dinero que tus profesores!
CARLOS: Todavía no me contratan permanentemente. Me pueden despedir después del entrenamiento.
PROF. YUJA: No creo. Tú eres muy inteligente. ¡Te deseo muy buena suerte!
CARLOS: Gracias, profesor Yuja.

**Answers for A escuchar.**
1) *"A".* 2) *Muñoz.* 3) *Nombres.* 4) *Colombia.* 5) *Comisión.* 6) *Después.*

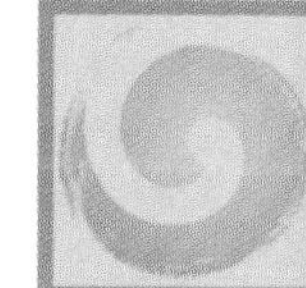

**A conversar.** Role-play an interview with a classmate in which one of you is the applicant, the other the employer. Discuss salary, past job experience, skills you have as they relate to this position, date you would be available to begin, educational background, how you learned of the position, and who has provided you with letters of recommendation.

**¿Lo sabía?**

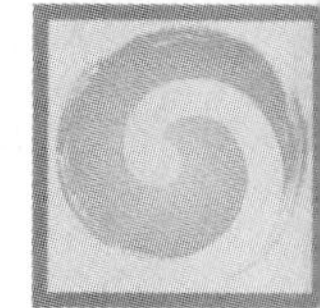

**Empresarios prósperos**

Gilberto S. Ocañas, nacido en Texas y con un título de ciencias políticas de la Universidad de Houston, es dueño de una compañía de imprenta para la Lotería del Estado de Texas. Su esposa, Ana M. "Cha" Guzmán, es vicepresidenta de Austin Community College y directora de la Comisión Presidencial de Excelencia en Educación para Hispanoamericanos. WinTex International Inc., que ahora se llama Ocañas Printing Company, tuvo 3.2 millones de dólares de ingresos en 1997 y ofrece servicios por todos los Estados Unidos. Antes, Ocañas y su mujer tenían no más del 40% de las acciones de la empresa; ahora tienen el 100%.

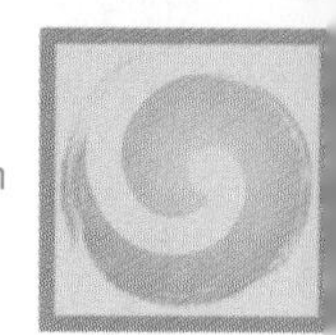

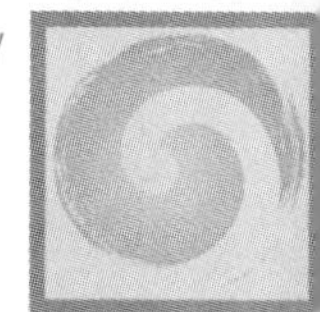

**¿Comprende Ud.?** Answer the following questions based on the article.

1. ¿Qué servicios ofrece esta empresa?
2. ¿De dónde es el título universitario del Sr. Ocañas?
3. ¿Cuánto dinero ganó la compañía en 1997?
4. ¿Este negocio ofrece servicios de imprenta mundialmente?

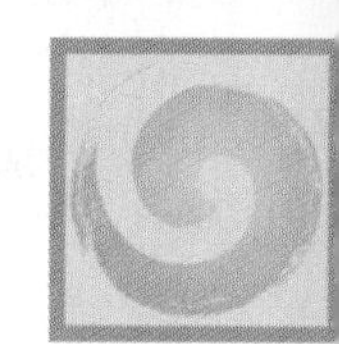

**A buscar.** Many multinational companies such as IBM, GTE, Motorola, and Pitney Bowes actively recruit Hispanic employees. Government agencies including the FBI, INS, and DEA also seek candidates with foreign language ability. Look for information on the Internet and locate at least three open positions geared mainly toward Spanish speakers. Then, share your findings with the class.

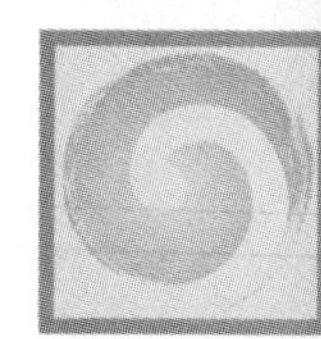

# ¡TRATO HECHO!

## Rincón profesional: Buscando trabajo en el Internet

¿Sabe usted cómo conseguir su empleo ideal? Si cree que es simplemente escribir su historia profesional en un currículum vitae y contestar anuncios en el periódico local, usted necesita entrar en el nuevo milenio. El método tradicional de buscar empleo cambió completamente. En el pasado, la estrategia principal prometió: "no es lo que sabe lo que abre las puertas profesionales... es a quién conoce." Pero ahora, la competencia intensa por los empleos más deseables, el desarrollo de una economía global, y más que nada, las comunicaciones electrónicas transforman la sabiduría tradicional.

Ahora se dice: "no es lo que usted sabe, ni a quién conoce... es a quién puede **llegar** a conocer... lo que abre las puertas profesionales". Por medio del Internet, la búsqueda del trabajo ideal ya no está limitada ni por la geografía, ni por los contactos o anuncios locales.

Al navegar por la red y "hacer click" un par de veces, los **internautas** que buscan empleo pueden ver lista tras lista de oportunidades profesionales por todas partes del mundo. Incluso es posible establecer contacto con personas con los mismos intereses profesionales en las "salas de charla" o *chat rooms* en cualquier idioma, en cualquier país. Estas salas sí pueden abrir puertas profesionales.

¿Quiere usted publicar su currículum vitae en su propia página en el Internet? No hay problema. Y ¡lo más interesante! Si Ud. acepta un empleo en Argentina, por ejemplo, hay gran posibilidad de que no tenga que ir nunca a Argentina. Por medio del Internet, usted puede ser uno de los nuevos **teletrabajadores**—profesionales que viven en una región geográfica y que por medios electrónicos: fax, correo electrónico y videoconferencias, se quedan trabajando tranquilamente en casa, que en ocasiones está al otro lado del mundo.

**¿Comprende Ud.?** Answer the following questions based on the reading.

1. What was the traditional wisdom about job hunting?
2. How has it changed?
3. Name two new ways to find out about interesting jobs.
4. Can you describe what **internauta** and **teletrabajador** mean? Does English have equivalent new words?
5. How is it possible to have a job in one country and live in another?

**Tapescript for A escuchar. Una computadora.**
AGUSTÍN: ¡Todos los días lo mismo! Hay muchos estudiantes que quieren usar las computadoras de la biblioteca. Hoy estuve esperando tres horas.
FRANCISCO: Sí, por eso acabo de comprar una computadora.
AGUSTÍN: Ya, pero son muy caras.
FRANCISCO: No, las computadoras están bajando de precio todos los días. Ahora hay una muy barata en Compumundo.
AGUSTÍN: Es que no tengo dinero.
FRANCISCO: Puedes pagar con tu tarjeta de crédito.
AGUSTÍN: Y, ¿qué voy a hacer ahora con los disquetes que tengo?
FRANCISCO: Eso no es problema, casi todas las computadoras son compatibles.

**A escuchar. Una computadora.** Agustín necesita comprar una computadora para hacer su tarea y está hablando con otro estudiante.

**¿Comprende Ud.?** Answer the following questions based on the dialog.

1. ¿Por qué está enojado Agustín?
2. ¿Qué sugiere Francisco?
3. ¿Por qué no puede comprar una computadora Agustín?
4. ¿Dónde venden una barata?
5. ¿Cómo puede pagar por la computadora?

**Answers for A escuchar.**
1) *Porque tuvo que esperar tres horas para usar la computadora.* 2) *Comprar una computadora.* 3) *Porque no tiene dinero.* 4) *En Compumundo.* 5) *Con su tarjeta de crédito.*

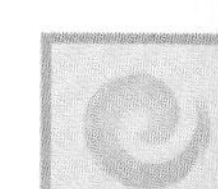

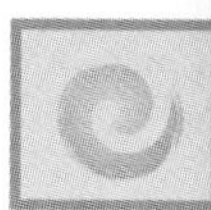

Activity in pairs. You may want to bring toy phones to make the activity more fun for the students.

**Una entrevista.** One student will call the head of personnel at a company he/she is interested in. The other student will act as the head of personnel. The student calling in will need to ask questions to find out whether they have any openings available, the requirements involved in this position, salary, etc. The head of personnel will need to find out the student's skills, strengths and weaknesses, date he/she would be available for work, salary requirements, job history, etc.

Group activity. You may want to work with the whole class to develop appropriate and interesting interview questions for the groups.

**Un currículum vitae.** Fill out the virtual resumé with personal information and interests. In groups of three or four classmates hold interviews asking pertinent questions based on the resumé.

MODELO: E1: *En el Hospital Buena Vida, ¿qué hizo usted?*
E2: *¿Dónde trabajó en 1995?*
E1: *¿Por qué dejó el trabajo?*

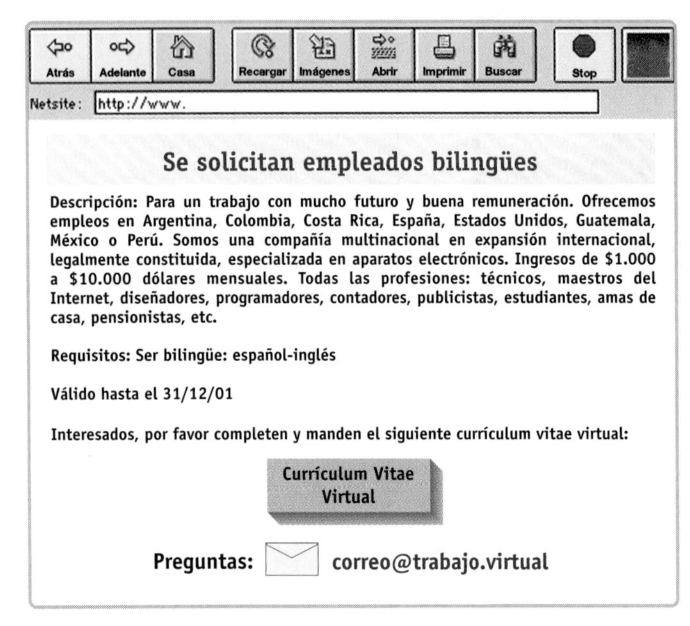

Atrás Adelante Casa Recargar Imágenes Abrir Imprimir Buscar Stop

Netsite: http://www.

**Se solicitan empleados bilingües**

Descripción: Para un trabajo con mucho futuro y buena remuneración. Ofrecemos empleos en Argentina, Colombia, Costa Rica, España, Estados Unidos, Guatemala, México o Perú. Somos una compañía multinacional en expansión internacional, legalmente constituida, especializada en aparatos electrónicos. Ingresos de $1.000 a $10.000 dólares mensuales. Todas las profesiones: técnicos, maestros del Internet, diseñadores, programadores, contadores, publicistas, estudiantes, amas de casa, pensionistas, etc.

Requisitos: Ser bilingüe: español-inglés

Válido hasta el 31/12/01

Interesados, por favor completen y manden el siguiente currículum vitae virtual:

Currículum Vitae Virtual

Preguntas: correo@trabajo.virtual

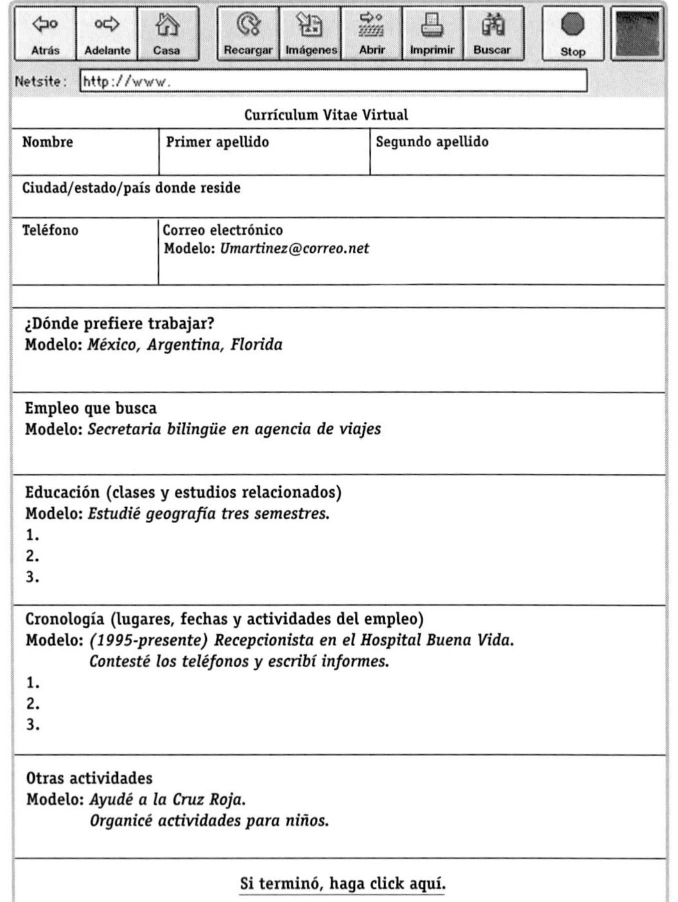

Atrás Adelante Casa Recargar Imágenes Abrir Imprimir Buscar Stop

Netsite: http://www.

Currículum Vitae Virtual

| Nombre | Primer apellido | Segundo apellido |
|---|---|---|

Ciudad/estado/país donde reside

| Teléfono | Correo electrónico<br>Modelo: *Umartinez@correo.net* |
|---|---|

¿Dónde prefiere trabajar?
Modelo: *México, Argentina, Florida*

Empleo que busca
Modelo: *Secretaria bilingüe en agencia de viajes*

Educación (clases y estudios relacionados)
Modelo: *Estudié geografía tres semestres.*
1.
2.
3.

Cronología (lugares, fechas y actividades del empleo)
Modelo: *(1995-presente) Recepcionista en el Hospital Buena Vida. Contesté los teléfonos y escribí informes.*
1.
2.
3.

Otras actividades
Modelo: *Ayudé a la Cruz Roja. Organicé actividades para niños.*

Si terminó, haga click aquí.

## A leer

Statistics once again! Use them to get a quick sense of the points the authors are making. Then, go back to read the article slowly and carefully. Pay special attention to the verbs in the preterite. Notice how the verbs take you back and forth between present and past tense and use that information to make sense of the article.

**Antes de leer.** Scan the introduction and conclusion of this article and see how much information you can derive from them. Then make a list of all the commercial names that appear and try to find a common link among them. When you're done look at all your findings: can you guess what the article will say?

**¡YA** no vivimos aislados! Ahora somos parte de una economía global y es necesario comunicarnos diariamente con personas que viven en los países más remotos. Las computadoras son nuestros mejores aliados: nos ayudan a tener una comunicación barata, fácil y rápida. Es por eso que la exportación de computadoras, en especial a Latinoamérica, aumenta cada día más. Según Computerworld[1], la venta de computadoras al mercado latinoamericano aumentó en un 22.7% el primer trimestre de 1997, comparado con un aumento del 15.4% en el mercado mundial en el mismo período.

Los países hispanoamericanos que compraron más computadoras fueron: Venezuela, Colombia, México y Chile. Luis Anavitarte, un analista que trabaja en Dataquest, dice que las agencias gubernamentales de esos países fueron los clientes más importantes. También compraron muchas computadoras las corporaciones, especialmente en el área de las telecomunicaciones. Este crecimiento se debe en gran parte a la inversión de capital extranjero en Latinoamérica.

Compaq Computer Corporation es la compañía americana que está en el primer lugar, con ventas de 104.863 unidades; después siguen The Acer Group e IBM. Se calcula que para el año 2001, el mercado latinoamericano para la compra de computadoras crecerá en un 18%.

[1]Publicado el 29 de mayo de 1997, www.computerworld.com

**¿Comprende Ud.?** Después de leer el texto anterior, conteste las siguientes preguntas:

1. ¿Por qué son importantes las computadoras?
2. ¿Cuáles son los países hispanoamericanos que compran más computadoras?
3. ¿Quiénes compran más computadoras en esos países?
4. ¿Cuáles son las compañías americanas que exportan más computadoras a Hispanoamérica?
5. ¿Piensas que en el futuro va a aumentar la exportación de computadoras a Hispanoamérica?

**Note.** You may want to review **ir a** + *infinitive* before assigning this activity.

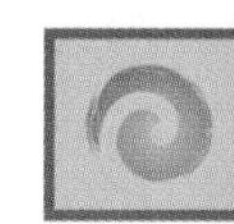
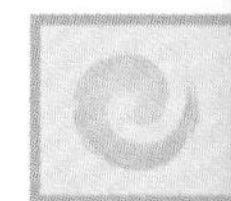

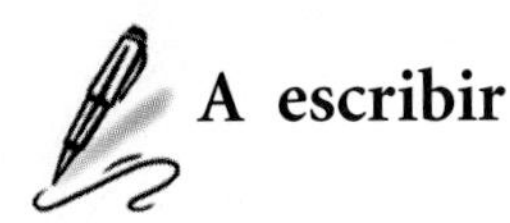

## A escribir

Explain what degree you're studying for, where you want to work in the future, and state the reasons why. Do you believe that computers will be important in shaping your professional future? Why? How influential do you think computers and technological advances in general will be to the professional future of the next two or three generations? Will all these changes be positive? negative? Explain your reasons in detail.

# 6 ¡Repaso!

LECCIÓN
SEIS

CHECK OUT THE *¡TRATO HECHO!* WEBSITE AND CD-ROM
FOR ACTIVITIES, GAMES, SELF-TESTS, AND MUCH MORE!

## LECCIÓN 1

**Tema 1** Las presentaciones
**Tema 2** En la clase
**Tema 3** Las cosas de la clase
**Tema 4** Los horarios

## LECCIÓN 2

**Tema 1** De tiendas
**Tema 2** En el centro comercial
**Tema 3** La comida
**Tema 4** La ropa

## LECCIÓN 3

**Tema 1** La familia
**Tema 2** El hogar
**Tema 3** Las cosas de la casa
**Tema 4** La guardería infantil

## LECCIÓN 4

**Tema 1** Las diversiones
**Tema 2** Las celebraciones
**Tema 3** La rutina diaria
**Tema 4** Los deportes

## LECCIÓN 5

**Tema 1** Cosas del trabajo
**Tema 2** Necesito un trabajo
**Tema 3** La entrevista de trabajo
**Tema 4** La carrera

REPASO REPASO REPASO REPASO REPASO REPASO REPASO REPASO REPASO

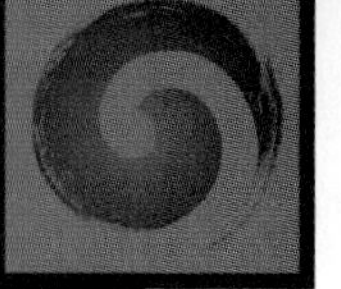

**Lección I**

# TEMA 1

## Las presentaciones

*¡Felicidades! You have been offered a teaching position in a bilingual school in Mexico. On your first day, you will have to meet and greet many new people.*

Answers for A. 1) *Buenos días.* 2) *Buenas tardes.* 3) *Buenas tardes.* 4) *Buenas noches.*

**A. ¡Hola!** Which greeting will you use at each of the following times of the day?

1. a las ocho de la mañana
2. al mediodía
3. a la una de la tarde
4. a las nueve de la noche

Answers for B. 1) *Tú.* 2) *Tú.* 3) *Ud.* 4) *Ud./Tú.* 5) *Ud.* 6) *Ud.*

**B. ¿Ud. o tú?** Will you greet the following people with **Ud.** or **tú**?

1. your nephew
2. a new student in your class
3. the new student's father
4. a new colleague
5. the school board director
6. an older woman who works in the cafeteria

Answers for C. 1) *¿Cómo se llama Ud.?* 2) *¿Cómo te llamas?* 3) *¿Cómo se llama Ud.?* 4) *¿Cómo se llama Ud.?* 5) *¿Cómo te llamas?* 6) *¿Cómo te llamas?*

**C. ¿Cómo se llama?** Ask the following people their names using formal or informal questions.

1. your new principal
2. your principal's 5-year-old daughter
3. a student's mother
4. an older colleague
5. your new roommate
6. your friend's little brother

Answers for D. *c, h, i.*

**D. Saludos.** It's Monday, 9:00 A.M. Which of these greetings are appropriate to greet the secretary your first day on the job?

a. Oye, ¿qué tal?
b. Buenas tardes.
c. Buenos días, señorita.
d. ¿Cómo estás, Adriana?
e. ¿Qué hay de nuevo?
f. Buenas noches, señorita.
g. ¡Hola!
h. ¿Cómo está Ud.?
i. Me llamo ________.

**E. ¿Y Ud.?** By now you should be able to greet anybody, anywhere, at any time. With a partner, role-play each of these situations. Chat briefly, then bring the conversation to a close.

- You work in a very formal school and you are greeting the principal for the first time in several weeks.
- You have just run into your best friend in the grocery store.
- You need to speak with a parent whom you have never met before.
- You have a friend in South America with whom you "chat" on the Internet.

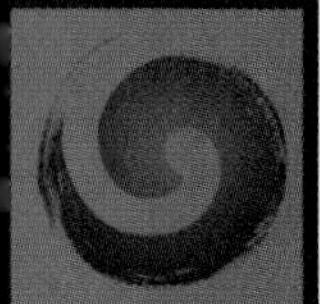

**Lección 1**

# TEMA 2

## En la clase

*You are starting a brand new semester with new classes, new professors, and new classmates. It may take time to get used to the new routine!*

**A. El primer día de clase.** You and a friend are waiting for class to start on the first day. As you look around the room, you imagine how everyone is feeling. Fill in the blank spaces with the appropriate form of **estar**.

Answers for A. 1) *Estoy.* 2) *Estás.* 3) *Estamos.* 4) *Está.* 5) *Está.* 6) *Están.* 7) *Están.*

Yo ____________(1) muy contenta esta mañana. Me gusta mucho estudiar español. Yo sé que tú ___________(2) nervioso porque crees que va a ser difícil. Pero no hay problema porque tú y yo ___________(3) en la misma clase y podemos estudiar juntos.

Aquí viene otro estudiante. Él mira un papel y mira el número del salón. Yo creo que él ___________(4) confundido. No sabe dónde ___________(5) su clase. Aquellas estudiantes que ___________(6) cerca de la puerta hablan de la gran fiesta de anoche. Es por eso que ellas __________(7) tan cansadas ahora.

**B. ¿Cómo están?** During the first week of classes people are beginning to settle into a routine. Change the phrases in parentheses to show how the following people are doing now.

Answers for B. 1) *Está contento.* 2) *Están preocupados.* 3) *Está ocupada.* 4) *Están confundidos.* 5) *Está mejor.* 6) *Están aburridas.*

1. El nuevo profesor (estar contento) con la clase.
2. Los estudiantes (estar preocupado) porque hay un examen.
3. Mi amiga Noelia (estar ocupado) con mucho trabajo y mucha tarea.
4. Los nuevos alumnos (estar confundido) con la gramática.
5. La alumna nueva (estar mejor) que la semana pasada.
6. Las chicas de la fiesta no (estar aburrido) en la clase de español.

**C. ¿Y Ud.?** With a classmate, role-play the following situations. One of you will ask *how are you?*, using a formal or informal question. The other will respond with an appropriate description.

Answers for C. 1) *Está contenta.* 2) *Está preocupada.* 3) *Está ocupado.* 4) *Están nerviosos.* 5) *Está mejor.* 6) *Están confundidos.*

MODELO: Your roommate. He has been studying all night without a break.
E1: *¿Cómo está tu compañero de cuarto?*
E2: *Está cansado.*

1. Your boss. She is very pleased with the new faculty.
2. Your mother's friend. Her sister is in the hospital.
3. Your best friend. He is taking three classes, working full time, and house-sitting for a relative.
4. Two colleagues. They have never taught before and the principal and other officials are going to observe their class today.
5. One of your new young students. Her cold is almost cured.
6. All of the students in the math class. They can't understand the concepts.

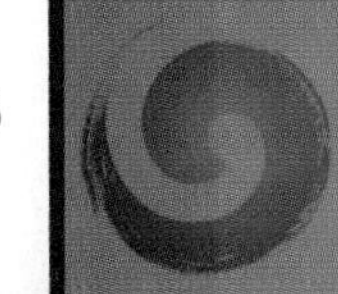

Lección I

# TEMA 3

## Las cosas de clase

*In Spanish brain teasers and puzzles are called* **rompecabezas.** *Here are some for you to try.*

Answers for A. 1) *Tres universidades.* 2) *Cincuenta bolígrafos.* 3) *Ochenta y una calculadoras.* 4) *Tres lápices.*

**A. Matemáticas.** Here are some word problems. Do the math and answer these questions.

MODELO: Hay veintidós libros en el estante. Diez alumnos y once alumnas sacan un libro cada uno. ¿Cuántos libros hay ahora?
*Hay un libro en el estante.*

1. Hay una universidad aquí y otras dos muy cerca, ¿cuántas hay en esta ciudad?
2. Yo tengo cien bolígrafos y les doy el 50% a los alumnos. ¿Cuántos tengo al final?
3. En la oficina hay una calculadora. Hay dos cajas más con cuarenta en cada una. ¿Cuántas calculadoras hay en la oficina?
4. Yo tengo un lápiz. Tú tienes dos. ¿Cuántos tenemos en total?

**B. ¿Qué hay en…?**

MODELO: el libro
*Hay páginas y palabras en el libro.*

1. el estante
2. el cuaderno
3. la mochila
4. la calculadora
5. la clase
6. la pizarra

Answers for C. 1) *La universidad está en la calle Universidad.* 2) *Las clases están en el edificio ML.* 3) *El lápiz está en la mochila.* 4) *El bolígrafo está en el escritorio.* 5) *Las computadoras están en el laboratorio.* 6) *El papel está en el cuaderno.* 7) *La comida está en la cafetería.* 8) *Los ejercicios están en el libro de texto.*

**C. El artículo definido.** One student will ask the question **¿Dónde está…?**, and another student will answer according to the cues given. Use definite articles to tell where these items are.

MODELO: E1: *¿Dónde está el libro?* (estante)
E2: *El libro está en el estante.*

1. universidad (calle Universidad)
2. clases (edificio ML)
3. lápiz (mochila)
4. bolígrafo (escritorio)
5. computadoras (laboratorio)
6. papel (cuaderno)
7. comida (cafetería)
8. ejercicios (libro de texto)

Answers for D. 1) *Hay sesenta minutos en una hora.* 2) *Hay veinticuatro horas en un día.* 3) *Hay siete días en una semana.* 4) *Hay cien centavos en un dólar.*

**D. Los números.** How quickly can you answer the questions below?

1. ¿Cuántos minutos hay en una hora?
2. ¿Cuántas horas hay en un día?
3. ¿Cuántos días hay en una semana?
4. ¿Cuántos centavos hay en un dólar?

**E. En la papelería.** You are going to buy school supplies. Make a list of ten items that you need for Spanish class, how many of each you need, the price for each, and the total you will spend. How much change will you get from $100?



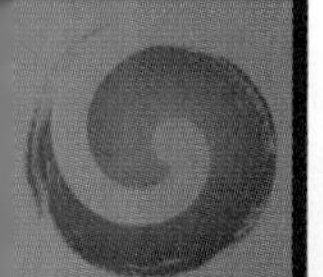

**Lección 1**

# TEMA 4

## Los horarios

*Tomás is a new student aide at his school. His schedule will be very busy between work and classes. Help him set up his calendar and schedule.*

**A. Mi horario.** Fill in Tomás's class schedule based on the following clues:

1. 8:00-10:00 (lunes/miércoles) Necesita una novela y un libro de poemas.
2. 8:00-10:00 (jueves) Necesita un microscopio.
3. 2:00-4:00 (miércoles) Necesita una calculadora de interés.
4. 11:00-1:00 (martes/jueves) Necesita un diccionario bilingüe.
5. 8:00-12:00 (viernes) Necesita una computadora.

**Answers for A.** 1) *Literatura.* 2) *Biología.* 3) *Matemáticas/contabilidad.* 4) *Español.* 5) *Informática.*

| | LUNES | MARTES | MIÉRCOLES | JUEVES | VIERNES | SÁBADO | DOMINGO |
|---|---|---|---|---|---|---|---|
| 8:00 am | | | | | | | |
| 9:00 am | | | | | | | |
| 10:00 am | | | | | | | |
| 11:00 am | | | | | | | |
| 12:00 noon | | | | | | | |
| 1:00 pm | | | | 1:30–Hablar con el jefe | | | |
| 2:00 pm | | | | | | | |
| 3:00 pm | | | | | | | |

**B. Reuniones de trabajo.** Tomás needs to meet with many people this week, and all meetings take place in the conference room (**la sala de reuniones**). First, complete these sentences and book the conference room for each of the following people. Fit the times in between Tomás's classes because he needs to be at each meeting.

MODELO: El jefe / hablar con Tomás.
*El jefe habla con Tomás el martes a la una y media en la sala de conferencias.*

1. Todos los estudiantes / practicar los verbos por una hora
2. Tomás y Eliana / estudiar por treinta minutos
3. El director / trabajar con los maestros por dos horas
4. El profesor de literatura / calcular las notas finales
5. Nosotros / preparar los exámenes por una hora
6. Las secretarias y Tomás/ tomar un café

**Answers for B.** 1) *Practican.* 2) *Estudian.* 3) *Trabaja.* 4) *Calcula.* 5) *Preparamos.* 6) *Toman.*

**C. Una reunión para todos.** See if there is an hour during the week when everyone can get together in the conference room at the same time for a meeting. Prepare a memo for all staff telling them about the meeting. Include when, where, and for what reason.

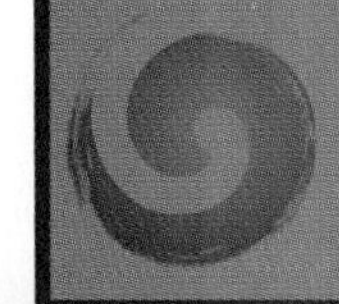

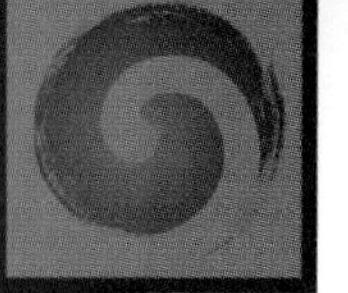

## Lección 2

# TEMA 1

### De tiendas

*You are a personal shopper working at a large Internet shopping service just before the holidays. Francisco is a very confused shopper who needs your help finding gifts for all of the people he included in the form below.*

1. **Mi madre:** A ella le gustan la música, el teatro y el vino tinto. No le gusta trabajar en casa. Va a muchas fiestas y recepciones.
2. **Mi hermana Rosa:** Ella estudia literatura. Siempre tiene un libro en la mano, que normalmente es de poesía.
3. **Mi sobrino Gregorio y mi padre:** Ellos se pasan todo el fin de semana con los deportes. Béisbol, fútbol, básquetbol... ¡No importa!
4. **Mis primos Glenn y Mariam:** Ellos trabajan mucho. Estoy preocupado. Ellos necesitan descansar y divertirse.
5. **Mi amigo Roberto:** Él nunca llega a la hora a ningún sitio. No es puntual.
6. **Mi amiga Adriana:** Ella trabaja como modelo. Le gusta mucho la ropa.

**A. El regalo perfecto.** For each person mentioned above, pick out the perfect gift and tell why it is perfect. Then, tell how much it will cost.

MODELO: *Para su madre: El regalo para su madre es una cena elegante para cuatro personas, entradas a un concierto y transporte en una limosina. Cuesta 500 dólares.*

**B. Para conocernos mejor.** As Francisco made a list of characteristics of his friends and family for the personal shopper, you will make a list of the characteristics of a classmate. First, ask your classmate if the following descriptions apply to him/her. Your classmate may agree with you or change the description to fit. Then ask what he or she likes.

MODELO: E1: *Tú eres... extrovertido/a y te gusta la literatura.*
E2: *No soy extrovertido/a. Soy tímido/a. Sí, me gusta la literatura.*

hablador/a, perezoso/a, pesimista, tímido/a, aficionado/a a..., romántico/a, pragmático/a, estudioso/a, divertido/a, inteligente, tonto/a

**C. El regalo ideal.** After you have an idea about your friend's likes and dislikes, imagine a perfect gift and explain why it is perfect for him or her. Remember that money is no object!

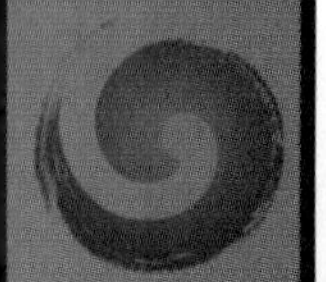

Lección 2

# TEMA 2

## En el centro comercial

*You and your friends have gone to the mall to shop for all kinds of gifts. Some people are happier shopping than others!*

**A. ¿Dónde?** One of you is gift shopping in the mall. The other is working at the information desk. The one who is shopping will have to ask the one at the information desk for directions to find the gifts he/she wants to buy.

**Directorio**

| | PISO | | PISO |
|---|---|---|---|
| Perfumería | 1º | Muebles y aparatos electrodomésticos | 6º |
| Zapatería | 2º | Librería/Discoteca | 7º |
| Ropa para dama | 3º | Cafetería | 8º |
| Ropa para hombre | 4º | Panadería | 9º |
| Joyería | 5º | Aparatos electrónicos | 10º |

MODELO: unos zapatos
E1: *¿Dónde puedo comprar… zapatos?*
E2: *Hay zapatos en la zapatería en el segundo piso.*

1. dos vestidos formales
2. un anillo de diamantes
3. un teléfono celular
4. unas botas vaqueras
5. una computadora
6. un libro de arte
7. un disco compacto de Luis Miguel
8. dulces y pasteles
9. un café y descanso
10. un perfume Paloma

**Answers for A.** 1) *Tercer piso.* 2) *Quinto piso.* 3) *Décimo piso.* 4) *Segundo piso.* 5) *Décimo piso.* 6) *Séptimo piso.* 7) *Séptimo piso.* 8) *Noveno piso.* 9) *Octavo piso.* 10) *Primer piso.*

**B. Después de comprar.** You and your friend have just returned from your shopping spree and are talking over the day and your purchases. One of you will ask the following questions using the correct form of **ser** or **estar**. The other will answer **no**, and then correct the statement with a logical response.

MODELO: la casa ¿sucia?
E1: *¿La casa está sucia?*
E2: *No, la casa está desordenada, no está sucia.*

1. los zapatos ¿de Italia?
2. nosotros ¿cansados?
3. los regalos ¿caros?
4. las botas ¿elegantes?
5. tú ¿contento?
6. las botas ¿en la bolsa?
7. los discos compactos ¿de Luis Miguel?
8. los regalos ¿debajo del árbol?
9. en las tiendas, los hombres ¿aburridos?
10. el anillo ¿de oro?

**Answers for B.** 1) *Son.* 2) *Estamos.* 3) *Son.* 4) *Son.* 5) *Estás.* 6) *Están.* 7) *Son.* 8) *Están.* 9) *Están.* 10) *Es.*

**C. ¿Listo? ¿Aburrido?** Read the following sentences about shopping and shoppers and decide by the context the correct form of **ser** or **estar** for each blank.

1. A mi padre no le gusta ir de compras con mi madre. En la tienda de ropa, él _________aburrido.
2. Para mi madre, no hay nada mejor que comprar ropa. Ella cree que pasar horas mirando los partidos de fútbol _________ totalmente aburrido.
3. Yo siempre encuentro el regalo perfecto para cada miembro de mi familia. Yo ________ muy lista para las compras.
4. Mañana hay rebajas. Si las tiendas abren a las ocho, yo puedo ________ lista para salir a las seis.

**Answers for C.** 1) *Está.* 2) *Es.* 3) *Soy.* 4) *Estar.*

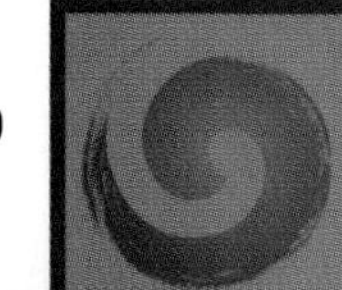

## Lección 2

# TEMA 3

### La comida

*Your home is very popular with visiting friends and family. You have to spend a great deal of time thinking about different foods, who likes to eat what, and whether you are prepared for your visitors' culinary quirks!*

**Answers for A.** 1) *No tengo ningún huevo sin yema.* 2) *No hay ningún restaurante....* 3) *No hay nadie....* 4) *No tengo ni caviar, ni champán, ni cacahuetes.* 5) *No hay nada en el refrigerador....*

**A. ¡No es posible!** A friend is looking for something to eat, but he/she wants the impossible. Answer his/her questions in the negative.

MODELO: ¿Tienes algún postre con menos de dos calorías?
*No, no tengo ningún postre con menos de dos calorías.*

1. ¿Tienes algunos huevos sin yema (*yolk*)?
2. ¿Conoces algún restaurante aquí con comida del Tibet?
3. ¿Hay alguien aquí con ganas de comer en Taco Bell?
4. ¿Tienes caviar, champán y cacahuetes para el desayuno?
5. ¿Hay algo en el refrigerador para traer a la clase de ciencia como proyecto?

**B. ¿Dónde está?** A friend can't find things in your refrigerator. Have a classmate ask where an item is. Then you show where.

MODELO: E1: *¿Dónde está la mantequilla?*
E2: *Está en la puerta al lado la mayonesa.*

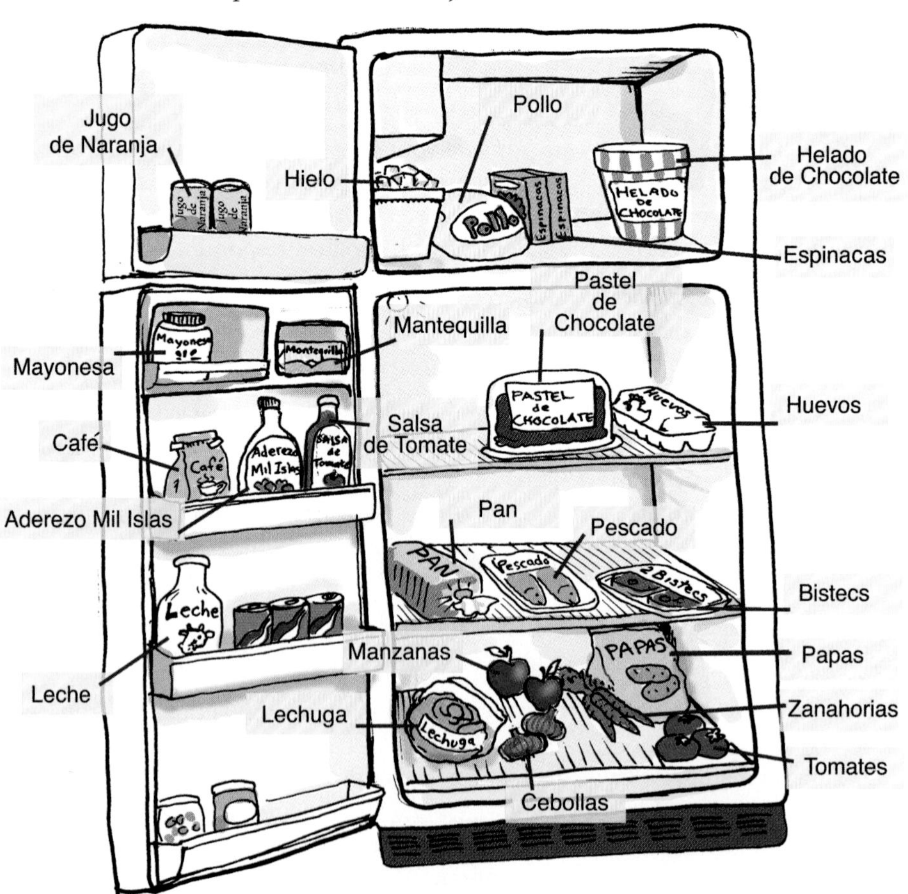

**C. Una comida.** With a partner, plan a complete breakfast, lunch, and dinner using the ingredients in the refrigerator.

## Lección 2

# TEMA 4

### La ropa

*You are out shopping with a friend for the day. As you wander through the different departments, you will point out different things that have caught your eye.*

**A. La moda personal.** Give the correct form of the indicated demonstrative adjective.

MODELO: Este: zapatos de tacón muy alto
*Estos zapatos.*

| **Este/a/os/as** | **Ese/a/os/as** | **Aquel/aquella/os/as** |
|---|---|---|
| 1. traje de baño | 5. botas de piel | 9. zapatillas Nike |
| 2. bata de toalla | 6. abrigo de piel | 10. pantalones anaranjados |
| 3. vestido largo, formal | 7. calcetines blancos | 11. camisetas blancas |
| 4. calzoncillos negros | 8. sandalias de plástico | 12. traje formal |

**Answers for A.** 1) *Este.* 2) *Esta.* 3) *Este.* 4) *Estos.* 5) *Esas.* 6) *Ese.* 7) *Esos.* 8) *Esas.* 9) *Aquellas.* 10) *Aquellos.* 11) *Aquellas.* 12) *Aquel.*

**B. De vacaciones.** A friend of the opposite sex is going to a fancy beach resort for a conference, some relaxation, and a possible meeting with the big boss. From the previous list of clothes, plan complete outfits for each of the following events. Add anything needed that is not on the list.

1. el viaje en avión
2. una reunión con el "gran" jefe
3. el sábado, para el tiempo libre durante el día
4. cena formal y baile el sábado por la noche

**C. ¡Me gusta más…!** You are on a tight budget while on vacation and will have to choose carefully how you spend your money. Tell which of the following options you like better.

MODELO: los pantalones de golf anaranjados o el traje formal negro.
*Me gusta más el traje formal.*

1. la camisa hawaiana o las sandalias para la playa.
2. un traje de baño muy bonito o dos pares de pantalones cortos.
3. las zapatillas de Nike o el abrigo de piel.
4. el viaje por la bahía en barco o los museos de historia y arte.
5. las tapas y el vino en un restaurante moderado o la comida cara en un restaurante elegante.
6. los boletos de avión de primera clase o un hotel caro.

**D. Modelos.** In groups of two, plan a spontaneous fashion show. One student will describe the complete outfit of another student who will model the clothing for the rest. Add as much detail as possible to the description.

## Lección 3

# TEMA 1

## La familia

*¡La nueva familia! Isabel has just married into a family from Peru. Tell who all of her new relatives are.*

**Answers for A.** 1) *Suegro.* 2) *Tíos.* 3) *Abuela.* 4) *Sobrinas.* 5) *Primos.* 6) *Cuñada.*

**A. Las relaciones.** Identify these family relationships.

1. El padre de su esposo/a es su ______________________.
2. Los hermanos de su padre son sus ______________________.
3. La madre de su madre es su ______________________.
4. Las hijas de sus hermanas son sus ______________________.
5. Los hijos de sus tías son sus ______________________.
6. La hermana de su esposo es su ______________________.

**Answers for B.** 1) *Su cuñado.* 2) *Sus primas.* 3) *Mi tío.* 4) *Sus hermanos.* 5) *Nuestra abuela.* 6) *Tus hermanas.*

**B. Mis parientes.** Use the correct possessive adjective to talk about these friends and family members.

MODELO: Tenemos un primo que está aquí.
*Nuestro primo está aquí.*

1. Eleanor tiene un cuñado que llega mañana.
2. María tiene dos primas que llegan mañana.
3. Yo tengo un tío que es soltero.
4. Usted tiene dos hermanos que son solteros.
5. Nosotros tenemos una abuela que es vieja.
6. Tú tienes dos hermanas que son casadas.

**C. ¿Cuántos años tienen?** Write out the ages of the following relatives.

MODELO: Mi hijo Gregorio nació el año pasado.
*Tiene un año.*

1. Nuestra abuela Lina nació en 1903.
2. Nuestra sobrina Eva nació en 1987.
3. Mi tío Gerardo nació en 1935.
4. Mis primas Melisa y Fé nacieron en 1966.
5. Mi suegro Claudio nació en 1928.
6. Mi cuñado Ricardo nació en 1950.

**Suggestion for D.** You may want to introduce a Spanish version of "Happy Birthday" (*Cumpleaños feliz, cumpleaños feliz, te deseamos todos, cumpleaños feliz*) or the traditional Mexican birthday song "Las mañanitas."

**D. Feliz, feliz en tu día...** Fill in the month and write out the full date of birth for three of your relatives. Then ask five classmates for their birthdates. Be prepared to sing "Happy Birthday."

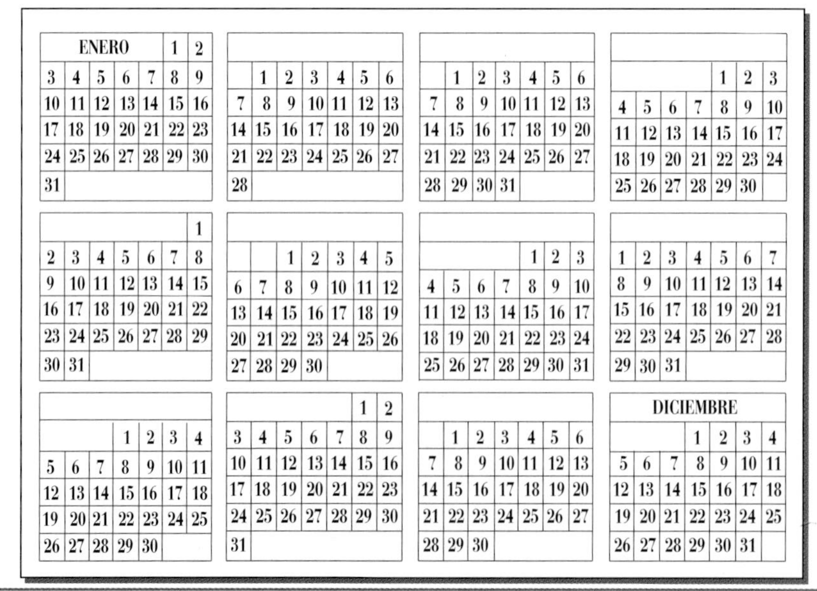

REPASO REPASO REPASO REPASO REPASO REPASO REPASO

# TEMA 2

## El hogar

*Home sweet home! ¡Felicidades! You are now a homeowner facing some of the joys, frustrations, and expenses of owning your own home. ¡Buena suerte!*

**A. La casa nueva.** One of you will play the role of a moving company driver, and the other will be the new homeowner. The movers have just arrived at the new home with the furniture. As they unload, the driver will ask where to put each item and the homeowner will indicate where in the house each item goes.

MODELO: E1: *¿Dónde ponemos la cama matrimonial?*
E2: *La cama matrimonial va en el dormitorio grande.*

1. la mesa y ocho sillas
2. el refrigerador
3. la computadora
4. el televisor
5. el sofá
6. la alfombra persa
7. el espejo grande
8. dos armarios
9. el estante grande
10. las plantas
11. la impresora
12. la cómoda
13. la lámpara
14. la caja con toallas

**B. El curioso.** One of the moving helpers is very curious and wants to know what you use the following rooms and items for. Be patient! Tell him/her two ways in which you plan to use each one of the following.

MODELO: E1: *¿Qué hacen en la cocina?*
E2: *En la cocina preparamos la comida y lavamos los platos.*

1. el televisor
2. la lámpara
3. el comedor
4. el dormitorio
5. la sala
6. el espejo grande
7. los estantes
8. la computadora

**Suggestion for B.** Give students a model using a piece of furniture to prompt them to use *con.*
E1: ¿Qué hacen con la mesa?
E2: Usamos la mesa para comer y para hacer la tarea.

**C. ¿Vende Ud. la casa?** You love your new home, but you still have to sell the old one. Write an advertisement describing the house that is for sale: describe the rooms, the yard, the kitchen. Put a price on it and justify the cost.

**D. Un mercadillo en el garaje.** You find you don't need all of the furniture and household items you brought to your new home. In a garage sale, negotiate with a classmate the sale of the items from the mover's list in exercise A.

MODELO: E1: *¿Cuánto cuesta el sofá?*
E2: *El sofá cuesta 100 dólares*
E1: *Es mucho. Sólo tengo 25 dólares.*
E2: *Está bien.* o *No, no vendo el sofá por 25 dólares.*

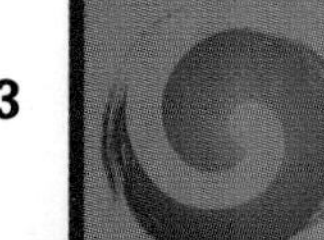

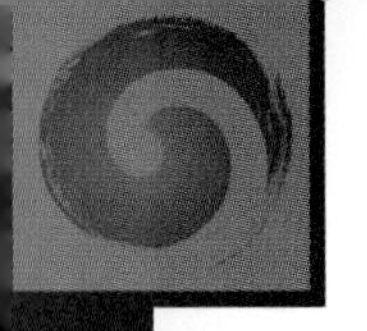



**Lección 3**

# TEMA 3

## Las cosas de casa

*Here's your chance to show off your new home. Everyone you know wants to see it.*

Answers for A. 1) *Pasamos la aspiradora.* 2) *Sacudimos/quitamos el polvo.* 3) *Lavamos/secamos.* 4) *Barremos.* 5) *Limpiamos/lavamos.* 6) *Limpiamos/ordenamos.*

**A. Los quehaceres domésticos.** You have just received word that out-of-town relatives are coming to see your new home. Quick! Clean it up. Tell what you do to each of the following. Use more than one verb where possible.

MODELO: la cama
*Hacemos la cama.*

1. la alfombra
2. los muebles
3. los platos sucios
4. el patio
5. la cocina
6. el refrigerador

**B. Nuestras casas.** Compare **mi casa** with **tu casa**. Give at least five comparisons of inequality (**más que…, menos que…**) and three of equality (**tan…como, tanto… como**).

MODELO: *Mi casa es más moderna que tu casa.*

**MI CASA**

**TU CASA**

**C. El vecino.** You live next door to the most extreme neighbor in the world: el Señor Extremo. His house is the biggest, the messiest, the oldest, etc. Make five extreme statements about your neighbor and his house.

MODELO: *Su casa es la más sucia de la cuadra/manzana* (block).

**D. ¿Cómo es tu casa?** Find out about a classmate's residence. How many rooms does it have, how many bathrooms, bedrooms? How far is it from the school? How many people live there? Now, make five statements comparing your two homes.

**Lección 3**

# TEMA 4

## La guardería infantil

*You and a friend have volunteered to help out today in a day-care center. Make sure that the children have what they need and that they are having fun!*

**A. Los niños.** One of you notices the children's behavior and asks what the following children need. The other will use a **tener** expression to explain.

MODELO: Paquito / caminar a la cocina / buscar galletas
E1: *Paquito camina a la cocina y busca galletas.*
E2: *Paquito tiene hambre.*

1. Maritza / buscar su chaqueta antes de salir a jugar
2. Elenita / querer jugo
3. Después del almuerzo, los niños / estar cansados
4. Después de dormir los niños / tener energía / no estar tranquilos en clase
5. Cuando los niños regresan / quitarse rápidamente las chaquetas

**Answers for A.** 1) *Busca/tiene frío.* 2) *Quiere/tiene sed.* 3) *Están/tienen sueño.* 4) *Ve/llora/tiene miedo.* 5) *Tienen/no están/ tienen ganas de...* 6) *Se quitan /tienen calor.*

**B. La hora de los cuentos.** After playing outside, the students ask you to tell them a story. Give the correct form of the verb.

En esta historia una niña _________ (1) (vivir) con su madrastra y sus dos hermanastras feas. Todos los días, esta niña, la Cenicienta, _________ (2) (tener) que limpiar la casa y lavar la ropa. Un día _________ (3) (llegar) a la casa una invitación al baile en el palacio.

La noche del baile, las hermanastras se _________ (4) (poner) sus mejores vestidos y _________ (5) (salir). La pobre Cenicienta sólo _________ (6) (llorar) y _________ (7) (limpiar). De repente, aparece el hada madrina. Ella le dice a Cenicienta: "Si tú _________ (8) (traer) aquí dos ratoncitos, una calabaza, una cortina y una ventana, yo te _________ (9) (hacer) dos caballos, un coche, un vestido elegante y unos zapatos de cristal. Entonces, tú _________ (10) (poder) ir al baile, pero _________(11) (tener) que regresar para la medianoche."

A las doce, cuando Cenicienta _________ (12) (salir) corriendo del palacio, ella _________ (13) (perder) un zapato. El príncipe _________(14) (ver) el zapato y _________ (15) (ir) a casa de Cenicienta. Cuando ella _________(16) (querer) saber cómo sabe el príncipe que es su zapato, él le dice: "Es fácil. Tu casa es la única que no _________ (17) (tener) ventana." Y ellos _________ (18) (vivir) felices para siempre.

**Answers for B.** 1) *Vive.* 2) *Tiene.* 3) *Llega.* 4) *Ponen.* 5) *Salen.* 6) *Llora.* 7) *Limpia.* 8) *Traes.* 9) *Hago.* 10) *Puedes.* 11) *Tienes.* 12) *Sale.* 13) *Pierde.* 14) *Ve.* 15) *Va.* 16) *Quiere.* 17) *Tiene.* 18. *Viven.*

REPASO REPASO REPASO REPASO REPASO REPASO REPASO REPASO REPASO REPASO

REPASO REPASO REPASO REPASO REPASO REPASO REPASO REPASO

## Lección 4

# TEMA 1

### Las diversiones

*Everyone is on vacation and has different ideas about how to spend the time off. What you do will depend on the weather, your friends, and just what you feel like doing and what you need to do.*

Answers for A. a) *Hace frío/nieva.* b) *Hace sol/hace calor/hace buen tiempo.* c) *Llueve/hace viento/hace mal tiempo.* d) *Hace fresco/hace buen tiempo.*

**A. El tiempo.** Tell what the weather is like and what you will do.

MODELO: *Hace calor. Vamos a la playa.*

1. ¿Qué tiempo hace?
   a. ________
   b. ________
   c. ________
   d. ________

2. ¿Adónde van Uds. hoy?
   a. ________
   b. ________
   c. ________
   d. ________

Answers for B. 1) *Van a ver una película.* 2) *Vamos a esquiar/caminar/acampar.* 3) *Van a limpiar/descansar.* 4) *Vas a comer/cocinar.* 5) *Van a nadar/tomar el sol.* 6) *Vamos a estudiar/hacer preguntas.*

**B. ¿Qué va a hacer?** Tell what the following people will do in these places.

MODELO: Yo/en el supermercado…
*Yo voy a comprar comida en el supermercado.*

1. Isabel y Lázaro/en el cine…
2. Nosotros/en las montañas…
3. Ustedes/en la casa…
4. Tú/en la cocina…
5. Mis amigos/en la playa…
6. Todos nosotros/en la clase…

**C. ¿Adónde van Uds. para…?** Tell where you go to do these things.

1. Para bailar…
2. Para pasar una noche romántica…
3. Para comer rápidamente…
4. Para comprar regalos…
5. Para esquiar en la nieve…
6. Para hacer un picnic…

**D. ¿Adónde?** Ask a classmate where he/she is going to do the following. If he/she has just done it, ask him/her to say so.

MODELO: almorzar
E1: *¿Adónde vas para almorzar?*
E2: *Voy a ir a la cafetería para almorzar.*

1. hacer la tarea para mañana
2. comprar la comida
3. sacar fotocopias
4. dormir la siesta
5. comprar ropa elegante
6. escapar de todas las preocupaciones

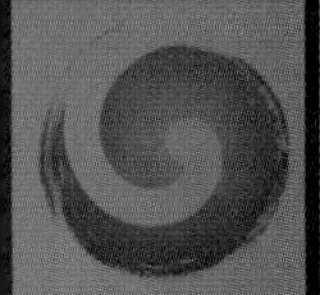

Lección 4

# TEMA 2

## Las celebraciones

*Your daughter is about to get married. Everyone is excited about the event, but the groom is a little nervous about the whole thing, including his new family. Let's help him get to know the family a little bit better.*

**A. Gente diferente.** You and your daughter are very much alike. Your spouse and your son are just the opposite. Explain how by finishing these sentences.

MODELO: dormir mucho
*Mi hija y yo dormimos mucho. Ellos duermen poco.*

1. preferir la comida rápida
2. perder las llaves siempre
3. volver tarde a casa
4. empezar el día temprano
5. servir cenas muy elegantes
6. querer ir a Disneylandia
7. pedir muchos favores
8. almorzar frecuentemente en casa

**Answers for A.** 1) *Preferimos/prefieren.* 2) *Perdemos/pierden.* 3) *Volvemos/vuelven.* 4) *Empezamos/empiezan.* 5) *Servimos/sirven.* 6) *Queremos/quieren.* 7) *Pedimos/piden.* 8) *Almorzamos/almuerzan.*

**B. ¿Qué quieren tomar?** You are at the wedding. Tell the waiter what these people want to drink.

MODELO: los novios
*Los novios quieren tomar champán.*

1. Los primos del novio (tienen seis años)...
2. La abuelita de la novia...
3. Mi compañero/a y yo...
4. Los miembros de la orquesta...
5. Los amigos del novio...
6. El padre de la novia...

**C. Para pedir...** These unusual guests are ordering from the menu. Tell what each one orders.

MODELO: los primos de la novia (tienen seis años)
*Los primos piden un sandwich de crema de cacahuete y mermelada.*

1. La tía gorda de la novia...
2. La amiga que está a dieta...
3. Los tíos muy elegantes del novio...
4. El primo borracho...
5. Mi gato y yo...
6. El perro chihuahua...

**D. Los regalos.** The bride and groom have registered for gifts, but their wedding guests prefer to give them other things. With a partner, choose five of the unusual guests from the lists in the previous two exercises and tell what they prefer to give.

MODELO: *La abuelita prefiere dar fotos viejas de la familia.*

REPASO REPASO REPASO REPASO REPASO REPASO REPASO REPASO REPASO



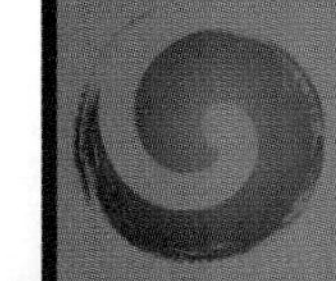

## Lección 4

# TEMA 3

### La rutina diaria

*In order to save money on rent, you have taken a room in a house with an unusual family. Each of you must explain your general routine to the other.*

Answers for A. 1) *Me lavo/me seco.* 2) *Me baño/me visto.* 3) *Me acuesto/me duermo.* 4) *Me caso/me divorcio.* 5) *Me enojo/me calmo.* 6) *Me siento/me levanto.*

**A. ¿Antes o después?** Tell which you do first.

MODELO: despertarse/levantarse
*Primero me despierto, después me levanto.*

1. secarse/lavarse
2. vestirse/bañarse
3. acostarse/dormirse
4. casarse/divorciarse
5. enojarse/calmarse
6. levantarse/sentarse

Answers for B. 1) *Me despierto.* 2) *Despierto.* 3) *Bañarme/me seco.* 4) *Se lavan.* 5) *Lavan.* 6) *Nos abrigamos.*

**B. La familia.** The head of the house will explain the activities. ¡OJO! Not all the verbs are reflexive.

1. Yo _________ (despertarse) a las cinco todas las mañanas.
2. A las siete, yo _________ (despertar) a mis hijos.
3. Después de (bañarse)_________, yo _________ (secarse).
4. Antes de desayunar, mis hijos _________(lavarse) las manos.
5. Usan tanta agua que ellos _________ (lavar) al perro también.
6. Cuando estamos listos para salir, _________ (abrigarse) todos.

Answers for C. 1) *Se despiertan/se duermen.* 2) *Se lava/se seca.* 3) *Me acuesto/me levanto.* 4) *Se divorcian/se casan.* 5) *Te quitas/te pones.* 6) *Nos dormimos/nos despertamos.*

**C. ¡No es cierto!** You have made the following observations about this unusual family, but they completely disagree with what you have said.

MODELO: Yo / acostarse a las ocho de la mañana
E1: *Yo me acuesto a las ocho de la mañana.*
E2: *Yo me levanto a las ocho de la mañana.*

1. Ustedes / despertarse tarde
2. Elena / lavarse el pelo
3. Yo / acostarse temprano
4. Ellos / divorciarse en febrero
5. Tú / quitarse la ropa antes de ir a clase
6. Nosotros / dormirse rápidamente

**D. ¡Ay! El amor.** The head of the household is throwing a party for the neighbors. Ricardo and María are both guests at the party when they see each other across the room and it's love at first sight. Work with a partner to narrate the story of their growing romance.

## Lección 4

# TEMA 4

## Los deportes

*It is New Year's Day and college football is about to declare the new champions. While everyone is gathered around the television, only half of the group is focused on sports.*

**A. Identidades.** Give the name of a famous person to finish each of these sentences.

1. Un gran jugador de fútbol es...
2. Una gran jugadora de básquetbol es...
3. Una gran actriz es...
4. Un gran actor es...
5. Un gran artista es...
6. Una gran artista es...

**B. Los mejores equipos...** Write the ranking of each team. Use ordinal numbers.

Answers for B. 1) *Segundo.* 2) *Décimo.* 3) *Cuarto.* 4) *Octavo.* 5) *Sexto.* 6) *Séptimo.* 7) *Primer.* 8) *Noveno.* 9) *Tercer.*

| Los diez mejores equipos del fútbol americano universitario | |
|---|---|
| 1. Tennessee | 6. Miami |
| 2. Florida State | 7. Florida |
| 3. Ohio State | 8. Wisconsin |
| 4. Arizona | 9. Texas A&M |
| 5. UCLA | 10. Nebraska |

MODELO: UCLA
*UCLA está en quinto lugar.*

1. Florida State
2. Nebraska
3. Arizona
4. Wisconsin
5. Miami
6. Florida
7. Tennessee
8. Texas A&M
9. Ohio State

**C. ¿Qué está(n) haciendo?** Everyone is doing something different during the long string of football games. Change the verbs to the present progressive.

Answers for C. 1) *Está preparando....* 2) *Están jugando....* 3) *Estoy durmiendo....* 4) *Te estás divirtiendo/ estás divirtiéndote....* 5) *Está almorzando....* 6) *Estamos haciendo....* 7) *Estamos limpiando/estamos quitando/están mirando....* 8) *Estoy comiendo....* 9) *Están gritando....* 10) *Están comprando....*

MODELO: Miro el partido de fútbol.
*Estoy mirando el partido de fútbol.*

1. Alejandro prepara las meriendas para la fiesta.
2. Jaime y Carlos juegan con los Game Boy.
3. Yo duermo antes de la fiesta.
4. Tú te diviertes con el perro.
5. Ud. almuerza con sus amigos durante el partido.
6. Hacemos ejercicio en el piso con la música de la banda.
7. Limpiamos la cocina y les quitamos el polvo a los muebles mientras ellos miran el partido.
8. Como una hamburguesa con papas fritas.
9. Roberto y Ricardo gritan por su equipo.
10. Elena y Catalina compran regalos por medio del otro televisor.

**D. Adivinanzas.** Ask a partner to pantomime simple activities or sports. You will tell what he/she is doing. Each does five, then switch.

MODELO: *Está jugando al fútbol.*

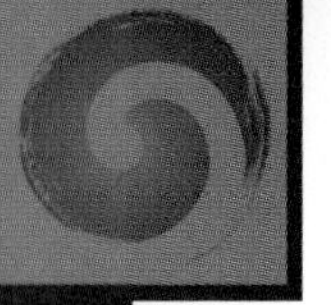



# Lección 5

# TEMA 1

## Cosas del trabajo

*You have just become the assistant to a very famous talent agent. Your first job is to organize a fund-raiser for a children's charity.*

**A. En la agencia de talentos.** Your boss wants to know if you can do these tasks. Tell her if you know how, then say whether it is difficult or easy for you.

MODELO: Sacar fotocopias
*Sí sé sacar fotocopias. Para mí es fácil.*

1. Buscar información en la red.
2. Meter folletos en los sobres.
3. Calcular intereses en las cuentas.
4. Preparar el café por la mañana.

**Answers for B.** 1) *Juega.* 2) *Gana.* 3) *Escribe.* 4) *Canta.* 5) *Es.* 6) *Inventa.*

**B. Un programa de caridad.** Your boss has written a list of areas to be represented by famous people at the fund-raiser for the children's charity. You will recommend a name and pretend to know the person.

MODELO: jugar al baloncesto
*Michael Jordan ya no juega al baloncesto. Para él es importante ayudar a los niños. Yo conozco a Michael Jordan.*

1. jugar al tenis
2. ganar campañas políticas
3. escribir novelas interesantes
4. cantar en inglés y en español
5. ser estrella de cine
6. inventar sistemas para computadoras

**C. ¿Cuánto paga?** Part of the benefit is an auctioned dinner with the following people. In pairs, estimate how much someone will donate for a dinner with each of these celebrities.

MODELO: Michael Jordan
*Un/a aficionado/a paga cinco mil dólares por una cena con Michael Jordan.*

1. Gloria Estefan
2. Hillary Rodham Clinton
3. Antonio Banderas
4. Pamela Anderson
5. Bill Gates
6. Ricky Martin

**D. La invitación.** In a group, create an invitation to this gala event including the following information. Invent the necessary details.

1. ¿Para cuándo es la invitación?
2. ¿Para quiénes son los fondos?
3. ¿Cuánto cuesta la cena?
4. ¿Qué personas famosas van a asistir?

# TEMA 2

## Necesito un trabajo

*Looking for work can be a full-time job in itself. It takes organization, motivation and time. Carlota's husband, Eduardo, wants to find his dream job. He needs some help.*

**A. Una discusión de familia.** When Carlota got home from work today, she asked her lazy husband what he did. Answer for him.

MODELO: ¿Limpiaste el apartamento?
*No limpié el apartamento.*

1. ¿Pagaste las cuentas?
2. ¿Preparaste la comida?
3. ¿Te comiste todo mi pastel?
4. ¿Buscaste trabajo?
5. ¿Escribiste tu currículum vitae?
6. ¿Dormiste toda la tarde?
7. ¿Miraste las telenovelas?
8. ¿Leíste los anuncios de empleo?
9. ¿Empezaste un artículo?
10. ¿Jugaste con el perro?

**Answers for A.** 1) *No pagué....* 2) *No preparé....* 3) *No me comí....* 4) *No busqué....* 5) *No escribí....* 6) *No dormí....* 7) *No miré....* 8) *No leí....* 9) *No empecé....* 10) *No jugué....*

**B. Por eso...** Eduardo did not look for work. Pretend you are Eduardo and give Carlota these excuses.

MODELO: Empecé a buscar trabajo pero... (perder / el periódico).
*Empecé a buscar trabajo pero perdí el periódico.*

1. (Llegar / dos hombres) para vender revistas.
2. (Salir / yo) para comprar un periódico.
3. (Dedicar / yo) mucho tiempo a leer los anuncios de empleo.
4. (Llamar / yo) por teléfono a mi mamá.
5. No (encontrar / yo) un lápiz para escribir mi currículum vitae.
6. (Dormirse / yo).

**Answers for B.** 1) *Llegaron.* 2) *Salí.* 3) *Dediqué.* 4) *Llamé.* 5) *Encontré.* 6) *Me dormí.*

**C. El jefe de Carlota.** Carlota's boss, Mr. Habib, wants to offer Eduardo a job. Pass the message from the boss's secretary to Carlota to Eduardo.

SECRETARIA: Carlota, tengo un mensaje _________(1) (*for you, formal*) del jefe.
CARLOTA: Eduardo, tengo un mensaje _________(2) (*for you, familiar*) del jefe.
SECRETARIA: El Sr. Habib tiene un trabajo para Eduardo. El Sr. Habib quiere hablar _________(3) (*with him*) a las 10:00 de la mañana.
CARLOTA: Eduardo, el jefe quiere hablar _________(4) (*with you, familiar*) a las 10:00 de la mañana.
SECRETARIA: Eduardo puede venir _________(5) (*with you, formal*) mañana.
CARLOTA: Puedes ir _________(6) (*with me*) mañana.

**Answers for C.** 1) *Para Ud.* 2) *Para ti.* 3) *Con él.* 4) *Contigo.* 5) *Con Ud.* 6) *Conmigo.*

Lección 5

# TEMA 3

## La entrevista de trabajo

*¡Pobre Eduardo! After the interview, he is so nervous that he goes to a friend's house to await the results.*

Answers for A. 1) *Me puse.* 2) *Puse.* 3) *Vine.* 4) *Quise/olvidé.* 5) *Pude.* 6) *Hice.*

**A. ¿Qué hizo Ud.?** You are Eduardo. Tell your friend what you did after your interview.

MODELO: (Despedirse) del Sr. Habib.
*Me despedí del Sr. Habib.*

1. (Ponerse) muy nervioso al final.
2. (Poner) mis papeles en el portafolios.
3. (Venir) aquí a tu casa para esperarte.
4. (Querer) llamar al Sr. Habib para decirle las cosas que yo (olvidar) durante la entrevista.
5. No (poder) llamar porque dejé el número en el coche.
6. (Hacer) una lista de cosas para mencionar en una nota de agradecimiento (*thank-you note*).

Answers for B. 1) *Cocinó.* 2) *Lloraron.* 3) *Gritaste.* 4) *Llamamos.* 5) *Hicieron.*

**B. ¿Qué hicieron todos?** What did these people do when they found out that you (Eduardo) got the job?

MODELO: Yo (querer) champán.
*Yo quise champán.*

1. Carlota (cocinar) una cena especial.
2. Los padres de Carlota (llorar).
3. Tú (gritar).
4. Mi hermana y yo (llamar) a nuestros padres.
5. Todos los amigos (hacer) una fiesta.

**C. La fiesta.** You (Eduardo) and the other classmates had a party to celebrate your accomplishment. Tell what you did to plan the party, what food you brought, and what happened at the party.

MODELO: *Yo hice una lista de invitados.*

Answers for D. 1) *Tuvieron.* 2) *Fueron.* 3) *Fue.* 4) *Llegaron.* 5) *Dijimos/Fuimos.* 6) *Pasaron.* 7) *Estuvieron.* 8) *Se quedó.*

**D. ¡Pobrecitos!** Some of your friends missed the party. Explain why.

MODELO: Patricia (estar) en San Francisco.
*Patricia estuvo en San Francisco.*

1. Noelia y Ricardo (tener) que trabajar.
2. Roberto y Gregorio (ir) al partido de futbol.
3. Daniel (ir) a México por negocios.
4. Kira y Érika (llegar) tarde del trabajo.
5. Mis amigos y yo (decir) que (ir) a otra fiesta.
6. Sus hermanas (pasar) horas en un atasco (*traffic jam*).
7. Sandra y Miguel (estar) en Miami.
8. Su tía (quedarse) en casa con su hijo.

## Lección 5

# TEMA 4

### La carrera

*Carlos and Alejandra are exploring career fields. Each has had some experience working while in college. Their career counselor has told them to make a list of experiences, skills, and abilities in order to start a search for their dream jobs.*

**A. La experiencia.** The counselor has provided a list of verbs to jog their memories about different skills that they have developed. Help them organize their work experience by telling which tasks they performed with each job.

| mesero | cajero | secretario | dependiente |
|---|---|---|---|

MODELO: cajero
*calcular las cuentas*

- servir a los clientes
- contar dinero
- escribir informes
- archivar documentos
- vender
- limpiar
- poner las mesas
- quitar las mesas
- hacer citas y reservaciones
- ir al banco
- leer muchos informes
- aprender y repetir de memoria muchas especialidades
- calmar a los clientes impacientes
- calcular las cuentas
- organizar la oficina
- traducir documentos bilingües
- operar computadoras
- navegar por la red
- pedir dinero y dar cambio

**B. En el futuro.** Tell which of their skills might be helpful in these professions. Add any other skills that you believe these professions require.

MODELO: actor
*Aprender y repetir de memoria…*

1. contador
2. ingeniero
3. administrador de empresas
4. agente de talentos
5. profesor
6. abogado

**C. ¿Y Ud.?** What profession are you thinking about for your future? Choose one and write a list of five tasks or skills required to do that job.

MODELO: *Asistente de vuelo: servir al público, limpiar, saber actuar en emergencias…*

# 7 La vida cotidiana

LECCIÓN SIETE

CHECK OUT THE *¡TRATO HECHO!* WEBSITE AND CD-ROM FOR ACTIVITIES, GAMES, SELF-TESTS, AND MUCH MORE!

TEMA 1

## La ciudad y el campo

- La vida urbana
- La vida rural
- El imperfecto
- Más sobre el imperfecto

TEMA 2

## Un accidente con el coche nuevo

- ¿Cómo funciona?
- Un accidente
- El pretérito y el imperfecto
- La narración en el pasado

TEMA 3

## Las emergencias

- En la sala de urgencias
- El tratamiento de José
- Contraste entre el pretérito y el imperfecto
- Más práctica con el pretérito y el imperfecto

TEMA 4

## En la calle

- ¿Dónde está...?
- Cómo protegerse
- *Se* impersonal
- Más práctica con *se* impersonal

# ¡TRATO HECHO!

- Rincón profesional: La ley
- A escuchar
- A leer
- A escribir

# La vida urbana

## La ciudad y el campo

*Los estudiantes del profesor Yuja hablan sobre la juventud de sus padres….*

PROF. YUJA: Todos ustedes tienen familiares que nacieron en el extranjero. ¿Cómo era la vida en sus países?

CARLOS: Mis abuelos son de Bogotá. Ellos dicen que la vida era muy tranquila y no había tantos peligros como ahora. Después de comer caminaban por el vecindario mientras los niños jugaban en la calle.

ISABEL: Mis padres vivían en un pueblo pequeño en Perú. Cuando eran novios las costumbres eran muy rígidas y dicen que nunca salían solos. Siempre tenían que llevar a un chaperón.

MARY: Mi padre nació en Inglaterra, pero no recuerda nada porque vino a los Estados Unidos cuando era niño. Conoció a mi mamá en España, cuando ella trabajaba en la Embajada Americana y mi papá estaba en el ejército.

ANA: Mis padres vinieron a los Estados Unidos cuando se casaron. Pensaban venir a trabajar a Los Ángeles sólo por un par de años, pero les gustó mucho la gran ciudad.

PROF. YUJA: ¿No les gustaba Costa Rica?

ANA: No mucho, porque vivían en una zona rural y se aburrían muchísimo. Dicen que no había nada que hacer. Ahora que se jubilaron, prefieren la tranquilidad de Costa Rica.

**A. ¿Comprende Ud.?** Conteste las siguientes preguntas según el diálogo.

**Answers for A.** 1) *Un chaperón.* 2) *Cuando se casaron.* 3) *En España.* 4) *Porque vivían en una zona rural.*

1. ¿Quién salía con los padres de Isabel cuando eran novios?
2. ¿Cuándo vinieron los padres de Ana a los Estados Unidos?
3. ¿Dónde se conocieron los padres de Mary?
4. ¿Por qué no les gustaba Costa Rica a los padres de Ana?

**B. Mi niñez.** Cambie las palabras en letra cursiva (*italics*) para describir su niñez (*childhood*).

MODELO: De niño/a mi familia vivía en *San Antonio.*
*De niña mi familia vivía en Miami.*

1. Era un/a niño/a *tímido/a.*
2. Tenía *muchos* amigos.
3. Mi mejor amigo/a se llamaba *Rebeca Morán.*
4. Nunca comía *frutas.*
5. No tenía *animales.*
6. Siempre quería tener *un perro.*
7. Para divertirme, me gustaba *leer.*
8. No me gustaba *practicar deportes.*

**C. A los diez años.** Cuando Ud. tenía diez años, ¿con qué frecuencia hacía estas cosas?

nunca | con frecuencia | casi nunca | todos los días | de vez en cuando | siempre

1. Escuchaba la radio.
2. Miraba la televisión.
3. Jugaba al ajedrez (*chess*).
4. Faltaba a la escuela.
5. Tocaba un instrumento musical.
6. Me peleaba con mis hermanos.
7. Leía.
8. Dormía hasta el mediodía.
9. Comía en McDonald's.
10. Obedecía a mis padres.

**D. ¡Antes las cosas eran diferentes!** Su abuela acaba de escribirle a Ud. una carta mencionando cómo era su vida hace cincuenta años. Había cosas mejores y peores. Escriba algunas de las cosas que su abuela mencionó en la lista y compare su lista con tres compañeros.

| Lo mejor | Lo peor |
| --- | --- |
| | |

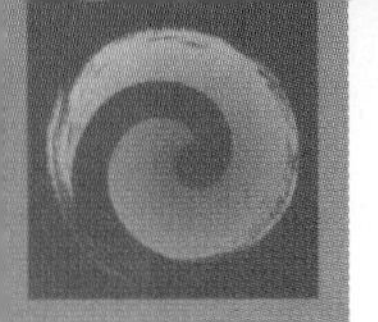

# La vida rural

## En el campo

*Lázaro pasa el día en el campo con sus estudiantes....*

LÁZARO: ¡Qué tranquilidad! ¡Qué paisaje tan bello! Vamos todos a respirar este aire tan puro. Raúl, ¿qué pasa?

RAÚL: Estoy un poco triste porque recuerdo el lugar en donde vivía en El Salvador. También allí había un lago. Mis padres tenían una granja con muchos animales. Mi papá sembraba maíz y teníamos muchos árboles frutales.

LÁZARO: ¿Qué hacían Miguel y tú?

RAÚL: Dábamos de comer a las gallinas.

LÁZARO: ¿Qué te gustaba más de ese lugar?

RAÚL: Me gustaba el lago. Los domingos venían mis tíos y mis primos e íbamos a comer y a nadar allí. Recuerdo que un día estábamos jugando cuando empezó a llover y tuvimos que recoger rápidamente toda la comida.

LÁZARO: ¿Pudieron comer después?

RAÚL: Sí, mientras llovía nosotros comimos y cantamos en la camioneta de mi tío Luis. ¡Nunca me divertí tanto!

**Answers for A.** 1) *En una granja.* 2) *Gallinas y otros animales.* 3) *Sus primos y tíos.* 4) *En el lago.*

**A. ¿Comprende Ud.?** Conteste las siguientes preguntas según el diálogo.

1. ¿Dónde vivían los padres de Raúl?
2. ¿Qué tipo de animales tenían en la granja?
3. ¿Quienes visitaban a Raúl los domingos?
4. ¿Dónde nadaban?

**B. En la escuela secundaria.** Lea las siguientes oraciones y decida cuál describe cómo era Ud. en la escuela secundaria.

1. a. Me gustaba la escuela.
   b. No me gustaba la escuela.
2. a. Llegaba tarde a la escuela a veces.
   b. Siempre llegaba a la escuela a tiempo.
3. a. Vivía cerca de la escuela.
   b. Vivía lejos de la escuela.
4. a. Practicaba deportes.
   b. No practicaba ningún deporte.
5. a. Tocaba un instrumento musical.
   b. No tocaba ningún instrumento musical.
6. a. Sacaba buenas notas.
   b. Sacaba malas notas.
7. a. Salía mucho con amigos/as.
   b. Me quedaba en casa.
8. a. Era muy activo/a.
   b. No hacía casi nada.

**C. Lo bueno y lo malo.** Tanto vivir en la ciudad como vivir en el campo tienen ventajas y desventajas. Hable con un/a compañero/a de lo mejor y lo peor de la ciudad y del campo. ¿Están de acuerdo? ¿Dónde prefiere vivir Ud.? ¿Y él/ella? Miren las fotos a continuación y utilícenlas para ayudar en su discusión.

**Follow up for C.** After students have shared their problem list in small groups, write on the board the most obvious problems mentioned in each group.

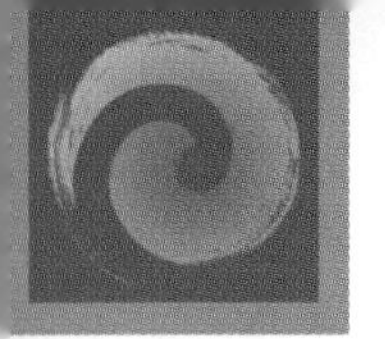

# El imperfecto
## (*What used to happen*)

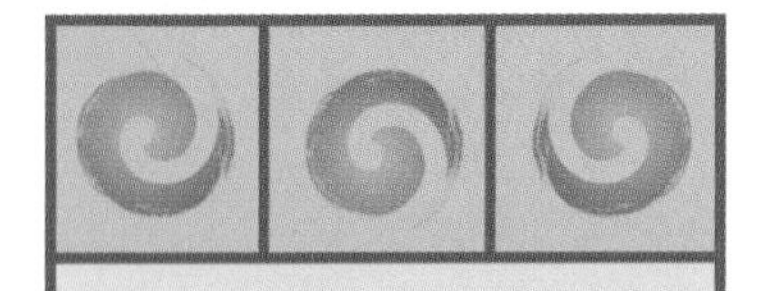

**Para averiguar**

1. What do you describe with the imperfect?
2. What are the imperfect endings for **-ar** verbs? And what are the endings for **-er** and **-ir** verbs? What is the imperfect of **hay**?
3. Which three verbs are irregular in the imperfect?
4. What are three different ways that **comíamos** might be expressed in English?

- To talk about how things *used to be*, use the imperfect. Unlike the preterite, which describes the completed aspect of an event, the imperfect describes the habitual or ongoing nature of past actions. Following are the forms of the imperfect.

| | trabajar | comer | vivir |
|---|---|---|---|
| yo | trabaj**aba** | com**ía** | viv**ía** |
| tú | trabaj**abas** | com**ías** | viv**ías** |
| él, ella, usted | trabaj**aba** | com**ía** | viv**ía** |
| nosotros/as | trabaj**ábamos** | com**íamos** | viv**íamos** |
| vosotros/as | trabaj**abais** | com**íais** | viv**íais** |
| ellos, ellas, ustedes | trabaj**aban** | com**ían** | viv**ían** |

- The imperfect of **hay** is **había**.

- There are only three irregular verbs in the imperfect.

| | ir | ser | ver |
|---|---|---|---|
| yo | **iba** | **era** | **veía** |
| tú | **ibas** | **eras** | **veías** |
| él, ella, usted | **iba** | **era** | **veía** |
| nosotros/as | **íbamos** | **éramos** | **veíamos** |
| vosotros/as | **ibais** | **erais** | **veíais** |
| ellos, ellas, ustedes | **iban** | **eran** | **veían** |

- The imperfect may be expressed in a variety of ways in English.

**Habitual actions**

**Iba** a la casa de mis abuelos. — *I (often)* ***went*** *to my grandparents' house.* / ***I used to go*** *to my grandparents' house.* / ***I would go*** *to my grandparents' house.*

Siempre **comíamos** temprano. — *We always* ***ate*** *early.* / *We always* ***used to eat*** *early.* / ***We would*** *always* ***eat*** *early.*

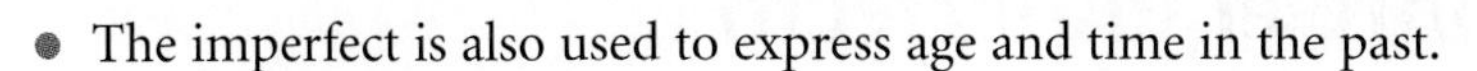

- The imperfect is also used to express age and time in the past.

| | |
|---|---|
| **Tenía** quince años entonces. | *I was fifteen then.* |
| **Eran** las diez de la noche. | *It was ten o'clock at night.* |

## A lo personal

**A. Ahora y entonces.** Indicate if the following statements are true regarding your present situation. Then say if they were also true in high school.

MODELO: Tengo una computadora.
*Sí, ahora tengo una computadora.*
*En la escuela secundaria no tenía una computadora.*

1. Vivo con mis padres.
2. Tengo que estudiar mucho.
3. Como en la cafetería.
4. Los estudiantes estudian mucho.
5. Los libros son caros.
6. Estoy en clase todo el día.
7. Saco buenas notas.
8. Siempre hago la tarea.
9. Conozco bien a mis profesores.
10. Hay clases todos los días.

**B. En estas ocasiones.** Ask a partner what he/she generally used to do as a child on the following occasions. Then switch roles.

MODELO: los fines de semana
E1: *De niño/a, ¿qué hacías los fines de semana?*
E2: *Jugaba con los otros niños que vivían en la misma calle.*

1. para su cumpleaños
2. los veranos
3. cuando hacía mal tiempo
4. cuando hacía buen tiempo
5. para divertirse
6. los domingos por la tarde
7. cuando tenía mucho dinero
8. cuando no tenía dinero

**C. ¿De niño?** Answer the following questions based on your childhood. Then use these questions to interview a classmate about his/her childhood and report to the class what you learned about your partner. (¡OJO! You will need to use third-person forms when you report what your partner answered to the questions.)

- ¿Dónde vivía?
- ¿Qué comía?
- ¿Con quiénes jugaba?
- ¿Cómo se llamaba su escuela primaria?
- ¿Quién era su maestro/a favorito/a?
- ¿Qué hacía en su tiempo libre?
- ¿Adónde iba de vacaciones?
- ¿Qué miraba en la televisión?

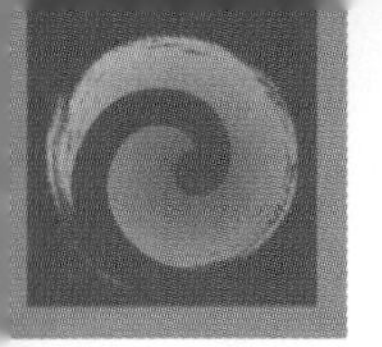

# Más sobre el imperfecto
## (*Interrupted actions*)

1. Do you use imperfect or preterite for events in progress in the past?
2. Which tense do you use for the action that interrupts the event in progress?

- Use the imperfect tense also to describe an activity in progress that was interrupted or stopped by another event in the past (often in the preterite tense).

  **Nadábamos** en el lago cuando empezó a llover.
  *We were swimming in the lake when it began to rain.*

  swimming ——————/——→
  rain

  Ustedes **estudiaban** cuando yo llamé.
  *You were studying when I called.*

  studying ——————/——→
  phone

  **Iba** a la tienda cuando vi el accidente.
  *I was going to the store when I saw the accident.*

  trip to the store ——————/——→
  crash!

- Another use of the imperfect tense expresses two activities in progress at the same time. These two activities are often joined by **mientras** (*while*).

  Mientras los niños **nadaban**, los padres **charlaban**.
  *While the children were swimming, the parents were chatting.*

  Mientras **llovía**, nosotros **jugábamos** en casa.
  *While it was raining, we played at home.*

  Lucero **silbaba** mientras **trabajaba**.
  *Lucero whistled while she worked.*

## A lo personal

**A. ¿Qué hacía?** Tell what you were doing when you were interrupted by the following events.

MODELO: me caí
*Yo corría por el parque cuando me caí.*

1. sonó el despertador
2. los amigos llegaron para comer
3. empezó a llover
4. encontré una bolsa de papel con 500 dólares
5. mis amigos gritaron "sorpresa"
6. oí un accidente en la calle
7. recordé que no traía dinero
8. se acabó la gasolina

**B. ¡Se apagaron las luces!** Tell what the following people were doing when the lights went out.

MODELO: el estudiante
*El estudiante estudiaba cuando se apagaron las luces.*

1. el profesor de matemáticas
2. la secretaria
3. el bibliotecario
4. los niños
5. nosotros en la clase de español
6. el cocinero
7. yo
8. la operadora de teléfonos
9. el gato
10. el mesero

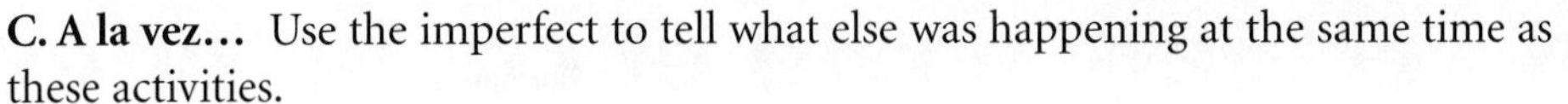

**C. A la vez...** Use the imperfect to tell what else was happening at the same time as these activities.

MODELO: Mientras mi mamá preparaba el desayuno...
*Mientras mi mamá preparaba el desayuno,* ***yo me vestía.***

1. Mientras los estudiantes hacían el examen, la profesora...
2. Mientras yo miraba la tele, yo...
3. Mientras el gato no estaba, los ratoncitos (*little mice*)...
4. Mientras los niños tomaban leche y galletas (*cookies*), los adultos...
5. Mientras yo estaba en clase hoy, el perro...
6. Mientras ustedes limpiaban la casa, nosotros...

**D. El saltamontes y la hormiga.** Use the imperfect tense to finish narrating the story of the grasshopper and the ant.

Hace muchos veranos, cerca de un lago muy popular entre turistas y sus familias, (1) ________ (vivir) dos enemigos: un saltamontes perezoso que (2) ________ (llamarse) Sam y una hormiga, Sally, que (3) ________ (ser) muy trabajadora.
A Sam le (4) ________ (gustar) pasar todos los días del verano bailando, jugando al tenis con los amigos y más que nada, durmiendo.
Todos los días Sam (5) ________ (dormir) hasta el mediodía, mientras Sally (6) ________ (despertarse) con el sol. Mientras Sam (7) ________ (bailar) hip hop y (8) ________ (burlarse) de Sally, ella (9) ________ (pensar) en el futuro y (10) ________ (cultivar) su jardín. Todas las tardes después de comer, ella (11) ________ (ir) al lago y (12) ________ (buscar) comida en los picnics de los turistas que siempre (13) ________ (traer) la comida más exquisita.
Al terminar el verano, Sally (14) ________ (tener) en su casa bastante comida para el invierno más cruel. El primer día que (15) ________ (hacer) frío, Sally escuchó un "por favoooor" muy triste. Cuando abrió la puerta, allí (16) ________ (estar) Sam. ¡Pobrecito! (17) ________(tener) miedo y hambre. Mientras Sam (18) ________ (pedir) perdón, también (19) ________(pedir) comida. La pobre Sally no (20) ________ (saber) qué hacer. ¡Tener compasión y compartir los frutos de su labor, o burlarse de él, como antes él se burlaba de ella!

**E. ¿Cómo se sentían?** With a classmate, use the imperfect to describe how Sally was feeling when she saw Sam, how Sam was feeling while he was talking to Sally, and finally, how they each spent the rest of the winter.

# TEMA 2 Un accidente con el coche nuevo

## ¿Cómo funciona?

Antes de salir de viaje, es importante…

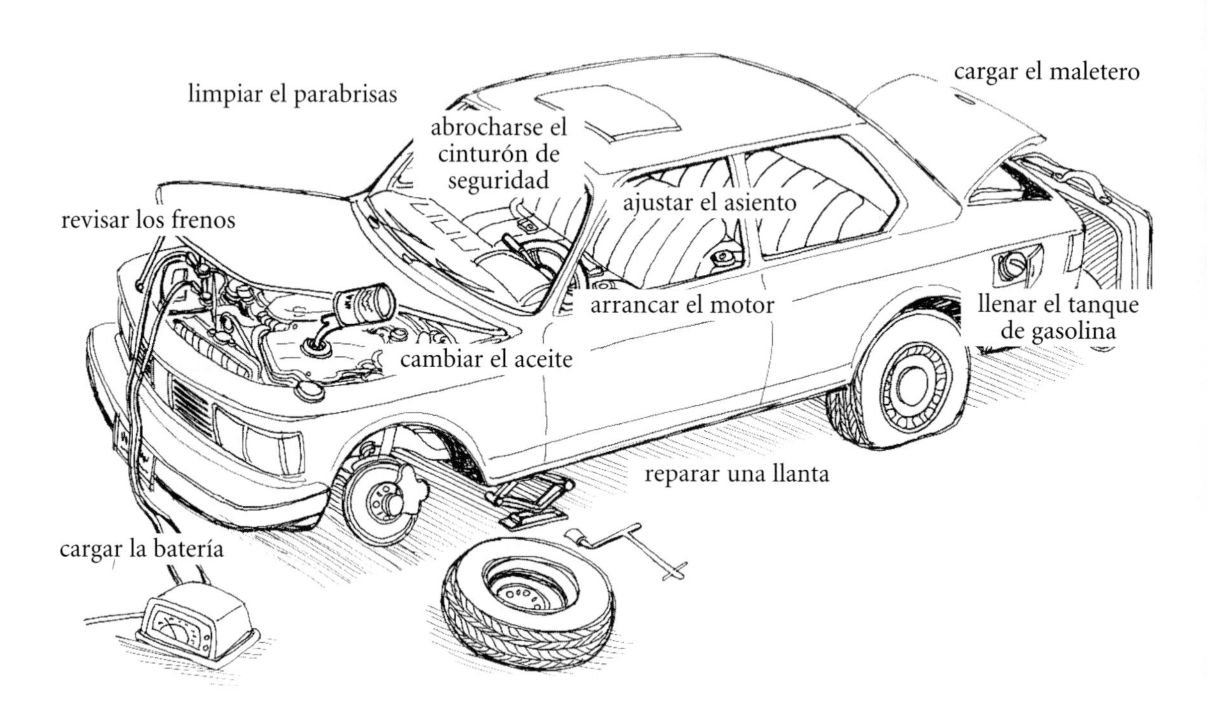


**New words:** condado, equipo de sonido, lujo.

### El coche nuevo de Ana

*Ana va a un concesionario para ver un coche que le interesa….*

VENDEDOR: Buenas tardes, ¿puedo ayudarla?

ANA: Sí, gracias. Necesito comprar un auto y leí en el periódico que ustedes tienen una gran venta.

VENDEDOR: Claro, además tenemos los mejores precios del condado. ¿Prefiere un auto pequeño o algo más grande? ¿Nuevo o de segunda mano?

ANA: Prefiero un auto mediano y nuevo.

VENDEDOR: Este rojo es una buena compra.

ANA: ¡Qué bonito! Vi la foto en el periódico. Pero aquí dice que cuesta 18.000 dólares y en el anuncio decía que costaba sólo 15.000. Además, en el anuncio se veía más grande, tenía un buen equipo de sonido y asientos de cuero.

VENDEDOR: Bueno, al pie del anuncio decía en letras pequeñas que el precio de algunos modelos empezaba en 15.000 dólares y que los accesorios de lujo eran opcionales. Es el último que tenemos y esta mañana vino una familia que estaba muy interesada.

ANA: Está bien. Voy a comprarlo.

**A. ¿Comprende Ud.?** Conteste las siguientes preguntas según el diálogo.

Answers for A. 1) *Un coche.* 2) *Mediano y nuevo.* 3) *15.000.* 4) *Rojo.*

1. ¿Qué quiere comprar Ana?
2. ¿Qué tipo de coche quiere Ana?
3. ¿Cuál era el precio del coche en el anuncio?
4. ¿De qué color es el coche que compra Ana?

**B. ¿Qué parte es?** Adivine la parte del coche según la descripción.

New word: *maleta*

1. Hay cuatro y son negras.
2. Se usan para parar el coche.
3. Es necesario cambiar esto cada 3.000 millas.
4. Se vende por galones en los Estados Unidos; por litros en México.
5. La ley dice que hay que abrocharse (*fasten*) esto.
6. Se ponen las maletas aquí.

a. la gasolina
b. el aceite
c. el maletero
d. las llantas
e. el cinturón de seguridad
f. los frenos

**C. Mi coche nuevo.** Ud. buscaba un auto nuevo y vio este anuncio en el periódico. ¡Éste es el coche perfecto para Ud., pero necesita dinero para el abono (*payment*)! Ud. quiere un préstamo (*loan*) del banco. Es importante explicar las ventajas de este modelo al empleado del banco. Escriba una lista indicando los accesorios de este modelo y luego, con su compañero/a que hace el papel de empleado del banco, explique por qué este coche es ideal.

**D. Una mirada hacia atrás.** El transporte de hoy es muy diferente del transporte de los años cuando sus abuelos y sus bisabuelos eran jóvenes. Hable con un/a compañero/a de cómo era el transporte en la época de la Primera Guerra mundial (*WWI*) y/o la Segunda Guerra mundial (*WWII*). ¿Cómo iban a la escuela? ¿Había aviones tan grandes como los de hoy?

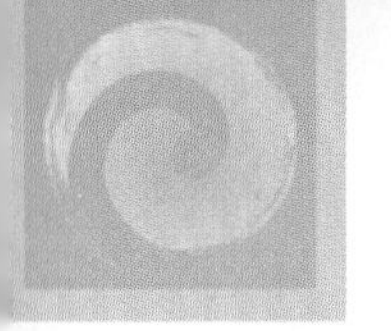

# Un accidente

## Ana tiene un choque

*Ana y José van en el coche nuevo cuando de pronto....*

JOSÉ: Me encanta tu coche nuevo. El papá de Fabiola tenía uno igual, pero lo vendió. Mira, ese señor está conduciendo muy rápido y va a perder el control.

ANA: ¡Ay, cuidado! Va a chocar con nosotros.

*Ana y el señor Antúnez chocan....*

JOSÉ: ¡Ay, me duele mucho la pierna!

ANA: ¡Pobrecito! Por favor, espera un minuto. ¿Alguien tiene un teléfono celular?

SR. ANTÚNEZ: Yo tengo uno. ¡Lo siento mucho! Estaba hablando por teléfono con un cliente y no vi su automóvil.

ANA: ¿Por qué hablaba por teléfono y conducía al mismo tiempo? Mi primo resultó herido y mire cómo está mi coche. Lo acababa de comprar. ¿Qué voy a hacer ahora?

SR. ANTÚNEZ: No se preocupe, yo tengo seguro. Ellos pueden pagar los gastos del hospital y arreglar su auto. Aquí tiene mi licencia de conducir y mi tarjeta del seguro. Voy a pedir una ambulancia.

**A. ¿Comprende Ud.?** Conteste las siguientes preguntas según el diálogo.

1. ¿Quién tenía un coche como el de Ana?
2. ¿Quién conducía el coche que chocó con ellos?
3. ¿Quién fue herido?
4. ¿Qué pidió el Sr. Antúnez?

**Answers for A.** 1) *El padre de Fabiola.* 2) *El Sr. Antúnez.* 3) *José.* 4) *Una ambulancia.*

**B. Mi accidente.** Describa un accidente que Ud. tuvo, quizás en coche o en bicicleta o esquiando en las montañas o... Escuche la historia del accidente de su compañero/a y decidan quién sufrió más.

**C. 911.** Ud. acaba de ser testigo de un accidente. Con otro/a estudiante, invente los detalles del accidente que Ud. vio, para contestar las preguntas de la operadora de emergencias del 911. Uno/a de Uds. debe hacer el papel de operadora y el/la otro/a debe contestar a todas las preguntas con todos los datos necesarios.

1. ¿Dónde ocurrió el accidente?
2. ¿Sabe Ud. exactamente a qué hora ocurrió este accidente?
3. ¿Hubo algún herido en el lugar del accidente?
4. ¿Qué hacía Ud. cuando ocurrió el accidente?
5. ¿Había más gente en la calle cuando pasó esto?
6. ¿Cuánto tiempo tardó en llegar la policía?
7. ¿Fue necesario llamar una ambulancia?
8. ¿Puede recordar otros detalles importantes de este accidente?

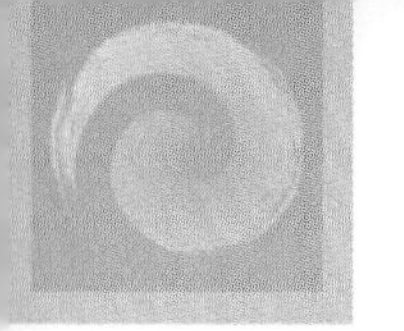

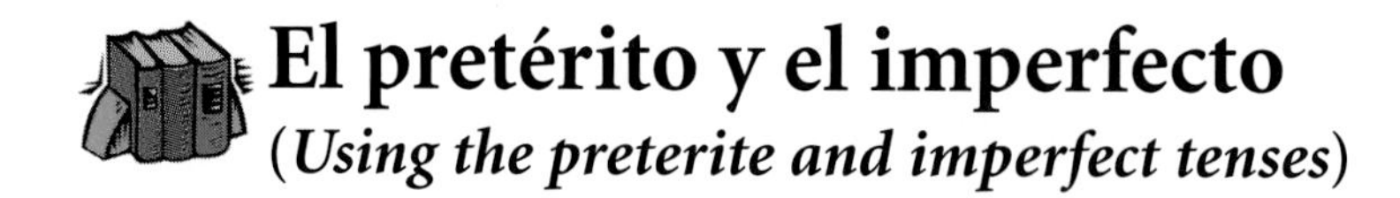

# El pretérito y el imperfecto
## (*Using the preterite and imperfect tenses*)

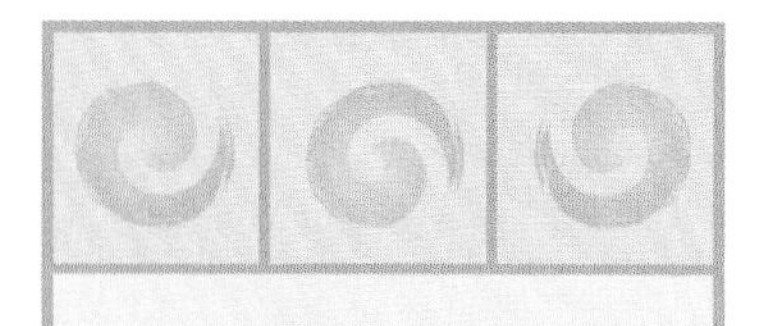

**Para averiguar**

1. Do you use the preterite or the imperfect to describe a completed action?
2. Which do you use to give background information against which an action takes place?
3. What is the difference between "**estaba enojado**" and "**se enojó**"?

**Expansion.** Point out to students that the preterite may describe mental or emotional reactions in the past, but not conditions.

**Use the preterite to:**

- describe single events in the past that are considered completed.

| | |
|---|---|
| **Nací** en Puerto Rico. | *I was born in Puerto Rico.* |
| **Vinimos** a Nueva York en 1981. | *We came to New York in 1981.* |

- describe events that took place a specific number of times.

| | |
|---|---|
| Tu amigo **llamó** cinco veces ayer. | *Your friend called five times yesterday.* |
| **Comí** en ese restaurante la semana pasada. | *I ate in that restaurant last week.* |

- express the beginning or end of an action.

| | |
|---|---|
| **Entré** a la escuela en 1982 y **me gradué** en 1994. | *I began school in 1982 and I graduated in 1994.* |
| La clase **terminó** temprano ayer. | *Class ended early yesterday.* |

- narrate a sequence of events.

| | |
|---|---|
| Esta mañana **me levanté, comí, me vestí** y **me fui** para la universidad. | *This morning I got up, ate, got dressed, and left for school.* |
| **Vi** el anuncio y **compré** el auto. | *I saw the ad and bought the car.* |

- describe mental or emotional *reactions* in the past.

| | |
|---|---|
| Me **enojé**. | *I got angry.* |
| Se **sorprendieron**. | *They were (became) surprised.* |

- While the preterite and the imperfect are both different aspects of the past, they are not interchangeable. Each gives a different "message" about time frames.

- The preterite is often described as an action that is "perfectly" complete within the sentence and captures an instant of time, like a photograph.

| | |
|---|---|
| Yo **leí** el anuncio. | *I read the ad.* (action complete) |
| Tú **compraste** el coche nuevo. | *You bought the new car.* (action complete) |

- The imperfect is often described in terms of a video camera. The focus is on the progression of the action through time, rather than on the completeness. In fact, use of the imperfect sometimes indicates that the activity may have been abandoned before completion. It serves to set the background to other actions.

| | |
|---|---|
| Yo **leía** el anuncio… cuando llegaste. | *I was reading the ad…when you arrived.* (action interrupted) |
| Yo **iba** a la tienda… cuando vi el accidente. | *I was on my way to the store…when I saw the accident.* (action interrupted) |

- Compare the following sentences and tell why the imperfect or preterite is used.

Mientras yo **hablaba** con el vendedor, otro cliente **compró** el coche.
**Hacía** calor y yo **estaba** enojada cuando el vendedor me **ofreció** otro coche.

## A lo personal

**A. De niño y ahora.** Tell if you used to do the following things on school days as a child. Then tell if you did them yesterday or the last day you went to class.

MODELO: ir a la escuela en autobús
*Sí, de niño/a iba a la escuela en autobús.* o *No, ayer no fui a la escuela en autobús.*

1. estar en la escuela todo el día
2. comer en la cafetería
3. llevar vaqueros a la escuela
4. perder su tarea
5. hacer preguntas en clase
6. jugar a un deporte después de las clases
7. regresar a casa después de las clases
8. salir por la noche

**B. Los diez primeros minutos.** In small groups, prepare a description of the first ten minutes of class today, adding as many details as possible. Compare your group's recollection with that of other groups.

- ¿Qué estaban haciendo todos cuando la clase empezó?
- ¿Qué había en el salón de clase? ¿Dónde estaba todo?
- ¿Hacía frío o calor en el salón de clase?
- ¿Qué hicieron primero? Luego, ¿qué hicieron?
- ¿Llegaron tarde algunos estudiantes?

**C. ¿Por qué?** Explain the circumstances that caused you to do these things the last time you did them.

MODELO: Estudié toda la noche porque...
*Estudié toda la noche porque tenía tres exámenes al día siguiente.*

1. Me puse un suéter porque...
2. Tomé una Coca-Cola porque...
3. Me dormí en clase porque...
4. No fui a clase porque...
5. Me puse nervioso/a en clase porque...
6. Fui a la biblioteca porque...
7. Trabajé todo el fin de semana porque...
8. Preparé una comida especial porque...
9. No dormí nada anoche porque...
10. Desayuné sólo leche esta mañana porque...

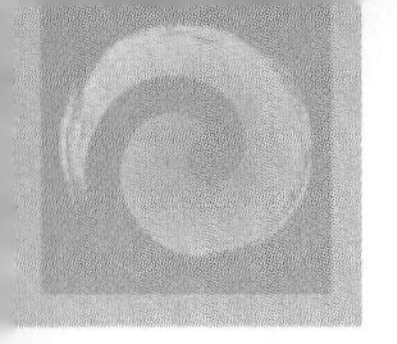

# La narración en el pasado
## (*Narration in the past*)

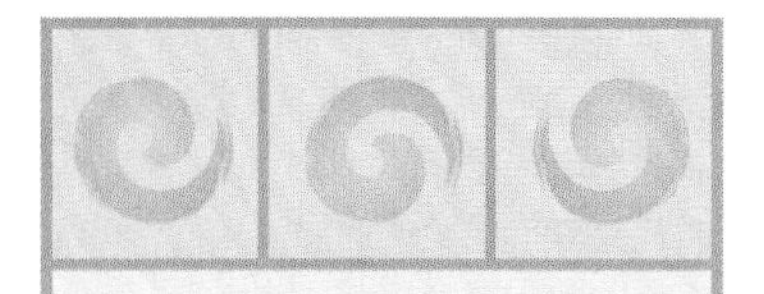

### Para averiguar

1. Do you use the preterite or the imperfect to describe events that took place in a certain order? Which tense do you use to give background information?
2. If you were describing a play that you saw, would you use the preterite or the imperfect to describe the scene where the curtain first went up? Which tense would you use to describe what the characters did, advancing the story?
3. Can you mix preterite and imperfect in the same sentence?

- When you tell a story in the past, you will often use both the preterite and imperfect aspects of the past. Use the preterite to describe events that took place in sequence. Use the imperfect to set the scene, giving background information to a sequence of several events. For example, if you were describing a play, you would use the imperfect to describe the stage when the curtain went up.

  Una mujer y un hombre **estaban** en una cocina. El hombre **hablaba** por teléfono y la mujer **leía** el periódico. La cocina **era** pequeña y **había** sólo una mesa con dos sillas. Según el reloj en la pared, **eran** las nueve de la mañana.

- In the preceding scene nothing has happened in the sense that no event occurred; however the scene has been set. The events that take place, which advance the story, are in the preterite.

  ...Según el reloj en la pared, eran las nueve de la mañana. Después de algunos minutos un muchacho **abrió** la puerta y **entró**. **Abrazó** a su madre pero no le **dijo** nada a su padre.

- The following diagram is useful to help visualize the use of the preterite and the imperfect when telling a story.

  Un muchacho **abrió** la puerta, **entró**, **se sentó** y **se comió** una manzana.
  **Tenía** el pelo rubio.

| abrió | entró | se sentó | se comió |
|---|---|---|---|
| x | x | x | x |

  ——————————————————————→
  tenía

  The X's represent events that can be sequenced in order (the preterite). The continuous line represents the background information, which cannot be ordered in the sequence of events, but rather is true throughout the scene (the imperfect). In the example, the boy's having blond hair cannot be ordered before or after the thing he does.

- In Spanish, another common way to talk about recurring events in the past is the imperfect of the verb **soler** (**solía**) + *infinitive*.

| | |
|---|---|
| **Solía** llover a las cuatro de la tarde en el verano. | *It used to rain at four o'clock in the summer.* |
| Nosotros **solíamos** ir a la playa. | *We used to go to the beach.* |
| Ella **solía** estudiar por las tardes. | *She used to study in the afternoons.* |
| Mis abuelos **solían** visitarnos en verano. | *My grandparents used to visit us during the summer.* |

## A lo personal

**A. ¿Qué historia?** In five sentences or less tell some of the main points of a favorite childhood fairy tale without naming the characters. After your description, your classmates should be able to guess which one it is.

MODELO: E1: *Había una muchacha que vivía en Kansas. Tenía un pequeño perro negro. Un día se enojó y se fue de la casa. Después regresó porque hacía muy mal tiempo. Ella se durmió y cuando se despertó, estaba en otro país con habitantes muy bajos.*
E2: *El mago de Oz.*

**B. Caperucita Roja.** Using your knowledge of Red Riding Hood and the cues provided, complete the story as indicated.

Érase una vez (1)__________ (haber) una muchacha que (2)__________ (llamarse) "Caperucita Roja". Ella y su mamá (3)__________ (vivir) en una casa que (4)__________ (ser) muy bonita en el desierto de Tucson. A Caperucita Roja le (5)__________ (gustar) caminar por el desierto y jugar con los animales. Un día su mamá le (6)__________ (decir): "Caperucita Roja, tu abuelita está muy enferma. Tú tienes que llevarle esta comida que yo (7)__________ (hacer)." Caperucita Roja (8)__________ (ponerse) sus nuevos zapatos LA Gear, (9)__________ (meter) toda la comida en una bolsa de Smith's y (10)__________ (empezar) a caminar en dirección a casa de su abuelita. Mientras (11)__________ (caminar), (12)__________ (cantar) la nueva canción de Enrique Iglesias. De repente *(suddenly)* (13)__________ (ver) al amigo coyote que seguramente (14)__________ (tener) ganas de comerla. Caperucita Roja, que probablemente no (15)__________ (saber) que era peligroso hablar con él, (16)__________ (decir): "Voy a casa de mi abuela que vive cerca de Skate Country North en la calle Stone, número 3435, para llevar estas enchiladas y estas tortillas que mi madre preparó".

**C. El Flautista de Hamelín.** Tell the story of the Pied Piper by using the correct preterite or imperfect form of the verb in parentheses.

En la ciudad de Hamelín (1)______ (haber) millones de ratones. De noche (2)______ (salir) y (3)______ (comer) todo. Una mañana todos los ciudadanos (4)______ (ir) a la casa del alcalde para quejarse. Nadie (5)______ (poder) matar a los ratones y todos (6)______ (sentirse) muy frustrados. Los ratones (7)______ (ser) demasiado numerosos.

Un día (8)______ (llegar) un caballero alto y guapo. (9)______ (llevar) un traje elegante y un sombrero con una pluma grande. En la mano (10)______ (tener) una flauta. Al ver que todos los ciudadanos (11)______ (estar) tristes, el flautista (12)______ (preguntar) por qué y el alcalde le (13)______ (explicar) que la ciudad (14)______ (estar) llena de ratones. El flautista (15)______ (decir) que (16)______ (poder) liberar la ciudad de los ratones y el alcalde le (17)______ (ofrecer) una bolsa de oro por sus servicios.

El flautista (18)______ (empezar) a tocar una melodía encantadora y los ratones (19)______ (salir) de todas partes del pueblo y (20)______ (correr) tras él. Cuando el flautista (21)______ (llegar) al río todos los ratones (22)______ (morir) porque no (23)______ (saber) nadar.

Al volver al pueblo, (24)______ (pedir) su bolsa de oro pero el alcalde no (25)______ (querer) darle el dinero. Así el flautista (26)______ (empezar) a tocar otra melodía aún más encantadora y todos los niños (27)______(salir) de sus casas y (28)______ (ir) con el flautista a la montaña donde (29)______ (desaparecer). Sin niños, el pueblo (30)______ (estar) muy triste. Todos los ciudadanos (31)______ (estar) furiosos y (32)______ (amenazar) al alcalde. El alcalde se arrepintió y (33)______ (pagar) la bolsa de oro. Al recibir el dinero, el flautista (34)______ (tocar) de nuevo su flauta y la montaña (35)______ (abrirse). Los niños (36)______ (salir) del interior de la montaña y (37)______ (ir) corriendo a sus padres.

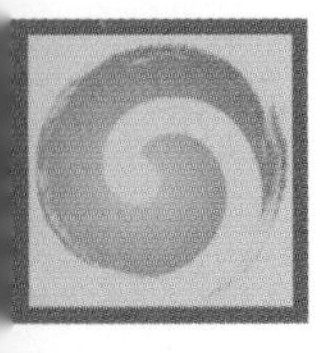

# Vocabulario

## TEMA 1
### La ciudad y el campo

**Sustantivos**

| | |
|---|---|
| **el aire** | *air* |
| **el árbol** | *tree* |
| **el banco** | *bank* |
| **el caballo** | *horse* |
| **la camioneta** | *pickup truck* |
| **la costumbre** | *custom* |
| **el ejército** | *army* |
| **la embajada** | *embassy* |
| **la gallina** | *chicken, hen* |
| **la gasolinera** | *gasoline station* |
| **la granja** | *farm* |
| **el lago** | *lake* |
| **el maíz** | *corn* |
| **el paisaje** | *landscape* |
| **el peligro** | *danger* |
| **la peluquería** | *barber shop/salón* |
| **el pueblo** | *town* |
| **el quiosco** | *kiosk, stall* |
| **el semáforo** | *traffic light* |
| **la vaca** | *cow* |
| **el vecindario** | *neighborhood* |
| **la vida** | *life* |

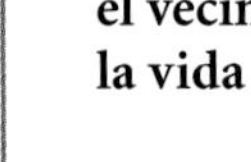

**Verbos**

| | |
|---|---|
| **aburrirse** | *to get bored* |
| **charlar** | *to chat* |
| **detenerse (g) (ie)** | *to stop* |
| **jubilarse** | *to retire* |
| **respirar** | *to breathe* |
| **sembrar (ie)** | *to sow, plant* |

**Adjetivos**

| | |
|---|---|
| **descompuesto/a** | *broken (down)* |
| **tranquilo/a** | *peaceful, tranquil* |
| **triste** | *sad* |

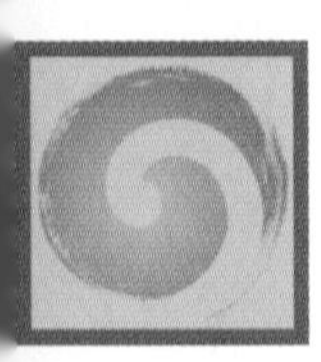

**Otras expresiones**

| | |
|---|---|
| **al pie de** | *at the foot of* |
| **antes** | *before* |
| **mientras** | *while* |
| **rápidamente** | *rapidly* |
| **todavía** | *still, yet* |
| **un par de** | *a couple of* |

## TEMA 2
### Un accidente con el coche nuevo

**Sustantivos**

| | |
|---|---|
| **el aceite** | *oil* |
| **la acera** | *sidewalk* |
| **el anuncio** | *advertisement* |
| **el asiento** | *seat* |
| **el autobús** | *bus* |
| **la batería** | *battery* |
| **la compra** | *purchase* |
| **el cuero** | *leather* |
| **el equipo de sonido** | *sound system* |
| **la esquina** | *corner* |
| **el estacionamiento** | *parking* |
| **el freno** | *brake* |
| **el gasto** | *expense* |
| **la grúa** | *tow truck* |
| **el letrero** | *sign* |
| **la licencia** | *license* |
| **la llanta** | *tire* |
| **el lujo** | *luxury* |
| **el maletero** | *trunk* |
| **el parabrisas** | *windshield* |
| **la parada** | *stop* |
| **el peatón** | *pedestrian* |
| **el periódico** | *newspaper* |
| **la pierna** | *leg* |
| **el seguro** | *insurance* |
| **el tanque** | *tank* |

**Verbos**

| | |
|---|---|
| **abrocharse** | *to buckle* |
| **ajustar** | *to adjust* |
| **arrancar** | *to start* |
| **cambiar** | *to change* |
| **cargar** | *to load, charge* |
| **chocar** | *to crash* |
| **doler (ue)** | *to hurt* |
| **encantar** | *to delight* |
| **reparar** | *to repair* |
| **revisar** | *to check* |

**Adjetivos**

| | |
|---|---|
| **derecho/a** | *right* |
| **herido/a** | *wounded* |

**Otras expresiones**

| | |
|---|---|
| **¡Cuidado!** | *Careful!* |
| **pobrecito/a** | *poor thing* |

# Reunión A

**A escuchar.** **Una llamada al 911.** Escuche la conversación entre la operadora de emergencia y el Sr. Antúnez. Marque las oraciones con **Cierto** (**C**) o **Falso** (**F**) según el diálogo.

1. _____ El Sr. Antúnez chocó con un árbol.
2. _____ El accidente fue en la Avenida Constitución, esquina con Azalea.
3. _____ Un niño se rompió una pierna.
4. _____ El niño estaba en el auto con el Sr. Antúnez.
5. _____ Una joven conducía el otro auto.
6. _____ Ya salieron los paramédicos y una patrulla de la policía.

**Tapescript for A escuchar.**
**Una llamada al 911.**
OPERADORA: Nueve uno uno. ¿Cuál es la emergencia?
SR. ANTÚNEZ: Tuve un accidente. Choqué con un auto. ¡Yo no quería chocar!
OPERADORA: ¿Dónde fue el accidente?
SR. ANTÚNEZ: En la Avenida Constitución, esquina con Azalea.
OPERADORA: ¿Hay heridos?
SR. ANTÚNEZ: Sí, un niño. Creo que se rompió una pierna.
OPERADORA: ¿Está consciente?
SR. ANTÚNEZ: Estaba consciente, pero ya se desmayó. Ay, ¿por qué tenía que pasar esto?
OPERADORA: No hay que ponerse nervioso, todo va a salir bien. ¿Dónde iba el niño? ¿Estaba en su auto?
SR. ANTÚNEZ: No, estaba en el otro auto con una joven. Ella está muy enojada conmigo, pero fue un accidente.
OPERADORA: ¿Ella conducía el otro auto?
SR. ANTÚNEZ: Sí, sólo había dos personas.
OPERADORA: Ya salieron los paramédicos y una patrulla de la policía.

**Answers for A escuchar.**
1) *F.* 2) *C.* 3) *C.* 4) *F.* 5) *C.* 6) *C.*

**A conversar.** Ud. es el/la paramédico/a que acaba de llegar a la escena de un accidente. Pregúntele a uno/a de los heridos (su compañero/a) qué pasó, si estaba consciente después del choque, si tiene alguna herida grave, etc.

**¿Lo sabía?**

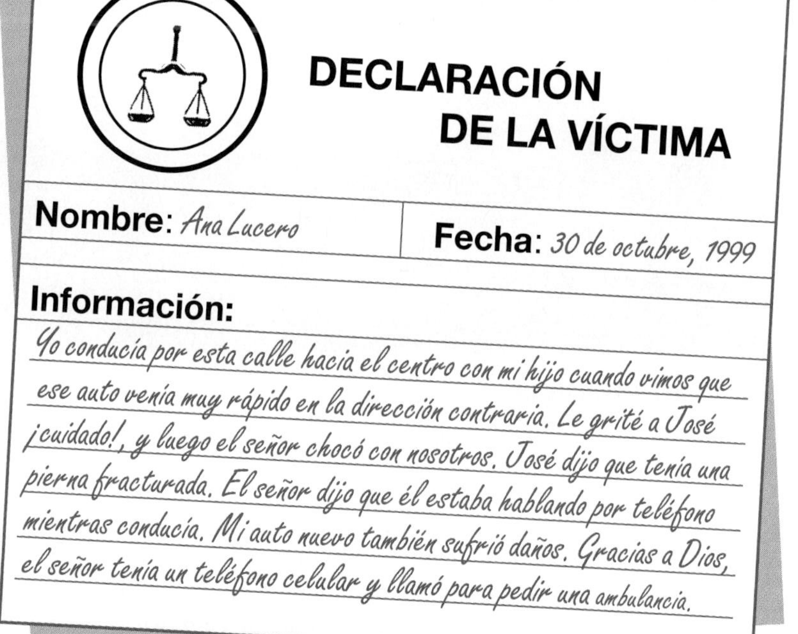

**DECLARACIÓN DE LA VÍCTIMA**

**Nombre:** *Ana Lucero*

**Fecha:** *30 de octubre, 1999*

**Información:**

*Yo conducía por esta calle hacia el centro con mi hijo cuando vimos que ese auto venía muy rápido en la dirección contraria. Le grité a José ¡cuidado!, y luego el señor chocó con nosotros. José dijo que tenía una pierna fracturada. El señor dijo que él estaba hablando por teléfono mientras conducía. Mi auto nuevo también sufrió daños. Gracias a Dios, el señor tenía un teléfono celular y llamó para pedir una ambulancia.*

**¿Comprende Ud.?** Conteste las preguntas según la declaración anterior.

1. ¿Quién conducía hacia el centro?
2. ¿Cómo conducía el señor?
3. ¿Qué hacía el señor en el momento del choque?
4. ¿Qué hizo el señor después del choque?

**A buscar.** En el Internet busque información estadística en español relacionada con el crimen, la polución, el número de accidentes, etc., de un barrio en su ciudad. Compare su información con otros compañeros y decidan cuál es el mejor lugar para vivir.

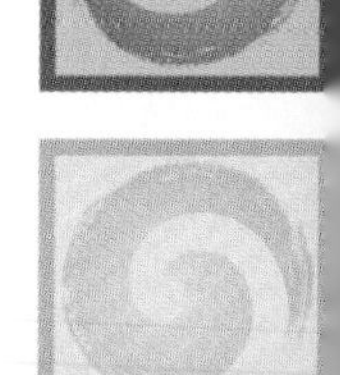

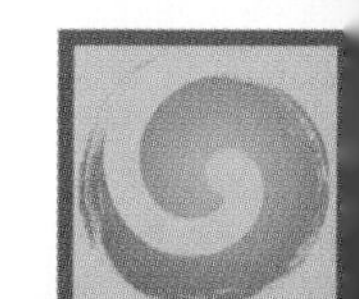

## En la sala de urgencias

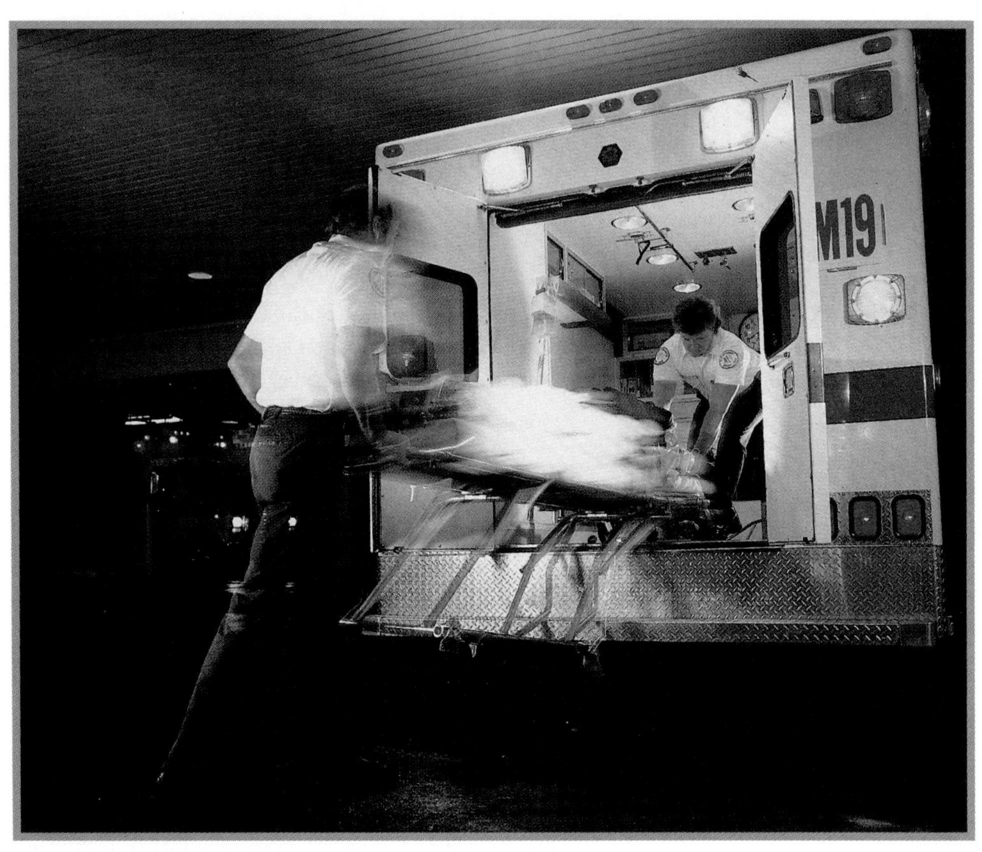


### En la ambulancia

*Después del accidente, la ambulancia lleva a José al hospital....*

JOSÉ: Me siento muy mal. ¿Dónde estoy? ¿Qué pasó?

SARGENTO: Ya estás recobrando el conocimiento. Hola, José, soy el sargento Arturo Manrique. Estás en la sala de urgencias del hospital.

JOSÉ: ¡Ay! Ahora recuerdo. Cuando ese auto chocó con nosotros, vi cómo se me rompía la pierna. ¡Pensaba que me iba a morir!

SARGENTO: No, no es nada serio. Te fracturaste la pierna derecha y te desmayaste. ¿Recuerdas algo más?

JOSÉ: Sí, era un auto azul que iba muy rápido. Un señor con el pelo blanco hablaba por teléfono y estaba distraído. No vio nuestro auto. ¿Cómo está Ana?

SARGENTO: Ella no resultó herida porque estaba sentada en el lado izquierdo. Estaba muy preocupada por ti y dijo que iba a venir al hospital más tarde.

JOSÉ: El señor que chocó con nosotros no mantenía el límite de velocidad. Yo creo que va a recibir una multa o va a ir a la cárcel, ¿verdad?

SARGENTO: No sé. Todavía estamos investigando. Ana se quedó en la escena del accidente con un policía para tomar las declaraciones de algunos testigos.

**A. ¿Comprende Ud.?** Conteste las siguientes preguntas según el diálogo.

1. ¿Quién está recobrando el conocimiento?
2. ¿Quién estaba sentado en el lado derecho del coche?
3. ¿Qué hacía el conductor del otro coche mientras conducía?
4. ¿Dónde está Ana ahora?

**Answers for A.** 1) *José.* 2) *José.* 3) *Hablaba por teléfono.* 4) *En la escena del accidente.*

**B. La descripción.** Ud. es la víctima del robo de su cartera (*wallet*) y habla con un policía para hacer una denuncia. Describa con detalle a la ladrona (*thief*), usando el dibujo. Conteste las preguntas con todos los detalles de la ropa, el pelo, la dirección en que iba, etc.

**C. ¿Qué pasó?** Ahora complete su informe con las circunstancias inmediatamente antes del robo. ¿Qué hacía Ud.? ¿Adónde iba? ¿Qué tenía en su cartera? ¿Cuánto dinero llevaba? ¿Había tarjetas de crédito? ¿Tenía la cartera en la mano? ¿en el bolsillo (*pocket*)?

**D. ¡Emergencia!** Piense en una emergencia que Ud. tuvo. ¿Dónde estaba? ¿Qué pasó? ¿De quién/es recibió ayuda? ¿Fue al hospital? Comparta su experiencia con su compañero/a.

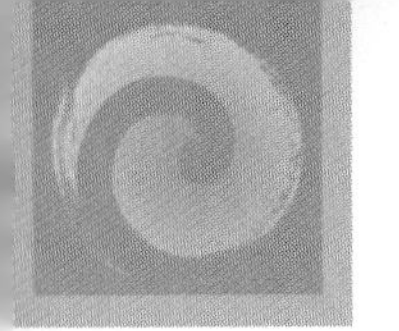

# El tratamiento de José

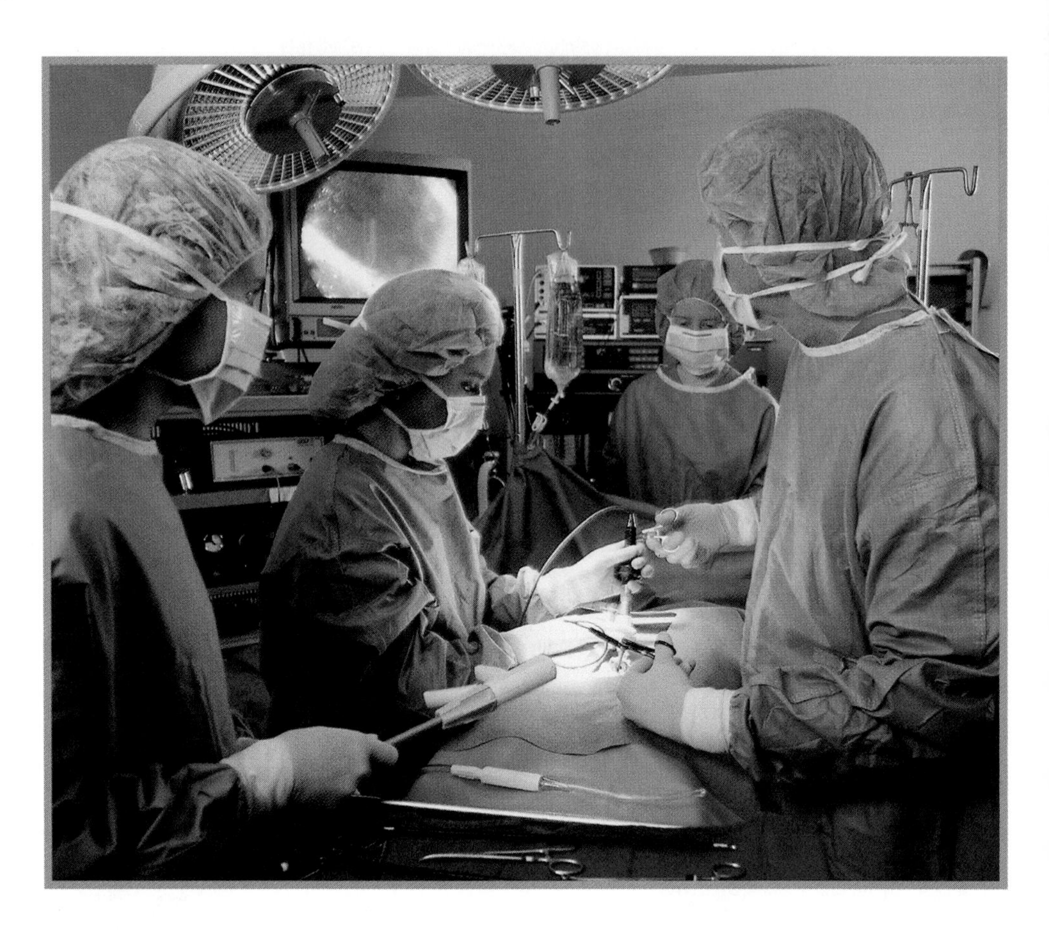

## En el hospital

*La Dra. Aguilar habla con Ana sobre la situación de José....*

DRA. AGUILAR: Señorita Castro, quiero hacerle unas preguntas antes de empezar el tratamiento de José. ¿Dónde están sus padres?

ANA: Ellos ya murieron, pero yo soy su madre adoptiva.

DRA. AGUILAR: Entonces, por favor firme estos papeles para autorizar el tratamiento médico. ¡No sabíamos si José era alérgico a alguna medicina!

ANA: No, creo que no es alérgico a nada. Aquí tiene los papeles.

DRA. AGUILAR: Gracias. José se fracturó una pierna y tenemos que operarlo. Le vamos a enyesar la pierna y no va a poder caminar por un tiempo.

ANA: Pero, ¿no va a poder ir a la escuela?

DRA. AGUILAR: Sí, pero primero tiene que usar una silla de ruedas y más tarde unas muletas (*crutches*). Después va a necesitar fisioterapia por unos seis meses para recuperarse totalmente.

ANA: Gracias, doctora Aguilar. Yo sabía que este hospital era muy bueno.

**A. ¿Comprende Ud.?** Conteste las siguientes preguntas según el diálogo.

1. ¿Qué problema tiene José?
2. ¿A qué es alérgico José?
3. ¿Qué debe hacer José por seis meses?
4. ¿Qué piensa Ana de este hospital?

**Answers for A.** 1) *Se fracturó una pierna.* 2) *A nada.* 3) *Fisioterapia.* 4) *Es muy bueno.*

**B. Pocahontas.** Mientras José está en el hospital, Ana quiere leerle este cuento famoso, pero, ¡hay un problema! Los párrafos no están en orden. Necesita ordenarlos de 1 a 5.

☐ Pero Pocahontas no olvidó a John Smith. Los ingleses no sabían cultivar la tierra como los indios y tenían mucha hambre. Pocahontas empezó a llevarles comida a John Smith y a sus hombres en Jamestown. Pero al padre de ella no le gustaba la amistad entre Pocahontas y los ingleses, y John Smith volvió a Inglaterra.

☐ Inglaterra le gustaba mucho a Pocahontas pero tenía muchas ganas de volver a América. En marzo de 1617 salieron para Jamestown, pero tuvieron que abandonar el viaje porque ella se enfermó. La pobre nunca volvió a ver su país y se murió a la edad de veintidós años.

☐ Érase una vez una princesa india que se llamaba Pocahontas. Era una muchacha muy inteligente y curiosa. Un día los guerreros de su padre regresaron del bosque con un prisionero extranjero. Cuando llegaron a la casa, Pocahontas vio por primera vez a un hombre blanco. Tenía los ojos azules y el pelo rubio. Se llamaba John Smith.

☐ Después de hablar un poco, el padre de Pocahontas dijo que John Smith tenía que morir. Pocahontas intercedió y le salvó la vida. John Smith se quedó con la tribu y habló mucho del rey James de Inglaterra. Ella se enamoró de él.

☐ En la primavera, nuevos hombres llegaron de Inglaterra. Uno de ellos era el Capitán Samuel Argall. Un día encontró a Pocahontas y la invitó a vivir en Jamestown. Allí conoció a John Rolfe, con quien se casó. Tres años después de casarse, Pocahontas fue a Inglaterra con Rolfe donde vio a John Smith otra vez.

**C. Cuentos favoritos.** José quiere escuchar más cuentos, pero Ana está cansada. Seleccione su cuento favorito del grupo que sigue y cuénteselo a José (su compañero/a) incluyendo por lo menos ocho líneas. Él/ella luego escoge su cuento favorito.

*La bella y la bestia* *La Cenicienta* *Caperucita roja* *Ricitos de oro y los tres osos*
*Los tres cerditos* *El patito feo* *Blancanieves y los siete enanitos* *La bella durmiente*

**D. En el hospital.** A veces es necesario ir al hospital. ¿Estuvieron Ud. o un pariente alguna vez en un hospital? ¿Por qué? ¿Eran buenos los médicos? ¿Tuvieron que pasar más de un día allí? ¿Cuántos? ¿Tenían seguro médico? ¿Cuánto costó? ¿Fue necesario recuperarse en casa después? Hable con su compañero/a y escuche su historia también.

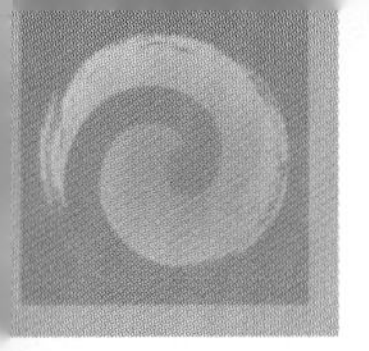

# Contraste entre el pretérito y el imperfecto
## (*Verbs with special connotations in the past*)

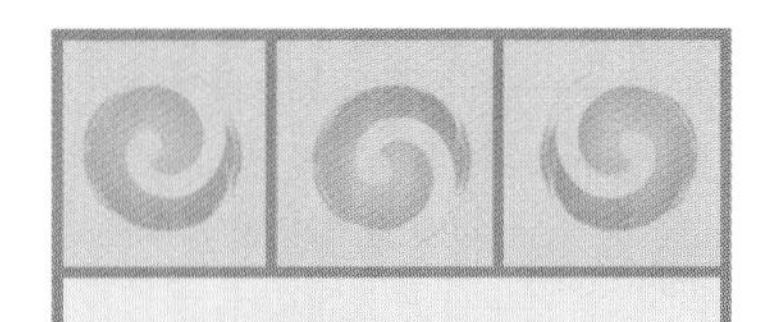

### Para averiguar

1. What are four verbs that have special connotations in the past?
2. What does **supe** imply? What does **sabía** imply?
3. What is the difference between **conocí** and **conocía**?

- As you learned in Lección 5, the verbs **conocer**, **saber**, **querer**, and **poder** may add special connotations when used in the preterite. In the preterite, use:

**conocer** → to say you met someone

**Conocí** a mi esposa en la universidad. — *I met my wife at the university.*

**saber** → to say you found something out

**Supe** que Ud. tuvo un accidente. — *I found out that you had an accident.*

**querer** → to say you tried

Yo **quise** llamar, pero no había teléfono. — *I tried to call, but there wasn't a phone.*

**no querer** → to say you refused to do something

Después del accidente, no **quise** ir al médico. — *After the accident, I refused to go to the doctor.*

**poder** → to say you managed to do something

No **pudieron** hacer ejercicio. — *They couldn't manage to exercise.*

- In the imperfect tense, **conocer**, **saber**, **querer**, and **poder** retain their original meanings.

Yo **conocía** a Antonio cuando todavía no era famoso. — *I knew Antonio when he wasn't yet famous.*
Yo **sabía** todas las respuestas del examen. — *I knew all the answers on the test.*
Yo **quería** preguntarte algo. — *I wanted to ask you something.*
Yo **podía** hacer la tarea sin problema. — *I was able to do the work without a problem.*

## A lo personal

**Note.** Activities in this section present an array of situations so that students can familiarize themselves with the contrast of preterite and imperfect in a variety of contexts.

**A. ¿Lo sabía Ud. o cuándo lo supo?** Read the following facts and tell if you already knew it or not. If you already knew it, tell when or how you found out.

MODELO: Jorge Washington fue el primer Presidente de los Estados Unidos.
*Lo sabía.* (I knew it) o *Lo supe cuando…leí este libro.* (I found out when I read this book.)

1. Hablan español en México.
2. Hablan portugués en Brasil.
3. La capital de Nicaragua es Managua.
4. Gloria Estefan es cubana.
5. Antonio Banderas es guapo.
6. El español es un idioma importante e interesante.
7. En España hablan muchos idiomas diferentes.
8. La población hispana es la minoría más numerosa en los Estados Unidos.
9. Los niños que aprenden otro idioma de pequeños tienen mejores notas en los exámenes de matemáticas.
10. El español es una lengua que deriva del latín.

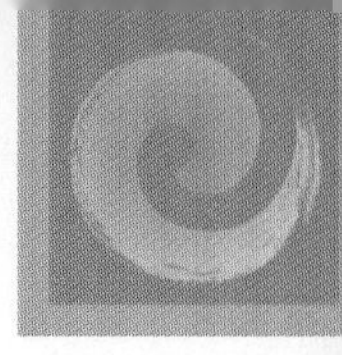

**B. ¿Qué?** Name the following things using complete sentences.

MODELO: una cosa que Ud. no pudo hacer ayer
*No pude hacer la tarea de matemáticas.*

1. la primera cosa que dijo Ud. hoy
2. una cosa que Ud. tuvo que hacer anoche
3. un lugar donde Ud. estuvo ayer
4. un viaje que quiso hacer, pero no pudo
5. la última cosa que no pudo Ud. comprender en la clase
6. su edad cuando Ud. supo que no existía Santa Claus
7. algo que Ud. quiso decirle a su profesor pero que no le dijo
8. una cosa que Ud. quiso hacer esta mañana pero que no pudo hacer

**C. Mi mejor amigo/a.** Answer the following questions about your best friend, your boyfriend or girlfriend, or your spouse. Then interview a classmate.

1. ¿Cómo se llama esta persona?
2. ¿Cuándo conoció Ud. a esa persona?
3. ¿Cómo conoció Ud. a esa persona?
4. ¿Dónde conoció Ud. a esa persona?
5. ¿Conocía Ud. a esa persona cuando estaban Uds. en la escuela primaria?

**D. Una boda terrible.** A friend of yours recently got married, but her wedding was a complete disaster. Read her statements below, which describe everything that went wrong. Then, rewrite each sentence replacing the italicized words to describe a perfect wedding.

1. El día de mi boda (*weddding*) *llovía y hacía muy mal tiempo.*
2. *Nadie* fue a la boda.
3. El novio llegó *tarde a la iglesia.*
4. Mi mamá *estaba muy triste y lloraba todo el tiempo.*
5. La madre de mi nuevo esposo *estaba histérica y no paraba de gritar durante la boda.*
6. Yo estuve enferma *durante toda la luna de miel* (*honeymoon*).
7. La comida de la recepción *estaba fría y mala.*
8. Los invitados *se pusieron enfermos* durante la recepción.
9. Mi hermanita *tenía que llevar las flores, pero ella se durmió en el coche.*
10. Mi nuevo esposo y yo *tuvimos que pasar nuestra luna de miel en nuestro apartamento.*

**E. Entrevista.** Interview one of your classmates using the questions below. If your classmate is married ask him/her the questions in the first group. Otherwise, use those in the second group.

1. ¿En qué año te casaste? ¿Cuántos años tenías? ¿Tuviste una boda grande? ¿Cuántas personas fueron a la boda? ¿Estabas nervioso/a cuando llegaste a la boda? ¿Dónde pasaron Uds. la luna de miel? ¿Tienes hijos? ¿Vivías aquí cuando nacieron? ¿En qué hospital nacieron?
2. ¿Quieres casarte algún día? Para ti, ¿es importante tener una boda grande? ¿Es importante tener un noviazgo largo? ¿Dónde te gustaría pasar la luna de miel? ¿Cuántos hijos te gustaría tener?

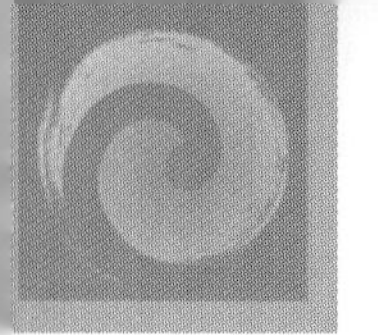

# Más práctica con el pretérito y el imperfecto
## (*Let's practice*)

### A lo personal

**A. ¿Qué hizo?** Here is information about how Francesca spent her day yesterday. The left column shows in what order she did things. The right column gives background information. Combine the sentences in a logical order to describe her day. Include connecting words such as **y**, **pero**, **luego**, **como**, or **por eso** where needed.

MODELO: *Se levantó a las siete y media ayer por la mañana. Tenía sueño y quería dormir un poco más. Su madre dormía todavía. Preparó el desayuno y comió cereal con fruta....*

| **PRETERITE (sequence of events)** | **IMPERFECT (background information)** |
|---|---|
| **Ayer por la mañana** | **Ayer por la mañana** |
| Se levantó a las siete y media. | Tenía mucho sueño y quería dormir un poco más. |
| Preparó el desayuno. | Su madre dormía todavía. |
| Comió cereal con fruta y tomó café. | No tenía tiempo para preparar más de comer. |
| Salió de la casa para el trabajo. | Hacía sol pero hacía un poco de frío. |
| Perdió el autobús y tuvo que esperar al siguiente. | En el autobús había mucha gente y no podía sentarse. |
| Llegó tarde a la oficina, a las nueve y cuarto. | Casi todos los pasajeros leían el periódico o dormían. |
| Trabajó de las nueve y veinte al mediodía. | Su jefe no estaba contento. |
| **Ayer por la tarde** | **Ayer por la tarde** |
| A la hora del almuerzo fue a la agencia de viajes. | La agencia no estaba muy lejos. |
| Compró un boleto para Puerto Rico. | La agente era muy simpática. |
| Regresó al trabajo a la una. | El boleto más barato costaba 500 dólares. |
| Trabajó sólo hasta las cuatro. | No había mucho que hacer en la oficina. |
| Después de trabajar, corrió por el parque por una hora. | Como hacía buen tiempo, tenía mucha energía. |
| Regresó a casa a las seis. | |
| **Ayer por la noche** | **Ayer por la noche** |
| Cenó pizza. | No tenía ganas de cocinar. |
| Después de cenar, descansó y miró la televisión. | Su madre estaba enferma y no quería comer. |
| Se acostó temprano. | No había muchos programas interesantes en la televisión. |
| | Estaba aburrida y tenía mucho sueño. |

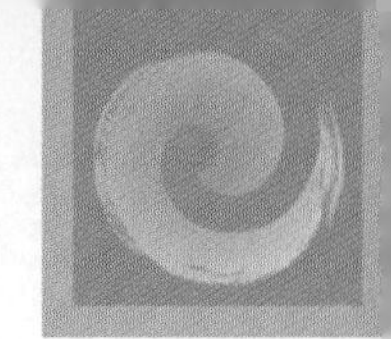

**B. Felicidades.** Look at your son Pablito. Yesterday was his graduation. Congratulations! During his years of school, what did he do every day to receive these honors? What did he do yesterday to celebrate? Write a short paragraph with this information and then compare it with that of a classmate.

**C. Al regresar.** Ask a partner about the first few minutes after he/she returned home yesterday. Add two questions of your own.

1. ¿A qué hora regresaste a casa?
2. ¿Cómo te sentías?
3. ¿Quién estaba en casa?
4. ¿Qué estaba haciendo esa persona?
5. ¿Qué ropa llevabas?
6. ¿Te cambiaste de ropa?
7. ¿Qué hiciste al llegar a casa?
8. ¿Comiste? ¿Miraste la televisión?
9. ¿Te acostaste?

**D. Una historia imaginaria.** In groups of four narrate a story about something that happened to one of you in the past. Two of you will be in charge of setting the scene, describing emotions and background. The other two will be in charge of narrating the actions that took place in the story, and providing information about specific times and places where actions occurred. You should sit in a circle and make up the story as you go, with each pair of students interjecting their comments where appropriate in the narration. Be as creative as possible and when you have completed the story, share with the rest of the class.

## ¿Dónde está...?

### Ana llama a la estación de policía

*Ana quiere estar segura de que la policía tiene todos los detalles del accidente....*

TENIENTE ALVÍDREZ: Soy la teniente Lorena Alvídrez. ¿En qué puedo servirle?
ANA: Tuve un accidente hace unos días y no sé si necesito hacer una declaración porque los dos conductores estamos asegurados.
TENIENTE ALVÍDREZ: Si los daños fueron de más de 500 dólares, la ley dice que tiene que hacer una declaración. ¿Hubo heridos?
ANA: Sí, mi hijo se fracturó una pierna.
TENIENTE ALVÍDREZ: ¿Preguntó en el hospital si ya se reportó el accidente?
ANA: No. ¿Se puede reportar dos veces?
TENIENTE ALVÍDREZ: Sí, no importa. Se llena un formulario que se puede recoger en la estación de policía o por medio de su agente de seguros.
ANA: ¿Se tiene que hacer en persona o se puede mandar por correo?
TENIENTE ALVÍDREZ: Se puede mandar por correo.

**A. ¿Comprende Ud.?** Conteste las siguientes preguntas según el diálogo.

1. ¿Ana tiene que hacer una declaración?
2. ¿Hubo más heridos además de José?
3. ¿Hay que llenar el formulario en persona?
4. ¿Estaba asegurado el coche de Ana?

**Answers for A.** 1) *Sí.* 2) *No.* 3) *No.* 4) *Sí.*

**B. En la calle Molino.** Usando estas indicaciones, determine el número de cada lugar.

MODELO: Al doblar a la derecha en la calle Molino, el hotel es el cuarto edificio a la derecha.
*El hotel es el 508.*

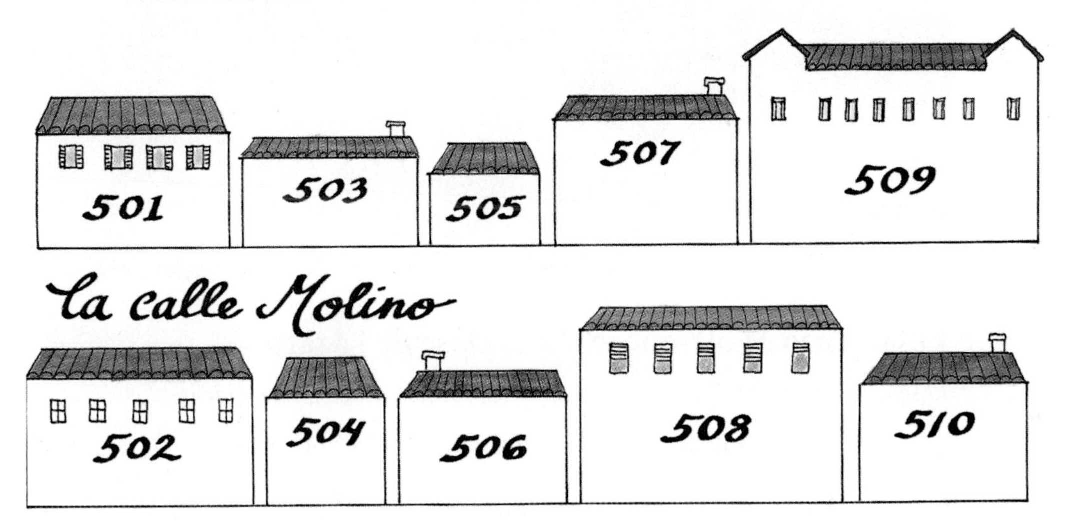


1. El restaurante La Paz está enfrente del hotel.
2. La farmacia está en la esquina, al lado del hotel.
3. Hay un hospital enfrente de la farmacia.
4. El banco está al otro extremo de la calle, al mismo lado que la farmacia.
5. Hay una pastelería al lado del banco.
6. La peluquería se encuentra entre la pastelería y el hotel.
7. La agencia de viajes está enfrente de la pastelería.
8. La oficina de correos está a la izquierda de la agencia de viajes, en la esquina.
9. Hay una pequeña tienda de artículos deportivos a la derecha de la agencia de viajes.

**C. Unos estudiantes perdidos.** Déle indicaciones a un estudiante nuevo para llegar a los lugares indicados.

MODELO: de la cafetería al salón de clase
*Se dobla a la derecha en la facultad de ciencias y se va derecho hasta llegar al salón.*

1. del salón de clase a la biblioteca
2. del edificio donde tienen clase a una parada de autobús
3. del campus a un banco
4. de la universidad a su apartamento/casa

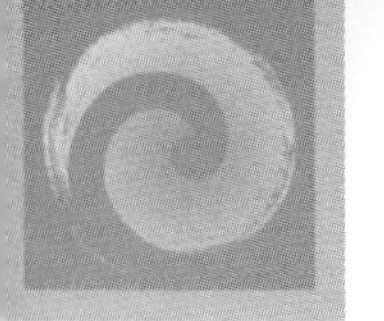

# Cómo protegerse

## El sargento Manrique visita la clase de Lázaro

*El sargento Manrique habla con los niños sobre la prevención de accidentes....*

LÁZARO: Atención, niños. Les presento al sargento Arturo Manrique. José lo conoció cuando tuvo su accidente.

SARGENTO: Buenos días. Quiero hablar de asuntos muy importantes para su seguridad. José, ¡qué bien que ya estás en la escuela! ¿Qué consejos nos puedes dar después de esa experiencia?

JOSÉ: Se debe llevar el cinturón de seguridad y se debe conducir con cuidado y mantener el límite de velocidad.

SARGENTO: ¡Muy bien! Fue un accidente muy serio pero sólo tuviste una fractura en una pierna porque llevabas el cinturón de seguridad. Los demás niños, ¿qué más pueden hacer para proteger su vida en la calle?

FABIOLA: No se habla con extraños.

JEANNE: Se tiene que hablar con los padres sobre los problemas.

RAÚL: Se aconseja alejarse de lugares oscuros y solitarios.

SARGENTO: ¡Muy bien! ¿Qué debo hacer si encuentro un arma de fuego o sustancias que no conozco?

TODOS: Se debe alejar del lugar y avisar a un adulto de confianza o llamar a la policía.

**Answers for A.** 1) *En clase de Lázaro.* 2) *De prevención de accidentes.* 3) *No hablar con extraños.* 4) *Con los padres.*

**A. ¿Comprende Ud.?** Conteste las siguientes preguntas según el diálogo.

1. ¿Dónde está el sargento?
2. ¿De qué va a hablar el sargento?
3. ¿Qué recomienda Fabiola?
4. ¿Con quién se debe hablar sobre los problemas?

**B. Los símbolos internacionales.** Ud. no está acostumbrado/a a los símbolos internacionales, pero la ley dice que es necesario aprenderlos antes de conducir en un país extranjero. ¿Puede determinar su significado?

1. Hospital
2. Aeropuerto
3. Donde se espera un taxi
4. No doblar a la izquierda
5. Velocidad máxima
6. No entrar
7. Parada del autobús
8. Lugar para acampar
9. Restaurante
10. Lugar para peatones solamente

**Expansion and answers for B.** Present the mile-to-kilometer comparison, mentioning that 1 mile equals 1.8 kilometers, roughly. Cite the maximum speed limit as 110 kph as compared to 65 mph.
1) *B.* 2) *E.* 3) *F.* 4) *I.* 5) *D.* 6) *J.* 7) *H.* 8) *A.* 9) *C.* 10) *G.*

**C. Los vigilantes del vecindario.** Ud. es un/a nuevo/a policía/mujer policía y esta noche es su primera reunión con un grupo de residentes. Prepare una lista de cinco sugerencias para la protección de todos. Compare su lista con la de su compañero/a.

MODELO: Se debe... *familiarizar con su rutina y conocer a sus vecinos.*

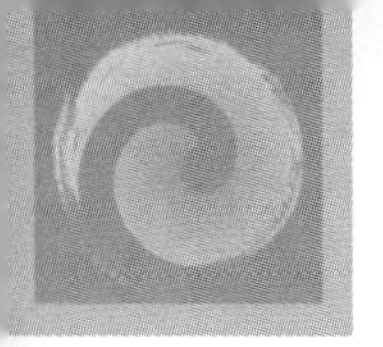

# *Se* impersonal
## (*Impersonal* "se")

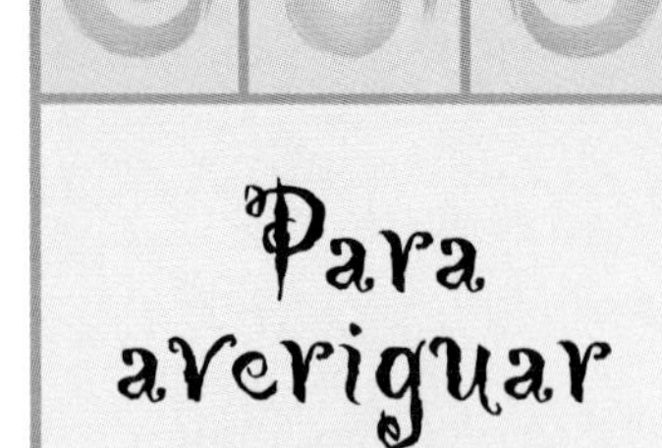

**Para averiguar**

1. What are three ways you might interpret the phrase **Eso no se dice**?
2. Which two verb forms are used with impersonal **se**?

- Use **se** to state generalizations about what is or is not done. Phrases with **se** may be expressed in a variety of ways in English.

| | |
|---|---|
| **Se habla** español allí. | *People speak Spanish there.*<br>*One speaks Spanish there.*<br>*Spanish is spoken there.* |
| Eso no **se hace** aquí. | *People don't do that here.*<br>*One does not do that here.*<br>*That is not done here.* |
| ¿**Se toma** vino tinto o blanco con eso? | *Do people drink red or white wine with that?*<br>*Does one drink red or white wine with that?*<br>*Is red or white wine drunk with that?* |
| ¿Cómo **se dice** "gato" en inglés? | *How is "cat" said in English?*<br>*How do you say "cat" in English?*<br>*How does one say "cat" in English?* |

- With **se**, use the third-person form (**él, ella, ellos, ellas**) of the verb. It may be singular or plural, depending on the subject. To make it plural, simply add **-n** to the verb.

| | |
|---|---|
| **Se vende** una casa en mi calle. | *A house is for sale on my street.* |
| **Se venden** dos casas en mi calle. | *Two houses are for sale on my street.* |
| **Se come** paella en España. | *Paella is eaten in Spain.* |
| **Se comen** tacos en México. | *Tacos are eaten in Mexico.* |

- Use a singular verb with people introduced by the personal **a** and with infinitive verbs used as subjects even when referring to more than one person or action.

| | |
|---|---|
| **Se puede** bailar allí. | *One can dance there.*<br>*(You can dance there.)* |
| **Se encuentra a** muchas personas en el parque los sábados. | *One finds many people in the park on Saturdays.*<br>*(You can find...; Many people are found...)* |

- When using an inherently reflexive verb in an impersonal **se** construction, the word **uno** must be added as the subject.

| | |
|---|---|
| **Uno se** divertía mucho. | *One used to have a good time.* |

## A lo personal

**A. ¿Dónde se vende?** Name a place in your area where the following are sold.

1. café
2. comida
3. flores
4. seguros para autos
5. ropa
6. computadoras
7. maletas
8. discos compactos
9. cerveza
10. hamburguesas

**B. El marciano vuelve.** You have a guest from Mars who does not understand our ways. Explain what we do with the following items.

MODELO: café
*El café se toma.*

1. hamburguesa
2. libros
3. televisor
4. música
5. autos
6. dinero
7. sombrero
8. anuncio

**C. ¿Qué se hace con...?** What does one do with...?

MODELO: Dawn
*Se lavan los platos con Dawn.*

- Windex
- Pledge
- Electrasol
- Dove
- Dirt Devil
- Tide
- Creot

**D. Un laberinto.** Sometimes a new city is like a maze. The Loya family is lost and needs your help to get around in this city. Follow the model and with a partner's help, tell the Loyas what they need to do in order to go from the hotel to the bank, to the travel agency and to the pharmacy.

MODELO: *Para ir a la Avenida Martí se sale del hotel y se dobla a la izquierda en la Calle Pizarro...*

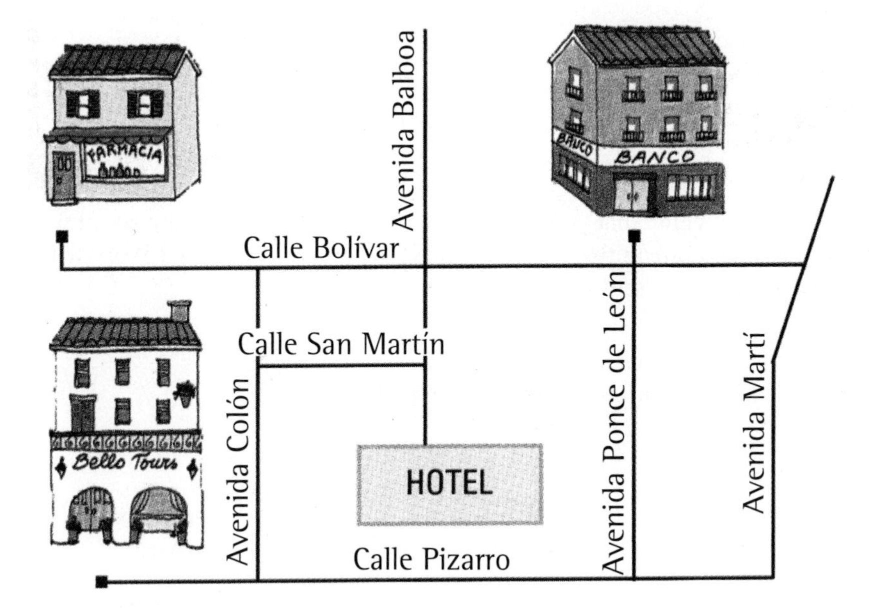

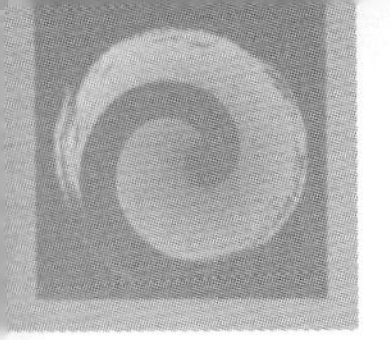

# Más práctica con *se* impersonal
## (*Let's practice*)

## A lo personal

**Note.** Activities in this section present different contexts to allow students to practice the impersonal *se* construction in a variety of situations.

**A. ¿Qué se puede hacer...?** You are helping a friend move into the university dorm. Have a classmate play the role of the dorm director and ask if the following are allowed or prohibited.

MODELO: pistolas
E1: *¿Se permiten o se prohiben las pistolas?*
E2: *Se prohiben las pistolas.*

1. fumar
2. animales
3. cocinar
4. cerveza
5. estudiar
6. amigos en el cuarto
7. música alta
8. plantas y flores
9. hornos de microondas
10. usar computadoras
11. navegar la red

**B. Hace cien años.** Imagine how life was different 100 years ago. Say whether or not people used to do the following things.

MODELO: viajar en avión
*No se viajaba en avión.*

1. mirar la televisión
2. comer mejor
3. vivir mejor
4. trabajar más
5. escuchar música
6. viajar mucho
7. jugar al béisbol
8. divertirse

Now, imagine that your parents or grandparents are talking about what was or was not done in the "good old days." What might they say? Work with a classmate to write five sentences.

MODELO: *Se obedecía a los padres.*
*Se podía encontrar trabajo fácilmente.*

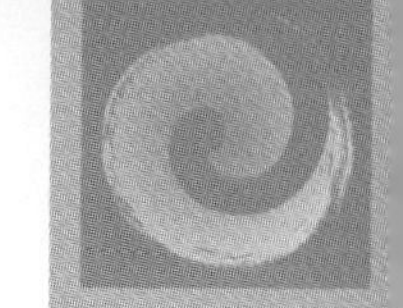

 **C. Entrevista.** Interview a classmate using the following questions.

1. ¿Se habla mucho español en la ciudad o en el pueblo donde vives? ¿Dónde se puede oír español cerca de tu casa? ¿Con qué tipo de trabajo se usa mucho español donde tú vives?
2. ¿Sabes cómo se dice *the environment* en español? ¿Cómo se escribe? ¿Uno se preocupa mucho por la contaminación aquí? ¿Se usa mucho el transporte público? ¿Se recicla?
3. ¿Se habla mucho del crimen en tu ciudad/pueblo? ¿Se siente uno seguro por la noche en la calle donde vives? ¿Se reportan muchos accidentes?

**D. Se necesitan artistas.** One of your professors has asked you and your partner to help a local school by creating an ad regarding traffic safety for elementary school students. With a partner, use the drawing below as a model, draw something, and come up with a traffic safety tip appropriate for elementary school students.

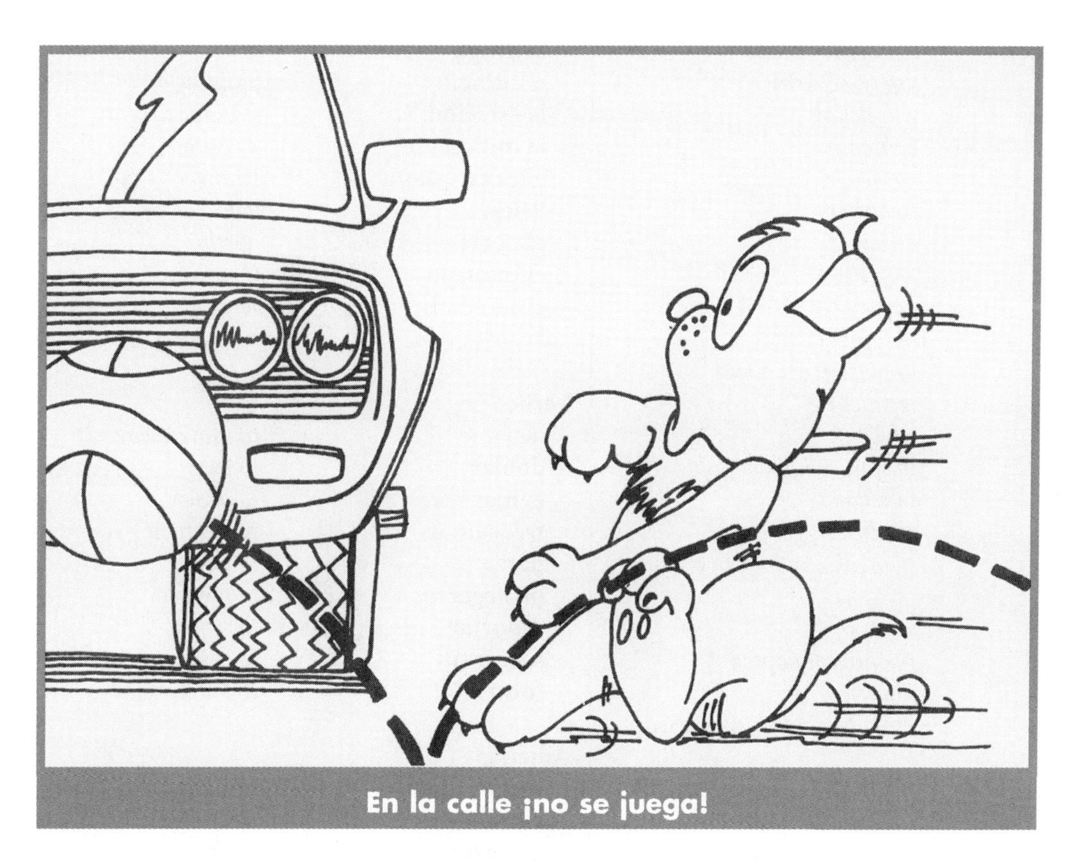


**E. ¿Qué se hace?** A South American exchange student will be studying at your university next semester. With a partner, make a list of five things that are done and five things that are not done in typical college classes in the United States. Then, compare your list with that of the group next to you. Report to the class any items that are on both lists.

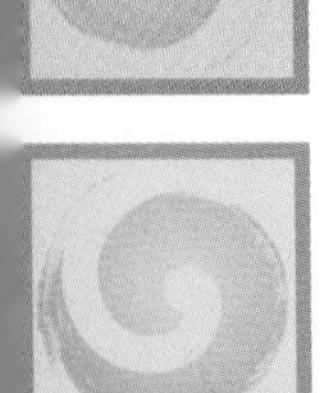
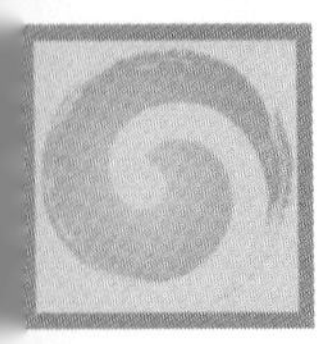

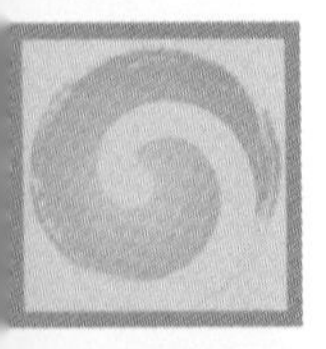

## TEMA 3
### Las emergencias

**Sustantivos**

| | |
|---|---|
| **la cárcel** | *jail* |
| **el cinturón** | *belt* |
| **el conocimiento** | *consciousness* |
| **la declaración** | *statement* |
| **la escena** | *scene* |
| **la fisioterapia** | *physical therapy* |
| **el límite** | *limit* |
| **las muletas** | *crutches* |
| **la multa** | *ticket, fine* |
| **la sala de urgencias** | *emergency room* |
| **la seguridad** | *safety, security* |
| **la silla de ruedas** | *wheelchair* |
| **el/la teniente** | *lieutenant* |
| **el/la testigo** | *witness* |
| **el tratamiento** | *treatment* |
| **la velocidad** | *speed* |

**Verbos**

| | |
|---|---|
| **desmayarse** | *to faint* |
| **enyesar** | *to plaster; set a cast* |
| **fracturarse** | *to fracture* |
| **morirse (ue)** | *to die* |
| **quedarse** | *to stay, remain* |
| **recobrar** | *to regain* |
| **recuperarse** | *to recover, get better* |
| **romperse** | *to break* |

**Adjetivos**

| | |
|---|---|
| **adoptivo/a** | *adoptive, adopted* |
| **alérgico/a** | *allergic* |
| **distraído/a** | *absent-minded, distracted* |
| **izquierdo/a** | *left* |
| **médico/a** | *medical* |

## TEMA 4
### En la calle

**Sustantivos**

| | |
|---|---|
| **el arma de fuego** | *firearm* |
| **el asunto** | *matter* |
| **la avenida** | *avenue* |
| **el/la conductor/a** | *driver* |
| **la confianza** | *confidence, trust* |
| **el consejo** | *advice* |
| **la cuadra, la manzana** | *block* |
| **el daño** | *damage* |
| **la dirección** | *address* |
| **la droga** | *drug* |
| **el edificio** | *building* |
| **la estación** | *station* |
| **la indicación** | *direction* |
| **el/la extraño/a** | *stranger* |
| **la ley** | *law* |
| **el norte** | *north* |
| **el informe** | *report* |
| **el sargento** | *sergeant* |
| **la sustancia** | *substance* |

**Verbos**

| | |
|---|---|
| **alejarse** | *to move away* |
| **doblar** | *to turn* |
| **evitar** | *to avoid* |
| **frecuentar** | *to frequent* |
| **parar** | *to stop* |
| **proteger** | *to protect* |
| **reportar** | *to report* |
| **seguir (i)** | *to continue, follow* |
| **tocar** | *to touch* |

**Adjetivos**

| | |
|---|---|
| **asegurado/a** | *insured* |
| **claro/a** | *clear, light* |
| **oscuro/a** | *dark* |
| **solitario/a** | *solitary* |

**Otras expresiones**

| | |
|---|---|
| **a la derecha** | *to the right* |
| **a la izquierda** | *to the left* |
| **hacia** | *toward* |
| **otra vez** | *again* |

# Reunión B

**A escuchar. La ciudad o el campo.** Escuche la conversación y complete cada oración con la información que escuche.

1. De joven, el Profesor Yuja prefería la ______________.
2. Carlos dice que en la ciudad hay teatros, cines, conciertos y mejores ______________.
3. Isabel comenta que los agricultores usan muchos ______________, insecticidas y otros químicos.
4. El profesor menciona la ______________ de la ciudad.
5. El examen final es escribir una ______________ sobre la vida en las zonas rurales y en la ciudad.

**Tapescript for A escuchar. La ciudad o el campo.**
PROF. YUJA: Cuando era joven prefería la ciudad, pero ahora no estoy seguro.
CARLOS: Escuche profesor, en la ciudad hay teatros, cines, conciertos y mejores trabajos.
PROF. YUJA: También muy buenos restaurantes y muchos centros comerciales.
MARY: Sí, pero estudie las estadísticas. Hay más crimen.
PROF. YUJA: Es verdad, las zonas rurales son más seguras, la vida es más tranquila y el aire es puro.
ISABEL: No sé. Lea las estadísticas y vea que los agricultores usan muchos fertilizantes, insecticidas y otros químicos muy malos para la salud.
PROF. YUJA: Pero en la ciudad hay más polución.
ANA: Miren, no sean injustos. Comparen diferentes ciudades y zonas rurales.
PROF. YUJA: Es una buena idea; para el examen final escriban una composición sobre la vida en las zonas rurales y en la ciudad. Investiguen cuáles son los mejores y los peores lugares para vivir.

**Answers for A escuchar.**
1) *Ciudad.* 2) *Trabajos.* 3) *Fertilizantes.* 4) *Polución.* 5) *Composición.*

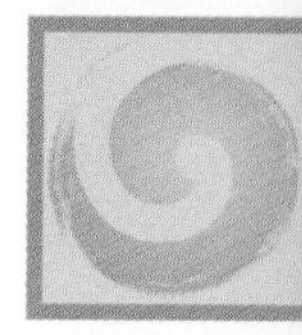

**A conversar.** Ud. es el/la médico/a que operó a un paciente con una fractura en la pierna causada por un accidente automovilístico. Hace mucho tiempo que Ud. no ve a este paciente (otro/a estudiante). Pregúntele cómo fue su recuperación y qué hizo para mejorarse.

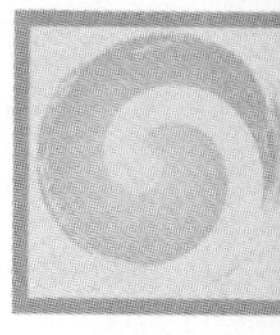

**¿Lo sabía?**

STATE OF CALIFORNIA
DMV
DEPARTMENT OF MOTOR VEHICLES
Una Agencia de Servicio Público

Solicitud de Licencia de Manejar,
Tarjeta de Identidad,
o Cambio de Nombre

NÚMERO DE SEGURO SOCIAL ___-__-____

| | |
|---|---|
| ¿Desea inscribirse para votar? | ☐ Sí. Por favor, complete el formulario adjunto.<br>☐ No. No complete el formulario. |
| Solicitud de Licencia de Manejar | ☐ A -Vehículos combinados y remolques con más de 10,000 libras<br>☐ B -Vehículos sencillos de 26,001 libras o más<br>☐ C -Clase básica<br>☐ D -Vehículos que transporten materiales peligrosos<br>☐ M1 -Motocicletas de dos ruedas de 150 cc o más<br>☐ M2 -Motocicletas de dos ruedas de 149 cc o menos |
| Solicitud de Tarjeta de Identidad | Anote el número de la tarjeta de identidad, si la tiene ________<br>Se vence en ______ |
| Información, Nombre y Dirección de todos los solicitantes | Nombre completo__________ Dirección __________<br>Apellidos__________ Ciudad__________<br>Sufijo (JR, SR)__________ Estado__________ |
| Información Personal | Sexo___ Color del cabello_____ Color de ojos _____ Estatura ___<br>Peso____ Fecha de nacimiento_____ (Día) _____ (Mes) _____ (Año) |
| Declaración de Perjurio | Certifico bajo pena de perjurio conforme a las leyes del Estado de California, que lo anterior es verdadero y correcto. |
| Firma del solicitante | Fecha ________ Firma ________ Teléfono (día) ________ |

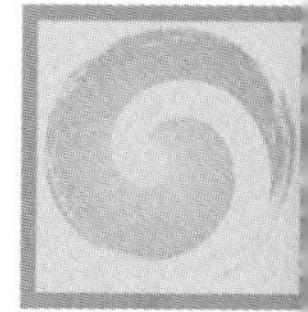

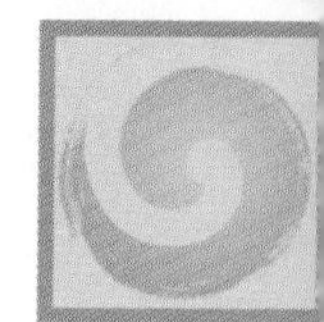

**¿Comprende Ud.?** Conteste según la solicitud.

1. ¿Cuáles son las tres razones para llenar esta solicitud (*application*)?
2. ¿Se puede usar también para inscribirse para votar?
3. ¿Cuál es la información básica para cada solicitante?
4. ¿Qué es una declaración de perjurio?

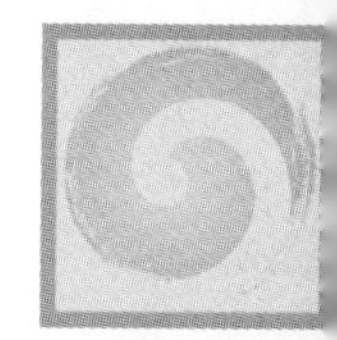

**A buscar.** En el Internet hay solicitudes de empleo y de tarjetas de crédito en español. Busque un ejemplo y traiga la solicitud a clase. Compare la que encontró con las de sus compañeros. ¿Para qué son las solicitudes? ¿Pueden descifrar la información requerida? ¿Es necesario entender todas las palabras para completarlas?

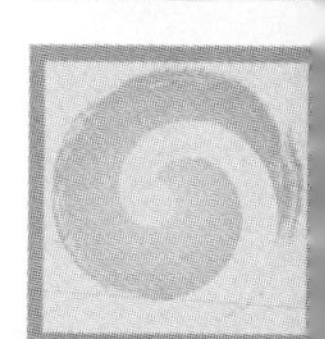

# ¡TRATO HECHO!

## Rincón profesional: La ley

**Oficina del Alguacil** *(Sheriff)* **del Condado de Marion**
*Palacio de Justicia del Condado Marion*
*100 High Street, N.E.*
*Salem, OR 97308*

"Una Fuerza en Nuestra Comunidad"

**EMERGENCIA – MARQUE 911**

Teléfono de emergencia – (503) 588-5032 Línea de Negocios – (503) 588-5094

**Raúl Ramírez, Alguacil**

### Información del Reclutamiento

**Solicitud**

Éste es un reclutamiento abierto-continuo para las categorías de Diputado Alguacil y Novicio Diputado Alguacil, con la Oficina del Alguacil del Condado de Marion. No se deben incluir cartas de recomendación y/o currículum vitaes con la solicitud. Se necesita ser mayor de edad y tener residencia legal en los Estados Unidos. No se exige experiencia anterior pero se prefiere a candidatos con conocimientos en este campo.

Preferencia: Todos los solicitantes cualificados están invitados a solicitar el puesto. Sin embargo, para cubrir las necesidades de la población diversa del Condado de Marion, el Alguacil ha determinado que la fluencia bilingüe en inglés y en español es una cualidad altamente deseada para llenar los puestos vacantes de Diputado Alguacil y Novicio Diputado Alguacil. Los solicitantes que declaren tener esta aptitud serán examinados sobre su habilidad bilingüe como parte del proceso de selección.

**¿Comprende Ud.?**

1. ¿A qué número se debe llamar en caso de emergencia?
2. ¿Deben mandar su currículum las personas interesadas?
3. ¿Cuál es la habilidad especial que se busca en un empleado? ¿Por qué es importante?
4. ¿Qué significado tiene el lema "Una fuerza en nuestra comunidad"?

**A escuchar. El encuentro.** Escuche la conversación entre Raquel y Melinda. Ellas estudiaron juntas en la escuela primaria, pero no se veían desde hace diez años.

**¿Comprende Ud.?** Conteste las preguntas según el diálogo.

1. ¿Dónde se conocieron Melinda y Raquel?
2. ¿A qué deporte jugaban juntas?
3. ¿Cómo se llamaba una de sus maestras?
4. ¿Cómo era el profesor de matemáticas?
5. ¿Quién es la esposa del profesor de matemáticas?

**Tapescript for A escuchar. El encuentro.**
RAQUEL: ¿Melinda Juárez? ¿No sabes quién soy?
MELINDA: ¡Claro, eres Raquel Iturriaga! Las dos fuimos compañeras en la escuela secundaria.
RAQUEL: Sí, también jugábamos en el mismo equipo de fútbol.
MELINDA: ¡Es verdad, perdíamos todos los partidos!
RAQUEL: ¿Recuerdas a la profesora Sansores? Siempre nos daba mucha tarea.
MELINDA: No quiero pensar en ella. Tenía que estudiar todos los fines de semana para sacar buenas notas.
RAQUEL: A mí me gustaba mucho el profesor de matemáticas. ¡Era muy guapo¡ Yo me quería casar con él. ¿No sabes con quién se casó?
MELINDA: Sí, se casó conmigo.

**Answers for A escuchar.**
1) *En la secundaria.* 2) *Al fútbol.* 3) *Sansores.* 4) *Muy guapo.* 5) *Melinda.*

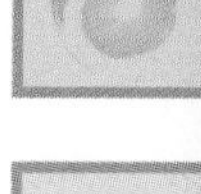

**El testigo.** Dos coches chocaron enfrente de su casa y Ud. fue testigo del accidente. Su compañero es un oficial de la policía y le va a preguntar cómo fue el accidente. Describa la escena con tanto detalle como sea posible.

**Proteja a los niños.** Ud. y otros tres compañeros más forman parte de un comité para la protección de los niños en su barrio. Elijan uno de los temas de la lista a continuación y creen un folleto (*brochure*) incluyendo recomendaciones útiles para los niños sobre ese tema en particular. ¡Sean creativos!

**Temas**

1. Tráfico en la ciudad
2. El peligro del fuego
3. Personas desconocidas
4. Accidentes en bicicleta

MODELO: Tráfico en la ciudad
1. *No se debe cruzar la calle cuando el semáforo está en rojo.*

## A leer

The selection that you are about to read is fiction. You will want to read literary pieces with a slightly different eye than you read non-fiction. Note first that the entire selection is made up of sentence fragments in the second person. The protagonist is giving quick impressions of what she is feeling. Read this selection more with your emotions than your head. It might even help if you read it aloud, to yourself, between clenched teeth, with full emotion!

**Antes de leer.** ¿Cómo se siente en situaciones como ésta?

MODELO: Está atrasado/a en el trabajo.
*No me gusta estar atrasado en el trabajo. Me pongo nervioso.*

1. Hay mucho tráfico.
2. El semáforo está en rojo en cada esquina.
3. Un conductor lo/la deja pasar para estacionar.
4. No puede encontrar lugar para estacionar.

## A escribir

Después de leer el artículo de la página 275, describa una situación similar a la de la historia que le ocurrió a Ud. Incluya detalles como:

1. ¿Dónde y cuándo ocurrió?
2. ¿Cuál era el estado de la carretera?
3. ¿Qué tiempo hacía?
4. ¿Había más gente involucrada (*involved*)?
5. ¿Cómo resolvió Ud. el problema?

*Life in big cities offers many amenities, like cultural activities and great shopping centers, but it also can be very stressful. One of the inconveniences of city life is the traffic, which not only can be heavy at times, but chaotic and unpredictable. When people drive, they generally become frustrated, and when they are helped, they are pleased. If you drive, you can identify with the narrator of* ***El arrebato****. This literary text you are going to read is one of many short stories that the young Spanish writer, Rosa Montero, has written for El País, a newspaper in Spain.*

# *El arrebato*

**por Rosa Montero**

Las nueve menos cuarto de la mañana. Semáforo en rojo, un rojo inconfundible. Las nueve menos trece, hoy no llego. Embotellamiento de tráfico. Doscientos mil coches junto al tuyo. Tienes la mandíbula tan tensa que entre los dientes[1] aún está el sabor del café del desayuno. Miras al vecino. Está intolerablemente cerca. La chapa[2] de su coche casi roza[3] la tuya. Verde. Avanza, imbécil. ¿Qué hacen? No arrancan. No se mueven los estúpidos. Están paseando, con la inmensa urgencia que tú tienes. Doscientos mil coches que salieron a pasear a la misma hora solamente para fastidiarte.[4] ¡Rojjjjo! ¡Rojo de nuevo! No es posible. Las nueve menos diez. Hoy desde luego que no llego-o-o-o (gemido desolado[5]). El vecino te mira con odio.[6] Probablemente piensa que tú tienes la culpa[7] de no haber pasado el semáforo (cuando es obvio que los culpables son los idiotas de delante). Tienes una premonición de catástrofe y derrota.[8] Hoy no llego. Por el espejo ves cómo se acerca un chico en una motocicleta, zigzagueando entre los coches. Su facilidad te causa indignación, su libertad te irrita. Mueves el coche unos centímetros hacia el del vecino y ves que el transgresor está bloqueado, que ya no puede avanzar. ¡Me alegro! Alguien pita por detrás. Das un salto, casi arrancas. De pronto, ves que el semáforo sigue aún en rojo. ¿Qué quieres, que salga con la luz roja, imbécil? Te vuelves en el asiento y ves a los conductores a través de la contaminación y el polvo[9] que cubre los cristales[10] de tu coche. Los insultas. Ellos te miran con odio asesino. De pronto, la luz se pone verde y los de atrás pitan desesperadamente. Con todo ese ruido reaccionas, tomas el volante, al fin arrancas. Las nueve menos cinco. Unos metros más allá la calle es mucho más estrecha;[11] sólo cabrá un coche. Miras al vecino con odio. Aceleras. Él también. Comprendes de pronto que llegar antes que el otro es el objeto principal de tu existencia. Avanzas unos centímetros. Entonces, el otro coche te pasa victorioso. Corre, corre, gritas, fingiendo gran desprecio:[12] ¿adónde vas, idiota?, tanta prisa para adelantarme sólo un metro... Pero la derrota duele. A lo lejos ves una figura negra, una vieja que cruza la calle lentamente. Casi la atropellas. "¡Cuidado, abuela!", gritas por la ventanilla; esas viejas son un peligro, un peligro. Ya estás llegando a tu destino y no hay posibilidades de aparcar. De pronto descubres un par de metros libres, un pedacito[13] de ciudad sin coche; frenas, el corazón te late apresuradamente.[14] Los conductores de detrás comienzan a tocar la bocina:[15] no me muevo. Tratas de estacionar, pero los vehículos que te siguen no te lo permiten. Tú miras con angustia el espacio libre, ese pedazo de paraíso[16] tan cercano y, sin embargo, inalcanzable.[17] De pronto, uno de los coches para y espera a que tú aparques. Tratas de retroceder, pero la calle es angosta[18] y la cosa está difícil. El vecino da marcha atrás[19] para ayudarte, aunque casi no puede moverse porque los otros coches están demasiado cerca. Al fin aparcas. Sales del coche, cierras la puerta. Sientes una alegría infinita, por haber cruzado la ciudad enemiga, por haber conseguido un lugar para tu coche, pero fundamentalmente, sientes enorme gratitud hacia el anónimo vecino que se detuvo[20] y te permitió aparcar. Caminas rápidamente para alcanzar al generoso conductor y darle las gracias. Llegas a su coche, es un hombre de unos cincuenta años, de mirada melancólica. Muchas gracias, insistes; soy el del coche azul, el que estacionó. El otro palidece y al fin contesta nerviosamente: "Pero, ¿qué quería usted? ¡No podía pasar por encima de los coches! No podía dar más marcha atrás". Tú no comprendes. "¡Gracias, gracias!" piensas. Al fin murmuras: "Le estoy dando las gracias de verdad, de verdad..." El hombre se pasa las manos por la cara y dice: "es que...este tráfico, estos nervios..." Sigues tu camino, sorprendido, pensando con filosófica tristeza, con genuino asombro[21] ¿Por qué es tan agresiva la gente? ¡No lo entiendo!

[1]teeth [2]license plate [3]scrapes [4]annoy [5]distressed moan [6]hate [7]fault [8]defeat [9]dust [10]windows [11]narrow [12]contempt [13]little piece [14]hurriedly [15]horn [16]paradise [17]unreachable [18]narrow [19]backs up [20]stopped [21]amazement

**¿Comprende Ud.?** Conteste las siguientes preguntas en relación a *El arrebato*.

1. ¿Dónde cree Ud. que ocurre esta historia?
2. ¿Qué tipo de personalidad cree Ud. que tiene el protagonista?
3. ¿Cuál es el tono de la historia? ¿Se identifica Ud. con el protagonista?

# 8

LECCIÓN OCHO

# Vámonos de viaje

CHECK OUT THE *¡TRATO HECHO!* WEBSITE AND CD-ROM FOR ACTIVITIES, GAMES, SELF-TESTS, AND MUCH MORE!

TEMA 1

## ¿Adónde vamos?

- De vacaciones
- En el aeropuerto
- Los complementos directos
- Más sobre los complementos directos

TEMA 2

## En el hotel

- En la recepción
- En la habitación
- Los complementos indirectos
- Los verbos como *gustar*

TEMA 3

## En el restaurante

- La cena
- El desayuno
- Dos pronombres juntos
- Resumen de los pronombres personales

TEMA 4

## Las indicaciones

- ¿Dónde está?
- Las excursiones
- Introducción a los mandatos formales
- Los pronombres con los mandatos

# ¡TRATO HECHO!

- Rincón profesional: Los viajes
- A escuchar
- A leer
- A escribir

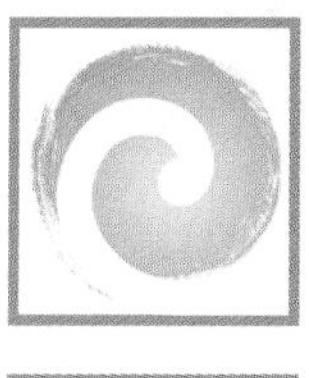

## De vacaciones

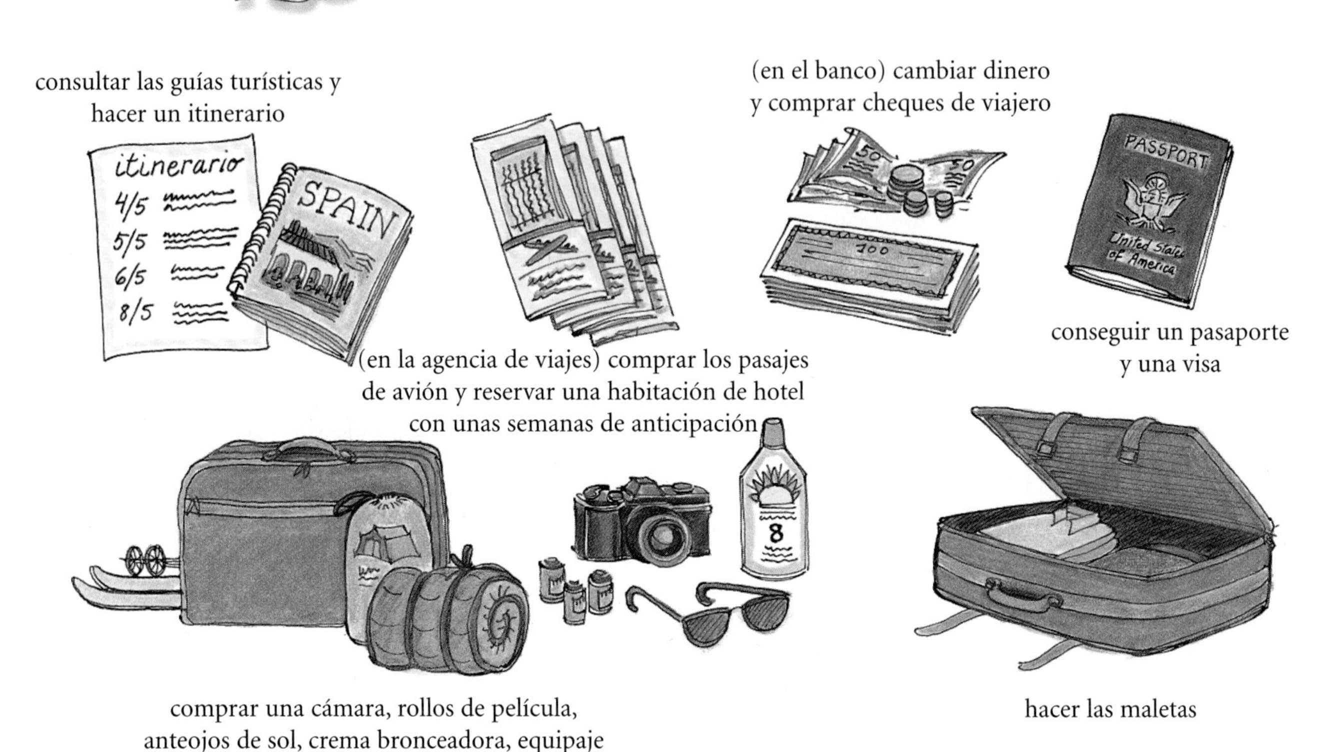


### De luna de miel

*Isabel y Lázaro van a la agencia de viajes para hacer reservaciones para un viaje....*

ANA: Lázaro, Isabel, ¡qué sorpresa verlos en la agencia!

LÁZARO: Queremos hacer reservaciones para nuestra luna de miel. Deseamos tomar un crucero. Lo queremos hacer al Caribe, por una semana.

ANA: La compañía Duquesa tiene una rebaja muy buena. ¿Prefieren un camarote interior o con vista al mar?

LÁZARO: Lo preferimos interior porque es más barato.

ANA: Tengo un viaje perfecto. El precio es de 1.200,00 dólares por persona. Incluye el pasaje de avión, el transporte al aeropuerto, el camarote y todas las comidas. ¿Quieren ver el folleto?

ISABEL: Sí. ¿Cuál es el itinerario?

ANA: Lo tengo en este folleto. Miren, el crucero dura quince días. Van a volar a Miami. Los recogen en el aeropuerto y los transportan al muelle para embarcarse. El barco se llama "La Duquesa del Pacífico" y los lleva a la República Dominicana, a Santo Tomás y a Puerto Rico. Allí desembarcan y los trasladan al aeropuerto.

ISABEL: Lo tomamos. Por favor, Ana ¿puedes hacer reservaciones para el 20 de junio?

ANA: Con mucho gusto. Yo las hago hoy mismo y los llamo en cuanto las confirme la compañía Duquesa.

**A. ¿Comprende Ud.?** Conteste las siguientes preguntas según el diálogo.

1. ¿Adónde quieren ir Isabel y Lázaro?
2. ¿Qué van a celebrar en el viaje?
3. ¿Por qué no piden un camarote con vista al mar?
4. ¿Cómo se llama el barco?

**Answers for A.** 1) *Al Caribe.* 2) *Su luna de miel.* 3) *Porque es caro.* 4) *La Duquesa del Pacífico.*

**B. ¿Cuándo?** Diga cuándo o cuántas veces Ud. hizo estas cosas la última vez que se quedó en un hotel. Pregúntele a su compañero/a también.

| con un mes de anticipación | dos días antes de salir | el día que salí |
|---|---|---|
| después de llegar / nunca | una vez / varias veces | dos veces |

1. reservar la habitación del hotel
2. hacer las maletas
3. tener que cambiar dinero
4. pasar el día entero en el hotel
5. tomar un taxi
6. llamar al servicio de habitación
7. lavar la ropa
8. leer el periódico
9. mirar la televisión en el hotel
10. pagar la cuenta

**Expansion for B.** Preview the use of direct object pronouns by paraphrasing student responses, e.g., *Leí el periódico después de llegar.—¿Lo leíste después de llegar?*

**C. Medios de transporte.** ¿Cuánto tiempo se necesita para hacer cada viaje? Calcule el tiempo aproximado para cada situación.

MODELO: ¿Para ir por metro del centro de México al Parque Chapultepec?
*En el metro toma aproximadamente veinte minutos.*

por avión

por autobús

en taxi

por barco/crucero

en tren/en metro

1. ¿Para ir de Miami a Puerto Rico en barco? ¿en avión?
2. ¿Para ir de Washington a Nueva York en tren? ¿en avión? ¿en autobús?
3. ¿Para ir de la universidad al centro de la ciudad a pie (*on foot*)? ¿en bicicleta? ¿en taxi?
4. ¿Para ir en crucero, desde San Juan, por el Canal de Panamá hasta Los Ángeles, después de parar en Acapulco?

**D. Entrevista.** Hable con su compañero/a de un viaje que cada uno/a de Uds. hizo.

1. ¿Qué hiciste? ¿Fuiste a un país extranjero? ¿Necesitabas un pasaporte? ¿una visa? ¿Con quién viajaste? ¿Por cuánto tiempo se quedaron allí? ¿Qué te gustó allí? ¿Qué no te gustó? ¿Te gustaría regresar a ese lugar?
2. ¿Usaste cheques de viajero? ¿Tuviste que cambiar dinero? ¿Cuánto gastaste? ¿Cuánto costó el pasaje de avión? ¿el crucero? ¿el hotel?
3. ¿Consultaste una guía turística? ¿Preparaste un itinerario antes de salir? ¿Seguiste el itinerario que preparaste o cambiaste de itinerario durante el viaje?
4. ¿Hiciste reservaciones antes de salir? ¿Con cuánto tiempo de anticipación las hiciste?

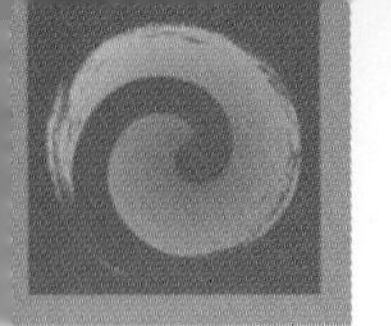

# ABC En el aeropuerto

## Facturando las maletas

*Isabel y Lázaro están a punto de subir al avión....*

DEPENDIENTA: Buenos días, bienvenidos a Aerolíneas Encanto. Sus pasajes, por favor.
ISABEL: Tú los tienes, Lázaro.
LÁZARO: No, yo no los tengo. Un momento, aquí están. Los puse con los pasaportes.
ISABEL: Queremos un asiento junto a la ventanilla y el otro en el centro.
DEPENDIENTA: Lo siento, pero no tenemos ningún asiento disponible en la ventanilla. ¿Cuántas maletas van a facturar?
LÁZARO: Estas cuatro grandes. También traemos dos maletas pequeñas. ¿Las podemos llevar en la mano?
DEPENDIENTA: Sólo si caben debajo del asiento. Aquí tienen los comprobantes de sus maletas y sus tarjetas de embarque. Los voy a poner dentro de este sobre, juntos con los pasajes de avión. La salida del vuelo 403 es por la puerta 18 y empiezan a embarcar a las diez de la mañana.

*En el avión, antes de despegar...*

AZAFATA: En nombre de toda la tripulación, les damos a todos una cordial bienvenida. Este es el vuelo 403 con destino a Miami. Aterrizamos en Miami aproximadamente a las 18:30 horas. En un momento vamos a servir bebidas. Más tarde servimos el almuerzo. Les deseamos un viaje muy placentero.

**Answers for A.** 1) *Lázaro.* 2) *Seis.* 3) *A las diez.* 4) *Miami.*

**A. ¿Comprende Ud.?** Conteste las siguientes preguntas con según el diálogo.

1. ¿Quién lleva los pasaportes?
2. ¿Cuántas maletas tienen Lázaro e Isabel en total?
3. ¿A qué hora comienzan a embarcar en el vuelo?
4. ¿Cuál es el destino del vuelo?

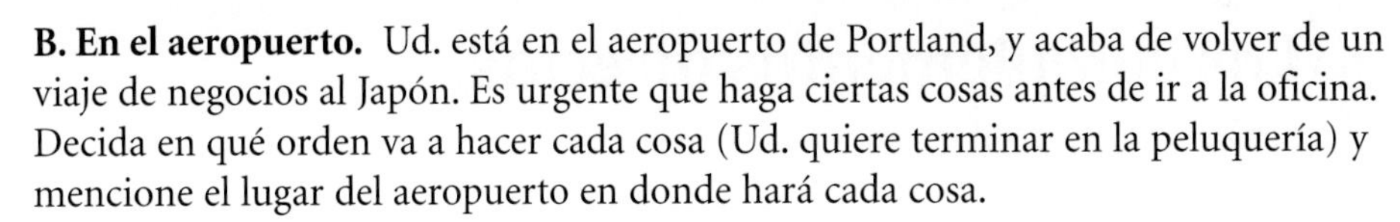

**B. En el aeropuerto.** Ud. está en el aeropuerto de Portland, y acaba de volver de un viaje de negocios al Japón. Es urgente que haga ciertas cosas antes de ir a la oficina. Decida en qué orden va a hacer cada cosa (Ud. quiere terminar en la peluquería) y mencione el lugar del aeropuerto en donde hará cada cosa.

MODELO: *Primero, voy a recoger el equipaje…*

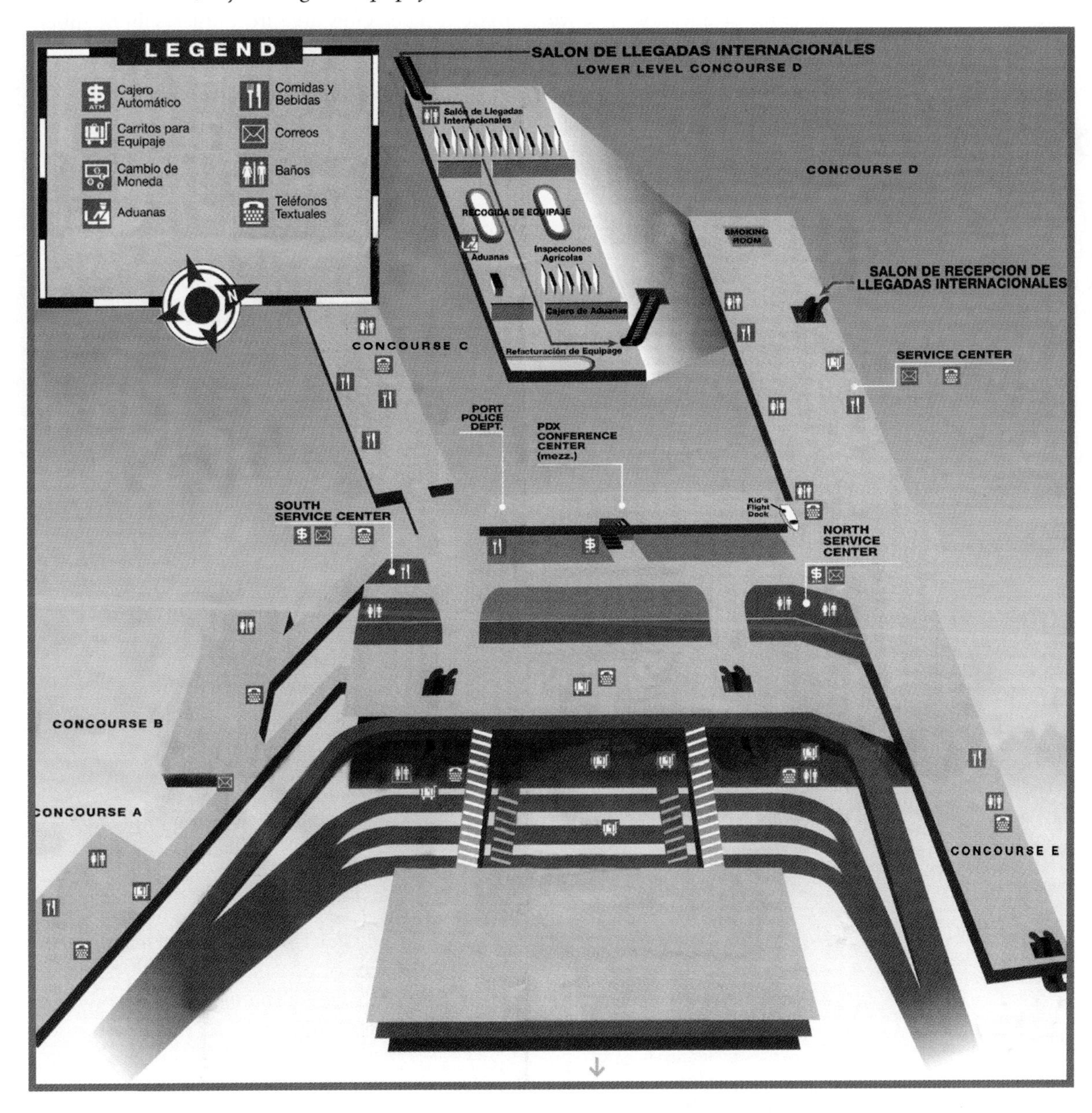


1. comer
2. cambiar dinero
3. usar el baño
4. recoger el equipaje (las maletas)
5. llamar a la oficina
6. poner las (tarjetas) postales en el correo
7. pasar por la aduana
8. sacar dinero del cajero automático

**C. En el mostrador del aeropuerto.** Uno/a de Uds. es el/la turista; el/la otro/a es el/la empleado/a de Aerolíneas Encanto. Están arreglando todo: pasaporte, pasajes, tarjetas de embarque (*boarding passes*), comprobantes de maletas, asientos, puerta de salida, hora de despegue, hora de aterrizaje, etc. El empleado tiene que asegurarse de que el turista tenga todos los documentos en regla y la información necesaria. ¡Dénse prisa porque el vuelo sale en media hora!

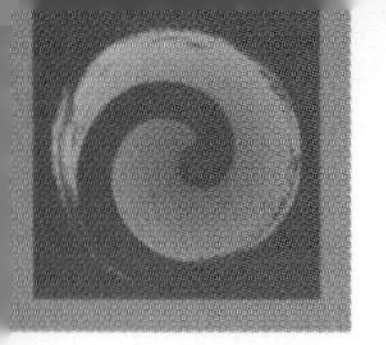

# Los complementos directos
## (*Direct objects*)

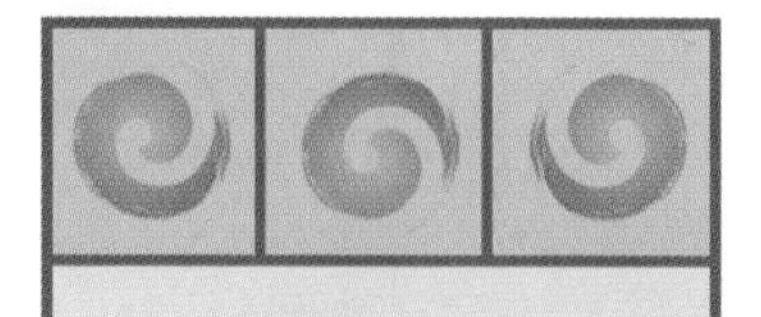

**Para averiguar**

1. What is a direct object?
2. What is a direct object pronoun?
3. What are the direct object pronouns in Spanish?
4. Where are direct object pronouns placed in a sentence?

- Direct objects are people, places, or things that are acted on by the subject of a sentence or question. The words in bold type below are direct objects. Remember that human direct objects are preceded by the personal **a**.

| | |
|---|---|
| Tengo **el folleto del crucero**. | *I have the cruise's pamphlet.* |
| Veo **el aeropuerto** desde esta ventana. | *I see the airport from this window.* |
| ¿Conoces **a mi amiga Mariam**? | *Do you know my friend Mariam?* |

- The following pronouns may replace nouns that function as direct objects.

| Direct object pronouns | | | |
|---|---|---|---|
| **me** | *me* | **nos** | *us* |
| **te** | *you* (familiar, singular) | **os** | *you* (familiar, plural) |
| **lo** | *him, it, you* (formal, singular, m.) | **los** | *them, you* (plural, m.) |
| **la** | *her, it, you* (formal, singular, fem.) | **las** | *them, you* (plural, fem.) |

- In English, direct object pronouns are placed after the verb. In Spanish, they are placed before a conjugated verb.

| | |
|---|---|
| —¿Conoces **este hotel**?<br>—Sí, **lo** conozco bien. | *Do you know this hotel?*<br>*Yes, I know it well.* |
| —¿Ves **el aeropuerto** desde tu ventana? | *Do you see the airport from your window?* |
| —Sí, **lo** veo muy bien desde mi cuarto. | *Yes, I see it very well from my room.* |
| —¿Hiciste **la reservación**?<br>—No, no **la** hice. | *Did you make the reservation?*<br>*No, I didn't make it.* |
| —¿Por qué nunca **me** invitas a tu casa? | *Why don't you ever invite me to your house?* |
| —Pues, **te** invito a cenar con nosotros mañana. | *I'm inviting you to have dinner with us tomorrow.* |

## A lo personal

**A. Para el viaje.** You are talking with your travel agent about what you will need to bring on your luxury cruise. Ask if you need these items.

MODELO: ropa formal
E1: *¿Necesito ropa formal?*
E2: *Sí, la necesita.*

1. un traje de baño
2. botas vaqueras
3. un abrigo
4. mucho dinero
5. toallas
6. comida
7. un suéter
8. una cámara
9. un vídeo de *Titanic*
10. mi pasaporte

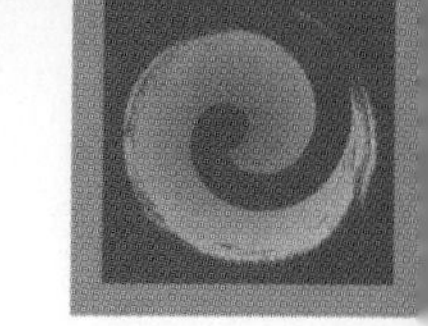

**B. ¿Dónde lo pusiste?** Your traveling companion wants to know whether you brought the following items or left them at home. Ask another student the following questions.

MODELO: el pasaporte
E1: *¿Trajiste el pasaporte?*
E2: *Sí, lo traje./No, lo dejé en casa.*

1. los boletos
2. el dinero
3. la ropa nueva
4. el gato
5. la cafetera
6. las sillas del comedor
7. el teléfono celular
8. las confirmaciones de las reservaciones

**C. La última vez.** When did you last do these things? Use a direct object pronoun in your response.

MODELO: hacer planes para un viaje
*Los hice la semana pasada./No los hago nunca.*

1. pedir un folleto de viajes
2. hacer reservaciones en un restaurante
3. consultar a su agente de viajes
4. celebrar su luna de miel
5. pedir un pasaporte
6. hacer un crucero
7. investigar lugares en el Internet
8. hacer las maletas para viajar
9. visitar a su familia
10. preparar un itinerario

**D. Los amigos.** Ask a classmate who does these things to him/her.

MODELO: llamar por teléfono con frecuencia
E1: *¿Quién te llama por teléfono con frecuencia?*
E2: *Mi hermana me llama dos o tres veces a la semana./Nadie me llama.*

1. hablar todos los días
2. invitar a salir
3. enojar a veces
4. visitar a veces
5. conocer muy bien
6. criticar
7. sorprender
8. ayudar con su tarea a veces
9. nunca comprender
10. aburrir

Now tell whether or not your Spanish teacher does the same things to you and your classmates.

MODELO: llamar por teléfono con frecuencia.
*Nunca nos llama por teléfono.*

**E. Los objetos.** With a partner, use as many verbs as you can to describe what we do with the following:

MODELO: dinero
*Lo ganamos, lo gastamos, lo ponemos en el banco…*

1. comida
2. ropa
3. libros
4. clases
5. folletos
6. agente de viajes
7. español
8. preguntas

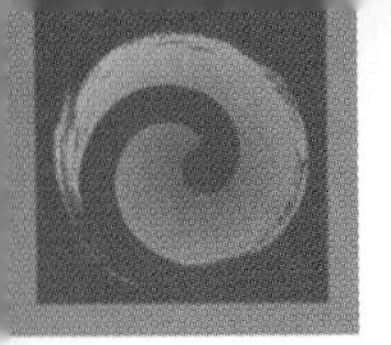

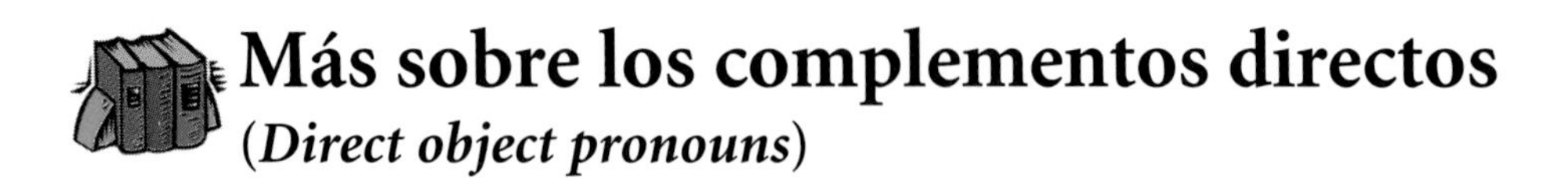

# Más sobre los complementos directos
## (*Direct object pronouns*)

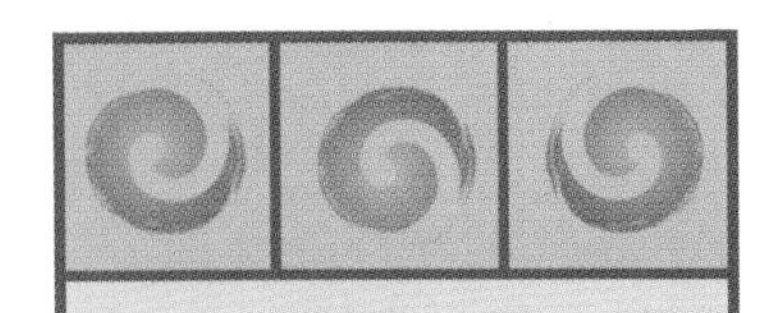

**Para averiguar**

1. Direct object pronouns may occur in either of two places when a conjugated verb is followed by an infinitive. What are these two positions?
2. What are the two possible positions of direct object pronouns with the present progressive **(estar + -ndo)**? When is there a written accent mark on the verb?

- You have seen that the direct object pronoun is placed before a conjugated verb. If an infinitive follows the conjugated verb and shares the same subject, the pronoun may be placed before the conjugated verb, or it may be attached to the end of the infinitive.

| | | |
|---|---|---|
| Voy a hacer **las reservaciones.** | → | **Las** voy a hacer.<br>Voy a hacer**las.** |
| Tengo que hacer **las reservaciones.** | → | **Las** tengo que hacer.<br>Tengo que hacer**las.** |

- In the present progressive, the direct object pronoun may be placed either before the conjugated form of **estar** or attached to the end of the **-ndo** form of a verb. In the latter case, a written accent is placed on the stressed vowel of the verb.

| | | |
|---|---|---|
| Estoy haciendo **las reservaciones** ahora. | → | **Las** estoy haciendo ahora.<br>Estoy hac**iéndolas** ahora. |

## A lo personal

**A. ¿Qué vas a hacer con ese...?** You want to know what your friend is going to do with these items. Your friend answers with a logical verb from the list below and a direct object pronoun.

MODELO: E1: *¿Qué vas a hacer con esas maletas?*
E2: *Voy a facturarlas./Las voy a facturar.*

leer mirar comer gastar tomar escuchar llevar comprar planear escribir

1. ese libro
2. esa película
3. ese café
4. esa pizza
5. esas revistas
6. esos casetes
7. ese suéter
8. esas tarjetas postales
9. ese itinerario
10. ese dinero

**B. Los novios.** With a classmate, role-play two young lovers arguing about their relationship. One partner reproaches the other for doing or not doing certain things. The other tries to appease his/her partner.

MODELO: llamar
E1: *¡Nunca me llamas!*
E2: *Te voy a llamar más.* o *Voy a llamarte más.*
criticar
E1: *¡Siempre me criticas!*
E2: *No te voy a criticar más.* o *No voy a criticarte más.*

1. invitar a salir
2. olvidar
3. tratar bien
4. abrazar
5. llevar al restaurante
6. escuchar
7. ponerse furioso/a
8. presentar a tus amigos
9. comprar cosas
10. tratar mal

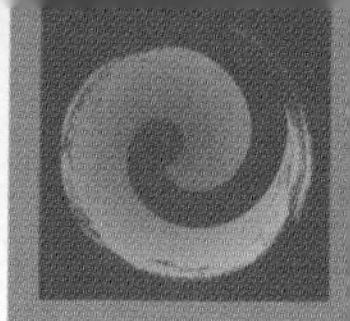

**C. ¿Qué estás buscando?** Your roommate is looking for the following items. You ask why, and he/she gives a logical answer.

MODELO: mis zapatos negros
E1: *¿Sabes dónde están mis zapatos negros?*
E2: *¿Por qué estás buscándolos?/¿Por qué los estás buscando?*
E1: *Los necesito porque voy a una boda.*

1. las maletas
2. las fotos de mi viaje
3. los boletos
4. mi traje de baño
5. mi ropa formal
6. mi calculadora
7. mi libro de español
8. mis anteojos
9. mis zapatos rojos
10. las llaves de mi coche

**D. ¿Me puedes ayudar?** Ask a classmate if he/she can or will do the following things for you.

MODELO: E1: *¿Me puedes ayudar con la tarea de cálculo?*
E2: *Claro que te puedo ayudar./No, no te puedo ayudar con el cálculo.*

1. ¿Me vas a llamar esta tarde?
2. ¿Me quieres acompañar a Puerto Rico este verano?
3. ¿Me puedes visitar este fin de semana?
4. ¿Me puedes ir a buscar a la biblioteca esta noche?
5. ¿Me quieres comprar un café?
6. ¿Me puedes ayudar a limpiar la casa?

**E. Una conversación.** You are ready for a trip and are afraid of forgetting something. With another student, role-play a discussion and make a to-do list. Then check off what you have to do.

MODELO: llamar al agente
*Yo ya lo llamé.* o
*Tengo que llamarlo.*

1. lavar la ropa
2. comprar los pasajes
3. hacer las reservaciones
4. buscar el equipaje
5. hacer las maletas
6. llamar un taxi
7. cerrar la casa
8. llevar al gato al veterinario
9. cancelar el periódico
10. llamar a mi madre

# TEMA 2 En el hotel

## ABC En la recepción

### En la recepción del Hotel Continental

*Isabel y Lázaro acaban de llegar al hotel donde van a quedarse....*

ISABEL: Buenas noches, tenemos una reservación a nombre del señor y la señora Frankel.

RECEPCIONISTA: Buenas noches. Sí, les reservé una habitación doble por una noche. ¿Me permiten su identificación?

ISABEL: No sé dónde están nuestros pasaportes. ¿Le podemos mostrar nuestra licencia de conducir?

RECEPCIONISTA: Claro, yo se la devuelvo inmediatamente. Les voy a dar una habitación preciosa en el décimo piso.

LÁZARO: A mí me gusta estar en la planta baja. ¿No se lo dijo nuestra agente de viajes?

RECEPCIONISTA: Sí, pero no le prometimos nada a su agente. Espero que no les moleste, pero el hotel está completamente lleno. Les di una habitación muy buena: tiene un balcón con vista al mar. Estoy seguro de que les va a gustar mucho.

LÁZARO: Bueno, no nos gusta, pero en fin. ¿Ya trajeron las maletas?

RECEPCIONISTA: No, no las ha traído la compañía Duquesa. Nosotros les subimos sus maletas en cuanto lleguen. Les voy a dar dos llaves para la habitación 1006. Los ascensores están detrás de la recepción. Doblen a la izquierda y allí los encuentran.

**A. ¿Comprende Ud.?** Conteste las siguientes preguntas según el diálogo.

1. ¿Qué tipo de habitación reservaron Lázaro e Isabel?
2. ¿En qué piso está su habitación?
3. ¿Qué se puede ver desde el balcón?
4. ¿Cuántas llaves tienen para la habitación?

**Answers for A.** 1) *Doble.* 2) *En el décimo.* 3) *El mar.* 4) *Dos.*

**B. Preferencias.** Diga cuál prefiere y hable con su compañero/a para saber sus preferencias.

¿Prefieres tú una habitación...

1. ...con baño por 8.000 pesetas o sin baño por 5.000?
2. ...con balcón por 12.000 pesetas o sin balcón por 11.000?
3. ...con el desayuno incluido por 10.000 pesetas o sin desayuno por 9.500?
4. ...con vista al mar o con vista a las montañas?
5. ...cerca del ascensor o lejos del ascensor?
6. ...en la planta baja, en el primer piso o en un piso más alto?

**Note.** Currency from different countries is introduced throughout the text in order to maximize student exposure. 1 dólar =158 pesetas.

**C. Un/a recepcionista.** Uno/a de Uds. es un/a empleado/a bilingüe en la oficina de reservaciones de los hoteles Londres. Hable por teléfono con un/a cliente/a (su compañero/a) que llama desde México para hacer una reservación. Hablen de:

- las fechas de llegada y salida
- el tipo de habitación deseado
- el precio
- características especiales del hotel/de la habitación

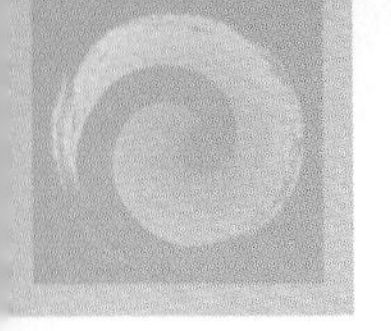

# En la habitación

## Problemas con la habitación

*Isabel y Lázaro están mirando la habitación del hotel....*

LÁZARO: No me gusta estar en el décimo piso. Me pongo muy nervioso.
ISABEL: Pero mira qué vista tan romántica. Te invito al balcón para ver el mar.
LÁZARO: No gracias. Me molesta la altura. ¿Te importa si bajamos a la piscina a nadar?
ISABEL: No nos permiten nadar a esta hora. Son las ocho de la noche. Además, no nos pusieron toallas. Voy a llamar a la recepcionista para pedirlas.

*Por teléfono...*

ISABEL: Señor, por favor, necesitamos toallas para la habitación 1006.
RECEPCIONISTA: ¿Le puedo llevar algo más?
ISABEL: Sí, jabón y unos vasos.
RECEPCIONISTA: Con mucho gusto, les pido que nos disculpen. La camarera les va a llevar todo inmediatamente.

**Answers for A.** 1) *Lázaro.* 2) *A la piscina.* 3) *A la recepcionista.* 4) *La camarera.*

**A. ¿Comprende Ud.?** Conteste las siguientes preguntas según el diálogo.

1. ¿Quién tiene miedo de la altura?
2. ¿Adónde quiere ir Lázaro?
3. ¿A quién llama Isabel?
4. ¿Quién lleva las toallas, el jabón y los vasos a la habitación?

**B. En el hotel.** ¿Qué puede estar diciendo un/a huésped del hotel? Complete las oraciones con una palabra lógica.

1. Hace mucho frío en la habitación. La ______________ no funciona.
2. Mi ropa está sucia. ¿Tiene el hotel ______________?
3. Quiero bañarme pero no hay ni ______________ ni ______________.
4. También quiero lavarme el pelo. ¿Hay ______________?
5. Pedí una habitación de no fumador. No comprendo por qué hay un ______________ en mi habitación.
6. Todavía no han hecho la cama. Necesitamos ______________ limpias.
7. Raramente hace calor aquí. Por eso, el hotel no tiene ______________.
8. No hay baño en la habitación pero pueden lavarse un poco porque hay un ______________.
9. Quiero cenar en la habitación esta noche. Voy a llamar al ______________.

**C. En un hotel de lujo.** Lea el anuncio para una cadena (*chain*) de hoteles de lujo en los Estados Unidos y después conteste las preguntas.

# Desde US $79, Para que no se incomode

Alcoba privada con cama tamaño king o dos camas matrimoniales, baño completo, vanity o peinador, televisor a color de control remoto y teléfono.

Sala de estar privada, con sofá-cama, televisor a color de control remoto, teléfono, mini-bar, horno de microondas, refrigerador, congelador y cafetera eléctrica.

Por el precio de una habitación angosta e incómoda en cualquier otro hotel, Royal le da una espaciosa suite, ideal para realizar sus negocios o disfrutar con la familia, y muchas otras agradables comodidades. Por ejemplo, todas las mañanas, en nuestro bello patio interior, le servimos un desayuno completo. Si en otros hoteles de habitaciones estrechas se siente incómodo, en nuestros hoteles de amplias suites, se va a sentir... ¡Verdaderamente a sus anchas!

ROYAL SUITES

Reservaciones:

1-800-555-3456

1. ¿Qué hay en la alcoba? ¿Cuál es otra palabra para **alcoba**? ¿Qué hay en la sala de estar?
2. ¿Cuánto cuesta la habitación más barata?
3. ¿Para qué es ideal una suite?
4. ¿A qué número pueden llamar si desean más información?
5. ¿Qué ofrecen todas las mañanas en el patio interior?
6. ¿Cómo se puede decir en inglés "¡Verdaderamente a sus anchas!"?

**D. Su luna de miel.** Ud. y su esposo/a están en su luna de miel. Al entrar a su habitación, ven que nada está bien. No hay toallas, no hay jabón, la cama está sin hacer (*unmade*), el televisor está encendido y ¡hay colillas (*butts*) en el cenicero! Llame al/a la recepcionista (su compañero/a) para resolver el problema.

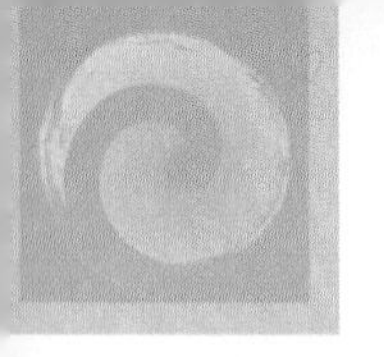

# Los complementos indirectos
## (*Indirect object pronouns*)

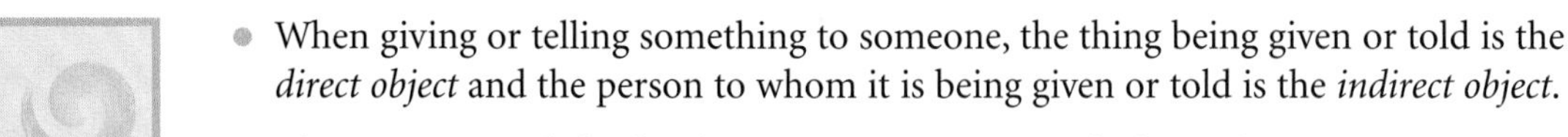

### Para averiguar

1. Which indirect object pronouns differ from the direct object pronouns?
2. Which two categories of verbs often have indirect objects? What is another common use of indirect objects?
3. Why do indirect object pronouns sometimes seem repetitive?
4. How do placement rules for indirect object pronouns compare with those for direct object pronouns?

- When giving or telling something to someone, the thing being given or told is the *direct object* and the person to whom it is being given or told is the *indirect object*.

They recommend *this hotel* ***to me.*** (*this hotel* = *d.o.*, ***to me*** = ***i.o.***)

I gave *the key* ***to him.*** (*the key* = *d.o.*, ***to him*** = ***i.o.***)

- Indirect object pronouns in Spanish are the same as direct object pronouns, except **le** is used instead of **lo** and **la**, and **les** is used instead of **los** and **las**.

| Indirect object pronouns | |
|---|---|
| **me** *(to, for) me* | **nos** *(to, for) us* |
| **te** *(to, for) you* (fam. sing.) | **os** *(to, for) you* (fam. pl.) |
| **le** *(to, for) him, her, you* (form. sing.) | **les** *(to, for) them, you* (form. pl.) |

- Indirect objects are frequently used with the following verbs that indicate exchange or communication.

| | | | |
|---|---|---|---|
| EXCHANGE: | **comprar** (*to buy*) | **dar** (*to give*) | **mandar** (*to send*) |
| | **ofrecer** (*to offer*) | **prestar** (*to lend*) | **regalar** (*to give as a gift*) |
| | **servir** (*to serve*) | **traer** (*to bring*) | **vender** (*to sell*) |
| COMMUNICATION: | **decir** (*to say, to tell*) | **enseñar** (*to teach*) | **recomendar** (*to recomm* |
| | **escribir** (*to write*) | **explicar** (*to explain*) | **hablar** (*to speak*) |
| | **leer** (*to read*) | **pedir** (*to ask for*) | **preguntar** (*to ask a questio* |

- Indirect objects are also used to request favors or to express for whom a favor is done.

¿**Me** trae una servilleta, por favor? — *Would you bring me a napkin, please?*
¿**Nos** hace un favor? — *Would you do us a favor?*
Siempre **le** preparo algo de comer. — *I always prepare him something to eat.*

- An indirect object noun that refers to a specific person or group of people is most often accompanied by the corresponding pronoun (clarifier) in the same sentence. Although this may seem repetitive, it is normal in Spanish. The clarifier and the noun must both refer to the same person or persons.

**Le** escribo cartas **a mi tío Eduardo.** — *I write letters to my uncle Eduardo.*
Nunca **les** presto dinero **a mis amigos.** — *I never lend money to my friends.*

- For clarification or emphasis, you may add the preposition **a** followed by a prepositional pronoun.

**Le** digo todo **a ella** pero no **le** digo nada **a él.** — *I tell her everything but I don't tell him anything.*
¿**Me** estás hablando **a mí**? — *Are you talking to me?*

- Indirect object pronouns follow the same placement rules as direct object pronouns or reflexive pronouns.

| | |
|---|---|
| SINGLE CONJUGATED VERB | ¿**Le** escribes una carta? |
| CONJUGATED VERB + *infinitive* | ¿**Le** vas a escribir una carta?/<br>¿Vas a escribir**le** una carta? |
| WITH **estar** + **-ndo** | ¿**Le** estás escribiendo una carta?/<br>¿Estás escribi**é**ndo**le** una carta? |

## A lo personal

**A. ¿Qué hace Ud.?** Some Chilean friends are coming for a visit. Indicate whether or not you would do these things. If you answer no, change the italicized words so that the statement is true.

1. Les recomiendo el hotel *Marriott.*
2. Les digo que *julio* es el mes más interesante.
3. Les digo que hace mejor tiempo aquí en *otoño.*
4. Les recomiendo el restaurante *Burger King.*
5. Les hablo en *español.*
6. Les enseño *la universidad.*

**B. Pronombres lógicos.** Complete each statement with the appropriate object pronoun.

**Suggestion for B.** Have students underline the indirect object in the sentence before they fill in the indirect object pronouns to aid comprehension.

MODELO: Siempre _____mando flores a mi madre para el Día de la Madre.
*Siempre* **le** *mando flores a mi madre para el Día de la Madre.*

1. Siempre ______ doy tarjetas a mis amigos para sus cumpleaños.
2. Con frecuencia _____ pido mucho dinero a mis padres.
3. A veces _____ presto mi coche a mi mejor amigo/a.
4. Cada semana _____ escribo un poema a mi novio/a.
5. Nunca ____ pido favores a mi compañero/a de cuarto.
6. A veces ______ doy las respuestas a mis compañeros de clase.
7. Nunca ______ traigo bebidas alcohólicas a mis amigos.
8. A veces _____ hablo a mi madre de cosas personales.

**C. ¿A quién?** To whom do you do the following things?

**New word:** *mentiras*

MODELO: pedirle ayuda con el español
*Les pido ayuda a mis amigas Teresa y Lupita.* o *No le pido ayuda a nadie.*

1. escribirle con frecuencia
2. darle consejos
3. decirle todo
4. hablarle en español
5. decirle mentiras a veces
6. pedirle favores

**D. Favores.** Make a list of three things that you have done for people and three things that others have done for you in the last few days.

MODELO: *Le mandé una tarjeta de cumpleaños a mi padre.*
*Mi novio/a me lavó la ropa anoche.*

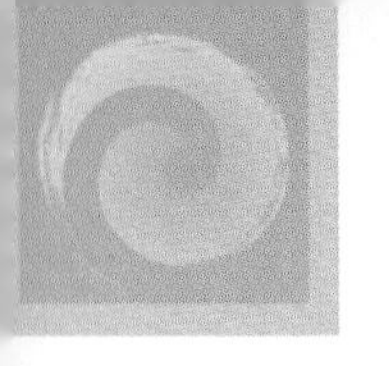

# Los verbos como *gustar*
## (*Verbs like* gustar)

### Para averiguar

1. What does **me gusta** literally mean?
2. When do you use the plural form **gustan**?
3. What are seven other verbs that are used like **gustar**?

- Since **Lección 2**, you have used the expression **me gusta** to say what you *like* and later, **me gustaría** to say what you *would like*. The **me** of **me gusta/me gustaría** is an indirect object pronoun.

  A phrase like **Me gustan los perros** literally means *Dogs are pleasing to me*. **Gustar** agrees with the subject **los perros**, and not with **me**. Note that the subject of **gustar** generally follows the verb and the definite article is generally used as well.

| | |
|---|---|
| **Les gusta** la playa. | *They like the beach.* *(The beach is pleasing to them.)* |
| **Le gustan** las ciudades grandes. | *She likes big cities.* *(Big cities are pleasing to her.)* |

- When followed by an infinitive or series of infinitives, **gustar** is used in the third person singular.

| | |
|---|---|
| **Les gusta** viajar. | *They like to travel.* |
| **Les gusta** comer, beber y bailar. | *They like to eat, drink, and dance.* |

- When you name a person who likes something, the name, noun, or pronoun must be preceded by **a**, since it is an indirect object. Remember that the indirect object pronoun will be included in your statement along with the indirect object noun or prepositional pronoun, even though this may seem redundant.

| | |
|---|---|
| **A** mí **me** gustan las películas. | *I like movies.* *(Movies are pleasing to me.)* |
| **A** mis padres **les** gusta pescar. | *My parents like to fish.* *(Fishing is pleasing to my parents.)* |
| **A** ti **te** gusta la nieve. | *You like snow.* *(Snow is pleasing to you.)* |

- The following verbs and expressions are used like **gustar**.

| | |
|---|---|
| **encantar** | *to delight, love (non-person)* |
| **hacer falta** | *to be lacking, in need* |
| **interesar** | *to interest* |
| **faltar** | *to be missing* |
| **molestar** | *to bother* |
| **importar** | *to be important, matter* |
| **quedar bien/mal** | *to fit well/badly* |
| **doler (ue)** | *to hurt, ache* |

| | |
|---|---|
| **Me encanta** Barcelona. | *I love Barcelona.* |
| **Le falta** el reloj. | *He's missing his watch.* |
| A los niños **no les interesan** los museos. | *Museums do not interest children.* |
| **Nos hace falta** dinero. | *We need money.* |
| ¿**Te molesta** si fumo? | *Does it bother you if I smoke?* |
| A mi amigo **no le importan** mis problemas. | *My problems don't matter to my friend.* |
| Este vestido **te queda** bien. | *This dress fits you well.* |
| ¿**Te duele** la cabeza? | *Does your head hurt?* |

## A lo personal

**A. ¿Quién es?** Which of your acquaintances or which celebrities do the following statements describe?

MODELO: Le(s) hace falta dinero.
*A mi hermano Javier siempre le hace falta dinero.* o
*A mí siempre me hace falta dinero.* o
*Nunca les hace falta dinero a mis amigos.*

1. Le(s) interesa mucho la política.
2. No le(s) importa la opinión de los demás.
3. Le(s) molesta mucho hablar de política.
4. Le(s) encanta hablar de cosas tontas.
5. Nunca le(s) gusta salir los fines de semana.
6. Le(s) interesan mucho los deportes.
7. Le(s) falta tiempo para estudiar.
8. Le(s) encanta comprar ropa.
9. Nunca le(s) queda bien la ropa.
10. No le(s) gusta mirar los deportes en la televisión.

**B. Los gustos.** Ask a classmate if he/she likes the following things associated with traveling. He/she will answer using one of the expressions below.

MODELO: los viajes en grupos grandes
E1: *¿Te gustan los viajes en grupos grandes?*
E2: *No, no me gustan nada los viajes en grupos grandes.*

Me encanta(n)... Me interesa(n) un poco... Me gusta(n) bastante... No me gusta(n) nada...

1. las ruinas antiguas
2. la playa
3. las montañas
4. las excursiones al campo
5. las discotecas
6. viajar en avión
7. broncearse
8. pescar
9. ir al teatro
10. escalar montañas

Now complete each of the four expressions listed above with other words to express your likes or dislikes while on vacation.

MODELO: *Me encanta probar la comida de otros países.*
*Me gustan bastante los cruceros.*
*Me interesa un poco visitar museos.*
*No me gusta nada viajar en autobús.*

**C. Entrevista.** Ask your classmate the following questions.

1. ¿A qué lugar te gustaría hacer un viaje? ¿Qué te encanta hacer durante las vacaciones? En un hotel, ¿te importa más el precio o el servicio?
2. En un hotel, ¿te gusta más llamar al servicio de habitación para la cena o salir a un restaurante?
3. ¿Te molesta si la gente (*people*) fuma en los vuelos internacionales? ¿Te gusta hablar con los pasajeros sentados a tu lado en el avión?
4. ¿Te gustaría pasar las vacaciones en una isla tropical este verano? ¿Cómo te queda tu traje de baño del verano pasado?
5. ¿Qué te falta para hacer un viaje ahora? ¿dinero? ¿tiempo? ¿ropa? ¿ganas?
6. Si haces caminatas por las montañas, ¿qué te duele después? ¿Te duele algo ahora?

# Vocabulario

## TEMA 1
### ¿Adónde vamos?

**Sustantivos**

| | |
|---|---|
| **la aduana** | *customs* |
| **el aeropuerto** | *airport* |
| **el alimento** | *food* |
| **el avión** | *airplane* |
| **la azafata** | *flight attendant* |
| **el barco** | *boat/ship* |
| **el bronceador** | *tanning lotion* |
| **el cajero automático** | *automatic teller* |
| **el camarote** | *ship's cabin* |
| **el comprobante** | *claim check* |
| **el crucero** | *cruise ship* |
| **el destino** | *destination* |
| **la duquesa** | *duchess* |
| **el equipaje** | *luggage* |
| **la guía** | *guidebook* |
| **el itinerario** | *itinerary* |
| **la luna de miel** | *honeymoon* |
| **la maleta** | *suitcase* |
| **la moneda** | *coin/currency* |
| **el muelle** | *pier* |
| **el pasaje** | *ticket* |
| **el pasaporte** | *passport* |
| **el pase** | *pass* |
| **la sorpresa** | *surprise* |
| **el transporte** | *transportation* |
| **la tripulación** | *crew* |
| **la ventanilla** | *window* |
| **el/la viajero/a** | *traveler* |
| **el vuelo** | *flight* |

**Verbos**

| | |
|---|---|
| **abordar/embarcar** | *to board, to embark* |
| **aterrizar** | *to land* |
| **despegar** | *to take off* |
| **facturar** | *to check (luggage)* |
| **incluir** | *to include* |
| **planear** | *to plan* |
| **transportar** | *to transport* |
| **volar (ue)** | *to fly* |

**Adjetivos**

| | |
|---|---|
| **placentero/a** | *pleasant* |
| **turístico/a** | *tourist* |

**Otras expresiones**

| | |
|---|---|
| **dentro** | *inside* |
| **en cuanto** | *as soon as* |

## TEMA 2
### En el hotel

**Sustantivos**

| | |
|---|---|
| **el aire acondicionado** | *air conditioning* |
| **la almohada** | *pillow* |
| **la altura** | *altitude/height* |
| **el ascensor** | *elevator* |
| **el botones** | *bellboy* |
| **el/la camarero/a** | *maid* |
| **el cenicero** | *ashtray* |
| **el champú** | *shampoo* |
| **la ducha** | *shower* |
| **el/la huésped** | *guest* |
| **el jabón** | *soap* |
| **la llave** | *key* |
| **el mar** | *sea* |
| **el papel higiénico** | *toilet paper* |
| **la planta baja** | *ground floor* |
| **el/la recepcionista** | *receptionist* |
| **la sábana** | *sheet* |
| **el servicio de lavandería** | *laundry service* |
| **la toalla** | *towel* |
| **el vaso** | *glass* |

**Verbos**

| | |
|---|---|
| **bajar** | *to go down* |
| **devolver (ue)** | *to return (something)* |
| **molestar** | *to bother* |
| **mostrar (ue)** | *to show* |
| **permitir** | *to permit, let* |
| **prometer** | *to promise* |
| **subir** | *to go up, get in* |

**Adjetivos**

| | |
|---|---|
| **doble** | *double* |
| **limpio/a** | *clean* |
| **lleno/a** | *full* |
| **precioso/a** | *lovely* |
| **seguro/a** | *sure, certain* |
| **sencillo/a** | *single* |

**Otras expresiones**

| | |
|---|---|
| **detrás** | *in back* |

# Reunión A

**A escuchar. Un buen restaurante.** Escuche la conversación entre el botones, Isabel y Lázaro. Marque las oraciones con **Cierto (C)** o **Falso (F)**.

1. _____ El botones recomienda un restaurante cubano.
2. _____ A Lázaro y a Isabel no les gusta la comida cubana.
3. _____ En el bar del Hotel Flamingo pueden bailar.
4. _____ Allí hay un grupo musical mexicano.
5. _____ Lázaro dice que les gusta caminar.
6. _____ Isabel dice que está cansada y quiere ir en taxi.

**Tapescript for *A escuchar*. Un buen restaurante.**
BOTONES: Buenas noches, señores. ¿Les puedo ayudar?
ISABEL: Sí, ¿nos puede recomendar un buen restaurante?
BOTONES: Si les gusta la comida cubana, en la Pequeña Habana hay muchos restaurantes buenos. ¿Conocen la comida cubana?
LÁZARO: Sí, la conocemos y nos encanta. También nos gusta la música cubana.
BOTONES: Entonces, yo sé dónde pueden bailar. Después de cenar, les sugiero ir al bar del Hotel Flamingo. Hay un grupo musical cubano muy bueno desde las nueve de la noche hasta las tres de la madrugada. ¿Les puedo conseguir un taxi?
LÁZARO: Gracias, nos gusta caminar.
ISABEL: Sí, nos gusta mucho, pero ahora estoy un poco cansada. Lázaro, ¿te importa si vamos en taxi?
LÁZARO: No, no me importa. Así vamos a poder bailar toda la noche.

**Answers for *A escuchar*.** 1) *C.* 2) *F.* 3) *C.* 4) *F.* 5) *C.* 6) *C.*

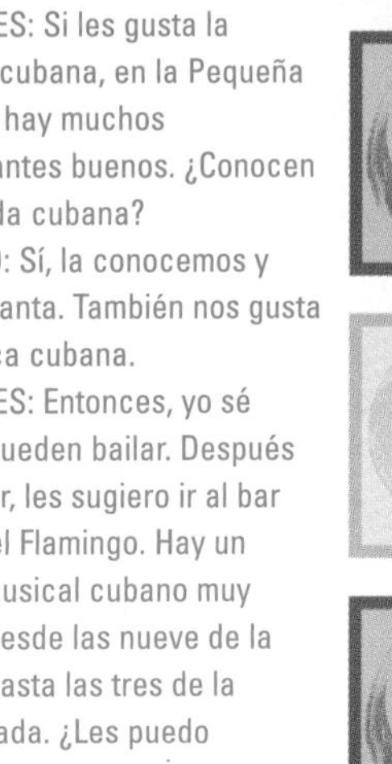

**A conversar.** Hoy es el cumpleaños de su compañero/a y Ud. quiere invitarlo/a a cenar en un restaurante. Pregúntele a dónde quiere ir y por qué. Ud. debe sugerir otro restaurante y entre los/as dos deben decidir cuál es mejor.

**¿Lo sabía?**

## Aerolíneas Imperiales

**tu aerolínea internacional**

Aerolíneas Imperiales, tu primera compañía aérea para viajar a Barcelona. Con más de 30 millones de pasajeros al año viajando de un punto a otro, Aerolíneas Imperiales te ofrece sus servicios para que disfrutes de una de las flotas más modernas del mercado.

Con más de 50 años volando y más de 30.000 personas trabajando para hacerte las distancias más cortas y el viaje más placentero.

Tenemos más de 900 vuelos diarios a todas partes del mundo. Entre éstos, te ofrecemos vuelos directos con salida diaria a ciudades tan interesantes como San Juan, Lima, Caracas, Buenos Aires, Valencia, Londres, Sevilla y París. Y estos son sólo algunos ejemplos de los lugares fascinantes que vas a poder visitar con nuestra aerolínea.

Estamos dispuestos a todo para llegar a ser los mejores, la primera compañía aérea en tu lista de viajes. Tú decides el destino, Aerolíneas Imperiales lo pone a tus pies.

**¿Comprende Ud.?**

1. Escriba por lo menos tres ventajas de viajar con Aerolíneas Imperiales.
2. Indique las naciones mencionadas basándose en los nombres de las ciudades—¡OJO! ¡Quizás sea necesario consultar un mapa!

**A buscar.** ¿Cuál es su destino soñado? Prepare su itinerario y comparta su viaje con el de otros en su grupo. Busque información en el Internet, revistas y/o periódicos. Incluya mapas, hoteles, restaurantes, sitios de interés, espectáculos, transporte y precios. Todos deben votar al final para escoger el mejor viaje de todos.

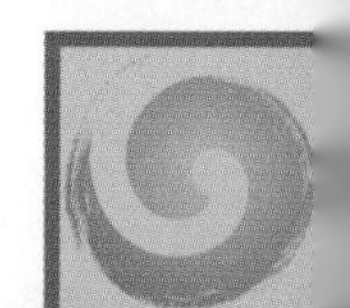

# TEMA 3 En el restaurante

## La cena

### La primera cena en "La Duquesa del Pacífico"

*Isabel y Lázaro ya están en el crucero disfrutando de los placeres de la vida....*

MESERO: Buenas noches, soy Casimiro. Voy a ser su mesero por toda la semana. Aquí tienen la carta. La compañía Duquesa los felicita por su boda y les regala una botella de champán.

ISABEL Y LÁZARO: Muchas gracias.

ISABEL: ¿Nos la puede mandar a nuestro camarote después de cenar?

MESERO: Con mucho gusto. Se la voy a poner en el refrigerador de su camarote. Hoy es la noche italiana y tenemos milanesas de ternera en salsa de tomate, acompañadas de brócoli con queso fundido. Se las recomiendo. ¡Están deliciosas!

LÁZARO: Está bien, me las puede traer, por favor, pero no me gusta el brócoli. ¿Me las puede acompañar con otra verdura?

MESERO: Sí, se las voy a servir con unas zanahorias. Señora, ¿se las traigo a usted también?

ISABEL: No, a mí me trae unos espaguetis con camarones en salsa blanca y una ensalada. También queremos dos cafés con leche. A mí me lo trae descafeinado.

MESERO: Gracias, les voy a traer sus bebidas.

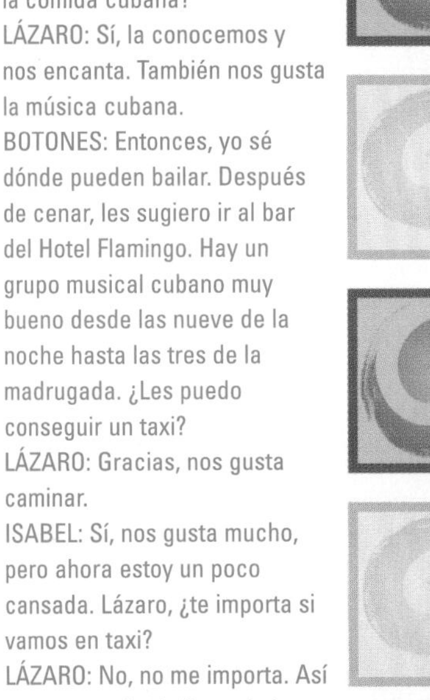

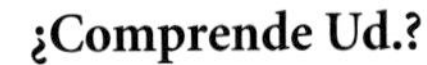

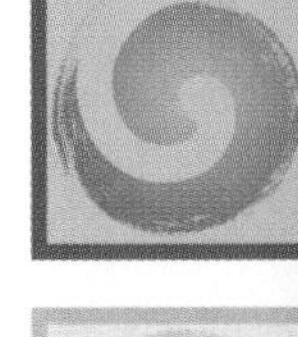

**A. ¿Comprende Ud.?** Conteste las siguientes preguntas según el diálogo.

1. ¿Qué les regala la compañía a Isabel y a Lázaro?
2. ¿Qué tipo de comida se sirve esta noche?
3. ¿A quién no le gusta el brócoli?
4. ¿Quién no quiere tomar cafeína?

**Answers for A.** 1) *Una botella de champán.* 2) *Italiana.* 3) *A Lázaro.* 4) *Isabel.*

**B. En el restaurante.** Escriba la palabra correcta para cada una de las definiciones de la lista siguiente.

MODELO: una lista de los platos que se sirven en un restaurante
*la carta/el menú*

1. la persona que prepara la comida
2. la persona que sirve la comida
3. la lista de vinos
4. el tenedor, el cuchillo y la cuchara para cada persona
5. el plato que se usa para llevar la comida a la mesa
6. la suma que se debe pagar
7. el lugar donde se paga la cuenta
8. el dinero adicional que se le da al camarero
9. la cosa que sirve para llevar los platos de comida a la mesa
10. la parte de un restaurante donde uno puede comer al aire libre (*outdoors*)

**C. ¡Listos?** Decida con su compañero/a quién dice cada una de estas expresiones, el camarero (**C**) o el cliente (**c**), y pónganlas en su orden correcto. Después, uno/a de Uds. debe leer las líneas del/de la cliente/a y el/la otro/a las líneas del/de la camarero/a. ¡OJO! Hay que añadir otras líneas para tener una conversación completa.

___ a. ___ ¿Están listos para pedir?
___ b. ___ Me trae la carta, por favor.
___ c. ___ ¡Buen provecho!
___ d. ___ ¿Qué recomienda Ud.?
___ e. ___ ¿Qué desean para beber?
___ f. ___ ¿Cuál es el plato del día?
___ g. ___ ¿Qué desea Ud. de plato principal?
___ h. ___ Otra taza de café, por favor.
___ i. ___ ¿Algo más?
___ j. ___ La cuenta, por favor.

**D. Una cita.** Ud. sale esta noche con un/a amigo/a. Acaban de terminar sus exámenes finales y Ud. quiere celebrarlo con una cena en un restaurante elegante. Pero su amigo/a prefiere un restaurante de servicio rápido. Hablen de las diferencias y tomen una decisión.

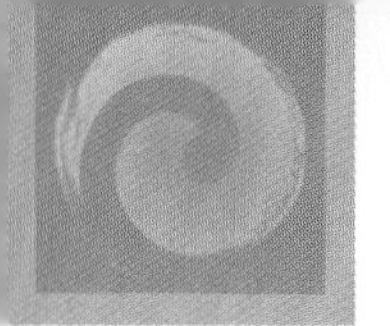

# ABC El desayuno

## Desayuno en "La Duquesa del Pacífico"

*Y a la mañana siguiente, Isabel y Lázaro van a desayunar....*

MESERO: Buenos días, señores. ¿Les sirvo algo?
ISABEL: Buenos días, Casimiro. Queremos dos jugos de naranja fríos, por favor.
MESERO: ¿Qué más desean? Tenemos como platillo especial unos crepes rellenos con queso en crema.
ISABEL: ¡Qué delicia! Me los trae, por favor.
LÁZARO: A mí también, por favor, pero con fruta fresca.
ISABEL: Lázaro, hoy es domingo y estoy pensando que en este momento Carlos y Mary están desayunando en su restaurante favorito. Me los imagino hablando de nuestra boda.
LÁZARO: Sí, ¿te los imaginas a ellos el día de su boda?
ISABEL: Sí, pero no se pueden casar por ahora. Tienen que acabar la carrera.
LÁZARO: Estoy de acuerdo. Yo siempre se lo digo. Ya nos trae el mesero el desayuno. Casimiro, se le olvidó mi café.
MESERO: No me lo pidió antes, señor, pero ahora mismo se lo traigo.

**Answers for A.** 1) *Fruta fresca.* 2) *Domingo.* 3) *En Carlos y Mary.* 4) *Acabar su carrera.*

**A. ¿Comprende Ud.?** Conteste las siguientes preguntas según el diálogo.

1. ¿Qué quiere Lázaro con sus crepes?
2. ¿Qué día es?
3. ¿En quién está pensando Isabel?
4. ¿Qué tienen que hacer Carlos y Mary antes de casarse?

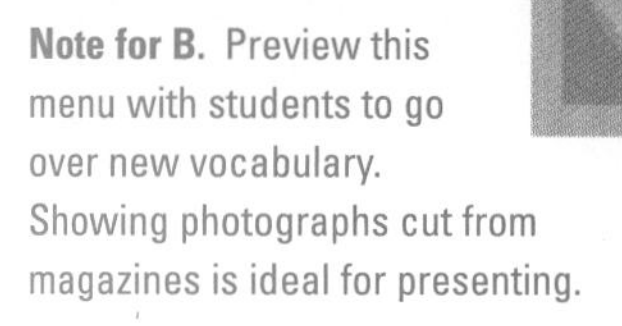

**B. ¡Tengo hambre!** Es la hora del almuerzo y Ud. y un/a amigo/a están en el Café Real. Hablen del menú del día y decidan qué van a pedir.

MODELO: *Tengo mucha hambre. Creo que voy a pedir una pizza clásica y un batido de chocolate.*

Note for B. Preview this menu with students to go over new vocabulary. Showing photographs cut from magazines is ideal for presenting.

**CAFÉ REAL**

**SÁNDWICHES**

| | |
|---|---|
| media luna | s/. 7.500 |
| cubano | s/. 8.500 |
| pavo (con lechuga y tomate) | s/. 8.000 |
| pernil (con lechuga y tomate) | s/. 7.800 |
| chorizo español | s/. 8.500 |

**PIZZAS**

| | |
|---|---|
| la clásica queso y tomate | s/. 10.000 |
| la Hawaiana jamón y piña | s/. 12.000 |
| la rústica hongos y berenjena | s/. 11.500 |

A cualquiera de las pizzas se le puede añadir...

cebolla, pimentón, ají, aceitunas, anchoas, hongos

**PASTELES Y POSTRES**

| | |
|---|---|
| tarta de frutas | s/. 3.000 |
| flan | s/. 2.500 |
| pastel de chocolate | s/. 3.400 |
| arroz con leche | s/. 2.800 |
| churros | s/. 3.000 |
| churros rellenos (crema, dulce de leche) | s/. 3.500 |
| helados varios | s/. 2.500 |

**BEBIDAS**

| | |
|---|---|
| café o té | s/. 2.000 |
| jugos (piña, mango, tomate de árbol, fresa, naranja) | s/. 3.200 |
| batidos (vainilla, chocolate, fresa) | s/. 3.500 |
| gaseosas | s/. 2.900 |
| agua mineral (con o sin gas) | s/. 2.000 |

**C. ¡Hay una mosca en la sopa!** Ud. está cenando en un restaurante elegante y encuentra una mosca (*fly*) en la sopa. Llame al camarero e insista en hablar con el/la dueño/a. Éste/a le pide una explicación al/a la cocinero/a. En grupos de cuatro, representen esta situación. No se olviden de incluir esta información:

- llamar la atención del/de la camarero/a
- explicar el problema
- pedirle al/a la dueño/a que descuente el precio de la sopa del total

**D. Entrevista.** Hable con su compañero/a de los restaurantes que frecuenta donde vive.

1. ¿Cuál es el restaurante más elegante de la ciudad donde vives? ¿Comes allí con frecuencia? ¿Qué pides cuando comes en un restaurante elegante? ¿Qué pides cuando comes en un restaurante de comida rápida?
2. ¿Te gusta la comida étnica? ¿Qué comidas étnicas te gustan? ¿la italiana? ¿la mexicana? ¿la china? ¿Hay restaurantes de otras nacionalidades en tu ciudad? ¿Qué pides cuando comes en un restaurante mexicano? ¿en un restaurante italiano?
3. ¿Tomas vino cuando comes en un restaurante? ¿Con qué comidas tomas vino tinto? ¿vino blanco? ¿Pides postre cuando comes en un restaurante? ¿Qué pides de postre normalmente? ¿Cuánto dejas de propina si el servicio es bueno? ¿Dejas propina si el servicio no es muy bueno? ¿si es muy malo?

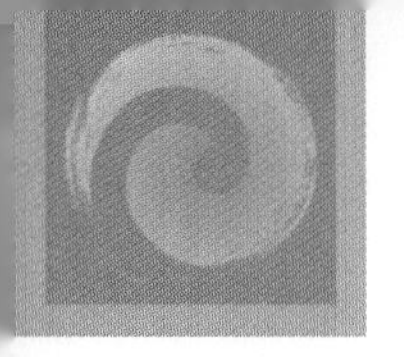

# Dos pronombres juntos
## (*Double object pronouns*)

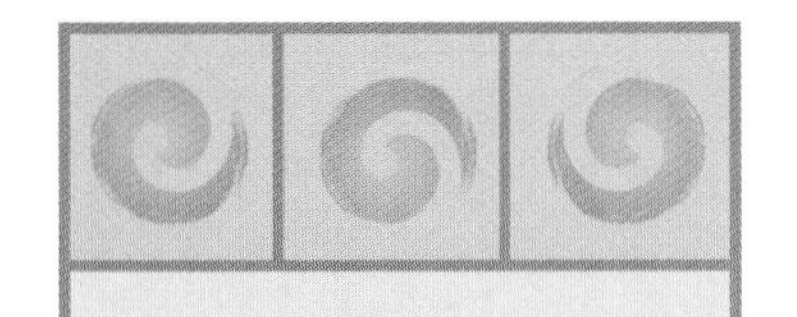

**Para averiguar**

1. Where are indirect object pronouns placed when used together with direct object pronouns?
2. What must you add to the stressed vowel of a verb when two pronouns are attached to the end of it?
3. What happens to the indirect object pronouns **le** and **les** when they are followed by the direct objects **lo**, **la**, **los**, or **las**?

- The indirect object pronoun always precedes the direct object pronoun when they are used together. A written accent must be added to the stressed vowel of an infinitive, or the **-ndo** form of the verb when two pronouns are attached to the end of it.

—¿**Me** puedes prestar tu coche?
—Por supuesto que **te lo** puedo prestar./Por supuesto que puedo prest**ártelo**.

—¿**Me** puedes traer leche?
—Sí, **te la** puedo traer./Sí, puedo tra**értela**.

- When both the direct and indirect object pronouns begin with the letter **l**, the indirect object pronoun changes to **se**.

—¿**Les** recomendaste **este hotel** a los turistas? — *Did you recommend this hotel to the tourists?*
—No, no **se lo** recomendé. — *No, I didn't recommend it to them.*

—¿**Le** diste **tu pasaporte** al recepcionista? — *Did you give your passport to the desk clerk?*
—Sí, **se lo** di. — *Yes, I gave it to him.*

- Since **se** can have a variety of meanings when it replaces **le** (*to you, to him, to her*) or **les** (*to you, to them*), you may add a prepositional phrase to clarify to whom you are referring.

**Se** lo dije **a Ud. (a él, a ella, a Uds., a ellos/as).** — *I told it to you (to him, to her, to you, to them).*

### A lo personal

**A. ¿Lo haces?** How would you answer your best friend if he/she asked you the following?

MODELO: —¿Le pides el recibo a la dependienta?
*—Sí, se lo pido a veces.* o *No, nunca se lo pido.*
—¿Me puedes prestar tu chaqueta?
*—Sí, te la puedo prestar.* o *No te la puedo prestar.*

1. ¿Les prestas tu(s) coche (ropa, dinero, apartamento, libros) a tus amigos?
2. ¿Me puedes prestar tu(s) coche (dinero, libro de español, apartamento, reloj, zapatos)?
3. ¿Me puedes comprar (almuerzo, flores, limonada, coche nuevo, boletos para el concierto)?
4. ¿Nos puedes preparar (café, cena, pastel, galletas)?

**B. En el restaurante.** Who does each activity, you or the waiter? Change the direct objects to pronouns and supply necessary indirect object pronouns accordingly.

MODELO: traer el menú
*El camarero nos lo trae.*
pedir la comida
*Nosotros se la pedimos al camarero.*

1. describir las especialidades
2. servir la comida
3. pedir la cuenta
4. traer la cuenta
5. dar la tarjeta de crédito
6. dar una propina

**C. Un día con el maitre d'.** Today is your first day working as a part-time waiter/waitress. The maitre d' is very demanding and is asking you questions to make sure everything is ready for dinner. Answer his questions according to the model.

MODELO: ¿Me preparaste las ensaladas que te pedí?
*Sí, se las preparé.* o
*No, no se las preparé.*

1. ¿Le trajiste los frijoles al cocinero?
2. ¿Les reservaste una mesa a mis hijos?
3. ¿Les compraste las flores exóticas a las recepcionistas?
4. ¿Le pediste el menú del día al cocinero?
5. ¿Le llevaste el periódico al jefe?
6. ¿Les preparaste el café a los otros camareros?
7. ¿Le cocinaste la sopa a la jefa?
8. ¿Me escribiste la carta que te pedí?
9. ¿Les diste el dinero de tu propina a los otros camareros?
10. ¿Me compraste la guía de restaurantes de la ciudad?

**D. De compras.** You are shopping for clothes for a trip to the coast. First, decide who is speaking, **el cliente** (**C**) or **el vendedor** (**V**). Then respond to each question or statement, replacing the direct object with a pronoun.

MODELO: _C_ ¿Me puede enseñar los trajes de baño?
*Por supuesto que se los puedo enseñar.*

1. ___ ¿Se va a probar este traje de baño?
2. ___ ¿Me puede enseñar las sandalias también?
3. ___ ¿Se va a probar estas sandalias?
4. ___ ¿Se va a llevar las sandalias? ¿y el traje de baño?
5. ___ ¿Me dio su tarjeta de crédito?
6. ___ ¿Me pone el traje de baño en una bolsa, por favor?
7. ___ ¿Le pongo las sandalias en la bolsa también?
8. ___ ¿Me dio el recibo?

**E. ¿Me puede ayudar?** A stranger stops you on campus and asks if you can do the following for him/her. Play the roles with a classmate.

**Suggestion for E.** Point out that in the model, *lo* is used as the pronoun for direct objects that are not specific nouns.

MODELO: explicar cómo ir al centro
E1: *¿Me puede explicar cómo ir al centro?*
E2: *Claro que se lo puedo explicar. Siga derecho por la calle Lavaca.*

1. decir cómo se llama esta universidad
2. escribir el nombre de la universidad
3. enseñar el campus
4. decir la hora
5. dar un dólar
6. leer este papel

# Resumen de los pronombres personales
## (*Summary of personal pronouns*)

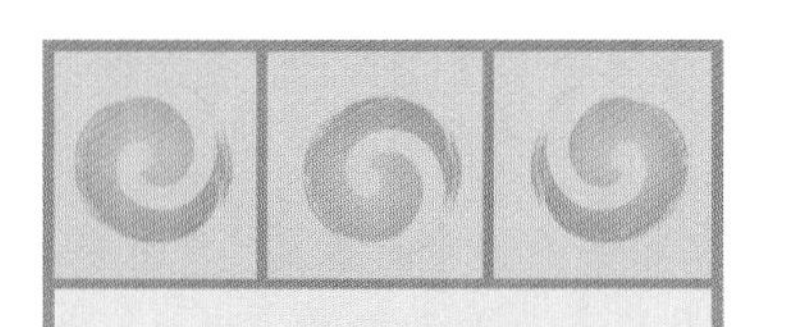

**Para averiguar**

1. When do you use subject pronouns such as **yo** or **tú**?
2. When may reflexive, direct object, and indirect object pronouns be attached to the end of the verb? When *must* they be attached to the end of the verb? When must they preceed the verb?

- The five sets of personal pronouns that you have learned are summarized below.

| Subject | Reflexive/ Reciprocal | Direct object | Indirect object | Prepositional |
|---|---|---|---|---|
| yo | me | me | me | mí |
| tú | te | te | te | ti |
| él | se | lo | le (se) | él |
| ella | se | la | le (se) | ella |
| usted | se | lo/la | le (se) | usted |
| nosotros/as | nos | nos | nos | nosotros/as |
| vosotros/as | os | os | os | vosotros/as |
| ellos | se | los | les (se) | ellos |
| ellas | se | las | les (se) | ellas |
| ustedes | se | los/las | les (se) | ustedes |

- Subject pronouns are generally used only when needed for clarity, to stress the subject, or to contrast the subject with someone else.

**Yo** me quedo pero **ellos** van a salir. *I'm staying but they are going out.*

- Reflexive/reciprocal, direct object, and indirect object pronouns all follow the same placement rules, which are summarized in the following chart.

| | Before a conjugated verb | Attached to the end of a verb |
|---|---|---|
| Single conjugated verb | ¿**Me** preparas **la cena**? | ———————— |
| Conjugated verb + infinitive | ¿**Me** vas a preparar **la cena?** | ¿Vas a preparar**me** la **cena?** |
| **estar** + **-ndo** form of the verb | ¿**Me** estás preparando **la cena**? | ¿Estás prepar**á**ndo**me** la cena? |

- Prepositional pronouns follow a preposition.

—¿Compraste algo **para nosotros**? *Did you buy something for us?*
—Compré algo **para ti** pero no **para él**. *I bought something for you but not for him.*

## A lo personal

**A. Recomendaciones.** For each category, make a recommendation to one of your classmates. Another student will agree or disagree with your recommendations.

MODELO: un hotel
E1: *Les recomiendo el hotel La Quinta.*
E2: *Se lo recomiendo también.* o
*No se lo recomiendo.* o
*No lo conozco.*

1. un parque de atracciones
2. una playa
3. una peluquería
4. un museo
5. una película
6. un país extranjero

Now ask a classmate to recommend a good place to do each of these things. Another student should agree or disagree.

MODELO: para acampar
E1: *Patricia, ¿nos puedes recomendar un buen lugar para acampar?*
E2: *Les recomiendo el lago Buena Vista.*
E3: *Se lo recomiendo también.* o *No se lo recomiendo.*

1. para esquiar
2. para comprar maletas
3. para comprar una tienda de campaña
4. para pescar
5. para bucear
6. para hacer un crucero

**B. En casa solo/a.** A student is describing a childhood vacation. Complete the paragraph with the correct pronouns.

A mi padre ________ (1) gustaban mucho las vacaciones de verano. Para ________ (2), eran muy importantes. El día de nuestra salida siempre ________ (3) despertaba a todos nosotros a las cinco de la mañana. Nunca entendí por qué a él ________ (4) importaba tanto salir antes de la salida del sol. Normalmente mis hermanos y yo ________ (5) sentábamos en el coche en el asiento de atrás. Mi hermano David estaba a la izquierda, mi hermana Gloria a la derecha y yo estaba entre ________ (6).

Una vez decidimos ir al Gran Cañón en Arizona. Mi madre no estaba con ________ (7) porque estaba con mi tía Delia. Como siempre, mi padre quería salir temprano. Sin despertar ________ (8), llevó a mi hermano y mi hermana al coche. No sé por qué, pero se les olvidó que yo dormía todavía y salieron sin ________ (9). Al salir el sol, mis hermanos ________ (10) despertaron y ________ (11) preguntaron a mi papá dónde estaba yo. Cuando mi papá por fin recordó que yo no estaba, ya estaban a ciento cincuenta millas de la casa. Regresaron para buscar ________ (12) y ________ (13) encontraron mirando dibujos animados en la sala.

**C. Entrevista.** Answer the questions with a partner using personal pronouns where appropriate.

1. ¿Quién te invita frecuentemente a cenar? ¿Dónde te gusta cenar? ¿Vas a cenar con esa persona esta noche?
2. Para ti, ¿qué es más importante en un restaurante? ¿la comida? ¿los precios? ¿el servicio? ¿el ambiente? ¿Les das una propina del 15 por ciento a los camareros, por lo general? ¿Cuándo no les das propina a los camareros?

## ABC ¿Dónde está?

### ¿Dónde está?

*Isabel y Lázaro le piden información al camarero sobre Puerto Rico....*

MESERO: ¿Les sirvo algo más?
LÁZARO: Sí, por favor sírvame más café y tráiga un poco de azúcar.
MESERO: Con mucho gusto. ¿Van a hacer alguna excursión a San Juan?
ISABEL: No, queremos ir por nuestra cuenta. Casimiro, yo sé que usted nació en Puerto Rico. Dígame qué podemos hacer en San Juan.
MESERO: Conozco muchos lugares pero, créanme, es mejor que se lo diga alguien del departamento de turismo. Ellos tienen mucha información y además les pueden proporcionar mapas.
LÁZARO: ¿Hay que pagar por los mapas?
MESERO: No, se los dan gratis. Acaba de subir a bordo un empleado y va a darles una charla en el teatro del barco. Dénse prisa, porque va a empezar en cinco minutos.
LÁZARO: ¿Cómo llegamos allí?
MESERO: Salgan del restaurante, doblen a la izquierda y tomen el ascensor hasta el tercer piso. Salgan del ascensor y doblen a la izquierda, después sigan derecho por el corredor hasta el final. Van a encontrar el vestíbulo inmediatamente al lado izquierdo.

**Answers for A.** 1) *A San Juan.* 2) *Casimiro.* 3) *Nada.* 4) *Un empleado.*

**A. ¿Comprende Ud.?** Conteste las siguientes preguntas según el diálogo.

1. ¿Adónde quieren ir Isabel y Lázaro?
2. ¿Quién nació allí?
3. ¿Cuánto cuestan los mapas?
4. ¿Quién va a hablar de San Juan?

**B. En el barrio.** Sus nuevos vecinos dicen que tienen que hacer unos recados (*errands*) ¿Adónde necesitan ir? ¿Pueden ir a pie? Con un/a compañero/a, y siguiendo el modelo, completen los recados indicados.

MODELO: Tengo que cambiar dinero...
E1: *Tengo que cambiar dinero. ¿Hay un banco cerca de aquí?*
E2: *Hay un banco en la calle 10.*
E1: *¿Puedo ir hasta allí a pie?*
E2: *No, está muy lejos. Tiene que tomar el autobús o un taxi.*

1. Tengo que comprar medicina...
2. Quiero comprar el periódico...
3. Tengo que cortarme el pelo...
4. Tengo que comprar comida...

**C. El mapa del Metro.** Ud. y un/a amigo/a de la universidad están de vacaciones en Madrid, pero nunca viajaron en metro porque no existe en su ciudad. Estudien el mapa, tratando de entender los colores diferentes y los números de las rutas. Planeen su viaje de...

1. la Ciudad Universitaria a la Gran Vía
2. la Gran Vía al Parque del Retiro
3. la Plaza de España a los Nuevos Ministerios
4. Atocha a la calle Chueca

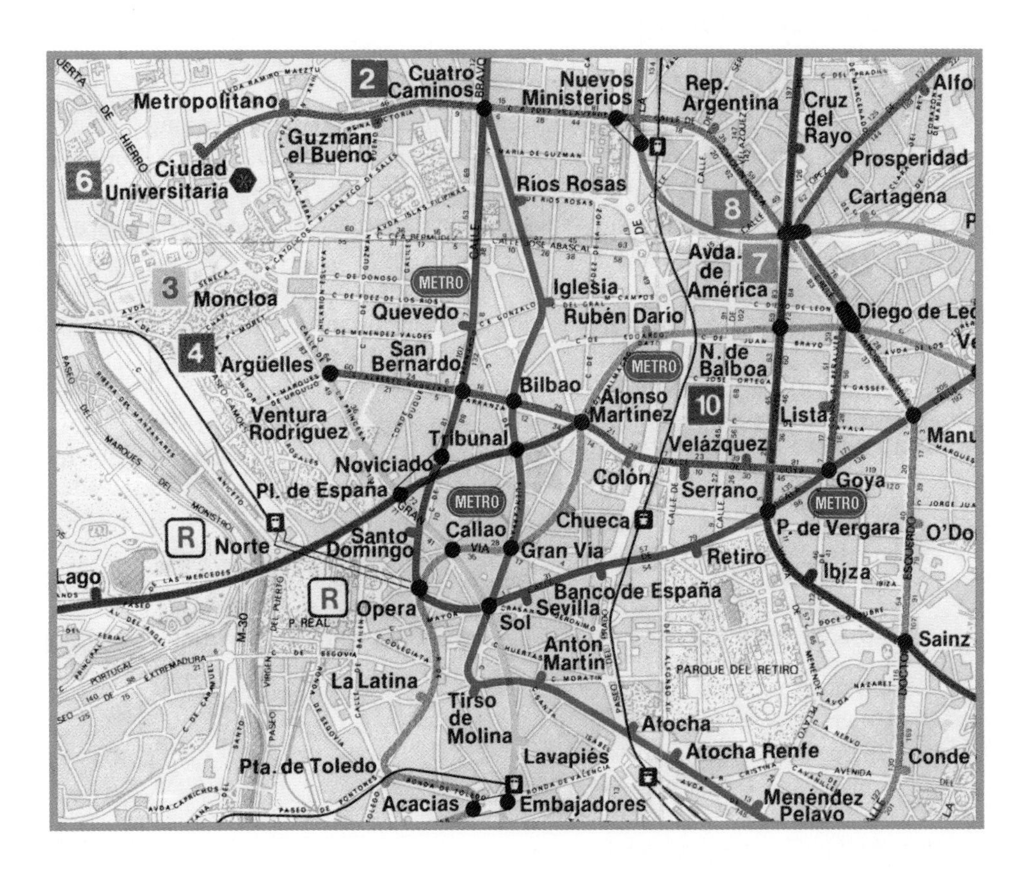

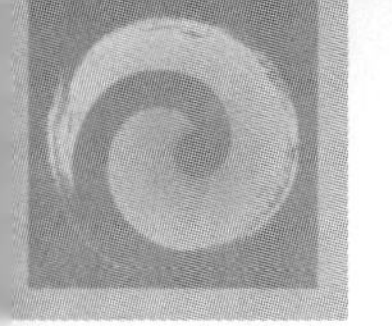

# ABC Las excursiones

## Lázaro e Isabel consiguen un taxi

*Isabel y Lázaro planean su itinerario turístico....*

LÁZARO: Isabel, vamos a alquilar un taxi porque no conocemos muy bien San Juan. Allí está la representante de la compañía Duquesa. Señorita Lola, por favor, consíganos un taxi.

REPRESENTANTE: Con mucho gusto. Vengan, súbanse a este taxi que está esperando en la calle.

TAXISTA: ¿Adónde los llevo?

ISABEL: Llévenos por favor a la oficina de turismo más cercana. ¿Cuánto nos cobra?

TAXISTA: Depende de lo que marque el taxímetro.

LÁZARO: Por favor, apúrese porque queremos visitar muchos lugares.

TAXISTA: No se preocupen. Yo los puedo llevar a donde quieran. Los espero afuera de la oficina de turismo. Contrátenme por todo el día. Así les sale más barato.

ISABEL: ¡Qué buena idea! Espérenos, no vamos a tardar mucho.

TAXISTA: Muy bien, señorita.

**Answers for A.** 1) *A la oficina de turismo.* 2) *La Srta. Lola.* 3) *Del taxímetro.* 4) *Por día.*

**A. ¿Comprende Ud.?** Conteste las siguientes preguntas según la información del diálogo.

1. ¿Adónde van Isabel y Lázaro en el taxi?
2. ¿Quién les consigue el taxi?
3. ¿De qué depende el precio del taxi?
4. ¿Es más barato pagar por viaje o por día?

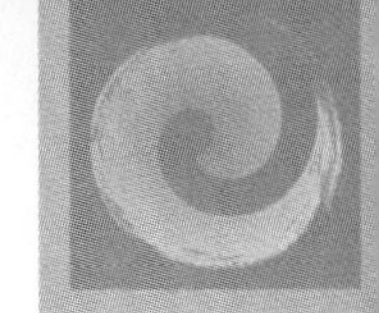

**B. Yo prefiero...** Es la primera vez que Ud. está en Madrid y quiere verlo todo, pero tiene sólo un día antes de irse. Tiene que escoger entre las excursiones indicadas. Hable con su compañero/a de lo que prefiere Ud. y pregúntele a él/ella cuál de las excursiones prefiere.

MODELO: *Me interesa mucho el baile flamenco. Yo quiero ir a ese espectáculo y prefiero la excursión con cena. Y tú, ¿qué opinas?*

## MADRID DE NOCHE

Salida a las 20,30 hrs.

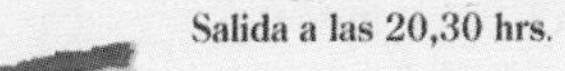

Espectáculo Scala — con copa **8.120** *ptas.*

con cena **13.000** *ptas.*

Recorrido panorámico por las avenidas más importantes de la ciudad iluminada antes de llegar a la mejor sala de fiestas de Madrid, **SCALA.**

**ESPECTACULO Y COPA:** Llegada a la Sala de Fiestas SCALA, donde se presenciará un espectáculo de variedades del más alto nivel internacional. Se servirá una consumición. Posteriormente regreso al hotel.

**ESPECTACULO Y CENA:** Llegada a la Sala de Fiestas Scala donde se servirá una cena con cava incluido y después se presenciará un grandioso espectáculo de variedades al más alto nivel internacional. Posteriormente regreso a los hoteles.

## MADRID FLAMENCO

Salida a las 20,30 hrs.

Espectáculo Florida Park — con copa **7.100** *ptas.*

con cena **11.020** *ptas.*

Recorrido panorámico por las avenidas más importantes de la ciudad iluminada antes de llegar a la sala de fiestas.

**FLAMENCO CON COPA:** Llegada a FLORIDA PARK para presenciar todo un recital de baile español y flamenco. Se servirá una consumición y aperitivos. Posteriormente regreso al hotel.

**FLAMENCO CON CENA:** A la llegada se servirá una cena con vino incluido, presenciando después un soberbio espectáculo de baile español y flamenco. Posteriormente, regreso al hotel. Antes del espectáculo habrá música de baile.

**C. Entrevista.** Hable con un/a compañero/a de sus vacaciones favoritas.

1. ¿Te gusta acampar? ¿Tienes una tienda de campaña (*tent*)? ¿un saco de dormir? ¿Necesitas electricidad cuando acampas? ¿Para qué? ¿Te bañas en el río (*river*) cuando acampas?
2. ¿Te gustan los parques de atracciones? ¿Cuál es tu parque de atracciones favorito? ¿Cuándo fue la última vez que estuviste allí?
3. ¿Prefieres pasar las vacaciones en el campo o en una ciudad grande? ¿Por qué? ¿Dónde pasaste tus últimas vacaciones? ¿Qué hiciste?

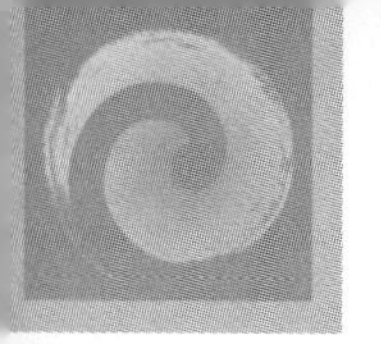

# Introducción a los mandatos formales
## (*Formal commands*)

**Para averiguar**

1. What stem do you use for the **Ud.** and **Uds.** commands of most verbs?
2. What endings do you add to the stem to form **Ud.** and **Uds.** commands of **-ar** verbs? of **-er/-ir** verbs?
3. Which five verbs have irregular **Ud.** and **Uds.** command forms?

**Note.** A variety of topics has been presented in these activities to allow student practice of formal commands in various contexts.

- Use commands (**los mandatos**) to tell people to do something. The command form of a verb is called the *imperative.* To give a command to someone you would address as **usted**, drop the final **o** of the **yo** form of the verb in the present tense and add these endings:

For **-ar** verbs, add **-e**:

| | | | |
|---|---|---|---|
| hablar | habl**o** | → | **¡Hable** más despacio, por favor!<br>*Speak more slowly, please!* |
| cerrar | cierr**o** | → | ¡No **cierre** la puerta!<br>*Don't close the door!* |

For **-er** and **-ir** verbs, add **-a**:

| | | | |
|---|---|---|---|
| leer | le**o** | → | **Lea** la página 278.<br>*Read page 278.* |
| hacer | hag**o** | → | ¡No **haga** eso!<br>*Don't do that!* |
| poner | pong**o** | → | **Ponga** el informe en la mesa.<br>*Put the report on the table.* |
| abrir | abr**o** | → | **¡Abra** la ventana, por favor!<br>*Open the window, please!* |
| venir | veng**o** | → | **Venga** mañana si puede.<br>*Come tomorrow if you can.* |
| seguir | sig**o** | → | **Siga** derecho.<br>*Keep going straight ahead.* |

- To give a command to more than one person, form the **ustedes** command by adding an **-n** to the **usted** command.

**Hagan** esos ejercicios para mañana. — *Do those exercises for tomorrow.*
No **hablen** durante los exámenes. — *Don't talk during exams.*

- These verbs have irregular command forms. You can easily remember which verbs they are because their **yo** forms do not end in **-o**.

| | dar | estar | ir | saber | ser |
|---|---|---|---|---|---|
| **usted** | **dé** | **esté** | **vaya** | **sepa** | **sea** |
| **ustedes** | **den** | **estén** | **vayan** | **sepan** | **sean** |

**Estén** aquí mañana a las seis. — *Be here tomorrow at six o'clock.*
**Vaya** a la estación de policía. — *Go to the police station.*

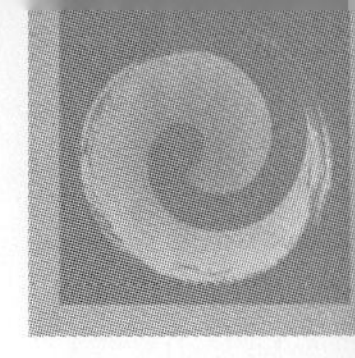

- For courtesy, you may insert the pronoun **usted** or **ustedes** after the verb.

| | |
|---|---|
| Vayan **Uds.** con ellos. | *Go with them.* |
| Diga **Ud.** todo. | *Tell everything.* |

## A lo personal

**A. ¿Cómo llego a...?** With a classmate, make a list of landmarks on your campus: **cafetería, baño, biblioteca, estacionamiento, librería, la oficina de su profesor/a**. Then ask your classmate how to get from your classroom to one of those sites. When you have received directions for all of your landmarks, trade roles with your partner and give or get directions from the landmark back to your classroom.

MODELO: el baño
E1: *¿Me puede decir cómo llegar al baño?*
E2: *Salga de la clase, doble a la derecha, siga hasta el final del pasillo y doble a la izquierda.*

**B. La declaración.** The following is a list of important things for a witness to an accident to do. Help the police finish the list by changing the infinitives to formal commands.

MODELO: describir la escena
*Describa Ud. la escena.*

1. hacer una declaración inmediatamente
2. contestar todas las preguntas honestamente
3. recordar todos los detalles
4. decir la verdad
5. no estar nervioso/a
6. estar tranquilo/a
7. volver a la escena
8. hablar claramente
9. dar todos los detalles
10. seguir las indicaciones del policía
11. ir a la estación de policía si es necesario
12. saber sus derechos (*rights*)

**C. Cuidando niños.** You are a substitute in an elementary school. Use formal Uds. commands to guide those students who...

MODELO: corren por la calle
*¡Niños, no corran por la calle!*

1. pelean
2. tienen que practicar matemáticas
3. quieren ir al baño
4. necesitan sacar sus libros
5. tiran aviones de papel
6. lloran
7. no quieren hacer la tarea
8. deben poner los libros en la mochila

**D. Los 10 mandatos de la clase.** Professors are always telling students what to do and how to do it. With a classmate, make a list of the 10 commands your teacher most commonly gives the class.

**E. ¡Una gran oportunidad!** For years you have been taking orders from all of your teachers. Finally, it is your turn to give orders to the teacher. Make a list of 10 commands you would like to give to your teacher.

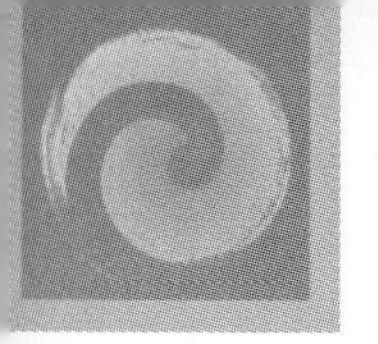

# Los pronombres con los mandatos (*Pronouns with commands*)

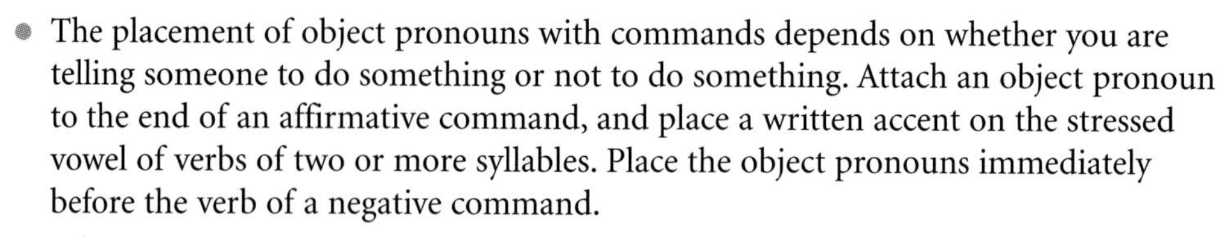

- The placement of object pronouns with commands depends on whether you are telling someone to do something or not to do something. Attach an object pronoun to the end of an affirmative command, and place a written accent on the stressed vowel of verbs of two or more syllables. Place the object pronouns immediately before the verb of a negative command.

| | |
|---|---|
| —¿Hacemos los ejercicios del cuaderno? | *Do we do the exercises from the workbook?* |
| —Sí, **há**gan**los**. o No, no **los** hagan. | *Yes, do them. or No, don't do them.* |
| —¿Puedo comer estos chocolates? | *May I eat these chocolates?* |
| —Sí, **có**ma**los**. o No, no **los** coma. | *Yes, eat them. or No, don't eat them.* |

- Reflexive pronouns follow the same placement rules as direct object pronouns.

| | |
|---|---|
| —¿Necesito levantar**me**? | *Do I need to get up?* |
| —Sí, lev**án**te**se**, por favor. / No, no **se** levante. | *Yes, get up, please. / No, don't get up.* |

## A lo personal

**A. Turismo.** Tell the tourists where to look for the following places in your city.

MODELO: el zoológico
*Búsquenlo en el mapa, cerca del Parque Central.* o *No lo busquen, no hay ninguno.*

1. Taco Bell
2. el museo de arte
3. la oficina de turismo
4. los almacenes grandes
5. el estadio de fútbol
6. la universidad
7. un restaurante muy elegante
8. mi casa
9. el supermercado

**B. El guía.** Now you are a tour guide and you must recommend interesting places where these tourists can get the following things.

MODELO: ropa
*Cómprenla en Macy's.*

1. pastel de cumpleaños
2. flores
3. cerveza
4. pizza
5. mariscos (*shellfish*)
6. boletos de teatro
7. recuerdos (*souvenirs*) de la ciudad
8. hamburguesas con queso
9. comida italiana
10. zapatos cómodos

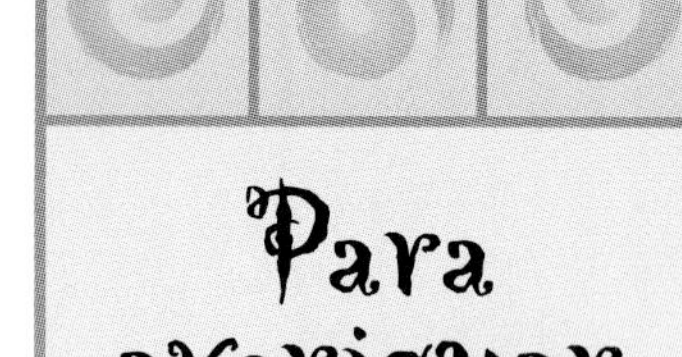

### Para averiguar

1. Where do you place direct object or reflexive pronouns with affirmative commands? With negative commands?
2. When do you add a written accent to the verb?

### ¡ojo!

Many Spanish speakers use the verbs **comer** and **beber** reflexively, when indicating what they *specifically* eat or drink.

**Me bebo un café.**
**Bebo mucho.**

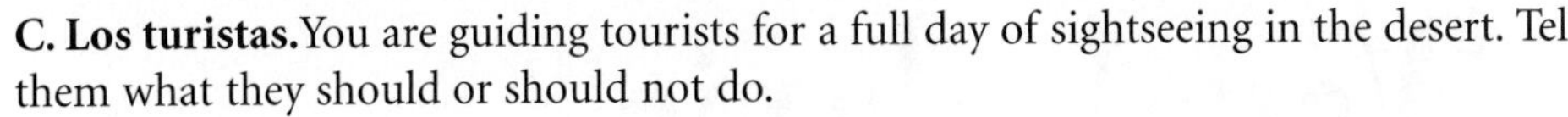

**C. Los turistas.** You are guiding tourists for a full day of sightseeing in the desert. Tell them what they should or should not do.

MODELO: acostarse tarde
*No se acuesten tarde.*

1. olvidarse de llevar sombrero
2. levantarse al mediodía
3. enojarse por el tráfico
4. prepararse para el calor
5. tomar mucha agua
6. preocuparse por las serpientes
7. ponerse repelente de insectos
8. traer su traje de baño.

**D. De vacaciones.** You and your partner are vacationing in Madrid and would like to get to know the city a little bit better. Pick two destinations from the map below. Then, one of you must give directions to the other to get to that destination. Then switch roles and pick a new destination. Your starting point will always be the Prado Museum.

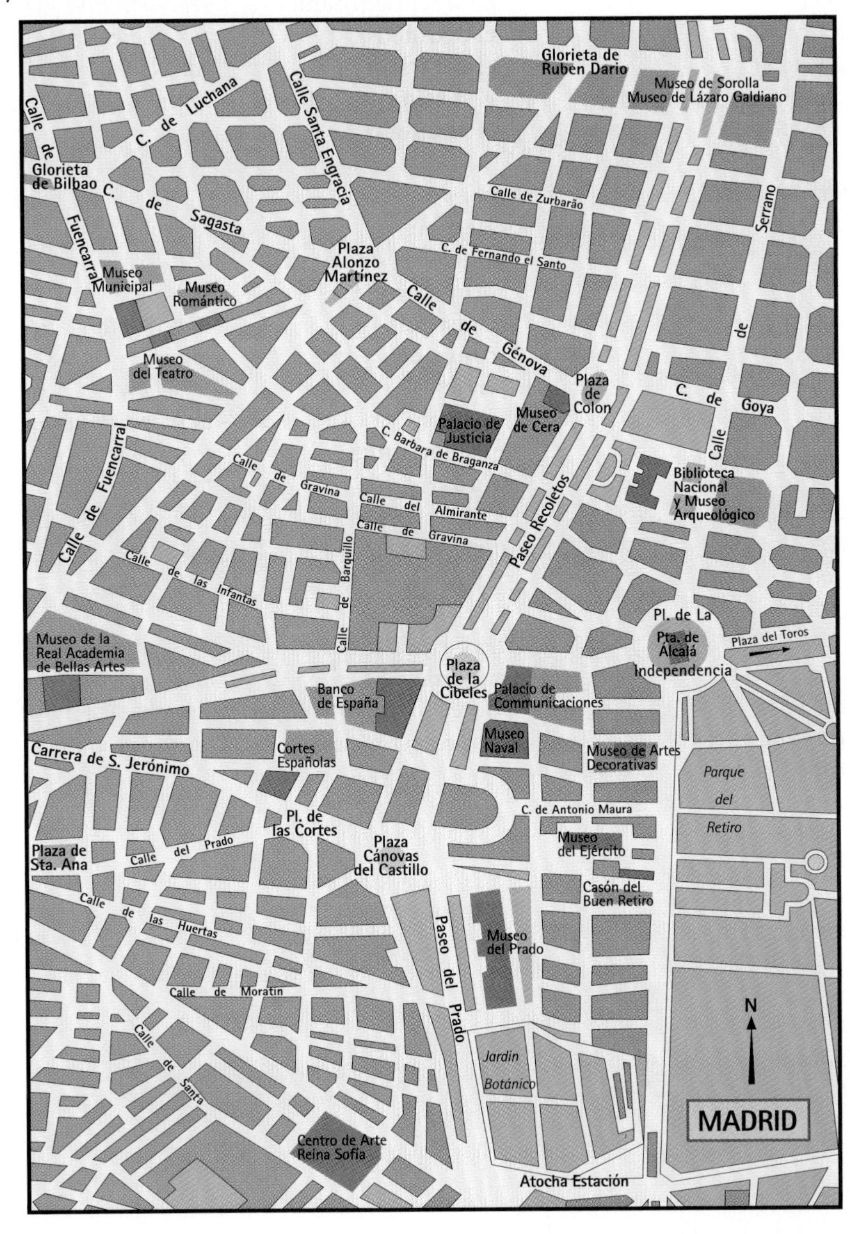


**E. El hotel.** Imagine that you are a tourist in your town and that your classmate is a taxi driver. Role-play the entire exchange with a classmate, making at least two stops.

# Vocabulario

## TEMA 3
### En el restaurante

| Sustantivos | |
|---|---|
| el azúcar | *sugar* |
| la bandeja | *tray* |
| la bebida | *drink* |
| la botella | *bottle* |
| el brócoli | *broccoli* |
| la carta de vinos | *wine list* |
| la cena | *dinner* |
| el champán | *champagne* |
| la chuleta | *chop/cutlet* |
| el crepe | *crepe* |
| los cubiertos | *place setting* |
| la cuchara | *spoon* |
| el cuchillo | *knife* |
| la cuenta | *bill* |
| el desayuno | *breakfast* |
| el/la dueño/a | *owner* |
| los espaguetis | *spaghetti* |
| la fruta | *fruit* |
| el menú/la carta | *menu* |
| el platillo | *course* |
| el postre | *dessert* |
| la propina | *tip* |
| el tenedor | *fork* |
| la ternera | *veal* |
| la terraza | *terrace* |
| la verdura | *vegetable* |

| Verbos | |
|---|---|
| acompañar | *to accompany* |
| cenar | *to eat dinner* |
| desayunar | *to eat breakfast* |
| imaginarse | *to imagine* |
| mandar | *to send* |
| olvidar | *to forget* |
| recomendar (ie) | *to recommend* |
| servir (i) | *to serve* |

| Adjetivos | |
|---|---|
| delicioso/a | *delicious* |
| descafeinado/a | *decaffeinated* |
| relleno/a | *stuffed* |

| Otras expresiones | |
|---|---|
| ahora mismo | *right now* |
| ¡Buen provecho! ¡Que aproveche! | *Enjoy your meal!* |

## TEMA 4
### Las indicaciones

| Sustantivos | |
|---|---|
| la charla | *chat* |
| el corredor, pasillo | *corridor/hall* |
| la excursión | *excursion* |
| el final | *end* |
| el mapa | *map* |
| el recado/mandado | *errand* |
| el/la representante | *representative* |
| el taxímetro | *taxi meter* |
| el/la taxista | *cab-driver* |
| el turismo | *tourism* |
| el vestíbulo | *lobby* |

| Verbos | |
|---|---|
| alquilar | *to rent* |
| apurarse, darse prisa | *to hurry* |
| broncearse | *to tan* |
| conseguir (i) | *to get, obtain* |
| contratar | *to hire* |
| creer | *to believe* |
| marcar | *to mark, indicate* |
| proporcionar | *to provide* |
| tardar | *to delay* |

| Adjetivos | |
|---|---|
| cercano/a | *nearby* |

| Otras expresiones | |
|---|---|
| a bordo | *on board* |
| derecho, recto | *straight* |
| por nuestra cuenta | *on our own* |

# Reunión B

**A escuchar.** **En la oficina de turismo.** Complete cada oración con palabras que escuche en la conversación.

1. El lugar más famoso de San Juan es ______________.
2. Está a la entrada de la ______________ de San Juan.
3. Las entradas para el teatro se acaban muy ______________.
4. Deben visitar también la ______________ de Puerto Rico.
5. En Ponce hay un ______________ importante.
6. Hay muchas ______________ bellísimas.

**A conversar.** Ud. va a hacer el papel de turista en la ciudad en donde vive. Su compañero/a va a ser un/a empleado/a de la Oficina de Turismo de la ciudad. El turista necesita averiguar qué lugares debe visitar, qué lugares debe evitar, qué tipo de transporte puede utilizar en la ciudad, etc. El/la empleado/a de la Oficina de Turismo debe contestar las preguntas del turista y recomendar lugares interesantes. Preparen la conversación y después, represéntenla enfrente de sus compañeros de clase.

**¿Lo sabía?** Un chef famoso en el mejor restaurante de Puerto Rico va a presentar su receta secreta de Salsa Mornay delante de un grupo de huéspedes del hotel.

**¿Comprende Ud.?** Conteste según la receta.

1. ¿Cuántas calorías tiene esta salsa por 1/3 de taza?
2. ¿Cuántos minutos antes de servir es necesario comenzar la preparación?
3. ¿Se agregan los quesos enteros?
4. ¿Cómo se sirve la salsa?

## Salsa Mornay

- Comience a prepararla 20 minutos antes de servir.
- Contiene 164 calorías por 1/3 tz.
- Es una buena fuente de calcio y vitamina A.

**Para preparar 2 1/3 tz:**
**3 cdas de mantequilla o margarina**
**2 cucharas de harina**
**1 tz de caldo de pollo**
**1 tz de mitad leche y mitad crema**
**1 yema de huevo**
**1/2 tz de queso Suizo natural rallado**
**1/4 tz de queso Parmesano rallado**

**1** En una olla de 2/4 de capacidad, a fuego mediano, derrita la mantequilla y agregue, revolviendo, la harina. Mezcle hasta que se unan bien.

**2** Viértale, poco a poco, y revolviendo, la leche y el caldo de pollo. Mezcle hasta que se espese.

**3** En un recipiente pequeño, y usando la escobilla de cocina o un batidor de alambre de mano, bata ligeramente la yema de huevo y agregue, revolviendo, un poquito de la mezcla anterior.

**4** Únala lentamente a la mezcla caliente, revolviendo vigorosamente para evitar que se le formen grumos.

**5** Agregue el queso y cocine a fuego de mediano a lento, revolviendo. Cocine hasta que se caliente bien, pero no lo deje hervir. Sirva caliente con vegetales cocinados, pescado, pollo asado o huevos poché.

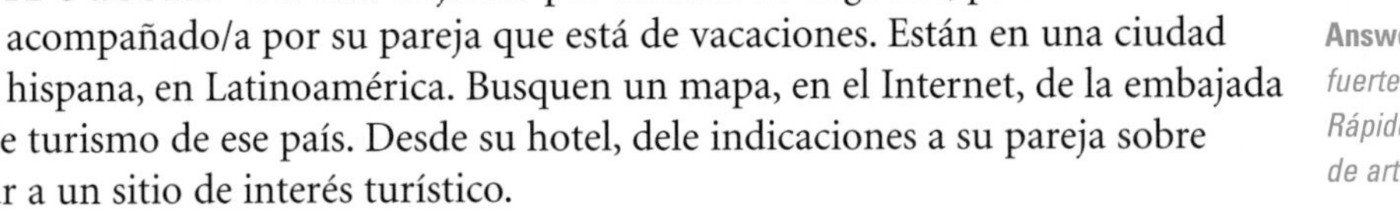

**A buscar.** Ud. está viajando por razones de negocios, pero acompañado/a por su pareja que está de vacaciones. Están en una ciudad hispana, en Latinoamérica. Busquen un mapa, en el Internet, de la embajada u oficina de turismo de ese país. Desde su hotel, dele indicaciones a su pareja sobre cómo llegar a un sitio de interés turístico.

**Tapescript for A escuchar. En la oficina de turismo.**
LÁZARO: Por favor, señora, ¿cuáles son los lugares de interés más importantes de Puerto Rico?
SEÑORA: Aquí tienen un mapa de la isla. Llévenselo y estúdienlo. El lugar más famoso en San Juan es el fuerte *El Morro*. ¿No lo recuerdan? Está a la entrada de la bahía de San Juan. ¿No lo vieron cuando el barco entraba al puerto? Visítenlo temprano porque por la tarde hace mucho calor.
LÁZARO: Sí, es hermosísimo. Dígame, ¿qué actividades hay?
SEÑORA: Este mes se celebra un festival de teatro muy importante en San Juan. Vayan a ver una obra. Pero escúchenme, las entradas se acaban muy rápido, cómprenlas ahora mismo. Vayan también a la Universidad de Puerto Rico. Tiene un edificio bellísimo.
ISABEL: Recomiéndenos también algo fuera de San Juan.
SEÑORA: Tenemos un museo de arte importantísimo en Ponce.
ISABEL: Díganos el nombre de la mejor playa.
SEÑORA: Hay muchas playas bellísimas, pero a mí me gusta Luquillo. No vayan en autobús, mejor pidan un taxi. Contrátenlo por todo el día. Llévense su traje de baño y alquilen un casillero para guardar sus cosas. Quédense allí todo el día. Compren algo para almorzar y cómanselo en las mesas que tienen para los turistas.

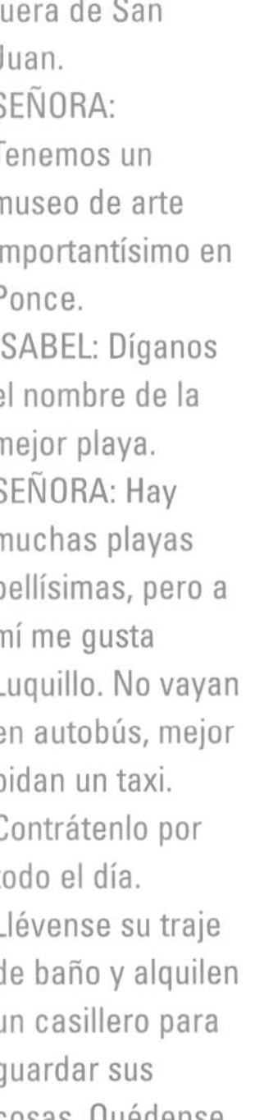

**Answers for *A escuchar.*** 1) *El fuerte El Morro.* 2) *Bahía.* 3) *Rápido.* 4) *Universidad.* 5) *Museo de arte.* 6) *Playas.*



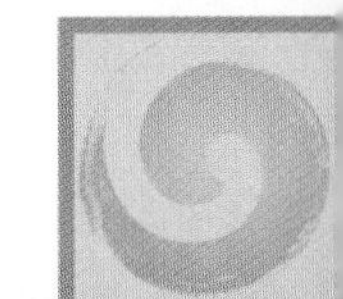

# ¡TRATO HECHO!

## Rincón profesional: Los viajes

¡Conozca el encanto y el esplendor del corazón ruso! Moscú le espera para abrirle las puertas a un mundo fascinante.

¿Le interesan a Ud. las profesiones relacionadas con el turismo? Pues, ¡prepárese ya! porque éste es uno de los sectores económicos que promete un futuro sumamente próspero para los que entienden el comercio global. No hay ningún país que no mande viajeros de negocios, estudiantes y turistas a otros países para conocer sus culturas y sus idiomas. Entre estos viajeros se cuentan muchos de España y de Hispanoamérica.

Si Ud. sabe dirigirse al creciente mercado de turistas, estudiantes, comerciantes y consumidores que hablan español, puede capturar un pedazo de esta prosperidad. Mire Ud. algunas de las invitaciones de bienvenida que desde todas partes del mundo, se extienden al turista que habla español.

¡Venga a descubrir los misterios de la selva africana! Nuestros safaris le ofrecen la oportunidad de vivir una gran aventura.

Australia le invita a sumergirse en sus aguas cristalinas y a nadar entre sus cientos de especies marinas.

¡Disfrute de unas vacaciones inolvidables en uno de los lugares más exóticos del país,el desierto de Arizona, lleno de peligros, placeres y bellos atardeceres!

**¿Comprende Ud.?**

1. ¿Qué sector de la industria está aumentando de forma global?
2. Dé dos razones por las cuales este crecimiento va a continuar en el futuro.
3. Para atraer a la población de habla hispana, ¿qué es lo que han hecho algunas de las empresas que viven del turismo?
4. ¿Qué anuncio le atrae más? ¿Por qué?

**A escuchar. Un viaje por Europa.** Gualberto y Eloísa hablan de sus planes para el verano.

**¿Comprende Ud.?** Conteste las preguntas según el diálogo.

1. ¿Adónde van a ir Gualberto y sus amigos este verano?
2. ¿Cómo van a viajar?
3. ¿Quién organiza el viaje?
4. ¿Dónde van a dormir?
5. ¿Qué pasa si algún ciclista sufre una emergencia?

**Tapescript for A escuchar. Un viaje por Europa.**
GUALBERTO: Todos nuestros amigos van a viajar por Europa en bicicleta este verano. ¿Por qué no vas con nosotros?
ELOÍSA: ¿No es muy peligroso?
GUALBERTO: No, una agencia de viajes lo organiza y vamos a tener un guía turístico a toda hora.
ELOÍSA: ¿Van a dormir en el campo?
GUALBERTO: No, la agencia ya hizo reservaciones en varios hoteles. Cuando viajas en bicicleta puedes conocer muy bien los países que visitas.
ELOÍSA: Pero yo ando en bicicleta muy despacio. ¿Qué pasa si todos los demás me dejan sola?
GUALBERTO: No hay problema. Nos sigue un camión, que recoge a los ciclistas que se cansan, se enferman o se quedan atrás. Lo llaman "la barredora".
ELOÍSA: Voy a pensarlo y después te digo.

**Answers for A escuchar.** 1) *A Europa.* 2) *En bicicleta.* 3) *Una agencia de viajes.* 4) *En varios hoteles.* 5) *Lo recoge un autobús.*

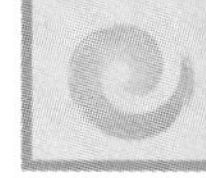

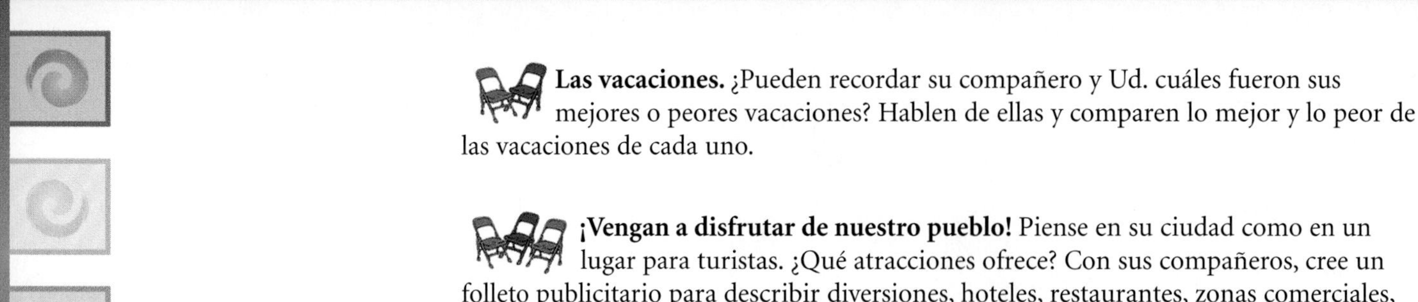

**Las vacaciones.** ¿Pueden recordar su compañero y Ud. cuáles fueron sus mejores o peores vacaciones? Hablen de ellas y comparen lo mejor y lo peor de las vacaciones de cada uno.

**¡Vengan a disfrutar de nuestro pueblo!** Piense en su ciudad como en un lugar para turistas. ¿Qué atracciones ofrece? Con sus compañeros, cree un folleto publicitario para describir diversiones, hoteles, restaurantes, zonas comerciales, etc. que se pueden encontrar en su ciudad. Deben incluir una descripción breve del área geográfica y del clima. Si quieren, pueden inventar atracciones nuevas. Al final del folleto, incluyan una lista con al menos cinco cosas que los turistas deben hacer en su ciudad. (Hagan esto en forma de mandato.)

MODELO: *Coma en nuestro famoso y exclusivo restaurante de McDonald's.*

## A leer

You can often guess the meaning of new words in readings because you already know another word from the same family. For example, you could probably guess that the verb **cansarse** means *to grow tired* because you know the adjective **cansado**. Or, knowing the verb **escalar**, you could guess that the noun **la escalada** means *the climbing*.

**Antes de leer.** Using the familiar words in parentheses, guess the meaning of the italicized words in each sentence.

1. (cerca) De alguna forma ha sentido la *cercanía* de esta gran ciudad.
2. (conjunto) Está dividida en cinco sectores que *en conjunto* tienen alrededor de quince millones de habitantes.
3. (conocer) Los *conocedores* dicen que la mejor comida china e italiana se prepara en estos barrios.
4. (descender) Los *descensos* de temperatura comienzan en noviembre.
5. (medio/a) Por lo regular, el 15% se considera como la propina *promedio.*

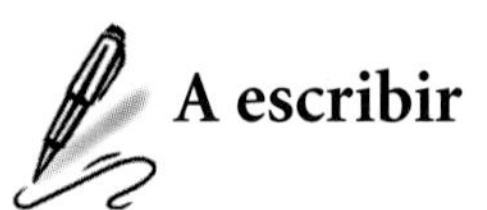

## A escribir

Utilizando la sección de *Recomendaciones* en el artículo como guía, escriba una lista similar de recomendaciones para algún lugar turístico que Ud. frecuenta durante sus vacaciones o que frecuentaba cuando era niño/a.

# NUEVA YORK
## la ciudad que nunca duerme

Si no ha estado nunca en Nueva York, seguramente de alguna forma ha sentido la cercanía de esta gran ciudad, también llamada "La Gran Manzana" o "La Urbe de Hierro".

**Un ambiente cosmopolita por excelencia**

Nueva York está dividida en cinco sectores (Manhattan, Brooklyn, Queens, Staten Island y el Bronx) que en conjunto tienen alrededor de quince millones de habitantes, y una zona suburbana, conocida como la Gran Nueva York, con unos veinte millones de personas.

Originalmente la fundaron los holandeses, pero al convertirse en una posesión británica se convirtió en Nueva York. Poco a poco comenzó a adquirir el carácter de una ciudad cosmopolita: en Nueva York viven más judíos que en Jerusalén, más irlandeses que en Dublín, y más italianos que en Venecia. Al caminar por la Quinta Avenida, no es raro oír hablar yiddish, alemán, árabe, español, francés y hasta inglés. Pasear por las calles de Nueva York es hacer un recorrido por diversas culturas; es admirar una ciudad con mil rostros que nunca deja de sorprender a los visitantes.

**Las tiendas y los restaurantes**

A menudo se dice que si algo no está a la venta en Nueva York, ese algo simplemente no existe. Como centro internacional de la moda, la joyería, las artes y la gastronomía, la ciudad ofrece todas las oportunidades imaginables en un mismo lugar. A los grandes almacenes como Macy's, Bloomingdale's y Saks Fifth Avenue, se agregan tiendas exclusivas como Burberry's, The Cockpit, Fendi, The Forgotten Woman, Polo/ Ralph Lauren, Tiffany's y muchas más.

Tras una jornada agotadora en las tiendas, no hay nada como una buena comida en uno de los innumerables restaurantes de Nueva York. ¡No se pierdan la comida del Barrio Chino y de la Pequeña Italia! Los conocedores dicen que la mejor comida china e italiana se prepara en estos barrios.

**La vida nocturna**

Como dice la canción que canta Frank Sinatra, Nueva York es una ciudad que nunca duerme. Disfrute de los atractivos y variados espectáculos que presentan los teatros en Broadway y fuera de Broadway. ¡Puede asistir cada noche a uno diferente! Un buen boleto para la sección de orquesta cuesta alrededor de sesenta dólares. Cómprelos con suficiente anticipación y de preferencia adquiéralos a través de una agencia de viajes para no quedarse sin función.

**Recomendaciones**

***Clima.*** Nueva York es una ciudad con temperaturas extremas. En el verano, vístase con ropa muy ligera. El frío comienza en noviembre y se prolonga hasta marzo. En esa época, lleve un abrigo o al menos una gabardina.

***Propinas.*** En los restaurantes la propina varía entre el 15% y el 20%, dependiendo del servicio. Por lo regular, el 15% se considera la propina promedio. En los taxis, dé un dólar por recorridos cortos, de diez minutos a media hora, o dé 2 dólares si se prolongan más de treinta minutos. En Nueva York y en general en los Estados Unidos, se debe dejar al menos 1 dólar diario a la camarera que asea nuestra habitación.

***Idioma.*** Si habla inglés, todo va a ser más fácil, pero si sólo habla español, despreocúpese, porque no va a tener dificultad alguna. En los hoteles, tiendas y restaurantes hay una o varias personas que hablan español.

***Costumbres.*** Al contrario de la imagen que difunden el cine y las series policiacas de televisión, los neoyorquinos son en general gente de lo más amable y apacible. En las noches, después de asistir al teatro, ir a cenar o escuchar música, es conveniente regresar al hotel en taxi. Si piensa alquilar un automóvil en Nueva York, recuerde las ventajas y desventajas de conducir en una ciudad grande como México, Los Ángeles o París. Decídalo usted.

***Dinero.*** Si lleva una cantidad importante para sus compras y gastos, procure llevar cheques de viajero. Deposítelos en la caja de seguridad que ofrecen gratis los hoteles y limítese a cambiar diariamente la cantidad que necesita. ■

**¿Comprende Ud.?** Indique si las siguientes afirmaciones son **Ciertas (C)** o **Falsas (F)** según el texto.

1. _____ Nueva York se divide en cuatro sectores.
2. _____ La ciudad de Nueva York siempre sorprende a los turistas.
3. _____ En Nueva York siempre hay personas que hablan español.
4. _____ Nueva York siempre tiene un clima cálido.
5. _____ En realidad, los neoyorquinos son más amables de lo que parecen en el cine o la televisión.

# 9

LECCIÓN NUEVE

# La salud y el bienestar

CHECK OUT THE *¡TRATO HECHO!* WEBSITE AND CD-ROM FOR ACTIVITIES, GAMES, SELF-TESTS, AND MUCH MORE!

TEMA 1

## El ejercicio

- El cuerpo
- La importancia del ejercicio
- Los mandatos (*tú*)
- Los mandatos (*nosotros*)

TEMA 2

## La dieta

- Comer bien es importante
- El buen comer significa buena salud
- Introducción al subjuntivo
- Más sobre el subjuntivo

TEMA 3

## La salud mental

- La depresión
- Las relaciones humanas
- Los verbos irregulares en el subjuntivo
- El subjuntivo: expresiones de emoción

TEMA 4

## Las enfermedades

- La atención médica
- En la farmacia
- El subjuntivo: expresiones de duda
- El subjuntivo: expresiones impersonales

# ¡TRATO HECHO!

- Rincón profesional: Salud, belleza y tranquilidad
- A escuchar
- El buzón de Doña Rosa
- A leer
- A escribir

# TEMA 1 El ejercicio

## El cuerpo

### Hay que ponerse en forma

*Ana acaba de llegar a clase, después de subir cuatro pisos por las escaleras….*

ANA: ¡Ay, que me sofoco! Los ascensores no funcionaban y tuve que subir cuatro pisos. ¿Por qué pusieron el salón de clases en el cuarto piso?

MARY: Siéntate, Ana. No hables más y descansa un poco. Estás en muy mala forma. ¿No haces ejercicio?

ANA: No, nunca tengo tiempo. Además, como no quiero engordar, como muy poco y me siento muy débil.

MARY: Ana, por Dios, come bien y haz más ejercicio.

PROF. YUJA: Sí, pero ten cuidado. Antes de comenzar cualquier plan de ejercicio, consulta con el médico. Por ahora, camina lentamente por una hora cada día y sube las escaleras en vez de tomar el ascensor.

MARY: Sí, compra un buen par de zapatos de tenis y usa ropa cómoda. Si no tienes tiempo de caminar durante el día, hazlo por la noche, después de cenar.

PROF. YUJA: Pero, ¡cuidado, puede ser peligroso! Por la noche usa ropa de colores claros y brillantes. Si llevas ropa oscura, compra una cinta fosforescente para reflejar la luz; pégatela en una parte visible, como la espalda o el pecho.

MARY: Comienza caminando despacio por unas semanas, una distancia pequeña, menos de una milla. Después, aumenta gradualmente la velocidad y la distancia. Pero no corras rápidamente, así no te lastimas las rodillas.

**A. ¿Comprende Ud.?** Conteste las siguientes preguntas según el diálogo.

1. ¿Por qué sufre Ana?
2. ¿Cómo se siente?
3. ¿Qué debe hacer ella antes de comenzar un plan de ejercicio?
4. ¿Cuándo debe caminar si no tiene tiempo durante el día?
5. ¿Por qué debe usar ropa de colores claros o una cinta fosforescente?
6. Por unas semanas, ¿qué debe hacer Ana?

**Answers for A.** 1) *Porque los ascensores no funcionaban.* 2) *Muy débil.* 3) *Consultar con el médico.* 4) *Por la noche.* 5) *Para reflejar la luz.* 6) *Caminar despacio.*

**B. ¡Yo mando!** Marque con una flecha (*arrow*) la parte del cuerpo indicada en cada mandato.

1. Lávate las manos.
2. Tócate los pies.
3. Cierra los ojos.
4. Tócate la cintura.
5. Lávate el pelo.
6. Cruza los brazos.
7. Lávate los dientes.
8. Abre la boca.

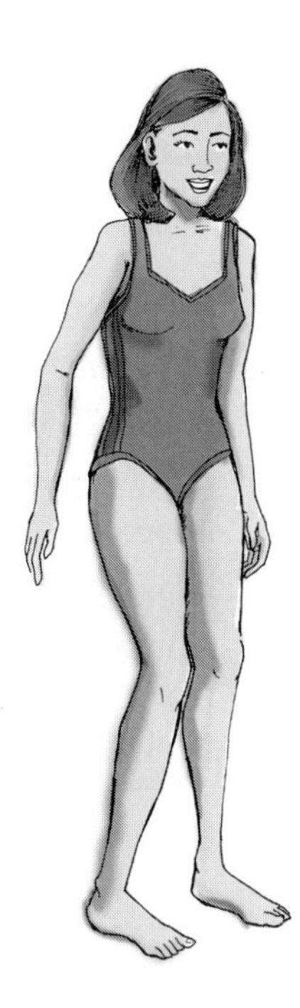

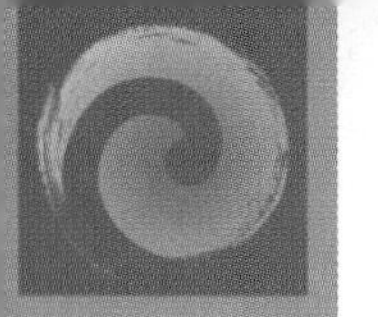

# La importancia del ejercicio

## Los ejercicios de calentamiento

*Lázaro y sus estudiantes se preparan para la clase de gimnasia....*

LÁZARO: Hagamos unos ejercicios de calentamiento antes de empezar la práctica de fútbol.

RAÚL: Vamos a esperar a José.

FABIOLA: No, José no puede hacer ejercicio. Todavía tiene que caminar con muletas.

LÁZARO: ¡Listos, empecemos! Pongámonos las manos en la cintura y subamos la pierna derecha. Ahora la izquierda. Subámoslas despacio: uno, dos, uno, dos.... Ahora de prisa: uno, dos, uno, dos... Volvamos a empezar y esta vez pongamos la espalda recta.

JEANNE: ¡Ay! Descansemos un poco. Me duelen las piernas.

LÁZARO: Está bien. Respiremos hondo para descansar. Llenemos los pulmones de oxígeno. Hagamos ejercicios con los brazos. Extendámoslos al frente, después hacia los lados y llevémoslos hacia abajo: uno, dos, tres, uno, dos, tres...

RAÚL: Me siento muy bien. Corramos un poco.

LÁZARO: ¿Vamos ya? Salgamos despacio y aceleremos la velocidad poco a poco. ¡Ay, no me dejen solo! ¡Espérenme! ¡Regresen!

**Answers for A.** 1) *Un ejercicio de preparación.* 2) *Porque tiene muletas.* 3) *Porque le duelen las piernas.* 4) *Los estudiantes lo dejan solo.*

**A. ¿Comprende Ud.?** Conteste las siguientes preguntas según el diálogo.

1. ¿Qué es un ejercicio de calentamiento?
2. ¿Por qué no puede hacer ejercicio José?
3. ¿Por qué quiere descansar Jeanne?
4. ¿Qué le pasa a Lázaro?

**B. El test de los Marines.** Hable con su compañero/a para contestar estas preguntas según la lectura.

New word: *nuca*

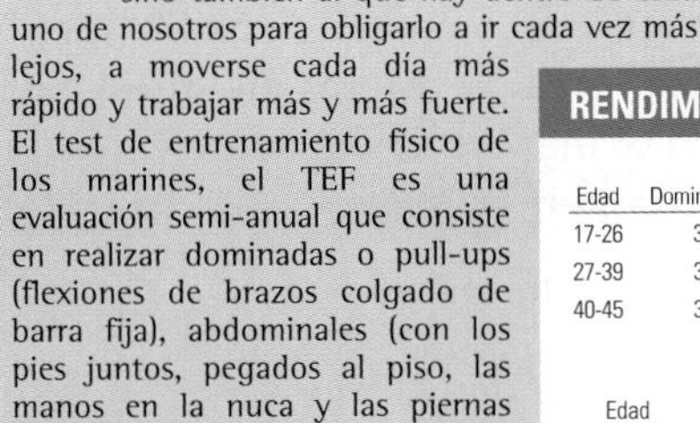

Desde 1775, el Cuerpo de Marines exige aptitud física y entrena a su gente para combatir no sólo al enemigo potencial, sino también al que hay dentro de cada uno de nosotros para obligarlo a ir cada vez más lejos, a moverse cada día más rápido y trabajar más y más fuerte. El test de entrenamiento físico de los marines, el TEF es una evaluación semi-anual que consiste en realizar dominadas o pull-ups (flexiones de brazos colgado de barra fija), abdominales (con los pies juntos, pegados al piso, las manos en la nuca y las piernas flexionadas, levantar el torso hasta llegar a las rodillas) y carrera de 5 kilómetros (3 millas).

Cada actividad tiene un puntaje que va de 0 a 100 y depende de la capacidad individual de cada marine. Un puntaje perfecto de 300 puntos se obtiene realizando 20 dominadas, 80 abdominales en dos minutos y recorriendo los 5 km. en 18 minutos.

Para las mujeres el máximo puntaje exige 70 posturales (colgarse de barra fija), 50 abdominales (idem hombres) y carrera de 2,5 kilómetros (aprox. 1 1/2 millas) en 10 minutos.

El puntaje obtenido es el factor más importante en la promoción para deter-minar sargentos y grados inferiores.

**RENDIMIENTO MÍNIMO ACEPTABLE (HOMBRES)**

| Edad | Dominadas | Abdominales | Carrera Minutos | Subtotal Puntos | Adicional Puntos | Supera el puntaje |
|---|---|---|---|---|---|---|
| 17-26 | 3 | 40 | 28 | 95 | 40 | 135 |
| 27-39 | 3 | 35 | 29 | 84 | 26 | 110 |
| 40-45 | 3 | 35 | 30 | 78 | 7 | 85 |

**Puntaje mínimo requerido**

| Edad | Insatisfactorio | 3ª clase | 2ª clase | 1ª clase |
|---|---|---|---|---|
| 17-26 | 0-134 | 135 | 175 | 225 |
| 27-39 | 0-109 | 110 | 150 | 200 |
| 40-45 | 0-84 | 85 | 125 | 175 |

**RENDIMIENTO MÍNIMO ACEPTABLE (MUJERES)**

| Edad | Colgarse de barra fija (Segundos) | Abdominales (repeticiones) | Carrera (minutos) | Total (puntos) |
|---|---|---|---|---|
| 17-26 | 16 | 22 | 15 | 100 |
| 27-39 | 13 | 19 | 16:30 | 73 |
| 40-45 | 10 | 18 | 18 | 56 |

**Puntaje mínimo requerido**

| Edad | Insatisfactorio | 3ª clase | 2ª clase | 1ª clase |
|---|---|---|---|---|
| 17-26 | 0-99 | 100 | 150 | 200 |
| 27-39 | 0-72 | 73 | 123 | 173 |
| 40-45 | 0-55 | 56 | 106 | 156 |

## POSTÚLESE PARA MARINE

Las tablas presentan los valores usados por el Cuerpo de Marines en evaluación de su rendimiento físico. Cada ejercicio se califica con un puntaje que va de 0 a 100. Estos subtotales se suman y dan un total general.

**HOMBRES:**

1. ¿Cuántos abdominales debe hacer un hombre de dieciocho años para tener 95 puntos?
2. Si un hombre de treinta años tiene solamente 105 puntos en total, ¿puede ser *Marine* de 2ª clase?

**MUJERES:**

1. ¿Cuántos minutos debe correr una mujer de veintiocho años para tener 73 puntos?
2. ¿Cuántos puntos necesita una mujer de veintidós años para ser *Marine* de 1ª clase?

**C. Entrevista.** En grupos de tres, contesten las siguientes preguntas.

1. ¿Cuántos abdominales pueden hacer? ¿Por cuánto tiempo pueden correr sin parar?
2. ¿Se estiran antes de hacer ejercicio? ¿Dónde prefieren hacer ejercicio? ¿en casa? ¿en un gimnasio?
3. Para Uds., ¿es difícil seguir un régimen? Para bajar de peso, ¿prefieren estar a dieta o hacer ejercicio? ¿Qué comen para subir de peso?
4. ¿Practican meditación? ¿Cuándo meditan? ¿Dónde? ¿Cómo se sienten después de meditar?

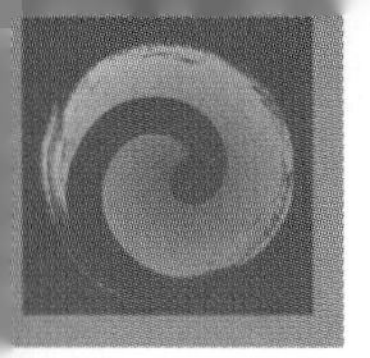

# Los mandatos (*tú*)
## (*Informal commands*)

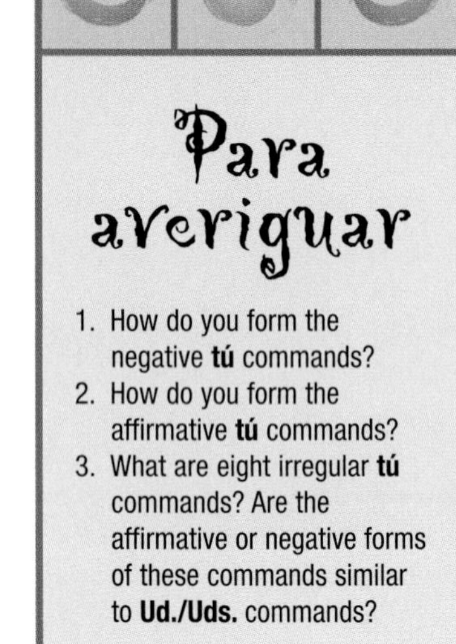

**Para averiguar**

1. How do you form the negative **tú** commands?
2. How do you form the affirmative **tú** commands?
3. What are eight irregular **tú** commands? Are the affirmative or negative forms of these commands similar to **Ud./Uds.** commands?

**Note:** A variety of topics has been included in activities within this section to allow practice of the command forms in several contexts.

- Unlike the **Ud.** commands, the form of the **tú** commands depends on whether you are telling a person to do something (an affirmative command) or not to do something (a negative command). Affirmative **tú** commands look like the **él/ella** form of the present indicative. As with all affirmative commands, direct object and reflexive pronouns are attached to the end of the verb, and a written accent is added to the stressed syllable of all verbs of two or more syllables.

| | |
|---|---|
| **Limpia** tu cuarto. | *Clean your room.* |
| **Levántate.** | *Get up.* |
| **Comienza** lentamente. | *Start slowly.* |
| **Vístete** con colores brillantes. | *Dress in bright colors.* |
| **Come** bien. | *Eat well.* |

- The negative commands are formed by adding **-s** to the **Ud.** command.

| Negative Ud. Command | Negative Tú Command | |
|---|---|---|
| ¡No **diga** eso! | ¡No **digas** eso! | *Don't say that!* |
| ¡No **se levante!** | ¡No **te levantes**! | *Don't get up!* |
| ¡No **lo haga!** | ¡No **lo hagas**! | *Don't do it!* |

- The affirmative **tú** commands of the following verbs are irregular. Note that as with all verbs, the negative **tú** commands are formed by adding **-s** to the **Ud.** command.

| | Affir. | Neg. | | Affir. | Neg. |
|---|---|---|---|---|---|
| **decir** | **di** | **no digas** | **salir** | **sal** | **no salgas** |
| **hacer** | **haz** | **no hagas** | **ser** | **sé** | **no seas** |
| **ir** | **ve** | **no vayas** | **tener** | **ten** | **no tengas** |
| **poner** | **pon** | **no pongas** | **venir** | **ven** | **no vengas** |

### A lo personal

**A. La maestra.** A teacher is talking to a young student. Which of the following would he/she more likely tell him to do?

MODELO: Juega con el cuchillo./No juegues con el cuchillo.
*No juegues con el cuchillo.*

1. Lávate las manos con frecuencia./No te laves las manos con frecuencia.
2. Escúchame bien./No me escuches.
3. Sigue las instrucciones./No sigas las instrucciones.
4. Cierra la puerta del salón./No cierres la puerta del salón.
5. Pégales a tus compañeros./No les pegues a tus compañeros.

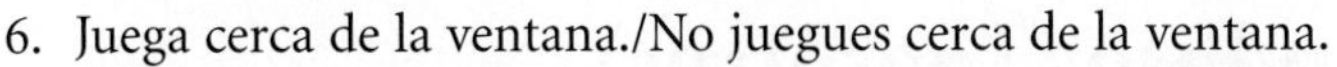

6. Juega cerca de la ventana./No juegues cerca de la ventana.
7. Mete el cuaderno en el microondas./No metas el cuaderno en el microondas.
8. Cómete todos los dulces./No te comas todos los dulces.
9. Tómate el vino./No te tomes el vino.
10. Habla durante las clases./No hables durante las clases.

**B. En la cocina.** Your best friend is out of shape and wants help sticking to a diet. You go through his/her refrigerator and tell him/her whether or not to put these items in the garbage (**basura**).

**Note.** In some Spanish-speaking countries, there is an alternate spelling for *cacahuete: cacahuate.*

MODELO: la leche
*No, no la tires a la basura.*

1. los huevos
2. los cacahuetes
3. la lechuga
4. el pastel de chocolate
5. el pollo
6. el helado
7. las papas fritas
8. las naranjas
9. el pan dulce
10. el azúcar

**C. Unos consejos.** Your younger cousin is about to start studying at the university. Give her advice about whether she should or shouldn't do the following things.

MODELO: tomar un curso de español
*Toma un curso de español./No tomes un curso de español.*
vivir sola
*Vive sola./No vivas sola.*

1. estudiar aquí
2. tomar los cursos más difíciles el primer año
3. hablar mucho en clase
4. comer en la cafetería universitaria
5. vivir cerca del campus
6. dormir en clase
7. salir hasta tarde todos los días
8. tener miedo de hacer preguntas
9. hacer la tarea
10. ir a todas las clases
11. dar su opinión en clase
12. ser tímida

**D. La Cenicienta.** With a classmate, role-play Cinderella and her stepmother discussing household chores. Use logical verbs.

MODELO: la aspiradora
E1: *Cenicienta, pasa la aspiradora.*
E2: *Acabo de pasarla.*

1. el piso
2. los platos
3. los muebles
4. la basura
5. la comida
6. el césped
7. la ropa
8. la mesa

**E. Felices para siempre.** After she marries the prince, Cinderella still wants to do the housework, but he refuses to let her. What does he say?

MODELO: la aspiradora
*No pases la aspiradora.*

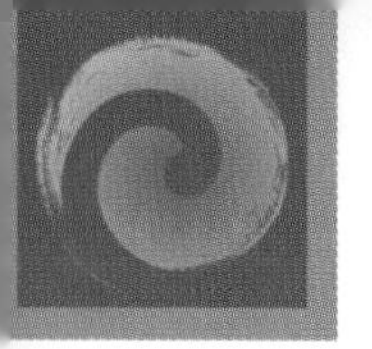

# Los mandatos (*nosotros*)
## (Nosotros *commands or "Let's"*)

**Para averiguar**

1. What are two ways to say *let's do something?*
2. Where do you place the object and reflexive pronouns with **nosotros** commands?

**¡ojo!**

Review the following Ud. command forms.

| Infinitive | Ud. command |
|---|---|
| conocer | conozca |
| dar | dé |
| decir | diga |
| estar | esté |
| hacer | haga |
| ir | vaya |
| oír | oiga |
| poner | ponga |
| saber | sepa |
| salir | salga |
| ser | sea |
| tener | tenga |
| traer | traiga |
| venir | venga |
| ver | vea |
| **-gar** verbs | |
| pagar | pague |
| **-car** verbs | |
| sacar | saque |
| **-zar** verbs | |
| empezar | empiece |

- One way to suggest doing something with other people in Spanish is to use **vamos a** + *infinitive.*

| | |
|---|---|
| ¡**Vamos a salir** esta noche! | *Let's go out tonight!* |
| ¡**Vamos a comer** a un restaurante! | *Let's go eat at a restaurant!* |
| **¡Vamos a practicar!** | *Let's practice!* |

- **Nosotros** commands are also expressed by adding **-mos** to the **Ud.** command form. The written accents of the **Ud.** commands **dé** and **esté** are not needed in the **nosotros** commands.

| | |
|---|---|
| ¡**Hagamos** ejercicio! | *Let's exercise!* |
| ¡**Comamos** en un restaurante vegetariano! | *Let's eat at a vegetarian restaurant!* |
| ¡**Seamos** pacientes! | *Let's be patient!* |
| No **salgamos** esta noche. | *Let's not go out tonight.* |
| ¡**Estemos** contentos con lo que tenemos! | *Let's be happy with what we have!* |

- The affirmative **nosotros** command of **ir** is **vamos** instead of **vayamos.** In the negative, however, you do say **no vayamos.**

| | |
|---|---|
| ¡**Vamos** a la playa! | *Let's go to the beach!* |
| ¡**No vayamos** allí! | *Let's not go there!* |

- Object pronouns are attached to the end of the verb in affirmative commands and an accent is written on the stressed vowel. Object pronouns are placed before the verb in negative commands. The final **-s** of the command is dropped before the indirect object pronoun **se.**

| | |
|---|---|
| ¡**Hagámoslo** mañana! | *Let's do it tomorrow!* |
| ¡No **lo hagamos** ahora! | *Let's not do it now!* |
| ¡**Digámoselo**! | *Let's tell it to them (him/her)!* |
| ¡No **se lo digamos**! | *Let's not tell it to them (him/her)!* |

- The reflexive pronoun **nos** is also attached to the end of the verb in affirmative commands. When this occurs, the final **-s** of the verb is dropped.

| | |
|---|---|
| ¡**Levantémonos** temprano! | *Let's get up early!* |
| **¡Vámonos!** | *Let's go!* |

### A lo personal

**A. Unas sugerencias.** You are determined to get into good shape. Accept or refuse the following suggestions made by a friend.

MODELO: ¡Vamos a comer a McDonald's esta noche!
*No, no comamos en McDonald's.*
¡Vamos a acostarnos temprano esta noche!
*Sí, acostémonos temprano.* o *No, no nos acostemos temprano.*

1. ¡Vamos a levantarnos a las seis de la mañana!
2. ¡Vamos a levantar pesas!
3. ¡Vamos a acampar en las montañas!

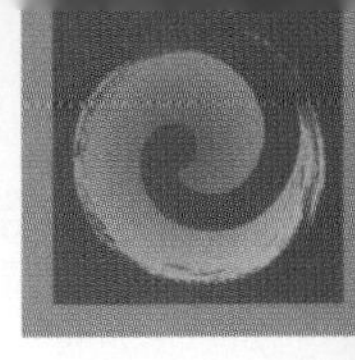

4. ¡Vamos a correr por dos horas y media!
5. ¡Vamos a hacer ejercicio!
6. ¡Vamos al bar esta noche!
7. ¡Vamos a quedarnos en la fiesta hasta las 4:00 A.M.!
8. ¡Vamos a escuchar mis casetes de Madonna todo el día!

**B. ¡Depende!** Under the following conditions, what might you suggest that you and your friends do tomorrow?

MODELO: Va a nevar.
*¡Vamos a esquiar!*

1. Va a hacer sol.
2. Va a hacer frío.
3. Va a llover.
4. Va a hacer mucho calor.
5. Uds. tienen mucho dinero.
6. Uds. no tienen dinero.

Give the same suggestions using the **nosotros** command.

MODELO: Va a nevar.
*¡Esquiemos!*

**C. ¿Qué quieres hacer?** Make an appropriate suggestion for each situation. Then, give the same suggestions using the nosotros command.

MODELO: Necesito hacer un poco de ejercicio.
*¡Vamos a correr en el estadio de la universidad!*
*¡Corramos en el estadio de la universidad!*

1. Quiero ganar un poco de peso.
2. Quiero adelgazar dos kilos.
3. Necesito hacer algo para controlar el estrés.
4. Hoy no tengo energía para trabajar.
5. No quiero pedir más comida rápida esta semana.
6. Hoy necesito comer algo sano; no quiero comer carne.
7. Quiero aprender alguna técnica para relajarme.
8. Hoy hace mucho frío afuera para hacer ejercicio.

# TEMA 2 La dieta

## Comer bien es importante

### La nutrición

*Ana visita a una dietista para mejorar su nutrición….*

SRA. ROSALES: Bienvenida, Ana. Soy Alma Rosales, la dietista. Tu doctor me envió tu historial clínico y veo que estás un poco anémica. ¡Es importante que te alimentes bien!
ANA: Sí, yo quiero tener buena salud. ¿Qué tengo que hacer?
SRA. ROSALES: Veo que nunca desayunas. Quiero que comas tres comidas diarias.
ANA: Voy a tratar de hacerlo.
SRA. ROSALES: Por ahora, te pido dos cosas: primero, que escribas todas las cosas que comas en los próximos diez días. Segundo, que llenes este cuestionario. Es muy importante que contestes la sección sobre tus alimentos favoritos. Quiero que anotes si eres alérgica a algún alimento y cuáles no te gustan o te hacen daño.
ANA: Gracias, le agradezco su ayuda. ¿Quiere que vuelva en dos semanas?
SRA. ROSALES: Sí, haz una cita con mi secretaria. No te preocupes, todo va a salir bien.

**Answers for A.** 1) *Está anemica.* 2) *Nada.* 3) *Si es alérgica a algún alimento y sus alimentos favoritos.* 4) *En dos semanas.*

**A. ¿Comprende Ud.?** Conteste las siguientes preguntas según el diálogo.

1. Según el historial clínico de Ana, ¿cuál es su problema físico?
2. ¿Qué desayuna Ana?
3. Al preparar su lista de alimentos, ¿qué debe incluir Ana?
4. ¿Cuándo debe regresar a ver a la dietista?

**B. ¿Cuál es mejor?** Usando la tabla de la revista *Mía,* dígale a su compañero/a qué comida o bebida es mejor para el problema indicado.

New words: *sangre, hierro*

MODELO: la fiebre del heno (el yogurt/la piña)
*El yogurt es mejor para la fiebre del heno.*

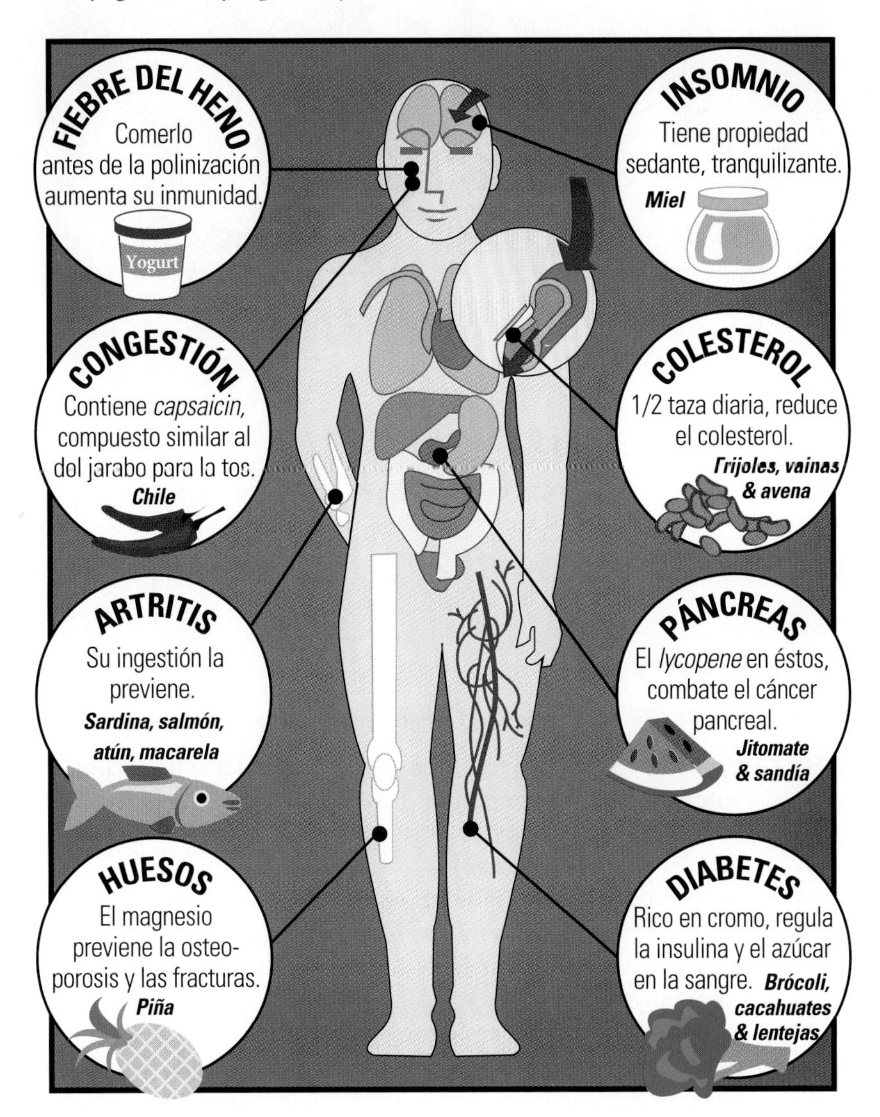


1. la diabetes (el brócoli/las papas)
2. el insomnio (el salmón/la miel)
3. la artritis (el pescado/la carne)
4. la congestión (las zanahorias/los chiles)
5. el colesterol (los frijoles/las bananas)
6. el páncreas (el ajo/la sandía)
7. los huesos (piña/manzana)

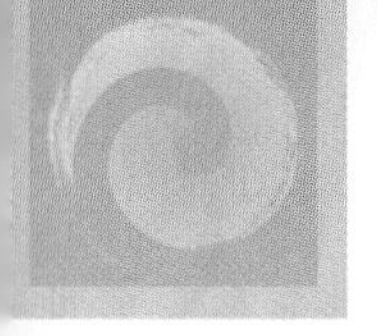

#  El buen comer significa buena salud

## La dieta para Ana

*Ana regresa a visitar a la dietista después de dos semanas....*

SRA. ROSALES: Primero, no quiero que comas tan desordenadamente. Es importante que tengas un horario fijo para las tres comidas.

ANA: Voy a decirle a Lucero que organicemos nuestro horario para comer siempre a la misma hora.

SRA. ROSALES: Me parece muy bien. También veo que te gusta comer entre comidas. Me imagino que tienes mucha hambre porque eres muy activa. Puedes tomar algo a media mañana y a media tarde, pero te aconsejo que comas frutas y verduras.

ANA: Pero me preocupa ganar peso si como mucho.

SRA. ROSALES: Bueno, todo depende de lo que comas. Te voy a dar este folleto. Mira, tiene una pirámide con los grupos de alimentos que son esenciales para una buena salud. Quiero que escojas un alimento de cada grupo para cada comida.

**Answers for A.** 1) *Come desordenadamente.* 2) *Tener un horario fijo de comidas.* 3) *Ganar peso.* 4) *Answers will vary.*

**A. ¿Comprende Ud.?** Conteste las siguientes preguntas según el diálogo.

1. ¿Cuál es el problema básico de la dieta de Ana?
2. ¿Qué necesita tener ella para mejorar su dieta?
3. ¿Cuál es la preocupación de Ana?
4. ¿Cuáles cree Ud. que son los grupos esenciales de alimentos?

**B. Mis alimentos favoritos.** Escriba por lo menos tres cosas que Ud. come de cada una de las categorías. Si no come bien, apunte lo que debe comer de ese grupo. ¿Cuáles son los alimentos favoritos de su compañero/a?

## LAS CUATRO FAMILIAS BÁSICAS DE ALIMENTOS

Las cuatro familias básicas incluyen los principales grupos en que pueden clasificarse la mayoría de los alimentos. El número y tamaño de porciones varía según la edad, la talla y la actividad física.

### Carnes y pescados

Como fuente esencial de proteína, se necesitan dos o más porciones de este grupo a diario. Dos o tres onzas de carne cocida, de pollo o de pescado constituyen una porción; o dos huevos; o una taza de frijoles secos o lentejas cocidas; o cuatro cucharadas de mantequilla de cacahuete.

### Frutas y verduras

Esta familia incluye frutas y verduras que son ricas en vitaminas A y C. La dieta diaria debe incluir por lo menos una porción de fruta o jugos cítricos, una porción de otra fruta y dos porciones de verduras (preferiblemente de color verde oscuro o amarillo).

### Leche y queso

Todos necesitamos leche o alimentos a base de leche cada día. Los niños menores de doce años necesitan por lo menos dos tazas de leche, los adolescentes, tres o más tazas; los adultos, dos tazas; las madres embarazadas o nodrizas, cuatro tazas. Algunas porciones de leche pueden sustituirse por alimentos lácteos como el queso.

### Pan y cereales

Pueden tomarse cuatro o más porciones de alimentos de este grupo, tales como pan, cereales secos o cocidos, fideos, arroz, o comidas horneadas a base de trigo entero o de harina enriquecida.

**C. La salud para los niños.** Ud. es maestro/a en una escuela primaria y ve que los niños siempre comen dulces (*sweets*) pero a veces ponen los vegetales en la basura. Prepare tres sugerencias para mejorarles la dieta y compare sus ideas con su compañero/a.

MODELO: *Cómanse las zanahorias—son buenas para los ojos.*

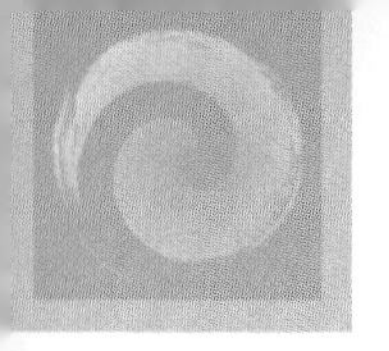

# Introducción al subjuntivo
## (*Introduction to the subjunctive*)

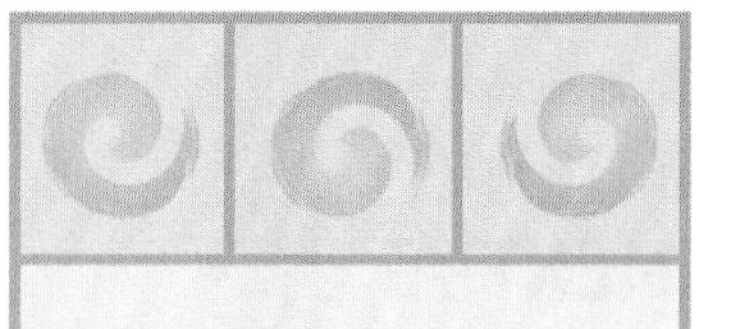

**Para averiguar**

1. When is the subjunctive used in a subordinate clause?
2. Which verb form that you have already learned is similar to the subjunctive?
3. When do you use an infinitive after verbs like **querer** or **preferir**?
4. When do you use the subjunctive after these verbs?

- Up to this point you have been using verb forms in the *indicative mood*. The indicative mood is used to describe what the speaker assumes to be true. There is another mood called the *subjunctive*. Using the subjunctive form of the verb often means that what is said is not considered a fact by the speaker. The subjunctive is used in the subordinate (*usually the second*) clause of a sentence when the main (*usually the first*) clause expresses a wish, doubt, emotion, or attitude. Compare these sentences.

**Indicative** Ana **come** tres comidas buenas todos los días.
(The speaker assumes that it is true that Ana eats three good meals every day.)

**Subjunctive** Quiero que Ana **coma** tres comidas buenas todos los días.
(The speaker does not assume it to be true that Ana eats three good meals every day. It is just what he/she wants to see happen.)

- The subjunctive is formed exactly like the **Ud.** command by changing vowels of the **-ar** verb endings to **e**, and the vowels of **-er** and **-ir** verbs to **a** on the **yo** form of the verb.

| | hablar | comer | vivir | ir | dar | estar |
|---|---|---|---|---|---|---|
| COMMAND → | hable | coma | viva | vaya | dé | esté |
| que yo | hable | coma | viva | vaya | dé | esté |
| que tú | hables | comas | vivas | vayas | des | estés |
| que él/ella/Ud. | hable | coma | viva | vaya | dé | esté |
| que nosotros/as | hablemos | comamos | vivamos | vayamos | demos | estemos |
| que vosotros/as | habléis | comáis | viváis | vayáis | deis | estéis |
| que ellos/ellas/Uds. | hablen | coman | vivan | vayan | den | estén |

- When there is only one subject that prefers, desires or hopes to do something, the verb is followed by an infinitive.

| | |
|---|---|
| Yo **quiero nadar**. | *I want to swim.* |
| Tú **necesitas caminar**. | *You need to walk.* |

- When one subject wants (prefers, desires or hopes) that a second subject do something, the two clauses are joined by **que** and the subjunctive is used in the second clause.

| | |
|---|---|
| (**Yo**) Quiero que (**tú**) **camines**. | *I want you to walk.* |
| (**Tú**) Esperas que (**yo**) **haga** ejercicio. | *You hope that I exercise.* |

- Note that while Spanish has two clauses connected by the conjunction **que**, English often has a different sentence structure.

| | |
|---|---|
| ¿Quieres que yo lo **haga**? | *Do you want me to do it?*<br>*Do you want that I do it?* |
| Desean que **nos quedemos** con ellos. | *They want us to stay with them.*<br>*They wish that we stay with them.* |

## A lo personal

**A. ¿El médico o los pacientes?** Does the doctor want the patients to do these things or do the patients want the doctor to do them? Begin each sentence with **Los pacientes quieren que el médico…** or **El médico quiere que los pacientes…**

MODELO: hablar con ellos después del examen físico
*Los pacientes quieren que el médico hable con ellos después del examen físico.*

1. describir bien los síntomas
2. hacer preguntas
3. contestar sus preguntas
4. volver el próximo año para su examen médico
5. dejar de fumar
6. pagar rápidamente
7. darles consejos para mejorarse pronto
8. recomendárselo a sus amigos
9. tomar la medicina según las indicaciones
10. prestarle atención a sus problemas

**B. ¿Cuáles prefiere?** When you are sick, which things do you prefer to do and which do you prefer that your roommate or spouse do?

MODELO: lavar el coche.
*Yo prefiero lavarlo.* o *Yo prefiero que mi compañero/a de cuarto lo lave.*

1. preparar la sopa de pollo
2. ir al supermercado
3. dormir
4. tomar la medicina
5. llevar la receta a la farmacia
6. mirar la televisión
7. lavar los platos
8. contestar el teléfono

**C. ¿Qué quieren?** Say whether or not the following people want the things indicated in parentheses.

MODELO: El médico (no) quiere que yo (tomar la medicina, pagarle, dormir, trabajar todo el día).
*El médico quiere que yo tome la medicina./El médico quiere que yo le pague./El médico quiere que yo duerma./El médico no quiere que yo trabaje todo el día.*

1. Mis padres (no) quieren que yo (venir a su casa, graduarme, ser feliz, estar enfermo/a).
2. Por lo general, los hijos (no) quieren que sus padres (darles dinero, ser muy estrictos, decirles cómo vivir).
3. (No) Queremos que nuestro/a profesor/a (venir a clase, hablar español en clase siempre, dar pruebas todos los días, hacer preguntas difíciles en los exámenes).
4. Nuestro/a profesor/a (no) quiere que nosotros (venir a clase tarde, estudiar, hacer la tarea, hablar mucho inglés en clase, comprender la lección).
5. Los pacientes de un hospital (no) quieren que su habitación (ser cómoda, estar limpia, tener muchas camas, costar mucho).
6. Los enfermeros (no) quieren que los pacientes (ser antipáticos, tener muchas visitas, desear mucha atención, tomar sus medicinas).

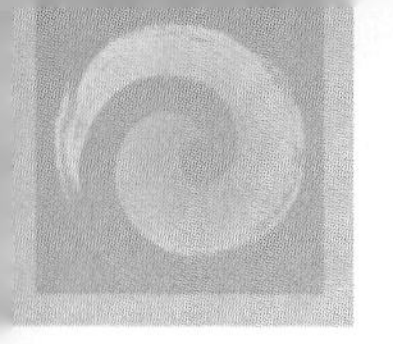

# Más sobre el subjuntivo
## (*More about the subjunctive mood*)

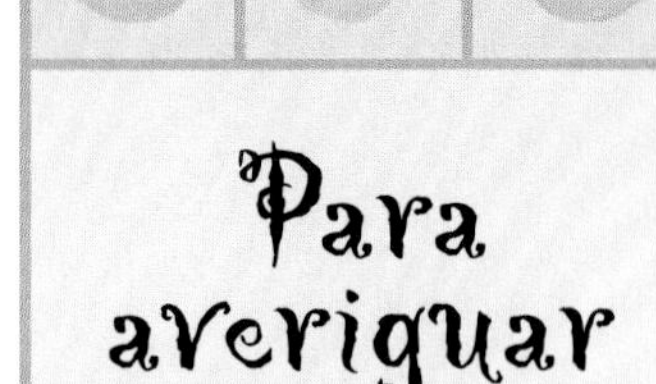

**Para averiguar**

1. Can you explain why expressions such as **recomiendo que** or **sugiero que** are followed by the subjunctive?
2. What other expressions of advice can you name?

- In Spanish, when one subject advises, recommends, suggests, permits, or prohibits that another subject do something, the subjunctive is used in the subordinate or second clause. The first clause verb is usually in the indicative, and the two clauses are joined by **que**.

**Yo** recomiendo **que** (**tú**) te cuides. — *I recommend that you take care of yourself.*
**Tú** me sugieres **que** (**yo**) vaya al médico. — *You suggest to me that I go to the doctor.*

- When the following verbs are used in the main clause and are followed by **que** and a change of subject, the verb in the second or subordinate clause will be subjunctive.

| | | | |
|---|---|---|---|
| aconsejar | desear | esperar | insistir en |
| pedir | permitir | preferir | prohibir |
| recomendar | sugerir | querer | |

Mi madre **insiste** en **que** yo **vuelva** a casa para la medianoche. — *My mother insists that I be home by midnight.*
El médico **aconseja que guardes** cama. — *The doctor advises that you stay in bed.*
Te **pido que** me **lleves** al médico. — *I am asking you to take me to the doctor.*
**Sugerimos que** Ud. **siga** las indicaciones del médico. — *We suggest that you follow the doctor's orders.*
Puedo hacer lo **que** tú **quieras.** — *I can do whatever you may want.*
Te prohíbo **que fumes** aquí. — *I forbid you to smoke here.*
Espero **que estés** mejor mañana — *I hope that you feel better tomorrow.*
Ellos prefieren **que** te **quedes** en casa. — *They prefer that you stay home.*

## A lo personal

**A. Sugerencias.** Your friend is very ill but insists on staying in class to get ready for a big test. Do you suggest that he/she do or not do the following?

MODELO: quedarse en clase
*Yo no te recomiendo que te quedes en clase.* o
*Yo te sugiero que te quedes en clase.*

1. regresar a casa
2. pasar todo el día en clase
3. ir a la biblioteca
4. guardar cama
5. hacer una cita con el médico
6. llamar a un compañero para pedirle la tarea
7. estudiar con un grupo en la cafetería
8. salir a bailar después de comer
9. cuidarse
10. dormir en clase

**B. ¿Qué podemos hacer?** You and your roommate are going to visit a friend in another city for the weekend. You are on the phone with your friend discussing what the three of you can do for fun while you visit, and your roommate wants to know what is being planned. Relay your friend's suggestions to your roommate.

MODELO: Podemos ir al cine.
*Sugiere que vayamos al cine.*
Podemos jugar al tenis.
*Quiere que juguemos al tenis.*

1. Podemos ver un partido de fútbol.
2. Podemos asistir al concierto de Ricky Martin.
3. Podemos salir el viernes por la noche.
4. Podemos hacer una cena en mi casa.
5. Podemos dar un paseo en bicicleta.
6. Podemos caminar por la playa.
7. Podemos ir al cine.
8. Podemos conocer a sus amigos.
9. Podemos visitar los museos.
10. Podemos hacer un picnic en el parque.

**C. La dieta correcta.** One of you is a nutritionist and the other is a client who wants to gain/lose weight. The client will explain to the nutritionist the reasons why he/she wants to lose/gain weight. Then, the nutritionist will suggest appropriate changes in lifestyle and diet.

**D. Lo que debemos comer.** In groups of three or four prepare a two-day menu for the client of Activity C. Make sure to include all the appropriate food groups in order to create a balanced diet that will serve the client's purpose and goal. You may want to include helpful suggestions so that the client may vary his/her diet to fit his/her personal needs.

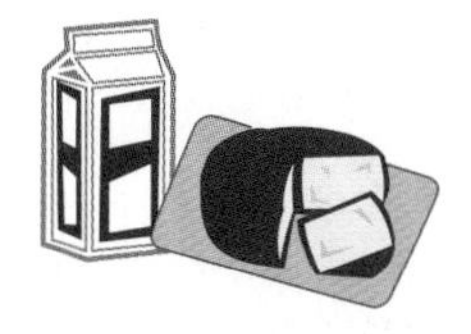

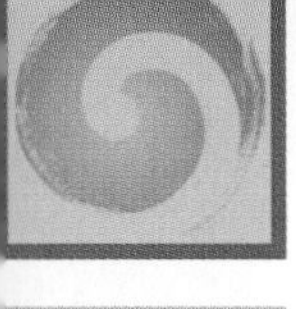

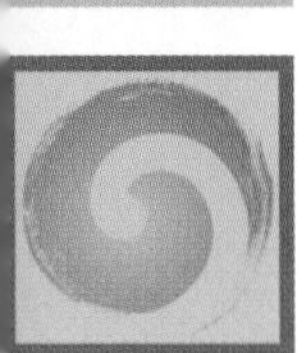
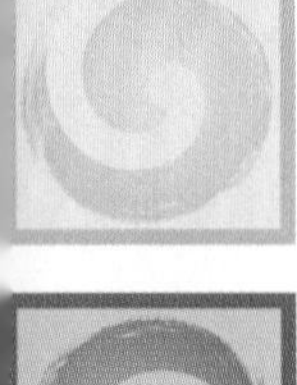
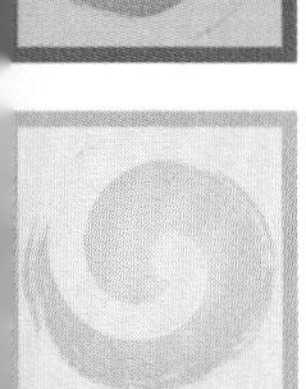
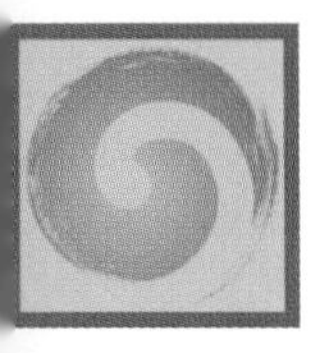

# Vocabulario

## TEMA 1

### El ejercicio

**Sustantivos**

| | |
|---|---|
| **la boca** | *mouth* |
| **el brazo** | *arm* |
| **el cabello** | *hair* |
| **la cabeza** | *head* |
| **la cadera** | *hip* |
| **la cinta** | *tape* |
| **la cintura** | *waist* |
| **el codo** | *elbow* |
| **el corazón** | *heart* |
| **el cuello** | *neck* |
| **el dedo** | *finger* |
| **la espalda** | *back* |
| **el estómago** | *stomach* |
| **la forma** | *shape* |
| **el muslo** | *thigh* |
| **la nalga** | *buttock* |
| **la nariz** | *nose* |
| **el ojo** | *eye* |
| **la oreja** | *ear* |
| **el pecho** | *chest* |
| **el pie** | *foot* |
| **la piel** | *skin* |
| **el pulmón** | *lung* |
| **la rodilla** | *knee* |
| **el talón** | *heel* |
| **el tobillo** | *ankle* |

**Verbos**

| | |
|---|---|
| **adelgazar** | *to lose weight* |
| **arriesgarse** | *to risk* |
| **aumentar** | *to increase* |
| **comenzar (ie)** | *to begin* |
| **engordar** | *to gain weight* |
| **estirarse** | *to stretch* |
| **lastimarse** | *to hurt oneself* |
| **reflejar** | *to reflect* |
| **reírse (i)** | *to laugh* |
| **sofocarse** | *to suffocate* |

**Adjetivos**

| | |
|---|---|
| **débil** | *weak* |

**Otras expresiones**

| | |
|---|---|
| **abajo** | *down there/here* |
| **en vez de** | *instead of* |
| **hondo** | *deep* |
| **lentamente** | *slowly* |

## TEMA 2

### La dieta

**Sustantivos**

| | |
|---|---|
| **los alimentos** | *food* |
| **el arroz** | *rice* |
| **la avena** | *oatmeal* |
| **el cacahuete** | *peanut* |
| **la calabaza** | *squash* |
| **la caloría** | *calorie* |
| **el camote** | *sweet potato* |
| **la carne** | *meat* |
| **la cita** | *appointment* |
| **el cromo** | *chromium* |
| **el cuestionario** | *questionnaire* |
| **la dieta** | *diet* |
| **el guisante/ el chícharo** | *pea* |
| **la harina** | *flour* |
| **los huevos** | *eggs* |
| **los fideos** | *noodles* |
| **la fiebre del heno** | *hay fever* |
| **el hueso** | *bone* |
| **el jarabe** | *syrup* |
| **el jitomate** | *tomato (small)* |
| **las lentejas** | *lentils* |
| **el maíz** | *corn* |
| **la mantequilla** | *butter* |
| **la miel** | *honey* |
| **la nutrición** | *nutrition* |
| **el pan** | *bread* |
| **el pescado** | *fish* |
| **el pollo** | *chicken* |
| **el queso** | *cheese* |
| **la tos** | *cough* |
| **el trigo** | *wheat* |

**Verbos**

| | |
|---|---|
| **aconsejar** | *to advise* |
| **agradecer (zc)** | *to be grateful* |
| **agregar** | *to add* |
| **alimentarse** | *to feed oneself* |
| **anotar** | *to make a note of* |
| **hacer daño** | *to hurt* |

**Adjetivos**

| | |
|---|---|
| **anémico/a** | *anemic* |
| **crudo/a** | *raw* |
| **embarazada** | *pregnant* |
| **frondoso/a** | *leafy* |
| **magro/a** | *lean* |

**Otras expresiones**

| | |
|---|---|
| **unos/as cuantos/as** | *a few* |
| **cualquier/a** | *any* |
| **¡Por Dios!** | *For heaven's sake!* |

# Reunión A

**A escuchar.** **José visita al ortopedista.** Escuche la conversación entre José y el Dr. Aguilar y complete las oraciones con la información que escuche.

1. José se pone impaciente porque quiere jugar ______________.
2. El Dr. Aguilar quiere que José ______________ otro mes.
3. Es importante hacer eso para que ______________ de la pierna sane bien.
4. José no quiere perder ______________ de fútbol.
5. Es probable que le quite ______________ dentro de dos semanas.
6. El doctor prohibe que ______________.

**Tapescript for A escuchar. José visita al ortopedista**
JOSÉ: Doctor Aguilar, ¿cuándo me recomienda que vuelva a jugar al fútbol?
DR. AGUILAR: José, no seas impaciente. Te pido que andes con muletas otro mes. Quiero que el hueso de tu pierna sane.
JOSÉ: Pero, voy a perder esta temporada de fútbol. Mis compañeros quieren que juegue con ellos. El año pasado fuimos los campeones nacionales.
DR. AGUILAR: Lo siento, pero no quiero que arriesgues tu salud. Me alegro de que el hueso esté sanando muy bien. ¿Te duele la pierna?
JOSÉ: No, no me duele. Entonces, ¿espero que me quite el yeso hoy?
DR. AGUILAR: Prefiero que esperes un poco. Si las radiografías salen bien, es probable que te lo quite en dos semanas.
JOSÉ: Entonces, ¿es posible que juegue con ellos en dos semanas?
DR. AGUILAR: No, José. Entiendo que tengas ganas de volver a jugar, pero te prohibo que hagas ejercicio. Te ordeno que descanses.

**Answers for A escuchar.**
1) *Al fútbol.* 2) *Ande con muletas.* 3) *El hueso.* 4) *La temporada.* 5) *El yeso.* 6) *Haga ejercicio.*

**A conversar.** Prepare Ud. cinco sugerencias (*suggestions*) para ayudar a un/a amigo/a (su compañero/a), a quien no le gusta hacer ejercicio, a ponerse en forma. Compare su lista con la de él/ella.

MODELO: *Te recomiendo que hagas ejercicio más a menudo.*

## ¿Lo sabía?

### Cuídese Ud. y cuide a su bebé

**Si Ud. fuma mientras está embarazada:**
- Ud. podría tener un aborto espontáneo o su bebé podría nacer muerto.
- Su bebé podría nacer prematuro o demasiado pequeño. Los bebés que nacen demasiado pequeños pueden tener problemas respiratorios y otros problemas de salud en general.
- Su bebé podría tener problemas de comportamiento y de aprendizaje más tarde en la niñez.
- Su bebé podría morir del síndrome de muerte súbita infantil. Esta enfermedad causa que un bebé aparentemente saludable muera sin indicación previa.

**¿Por qué conviene dejar de fumar mientras está embarazada?**
- Ud. va a tener un embarazo más saludable.
- Su bebé se desarrollará mejor porque le llegarán más oxígeno y sustancias nutritivas.

- Su bebé tiene más probabilidades de nacer sano.

**Ud. puede dejar de fumar. Siga estos consejos:**
- Escriba en un papel las razones por las cuales quiere dejar de fumar.
- Elija un "día sin fumar" que caiga en las próximas dos semanas.
- Pídale a una persona muy allegada a Ud. y que no fume—puede ser su pareja o una amistad—que le ayude a dejar de fumar.
- Tire a la basura todos sus cigarrillos, ceniceros, fósforos y encendedores.
- Manténgase alejada de los sitios y las actividades que le provocan el deseo de fumar.

**Cuando sienta deseos de fumar, haga una de las cosas que siguen:**
- Cepíllese los dientes.
- Salga a caminar.
- Llame a un/a amigo/a.
- Mastique chicle sin azúcar o coma trocitos de zanahoria.
- Lea de nuevo su lista de razones para dejar de fumar.
- Mantenga las manos ocupadas. Busque cosas que pueda hacer con las manos para que no tenga que sostener el cigarrillo.

**¿Comprende Ud?** Según la información del boletín, dé una respuesta.

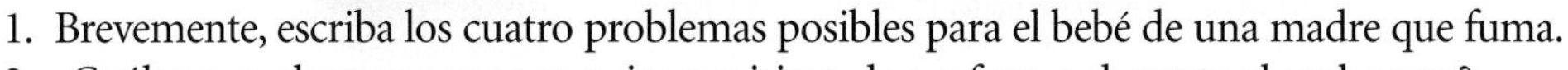

1. Brevemente, escriba los cuatro problemas posibles para el bebé de una madre que fuma.
2. ¿Cuáles son algunas consecuencias positivas de no fumar durante el embarazo?
3. ¿Cuáles son los consejos más importantes para dejar de fumar?

**A buscar.** Busque un programa de ejercicio o mejoramiento de salud en español en el Internet, en los periódicos de su barrio o en revistas populares para traer a la clase. Compare sus artículos con los de sus compañeros en grupos de cuatro. ¿Cuál es el mejor? ¿Por qué?

## La depresión

*Después de clase, el profesor Yuja habla con Mary de una muerte en su familia....*

MARY: Profesor Yuja, ¿qué le pasa? Lo veo muy triste.
PROF. YUJA: Mi papá murió hace dos meses de leucemia. Lo extraño mucho.
MARY: Lo siento. ¿Qué va a hacer su mamá?
PROF. YUJA: Me preocupa que no quiera hacer nada. Siempre era muy activa y ahora no desea ver a nadie.
MARY: Siento mucho que no esté bien su mamá. ¿Por qué no se muda con ustedes?
PROF. YUJA: Ella dice que quiere ser independiente. Temo que se vaya a enfermar. Antes comía muy bien pero ahora está débil porque se alimenta mal.
MARY: Tiene síntomas de depresión. Le recomiendo que la lleve a un terapeuta.
PROF. YUJA: Es una buena idea. Voy a hacer una cita con un amigo que trabaja para el hospital del condado. Espero que no esté muy ocupado.

**Answers for A.** 1) *Está triste.* 2) *De que su mamá se enferme.* 3) *Come mal.* 4) *Que la lleve a un terapeuta.*

**A. ¿Comprende Ud.?** Conteste las siguientes preguntas según el diálogo.

1. ¿Qué le pasa al Profesor Yuja?
2. ¿De qué tiene miedo el profesor?
3. ¿Cómo come su mamá ahora?
4. ¿Qué recomienda Mary?

# LA DEPRESIÓN HABLA TODOS LOS IDIOMAS

¿Cómo se puede saber si uno sufre de depresión? ¿Cómo se sabe si hay que hablar con el médico? Una forma de averiguar las respuestas es empezar con la lista incluida aquí.

La depresión tiene síntomas específicos con los que su médico está familiarizado. Lea la lista y marque los elementos que mejor describan su situación. Si Ud. sufre o ha sufrido cinco o más de estos síntomas por más de dos semanas, necesita visitar a su médico.

Lista de síntomas asociados con la depresión:

- ❑ Me siento triste y/o irritable.
- ❑ No disfruto de las cosas de las que antes disfrutaba (trabajo, pasatiempos, deportes, amigos, vida sexual).
- ❑ Mi apetito y/o peso ha(n) cambiado.
- ❑ Duermo mucho o no duermo lo suficiente.
- ❑ Siempre estoy cansado/a y no tengo energía.
- ❑ Me siento culpable, sin esperanza y siento que no valgo nada.
- ❑ No puedo concentrarme ni recordar cosas ni tomar decisiones.
- ❑ Mis amigos dicen que estoy intranquilo/a y que mi energía ha disminuido.
- ❑ A menudo pienso en la muerte y/o he intentado suicidarme.



**B. La depresión habla todos los idiomas.** Todos sufrimos de depresión a veces. Marque los síntomas de la lista anterior y hable con un/a compañero/a para ver las semejanzas (*similarities*) entre la información presentada y su propia (*own*) experiencia

MODELO: *Cuando estoy deprimido/a, no puedo concentrarme.*

**C. Consejos.** Uno/a de Uds. es locutor/a de un programa de radio y los/as otros/as tres son personas que llaman pidiendo consejo. Hagan los papeles oralmente.

1. ¿Qué debo hacer cuando mi jefe me enoja en el trabajo?
2. Siempre me molesta cuando los hijos de mi vecino hacen ruido. ¿Qué debo hacer para mejorar la situación?
3. Mi novio/a siempre se enoja cuando estoy con mis amigos. ¿Qué puedo hacer?
4. La tensión en mi vida no me permite dormir. ¿Qué sugiere?
5. ¿Cuáles son los síntomas de la depresión? Creo que mi madre está deprimida y no sé qué hacer.

**Expansion for C.** Ask students to name organizations in the community that offer counseling services/ support groups.

**D. Un momento terrible.** Hable con dos compañeros/as sobre un mal momento en su vida. ¿Su familia y sus amigos le ofrecieron apoyo? ¿Ud. trató de esconder (*hide*) su problema? ¿Era una enfermedad física o mental? ¿Cómo resolvió esta crisis?

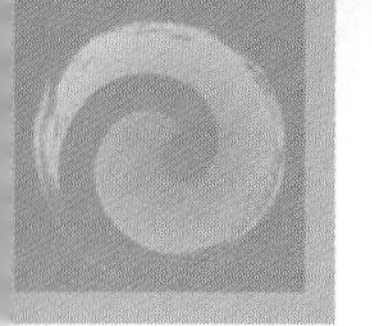

# Las relaciones humanas

## En la oficina del Dr. Ocampo

*El profesor Alberto Yuja visita a un psicólogo para hablar sobre su madre....*

DR. CAMPO: Alberto, me temo que tu mamá tiene síntomas de depresión. Por ahora, no quiero que tome medicinas. Es normal que se sienta así después de la muerte de su esposo.

PROF. YUJA: ¡Imagínate! Estuvieron casados por cincuenta años. ¿Qué puedo hacer para que se sienta mejor?

DR. CAMPO: No me gusta que viva sola. ¿Es posible que le haga compañía alguien?

PROF. YUJA: Voy a pedirle a mi hija Elenita que se quede con ella por un tiempo.

DR. CAMPO: Muy bien. Es muy importante que le prepare la comida y que la obligue a comer bien. Organicen actividades con la familia para que tu mamá salga de la casa.

PROF. YUJA: ¿Crees que se puede aliviar pronto?

DR. CAMPO: Sí, pero necesita terapia psicológica. En el hospital tenemos un grupo de apoyo para viudas. Quiero que asista una vez por semana.

PROF. YUJA: Claro, le voy a pedir a mi esposa que la lleve.

**A. ¿Comprende Ud.?** Conteste las siguientes preguntas según el diálogo.

1. ¿Cómo sabe Ud. que el Dr. Ocampo conoce ya al profesor Alberto Yuja?
2. ¿Qué medicinas quiere el doctor que tome la madre de Alberto?
3. ¿Cuánto tiempo duró el matrimonio de los padres de Alberto?
4. ¿Qué debe organizar Alberto?

**Answers for A.** 1) *Porque lo llama Alberto.* 2) *Ninguna.* 3) *Cincuenta años.* 4) *Actividades con la familia.*

**B. Voy al psicólogo.** Prepare una lista de posibles preocupaciones de una persona deprimida. Compare su lista con la de un/a compañero/a.

MODELO: *Espero que mi novio/a me quiera, pero no sé.*
*Él/ella me dice que haga todo en la casa y…*

**C. El grupo de apoyo.** Con tres compañeros/as, discuta los efectos del abuso doméstico en la familia. ¿Cuáles son algunas características del abuso? ¿Hay soluciones posibles?

MODELO: *Los niños tienen miedo y se sienten culpables.*
*Los padres necesitan comunicarse mejor.*

## UN EXAMEN:

### ¿Cómo va tu relación con tu pareja?

**¿Has observado que tu pareja…**

- ❑ …te insulta y te humilla constantemente?
- ❑ …te da miedo por la forma en que te mira?
- ❑ …controla lo que haces, con quién hablas y adónde vas?
- ❑ …no te permite ver a tus amistades y/o familia?
- ❑ …no te permite trabajar?
- ❑ …te quita el dinero o se niega a compartirlo contigo?
- ❑ …toma todas las decisiones sin consultarte?
- ❑ …te dice que eres una mala madre o te amenaza con quitarte a tus hijos?
- ❑ …te trata como a una sirvienta?
- ❑ …dice que tú siempre tienes la culpa de todo?
- ❑ …destruye tus pertenencias?
- ❑ …te intimida con el uso de fuerza física o armas de cualquier tipo?
- ❑ …te fuerza a retirar los cargos si lo denuncias a la policía?
- ❑ …te empuja o te golpea?
- ❑ …te amenaza con matar o lastimar a tus animales domésticos?
- ❑ …te amenaza con suicidarse?
- ❑ …te amenaza con matarte?

***Incluso si marcaste sólo una de las preguntas, es posible que estés en una relación abusiva. Llama a nuestra línea confidencial sin costo alguno.***

**Línea Nacional sobre la Violencia Doméstica**

**1•800•799•7233**

***Opciones - Apoyo - Conexiones - Te atenderemos las veinticuatro horas del día.***

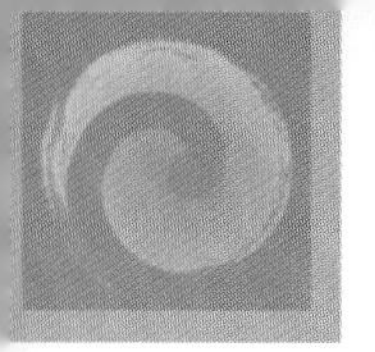

# Los verbos irregulares en el subjuntivo
## (*Irregular subjunctive forms*)

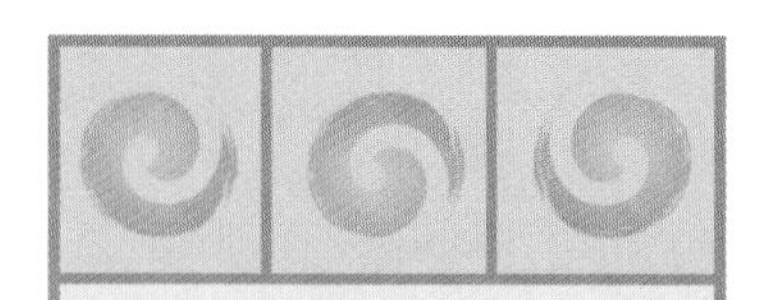

### Para averiguar

1. What five verbs have irregular forms in the formal commands?
2. Are they the same or different in the subjunctive form?
3. In **-ir** stem-changing verbs, what happens to the **e** in the stem of the **nosotros** and **vosotros** forms?
4. Do **-ar** and **-er** stem-changing verbs have a spelling change in the **nosotros** and **vosotros** forms of the subjunctive?
5. How does pronoun placement differ in the command and subjunctive forms?

- The five verbs with irregular formal command forms are:

| | |
|---|---|
| ir | **vaya** |
| ser | **sea** |
| dar | **dé** |
| estar | **esté** |
| saber | **sepa** |

These Ud. command forms are also the basis for the subjunctive forms of the verbs:

| | | | | | | |
|---|---|---|---|---|---|---|
| ir | **vaya** | **vayas** | **vaya** | **vayamos** | **vayáis** | **vayan** |
| ser | **sea** | **seas** | **sea** | **seamos** | **seais** | **sean** |
| dar | **dé** | **des** | **dé** | **demos** | **deis** | **den** |
| estar | **esté** | **estés** | **esté** | **estemos** | **estéis** | **estén** |
| saber | **sepa** | **sepas** | **sepa** | **sepamos** | **sepáis** | **sepan** |

- An **e** in the stem of the **nosotros** and **vosotros** forms of stem-changing **-ir** verbs changes to **i** and an **o** changes to **u** in the subjunctive. Note that this change occurs only with stem-changing **-ir** verbs, and not with **-ar** and **-er** verbs.

| INFINITIVE | | SUBJUNCTIVE |
|---|---|---|
| -ar | cerrar | **cierre**, **cierres**, **cierre**, cerremos, cerréis, **cierren** |
| -er | volver | **vuelva**, **vuelvas**, **vuelva**, volvamos, volváis, **vuelvan** |
| but ¡OJO! | | |
| -ir | sentir | sienta, sientas, sienta, **sintamos**, **sintáis**, sientan |
| | dormir | duerma, duermas, duerma, **durmamos**, **durmáis**, duerman |

- In subjunctive constructions, pronoun placement follows the same rules as in indicative sentences, rather than those of commands. Pronouns are placed before conjugated verbs.

| | |
|---|---|
| infinitive | **comerse** el pan |
| command | ¡**Cómaselo**!/¡No **se lo coma**! |
| subjunctive | Quiero que **se lo coma**/No quiero que **se lo coma.** |

**A. Madre sólo hay una.** Your mother just had a conversation with your doctor about your health. Now, she wants to make sure that you do everything the doctor recommended. Complete her statements according to the model.

MODELO: hacer deporte
*El doctor quiere que hagas deporte.*

1. acostarse temprano
2. comer comidas naturales
3. buscar cosas interesantes para pasar el tiempo libre
4. darle más importancia a la salud
5. estar más tranquilo/a durante los períodos de exámenes
6. dormir 8 horas todas las noches
7. ser responsable cuando maneja
8. ir a visitar a la familia cuando está deprimido/a

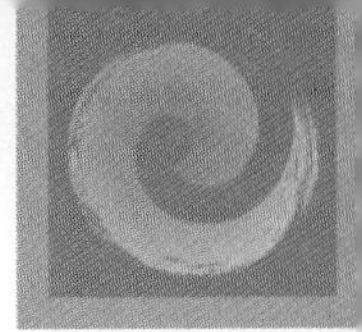

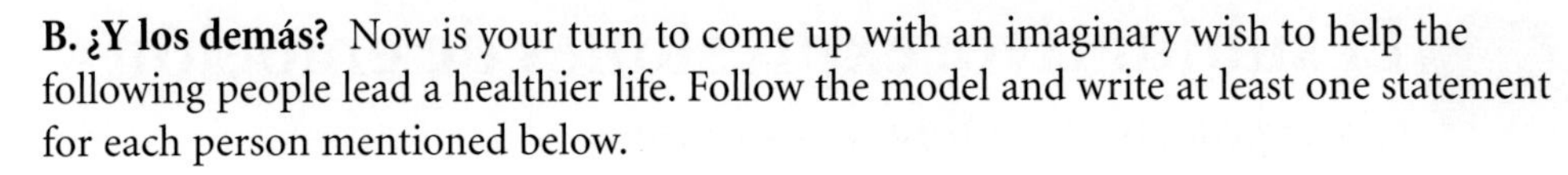

**B. ¿Y los demás?** Now is your turn to come up with an imaginary wish to help the following people lead a healthier life. Follow the model and write at least one statement for each person mentioned below.

MODELO: mi hermano
*Quiero que mi hermano coma más vegetales y menos dulces.*

1. mis padres
2. mi mejor amigo/a
3. mi profesor/a de español
4. mi novio/a
5. mi peor enemigo/a
6. mis vecinos
7. el presidente de los Estados Unidos
8. mi perro/a o mi gato/a
9. mis amigos/as de la escuela secundaria
10. mis compañeros/as de clase de español

**C. ¡Qué chica tan exigente!** Your sister is ill and has to stay in bed for several days. At first, you tried to help her out but lately she's become very bossy. Look at the following sentences and change them to a command in the **tú** form, to reflect your sister's bossiness.

MODELO: Quiero que me traigas un vaso de agua.
*¡Tráeme un vaso de agua!*

1. Quiero que me leas una revista de moda.
2. Espero que vuelvas temprano de la universidad para ayudarme.
3. Necesito que me compres las medicinas que me recetó el médico.
4. No quiero que traigas aquí a tu perro.
5. Quiero que nos prepares una comida dietética a mi amiga y a mí.
6. Prefiero que no mires la televisión cuando yo esté descansando.
7. Quiero que limpies toda la casa hoy por la tarde.
8. Necesito que vayas a la tienda de la esquina ahora mismo.
9. Quiero que tengas paciencia conmigo porque estoy enferma.
10. Quiero que me digas cuánto te gusta estar conmigo.

**D. Entrevista.** Take turns asking and answering the following questions with a classmate.

1. ¿Hay alguna meta que quieras alcanzar respecto a tu salud? ¿Cuál es? ¿Cómo esperas poder alcanzar esa meta?
2. ¿Llevas una vida más o menos sana (*healthy*)? ¿Mantienes una dieta equilibrada? ¿Qué crees que necesitas para poder llevar una vida más saludable (*healthy*)?
3. ¿Qué tipo de situaciones te ponen de mal humor? ¿Qué haces para sentirte mejor? ¿Qué recomendación le harías a alguien que siempre está de mal humor?
4. ¿Qué haces para combatir el estrés en tu vida? ¿Cuáles crees que son algunas de las consecuencias del estrés en la vida diaria?
5. ¿Hay alguien en tu familia que lleve una vida más tranquila que los demás? ¿Qué crees que hace esa persona para combatir las tensiones y los problemas de todos los días? ¿Crees que tú puedes aprender algo de esta persona?

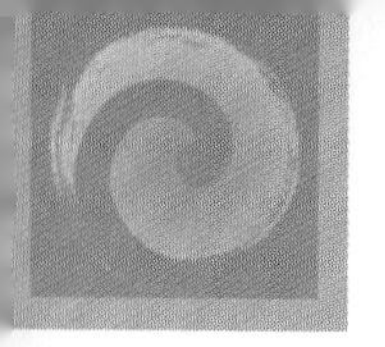

# El subjuntivo: expresiones de emoción
## (*Expressions of feeling or judgment*)

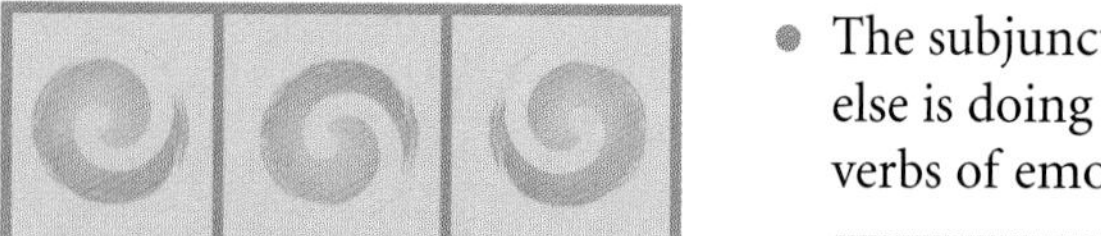

**Para averiguar**

1. You have learned to use the subjunctive to describe something that may or may not be factual. What is an additional use of the subjunctive?
2. What are ten expressions of emotion that are usually followed by the subjunctive?

- The subjunctive can be used to express the way someone feels about what someone else is doing or about what is happening to someone else. Here are some common verbs of emotion that are commonly followed by the subjunctive.

| | |
|---|---|
| **me (te, le...) gusta que...** | **me (te, le...) molesta que...** |
| **me (te, le...) encanta que...** | **me (te, le...) sorprende que...** |
| **alegrarse de que...** | **sentir que...** |
| **estar contento/a de que...** | **temer que...** |
| **estar triste de que...** | **tener miedo de que...** |

**Me alegro de que vayas** con nosotros. — *I am happy that you are going with us.*

**Siento que** los demás **tengan que** quedarse aquí. — *I am sorry that the others have to stay here.*

—¿**Les gusta** a tus padres **que estudies** música? — *—Do your parents like that you study music?*

—Sí, pero **les molesta que toque** el violín en casa. — *—Yes, but it bothers them that I play the violin at home.*

## A lo personal

**A. Una llamada telefónica.** You are talking on the phone with a friend whose mother has been depressed. Express your emotions about what his/her mother is doing, using **me alegro de que..., estoy contento/a de que..., estoy triste de que...,** or **siento que...**

MODELO: No se divierte mucho.
*Siento que no se divierta mucho.*

1. No quiere comer.
2. Habla muy poco con sus amigos.
3. No sale con la familia.
4. Recibe muchas visitas.
5. Tiene suficiente dinero.
6. Va a un grupo de apoyo una vez a la semana.
7. Llora mucho.
8. Está un poco enferma hoy.

**B. ¡Pobrecito/a!** The same friend calls two days later to tell that he/she has had an accident. React to each statement using a verb that expresses your feelings.

1. El choque no es tan grave.
2. Yo estoy bien.
3. El otro conductor tiene la culpa.
4. El otro conductor no tiene seguro.
5. Él dice que yo tengo la culpa.
6. Hay muchos testigos.
7. La policía le da una multa al otro.
8. No puedo usar mi coche.

**C. Gustos y molestias.** With a partner, list the things that these people generally like those named in parentheses to do, and things that bother them.

MODELO: a los profesores (los estudiantes)
*A los profesores les gusta que los estudiantes escuchen en clase.*
*Les molesta que los estudiantes duerman en clase.*

1. a los estudiantes (los profesores)
2. a los padres (sus hijos)
3. a los hijos (los padres)
4. a las mujeres (los hombres)
5. a los hombres (las mujeres)
6. a los meseros (los clientes)

**D. Los titulares.** Express your feelings about the following headlines in your school newspaper.

MODELO: La matrícula sube.
*No me gusta que la matrícula suba.*

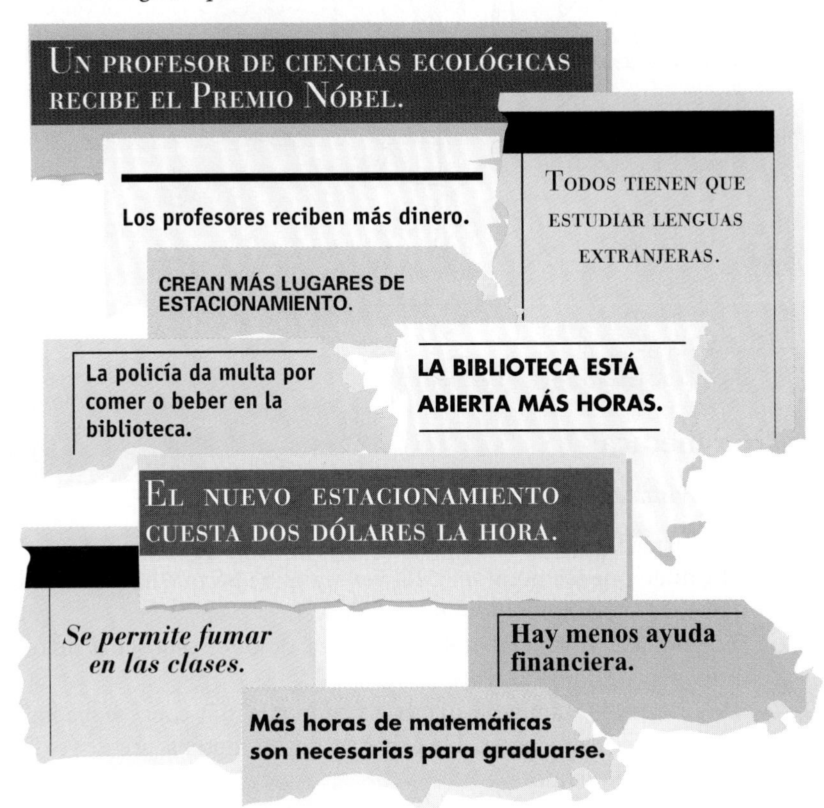


**E. Deseos.** Express your feelings about the following people by completing each sentence in a creative manner.

MODELO: Estoy contento de que mis padres…
*Estoy contento de que mis padres puedan hacer un viaje este verano.*

1. Temo que mi mejor amigo/a…
2. Espero que el/la profesor/a…
3. Me alegro de que mis padres…
4. Prefiero que nadie…
5. Me gusta que todos mis amigos…
6. Ojalá que yo…

**F. Compañeros/as de cuarto.** Role-play an argument with your roommate in which you tell each other what you don't like about each other's habits and behavior and what bothers you.

## La atención médica

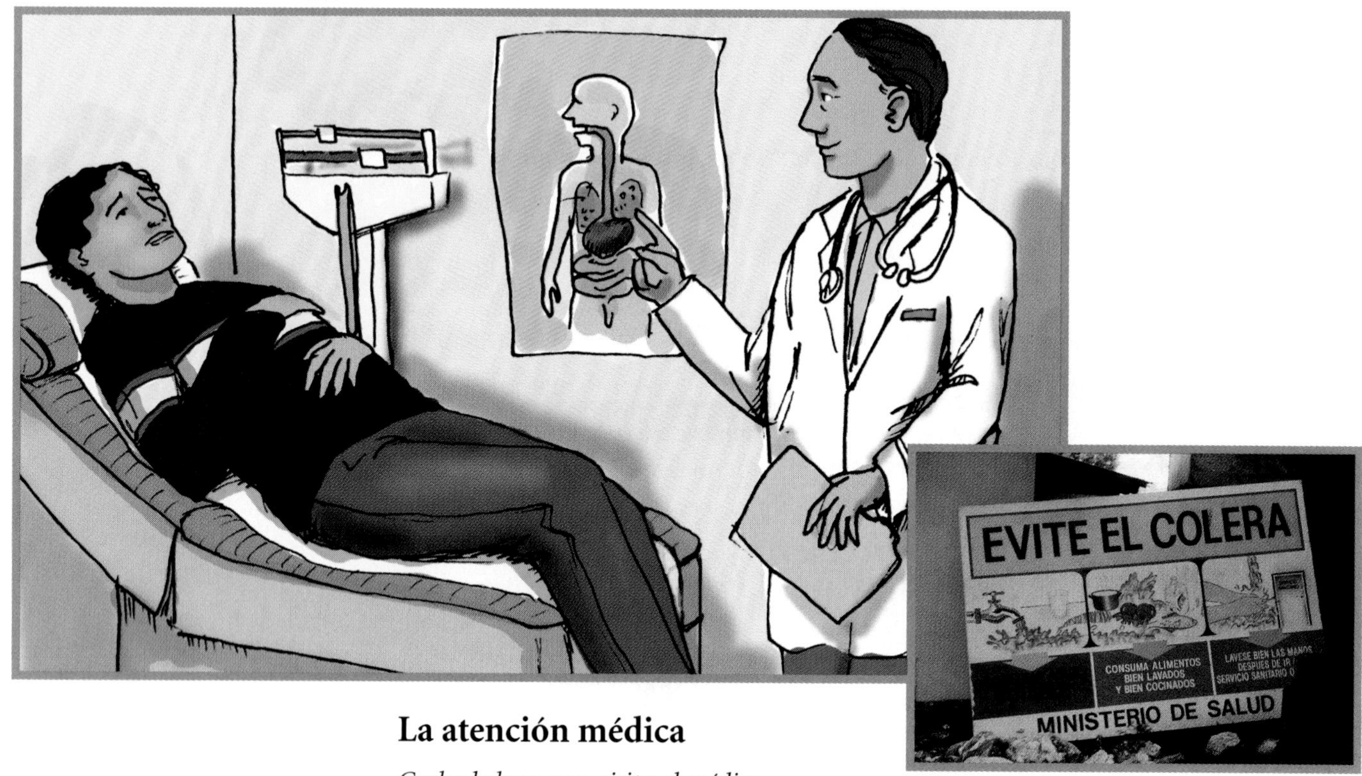


### La atención médica

*Carlos le hace una visita al médico....*

CARLOS: Dr. Lárraga, me siento muy mal. ¿Cree usted que es pulmonía?

DR. LÁRRAGA: No, dudo que sea pulmonía. Tal vez sea gripe porque hay una epidemia por toda la ciudad ¿Qué síntomas tienes?

CARLOS: Tengo malestar general: dolor de cabeza, dolor de oídos, tos, dolor muscular y no puedo respirar bien.

DR. LÁRRAGA: Déjame que te examine. Sí, tienes los pulmones muy congestionados. Tienes 39 grados de temperatura. No te has vacunado contra la gripe, ¿verdad?

CARLOS: No, no tuve tiempo.

DR. LÁRRAGA: Quiero que te cuides mucho porque eres asmático. Espero que no salgas a la calle por un par de días. Te voy a recetar unas inyecciones. ¿Eres alérgico a algo?

CARLOS: Sí, soy alérgico a la penicilina.

DR. LÁRRAGA: Entonces te voy a recetar otro antibiótico. Aquí tienes una receta para unas cápsulas y para un jarabe para la tos. Dudo que puedas trabajar con esta gripe tan fuerte. Te recomiendo que tomes muchos líquidos y que guardes cama.

**Answers for A.** 1) *Que sea pulmonía.* 2) *Malestar general.* 3) *Sí, a la penicilina.* 4) *Para cápsulas y jarabe.*

**A. ¿Comprende Ud.?** Conteste las siguientes preguntas según el diálogo.

1. ¿Qué teme Carlos?
2. ¿Cuáles son sus síntomas?
3. ¿Carlos es alérgico? ¿A qué?
4. ¿Para qué es la receta?

**B. ¿Qué le pasó?** Complete cada oración describiendo la situación.

MODELO: La profesora anda con muletas porque...*tiene una pierna fracturada.*

1. Pobre señor, tuvo un accidente y tiene...
2. En el invierno siempre tengo problemas con...
3. Comí demasiado y tengo dolor de...
4. Uno de los síntomas del catarro (*cold*) es...
5. Un síntoma de un infarto es...
6. Una causa posible del cólera es...

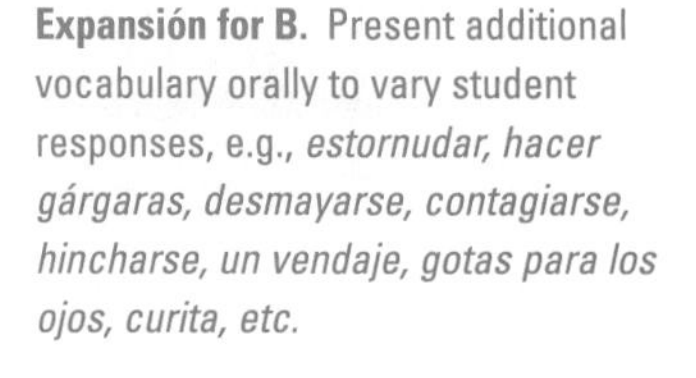
**Expansión for B.** Present additional vocabulary orally to vary student responses, e.g., *estornudar, hacer gárgaras, desmayarse, contagiarse, hincharse, un vendaje, gotas para los ojos, curita, etc.*

**C. En caso de infarto.** Después de leer, conteste las preguntas con un compañero/a. ¿Alguno/a de Uds. se encontró alguna vez en una situación así?

1. ¿Qué se debe hacer si uno no puede ponerse en contacto con el médico?
2. ¿En qué posición debe estar el paciente? ¿Qué no debe hacer?
3. ¿Qué se debe hacer si el paciente no respira y no tiene pulso?
4. ¿Cuáles son los síntomas de un infarto?

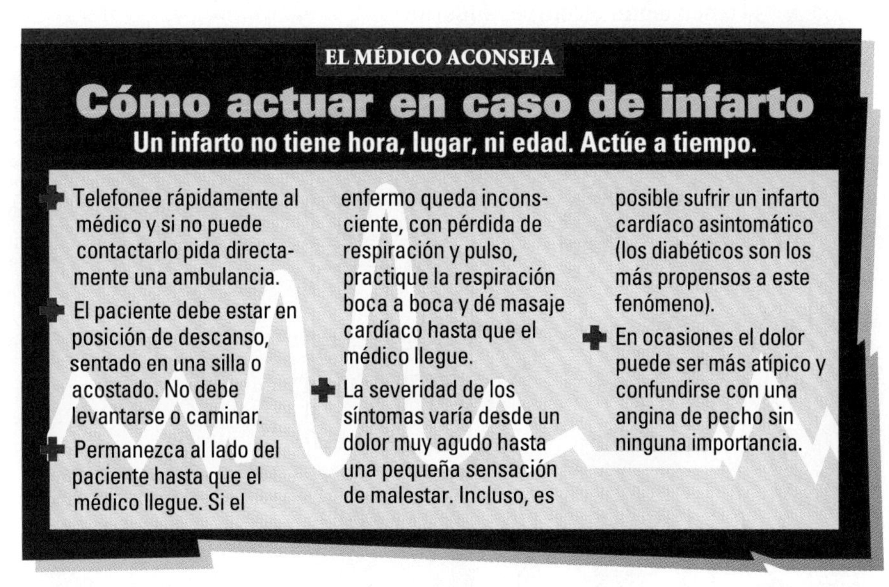
EL MÉDICO ACONSEJA

**Cómo actuar en caso de infarto**

**Un infarto no tiene hora, lugar, ni edad. Actúe a tiempo.**

- Telefonee rápidamente al médico y si no puede contactarlo pida directamente una ambulancia.
- El paciente debe estar en posición de descanso, sentado en una silla o acostado. No debe levantarse o caminar.
- Permanezca al lado del paciente hasta que el médico llegue. Si el enfermo queda inconsciente, con pérdida de respiración y pulso, practique la respiración boca a boca y dé masaje cardíaco hasta que el médico llegue.
- La severidad de los síntomas varía desde un dolor muy agudo hasta una pequeña sensación de malestar. Incluso, es posible sufrir un infarto cardíaco asintomático (los diabéticos son los más propensos a este fenómeno).
- En ocasiones el dolor puede ser más atípico y confundirse con una angina de pecho sin ninguna importancia.

**D. Entrevista.** Hable con su compañero/a para contestar las preguntas.

1. ¿Conoces a algún médico? ¿Tienes un/a médico favorito/a? ¿Por qué te gusta? ¿Cuántas veces al año visitas al médico? ¿Prefieres ir a su consultorio o al hospital? ¿Fuiste a un cirujano (*surgeon*) alguna vez? ¿Para qué?
2. ¿Qué debes hacer si tienes fiebre? ¿Cómo puedes evitar un infarto?
3. ¿Cuándo se enyesa un brazo? ¿Tuviste un brazo enyesado alguna vez? ¿Por cuánto tiempo?
4. ¿Para qué son las muletas? ¿y una silla de ruedas? ¿Hay acceso para sillas de ruedas en todos los edificios de la universidad?
5. ¿Te llevaron alguna vez en una camilla (*stretcher*)? ¿Por qué? ¿Te atendieron en una sala de urgencias?

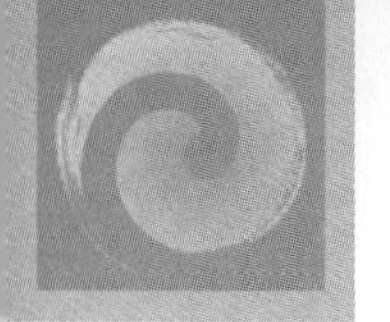

# En la farmacia

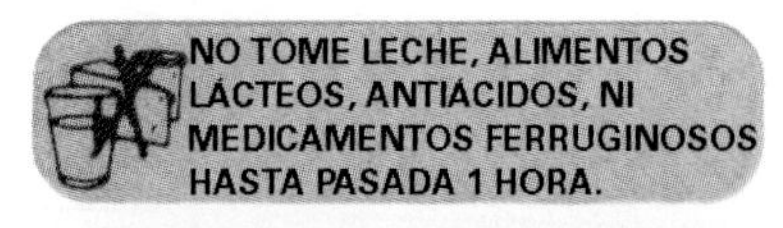


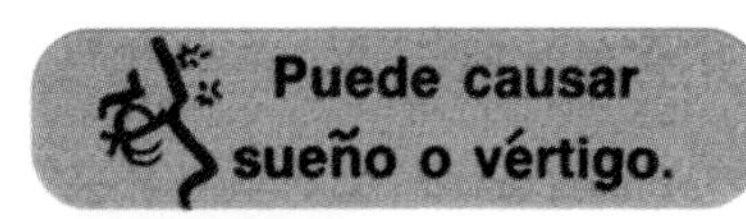


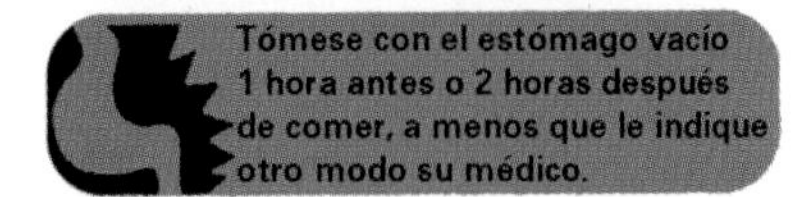


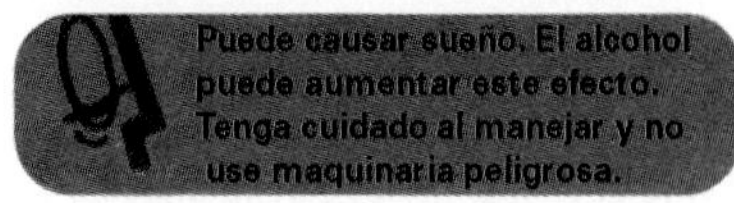

## Comprando medicamentos

*Carlos acaba de llegar a la farmacia para comprar lo que necesita....*

CARLOS: Buenas tardes, necesito esta receta. ¿Sabe usted si mi seguro paga por estos medicamentos?

FARMACÉUTICO: Déjeme ver su tarjeta de seguro.

CARLOS: Aquí la tiene, ojalá que sea posible.

FARMACÉUTICO: No dice nada y yo no estoy seguro. La computadora no funciona. ¿Puede regresar más tarde?

CARLOS: No, no creo que pueda volver. El doctor quiere que me acueste lo más pronto posible. Es mejor que pague ahora y después yo mando la cuenta a mi compañía de seguros.

FARMACÉUTICO: Está bien. Aquí tiene las medicinas. En este frasco están las cápsulas. El médico quiere que se tome una cada cuatro horas.

CARLOS: ¿Tienen algún efecto secundario?

FARMACÉUTICO: Pueden causarle diarrea. Es mejor que se las tome antes de comer. Cuando tenga mucha tos, tome una cucharada del jarabe. Pero ¡cuidado, no maneje porque le puede entrar sueño o mareo!

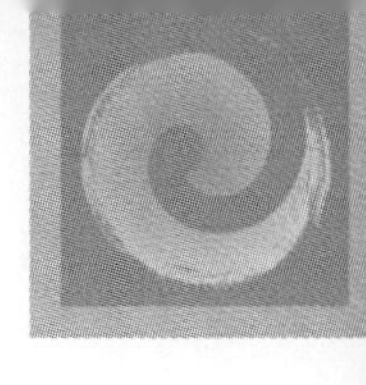

**A. ¿Comprende Ud.?** Conteste las siguientes preguntas según el diálogo.

1. ¿Qué quiere el doctor que haga Carlos?
2. ¿Cuándo va a tomar las cápsulas?
3. ¿Cuál es un posible efecto secundario de la medicina?
4. ¿Para qué es el jarabe?

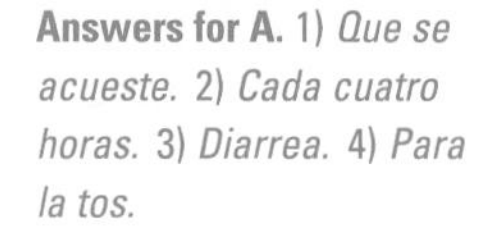

**Answers for A.** 1) *Que se acueste.* 2) *Cada cuatro horas.* 3) *Diarrea.* 4) *Para la tos.*

**B. ¿Qué sabe Ud. de la diabetes?** ¿Representan las oraciones siguientes condiciones relacionadas con la diabetes o no?

1. Es importante que coma menos azúcar.
2. Es necesario que verifique el nivel de la insulina.
3. Es cierto que siempre tiene hambre.
4. Es probable que orine a menudo.
5. Es posible que tenga sed.
6. Es verdad que las heridas no sanan.

**C. Entrevista.** Hágale Ud. las preguntas a su compañero/a.

1. ¿Qué vitamina se recomienda para evitar el catarro (*cold, flu*)? ¿Qué vitamina se encuentra en la leche? ¿Para qué necesitas esta vitamina?
2. ¿Cómo le tomas el pulso a alguien? ¿Cuándo fue la última vez que alguien te tomó el pulso? ¿Quién te lo tomó?
3. ¿Para qué se usa un vendaje (*bandage*)?
4. ¿Cómo consigues antibióticos? ¿Dónde los puedes comprar? ¿Para qué son?

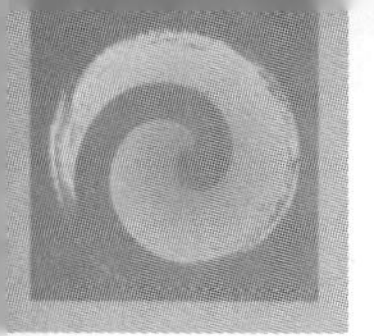

# El subjuntivo: expresiones de duda
## (*Expressing doubt or uncertainty*)

## Para averiguar

1. What are ten expressions of doubt that are followed by the subjunctive?
2. Why do you not use the subjunctive after **creer que, estar seguro/a que, es cierto que,** and **es verdad que** in an affirmative statement?
3. When do you use the subjunctive after those phrases?
4. What are two ways to say *perhaps* or *maybe*? When do you use the subjunctive with them?

- The subjunctive is also used to question the truth about something. It is used after the verbs and expressions of doubt or uncertainty.

| VERBS | | EXPRESSIONS OF DOUBT |
|---|---|---|
| **dudar que...** | → | **es dudoso que...** |
| **no creer que...** | → | **es posible/imposible que...** |
| **no estar seguro/a de que...** | → | **es probable/improbable que...** |
| **no es cierto que...** | → | **no es verdad que...** |

**Dudo que haya** pastillas contra esta gripe. *I doubt that there are pills for this flu.*
**Es posible que tengan** una inyección que alivie los síntomas. *It's possible that they might have an injection to ease the symptoms.*

- Since **creer que, estar seguro de que, es cierto que,** and **es verdad que** indicate that the speaker considers his or her assumptions to be true, they take the indicative in affirmative statements. When these verbs and expressions are used negatively, doubt is implied, and therefore they take the subjunctive.

**Creo que** ella **viene** esta noche. *I believe she's coming tonight.*
**No creo que** él **llame.** *I don't think he'll call.*

- When these expressions are used in a question, they take the indicative if the speaker is merely seeking information, but use the subjunctive if the speaker is expressing doubt as to the answer.

—¿**Es verdad que te sientes** mal? *Is it true that you feel bad?*
—Sí, **creo que es** pulmonía. *Yes, I think it's pneumonia.*

—¿**Crees que sea** pulmonía? *Do you think it's pneumonia?*
—No, **no creo que sea** pulmonía. *No, I don't think it's pneumonia.*

**Note.** Point out to students that if the main verb precedes *tal vez* or *quizás*, the indicative is used.

- Use **quizás** or **tal vez** to say *maybe, perhaps*. The subjunctive is used after these expressions, unless the speaker feels quite sure that the assertion is true.

**Quizás venga** el médico. *Perhaps the doctor might come.*
(The speaker has some doubt.)
**Viene** el médico mañana, **quizás.** *Perhaps the doctor is coming tomorrow.*
(The speaker thinks it is true.)

## A lo personal

**A. ¿Mito o verdad?** Tell whether you believe the following sayings about health to be true or false.

MODELO: El té verde fortifica la memoria.
*No creo que sea cierto.* o *Creo que es cierto.*

1. El caldo de pollo es la mejor medicina contra la gripe.
2. La aspirina ayuda a las personas con problemas del corazón.
3. Una copa de vino tinto cada día evita los problemas del corazón.
4. Para bajar de peso, debemos eliminar dos comidas diarias.
5. Contra la gripe, tomamos tequila, limón y sal.

6. Para el dolor de garganta (*throat*) es bueno tomar té con miel.
7. Vivir con animales alivia mucho el estrés.
8. El pescado alimenta el cerebro.
9. El chocolate es bueno para las emociones.
10. Las espinacas transforman a las personas en Popeye.

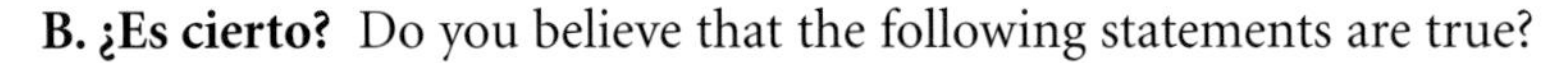

**B. ¿Es cierto?** Do you believe that the following statements are true?

MODELO: Las medicinas de hierbas son mejores que las recetas del médico.
*Sí, es cierto que las medicinas de hierbas son mejores.* o
*No es verdad que las medicinas de hierbas sean mejores.*

1. Las medicinas nuevas son más eficientes que las viejas.
2. Siempre se debe aceptar la primera opinión del médico.
3. Necesitamos más hospitales en esta ciudad.
4. Los médicos ganan mucho dinero.
5. Los médicos siempre saben cuál es el mejor tratamiento.
6. Hay más ataques de corazón por las mañanas.
7. El médico siempre tiene la razón.
8. Las mujeres son mejores pacientes que los hombres.

**C. En España.** You are going to Spain with a friend and are discussing what you know about health care in case one of you gets sick. Give your opinion about these statements.

**Suggestion for C.** Have students exchange affirmations and doubts about the hospital in the photo. For example, *Creo que tienen un laboratorio muy bueno. No creo que haya que esperar mucho en la sala de urgencias.*

MODELO: Hay muchos hospitales.
*Dudo que haya muchos hospitales.* o
*Creo que hay muchos hospitales.*

1. Los hospitales están abiertos sólo hasta las nueve de la noche.
2. A veces los farmacéuticos recetan medicinas.
3. Muchos médicos saben hablar inglés.
4. Se aceptan nuestros seguros en los hospitales.
5. Tienen hospitales muy modernos.
6. Hay muchas enfermedades tropicales en Valencia.

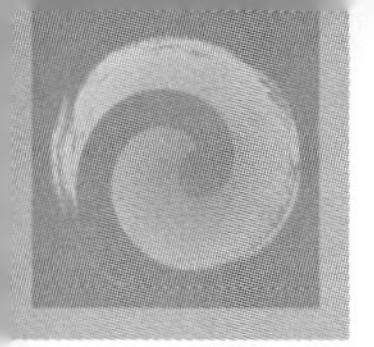

# El subjuntivo: expresiones impersonales (*Impersonal expressions*)

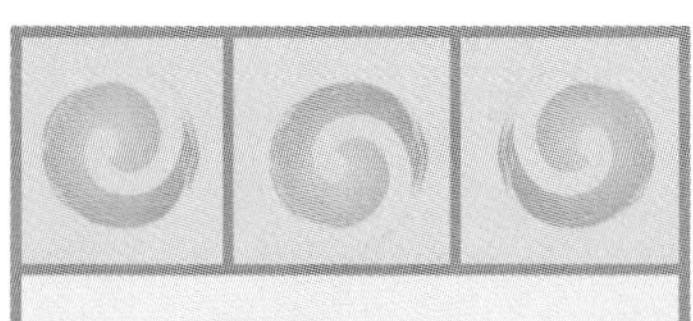

**Para averiguar**

1. Name eight of the sixteen expressions that are followed by the subjunctive. What do they express?
2. What does **ojalá** mean?
3. When do you use the subjunctive after impersonal expressions? The indicative?

**Suggestion.** Point out that *ojalá* is one of many Spanish words of Arabic origin. *Ojalá* comes from an Arabic expression meaning *may it be Allah's will.*

- As you have seen, you use the indicative to describe what actually happens and the subjunctive to express desire for something to happen. The subjunctive is also used after the following expressions when they make a subjective comment on whatever follows them.

| | |
|---|---|
| **Es bueno/malo/mejor que...** | **Es preferible que...** |
| **Es común que...** | **Es raro que...** |
| **Es increíble que...** | **Es ridículo que...** |
| **Es lógico que...** | **Es triste que...** |
| **Es importante que...** | **Es una lástima que...** |
| **Es necesario que...** | **Es urgente que...** |
| **Es normal que...** | **Ojalá (que)...** |

**Es bueno que** vayas al médico. — *It's good that you are going to the doctor.*
**Es una lástima que** no haya farmacia aquí. — *It's a shame that there is no pharmacy here.*
**¡Ojalá que** el médico pueda verme! — *Let's hope that the doctor can see me!*

- With impersonal expressions such as these, use the subjunctive to express an opinion about specific people's actions. When the emphasis is not on a specific person, use the infinitive.

**Opinion about specific people**
Es mejor que los niños descansen. — *It's better for the children to rest.*

**General opinion**
Es mejor descansar. — *It's better to rest.*

## A lo personal

**A. ¿Es importante?** Your patient is asking you about his/her recovery from the flu. Tell him/her how important it is to do the following.

MODELO: ¿Necesito guardar cama?
*Sí, es preferible que guardes cama.*

Es necesario... Es importante... Es mejor... Es preferible... Es bueno... No es necesario...

1. ¿Necesito comprar la receta inmediatamente?
2. ¿Necesito descansar mucho?
3. ¿Debo tomar muchos líquidos?
4. ¿Necesito abrigarme mucho?
5. ¿Necesito quedarme en casa?
6. ¿Puedo trabajar?
7. ¿Debo aislarme de otras personas?
8. ¿Puedo conducir si tomo la medicina?
9. ¿Debo tomar la medicina con comida?
10. ¿Debo pagarle ahora?

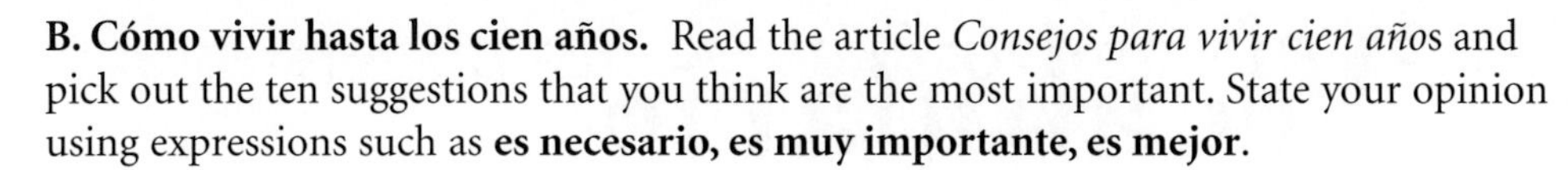

**B. Cómo vivir hasta los cien años.** Read the article *Consejos para vivir cien años* and pick out the ten suggestions that you think are the most important. State your opinion using expressions such as **es necesario, es muy importante, es mejor.**

MODELO: *Es muy importante mantener una dieta rica en frutas y verduras.*

Now name five areas in which it is important for you to change your ways.

MODELO: *Es importante que yo coma más frutas y verduras.*

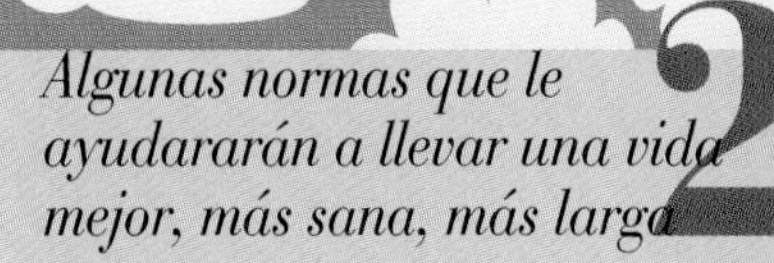

*Algunas normas que le ayudararán a llevar una vida mejor, más sana, más larga*

## 25 Consejos para vivir 100 años

1. Mantenga una dieta rica en frutas y verduras.
2. Nunca duerma menos horas de las que necesita.
3. Si no puede perdonar, por lo menos olvide.
4. Tenga siempre un libro junto a su mesa de noche.
5. Camine un poquito diariamente.
6. Reúnase con frecuencia con sus viejos amigos.
7. No esconda sus sentimientos. Exprese lo que siente.
8. Para los que viven solos, una mascota es la mejor compañía.
9. Si se da baños de sol, escoja las horas en que es más benigno tomarlo.

10. Los chistes y la risa en general son una medicina maravillosa.
11. En la calle, conduzca siempre su auto a la velocidad indicada.
12. No olvide ponerse el cinturón de seguridad siempre que conduzca o permanezca en un auto.
13. Todos los días tome cinco o seis vasos de agua fresca.
14. Limite su consumo de carnes rojas.
15. Si no sabe mucho de electricidad, llame a un electricista.
16. Hágase un chequeo médico por lo menos una vez cada dos años, aunque no tenga ningún malestar.
17. Sométase a una prueba de mamografía una vez al año.
18. Duerma en un colchón duro para cuidar la espalda.
19. Al respirar, trate de hacer siempre inspiraciones profundas.
20. Medite todos los días por lo menos unos 15 minutos.
21. Manténgase en contacto directo con la naturaleza.
22. Báñese con jabones suaves y aceitosos para proteger su piel.
23. Pruebe las yerbas y los remedios naturales.
24. Dese un buen masaje de vez en cuando.
25. Si fuma, deje de hacerlo.

**C. Consejos.** Give advice as your friend tells you one of his/her problems or something he/she wants.

MODELO: Estoy enfermo/a y tengo poca energía.
*Es necesario que vayas al médico y cambies tu dieta.*

1. Me siento muy mal y tengo fiebre.
2. Quiero bajar de peso.
3. Quiero vivir muchos años.
4. Discutí con mi novio/a. Estoy muy estresado/a.
5. Tomo mucha medicina y estoy mareado/a.
6. ¡Tengo un dolor en el pecho!

# Vocabulario

## TEMA 3
### La salud mental

**Sustantivos**

| | |
|---|---|
| **el animal doméstico** | *household pet* |
| **la amistad** | *friendship* |
| **el apoyo** | *support* |
| **el asunto** | *matter* |
| **la cachetada/el cachete** | *slap on the face* |
| **la debilidad** | *weakness* |
| **la esperanza** | *hope* |
| **el éxito** | *success* |
| **la falta** | *lack* |
| **el fracaso** | *failure* |
| **el idioma** | *language* |
| **la muerte** | *death* |
| **la pena** | *grief* |
| **la pertenencia** | *belonging* |
| **la tensión arterial** | *blood pressure* |
| **la señal** | *sign* |

**Verbos**

| | |
|---|---|
| **aliviar** | *to alleviate* |
| **aprovecharse (de)** | *to take advantage of* |
| **cuidar** | *to take care of* |
| **disfrutar** | *to enjoy* |
| **empujar** | *to push* |
| **golpear** | *to hit* |
| **hallar** | *to find* |
| **matar** | *to kill* |
| **negar (ie)** | *to deny* |
| **reconocer (zc)** | *to recognize* |
| **sufrir** | *to suffer* |
| **temerse** | *to be afraid of* |
| **valer (g)** | *to have value* |

**Adjetivos**

| | |
|---|---|
| **avergonzado/a** | *ashamed* |
| **culpable** | *guilty* |
| **deprimido/a** | *depressed* |
| **desconcertado/a** | *bewildered* |
| **enfermo/a** | *sick* |
| **entendido/a** | *understood* |
| **escondido/a** | *hidden* |
| **tratado/a** | *treated* |

**Otras expresiones**

| | |
|---|---|
| **de hecho** | *as a matter of fact* |
| **sin embargo** | *nevertheless* |

## TEMA 4
### Las enfermedades

**Sustantivos**

| | |
|---|---|
| **el antibiótico** | *antibiotic* |
| **la cápsula** | *capsule* |
| **la cucharada** | *spoonful* |
| **el dolor** | *pain* |
| **el efecto secundario** | *side effect* |
| **la enfermedad** | *illness* |
| **el/la farmacéutico/a** | *pharmacist* |
| **el frasco** | *bottle (of medicine)* |
| **la gripe** | *flu* |
| **la herida** | *wound* |
| **el hormigueo** | *pins and needles* |
| **el infarto** | *stroke* |
| **la inyección** | *injection* |
| **el malestar** | *discomfort* |
| **el masaje** | *massage* |
| **el/la paciente** | *patient* |
| **el peso** | *weight* |
| **la pulmonía** | *pneumonia* |
| **la receta** | *prescription* |
| **el síntoma** | *symptom* |
| **el sueño** | *sleep* |
| **el termómetro** | *thermometer* |
| **el vendaje** | *bandage* |

**Verbos**

| | |
|---|---|
| **agitar** | *to shake* |
| **agotar** | *to use up* |
| **cubrir** | *to cover* |
| **desobedecer (zc)** | *to disobey* |
| **orinar** | *to urinate* |
| **prohibir** | *to forbid* |
| **recetar** | *to prescribe* |
| **vacunarse** | *to be vaccinated* |

**Adjetivos**

| | |
|---|---|
| **agudo/a** | *sharp* |
| **asmático/a** | *asthmatic* |
| **borroso/a** | *blurred* |
| **congestionado/a** | *congested* |
| **fuerte** | *strong* |
| **mareado/a** | *nauseous/dizzy* |

**Otras expresiones**

| | |
|---|---|
| **¡Ojalá!** | *I hope so! I wish!* |
| **tal vez** | *perhaps* |

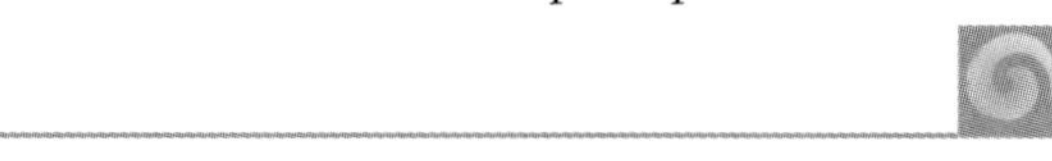

# Reunión B

**A escuchar. Otra visita al ortopedista.** Escuche la conversación y complete las oraciones con la información que escuche.

1. José se puso a jugar al fútbol y _______________ la pierna.
2. El doctor quiere que le tomen inmediatamente _______________.
3. No cree el doctor que haya _______________.
4. Le prohibe a José que _______________.
5. Además, le recomienda que no _______________.
6. Le dice que esté en cama por _______________.

**A conversar.** Uno/a de Uds. es el/la doctor/a, el/la otro/a es un/a paciente con problemas del corazón. Fuma, tiene el colesterol alto, pesa demasiado y no hace ejercicio. Después de hacerle algunas preguntas, el/la doctor/a le va a hacer sugerencias para lograr una vida mejor.

MODELO: Paciente: *Doctor/a, estoy preocupado/a por mi salud.*
Doctor/a: *Es necesario que baje de peso. Haga ejercicio todos los días.*

## ¿Lo sabía?

**¿Comprende Ud.?** Según la información indicada, dé la respuesta.

1. ¿Cuáles son algunas de las técnicas para estar mejor?
2. En tres oraciones, escriba un resumen de la meditación (sin copiar del texto).
3. ¿Qué aprendió de "stretching" o estiramientos?

### LA MEDITACIÓN

**¿Qué es?**
Es una técnica excelente para combatir el estrés, el insomnio, la falta de concentración, la capacidad de memoria e, incluso, con la práctica, los dolores físicos.

**¿Dónde practicarla?**
Es aconsejable escoger un lugar tranquilo y procurar practicarla siempre a la misma hora para que la mente coja el hábito y se predisponga al estado adecuado.

**¿Cómo hacerlo?**
Mantén la espalda recta sin necesidad de adoptar posturas que resulten incómodas. Basta con apoyarte en una pared. Cierra los ojos y realiza respiraciones profundas durante cinco minutos. Luego deja que la respiración se normalice. Concéntrate en un punto en el entrecejo o en el corazón, según seas más cerebral o emocional. Deja que los pensamientos pasen sin intentar detenerlos. Vuelve a tu centro de atención. Cuando quieras terminar, hazlo utilizando la respiración para volver a sentir el cuerpo y tu entorno.

### EL "STRETCHING" O ESTIRAMIENTOS

**¿Qué es?**
Es un método efectivo para mejorar migrañas, dolores de espalda, hipertensión, fatiga o insomnio. Al eliminar la rigidez permite mantener el cuerpo en buena forma.

**¿Dónde practicarlo?**
Esta técnica se puede adquirir en un gimnasio con un especialista. Luego se puede practicar en casa y en todas partes.

**¿Cómo hacerlo?**
Consiste en la realización de ejercicios suaves de estiramiento con el objetivo de conseguir que cualquier parte de nuestro cuerpo que esté rígida recupere su elasticidad y flexibilidad.

**A buscar.** Busque información en español sobre enfermedades y/o salud mental (grupos de apoyo para dejar de fumar, abuso de droga/alcohol, depresión, cáncer de mama (*breast*), etc.) en el Internet o en periódicos y revistas. Hable con dos compañeros/as sobre el valor de participar en tales grupos.

**Tapescript for A escuchar. Otra visita al ortopedista.**

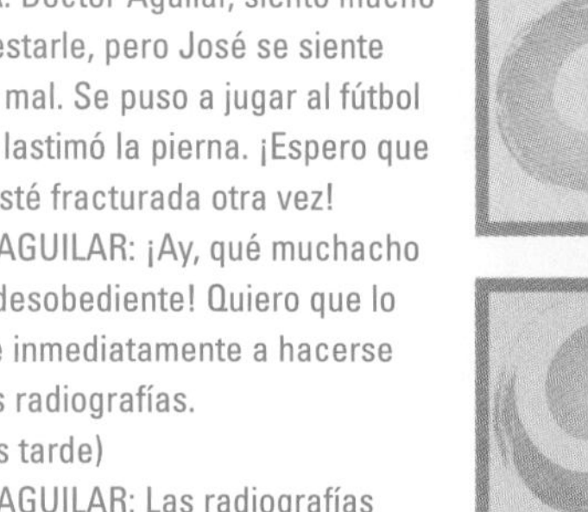

ANA: Doctor Aguilar, siento mucho molestarle, pero José se siente muy mal. Se puso a jugar al fútbol y se lastimó la pierna. ¡Espero que no esté fracturada otra vez!
DR. AGUILAR: ¡Ay, qué muchacho tan desobediente! Quiero que lo lleve inmediatamente a hacerse unas radiografías.
(Más tarde)
DR. AGUILAR: Las radiografías salieron bien. No creo que haya fractura. Pero José, espero que esta vez no me desobedezcas. Te prohibo que hagas ejercicio. Quiero que me lo prometas.

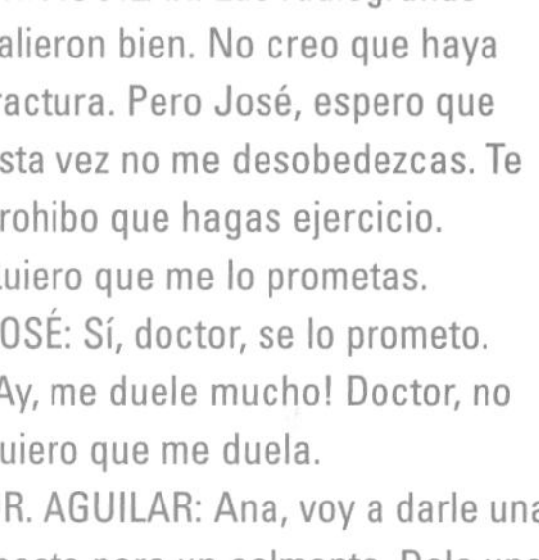

JOSÉ: Sí, doctor, se lo prometo. ¡Ay, me duele mucho! Doctor, no quiero que me duela.
DR. AGUILAR: Ana, voy a darle una receta para un calmante. Dele una tableta cada cuatro horas. Le recomiendo que no asista a la escuela por unos días.

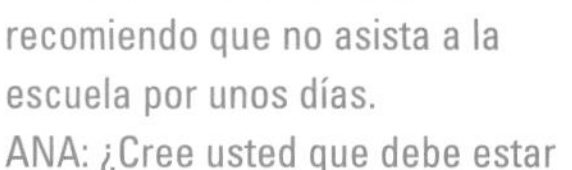

ANA: ¿Cree usted que debe estar en cama?
DR. AGUILAR: Sí, por un par de días. Después quiero que se mueva en silla de ruedas por una semana.

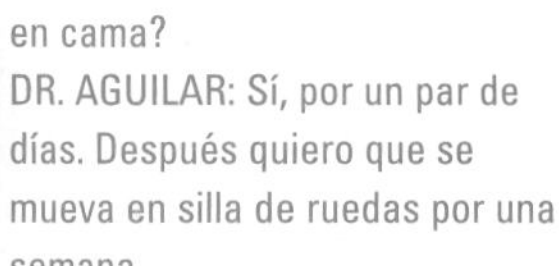

ANA: ¡Dios quiera que no sea nada serio! Gracias, Dr. Aguilar.

**Answers for A escuchar.**
1) *Se lastimó.* 2) *Unas radiografías.* 3) *Fractura.* 4) *Haga ejercicio.* 5) *Asista a la escuela.* 6) *Unos días.*

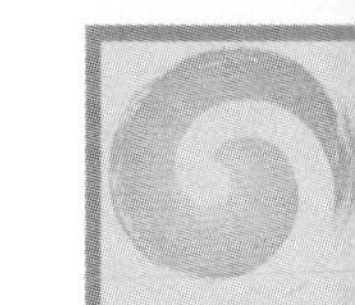

# ¡TRATO HECHO!

## Rincón profesional: Salud, belleza y tranquilidad

Son cada día más comunes las vacaciones dedicadas al alivio del estrés por medio de la meditación y el desarrollo de la salud y la belleza. En Tucson, Arizona, *Miraval* es un balneario que ofrece además de servicios de hotel, los servicios estéticos de los más elegantes salones de belleza, las técnicas y equipo de los más modernos gimnasios y las prácticas de los más antiguos sistemas de salud basados en el equilibrio entre el espíritu y el cuerpo.

**Tranquilidad, Serenidad, Sencillez y Felicidad**

*Miraval* es un lugar como ningún otro en el mundo. Ofrece los métodos más sofisticados del nuevo milenio.

Todo el personal de *Miraval*—desde el chofer que le espera en el aeropuerto de Tucson, hasta su entrenador personal y el cocinero ejecutivo—tienen en común la profunda creencia de que la salud y la felicidad nacen de la armonía entre el cuerpo, la mente y el espíritu. Aquí no sólo se enseña a vivir de manera equilibrada, aquí todos la vivimos.

La vida en *Miraval* es una combinación seductora de placeres sencillos y experiencias extraordinarias. Aquí, Ud. puede experimentar lo que jamás se había imaginado.

Suba una escarpada casi vertical. Pruebe *vaulting*—acrobacias a caballo. Descubra las técnicas de respiración que alivian el estrés y a la vez, mejore su técnica de tenis. Aprenda una filosofía nueva que cambie para siempre su aprecio por la comida saludable.

O sencillamente, descanse con un masaje de piedras calientes, una comida maravillosa o unos momentos serenos en la piscina a la luz de la luna. Es siempre, lo que Ud. desee…

*Hospitalidad, esmero*
*y atención personal*
*definen la vida en Miraval.*
*No importa si Ud. ha venido*
*para encontrar equilibrio*
*al fortalecer el cuerpo,*
*encajar la mente o enriquecer el espíritu.*
*Estamos aquí para apoyarle en*
*su viaje al autodescubrimiento...*

**¿Comprende Ud.?**

1. ¿Qué es lo que la mayoría de la gente quiere hacer durante sus vacaciones?
2. Los servicios ofrecidos en *Miraval* presentan técnicas modernas y antiguas. ¿Cuáles son modernas y cuáles son antiguas?
3. ¿Cuál es la filosofía de todos los empleados de *Miraval*?
4. Mencione tres formas en las que Ud. se puede relajar en *Miraval*.

**A escuchar. De compras.** Conteste las preguntas según la información del diálogo entre Georgina y Rubén.

**¿Comprende Ud.?**

1. ¿Por qué le habla Georgina a Rubén?
2. ¿Rubén va a ir con Georgina?
3. ¿Por qué?
4. ¿Qué le recomienda Georgina?
5. ¿Qué decide Rubén al final?

**Tapescript for A escuchar. De compras.**
GEORGINA: Hola, Rubén. ¡Me alegro de que estés en casa! Quiero pedirte que me acompañes a comprar unos libros.
RUBÉN: ¡Ay, lo siento pero no puedo ir! Tengo un dolor de cabeza fuertísimo.
GEORGINA: Toma una aspirina para que se te quite y vámonos a la calle.
RUBÉN: No, me dijo el doctor que no las tome porque me irritan el estómago. Los otros analgésicos no me ayudan.
GEORGINA: Bueno, no es necesario que vayamos ahora mismo. Puedo esperar un par de horas.
RUBÉN: Dudo que se me quite tan pronto. Vamos mañana.
GEORGINA: No, porque mi profesor de literatura quiere que los lleve a clase esta noche.
RUBÉN: Entonces, dile a tu hermana que te acompañe porque yo necesito descansar.

**Answers for A escuchar.**
1) *Para invitarlo a ir de compras.* 2) *No.* 3) *Porque le duele la cabeza.* 4) *Que se tome una aspirina.* 5) *Decide quedarse en casa.*

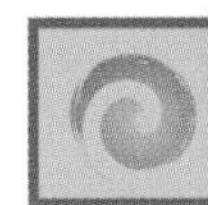

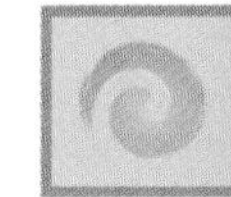
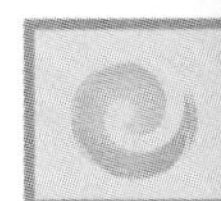

## El buzón de Doña Rosa

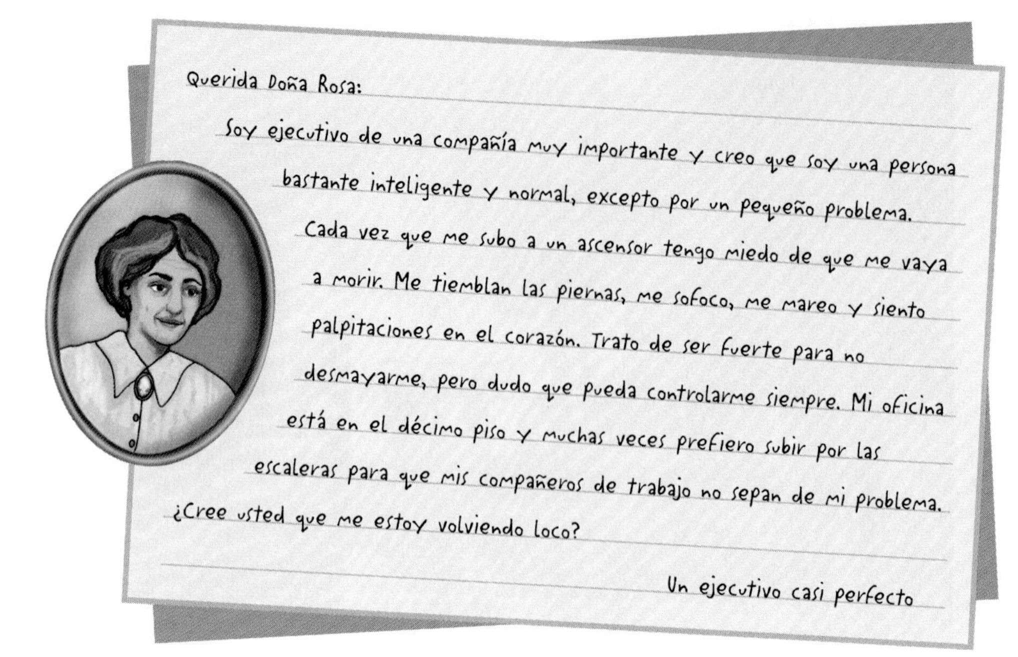

Querida Doña Rosa:

Soy ejecutivo de una compañía muy importante y creo que soy una persona bastante inteligente y normal, excepto por un pequeño problema. Cada vez que me subo a un ascensor tengo miedo de que me vaya a morir. Me tiemblan las piernas, me sofoco, me mareo y siento palpitaciones en el corazón. Trato de ser fuerte para no desmayarme, pero dudo que pueda controlarme siempre. Mi oficina está en el décimo piso y muchas veces prefiero subir por las escaleras para que mis compañeros de trabajo no sepan de mi problema. ¿Cree usted que me estoy volviendo loco?

Un ejecutivo casi perfecto

**¿Qué dice Doña Rosa?** Ud. y otro/a estudiante van a ayudar a Dña. Rosa a contestar esta carta. ¿Creen Uds. que *Un ejecutivo casi perfecto* está loco? Si no, ¿qué problemas tiene? ¿Qué puede hacer para cambiar? ¿Dónde puede encontrar a alguien que le ayude?

**¡Vamos a publicar!** Uds. forman parte de un grupo de autores que va a escribir un libro de autoayuda para personas que quieren un cambio total de salud y belleza. Diseñen los títulos de diez capítulos y escriban a una casa editorial para convencer a los editores de que deben publicar su libro. También pueden sugerir ideas que ayuden a promocionar el libro en el mercado.

## A leer

The roots of most words we use nowadays in Western medicine come from the Latin or Greek languages. For example, the word migraine comes from the Greek word "hemicrania", which means "half of the skull". This makes it easier for doctors to read articles in different languages. In the following text, can you identify some words that are also used in the English language?

**Antes de leer.** En el texto de la página 359, subraye los términos médicos que vienen de la misma raíz en inglés y en español. ¿Cuántas palabras son idénticas? ¿Cuántas palabras son similares? ¿Sabe el significado de esas palabras? Busque en el diccionario las palabras que no comprenda.

## LAS MIGRAÑAS

**¿Tiene** una migraña? ¿Teme que su cabeza explote? Usted no es la única persona: nueve de cada diez mujeres y siete de cada diez hombres padecen dolores de cabeza constantes. Las migrañas son la forma más severa del dolor de cabeza.

¿Cuáles son sus causas? Es posible que casi todas las migrañas sean de origen hereditario. Causas relacionadas con la tensión emocional pueden precipitarlas: el estrés, la depresión, la baja autoestima, la soledad, el temor y el cansancio extremo. Hay también causas fisiológicas, como los cambios hormonales, sobre todo en el nivel de estrógeno en las mujeres. En algunas personas las migrañas son de origen alérgico. Hay sustancias y alimentos que las precipitan: el chocolate, el queso, la grasa, los cítricos, el alcohol y algunos conservantes, como el glutamato de sodio.

**Síntomas relacionados con las migrañas:** un dolor punzante que empieza en el ojo y se extiende hasta la mitad del cráneo, náusea, vómito, rigidez en el cuello, aversión a la luz, distorsiones visuales (manchas, estrellas) y escalofríos.

**Tratamiento:** es importante que lleve una vida tranquila, pero si no puede, hay analgésicos como la aspirina, medicamentos que contienen ergotamina, relajantes musculares, tranquilizantes, antidepresivos, vasodilatadores y beta-bloqueadores.

¿Es posible curar las migrañas? No, nunca se curan, pero se pueden controlar. Es importante que usted ayude. Haga una lista de los alimentos que come cuando aparecen las migrañas. Si es posible, incluya los nombres de los conservantes que contienen. Lleve una lista de cuándo aparecen las migrañas: ¿cuando viaja o come fuera? ¿A qué hora? ¿Qué días? ¿los fines de semana? ¿cuando tose o tiene una infección? ¿Cree que son efectos secundarios de las medicinas que está tomando?

Si persisten las migrañas a pesar de todo lo que haga, consulte con un neurólogo. Pídale que le tome rayos X o que le haga una tomografía cerebral para estar seguro de que no tiene un abceso o un tumor cerebral.

**¿Comprende Ud.?** Responda a las siguientes preguntas según el texto anterior:

1. ¿Cuáles son las causas emocionales de las migrañas?
2. ¿Por qué las mujeres padecen migrañas más frecuentemente que los hombres?
3. ¿Cuáles son los alimentos que pueden causar una migraña?
4. ¿Conoce algunos alimentos o sustancias que le produzcan migrañas a usted?
5. Si no padece de migrañas, ¿es alérgico/a a algún alimento o a alguna sustancia?
6. ¿Qué síntomas tiene cuando reacciona a alguna alergia?
7. ¿Qué hace para tratar esos síntomas?

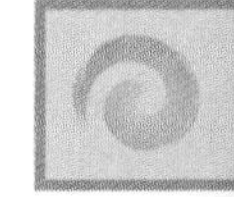

## A escribir

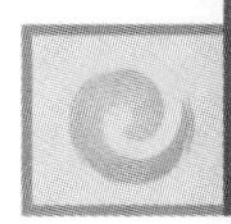

¿Conoce a alguien que tenga una enfermedad crónica? ¿Qué enfermedad es? ¿Cuáles son los síntomas? ¿Cuál es el tratamiento que recibe? Por escrito, explique todo lo que sepa sobre esta situación, incluyendo tantos detalles como sea posible.

# 10 El comercio y las finanzas

LECCIÓN DIEZ

CHECK OUT THE *¡TRATO HECHO!* WEBSITE AND CD-ROM FOR ACTIVITIES, GAMES, SELF-TESTS, AND MUCH MORE!

TEMA 1

## Los empleos

- El mundo de los negocios
- El poder de la economía hispana
- Los adverbios
- Otros usos de *se*

TEMA 2

## La propiedad privada

- La casa ideal
- En la agencia inmobiliaria
- Los pronombres relativos
- El subjuntivo en cláusulas adjetivales

TEMA 3

## El banco

- Los servicios bancarios
- Los consejos legales
- El participio pasado como adjetivo
- El presente perfecto de indicativo

TEMA 4

## Los preparativos

- Los problemas posibles
- Hay mucho que hacer
- El presente perfecto de subjuntivo
- El pluscuamperfecto

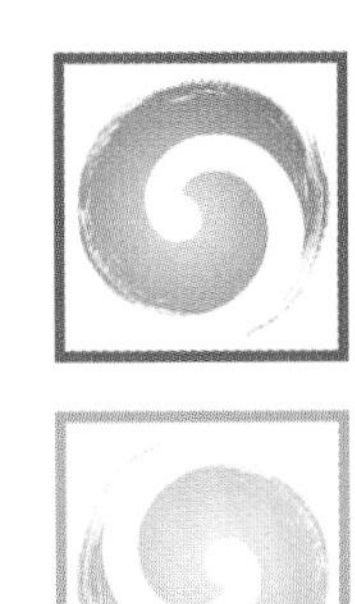

# ¡TRATO HECHO!

- Rincón profesional: La casa del futuro
- A escuchar
- A leer
- A escribir

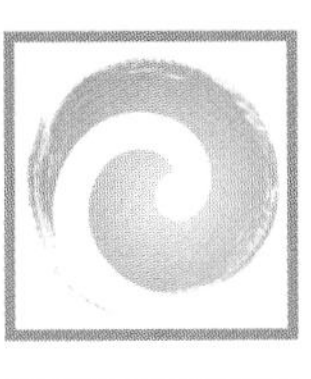

# TEMA 1 Los empleos

## ABC El mundo de los negocios

### Oportunidades profesionales

*Isabel, Ana y José asisten a una feria del trabajo….*

ISABEL: ¡Qué interesante está la feria del trabajo de la universidad!
ANA: Estoy completamente de acuerdo. Por eso traje a José; es importante que decida pronto qué carrera va a estudiar en el futuro.
ISABEL: ¡Qué bien! José, ¿te gusta algo en especial?
JOSÉ: Sí, me interesan verdaderamente las finanzas. Tal vez sea corredor de bolsa para comprar y vender acciones.
ANA: Mira aquí hay una representante de una compañía financiera. Señorita, ¿qué requisitos se necesitan para trabajar con ustedes?
REPRESENTANTE: Decididamente, se prefieren las carreras de economista, analista financiero o informático. También tenemos muchos puestos para programadores de computadoras.
ISABEL: Yo estudié negocios internacionales y hablo inglés y español.
REPRESENTANTE: Es bueno que sea bilingüe porque nosotros tenemos muchos clientes en el extranjero. Ellos invierten muchos fondos en nuestro país.

**Answers for A.** 1) *En la feria del trabajo.* 2) *Las finanzas.* 3) *Carreras relacionadas.* 4) *Fondos de inversión.*

**A. ¿Comprende Ud.?** Conteste las siguientes preguntas según el diálogo.

1. ¿Dónde están Isabel y Ana?
2. ¿Qué carrera le interesa a José?
3. ¿Cuáles son los requisitos para trabajar con una compañía financiera?
4. ¿Qué ofrecen los clientes de una compañía financiera a la compañía?

**B. La bolsa de valores.** Sus abuelos le dieron a Ud. mil dólares para comprar acciones. Ellos quieren que Ud. aprenda un poco antes de comprar y quieren ver los resultados de su inversión en seis meses. Seleccione la respuesta correcta según la información del artículo.

**Expansion for B.** Bring in current stock quotes and/or currency exchange rates for comparison.

1. Según el índice de Dow Jones, los valores del once al doce de julio han *subido/bajado* por 12.400.
2. Y los del Nikkei han subido por *16.000/17.000.*
3. En contraste con los otros dos, los precios de Financial Times han *subido/bajado* por 13.400.
4. Estas cifras representan las bolsas *nacionales/internacionales.*

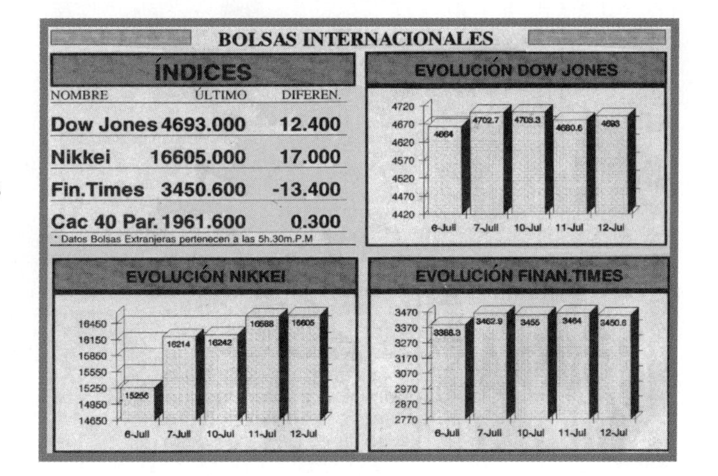

BOLSAS INTERNACIONALES

ÍNDICES

| NOMBRE | ÚLTIMO | DIFEREN. |
|---|---|---|
| Dow Jones | 4693.000 | 12.400 |
| Nikkei | 16605.000 | 17.000 |
| Fin.Times | 3450.600 | -13.400 |
| Cac 40 Par. | 1961.600 | 0.300 |

* Datos Bolsas Extranjeras pertenecen a las 5h.30m.P.M



**C. El invitado de honor.** Steve Fuentes es un invitado en su clase de economía y va a hablar de su carrera como hombre de negocios. Ud. tiene que presentarlo. Prepare una introducción breve, de cuatro a cinco líneas, con información biográfica de él. Compare sus notas con las de un/a compañero/a y decidan cuál de las dos es mejor.

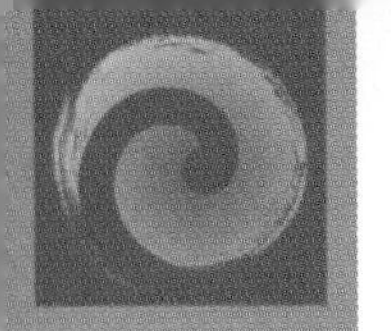

# El poder de la economía hispana

## En la feria del trabajo

*Isabel busca trabajo en la feria....*

ANA: En las ferias del trabajo se pueden conseguir buenos trabajos.
ISABEL: Efectivamente. Vamos a ver qué se ofrece en la bolsa de trabajos.
ANA: Se ofrecen muchos puestos en negocios internacionales. Mira, se necesitan muchos empleados bilingües en la fábrica de refrescos Doctor Pimienta.
ISABEL: Se dice que esa compañía paga muy generosamente.
ANA: Pues, se están haciendo entrevistas continuamente en el salón de conferencias. ¿Por qué no vas?
ISABEL: Porque se me olvidaron mis papeles de la universidad, pero puedo hacer una cita para mañana.
ANA: Vamos a hacerla y así también puedes recoger una solicitud para traerla completamente llena.
ISABEL: Perfecto. Después, te acompaño a buscar la sección de agencias de viajes para ver qué hay de nuevo.

**Answers for A.** 1) *Conseguir trabajo.* 2) *Trabajos internacionales.* 3) *Continuamente.* 4) *Los papeles de la universidad.*

**A. ¿Comprende Ud.?** Conteste las siguientes preguntas según el diálogo.

1. ¿Cuál es la razón principal para asistir a una feria de trabajo?
2. ¿Qué trabajos se ofrecen en la feria?
3. ¿Cuándo tienen entrevistas?
4. ¿Qué se le olvidó a Isabel?

**B. El desempleo en Chile.** Complete las oraciones con la información del artículo.

19

## Indicadores Económicos

### Desempleo

**Chile**
La tasa de desempleo en Chile descendió al 5.1 por ciento en el trimestre de diciembre de 1997 a febrero de 1998, en contraste con el 5.4 por ciento del mismo trimestre en el año anterior, informó el Instituto Nacional de Estadísticas (INE). En el trimestre de diciembre de 1997 a febrero de 1998, la fuerza laboral se estimó en 5.667.650 personas, lo que representa un aumento del 1.3 por ciento con respecto al mismo trimestre en el año anterior. El INE puntualizó que en este mismo período el desempleo de jóvenes entre quince y diecinueve años bajó al 14.3 por ciento en comparación con el 15.2 por ciento observado en el mismo trimestre del año anterior. Por sexo, la tasa de desempleo es del 6.9 por ciento para las mujeres y del 4.3 por ciento para los hombres.

1. La tasa de desempleo en Chile ______________ al 5.1% en el trimestre de diciembre 97–febrero 98.
2. La información vino del ______________.
3. La abreviatura del Instituto Nacional de Estadísticas es ______________.
4. El número de personas con empleo es ______________.
5. Esto representa un ______________ de 1.3% con respecto al igual trimestre del año anterior.
6. La tasa de desocupación para las mujeres es de ______________ y para los hombres ______________.

**C. Las contribuciones de los hispanos.** Prepare una presentación sobre el poder económico de los hispanos en los Estados Unidos. Escriba un informe breve indicando el número de compañías con dueños hispanos, los estados en que se encuentran (en orden de importancia) y los ingresos anuales (en dólares) de las compañías más importantes. Trabaje con un/a compañero/a para estar seguro/a de tener toda la información necesaria.

**Note for C.** Point out to students the differences between *billion* and *billón*. (1.000.000.000 = 1 billion) (1.000.000.000.000 = *1 billón*).

## El motor de 152 millones de dólares

**Los diez estados superiores según ingresos de compañías con dueños hispanos**

| Orden | Estado | No. de compañías | Ingresos (en 1.000 dólares) |
|---|---|---|---|
| | **Total EE. UU.** | **771,708** | **$72,824,270** |
| 1 | California | 249,717 | $19,552,637 |
| 2 | Florida | 118,208 | $16,127,202 |
| 3 | Texas | 155,909 | $11,796,301 |
| 4 | Nueva York | 50,601 | $4,732,279 |
| 5 | Nueva Jersey | 22,198 | $2,827,937 |
| 6 | Illinois | 18,368 | $1,950,685 |
| 7 | Nuevo México | 21,586 | $1,479,650 |
| 8 | Arizona | 17,835 | $1,298,084 |
| 9 | Colorado | 13,817 | $1,212,137 |
| 10 | Virginia | 7,654 | $957,962 |

Source: U.S. Census Bureau, "Survey of Minority-owned Business Enterprises – Hispanic 1992 (MB92-2)"

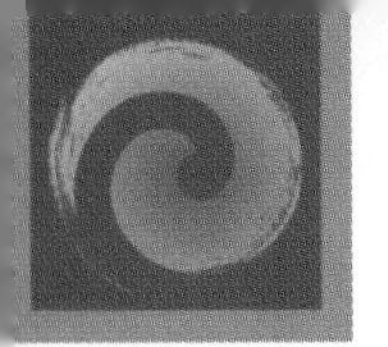

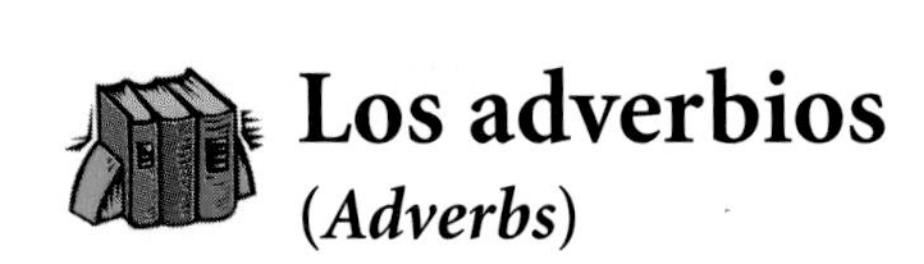

# Los adverbios
## (*Adverbs*)

**Para averiguar**

1. What is the English equivalent of the Spanish ending **-mente**?
2. To what form of the adjective do you add **-mente** to form an adverb?

**Expansion.** Have students practice adverb formation from the following: *fácil, difícil, feliz, temprano, perfecto, primero.*

Remind students that when an adjective has a written accent, the adverb maintains it: *fácil = fácilmente.*

- Adverbs are words that qualify or modify an adjective, a verb, or another adverb. Use an adverb to describe how an action happens. Many adverbs in Spanish end in **-mente**, which corresponds to the *-ly* ending in English.

- The **-mente** ending is added to the *feminine* and/or *singular* form of the adjective. Keep in mind that some feminine adjectives end in **-e** or a consonant.

| | | | |
|---|---|---|---|
| rápido | rápida | rápidamente | *rapidly* |
| libre | | libremente | *freely* |
| normal | | normalmente | *usually* |

- If you are using two or more adverbs in a row, the **-mente** ending is used on the last adverb only.

  Ellos hablan **clara** y **lentamente**. *They speak clearly and slowly.*

## A lo personal

**A. ¿Completa o parcialmente?** Say whether you do the following activities completely or partially.

MODELO: limpiar la casa
*Yo limpio la casa parcialmente.*

1. comer un helado enorme
2. leer el periódico el domingo
3. hacer la tarea de español
4. decir la verdad
5. pagar la tarjeta de crédito cada mes
6. prestar atención a un/a profesor/a aburrido/a

**B. ¿Cómo lo hace Ud.?** Indicate how you do the following activities. Draw on some of the adverbs in this section.

MODELO: ducharse
*Me ducho lentamente.*

1. limpiar la casa
2. estudiar para los exámenes
3. comer
4. despertarse
5. manejar
6. gastar dinero
7. divertirse
8. escribir a máquina
9. hablar por teléfono
10. hablar español

**C. ¿Qué le gusta hacer…?** Tell what activities you like to do in the following ways.

MODELO: rápidamente
*Me gusta comer rápidamente.*

1. tranquilamente
2. intensamente
3. alegremente
4. lentamente
5. diariamente
6. perfectamente

**D. La liebre y la tortuga.** Turn the following adjectives into adverbs to tell a new version of the famous story of the Tortoise and the Hare.

Érase una vez una tortuga que (1) ________ (normal) terminaba el día de trabajo y andaba (2) ________ (feliz) a su casa. También había una liebre acostumbrada a correr (3) ________ (rápido y loco) por todas partes.

Un día la tortuga saludó (4) ________ (amable) a la liebre quien le respondió (5) ________ (rudo): "Amiga tortuguita, caminas y hablas tan (6) ________ (lento) que aquí te espero (7) ________ (impaciente)." La pobre tortuga, que (8) ________ (general) era muy tímida, se enojó y le desafió a una carrera.

La liebre sabía (9) ________ (perfecto) bien que podía ganar (10) ________ (fácil). Corrió (11) _________ (directo) a su cantina favorita donde (12) _________ (tranquilo) tomó unas cervezas con sus amigos. La tortuga, que estaba acostumbrada a trabajar (13) _________ (inteligente), se puso sus nuevas zapatillas deportivas *Nike* y llegó (14) _________ (instantáneo) a la meta. ¡Qué sorpresa tuvo la liebre borracha al saber que la tortuga se convirtió (15) _________ (claro y definitivo) en la nueva campeona!

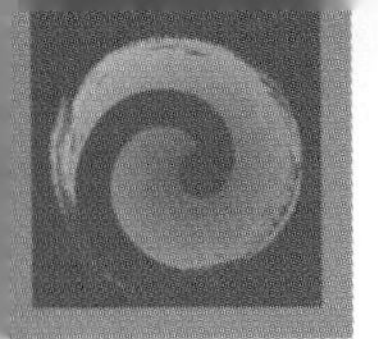

# Otros usos de *se*
## (*More uses of* se: *unplanned or accidental events*)

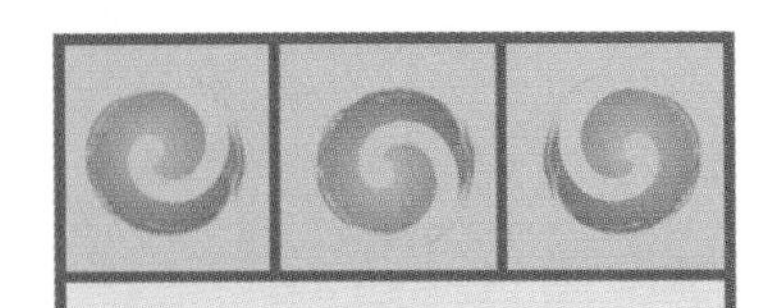

**Para averiguar**

1. How can you make certain actions impersonal or passive?
2. How do you show that an action or event was unintentional?
3. How do you indicate the person that the unplanned event happened to?
4. How do you show that an action may have been deliberate?

**Expansion.** Point out that as with *gustar* and such verbs, if the indirect object is mentioned or if clarification is needed, a prepositional phrase will be included: ***A mí** se me cayó el vaso.*

- You have seen that the use of **se** + certain verbs can make an action passive or impersonal:

| | |
|---|---|
| **Se** habla español en México. | *Spanish is spoken in Mexico.* |
| **Se** venden libros aquí. | *Books are sold here.* |

- This construction is also used for accidental or unplanned events (something got broken, left behind, lost, forgotten, used up, dropped) to show that the event was unintentional and no one is really responsible. ¡OJO! Don't forget that the verb will be plural if the lost, broken, etc. object is plural.

| | |
|---|---|
| **Se** romp**ió la puerta**. | *The door broke.* |
| **Se** perd**ieron las llaves**. | *The keys got lost.* |

- By placing an indirect object pronoun (**me, te, le, nos, les**) before the verb, you can indicate who the person most affected by the accident or event was.

| | |
|---|---|
| **Se me** rompió la puerta. | *The door broke (on me).* |
| **Se te** perdieron las llaves. | *The keys got lost (on you).* |

- Use of the active voice can make the action seem more deliberate:

| | |
|---|---|
| **Yo** rompí los vasos. | *I broke the glasses.* |
| **Tú** olvidaste mis libros. | *You forgot my books.* |

- Here are some common "unplanned events":

| | | |
|---|---|---|
| **quedarse** | (A mí) Se me **quedó** la tarea en casa. | *I left my homework at home.* |
| **romperse** | (A ti) Se te **rompieron** los pantalones. | *Your pants got torn.* |
| **acabarse** | (A nosotros) Se nos **acabó** la gasolina. | *We ran out of gas.* |
| **olvidarse** | (A él) Se le **olvidaron** los libros. | *He forgot his books.* |
| **descomponerse** | (A ellos) Se les **descompuso** el coche. | *Their car broke down.* |
| **ocurrirse** | (A mí) Se me **ocurrió** una idea. | *An idea occurred to me.* |
| **caerse** | (A María) Se le **cayó** el espejo. | *María dropped her mirror.* |

## A lo personal

**A. ¿Dónde tengo la cabeza?** Yesterday you were so forgetful that you are surprised you remembered your own name! Tell what you forgot.

MODELO: los libros
*Se me olvidaron los libros.*

1. los zapatos
2. el almuerzo
3. las llaves
4. la cita con el dentista
5. las lentes de contacto

6. la tarea de español
7. la cita con mi novio/a
8. las entrevistas del empleo
9. el número de teléfono de mi casa
10. mi propio nombre

**B. ¿A quién?** Tell who forgot the keys to the new house according to the cues.

MODELO: a mí
*A mí se me olvidaron las llaves.*

1. a ti
2. al agente
3. a los novios
4. a nosotros
5. a mi hermana
6. a mis padres

**C. ¿Qué te pasó?** Use the clues in the second column to explain why you are in the following situations.

MODELO: ¿Por qué no almuerzas? → acabarse el dinero
*No almuerzo porque se me acabó el dinero.*

1. ¿Por qué llegaste tarde? → descomponerse el coche
2. ¿Por qué no tienes la tarea? → quedarse en casa
3. ¿Por qué no vienes en coche? → acabarse la gasolina
4. ¿Por qué no entras en la casa? → perderse las llaves
5. ¿Por qué no te quitas el abrigo? → romperse los pantalones
6. ¿Por qué no te peinas? → caerse el espejo

**D. ¡Excusas!** With a classmate, come up with a list of the ten best excuses students give for not coming to class or for not being prepared.

MODELO: *No vine a clase ayer porque se me descompuso* (broke) *el coche.*

EXCUSAS

1.
2.
3.
4.
5.
6.
7.
8.
9.
10.

# TEMA 2 La propiedad privada

## La casa ideal

### Se busca casa

*Isabel y Lázaro visitan la casa de sus sueños....*

ISABEL: Lázaro, te presento a la señora Miller, la agente inmobiliaria de quien te hablé.
LÁZARO: Mucho gusto. Isabel dice que habla usted el español muy bien.
SRA. MILLER: Gracias, aprendí español porque tenemos muchos clientes que son hispanos.
ISABEL: Su jefe, a quien conocí ayer, sabe hablar cuatro lenguas.
SRA. MILLER: Sí, a los clientes les gusta que nos podamos comunicar con ellos en su propia lengua. Por eso las ventas de la agencia son las más altas de la ciudad. Ya llegamos a la casa.
ISABEL: Lázaro, ésta es la casa que me gustó. ¡Es preciosa!
LÁZARO: Sí, es muy bonita, pero me parece un poco grande.
ISABEL: Por ahora sí, pero pensamos tener varios hijos. Ellos son quienes van a disfrutar de la casa. Señora Miller, lo vamos a pensar brevemente y nos comunicamos con usted.

**Answers for A.** 1) *Con la Sra. Miller.* 2) *Porque hablan español y otras lenguas.* 3) *Tener varios hijos.* 4) *Answers will vary.*

**A. ¿Comprende Ud.?** Conteste las siguientes preguntas según el diálogo.

1. ¿Con quién hablan Lázaro e Isabel?
2. ¿Por qué son muy altas las ventas de esa agencia?
3. ¿Qué piensan Lázaro e Isabel en cuanto a su futura familia?
4. ¿Cuál es una ventaja *(advantage)* de comprar una casa?

**B. ¿Mi propia casa?** Después de vivir en varios apartamentos por los últimos cinco años, Ud. ya se cree listo/a para comprar su propia casa, pero todavía tiene dudas. Prepare una lista de cinco razones por las cuales debe buscar la casa perfecta para comprar.

MODELO: *Ya no voy a tirar el dinero por la ventana.*

**C. El/la agente inmobiliario.** Uno/a de Uds. es agente inmobiliario de la agencia más grande de la ciudad. El/la otro/a es un/a cliente/a que busca una casa. Hablen de qué busca, el precio necesario, el lugar deseado, el número de cuartos, cuánto puede pagar de enganche y otros detalles necesarios. Los/as dos pueden traer anuncios de casas en venta de periódicos o revistas para tener una idea más clara.

MODELO: *La casa que busco tiene que estar en las afueras de la ciudad, cerca de un parque. Es necesario que tenga dos baños y tres dormitorios.*

**Note for C.** Mention that houses in Hispanic countries are measured in square meters, not square feet. Thus an ad showing the lot and/or house size would need to be multiplied by 10 (for easy conversion) to equal square feet. 200 ms. ($m^2$) equals approximately 2,000 square feet.

**D. Mi palacio personal.** Haga el papel de Guillermo Puertas, dueño de una compañía internacional de computadoras con billones de dólares en el banco. Él diseñó su casa personal (un palacio) en Costa Rica, pero a causa de la competencia fuerte el año pasado y de pasar muchas horas en la playa en vez de en la oficina, ya está en bancarrota (*bankruptcy*) y tiene que vender su palacio. Dibuje su casa o saque una foto de ella y escriba toda la información importante para la venta. Luego, enséñeles a tres compañeros su anuncio, a ver si ellos están interesados en comprarla.

Dirección ______

Precio ______

Nº de cuartos ______

Detalles especiales ______

Más información ______

______

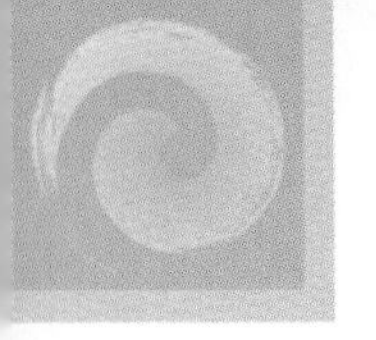

# ABC En la agencia inmobiliaria

## Nuestra vivienda

*Isabel y Lázaro deciden comprar la casa....*

SRA. MILLER: ¡Qué bien que decidieron comprar la casa! No hay otra que sea tan bonita.
ISABEL: Tampoco creo que sea cara. Vimos muchas casas que eran más caras y no tan bonitas. ¡Espero que el enganche no sea mucho!
SRA. MILLER: No, solamente el 20%.
LÁZARO: Bueno, no creo que nuestra oferta sea muy baja. Ojalá que los dueños la acepten.
SRA. MILLER: Sí, no creo que haya ningún problema. Dicen que los dueños se mudan a otro estado en dos meses y necesitan que la casa se venda rápidamente.
ISABEL: Nosotros vivimos en un apartamento muy pequeño con un amigo de Lázaro.
LÁZARO: Además, me gusta el sitio, está cerca de la escuela donde trabajo. Si se me pierden las llaves del coche, puedo caminar.

**Answers for A.** 1) *Porque van a comprar la casa.* 2) *El 20 por ciento.* 3) *Se mudan a otro estado.* 4) *En un apartamento pequeño.*

**A. ¿Comprende Ud.?** Conteste las siguientes preguntas según el diálogo.

1. ¿Por qué está contenta la señora Miller?
2. ¿Cuánto es el enganche?
3. ¿Por qué venden la casa los dueños?
4. ¿Dónde viven Lázaro e Isabel ahora?

**B. ¡Es el momento de comprar!** Complete las oraciones con información del artículo.

1. Los bajos ______________ son un incentivo importante para comprar una casa.
2. Las tasas bancarias no han aumentado a causa de la ______________ en Asia y la ______________ en Rusia.
3. Las ventas de casas registraron un ______________ en relación con el mismo período del año pasado.
4. Se vendieron ______________ casas seminuevas, ______________ condominios y ______________ residencias de nueva construcción.
5. El mayor incremento en ventas correspondió a los ______________.

## Bajos intereses estimulan a los nuevos propietarios

**Redacción Latinoamericana**

Los bajos intereses hipotecarios continúan siendo el mayor incentivo para alentar a la compra de viviendas, desde que la Reserva Federal decidió mantener sin cambio las tasas bancarias durante su última reunión.

La crisis económica que azota a varios países asiáticos, la recesión rusa y otros fenómenos económicos que repercuten en Latinoamérica han influido en la economía estadounidense, haciendo innecesario el aumento de las tasas bancarias para frenar la inflación.

Durante las últimas cuatro semanas que terminaron el 10 de agosto, las ventas de casas en la región registraron un incremento de cerca del 34 por ciento en relación con un mismo período el año pasado, mientras que el precio promedio reportó un aumento del 14.5 por ciento.

Las transacciones de compra y venta incluyeron 3.523 casas seminuevas, 1.251 condominios y 423 residencias de nueva construcción.

El mayor incremento en ventas correspondió a los condominios, al registrar un índice del 68.8 por ciento más respecto a 1997; le siguieron las casas ya construidas, con un aumento del 31 por ciento, y curiosamente tratándose de residencias nuevas, las transacciones sufrieron una caída del 8.6 por ciento en comparación con el año pasado.

**C. Necesitamos aprender más.** Con un/a compañero/a, hagan el papel de una pareja con ganas de comprar una casa. Hablen de por qué sería buena idea asistir a este seminario. Pueden mencionar otras razones también que no se incluyen en el boletín.

MODELO: *Querido/a, sabemos muy poco de los precios en esta ciudad. Es posible que nos hablen de los precios de casas que se han vendido últimamente.*

## Seminario para comprar casa

La compañía Casa Linda ofrecerá un seminario gratuito en español a primeros compradores de casa, este sábado 29 de las once de la mañana hasta la una de la tarde, en el n° 300 de la calle Conquistador, en Ventura, CA.

Para quienes todavía sueñan con vivir en casa propia, el cambio de inquilino a propietario quizás parezca complicado y largo, pero puede ser fácil si reciben adecuada orientación para conocer ese procedimiento paso a paso.

Según informó Beatriz Pérez, portavoz de dicha compañía, el seminario fue organizado para abrir sus puertas a la comunidad hispana y demostrar lo sencillo que puede ser convertirse en propietario.

Durante el evento, los asistentes podrán preguntar con toda libertad y así despejar sus dudas y temores. Sólo por asistir, se les dará un certificado de pre-cualificación y un descuento para hacerlo efectivo al comprar su casa.

Para más detalles llame al teléfono Nº 781-7756.

**D. La oferta de Lázaro e Isabel.** En grupos de tres (Lázaro, Isabel y la Sra. Miller), escriban la oferta que van a presentarle al agente de los dueños de la casa. Deben incluir cuánto dinero ofrecen, el número de días para cerrar el trato, las condiciones que esperan, tales como: la inspección de la casa, la necesidad de conseguir el préstamo del banco…

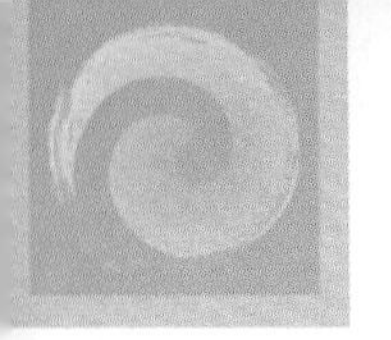

# Los pronombres relativos
## (*Relative pronouns*)

### Para averiguar

1. What is the purpose of a relative pronoun?
2. Name the most common relative pronoun in Spanish.
3. When must you use **quien** rather than **que**?
4. Can you explain the difference between **que** and **lo que**?
5. What Spanish adjective means *whose*?

**Note.** Point out that relative pronouns have no accents.

**Clarification.** Tell students that in a sentence like *The woman who came was my mom, que* and not *quien* is used to mean *who: La mujer que llamó era mi madre.*

- Use a relative pronoun to join two *related* clauses into a single sentence. **Que** is probably the most common relative pronoun. It can often be used for persons or things.

| | |
|---|---|
| Ésta es la casa. La casa me gusta. | *This is the house. I like the house.* |
| Ésta es la casa **que** me gusta. | *This is the house that I like.* |
| El agente habla español. El agente tiene muchos clientes. | *The realtor speaks Spanish. The realtor has many clients.* |
| El agente **que** habla español tiene muchos clientes. | *The realtor who speaks Spanish has many clients.* |

- **Quien** is used only for people. **Quien** must be used after a preposition, if the clause refers to people. After a preposition referring to objects, **que** is used.

| | |
|---|---|
| El agente **con quien** hablamos ayer tiene unas sugerencias. | *The agent with whom we spoke yesterday has some suggestions.* |
| Las chicas **con quienes** fuiste a la escuela están allí. | *The girls with whom you went to school are over there.* |
| El coche **en que** llegaron es enorme. | *The car they arrived in is huge.* |

- To say *what* as a statement, rather than as a question, use **lo que** (*that which*) (for unidentified things or nouns) instead of **que. Lo que** is a neuter form that refers to an idea or a previous situation or event. Relative pronouns, unlike question words, do not have accents.

| | | |
|---|---|---|
| Question: | ¿**Qué** buscas? | *What are you looking for?* |
| Statement: | Yo sé **lo que** buscas. | I *know what you are looking for.* |
| Question: | ¿**Qué** pasa? | *What's happening?* |
| Statement: | **Lo que** pasa es esto. | *This is what's happening.* |

- In Spanish, to say the possessive *whose,* match the relative pronoun **cuyo/a/os/as** to the noun following it.

| | |
|---|---|
| El señor **cuya casa** visitamos es amigo de mi padre. | *The man whose house we visited is a friend of my father.* |
| Mi amiga, **cuyos libros** están allí, regresa en seguida. | *My friend, whose books are over there, will be right back.* |

## A lo personal

**A. ¿Que o quien?** Use either **que** or **quien/es** to finish the following sentences.

MODELO: La casa ________ me enseñaste es elegante.
*La casa* ***que*** *me enseñaste es elegante.*

1. Las señoras ________ vinieron ayer con tus padres, quieren comprar la casa.
2. Las señoras con ________ vinieron ayer tus padres, quieren comprar la casa.
3. El coche en ________ llegaron es una limosina elegante.

4. La chica, a ________ conociste anoche, quiere hablarte.
5. El dormitorio más grande tiene un baño ________ me gusta mucho.
6. La residencia estudiantil en ________ vivo yo, no tiene baños particulares.
7. La compañera de cuarto con ________ vives tú es muy simpática.
8. Tengo una amiga ________ habla perfectamente tres idiomas.

**B. Una oración de dos.** Use the relative pronoun **que** or **quien/es** to combine the following sentences into one.

MODELO: El hombre está en la sala. El hombre es agente inmobiliario.
*El hombre que está en la sala es agente inmobiliario.*

1. Necesito el libro. El libro está en el coche.
2. Trabajo con un agente. El agente sabe mucho.
3. Los agentes hablan español. Los agentes tienen muchos clientes.
4. El agente vendió la casa. La casa era de mi hermana.
5. Llegamos en una limosina. La limosina es enorme.
6. Hablamos con un consejero. El consejero nos dio buenos consejos.
7. Te hablé de un agente. El agente llegó.
8. Estudio con varios amigos. Mis amigos son inteligentes.
9. Tengo tres gatos. Mis gatos son cómicos.
10. Invito a muchos de mis amigos a mi casa nueva. Mis amigos están contentos.

**C. ¿De quién?** Join the following sentences with the proper form of **cuyo/a/os/as**.

MODELO: McDonald's es un restaurante. Su fama es internacional.
*McDonald's es un restaurante cuya fama es internacional.*

1. Pinocho es un muchacho. Su nariz crece cuando dice mentiras.
2. Stephen King es un autor. Sus novelas dan miedo.
3. Taco Bell es una compañía. Sus anuncios tienen al perro chihuahua que habla español.
4. Michael Jordan es un deportista. Sus zapatos son enormes.
5. La persona que enseña esta clase es un/a profesor/a excelente. Sus estudiantes son muy inteligentes.
6. Gaudí era un arquitecto español. Sus diseños son interesantísimos.

**D. ¿Qué necesita Ud?** Tell what you will need in order to be able to do the following.

MODELO: sacar una "A" en la clase de español
*Lo que necesito es más tiempo para estudiar.*

1. ir de vacaciones por un mes
2. comprar una casa fabulosa
3. tocar el piano o cantar en Carnegie Hall
4. ganar la lotería
5. mantener la buena salud

**E. Lo que tengo… lo que quiero.** Describe to a classmate what you have now and what you want to have in a car, a job and a home. Switch roles and then compare your preferences.

MODELO: *Lo que tengo es un apartamento pequeño. Lo que quiero es una casa grande con piscina y televisor de pantalla grande…*

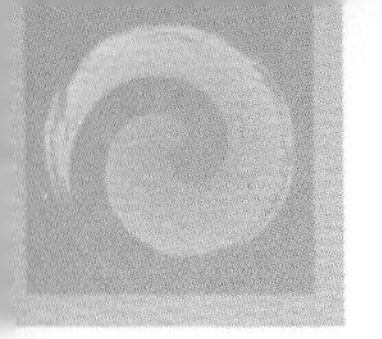

# El subjuntivo en cláusulas adjetivales
## (*Using the subjunctive to show what may or may not exist*)

**Para averiguar**

1. What is an adjective clause?
2. When do you use the indicative in an adjective clause? When do you use the subjunctive?
3. Do you use the indicative or the subjunctive in an adjective clause to describe a nonexistent noun after **nadie** or **nada**?

**Expansion.** Emphasize the role of the speaker's perception in determining what is a fact and what is not, and how that determines the choice of indicative/subjunctive mood when speaking.

- An adjective clause is a subordinate clause that describes a noun in the main clause.

  Tengo una **casa** (*main clause-noun*) que es muy **elegante.** (*subordinate clause-adjective*)
  *I have a house that is very elegant.*

- Use the indicative in an adjective clause to describe a person, place, or thing that is known to exist.

  Tengo una casa (*I own it, I know it exists*) que **es** muy elegante.

- Use the subjunctive to describe a person, place, or thing that doesn't exist or is only assumed to exist by the speaker.

  Quiero una casa **que sea** muy elegante.
  *I want a house (I don't know if there is one) that is very elegant.*

  Viven en una casa **que tiene piscina**.
  *They live in a house that has a pool.*
  (The house is specific and known to exist.)

  Buscan una casa **que tenga piscina**.
  *They're looking for a house that has a pool.*
  (The house is indefinite and only assumed to exist.)

  Conozco un restaurante **donde sirven buena paella.**
  *I know a restaurant that serves good paella.*
  (The speaker has a specific restaurant in mind.)

  ¿Conoces un buen restaurante **donde sirvan buena paella**?
  *Do you know a restaurant that may serve good paella?*
  (The speaker does not have a specific restaurant in mind.)

- The subjunctive is also used to describe a nonexistent noun.

  No he visto a nadie **que tenga tu maleta.** — *I haven't seen anyone who might have your suitcase.*

  No conozco a nadie **que lo haya hecho.** — *I don't know anyone who may have done it.*

### A lo personal

**A. ¿De qué tipo?** Complete the following sentences with the options in parentheses to describe what you would or would not like to have.

MODELO: Quiero una casa que... (ser grande, tener ocho dormitorios)
*Quiero una casa que sea grande.*
*Quiero una casa que tenga ocho dormitorios.*

1. Quiero una casa que... (tener aire acondicionado central, limpiarse fácilmente, no costar mucho dinero, estar en el campo).
2. Prefiero un apartamento que... (costar mucho, estar cerca de la universidad, estar en la planta baja, ser muy grande).
3. Quiero un trabajo que... (ser difícil, pagar bien, interesarme, ponerme nervioso/a).
4. Quiero tener profesores que... (dar mucha tarea, hacerme muchas preguntas, perder la paciencia, ser aburridos).

**B. ¿Conoces a alguien que…?** Tell whether or not you know someone who has or does the following things.

MODELO: una motocicleta
*Sí, tengo un amigo que tiene una motocicleta.* o
*No conozco a nadie que tenga una motocicleta.*

1. limpiar su casa todos los días
2. vivir en un monasterio
3. llevar botas de piel
4. hacer cruceros dos veces al año
5. manejar una ambulancia
6. ponerse anillos en la lengua
7. estudiar español
8. tener un trabajo maravilloso

**C. Cerca del campus.** Ask a classmate if he/she knows of the following places near the campus.

MODELO: una librería/vender revistas en español
E1: *¿Conoces una librería que venda revistas en español cerca de aquí?*
E2: *Sí, Barnes & Noble vende revistas en español.* o
*No conozco ninguna librería que venda revistas en español.*

1. un restaurante/servir cocido (*stew*)
2. una tienda/vender ropa usada
3. unos apartamentos/no ser muy caros
4. una tienda de vídeos/tener películas en español
5. un supermercado/estar abierto toda la noche
6. un cine/dar películas extranjeras
7. un mecánico/ser honesto
8. un taller/arreglar los frenos

**D. ¿En tu familia?** Ask a classmate if someone in his/her family is doing the following things currently.

MODELO: casarse
E1: *¿Hay alguien en tu familia que se case este año?*
E2: *Sí, mi hermano mayor se casa en mayo.* o
*No, no hay nadie en mi familia que se case este año.*

1. comprar una casa
2. tener un bebé
3. estar enfermo
4. buscar un nuevo apartamento
5. ir a Sudamérica
6. hacer algo extraordinario
7. divorciarse
8. vender su casa

**E. En la agencia.** You are describing to a real estate agent how you want your new house to be. Complete each sentence logically.

MODELO: Me gusta nadar. Quiero una casa que…
*Quiero una casa que tenga piscina.*

1. Me gusta ir de compras. Quiero una casa en un lugar donde…
2. Me gusta la tranquilidad. No quiero una casa en un lugar donde…
3. Tengo dos gatos. Quiero una casa que…
4. No me gusta arreglar casas. No quiero una casa que…
5. Me gustan los electrodomésticos. Quiero una casa que…
6. No tengo mucho dinero para el enganche. Prefiero una casa que…

## Los empleos

### Sustantivos

| | |
|---|---|
| **las acciones** | *shares, stock* |
| **el/la analista** | *analyst* |
| **la bolsa de trabajo** | *job market* |
| **la bolsa (de valores)** | *stock market* |
| **la carrera** | *major* |
| **el comercio** | *trade* |
| **el/la corredor/a de bolsa** | *stockbroker* |
| **el/la economista** | *economist* |
| **la entrevista** | *interview* |
| **el extranjero** | *abroad* |
| **la feria** | *fair* |
| **las finanzas** | *finance* |
| **los fondos** | *funds* |
| **el mercadeo** | *marketing* |
| **la solicitud** | *application* |
| **la sucursal** | *branch office* |

### Verbos

| | |
|---|---|
| **invertir (ie)** | *to invest* |
| **ofrecer (zc)** | *to offer* |
| **recoger** | *to pick up* |

### Adjetivos

| | |
|---|---|
| **financiero/a** | *financial* |
| **interesante** | *interesting* |

### Adverbios

| | |
|---|---|
| **completamente** | *completely* |
| **continuamente** | *continuously* |
| **decididamente** | *decidedly* |
| **efectivamente** | *certainly* |
| **especialmente** | *especially* |
| **fuertemente** | *strongly* |
| **generosamente** | *generously* |
| **verdaderamente** | *truthfully, truly* |

### Otras expresiones

| | |
|---|---|
| **por eso** | *that's why* |

# TEMA 2

## La propiedad privada

### Sustantivos

| | |
|---|---|
| **la cochera** | *carport* |
| **el enganche/la entrada** | *down payment* |
| **el financiamiento** | *financing* |
| **el/la inquilino/a** | *tenant* |
| **la agencia inmobiliaria** | *real estate agency* |
| **el interés** | *interest* |
| **la lengua** | *language* |
| **la oferta** | *offer* |
| **el/la portavoz** | *spokesperson* |
| **la propiedad** | *real estate/property* |
| **el/la propietario/a** | *property owner* |
| **la tasa** | *rate (of interest)* |
| **el trato** | *deal* |
| **las ventas** | *sales* |

### Verbos

| | |
|---|---|
| **alentar (ie)** | *to encourage* |
| **despejar** | *to clear up* |
| **disfrutar** | *enjoy* |
| **golpear** | *to hit* |
| **parecer (zc)** | *to seem* |
| **tirar** | *to throw away* |

### Adjetivos

| | |
|---|---|
| **amplio/a** | *ample* |
| **amueblado/a** | *furnished* |
| **dicho/a** | *said* |
| **dilatado/a** | *prolonged* |
| **gratuito/a** | *free of cost* |
| **hipotecario/a** | *mortgage (related to)* |
| **paciente** | *patient* |

### Otras expresiones

| | |
|---|---|
| **brevemente** | *briefly* |
| **paso a paso** | *step by step* |

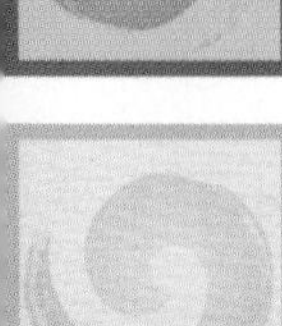

# Reunión A

A escuchar. **La oferta de Lázaro e Isabel.** Complete las oraciones con la información que escuche en el diálogo.

1. Los dueños aceptaron su ______________________________.
2. Lázaro e Isabel necesitan firmar unos papeles para que se cierre el _________.
3. Ellos quieren que su __________________________ los revise primero.
4. También insisten en que se haga una __________________________.
5. El papá de un estudiante de Lázaro inspecciona las _________ y el sistema eléctrico para el condado.
6. Además es importante una inspección para detectar ____________.

**Tapescript for A escuchar.**
**La oferta de Lázaro e Isabel.**
SRA. MILLER: ¡Los felicito! Los dueños aceptaron su oferta. Antes de que se me olvide, quiero que firmen estos papeles para que se cierre el trato.
LÁZARO: Primero queremos que nuestro abogado los revise cuidadosamente.
SRA. MILLER: Claro, es una buena idea. Llévenselos a su casa y me los traen cuando estén listos.
ISABEL: ¡Ay, se me olvidaba! Antes de firmar los papeles queremos que se haga una inspección.
LÁZARO: El papá de uno de mis alumnos inspecciona las tuberías y el sistema eléctrico para el condado. Quizá él pueda ayudarnos.
ISABEL: Claro. También queremos que se haga una inspección para detectar termitas y otras pestes caseras.
LÁZARO: ¿Conoce alguna compañía exterminadora que sea buena?
SRA. MILLER: Sí, ellos inspeccionan la casa y fumigan si es necesario. Se me perdió el número de teléfono, pero yo les llamo para que vayan a la casa.

**Answers for A escuchar.**
1) *Oferta.* 2) *Trato.* 3) *Abogado.* 4) *Inspección.* 5) *Tuberías.* 6) *Termitas.*

**A conversar.** Desgraciadamente (*unfortunately*), Ud. y su amigo/a (su compañero/a) han perdido su trabajo, pero rápidamente se les ocurre un plan. Uds. leyeron que mañana hay una feria de trabajo en la universidad. Hablen de qué empleo van a buscar en la bolsa de trabajo, qué necesitan preparar antes de ir, con quién piensan hablar, qué empleos pueden tener requisitos como un título o experiencia y...

## ¿Lo sabía?

### El hombre del libro

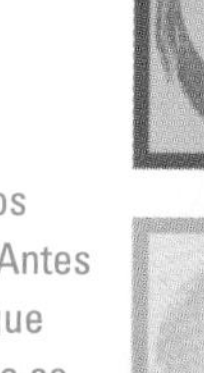

Jeff Bezos, el hombre del ciberespacio, creó un paraíso para compradores en el Internet con www.amazon.com. A los tres años, Jeff decidió que quería una cama y no su cuna (*crib*). Su mamá, que le dijo que no, volvió a casa un día para encontrarlo con un destornillador (*screwdriver*), tratando de desmontar la cuna. Según ella, siempre era difícil prever sus acciones.

Ahora a los treinta y cuatro años, Jeff es el jefe de la compañía más conocida del Internet que vende libros y música. Tiene 3.1 millones de clientes y 1.100 empleados. Sus ganancias de los últimos tres meses han sido de 116 millones de dólares. ¡Y pensar que empezó en su garaje! Él dice que "...las computadoras son el instrumento máximo".

El mayor de tres hijos de un inmigrante cubano—ingeniero de petróleo—y un ama de casa, se crió en Miami y Houston. Después de estudiar informática en Princeton, diseñó sistemas de programas financieros, pero se le ocurrió aprovechar el crecimiento (*growth*) del Internet. Su valor financiero personal ahora es de dos billones de dólares.

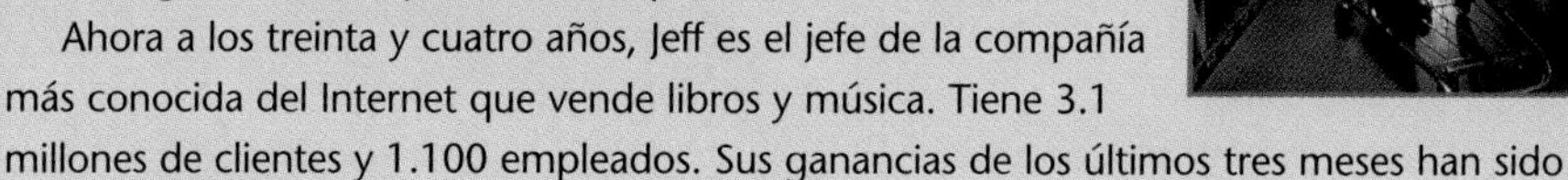

**¿Comprende Ud?** Conteste según la información del artículo.

1. ¿Quién es este hombre?
2. ¿Qué hizo a los tres años?
3. ¿Puede Ud. dar una descripción de www.amazon.com?
4. ¿A qué se debe parte de su éxito?
5. ¿Quiénes son sus padres?
6. ¿Cuál es su valor financiero ahora?

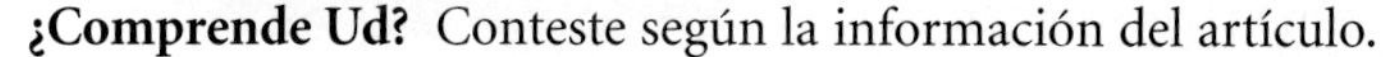

**A buscar.** Busque información en el Internet sobre una casa o condominio que se venda en su ciudad hispana favorita. Hable con dos compañeros de lo bueno y lo malo de cada oferta que encontraron, incluyendo el precio, el lugar y la descripción de la propiedad. ¿Hay detalles especiales? ¿Cuál les gustaría comprar? Decidan cuál de las tres propiedades es mejor y expliquen por qué.

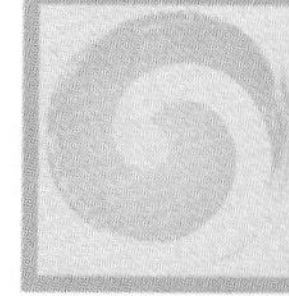

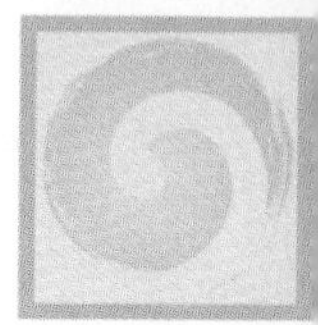

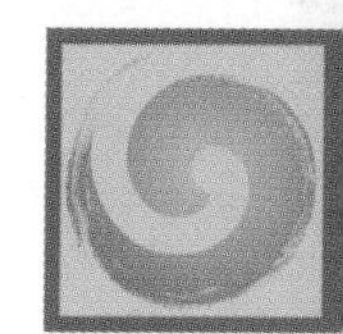

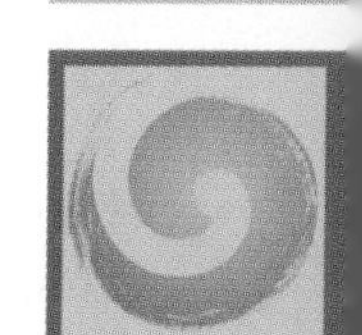

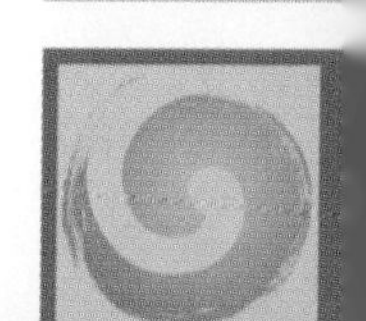

## Los servicios bancarios

Note. Discuss this article in class, asking questions such as, *¿Por qué empezó Barnett Bank el Super Mobile? ¿Cómo va a servir a la gente del Condado de Dade?*

***Barnett Bank Inaugura el Super Mobile***

Barnett Bank, N.A., South Florida, cumple su compromiso con las comunidades del Condado de Dade que no tienen acceso a servicios bancarios. Esta empresa ha inaugurado el nuevo Super Mobile, un banco ambulante de 38 pies de largo que servirá como centro bancario temporal hasta que se construyan sucursales permanentes.

### Necesitamos un préstamo

*Lázaro e Isabel piden un préstamo para comprar la casa....*

ISABEL: Sr. Tapia, disculpe que lleguemos tarde, pero se nos descompuso el coche.

SR. TAPIA: No se preocupen, no tengo otra cita. Es la una de la tarde y el banco está abierto hasta las cinco. ¿En qué puedo servirles?

LÁZARO: Estamos decididos a comprar una casa y esperamos que nos ayude a encontrar una buena hipoteca.

SR. TAPIA: ¡Qué bien que estén resueltos a comprarla! Yo les consigo un préstamo que tenga un interés razonable. ¿Lo prefieren a quince o a treinta años?

ISABEL: Nuestro contador dice que es mejor que paguemos el préstamo en treinta años.

SR. TAPIA: Estoy de acuerdo, porque todavía son jóvenes. ¿Los dos trabajan?

LÁZARO: Solamente yo, pero Isabel está resuelta a conseguir un trabajo.

SR. TAPIA: Entonces, no se preocupen. No creo que haya ningún problema. Llenen esta solicitud y vuelvan tan pronto como sea posible.

Answers for A. 1) *Se les descompuso el coche.* 2) *Una hipoteca.* 3) *Por treinta años.* 4) *No trabaja.*

**A. ¿Comprende Ud.?** Conteste las siguientes preguntas según el diálogo.

1. ¿Por qué llegan tarde Isabel y Lázaro al banco?
2. ¿Qué desean ellos?
3. ¿Por cuántos años quieren el préstamo?
4. ¿Dónde trabaja Isabel?

**B. Los préstamos estudiantiles.** Complete las oraciones según la información del folleto. Luego, hable con su compañero/a de cómo pagan Uds. sus costos universitarios.

## GUÍA DE AYUDA FINANCIERA

### ¿Está Ud. preocupado sobre cómo financiar sus estudios universitarios?

**Casi todas las personas en los Estados Unidos lo están. Wells Fargo puede ayudarle a tomar decisiones correctas para financiar el costo de su educación.**

### ¿Cómo puede empezar?

**Primero los estudiantes tienen que completar y enviar la Solicitud Gratuita para Ayuda Financiera Federal (FAFSA) inmediatamente después del primero de enero. La solicitud FAFSA se utiliza en toda la nación para determinar la elegibilidad para ayuda federal. Casi todos los estados usan la misma solicitud para determinar la elegibilidad para ayuda estatal. Ésta, por lo general, se puede obtener por medio de los consejeros vocacionales de las escuelas secundarias, la biblioteca pública, las oficinas de ayuda financiera en las universidades, o llamando al 1-800-433-3243. FAFSA viene en versión electrónica en el programa FAFSA Express o se puede utilizar la solicitud impresa. Algunas escuelas pueden enviar solicitudes de forma electrónica desde sus oficinas de ayuda financiera.**

### ¿Qué tipo de ayuda se ofrece?

**El Departamento de Educación de los Estados Unidos mantiene los siguientes programas principales de ayuda financiera para estudiantes:**

- **Préstamo Federal Pell Grant**
- **Préstamo Federal Suplementario de Oportunidad Educativa (FSEOG)**
- **Préstamo de Trabajo/Estudio (FWS)**
- **Préstamo Federal Perkins**
- **Préstamo Federal Stafford (con y sin subvención)**
- **Préstamo Federal Plus**

WELLS FARGO

1. El propósito (*purpose*) del folleto es cómo __________ sus estudios universitarios.
2. Si tiene más preguntas, es posible __________.
3. Se puede conseguir la solicitud de __________, __________, __________ o __________.
4. FAFSA significa __________.
5. En algunas escuelas se pueden enviar solicitudes __________.
6. Hay __________ tipos de préstamos federales apoyados por el Departamento de __________ de los EE. UU.

**C. ¿Un préstamo fácil?** Ud. ha encontrado la casa ideal, pero ahora hay que buscar el mejor préstamo. ¡Es tan complicado! Ud. ve este anuncio en el periódico y se sienta a apuntar lo que *Siglo XXI* ofrece. Escriba cinco razones por las cuales Ud. piensa llamar a *Siglo XXI*. Entonces compare su lista con la de un/a compañero/a para ver si encontraron las mismas razones.

MODELO: 1. *Siglo XXI es un líder en préstamos hipotecarios.*

EN SIGLO XXI TODO ES TAN FÁCIL
¡QUE YA HASTA ME SIENTO EN CASA!

En Siglo XXI somos el líder en préstamos hipotecarios para hispanos y queremos hacer todo lo posible para facilitarle la experiencia de comprar una casa. Contamos con varias oficinas en su área y expertos en préstamos hipotecarios que hablan español y entienden sus necesidades.

Y en Siglo XXI, su transacción nunca sale de nuestra oficina para ser procesada. Las perso-nas con quienes trata desde un principio, ¡son las mismas personas autorizadas para aprobar su préstamo! Visite o llámenos hoy mismo. ¡Y siéntase como en su casa!

Llame gratis a Siglo XXI al 1-888-SU-CASA5

**Prestamos Hipotecarios de Siglo XXI. Haciendo Realidad Sus Sueños**

# ABC Los consejos legales

## La consulta con el abogado

*Isabel y Lázaro van a la oficina de su abogado….*

ISABEL: Licenciado Rangel, ¿ha tenido tiempo para revisar el contrato de compra de la casa?

LIC. RANGEL: Sí, lo he visto cuidadosamente y estoy satisfecho con los términos.

LÁZARO: No ha dicho si le parece que es un buen precio.

LIC. RANGEL: No he visto la casa, pero creo que han hecho una buena compra. Han escogido un buen vecindario.

ISABEL: Además, la casa es grande y está bien cuidada.

LÁZARO: Ya la han inspeccionado y solamente necesita unas reparaciones menores, pero no hay problemas graves.

LIC. RANGEL: Es importante que la señora Miller tenga por escrito los resultados de la inspección.

LÁZARO: Ya hemos hablado con ella y dice que va a ponerlos en el contrato de compra.

**Answers for A.** 1) *Es satisfactorio.* 2) *Grande y cuidada.* 3) *Reparaciones menores.* 4) *Will vary.*

**A. ¿Comprende Ud.?** Conteste las siguientes preguntas según el diálogo.

1. ¿Cuál es la opinión del Licenciado Rangel sobre el contrato?
2. ¿Cómo es la casa, según Isabel?
3. ¿Qué se necesita hacer en la casa?
4. En su opinión ¿por qué es necesario tener los resultados de la inspección por escrito?

**B. Necesito un abogado.** Lea los anuncios de los dos abogados. Analice las especialidades de cada uno. Luego, hable con un/a compañero/a de cuatro situaciones posibles por las cuales tendrían (*would have*) que llamar al uno o al otro.

MODELO: *Mi amigo ha sufrido dolor de espalda desde su accidente el mes pasado. No tiene abogado ahora, pero creo que es necesario que busque uno porque no le pagan sus cuentas médicas.*

**OFICINAS LEGALES DE ROMANO Y ECHEVARRIA**

**LE ASEGURAMOS QUE NUESTRA OFICINA LEGAL ES LA MÁS EFICIENTE EN**

**Inmigración:**
- ❐ Consultas sobre patrocinadores familiares o de trabajo
- ❐ Consultas y defensa legal por problemas de residencia y de visas
- ❐ Tramitamos todos los papeles necesarios para su Tarjeta Verde
- ❐ Casos de naturalización y defensa contra deportación

**Deudas:**
- ❐ Problemas de crédito y débito
- ❐ Embargos de casas o automóviles
- ❐ Embargo del sueldo por el IRS

La primera consulta es gratis.
Ofrecemos precios módicos y planes de pago.
Citas disponibles por las tardes después del trabajo y los fines de semana.

Llame al (714) 599-9204 y nosotros estaremos a su disposición.

**ABOGADOS ALERO Y BUENAVISTA**

**Le ofrecemos ayuda con todo tipo de problemas legales.**

- ➤ Divorcios
- ➤ Disputas Familiares
- ➤ Custodia de niños
- ➤ Testamentos
- ➤ Bancarrota
- ➤ Accidentes de coche
- ➤ Problemas laborales
- ➤ Acoso sexual en el trabajo

**Póngase en contacto con nosotros hoy mismo. Máxima discreción y eficiencia. Llame al (312) 382-3825 para concertar una visita**

**¡Le estamos esperando!**

**C. La planificación financiera.** Lea el artículo, complete las oraciones y luego hable con un/a compañero/a sobre algunas de las razones importantes para planear su futuro, incluyendo la necesidad de escribir un testamento.

1. Visto que las mujeres viven más años que los hombres, necesitan ______________.
2. Una tercera parte de las mujeres en EE. UU. no tiene ______________.
3. Para una mujer de veinte a treinta años, es necesario ______________.
4. A los cuarenta hay que ______________.
5. A los cincuenta es importante ______________.
6. Se debe buscar información de ______________.

Tanya Pages es una agente de seguros en la agencia del sur de Florida de Principal Mutual Life Insurance Company. Tanya dice que las latinas están ganando más dinero que antes y que son más independientes a la vez. Pero ganar más dinero no quiere decir ahorrar (*save*) más. Las mujeres tienen necesidades económicas únicas que muchas veces no son reconocidas. Es posible que sean pobres al jubilarse.

Una tercera parte de las mujeres en los EE. UU. no tiene seguro de vida. Por lo general viven diez años más que los hombres, necesitando más fondos en el futuro para su salud y sus años jubilados. Además ganan menos sueldo.

Por eso es importante tomar decisiones temprano para lograr la independencia financiera. Hay que educarse en la planificación de sus recursos. Para una mujer de veinte o treinta años, es necesario empezar un plan de ahorros y de seguros. Se debe tener cuidado con tarjetas de crédito y préstamos. Después de casarse o empezar una familia es aún más importante planear su patrimonio (*estate*) personal y escribir un testamento.

A los cuarenta ya es momento de medir sus necesidades para después de jubilarse. Hay que

evaluar con cuidado sus inversiones. ¡No se olvide de pensar en el precio de la educación universitaria de sus hijos! ¿A los cincuenta? Una mirada final a ver si todo va bien.

La independencia financiera empieza por aceptar responsabilidad por el futuro propio. Busque información de los expertos.

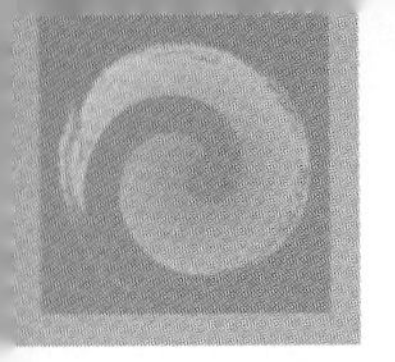

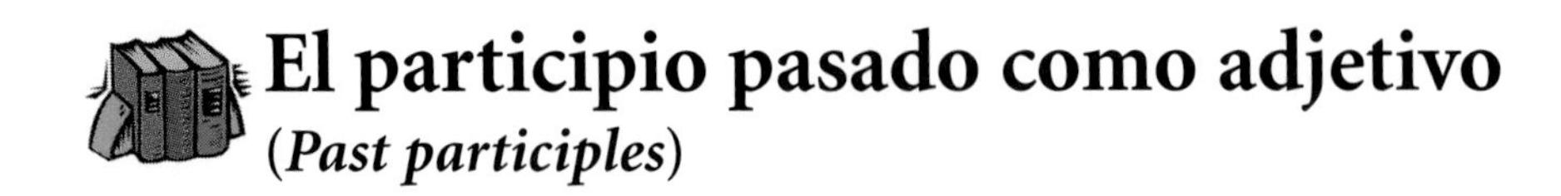

# El participio pasado como adjetivo
## (*Past participles*)

**Para averiguar**

1. What form of the verb can be used as an adjective?
2. What is the regular past participle ending in English? Which endings are used to form the regular past participles of **-ar** and **-er/-ir** verbs in Spanish?
3. What are ten Spanish verbs that have irregular past participles?

- Regular past participles are formed in Spanish by adding these endings to the verb stem:

| Infinitive | Stem | Ending | Past Participle |
|---|---|---|---|
| prepar**ar** | prepar | -ado | prepar**ado** |
| conoc**er** | conoc | -ido | conoc**ido** |
| dorm**ir** | dorm | -ido | dorm**ido** |

- When the verb stem ends with **-a, -e,** or **-o,** a written accent is added to the **-ido** ending of **-er** and **-ir** verbs.

| | |
|---|---|
| traer | **traído** |
| creer | **creído** |
| oír | **oído** |

- The following verbs have irregular past participles:

| | | | |
|---|---|---|---|
| abrir | **abierto** | morir | **muerto** |
| decir | **dicho** | poner | **puesto** |
| escribir | **escrito** | resolver | **resuelto** |
| freír (*to fry*) | **frito** | romper | **roto** |
| hacer | **hecho** | ver | **visto** |
| imprimir (*to print*) | **impreso** | volver | **vuelto** |

- The past participle is a verb form that can be used as an adjective. In English, regular past participles end in *-ed*. Note how the verbs *to reserve* and *to surprise* are used as adjectives in the following sentences.

| | |
|---|---|
| Las habitaciones están **reservadas**. | *The rooms are reserved.* |
| Estoy muy **sorprendido**. | *I am very surprised.* |

- When a past participle is used as an adjective, it agrees in number and gender with the noun that it modifies.

| | |
|---|---|
| Las maletas están hech**as**. | *The bags are packed.* |
| Los niños están emocionad**os**. | *The children are excited.* |

### A lo personal

**A. ¿Cómo está Ud.?** Use the past participle of each verb to describe yourself at the present moment.

MODELO: cansar
*Estoy cansado/a.* o *No estoy cansado/a.*

1. confundir
2. preocupar
3. ocupar
4. perder
5. preparar
6. frustrar
7. sorprender
8. aburrir
9. dormir
10. relajar

11. deprimir
12. encantar
13. disgustar
14. acostar
15. sentar
16. enojar
17. vestir
18. broncear

**B. Ayer cuando regresé.** Use the past participle of the verb to tell in what state you found each thing when you returned home yesterday.

MODELO: las llaves/perder
*Las llaves no estaban perdidas.*

1. las camas/hacer
2. la mesa/poner
3. la cena/preparar
4. el teléfono/ocupar
5. la puerta/abrir
6. las ventanas/cerrar
7. el televisor/poner
8. los platos/lavar
9. las plantas/morir
10. las papas/freír

**C. Los gustos.** Use a past participle to say whether or not you like the following things.

MODELO: ¿Le gusta la comida que se prepara en el microondas?
*Sí, (No, no) me gusta la comida preparada en el microondas.*

¿Le gusta(n)...

1. ...la ropa que se vende en Sears?
2. ...la comida que se sirve en la cafetería de aquí?
3. ...los libros que se leen en la clase de historia?
4. ...la música que se oye en las discotecas?
5. ...los ejercicios que se escriben en el cuaderno?
6. ...las actividades que se hacen en grupo en clase?
7. ...el grafiti que se ve en las ciudades grandes?
8. ...las cosas que se dicen en el show de Howard Stern?

**D. ¿Está hecho?** Your instructor wants to know if these things have been done. Answer each question using a past participle.

MODELO: ¿Preparó Ud. los ejercicios en el cuaderno para hoy?
*Sí, están preparados.*

1. ¿Abrió Ud. el libro en la página 284?
2. ¿Cerró alguien la puerta?
3. ¿Escribió alguien las respuestas en la pizarra?
4. ¿Perdió Ud. su tarea?
5. ¿Rompió Ud. la silla?
6. ¿Hizo Ud. la tarea para hoy?
7. ¿Rompió alguien la tiza?
8. ¿Resolvieron Uds. el problema?

**E. ¡Qué día tan horrible!** You and your roommate tried to get to Spanish class for the exam, but everything went wrong. Together, come up with a list of at least eight things that went wrong using the past participle.

MODELO: *El despertador estaba roto.*

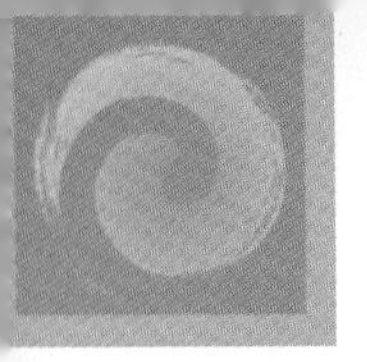

# El presente perfecto de indicativo
## (*The present perfect indicative*)

**Para averiguar**

1. Which auxiliary verb do you use with a past participle to say that you have done something?
2. Where do you place the object and reflexive pronouns with the present perfect?

**Note.** Point out to students that the present perfect is used to express something occurring in the past that is related to the present.

- The present perfect (**el presente perfecto**) is used to say that you have done something. It is composed of the present tense of the *auxiliary verb* **haber** and the *past participle.* In the present perfect, the past participle is a verb form and does not show agreement as it does when used as an adjective.

| | Auxiliary verb | Past participle | |
|---|---|---|---|
| yo | **he** | hablado | *I have spoken* |
| tú | **has** | hablado | *you have spoken* |
| él, ella, Ud. | **ha** | hablado | *he/she has spoken, you have spoken* |
| nosotros/as | **hemos** | hablado | *we have spoken* |
| vosotros/as | **habéis** | hablado | *you have spoken* |
| ellos, ellas, Uds. | **han** | hablado | *they have spoken, you have spoken* |

—¿Cuántas veces **has visitado** la casa? — *How many times have you visited the house?*
—**He estado** tres veces allí. — *I have been there three times.*
—¿Tus padres la van a ver? — *Are your parents going to see it?*
—Ya la **han visto.** — *They have already seen it.*

- Object and reflexive pronouns are placed before the conjugated auxiliary verb.

—¿**Has comprado** la casa? — *Have you bought the house?*
—No, todavía no **la he comprado.** — *No, I haven't bought it yet.*

## A lo personal

**A. ¿Lo has hecho?** Ask a classmate if he/she has ever done these activities. Your classmate will then tell how many times he/she has done them.

MODELO: visitar España
E1: *¿Has visitado España?*
E2: *Sí, he visitado España dos veces.* o *No, nunca he visitado España.*

1. comprar una casa
2. romper la ventana de un vecino
3. arreglar la tubería (*plumbing*)
4. pedir un préstamo
5. hacer muebles
6. pintar toda la casa
7. volver a tu primera casa
8. subir al techo
9. alquilar un apartamento
10. hacer pagos para una hipoteca

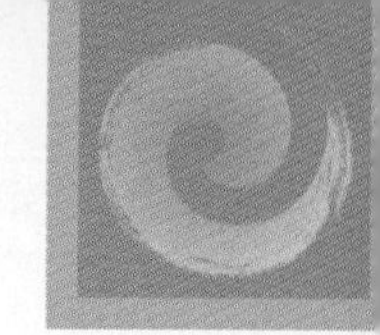

**B. Consejos.** Your friend has several problems. With a partner, think of questions to ask in order to find out what might have caused each problem and what your friend has done to resolve it.

MODELO: Hace frío en mi apartamento.
*¿Has puesto la calefacción?*
*¿Has cerrado las ventanas?*
*¿Has hablado con el dueño?*

1. No comprendo nada en la clase de español.
2. Salgo de vacaciones en dos días y nada está listo.
3. Mi novio/a no quiere salir más conmigo.
4. Mi esposo/a no quiere que yo trabaje fuera de casa.

**C. Antes de mudarse.** Today you move into your new house. Tell if you have done the following things or will do them.

**Note for C.** Remind students that the object pronoun must come before the auxiliary verb in Spanish.

MODELO: poner las cosas en cajas
*Sí, las he puesto en cajas.* o
*No, voy a ponerlas en cajas después.*

1. conseguir una hipoteca
2. consultar a un agente
3. hacer una lista de posesiones
4. cambiar el número de teléfono
5. conseguir una compañía de mudanzas
6. comprar una cama
7. hacer las maletas
8. olvidarse de hacer algo
9. llamar a la compañía eléctrica
10. cancelar la suscripción del periódico

**D. Entrevista.** Use the following questions to interview a classmate.

1. ¿Has pensado en dónde quieres vivir después de graduarte? ¿Has soñado con la casa ideal? ¿Alguna vez has visto la casa ideal?
2. Antes de vivir en esta ciudad, ¿dónde has vivido? ¿Has pensado en volver?
3. ¿Has vivido en una casa con piscina? ¿Te gustaría hacerlo?
4. ¿Has pedido una hipoteca alguna vez? ¿la conseguiste?
5. ¿Qué países extranjeros has visitado? ¿Has visto las casas típicas de allí? ¿Te gustaría vivir allí por un tiempo?

**E. Una conversación.** You and your roommate are moving tomorrow into a new apartment. Make a checklist of ten things that need to be done. Then discuss if you have or have not done them.

COSAS POR HACER

1.
2.
3.
4.
5.
6.
7.
8.
9.
10.

# TEMA 4 Los preparativos

## ABC Los problemas posibles

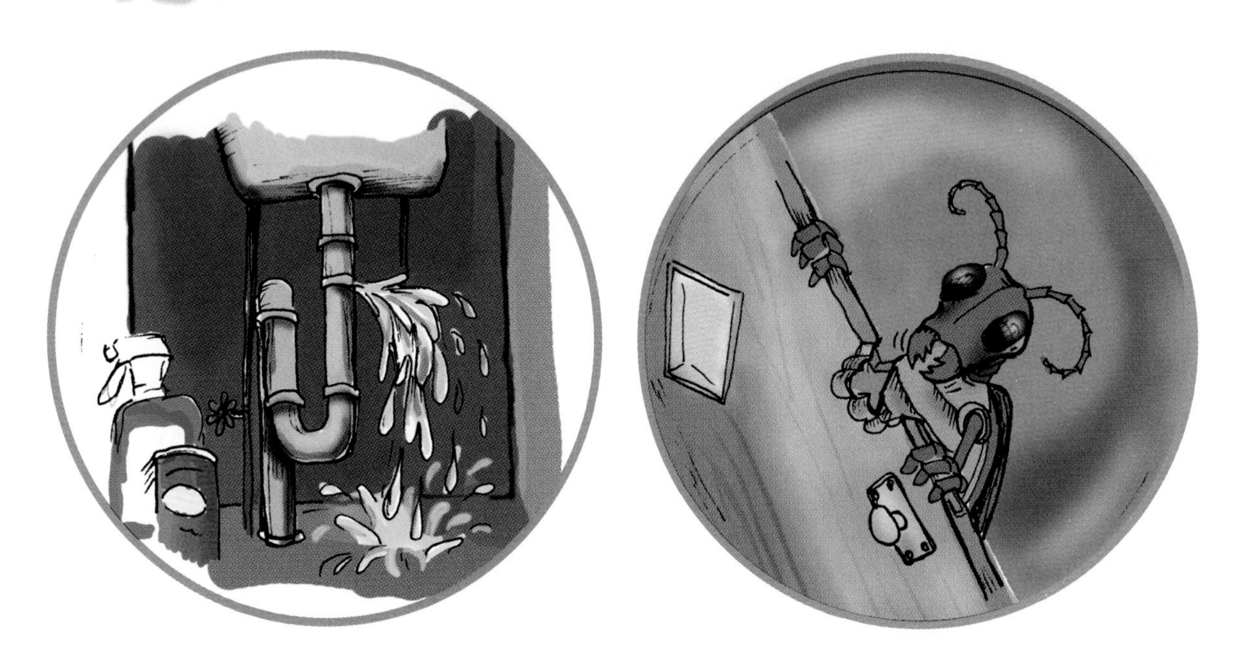

### El diseño

*El arquitecto Rigual visita la casa nueva de Isabel y Lázaro....*

ISABEL: Lázaro, éste es el arquitecto de quien te había hablado. No creo que lo hayas conocido en la feria del trabajo.

LÁZARO: Mucho gusto. Isabel estaba encantada con las fotos de sus diseños. Me dijo que nunca había visto casas tan bonitas.

ARQ. RIGUAL: Gracias. Todas eran casas viejas. Me especializo en redecorar. Dudo que Uds. hayan podido comprar una casa mejor.

LÁZARO: Sí, nunca he visto una casa tan bien cuidada. Isabel, ¿cuánto tiempo vivieron aquí los dueños anteriores?

ISABEL: La señora Miller me dijo que habían vivido aquí por veinte años y nunca tuvieron hijos.

ARQ. RIGUAL: Eso explica por qué está en buenas condiciones. ¿Cuál fue el resultado de la inspección?

LÁZARO: El inspector dijo que las termitas habían dañado la puerta de la cocina y que probablemente había que cambiarla.

ISABEL: Y que se ha dañado la tubería de uno de los baños.

**Answers for A.** 1) *Un arquitecto.* 2) *En la feria del trabajo.* 3) *A redecorar.* 4) *Veinte años.*

**A. ¿Comprende Ud.?** Conteste las siguientes preguntas según el diálogo.

1. ¿Quién va a la casa nueva de Lázaro e Isabel?
2. ¿Dónde lo conoció Isabel?
3. ¿A qué se dedica el arquitecto Rigual?
4. ¿Por cuánto tiempo vivieron los dueños anteriores en la casa?

**B. ¡Ladrones en mi casa!** Lea el artículo, conteste las preguntas y hable con su compañero/a de qué tipo de seguridad hay en sus casas.

**New word:** maniatar = *to tie up*

1. ¿Dónde no debe Ud. esconder la llave de su casa, según este artículo?
2. ¿Qué tipo de puertas se recomiendan?
3. ¿Qué tipo de programas de vigilancia se sugieren en este artículo? ¿Cree Ud. que estos programas son útiles (*useful*)?

## CUÁN SEGURO ES EL HOGAR...

(por R. Cores)

*Aníbal Prieto llegó a su casa después de un duro día de trabajo, y en la puerta de su garaje en Queens, NY, lo asaltaron. Los ladrones se llevaron su reloj, una cadena de oro, su cartera y todo lo que pudieron encontrar en la casa. A Aníbal lo encontraron horas después, golpeado y maniatado.*

Este tipo de robo puede suceder dondequiera. Aunque informes del FBI indican que el crimen ha disminuido en el país, de nada le sirven a Ud. las estadísticas si se encuentra en el porcentaje de víctimas. ¿Qué hacer? Expertos en la materia sugieren las siguientes precauciones:

**Cerraduras:**
- Cierre puertas y ventanas aunque sólo salga de casa por poco tiempo.
- No deje la llave escondida en ningún lugar cerca de la puerta.

**Objetos de valor:**
- Mantenga objetos de valor fuera de la vista, para que no se vean por las ventanas.
- Identifique sus objetos de valor con un número para reconocerlos después.
- Tenga un inventario al día, del contenido de su hogar. Guárdelo en una caja de seguridad.

**Puertas y ventanas:**
- Sustituya puertas de madera débil por madera sólida o metal.
- Asegúrese de que las bisagras están hacia dentro. Si quedan por fuera, los ladrones pueden quitar los tornillos y tumbar la puerta.
- Asegure las ventanas dobles con cerrojos o poniendo barras de metal.
- Instale barras de metal detrás de las puertas del sótano y del garaje.

Los programas de vigilancia de vecinos son excelentes y defienden contra el crimen. Es una buena idea aliarse con sus vecinos para comenzar un programa en su barrio en caso de que no exista uno. Trate de comunicarse con los que viven a su alrededor y notifique a la policía de cualquier movimiento sospechoso de autos o personas ajenos a su área. Nunca abra la puerta a desconocidos ni informe sobre sus planes de viaje a personas que no sean de absoluta confianza.

*Vista* Magazine, June 1998.

**C. Los seguros imprescindibles.** Lea el anuncio de seguros y hable con su compañero/a de qué tipo de seguro es imprescindible (*indispensable*): el de casa, el de auto, el de vida o todos. ¿Y el seguro médico? Mencionen los límites apropiados, el precio que hay que pagar para tenerlos y cuáles tienen Uds. ¿Han tenido la necesidad de presentar una demanda (*claim*)? ¿Por qué? ¿Cómo salió?

MODELO: *La hipoteca de mi casa requiere que tenga seguro para la casa.*

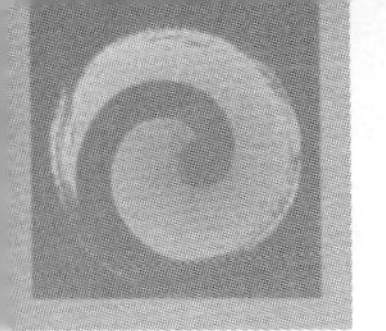

# ABC Hay mucho que hacer

## Haciendo cambios

*El arquitecto Rigual sugiere algunos cambios en la casa de Isabel y Lázaro....*

ARQ. RIGUAL: Es obvio que nunca habían modernizado esta casa. ¿Han pensado en cambiar el estilo?

ISABEL: No, nos ha gustado así. La señora Miller nos había sugerido cambiar la alfombra y pintar la casa de colores más modernos.

ARQ. RIGUAL: Sí, es buena idea, pero yo había pensado hacer otros cambios. ¿No han visto que la cocina es muy pequeña?

ISABEL: Sí, ya lo había notado, pero había pensado pintarla de un color claro para que parezca más grande.

ARQ. RIGUAL: No, eso no. Yo había diseñado una cocina con el techo muy alto. Miren, aquí tengo los planos. ¿No es preciosa?

LÁZARO: Sí, pero me parece muy cara. No habíamos pensado gastar mucho dinero.

ARQ. RIGUAL: Yo tengo un amigo que es contratista y puede darles un buen precio.

ISABEL: No sé, no hemos resuelto nada. Vamos a pensarlo.

**Answers for A.** 1) *Pintarla de color claro.* 2) *Poner un techo alto.* 3) *No tienen dinero.* 4) *Pensarlo.*

**A. ¿Comprende Ud.?** Conteste las siguientes preguntas según el diálogo.

1. ¿Cuáles son los planes de Lázaro e Isabel para cambiar la cocina?
2. ¿Y los planes del señor Rigual?
3. ¿Por qué no han pensado Lázaro e Isabel en cambiar el estilo de la casa?
4. ¿Qué deciden hacer ellos?

**B. La electricidad y...** Acaba de mudarse a una casa nueva y necesita organizar todos los servicios. Estudie el boletín de la compañía de electricidad y conteste las preguntas.

1. ¿Cómo se puede pagar?
2. ¿Qué es un plan de pago en cuotas iguales?
3. ¿Dónde se puede pagar su cuenta eléctrica?
4. ¿Qué se debe buscar para saber que es un lugar de pago autorizado?

**Pago directo**

Simplifique su vida y haga el pago mensual de sus cuentas sin problemas. Con el sistema de Pago Directo, esta práctica opción pagará su cuenta eléctrica mediante un débito mensual automático en su cuenta corriente, que será cobrado diez días después de que Ud. reciba la factura por correo. Llame al 1-800-950-2356 para solicitar un formulario de inscripción. Este servicio es gratis.

**Pago telefónico**

Goce de las ventajas de poder pagar su factura directamente desde su cuenta corriente, desde cualquier lugar en donde Ud. tenga acceso a un teléfono, a cualquier hora del día o de la noche. Llámenos para solicitar un formulario de inscripción. Ud. estará a tan sólo unas cuantas teclas telefónicas de poder pagar su cuenta mensual sin problemas. El coste de este servicio es de 20 centavos por transacción.

**Plan de pago en cuotas iguales**

Este plan le permite crear un presupuesto para su cuenta eléctrica y dividirlo en pagos iguales. Hay algunas restricciones en este programa, basadas en la elegibilidad del cliente. Llámenos para mayor información.

**Lugares de pago autorizados**

Ahora Ud. puede pagar su cuenta en más lugares que nunca, con más de 425 lugares de pago autorizados por la compañía. Para localizar el lugar más cercano a su residencia, llame a nuestro sistema automático de respuesta. Acuérdese de buscar el logotipo de Edison en los letreros colocados en nuestros lugares de pago autorizados.

**C. Un mundo pequeño.** El comercio ya es internacional. Lea el artículo y luego hable con su compañero/a de otros negocios con sucursales en el extranjero. Busquen más información sobre otras compañías internacionales en el Internet y preséntenla en la clase.

MODELO: *Yo sé que hay Costco en Madrid, España y Smart & Final en Tijuana, México. ¡En San José, Costa Rica hay KFC, McDonald's, Domino's Pizza y Burger King!*

## Home Depot y Ace Hardware en Latinoamérica

Dos compañías norteamericanas, Home Depot y Ace Hardware ya se han metido en el mercado latinoamericano. Home Depot, fundada en 1978, abrió su primera tienda en Santiago, Chile con planes de estar en Argentina en 1999. Dicen que quieren aprovechar el *boom* en el área de renovación de casas y piensan comprar su mercancía (*merchandise*) a vendedores regionales.

Ace Hardware, de gran competencia con Home Depot, se ha juntado con Sodimac, S.A. para crear una alianza de mercadeo por toda la América del Sur. Empiezan sus sucursales en Chile, Colombia y Perú. Los ingresos de Sodimac el año pasado fueron de 700 millones de dólares. En los EE. UU. y en otras sesenta naciones en seis continentes Ace Hardware opera 5.100 tiendas. Sus ingresos fueron de doce billones en 1997.

# El presente perfecto de subjuntivo
## (*The present perfect subjunctive*)

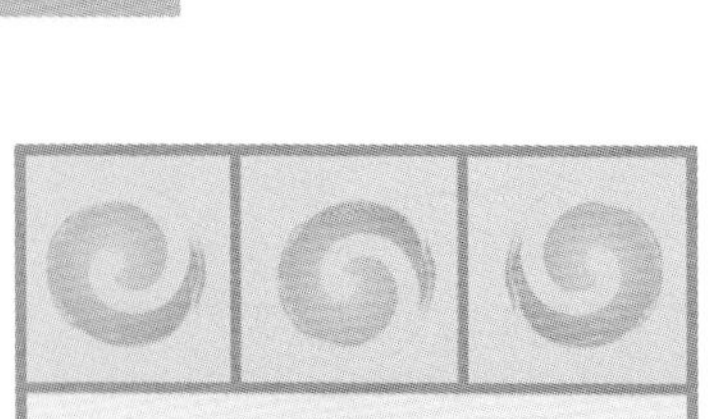

**Para averiguar**

1. What two tenses does the present perfect subjunctive bridge?
2. How do you form the present perfect subjunctive?

**Note.** Remind students that when expressing emotion, doubt, etc., in the present about something that occurred in the past, the present perfect subjunctive is used.

- The present perfect subjunctive is formed by using the subjunctive of the auxiliary verb **haber** and the *past participle*.

| Present Perfect Subjunctive | | | | | | | |
|---|---|---|---|---|---|---|---|
| yo | **haya** | | | nosotros/as | **hayamos** | | |
| tú | **hayas** | + | **hablado** | vosotros/as | **hayáis** | + | **hablado** |
| él, ella, Ud. | **haya** | | | ellos, ellas, Uds | **hayan** | | |

- Use the present perfect subjunctive as a bridge between an observation, judgment or feeling in the *present* about an event in the *past*.

Es bueno que **hayan** llegado. *It's good that you (have) arrived.*

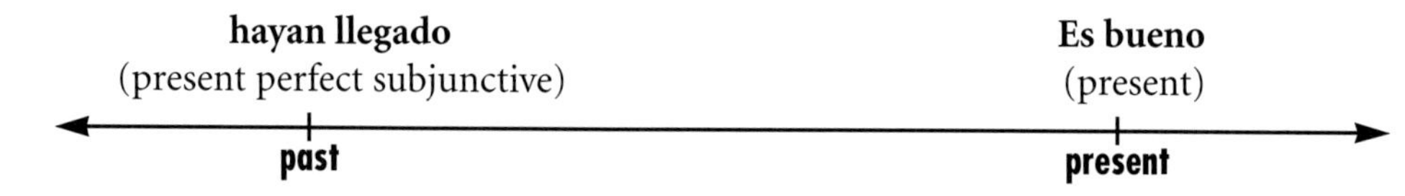


## A lo personal

**A. ¡Desapareció!** You stop by your best friend's house at a time when he/she is usually there, but nobody answers. Say whether or not you think he/she might have done the following things.

MODELO: ir a la iglesia
*Quizás haya ido a la iglesia.*
*Dudo que haya ido a la iglesia.*

1. salir con amigos
2. ir de compras
3. ir a la biblioteca
4. mudarse
5. dormirse en el baño
6. ponerse enfermo/a
7. irse de vacaciones
8. volver a vivir con sus padres

**B. ¿Buenas noticias o malas noticias?** Ask a classmate if he/she has done the following things lately. Then express your feelings about the answer.

MODELO: ¿Has estado enfermo/a recientemente?
E1: *Sí, he estado enfermo/a.*
E2: *Es una lástima que hayas estado enfermo/a.*

1. ¿Has recibido una "A" en la clase de español esta semana?
2. ¿Has comprado una casa nueva este año?
3. ¿Has tenido muchos problemas con tu novio/a o esposo/a?
4. ¿Has roto algo de valor esta semana?

5. ¿Te has gastado todo el dinero antes de terminar el mes?
6. ¿Te has divertido en la clase de español?

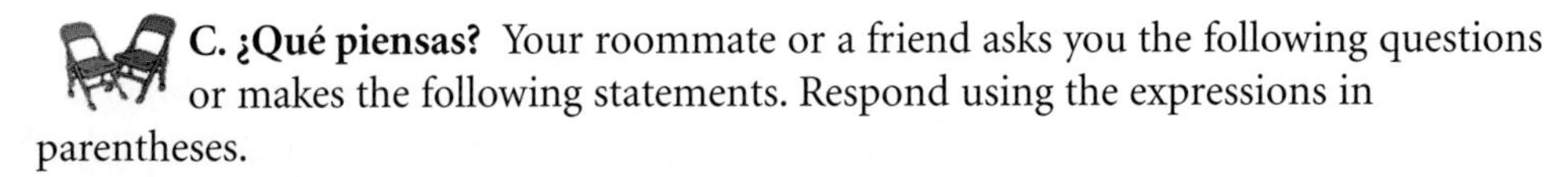

**C. ¿Qué piensas?** Your roommate or a friend asks you the following questions or makes the following statements. Respond using the expressions in parentheses.

MODELO: Saqué una mala nota en el examen de cálculo. (es una lástima que)
*Es una lástima que hayas sacado una mala nota.*

1. ¿Me llamó mi papá hoy? (no creo que)
2. Nuestro equipo perdió el partido. (es una lástima que)
3. ¿Ya llegaron mis amigos? (dudo que)
4. La fiesta fue anoche. (no es cierto)
5. El policía me puso una multa esta mañana. (siento que)
6. ¿Tus amigos fueron al cine? (dudo que)
7. Tu novio/a salió con otro/a anoche. (me molesta que)
8. El profesor nos dijo que no había clase mañana. (quizás)
9. Conocí a dos de tus amigos ayer. (me alegro de que)
10. ¿Cancelaron las clases por el mal tiempo? (es posible que)

**D. La vida es una telenovela.** You have been away on a long trip and when you return you find that the following things have happened. Express your feelings.

MODELO: Su compañero/a de cuarto ha tenido un accidente con el coche de usted.
*Me molesta que haya tenido un accidente con mi coche.*

1. Su compañero/a de cuarto ha reparado el coche de usted.
2. Su novio/a ha encontrado un buen trabajo.
3. Su novio/a se ha casado con otro/a.
4. Su perro ha tenido cachorros (*puppies*).
5. Todas sus plantas se han muerto.
6. A sus padres les ha tocado la lotería.
7. Su profesor/a le ha dado una "A" en el examen final.
8. Su préstamo de estudiante no ha sido aceptado.
9. Su vecino se ha mudado a vivir con Ud.
10. Su mamá se ha ido de safari a Kenia.

Now make a list of things that you hope have or have not happened when you return home today.

MODELO: *Espero que mis hijos hayan limpiado su cuarto.*
*¡Ojalá que no haya habido un incendio!*

**E. Es increíble.** Name one interesting thing you have done and one thing you have not done. Your classmate will say which one he/she believes.

MODELO: E1: *He visto al presidente en persona. He visitado Europa dos veces.*
E2: *No creo que hayas visto al presidente. Creo que has visitado Europa dos veces.*
E1: *Tienes razón. No he visto al presidente.*

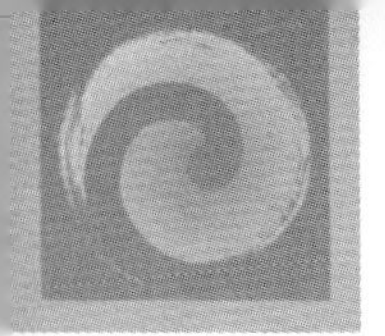

# El pluscuamperfecto
## (*The pluperfect tense*)

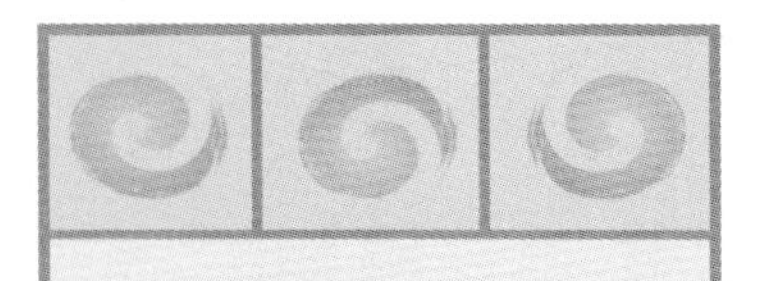

**Para averiguar**

1. What is the English equivalent of había in the pluperfect tense?
2. Does an action in the pluperfect tense take place before or after an action in the preterite?
3. What does the pluperfect tense share with the present perfect tense?

- The pluperfect tense is used to say that you *had done* something by the time something else happened. It is composed of the imperfect tense of the auxiliary verb **haber** and the past participle. Use the same past participle as in the present perfect tense.

| | Auxiliary verb | Past participle |
|---|---|---|
| yo | **había** | hablado |
| tú | **habías** | hablado |
| él, ella, Ud. | **había** | hablado |
| nosotros/as | **habíamos** | hablado |
| vosotros/as | **habíais** | hablado |
| ellos, ellas, Uds. | **habían** | hablado |

- Think of the pluperfect as the past of the past. It is used to talk about a time even earlier than another event in the past.

Ayer cuando yo **llegué** a las siete, ellos ya **habían llegado**. — *Yesterday when I arrived at seven, they had already gotten here.*

**habían llegado** (even earlier past) — **yo llegué** (past event) — (telling the story)

**earlier past** — **past** — **present**

Ayer **conocí** a la arquitecta Vela. Yo **te había hablado** de ella el año pasado. — *Yesterday, I met the architect Vela. I had spoken to you about her last year.*

**te había hablado** (even earlier past) — **conocí** (past event) — (telling the story)

**earlier past** — **past** — **present**

- Note that with compound tenses in Spanish nothing may be inserted between the auxiliary **haber** and the past participle. The auxiliary verb must agree in number with the subject of the sentence and the past participle remains unchanged regardless of the subject.

Nosotras **habíamos** comprado un coche. — *We had bought a car.*
Ella **había** vivido en Madrid. — *She had lived in Madrid.*
Yo **había** estado en tu casa. — *I had been in your house.*
Tú **habías** escrito la carta. — *You had written the letter.*

## A lo personal

**A. ¿Antes de 1999?** Say whether or not you had done the following things before 1999.

MODELO: usar una computadora
*Sí, yo había usado una computadora.*
*No, yo no había usado una computadora.*

1. ir a la escuela primaria
2. estudiar matemáticas
3. comprar un auto
4. romper un espejo
5. ver una película
6. decir una mentira
7. vivir solo/a
8. escribir en español
9. conocer a su profesor/a de español
10. abrir el texto *¡Trato hecho!*

**B. ¿Antes o después?** Everyone had a lot to do today. Tell which activity each of these people had done before doing the other.

MODELO: Mi papá → levantarse/bañarse
*Mi papá se había levantado antes de bañarse.*

1. Mi hermana → ducharse/peinarse
2. Yo → secarme/bañarme
3. Mi mamá → vestirse/salir
4. Mi abuela → preparar el desayuno/lavar los platos
5. Mi hermano → llegar a su clase/hacer su tarea
6. Mi novio/a → llamarme/encontrar un teléfono
7. Mis otros hermanos → romper la ventana/tirar la pelota
8. Mi otra hermana y yo → salir de la casa/abrir la puerta

**C. ¡Se le había olvidado!** Poor Lázaro! He has been so distracted that he has not been paying attention to what needed to be done. Today was a disaster. Tell what he had or had not done to cause each of the following situations.

MODELO: Se le acabó la gasolina.
*No había ido a la gasolinera.*

1. No estuvo preparado para la clase.
2. Se le quedaron los papeles en el escritorio.
3. Se le olvidó la cita con el dentista.
4. Se cayó por la escalera.
5. No tuvo dinero para el almuerzo.
6. Se le perdieron las lentes de contacto.
7. Se le olvidaron las respuestas en el examen.
8. No pudo abrir la puerta de su casa.
9. No recordó el número de teléfono de su amigo.
10. Lo atropelló (*ran over*) un coche al cruzar la calle.

**D. Antes de venir a la universidad.** Make a list of eight things that you had never done before coming to school here. Compare lists with a classmate and decide if the new experience is good or bad.

MODELO: Nunca había comprado libros tan caros.
*Es malo que los libros sean tan caros.*

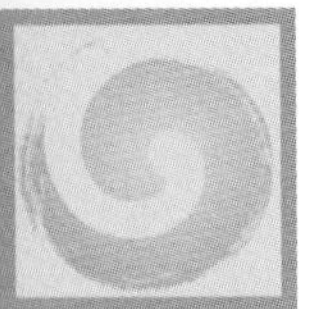
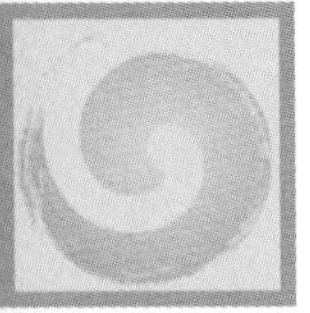

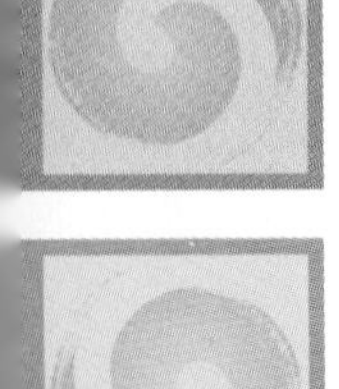

## TEMA 3
### El banco

**Sustantivos**

| | |
|---|---|
| **el/la acreedor/a** | *creditor* |
| **el/la banquero/a** | *banker* |
| **el embargo** | *seizure* |
| **la entrega** | *delivery* |
| **la hipoteca** | *mortgage* |
| **el juicio** | *judgment* |
| **el/la patrocinador/a** | *sponsor* |
| **la planificación** | *planning* |
| **el préstamo** | *loan* |
| **la reparación** | *repair* |
| **el resultado** | *result* |
| **el término** | *term* |
| **el testamento** | *will* |
| **el vecindario** | *neighborhood* |

**Verbos**

| | |
|---|---|
| **aprobar** | *to approve* |
| **descomponerse** | *to break down* |
| **escoger** | *to choose* |
| **inspeccionar** | *to inspect* |

**Adjetivos**

| | |
|---|---|
| **ambulante** | *traveling* |
| **atrasado/a** | *delayed* |
| **cuidado/a** | *cared for* |
| **decidido/a** | *decided* |
| **grave** | *serious* |
| **impreso/a** | *printed* |
| **menor** | *minor* |
| **razonable** | *reasonable* |
| **resuelto/a** | *resolved* |
| **satisfecho/a** | *satisfied* |

**Otras expresiones**

| | |
|---|---|
| **por escrito** | *in writing* |
| **pronto** | *soon* |

## TEMA 4
### Los preparativos

**Sustantivos**

| | |
|---|---|
| **la alfombra** | *carpet* |
| **el/la arquitecto/a** | *architect* |
| **la cerradura** | *lock* |
| **el/la contratista** | *contractor* |
| **la cuota/el plazo** | *installment* |
| **el diseño** | *design* |
| **el hogar** | *home* |
| **el/la inspector/a** | *inspector* |
| **el/la ladrón, ladrona** | *thief* |
| **el plano** | *plan* |
| **la sucursal** | *branch* |
| **la tubería/plomería** | *plumbing* |
| **el techo** | *roof* |
| **la termita** | *termite* |

**Verbos**

| | |
|---|---|
| **asaltar** | *to assault* |
| **dañar** | *to damage* |
| **diseñar** | *to design* |
| **especializarse** | *to specialize* |
| **gastar** | *to spend* |
| **maltratar** | *to mistreat* |
| **modernizar** | *to modernize* |
| **notar** | *to notice* |
| **pintar** | *to paint* |
| **redecorar** | *to redecorate* |
| **resolver (ue)** | *to resolve* |
| **sugerir (ie)** | *to suggest* |

**Adjetivos**

| | |
|---|---|
| **anterior** | *previous* |
| **imprescindible** | *indispensable* |
| **moderno/a** | *modern* |
| **obvio/a** | *obvious* |
| **util** | *useful* |

**Otras expresiones**

| | |
|---|---|
| **probablemente** | *probably* |

# Reunión B

**A escuchar. Los vecinos.** Complete las oraciones con la información que escuche en la conversación.

1. ¿Quién vive en la casa de enfrente?
2. ¿Qué comida les trajo Cristina?
3. ¿Cuándo conocieron Lázaro e Isabel a Harold y a Susana?

**A conversar.** Uno/a de ustedes es el/la director/a de un banco. Un/a cliente/a, su compañero/a, ha cerrado su cuenta corriente (*checking account*) y Ud. quiere saber por qué. Creen una conversación entre los/las dos.

## ¿Lo sabía?

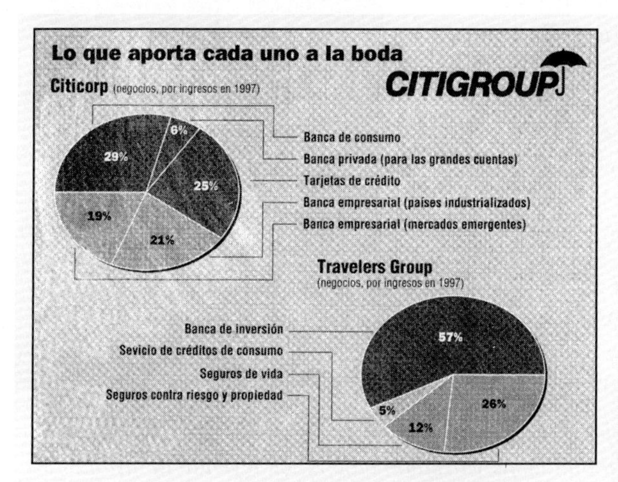


**CITICORP Y TRAVELERS ESTREMECEN AL MUNDO FINANCIERO CON SU ACUERDO DE FUSIÓN**

*Sería la mayor alianza en la historia, valorada en 82.600 millones de dólares.*

Por Michael Siconolfi
Redactor de The Wall Street Journal

El mundo de las finanzas sufrió ayer una gran sacudida luego de enterarse del mayor acuerdo en la historia: el plan de fusión entre Travelers Group Inc. y Citicorp, valorado en ochenta y dos mil seiscientos millones de dólares.

Pero es mucho más que un pacto que creará la mayor compañía de servicios financieros del mundo, con activos que llegan a los 700.000 millones de dólares americanos. El acuerdo también podría marcar el final de la ley que data de la era de la Depresión y que previene la unión entre compañías de seguros, bancos, y otras firmas. De hecho, el convenio se basa en el entendimiento de que el congreso estadounidense abolirá la ley Glass-Steagall en los próximos años. Citigroup, el nombre que adoptará la nueva empresa, ofrecerá banca tradicional, créditos de consumo y tarjetas de crédito (sobre todo mediante la división Citibank de Citicorp), seguros a todo riesgo, de propiedad y de vida (en la división de seguros Travelers), banca de inversión, intermediación financiera y gestión de activos (a través de la división de valores de Travelers Salomon Smith Barney Holdings).

**¿Comprende Ud.?**

1. ¿Por qué es importante la fusión de Citicorp y Travelers?
2. ¿Cuánto es el valor total de este acuerdo?
3. ¿Cuáles son los servicios que ofrecerá Citigroup?
4. ¿Qué parte de los ingresos de Citicorp es de tarjetas de crédito?
5. ¿Cuál es el porcentaje de negocios de seguros de Travelers?

**A buscar.** Busque información en español de préstamos que se ofrecen en los bancos de su ciudad y/o en el Internet. ¿Qué tipos hay? ¿Se puede conseguir un préstamo para comprar una casa? ¿un coche? ¿para renovar su casa? ¿para la educación? Hable con dos compañeros/as de los términos que se ofrecen, incluyendo el interés. ¿Es buena idea pedir un préstamo? ¿Para qué?

**Tapescript for A escuchar. Los vecinos.**

ALBERTO: ¡Bienvenidos! Me llamo Alberto y éstos son Giorgio y Sandra. Somos los tres estudiantes de la casa de enfrente. Les hemos traído unas frutas.
CRISTINA: Soy Cristina, la vecina de la casa de la derecha. Les he cocinado un pollo con macarrones. Están cubiertos con salsa de tomate.
SUSANA: Nosotros somos Harold y Susana. Ya nos habíamos conocido cuando vinieron a inspeccionar la casa. Les cociné unas enchiladas. Ojalá que estén buenas.
LÁZARO: Muchas gracias a todos. Creo que se vive muy tranquilamente en este vecindario. Siento mucho que no hayamos comprado unos refrescos.
ISABEL: ¡Sí, los había comprado ayer, pero no sé dónde están! Lo siento, todo está tan desordenado.
LÁZARO: Harold, ¿habla español?
HAROLD: Un poquito. Susana y yo nos casamos hace tres años y me ha estado enseñando muy pacientemente a hablar español.
ISABEL: Lo habla perfectamente. ¡Bien, Lázaro ha encontrado los refrescos! ¡A comer! Todos estamos muertos de hambre.

**Answers for A escuchar.**
1) *Tres estudiantes.* 2) *Un pollo con macarrones.* 3) *Cuando inspeccionaron la casa.*

# ¡TRATO HECHO!

## Rincón profesional: La casa del futuro

Cierre Ud. los ojos e imagínese una casa futurista. ¿Qué ve Ud.? ¿Una casa en forma de cúpula? ¿Una caverna subterránea como la residencia ideada por los diseñadores de *La Guerra de las Galaxias?* ¿O simplemente un domicilio que en realidad es una especie de platillo volante?

Según los arquitectos que empiezan a formular las casas del nuevo milenio, los cambios en el diseño de nuestras residencias no serán tan dramáticos. En realidad, la casa del nuevo milenio visualmente, se parece mucho a las casas en que vivimos hoy. Lo que sí va a cambiar es la "inteligencia" de la casa, no la apariencia.

—¿Qué quiere decir—Ud. se estará preguntando—una casa inteligente? Usemos otra vez la imaginación.

*Cierre los ojos. Piense en un día en la playa. Ud. y sus seres queridos están tomando limonada, descansando bajo el sol, leyendo la última novela de su*

*autor favorito o simplemente mirando pasar el mundo. Mientras tanto, allí en la casa, una computadora está cortando el césped, lavando la ropa y el piso y comprando comida del supermercado.*

Dicen los expertos del diseño futurista, que la posibilidad de tener una casa "inteligente" no es tan remota. Estas casas existen actualmente y pronto vendrá el momento en que veremos casas aún más inteligentes. Con las computadoras que son cada vez más comunes en nuestras casas, imagine que un día su buscapersonas le transmita una carta eléctronica de parte de su refrigerador para recordarle que necesita comprar más leche.

—Perdone Ud. mientras dejo un mensaje en el "busca" para mi nueva casa:

"Querida casa tan inteligente, te pido que encuentres la manera de pagar tu hipoteca. Yo voy al club para jugar un partido de golf."

**¿Comprende Ud?**

1. Describa las casas futuristas que la mayor parte de la gente se imagina.
2. ¿Cree que va a haber una gran diferencia entre la apariencia de nuestras casas de hoy en día y la apariencia de las casas del futuro?
3. En el ejemplo presentado anteriormente, ¿qué hace la "casa inteligente" mientras la familia está en la playa?
4. ¿Qué mensaje le deja el dueño a la casa en su "bíper"?

**A escuchar.** **Socorro va al banco.** Escuche la conversación entre Socorro y un empleado del banco y conteste las preguntas según lo que escuche.

**¿Comprende Ud.?**

1. ¿Para qué ha pedido un préstamo Socorro?
2. ¿Qué papeles ha traído Socorro para pedir el préstamo?
3. ¿Trabaja ahora?
4. ¿Cuánto dinero necesita para iniciar su negocio?

**Tapescript for A escuchar. Socorro va al banco.**
En el banco, Socorro pide un préstamo para iniciar su propio negocio
SR. TAPIA: Bien, ha traído la solicitud que le había pedido. Su jefe, que la conoce desde hace diez años, me ha dado muy buenas referencias suyas.
SOCORRO: Él no quiere que me vaya y me ofreció un aumento de sueldo. En su negocio se necesitan personas que hablen correctamente español e inglés.
SR. TAPIA: Pero usted está resuelta a trabajar independientemente, ¿verdad?
SOCORRO: Sí, quiero iniciar una agencia de publicidad. ¿Cree usted que tenga problemas para conseguir el préstamo?
SR. TAPIA: No, ya hemos recibido el informe de su crédito y es excelente. Su préstamo ya está aprobado.
SOCORRO: Gracias, pienso que es muy importante que las cuentas se paguen puntualmente. Necesito que me preste aproximadamente 30.000 dólares. ¿Qué interés cobra por esa cantidad?
SR. TAPIA: El 19 por ciento al año. Le vamos a dar una chequera y solamente le cobramos interés sobre la cantidad que gaste.
SOCORRO: Espero que sea una buena idea tener mi propio negocio.

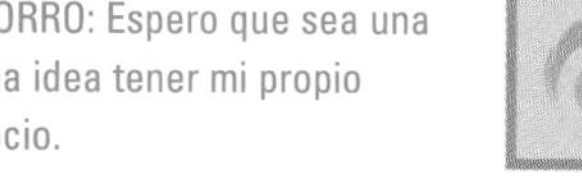

**Answers for A escuchar.**
1) *Para abrir su propio negocio.* 2) *La solicitud y referencias.* 3) *Sí.* 4) *30.000 dólares.*

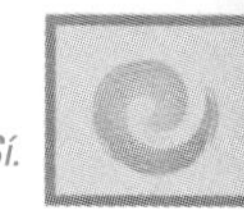

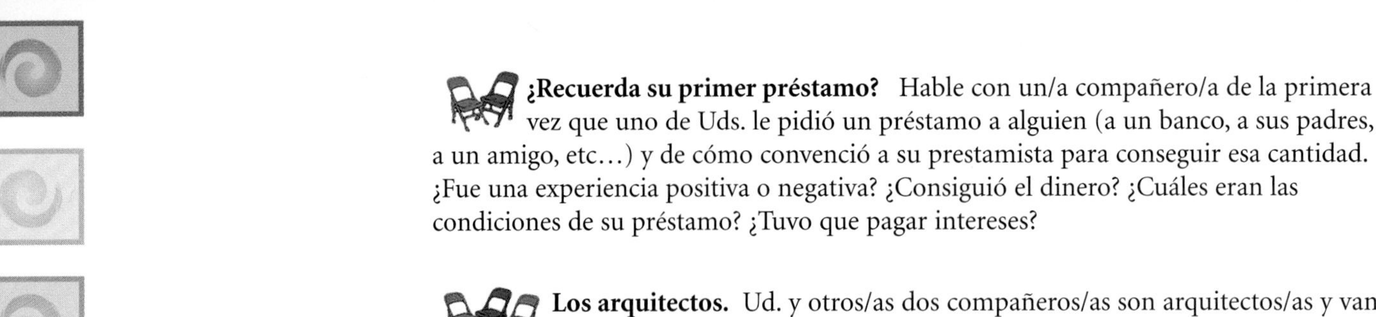

**¿Recuerda su primer préstamo?** Hable con un/a compañero/a de la primera vez que uno de Uds. le pidió un préstamo a alguien (a un banco, a sus padres, a un amigo, etc...) y de cómo convenció a su prestamista para conseguir esa cantidad. ¿Fue una experiencia positiva o negativa? ¿Consiguió el dinero? ¿Cuáles eran las condiciones de su préstamo? ¿Tuvo que pagar intereses?

**Los arquitectos.** Ud. y otros/as dos compañeros/as son arquitectos/as y van a diseñar una casa futurista. Decidan qué tipo de diseño quieren crear y usen la imaginación para crear la "casa más inteligente" que sea posible. Cuando tengan el diseño deben presentárselo a otro grupo de estudiantes y pedirles un préstamo para financiar la construcción. ¡A ver si se lo dan!

## A leer

When you read a text in Spanish, it is a good idea to scan it for expressions that are similar in English and in Spanish. When you find them, you may underline them, and that would make it easier for you to understand the general idea behind it.

**Antes de leer.** Before reading *¡Hablemos de negocios!*, try to guess the meaning of the following phrases:

1. Oportunidades para la mujer latina
2. Habilidad para organizar
3. El número está creciendo rápidamente
4. El porcentaje de negocios
5. La elección de candidatas hispanas
6. Ha tenido un impacto positivo
7. Un cambio gradual
8. Los roles sexuales

ALGUNAS DE LAS MEJORES COMPAÑÍAS PARA MUJERES HISPANAS

**Whirlpool Corporation**
Gloria Zamora
General Director of Sales, LASSCO/SASCO (Miami)

**US West**
Remedios Díaz-Oliver
Member, Board of Directors

**United Parcel Service**
Jovita Carranza
District Manager

**Trans World Airlines**
Teresa M. Preciado
Manager-Budget/Contracts, Hotel Administration

**Texas Instruments**
Billie Meador
Manager, State Government Relations

**Student Loan Mortgage Corporation (Sallie Mae)**
Regina Montoya
Member, Board of Directors

**Procter & Gamble**
Martha Feller
Associate Director, Product Development

**Pitney Bowes**
Linda Alvarado
Member, Board of Directors

**NYNEX**
Gail Z. Cardona
Director of Corporate Safety

**New York Life**
Barbara Senatore
Associate Medical Director

**NBD Bancorp.**
María Elena Gisser
Vice President, Commercial Lending

**MTV Latino**
Antoinette Marie Zel
Vice President, Law, Business Affairs & New Business Development

## ¡Hablemos de negocios![1]

En las últimas décadas han habido más oportunidades para que la mujer latina se eduque o inicie su propio negocio. Esto ha generado cambios muy importantes en su vida. Antes se creía que la mujer debía manejar las cosas desde atrás, a la sombra; ahora sale a la luz, para ponerse al frente de su propio negocio. Su tenacidad, su energía, su habilidad para organizar y dirigir han sido cualidades importantes en el mundo de los negocios.

A pesar de que las latinas solamente son dueñas del 5 por ciento de todos los negocios que tienen las mujeres, el número está creciendo más rápidamente que en cualquier otra categoría. Entre 1987 y 1996 el porcentaje de negocios pertenecientes a mujeres latinas aumentó en un 206 por ciento, comparado con un aumento del 47 por ciento en todos los negocios. El crecimiento más rápido fue en áreas en donde típicamente no trabaja la mujer latina: 428 por ciento en construcción, 389 por ciento en agricultura y 338 por ciento en ventas al por mayor.[2]

Para las mujeres de negocios latinas ha sido muy importante el nombramiento de una mujer al frente de la Administración de Pequeños Negocios: Aída Álvarez, que es la primera mujer latina en el Gabinete Presidencial. La participación de la mujer hispana en la política también ha aumentado: la elección de candidatas hispanas ha aumentado en un 400 por ciento desde 1984.

El aumento del número de mujeres hispanas en la política y en los negocios ha tenido un impacto positivo en las nuevas generaciones. Entre 1973 y 1996, el porcentaje de mujeres latinas que no terminaron la educación secundaria bajó del 55 por ciento al 33 por ciento y el número de hispanas con títulos universitarios aumentó del 4 por ciento al 10 por ciento[3].

La tendencia de la mujer latina a continuar su educación y a tener su propio negocio, refleja un cambio gradual en la cultura latina. Puede haber muchas causas: el aumento de la tasa de divorcio, el espíritu emprendedor de las emigrantes, los cambios en los roles sexuales y la transformación de los valores culturales. Las estadísticas proyectan que en los próximos diez años va a haber un progreso considerable para la mujer latina.

[1]La mayoría de las ideas están tomadas del artículo de Lee Romney, "Latinas Get Down to Business," *L.A. Times,* Friday, Nov. 13, 1998.
[2]Romney cita estas estadísticas de National Foundation for Women Business Owners.
[3]Anthony P. Carnevale de Educational Testing Service proporcionó estos datos para Romney.

**¿Comprende Ud.?** Conteste las preguntas siguientes según la lectura.

1. Mencione dos cambios recientes en las oportunidades de la mujer latina en los negocios.
2. ¿Qué consecuencias positivas pueden tener estos cambios?
3. ¿Cuáles son algunas de las causas que han producido este cambio general?

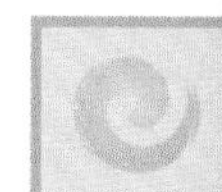

## A escribir

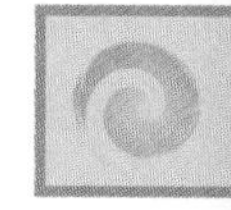

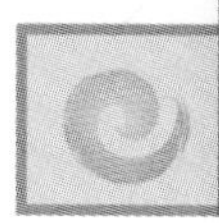

¿Conoce a alguna mujer hispana que tenga su negocio propio? ¿Qué tipo de negocio es? ¿Piensa que el número de negocios de latinas va a aumentar en el siglo XXI? ¿Por qué? ¿Qué piensa de la participación de la mujer en general, en terrenos que han estado reservados para los hombres? ¿Cree que va a haber consecuencias positivas y negativas a raíz de este cambio o solamente positivas? Explique sus razones por escrito.

# 11 Los medios de comunicación

LECCIÓN ONCE

CHECK OUT THE *¡TRATO HECHO!* WEBSITE AND CD-ROM FOR ACTIVITIES, GAMES, SELF-TESTS, AND MUCH MORE!

TEMA 1

## La publicidad

- La comunicación de hoy
- Las carreras en comunicación
- El futuro
- El futuro: probabilidad y concesión

TEMA 2

## Un reportaje

- La comunicación instantánea
- Lo moderno
- El subjuntivo en cláusulas adverbiales
- Más sobre el subjuntivo en cláusulas adverbiales

TEMA 3

## Una entrevista

- La tecnología
- El mundo electrónico
- El imperfecto del subjuntivo
- Más práctica con el imperfecto del subjuntivo

TEMA 4

## Nuevas vías de comunicación

- El nuevo milenio
- La Supercarretera de información
- El condicional
- Las cláusulas con *si*

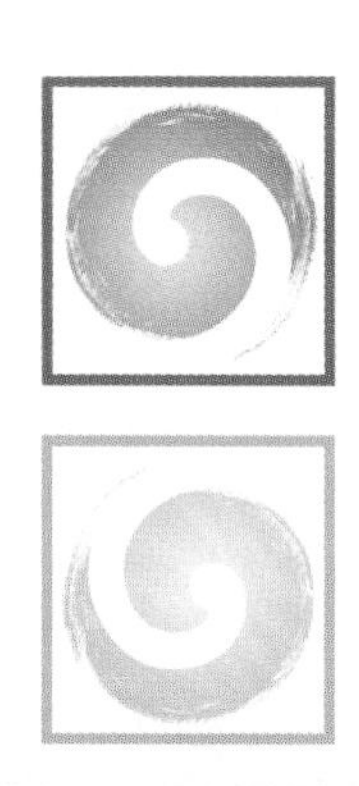

# ¡TRATO HECHO!

- Rincón profesional: El euro
- A escuchar
- El buzón de Dña. Rosa
- A leer
- A escribir

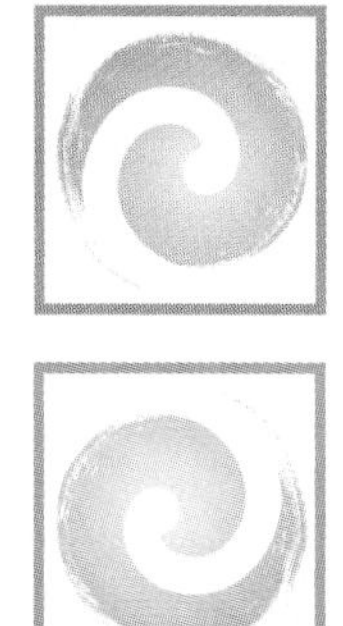

## La comunicación de hoy

La Opinión

Final Fundado en 1926 • Año 65, Número 350 Los Angeles, California • Jueves 31 de agosto de 1995 35¢

DEPORTES

Pospuesto el campeonato salvadoreño

Diferencias entre clubes y Federación por la competencia

Concejo condena también declaraciones de Fuhrman

☐ Pide a Williams tomar medidas contra el descrédito público

ESTATAL

No quieren aguacates

☐ Estados Unidos teme a competencia mexicana, 8A

Padres de joven muerto por policía presentan una demanda federal

☐ Aducen uso de fuerza excesiva y violación de los derechos civiles

### ¿Y ahora qué?

*¿Qué hará Isabel en el futuro…?*

Expansion. Discuss NAFTA and the goal of expanding the free trade agreement to all of Latin America. If possible, bring in news articles on meetings of government leaders to bring closer a hemispheric accord.

ANA: Isabel, ¿qué harás ahora que terminaste tu carrera y te casaste?

ISABEL: Pues buscaré trabajo, pero no en el campo de los negocios internacionales porque no quiero viajar mucho. Me gusta mucho California y quiero quedarme aquí.

ANA: Con el Tratado de Libre Comercio supongo que habrá varios campos en donde se necesiten especialistas que sean bilingües.

ISABEL: Sí, tengo ganas de trabajar en algo que me guste, como en los medios de comunicación. En el sur de California hay un diario que se publica en español y varias estaciones de radio y televisión.

ANA: Ahora recuerdo, tengo un cliente que trabaja para el Canal 6. Él siempre dice que necesitan personas que hablen y escriban bien inglés y español.

ISABEL: Ana, ¿me harás el favor de ponerme en contacto con él?

**A. ¿Comprende Ud.?** Conteste las siguientes preguntas según el diálogo.

1. ¿Qué planes tiene Isabel?
2. ¿Por qué no piensa trabajar ella en el campo de negocios internacionales?
3. ¿Qué es el Tratado de Libre Comercio?
4. ¿En qué tiene interés Isabel?

**Answers for A.** 1) *Buscar trabajo.* 2) *No quiere viajar mucho.* 3) *Un acuerdo de comercio con los EE. UU., Canadá y México.* 4) *En los medios de comunicación.*

**B. Mis planes para el futuro.** Termine cada oración según sus deseos para el futuro y póngalas en orden lógico.

Ganaré ____________ de dólares e invertiré mi dinero en ________________.
Conseguiré un buen trabajo con ____________. Mi posición será ____________.
Compraré la casa de mis sueños en ______________. Tendrá ______________.
Me graduaré de la universidad en ____________ con un título de ___________.
Después de jubilarme, pasaré los días en la playa de ____________ o quizás en ___________.
Viajaré por todo el mundo con ____________, especialmente por ____________.

**C. ¿Servicio celular prepagado o no?** Lea la propaganda de *AirTouch*. Luego, con dos compañeros, hablen de las (des)ventajas de pagar sus llamadas celulares antes de hacerlas. ¿Qué tipo de servicio prefieren Uds.? ¿Por qué? ¿Todos usan un teléfono celular? ¿Cuánto pagan mensualmente? ¿Por cuántos minutos hablan? ¿Es para uso personal o profesional?

Es muy fácil

- Las tarjetas pre-pagadas están disponibles en denominaciones de $30. Puede comprar una tarjeta nueva para agregar dinero a su cuenta.
- Un cargo de $30 (incluyendo impuestos) será cobrado por su representante de ventas de AirTouch, quien le dará un número móvil que será programado en su teléfono celular.
- El costo de cada llamada que haga o reciba será deducido de su cuenta, basado en los precios explicados en este folleto. (Los precios están sujetos a cambios).
- Los recordatorios de su balance de cuenta al principio de cada llamada, le informarán cuantos minutos le quedan en su tarjeta. Al terminar su llamada, le informarán de cuánto dinero le queda en su cuenta.

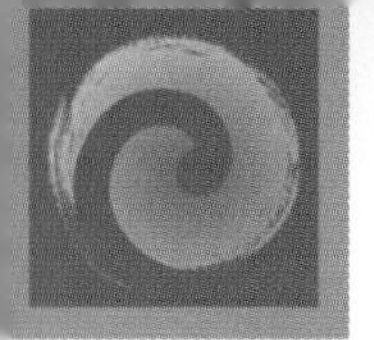

# Las carreras en comunicación

## La entrevista en el Canal 6

*Isabel se entrevista con el jefe de personal del Canal 6....*

ISABEL: No sé si Ana le ha dicho que me interesa trabajar en los medios de comunicación.

SR. BACATÁ: Sí, tenemos un puesto en el departamento de publicidad. A pesar de que transmitimos en inglés, un gran porcentaje de nuestra audiencia es hispano y por eso necesitamos personal bilingüe.

ISABEL: No sé mucho de mercadotecnia. Me pregunto si habrá algún otro puesto.

SR. BACATÁ: En un mes, tendremos un puesto en el departamento de noticias. Los productores del noticiero buscan a alguien que sea bilingüe.

ISABEL: ¿Qué haré si consigo este puesto con ellos?

SR. BACATÁ: Recibirá los cables de las agencias de noticias hispanas, analizará su contenido y seleccionará los más importantes. Después los traducirá y escribirá un resumen para las noticias.

ISABEL: Me parece muy interesante y podré hacerlo bien porque me especialicé en Latinoamérica. Tomé varios cursos sobre su política y cultura.

SR. BACATÁ: Nos encantará tenerla. Aquí tiene una solicitud. La traerá lo más pronto posible, ¿verdad?

**A. ¿Comprende Ud.?** Conteste las siguientes preguntas según el diálogo.

1. ¿Por qué se necesita personal bilingüe?
2. ¿Cuál es el puesto que tendrán en un mes?
3. ¿Qué hará Isabel en ese departamento?
4. ¿Qué le da el Sr. Bacatá a Isabel?

**Answers for A.** 1) *Un porcentaje de la audencia es hispano.* 2) *Un puesto en el departamento de noticias.* 3) *Recibirá los cables de las agencias hispanas, analizará su contenido, seleccionará los más importantes, los traducirá y escribirá un resumen.* 4) *Una solicitud.*

**B. Que será, será.** Con tanto hablar del futuro, no nos olvidemos de la riqueza del pasado. Hay muchos proverbios populares que nos ofrecen una moraleja. Con un/a compañero/a, piensen en un dicho parecido en inglés. ¡OJO! Muchas veces hay que cambiar las palabras. Después, escriban la moraleja.

MODELO: Más vale pájaro en mano que cien volando.
*A bird in hand is worth two in the bush.*
*Lesson: Stick with a sure thing.*

1. Quien supo empezar bien sabrá acabar.
2. Entre padres y hermanos no metas las manos.
3. Quien te engañó, te engañará (*deceive*), y si repite, bien te estará.
4. Quien hoy llora, mañana canta.
5. En la casa del pobre todos pelean sin saber por qué, y es porque no tienen de qué comer.
6. Lo que se aprende en la cuna siempre dura.
7. Una onza de práctica vale una libra de gramática.
8. Quien da primero da dos veces.

**C. ¿Una carrera en publicidad?** El Sr. Lizaur, dueño de la agencia de publicidad Medialuna en Pamplona, España, le ofrece un puesto de diseñador/a de propaganda para varios clientes suyos. Durante la entrevista, Ud. quiere demostrarle su capacidad creativa. Diseñe publicidad para dos clientes posibles—una compañía de ropa deportiva y una estación de radio de música rock. Después, cambie de papel (*roles*) con su compañero/a.

MODELO: E1: *Sr./Srta./Sra., ¿me puede enseñar ejemplos de su trabajo?*
E2: *Con mucho gusto, Sr. Lizaur. Aquí tengo un programa que he preparado para la venta de ropa deportiva.*

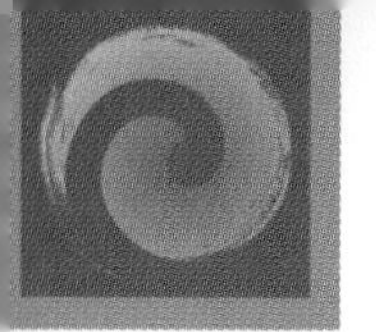

# El futuro
## (*The future tense*)

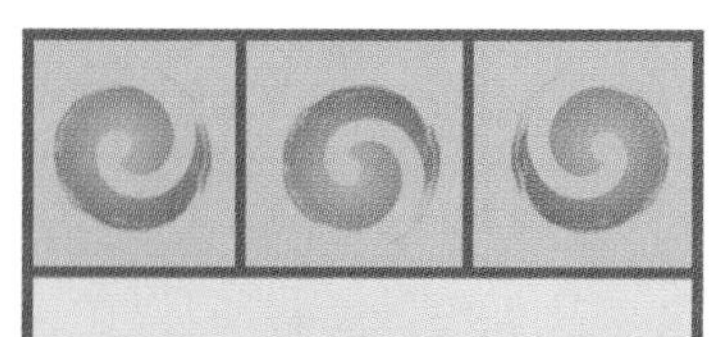

**Para averiguar**

1. What is the future tense stem for most verbs in Spanish? What is a good way to remember the future tense endings?
2. Which ten verbs have irregular future tense stems?

- You have learned to say what someone *is going to do* using **ir a** + *infinitive.* Use the future tense to say what someone *will do.* The stem of the future tense for most verbs is the same as the infinitive. There is a written accent on all of the endings, except the **nosotros** form.

| | **hablar** | **comer** | **vivir** |
|---|---|---|---|
| yo | hablar**é** | comer**é** | vivir**é** |
| tú | hablar**ás** | comer**ás** | vivir**ás** |
| él, ella, Ud. | hablar**á** | comer**á** | vivir**á** |
| nosotros/as | hablar**emos** | comer**emos** | vivir**emos** |
| vosotros/as | hablar**éis** | comer**éis** | vivir**éis** |
| ellos, ellas, Uds. | hablar**án** | comer**án** | vivir**án** |

- The following verbs have irregular stems in the future:

| **Infinitive** | **Stem** | **Future** |
|---|---|---|
| decir | **dir-** | dir**é**, dir**ás**,... |
| querer | **querr-** | querr**é**, querr**ás**,... |
| haber | **habr-** | habr**é**, habr**ás**,... |
| saber | **sabr-** | sabr**é**, sabr**ás**,... |
| hacer | **har-** | har**é**, har**ás**,... |
| salir | **saldr-** | saldr**é**, saldr**ás**,... |
| poder | **podr-** | podr**é**, podr**ás**,... |
| tener | **tendr-** | tendr**é**, tendr**ás**,... |
| poner | **pondr-** | pondr**é**, pondr**ás**,... |
| venir | **vendr-** | vendr**é**, vendr**ás**,... |

—¿Qué decisiones vas a tomar para el próximo año? ¿Qué **harás** para vivir mejor?
*What resolutions are you going to make for next year? What will you do to live better?*

—No **comeré** azúcar, no **tomaré** alcohol y **trabajaré** más.
*I won't eat sugar, I won't drink alcohol and I'll work more.*

—No **podrás** mantener esas decisiones más de una semana.
*You won't be able to keep those resolutions more than a week.*

—**Haré** todo lo que sea necesario.
*I will do whatever it takes.*

—Pues yo **tendré** A's en todas mis clases.
*I will have A's in all my classes.*

## A lo personal

**A. Resoluciones.** A friend is making resolutions of how he will improve his life this year. Does he say that he will do the following things more or that he will do them less?

MODELO: hacer ejercicio
*Haré más ejercicio.*

1. tomar alcohol
2. comer grasa
3. trabajar
4. ayudar a mi familia
5. ser egoísta
6. salir hasta tarde entre semana
7. mirar la televisión
8. estudiar español
9. viajar más
10. conocer nuevas culturas

Now make a list of four resolutions for yourself for the next few months.

**B. Predicciones.** Predict whether or not the indicated people will do the indicated activity during the next six months.

MODELO: (mi novio/a y yo) casarnos
*Sí, nos casaremos.* o *No, no nos casaremos.*

1. (yo) publicar un libro
2. (mi padre) comprar un coche
3. (mi hermana) tener un programa de radio o televisión
4. (yo) empezar un nuevo trabajo
5. (mi compañero/a de cuarto) mudarse a México
6. (mis padres y yo) hacer un viaje juntos
7. (mi profesor/a de español) darme una A
8. (mi madre) viajar por Europa
9. (mi perro) dormir todo el día
10. (mi jefe/a) darme un aumento (*raise*) de sueldo.

**C. En el futuro.** Think about your future dream career and make a list of ten activities you will do on the job. If you haven't chosen a profession, imagine your life as a teacher.

MODELO: *Profesión: Estrella de rock*
*1. Cantaré muchas canciones.*
*2. Escribiré nuevas canciones.*
*3. Practicaré con mi grupo.*

**D. Su pareja.** Your partner/spouse will keep things running at home so that your career will thrive. Make a list of ten activities that your spouse will do to help you.

MODELO: *Mi pareja limpiará la casa.*

**E. Buscando trabajo.** It is time to look for a new job. With a partner, make a list of eight steps you will take to prepare to job-hunt.

MODELO: *Compraré el periódico.*

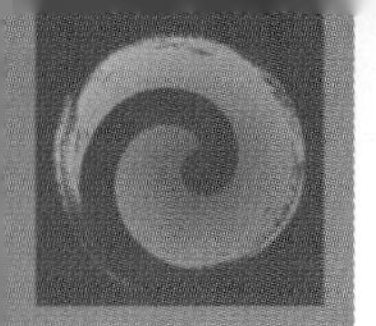

# El futuro: probabilidad y concesión
## (*The future to express probability and concession*)

- The future tense can be used to express probability in Spanish. When used to express probability, the future is translated using a variety of words in English: *probably, could, might, must, wonder, think,* and *bet* are some examples.

| | |
|---|---|
| —¿Dónde **estarán** los demás? | *Where might the others be?* |
| —**Estarán** perdidos. | *They are probably lost.* |
| —Me imagino que **llegarán** pronto. | *I guess that they will arrive soon.* |
| —¿**Habrán** tenido un accidente? | *Could they have had an accident?* |
| —¿Qué **estará** haciendo José? | *What do you think José is doing?* |
| —**Estará** estudiando. | *I bet he's studying.* |

- The future tense can also be used to express a concession. In this case it is usually translated into English using the words *may* and *might*.

| | |
|---|---|
| —Tú **serás** la mayor pero tu hermana es más alta. | *You may (might) be the oldest, but your sister is taller.* |
| —**Estará** nublado, pero hace calor. | *It may be cloudy, but it's hot.* |

## A lo personal

**A. ¿Qué estarán haciendo?** Based on the information given, say what the following people are probably doing.

MODELO: Carmen está en la biblioteca.
*Estará estudiando.*

1. Jorge está en la cocina.
2. Ellos están en el aeropuerto.
3. Los padres de Daniela vienen a visitarla esta noche.
4. Luisa va a correr en un maratón mañana.
5. Las chicas están en la oficina de correos.
6. Patricio está en el salón de clase.
7. Nuria va a salir a bailar.
8. Gregorio tiene una entrevista mañana.
9. Mi novio/a está en el centro comercial.
10. Mi jefe está en la cafetería.

**B. Algún día.** Make a list of the things you will probably do and how you will probably feel on the following occasions.

MODELO: el día del examen final
*Estudiaré, vendré a clase, llegaré temprano, estaré un poco nervioso/a, saldré con mis amigos después del examen…*

1. el día de su graduación
2. durante las próximas vacaciones
3. el 31 de diciembre
4. antes de acostarse esta noche
5. el último día de clase de español
6. el día de una entrevista importante de trabajo

**C. Entrevista.** Interview your classmate about his/her views of the future.

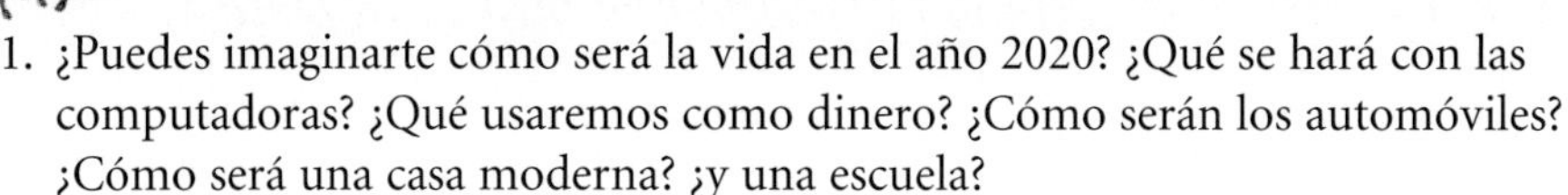

1. ¿Puedes imaginarte cómo será la vida en el año 2020? ¿Qué se hará con las computadoras? ¿Qué usaremos como dinero? ¿Cómo serán los automóviles? ¿Cómo será una casa moderna? ¿y una escuela?
2. Dentro de veinticinco años, ¿qué pasará con los problemas sociales como la violencia y la delincuencia? ¿Habrá curas para alguna de las enfermedades de hoy? ¿Para cuáles?
3. ¿Qué pasará con nuestro planeta en veinticinco años?
4. ¿Crees que algún día podremos viajar a otros planetas? ¿Querrás viajar al espacio? ¿Por qué?

**D. La mejor propaganda.** Three of you have been assigned to design an ad campaign for TELECAB, a company offering cable television in your area. GTE is the strongest competitor of TELECAB. Read the publicity from GTE and plan your counterattack, mentioning what services you will offer clients so that they will select TELECAB over GTE for their cable needs.

## GTE americast™

**Le Ofrece Una Programación Más Innovadora, Recepción Superior, Excepcional Confiabilidad y Servicios Exclusivos.**

GTE **americast** televisión por cable le ofrece una amplia variedad de opciones para la total satisfacción de su familia.

El servicio Básico **americast** localcast™ le ofrece acceso a su comunidad y Superstations.

Más de 60 canales **americast** premiercast™ le dan una gran variedad de más opciones incluyendo The Disney Channel sin costo extra.

GTE **americast** le ofrece una imagen súper clara en su televisor y una calidad en el sonido fabulosa que es solamente posible con la tecnología de fibra óptica.

GTE le revisa su sistema de cable constantemente, le revisan la señal de dos a tres veces por segundo para que usted no reciba interrupciones en el servicio.

**Disfrute la Conveniencia de Nuestro Sistema StarSight Teleguía Programada Electrónicamente y un Centro de Control de Vídeo con Control Remoto.**

Con StarSight usted puede grabar programas en su videograbadora con sólo el toque de un botón y ordenar programas y eventos de pay-per-view (eventos de pagar-por-ver) sin tener que hacer ni una llamada telefónica.

Los televidentes de GTE americast obtienen todo el uso y el beneficio del centro de control de video y el uso del control remoto universal sin cargo extra.

Descubra la forma interactiva de su televisor con GTE mainStreet™ donde usted puede jugar, ganar premios, hacer compras, ver precios de la bolsa de valores o planear las vacaciones familiares - más de 80 servicios interactivos.

Además, futuros servicios digitales le abrirán un mundo de oportunidades incluyendo una gran variedad de canales y una excelente calidad en la imagen.

**It's for you!**



### Precios
(El precio final incluirá impuestos)

**Básico**

**Localcast (sólo) = $10.95**
- 27 canales
- una guía de programación impresa

**Básico Extendido**

**Localcast + Premiercast = $26.95**
- 64 canales con Fox Sport West 2, Disney
- incluye uno de nuestros convertidores con un control remoto universal
- guía electrónica de programación en la pantalla
- acceso a peleas y películas nuevas
- una guía de programación impresa

**Canales Premier**

| | |
|---|---|
| HBO 1 HBO 2 | $10.95 |
| Cinemax 1 & Cinemax 2 | $10.95 |
| Showtime + Sundance + TMC + Flix | $10.95 |
| Starz & Encore | $ 7.95 |

**mainStreet™**

**mainStreet (sólo)** **$7.95**
- 80 actividades interactivas, ¡Juegos, Niños, Ahora!, Finanzas, Ir de compras, Noticias, Inteligencia
- No compre software. El sistema es autosuficiente y está listo para usarse.
- Tenemos un sistema seguro. Todas las actividades son apropiadas para toda la familia.

**Haga Sus Propias Combinaciones de Canales Premier y Ahorre**

| | |
|---|---|
| **Dos paquetes de películas** (4 a 6 canales) | $17.95 |
| **Tres paquetes de películas** (6 a 8 canales) | $22.95 |
| **Cuatro paquetes de películas** (10 canales) | $25.95 |
| **MainStreet** (con un paquete premier) | $ 3.95 |
| **MainStreet** (con dos o más paquetes) | $ 1.95 |

Reprinted with permission of Corporate Media Partners d/b/a americast.

# TEMA 2 Un reportaje

## La comunicación instantánea

### El primer día de trabajo

*Isabel llega a su casa después de su primer día de trabajo....*

ISABEL: ¡Ay, Lázaro! Hoy fue mi primer día en el Canal 6. Ojalá que todo salga bien.
LÁZARO: Todo va a salir bien. No quiero que te preocupes.
ISABEL: Me preocupa hacer las cosas mal.
LÁZARO: No creo que las hagas mal. Tú eres muy inteligente. No estés nerviosa.
ISABEL: No estoy nerviosa, pero quiero que entiendas que ésta es una oportunidad muy buena para mí.
LÁZARO: Lo entiendo perfectamente, mi amor. Estás en el período de prueba. Espera a que ellos te entrenen bien.
ISABEL: ¿Qué pasará si me entrenan y no lo hago bien?
LÁZARO: No creo que eso pase. Lo harás muy bien.

**Answers for A.** 1) *Fue su primer día de trabajo.* 2) *No quiere hacer las cosas mal.* 3) *No cree que las haga mal.* 4) *Es muy buena.*

**A. ¿Comprende Ud.?** Conteste las siguientes preguntas según el diálogo.

1. ¿Qué le pasó a Isabel hoy?
2. ¿Por qué está preocupada?
3. ¿Cuál es la opinión de Lázaro?
4. ¿Qué le parece a Isabel esta oportunidad?

**B. ¿Necesita un buscapersonas?** Su amigo/a (su compañero/a) acaba de enseñarle su nuevo buscapersonas—¡puede recibir mensajes también! Apunte tres razones por las cuales el buscapersonas es útil, y algunos de sus inconvenientes. Comparta su lista con la de su compañero/a.

**Expansion for B.** Mention that the word for beeper in Spanish is *buscapersonas,* but that Spanglish has caused *bíper* to be used also!

MODELO: E1: *Con mi buscapersonas, mis hijos pueden contactarme (reach me) dondequiera que esté.*
E2: *Mi profesora no quiere que lo traiga para no interrumpir la clase.*

**C. Las necesidades básicas.** Un brindis (*toast*) famoso en español es: *Salud, pesetas, amor y tiempo para gozarlos.* Pacific Bell declara que debemos decir: *Salud, dinero, amor y... TELÉFONO.* La competencia es fuerte en el mundo de la comunicación. Busque propaganda de otras compañías para comparar sus precios en cuanto al número de minutos, servicio de larga distancia, modelo de teléfono, precio mensual, período del contrato, etc.... Con dos compañeros, discutan la mejor oferta.

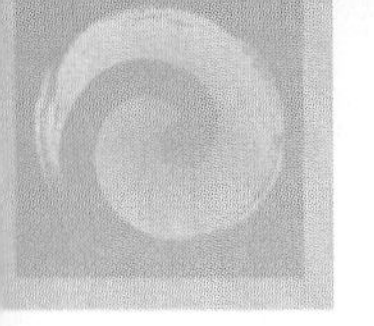

# ABC Lo moderno

## Recaudando fondos

*Lázaro habla con sus estudiantes....*

LÁZARO: Es muy importante que haya libertad de prensa. Todos tenemos derecho a la libre expresión.

JOSÉ: ¿Los niños también?

LÁZARO: Claro, aunque no sean adultos y no voten, tienen derecho a expresarse libremente.

JOSÉ: Bueno, lo que yo quiero es que tengamos una buena educación. Pero nuestra escuela necesita modernizar su equipo. Por ejemplo, nos faltan computadoras.

LÁZARO: Es verdad, pero el distrito escolar no tiene fondos. Niños, ¿qué podemos hacer para modernizar nuestra escuela?

FABIOLA: Usted siempre ha dicho que usemos los medios de comunicación para lograr cosas positivas. Podemos escribir una carta al editor del periódico para que los demás lo sepan y nos ayuden lo más pronto posible.

JEANNE: Para que nos escuchen atentamente, podemos pedir firmas a los niños, a los maestros y a los padres.

RAÚL: Sí, también podemos escribir a las compañías que fabrican y venden computadoras.

LÁZARO: Han tenido una idea excelente. Espero que empiecen inmediatamente.

**Answers for A.** 1) *Que haya libertad de prensa.* 2) *El derecho a expresarse.* 3) *El distrito escolar no tiene fondos.* 4) *Escribir una carta al editor.*

**A. ¿Comprende Ud.?** Conteste las siguientes preguntas según el diálogo.

1. ¿Qué es importante para Lázaro?
2. ¿Cuál es uno de los derechos de los niños?
3. ¿Por qué no hay más computadoras en la escuela?
4. ¿Cuál es la idea de Fabiola?

**B. Instrucciones para el/la tonto/a.** Uno/a de Uds. es vendedor/a de teléfonos celulares y el/la otro/a es un/a cliente/a que no sabe nada de tecnología. Usando la información del manual de instrucciones, explíquele los datos básicos de su teléfono a este/a cliente/a.

MODELO: E1: *¿Para qué es la tecla RCL?*
E2: *Esa tecla es para marcar otra vez un número de teléfono de la memoria.*
E1: *¿La memoria mía?*
E2: *No, de la memoria del teléfono.*

Español

## TELÉFONO CELULAR PORTÁTIL DE MANO

MANUAL DE INSTRUCCIONES DEL PROPIETARIO

•Información clave y datos varios

(10) El interruptor PWR (tecla de Encendido/Apagado) se utiliza para encender o apagar la unidad.

(11) La tecla SEND (Enviar) sirve para hacer una llamada.

(12) La tecla END (Fin) sirve para terminar una llamada.

(13) La tecla CLR (Borrar) sirve para borrar los dígitos del visor.

(14) La tecla RCL (Rellamar) sirve para volver a marcar los números de teléfono de la memoria.

(15) La tecla STO (Memorizar) se usa en combinación con las teclas de dígitos para guardar números de teléfono en la memoria.

(16) La tecla FNC (Función) se usa en combinación con las teclas de dígitos y sirve para usar las funciones adicionales.

**C. El robo es un problema.** Las tiendas pierden mucho dinero a causa de los robos, y nosotros, los clientes, sufrimos las consecuencias. Tres de Uds. van a buscar soluciones posibles y van a hacer una lista de ideas para evitar la ratería (*petty theft*). Una posibilidad es el sistema de *Sensormatic*. Digan si creen que ese sistema puede resolver el problema y mencionen otras sugerencias.

**TODOS NOS BENEFICIAMOS CUANDO LOS ROBOS EN LAS TIENDAS SE ACABAN.**

Protegemos nuestra mercancía con el sistema Sensormatic contra la ratería en las tiendas.

**Porque nosotros nos preocupamos por usted.**

En un esfuerzo por modernizar los procesos operativos nuestra tienda ha instalado un sofisticado sistema electrónico "Sensormatic" para prevenir el robo de artículos y controlar los inventarios.

De esta manera nuestros costos no aumentarán innecesariamente y los precios al público podrán mantenerse bajos, con lo cual usted, nuestro cliente, resultará favorecido.

Contamos con su comprensión y colaboración en el logro de estos objetivos.

Gracias por elegirnos para sus compras y, por favor, regrese pronto.

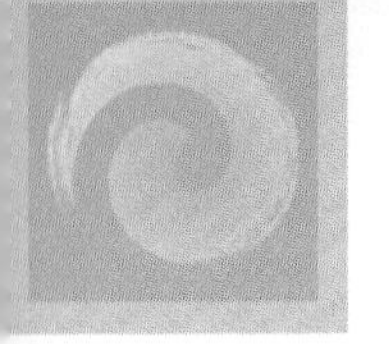

# El subjuntivo en cláusulas adverbiales
## *(Using the subjunctive with certain adverbial phrases)*

**Para averiguar**

1. Which adverbial phrases always require the subjunctive?
2. Which phrases drop the **que** and use the infinitive if the subject is the same for both clauses?

- Certain adverbial phrases always form a subordinate clause with a verb in the subjunctive because they set up conditions for events that may or may not result in the expected outcome.

| | |
|---|---|
| **antes (de) que** | *before* |
| **para que** | *so that* |
| **con tal (de) que** | *provided that, as/so long as* |
| **a menos que** | *unless* |
| **sin que** | *without* |

| | |
|---|---|
| Saldré del trabajo temprano **antes de que llegue** mi jefa. | *I'll leave work early before my boss arrives.* |
| Saldré del trabajo temprano **para que tú tengas** el coche. | *I'll leave work early so that you can have the car.* |
| Saldré del trabajo temprano **con tal de que mi jefa me permita** salir. | *I'll leave work early provided that my boss lets me leave.* |
| Saldré del trabajo temprano **a menos que no termine** el proyecto. | *I'll leave work early unless I don't finish the project.* |
| Saldré del trabajo temprano **sin que mi jefa lo sepa**. | *I'll leave work early without my boss knowing about it.* |

- With **sin que, para que, antes de que** and **con tal de que,** if the same person is the subject of both clauses, drop the **que** and use the infinitive form of the verb.

| | |
|---|---|
| Saldré del trabajo temprano **para limpiar** la casa. | *I'll leave work early in order to clean the house.* |
| Pasaré por el supermercado **antes de ir** a casa. | *I'll stop by the grocery store before going home.* |
| Saldré temprano **sin decirle** nada a la jefa. | *I'll leave early without saying anything to the boss.* |
| Saldré temprano **con tal de terminar** rápido. | *I'll leave early as long as I finish quickly.* |

## A lo personal

**A. Condiciones.** Use the correct form of the verb in parentheses to complete these sentences.

MODELO: Quiero salir de clase temprano…
a. sin que el profesor (saberlo).
*Quiero salir de clase temprano sin que el profesor lo sepa.*

1. Quiero salir de clase temprano…
   a. antes de que el profesor (devolvernos) el último examen.
   b. a menos que (haber) una pruebita.
   c. con tal de que no (verme) el profesor.
   d. para que el profesor no (saber) que no he estudiado.

2. Esta noche voy a estudiar español...
   a. antes de que (llamarme) mis amigos.
   b. para que (estar) sorprendido mañana el profesor.
   c. para (aprenderlo) bien.
   d. con tal de que no (haber) nada en la tele.
   e. a menos que (venir) mi novio/a.

3. Este verano iremos a México...
   a. antes de que (empezar) las lluvias.
   b. para que mis amigos lo (conocer).
   c. con tal de que no (tener) que repetir la clase de español.
   d. sin que nadie (saberlo).

**B. El primer día.** Today you are starting a new job and want to make a good impression on your boss, Dr. Durán. Complete the following sentences.

MODELO: Yo ya estoy en la oficina antes de que el jefe...
*Yo ya estoy en la oficina antes de que el jefe llegue.*

1. Yo prepararé el café para que el jefe...
2. Yo almorzaré a las doce a menos que el jefe...
3. Yo trabajaré muchas horas con tal de que el jefe...
4. Yo haré muchas preguntas a menos que el jefe...
5. No saldré temprano a menos que el jefe...
6. No haré llamadas personales sin que el jefe...
7. Terminaré todo mi trabajo antes de que el jefe...
8. Llegaré muy temprano todos los días a menos que...

**C. Necesito un teléfono.** Now that you've landed a good job, you want to convince your mom to buy you a cellular phone. With a classmate role-play a situation where one of you expresses the reasons why you need the phone, and the other (as the mother) sets conditions you have to meet before she buys it for you.

MODELO: E1: *Necesito el teléfono celular para poder llamar si el coche se me descompone.*
E2: *No te compraré el teléfono a menos que me prometas que no hablarás mientras conduzcas.*

## EN CONTACTO CON TODO EL MUNDO

*Desde que tuve a mi nueva bebé, el tiempo no me alcanza para nada, pero usando los servicios de AT&T he podido simplificar mi vida. Ahora estoy más en contacto con toda mi familia, no importa donde me encuentre. Con el teléfono celular de AT&T, puedo llamar desde cualquier lugar y avisarle a mi esposo que yo llevaré a Carlitos a su partido de fútbol. Y con la tarjeta de llamadas AT&T Calling Card, Marilú, nuestra niña mayor, puede llamarnos desde cualquier teléfono sin necesidad de usar monedas. Así no tiene excusas para no avisarnos que llegará tarde. Además, con* AT&T **True Reach International**℠ Savings *recibimos ahorros cada vez que llamamos a nuestro país y dentro de los Estados Unidos. Con AT&T me siento más segura, porque siempre estoy en contacto con todo el mundo.*

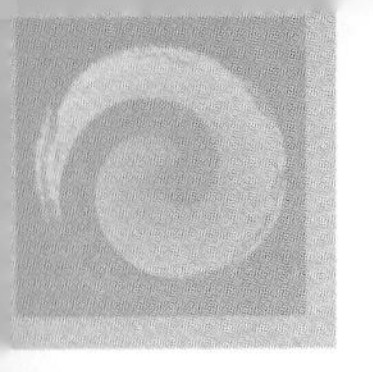

# Más sobre el subjuntivo en cláusulas adverbiales (*Subjunctive or indicative with completed or potential events*)

## Para averiguar

1. Which adverbial phrases can be followed by either the subjunctive or the indicative?
2. What is the grammatical cue to let you know to use subjunctive or indicative?

- Use the subjunctive after the following adverbial phrases when they refer to future or potential events that may or may not happen. The main verb will be in a future tense.

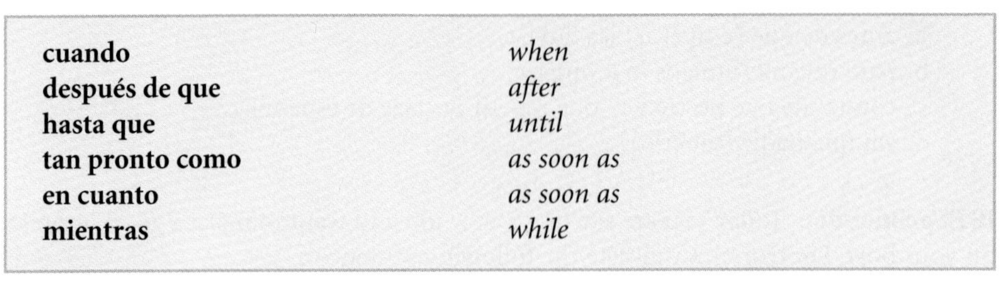

| | |
|---|---|
| **cuando** | *when* |
| **después de que** | *after* |
| **hasta que** | *until* |
| **tan pronto como** | *as soon as* |
| **en cuanto** | *as soon as* |
| **mientras** | *while* |

**Cuando me toque** la lotería (this may or may not come true), yo **compraré** una computadora para cada estudiante en la clase (cannot happen until I do win).
*I will buy a computer for each student in the class when I win the lottery.*

Todos los estudiantes **sacarán** una "A" **después de que lleguen** las computadoras.
*Every student will get an "A" after the computers arrive.*

**Trabajaremos** con lápiz y papel **hasta que lleguen** las computadoras.
*We will work with pencil and paper until the computers arrive.*

**Tan pronto como** (**En cuanto**) **lleguen** las computadoras, **aprenderemos** a navegar en el Internet.
*As soon as the computers arrive, we will learn to surf the Internet.*

**Mientras** él **esté** aquí, **podremos** ir a México.
*While he is here, we will be able to go to Mexico.*

- Use the indicative after these adverbial phrases when the sentence indicates a completed, in progress, or recurring activity. The main verb will be in a past or present tense.

El año pasado, **cuando me tocó** la lotería, **compré** computadoras para la clase.
*Last year when I won the lottery, I bought computers for the class.*
(both actions have happened and are complete. No subjunctive.)

Todos los días, **tan pronto como llego** a la clase, **leo** mi correo electrónico.
*Everyday, as soon as I get to class, I read my E-mail.*
(describes what does happen on a regular basis. Nothing is uncertain. No subjunctive.)

- At times, **hasta que** and **después (de) que** may drop the **que** and take an infinitive if there is no change of subject. In some cases, both options are accepted.

| | |
|---|---|
| Estaremos aquí **hasta terminar** la tarea. | *We will be here until we finish the work.* |
| Estaremos aquí **hasta que terminemos** la tarea. | *We will be here until we finish the work.* |
| **Después de terminar** el trabajo, irás a casa. | *After (you) finish the work, you will go home.* |
| **Después de que termines** el trabajo, irás a casa. | *After you finish the work, you will go home.* |

## A lo personal

**A. En la clase.** There are two minutes left in your Spanish class and the teacher shows no signs of giving you the assignment and letting you go. Decide whether the following sentences refer to the patient or impatient students.

MODELO: Los estudiantes se quedarán **hasta que** termine el profesor.
*Los estudiantes* ***pacientes*** *se quedarán hasta que termine el profesor.*

1. Van a salir después de que termine el profesor.
2. No esperarán hasta que el profesor termine de hablar.
3. Saldrán tan pronto como el profesor se voltee (*turn around*) para escribir en la pizarra.
4. Escucharán cuando el profesor les dé la tarea.
5. Sacarán sus mochilas después de que el profesor termine.
6. Sacarán sus mochilas mientras esté hablando el profesor.
7. Saldrán cuando no los mire el profesor.
8. No esperarán a que el profesor les devuelva el examen.
9. No mirarán el reloj mientras hable el profesor.
10. Esucharán todo hasta que los despida el profesor.

**B. La próxima clase.** During the next class, you tell the teacher what happened yesterday while he was talking. Rewrite your answers from Activity B in the past tense.

MODELO: Los estudiantes pacientes **se quedarán** hasta que **termine** el profesor.
*Ayer, los estudiantes pacientes se quedaron hasta que Ud. terminó.*

**C. Los planes.** Finish these statements about your future plans and share your thoughts with a classmate.

MODELO: Estudiaré español hasta que…
*Estudiaré español hasta que lo aprenda.*

1. Cuando me toque la lotería…
2. Viviré en esta ciudad mientras…
3. Iré de vacaciones después de que…
4. Estudiaré hasta que…
5. Después de que me case… (divorcie)…
6. Tan pronto como termine el semestre, yo…
7. Compraré una computadora nueva para cada compañero cuando…
8. En cuanto salga de clase hoy, yo…

# Vocabulario

## TEMA 1
### La publicidad

| Sustantivos | |
|---|---|
| la audiencia | *public* |
| el cable | *cable* |
| el campo | *field* |
| el canal | *channel* |
| el contacto | *contact* |
| el contenido | *content* |
| la cultura | *culture* |
| el departamento | *department* |
| el diario | *newspaper* |
| el/la especialista | *specialist* |
| los medios de comunicación | *media* |
| la mercadotecnia | *marketing* |
| las noticias | *news* |
| el noticiero | *news (program)* |
| la política | *politics* |
| el porcentaje | *percentage* |
| el/la productor/a | *producer* |
| la radio | *radio* |
| el resumen | *summary* |
| la televisión | *television* |

| Verbos | |
|---|---|
| analizar | *to analyze* |
| suponer (g) | *to suppose* |
| transmitir | *to broadcast* |

| Otras expresiones | |
|---|---|
| a pesar de | *in spite of* |

## TEMA 2
### Un reportaje

| Sustantivos | |
|---|---|
| el/la adulto/a | *adult* |
| los/las demás | *the rest* |
| el derecho | *right* |
| el distrito | *district* |
| el/la editor/a | *editor* |
| la encuesta | *survey* |
| el equipo | *equipment* |
| la expresión | *expression* |
| la firma | *signature* |
| la libertad | *liberty* |
| el período | *period* |
| la prensa | *press* |
| la prueba | *proof* |
| el reportaje | *article, report* |

| Verbos | |
|---|---|
| entrenar | *to train* |
| expresarse | *to express oneself* |
| fabricar | *to manufacture* |
| lograr | *to attain, achieve* |
| recaudar | *to collect (money)* |
| votar | *to vote* |

| Adjetivos | |
|---|---|
| instantáneo/a | *instantaneous* |
| escolar | *scholastic* |

| Otras expresiones | |
|---|---|
| atentamente | *attentively* |
| aunque | *even though* |
| libremente | *freely* |
| mi amor | *sweetheart* |
| por ejemplo | *for example* |

# Reunión A

**A escuchar.** **Una visita a la escuela.** Lourdes Abad, locutora del Canal 32, visita la escuela California. Conteste las preguntas según la información que escuche.

1. ¿Qué han organizado los estudiantes?
2. ¿Para quién habrá más oportunidades?
3. Según Fabiola, ¿cuántas computadoras tiene la escuela?
4. Según Jeanne, ¿de quién necesitan ayuda?

**Tapescript for A escuchar. Una visita a la escuela.**
SRTA. ABAD: Estoy con unos estudiantes que han organizado un movimiento para mejorar su escuela. José Galván-Rossi, quiero que resuma brevemente lo que está pasando.
JOSÉ: El señor Frankel, nuestro profesor, nos enseñó un reportaje del canal 32 acerca de los cambios que vendrán en el año 2000. Tendrán más oportunidades de trabajo los que sepan manejar las computadoras.
SRTA. ABAD: Fabiola Reyes, ¿será posible que su escuela no tenga computadoras?
FABIOLA: Bueno, tenemos dos, pero no serán suficientes para entrenar a toda la escuela. Habrá que comprar más.
SRTA. ABAD: Jeanne Girardot, ¿qué harán para cambiar las cosas?
JEANNE: Para que tengamos un buen laboratorio de informática será necesario que nos ayude el público.
SRTA. ABAD: Pues ya han visto a este grupo de niños que desean que su comunidad mejore. Los televidentes que quieran ayudar, envíen su donativo a la dirección que está en la pantalla. Para el canal 32, reportó Lourdes Abad.

**Answers for A escuchar.**
1) *Un movimiento.* 2) *Para los que sepan manejar las computadoras.* 3) *Dos.* 4) *Del público.*

**A conversar.** Algunos inmigrantes les envían a sus familiares parte del dinero que ganan. A veces estas personas mandan el dinero en efectivo (*cash*) y no llega. Hable con un/a compañero/a del programa de *Dinero seguro*. ¿Qué les parece? ¿Es una buena solución al problema? ¿Hay otras compañías con programas similares en su ciudad? ¿Cobran por el servicio? ¿Cuánto?

**SEGURO**
El dinero llega directo a cualquiera de las 1.200 sucursales de Bancomer en todo México.

**RÁPIDO**
Está disponible en quince minutos o menos.

**GARANTIZADO**
Es el único servicio que cuenta con el respaldo del Servicio Postal de los Estados Unidos y de Bancomer en México.

**¡LLAME GRATIS A MÉXICO!**

Cada vez que utilice **Dinero Seguro®** usted recibe una tarjeta para llamar gratis a México.

## ¿Lo sabía?

New word: *cuán.*

### ¿Comprende Ud?

1. ¿Qué son los "ratings"?
2. ¿Ud. ha participado en una encuesta?
3. ¿Ud. cree que los resultados de tales encuestas tienen valor? ¿Por qué?

**¡Esta es su oportunidad de contar en los "ratings" de la radio!**

No importa cuán poco o mucho usted escucha la radio, usted es parte importante de la encuesta de "Ratings" de la Radio de Arbitron. Su hogar es uno de los pocos que hemos escogido en su área. Ahora usted, y las otras personas de su casa, pueden asegurarse de que la radio que escuchan realmente cuenta en los "ratings".

**A buscar.** El Internet nos ofrece un mundo nuevo de información. Busque información sobre un tema específico usando un motor de búsqueda (*search engine*) en español y comparta lo que encuentre con tres compañeros. Posibilidades: deportes, noticias de hoy, el tiempo, la bolsa de valores, arte, literatura, venta de autos, casas,... Lea las notas de sus compañeros y hágales dos o tres preguntas específicas de la información de cada uno.

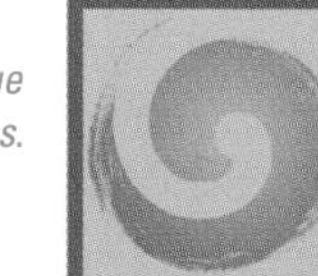

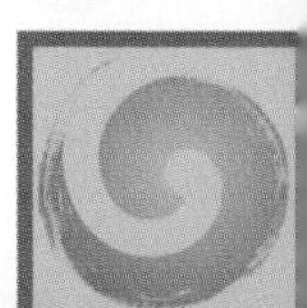

# TEMA 3 Una entrevista

## La tecnología

### Buenas noticias

*Carlos llama por teléfono a Lázaro....*

CARLOS: Hola, Lázaro. Te vi en el Canal 32 el viernes pasado. ¡No creía que tus estudiantes fueran tan listos!

LÁZARO: Yo no les pedí que lo hicieran. José y Fabiola tuvieron la idea.

CARLOS: Sí, Mary me dijo que ellos se pusieron en contacto con Lourdes Abad para pedirle que viniera a la escuela.

LÁZARO: Y claro, a ella le gustó que se pudiera hacer un reportaje positivo de un grupo de jóvenes. Hemos tenido muchos donativos.

CARLOS: Pues, tengo una buena noticia. Mi jefe vio el reportaje y me pidió que te hablara porque quiere ayudarlos.

LÁZARO: ¿De verdad? No creí que tantas personas lo hubieran visto.

CARLOS: La junta directiva de nuestra compañía decidió que les donáramos 20 computadoras. También hablamos con *Computadoras del Sol* para que donaran otras 20.

LÁZARO: ¡Qué bien! Ahora podremos usar el dinero de los donativos para construir un salón para las clases de informática.

**A. ¿Comprende Ud.?** Conteste las siguientes preguntas según el diálogo.

1. ¿Dónde vio Carlos a Lázaro?
2. ¿Qué le gustó a Lourdes Abad, la locutora?
3. ¿De dónde recibirán las computadoras?
4. ¿Para qué piensan usar el dinero de los donativos?

**Answers for A.** 1) *En el canal 32.* 2) *Que se pudiera hacer un reportaje positivo.* 3) *De Computadoras del Sol.* 4) *Para construir un salón para las clases de informática.*

**B. ¡Qué pesadilla de entrevista!** Ud. tuvo una entrevista para el puesto de sus sueños, pero todo salió mal. Termine las oraciones con una posibilidad malísima y enséñele sus respuestas a su compañero/a.

MODELO: ¡El jefe esperaba que supiera manejar ______________!
*¡El jefe esperaba que supiera manejar aviones F–16!*

1. ¡Quería que empezara ______________________________!
2. ¡Dudaba que pudiera ______________________________!
3. ¡Era necesario que trabajara ____________________________!
4. ¡Tal vez tuviera que trabajar en ______________________!
5. ¡Se alegraba de que hablara ________________ solamente!

**C. El poder del inmigrante.** Después de leer la cita de Thomas Castro, presidente de *El Dorado Communications*, Los Ángeles, haga el papel de locutor/a del Canal 6. Entreviste a un/a político/a (su compañero/a) en cuanto a su opinión del poder del voto del inmigrante. ¿Cuáles son los asuntos de mayor interés para él/ella? ¿la economía? ¿la educación? ¿el desempleo? ¿la salud? ¿el cuidado de los niños? ¿los "secretos públicos" de los líderes? ¿Hay algún tema que sea de mayor interés para los inmigrantes que para el resto de la población?

MODELO: E1: *En su opinión, ¿qué asuntos son de mayor importancia para la población de inmigrantes en este país?*
E2: *Pues, yo opino que…*

**Variation for C.** Invite someone connected with media in the community to speak to the class. It would be particularly useful if there were a Spanish connection. Mention the importance of the Hispanic population with respect to buying power, number of voters, etc.

"El enorme cambio ocurrido en este país se refleja en el hecho de que los inmigrantes decidan hacerse ciudadanos. Los medios de comunicación en español son capaces de educar a los nuevos inmigrantes y de comunicarles lo que les espera en esta nación."

Thomas Castro, CEO
*El Dorado Communications, Los Angeles*

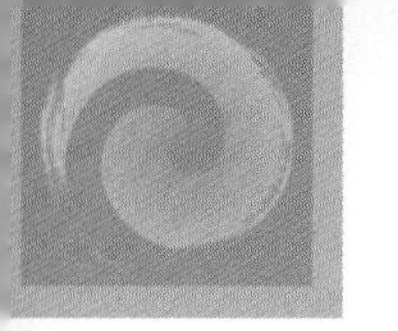

# ABC El mundo electrónico

## Las inversiones

*Mary y Carlos visitan a Isabel y Lázaro en su casa nueva....*

ISABEL: Me alegro de que viéramos ese seminario de negocios que ofrecieron por la televisión.
CARLOS: Yo no lo vi. ¿Estuvo bien?
LÁZARO: Excelente. Estábamos muy interesados porque Isabel quiere que invirtamos dinero en acciones.
MARY: Yo ya lo había visto y estuvo muy interesante. El doctor Sacal es una autoridad mundial en el tema.
ISABEL: Sí, hablaba como si supiera mucho de la bolsa de valores. Insistía en que se invirtiera en el campo de la tecnología. Carlos, ¿será una buena idea?
CARLOS: Me parece que sí. ¿Dónde sugirió que compraran las acciones?
LÁZARO: Recomendó que las compráramos y vendiéramos por medio del Internet porque se ahorra mucho dinero.
ISABEL: Dijo que era importante que observáramos las fluctuaciones de los precios para que compráramos cuando los precios estuvieran bajos y vendiéramos cuando subieran.

**Answers for A.** 1) *Un seminario.* 2) *Isabel deseaba que invirtieran dinero en acciones.* 3) *Por medio del Internet para ahorrar dinero.* 4) *Las fluctuaciones de los precios, para comprar cuando estén bajos y vender cuando estén altos.*

**A. ¿Comprende Ud.?** Conteste las preguntas con información del diálogo.

1. ¿Qué vieron Isabel y Lázaro por la televisión?
2. ¿Por qué estaban interesados?
3. ¿Cómo recomendó el Dr. Sacal que compraran las acciones? ¿Por qué?
4. ¿Qué deben observar en el Internet? ¿Para qué?

**B. ¿Juguete o salvación?** La tecnología ha revolucionado el mundo de los negocios a fines del siglo XX. No se puede ir en un vuelo de Los Ángeles a Nueva York sin notar la cantidad de computadoras portátiles que se usan. Su jefe le va a comprar una computadora nueva para sus viajes, y Ud. necesita preparar su lista de requisitos. Intercambie su lista con la de su compañero/a a ver quién quiere más cosas. ¡Acuérdese! La persona con el mejor "juguete" gana.

MODELO: *Modem de 56.6 K, pantalla en color de 12 pulgadas...*

**C. Los hispanos en la comunicación.** Rosana Rosado, la editora en jefe de *El Diario-La Prensa* de Nueva York, reconoce el valor de los hispanos en la vida norteamericana de hoy. Lea su cita y hable con un/a compañero/a de las contribuciones de los hispanos a los Estados Unidos. Pueden hablar de los medios de comunicación y de la vida política, pero no se olviden de incluir su impacto en otras áreas como los espectáculos, los deportes, la arquitectura, la comida....

"Aparte del terreno político, los latinos como grupo hemos dado pasos gigantescos en otros campos. Estamos haciendo cosas importantes en los medios de comunicación, en el gobierno y en la política. Pero lo hacemos de manera callada."

Rosana Rosado,
**Editora en Jefe**
*El Diario-La Prensa, New York City*

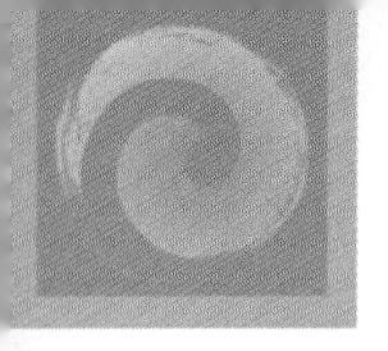

# El imperfecto del subjuntivo
## *(Imperfect subjunctive)*

**Para averiguar**

1. What form of the subjunctive do you use when the main verb is in the present or future tense?
2. What form of the subjunctive do you use when the main verb is in the past tense?
3. What verb form is the basis for the formation of the imperfect subjunctive?
4. Which is the only form of the imperfect subjunctive to have a written accent?

- Just as the indicative mood has tenses that refer to the past, present and future, so does the subjunctive. Use the present subjunctive to talk about the present and future. Use the imperfect subjunctive to talk about the past.

- To form the imperfect subjunctive, take the third person plural of the preterite, remove the **-on** and add the following endings: **-a, -as, -a, -amos, -ais, -an.** ¡OJO! The **nosotros** from always has an accent.

- Many Spanish speakers use these alternate endings for the imperfect

  subjunctive: **-se, -ses, -se, -semos, -seis, -sen**
  **Ir:** fuese, fueses, fuese, fuésemos, fueseis, fuesen

| Formation of the imperfect subjunctive | | |
|---|---|---|
| **verb** | **3rd person preterite** | IMPERFECT SUBJUNCTIVE |
| ir | fueron | **fuera, fueras, fuera, fuéramos, fuerais, fueran** |
| saber | supieron | **supiera, supieras, supiera, supiéramos, supierais, supieran** |
| hablar | hablaron | **hablara, hablaras, hablara, habláramos, hablarais, hablaran** |
| vivir | vivieron | **viviera, vivieras, viviera, viviéramos, vivierais, vivieran** |
| haber | hubieron | **hubiera, hubieras, hubiera, hubiéramos, hubierais, hubieran** |
| tener | tuvieron | **tuviera, tuvieras, tuviera, tuviéramos, tuvierais, tuvieran** |
| poder | pudieron | **pudiera, pudieras, pudiera, pudiéramos, pudierais, pudieran** |
| venir | vinieron | **viniera, vinieras, viniera, viniéramos, vinierais, vinieran** |

- Use the imperfect subjunctive as you would the present subjunctive. Whether you use the present subjunctive or imperfect subjunctive in a sentence will depend on whether the main verb is in the past tense or the present tense.

Yo **quiero** que tú **vengas.** — *I want you to come.*
Yo **quería** que tú **vinieras.** — *I wanted you to come.*

No **creo** que ellos **sepan** la verdad. — *I don't believe that they know the truth.*
No **creía** que ellos **supieran** la verdad. — *I didn't believe that they knew the truth.*

Te lo **digo** para que nos **ayudes.** — *I am telling you so that you will help us.*
Te lo **dije** para que nos **ayudaras.** — *I told you so that you would help us.*

## A lo personal

**A. De niño/a.** When you were in elementary school, did your teacher want you to do or not do the following things?

MODELO: La maestra quería que nosotros...pegar a los otros niños.
*La maestra no quería que les pegáramos a los otros niños.*

La maestra (no) quería que nosotros...

1. ...traer dinero para la leche
2. ...masticar chicle en la clase
3. ...tener juguetes eléctronicos en la clase
4. ...leer muchos libros
5. ...levantar la mano para pedir permiso para salir
6. ...dormir la siesta en la clase
7. ...tirar aviones de papel
8. ...prestarle mucha atención cuando hablaba

**B. De adulto.** Think back to high school and the things that you thought were important. Tell whether they were or were not really important from today's perspective.

MODELO: sacar buenas notas.
*Sí, era importante que yo sacara buenas notas.*

1. llevar ropa cara
2. fumar
3. ser futbolista o animadora
4. estudiar matemáticas
5. manejar un coche rápido
6. tener el peinado perfecto
7. salir con las personas más populares
8. burlarse de los estudiantes inteligentes
9. tener una cita para el baile de fin de curso
10. participar en actividades sociales

**C. ¡Feliz cumpleaños!** Since you were away at school on your birthday last year, your friends and family sent your gifts to you. They didn't finish writing the card because they were sure that you'd know why they chose the gifts. Finish the card for each of the gifts.

MODELO: tu mamá: "Te compré un boleto de avión para que tú...*vinieras a visitarnos*".

1. tu papá: "Te mandé una computadora para que tú...
2. tu abuela: "Te mandé un pastel para que tú...
3. tu mejor amigo: "Te compré mucha cerveza para que tú...
4. tu primer maestro de español: "Te mandé un diccionario de español para que tú...
5. tu novio/a "Te mandé una foto romántica para que tú...
6. tu abuelo: "Te compré un automóvil deportivo para que tú...

**D. Mi novio/a ideal...** Back in high school you probably had very definite ideas about what you wanted. Make a list of what you were looking for in a sweetheart. Then compare your list to a classmate's list. Try to compare with someone you find interesting!

MODELO: *Yo buscaba a alguien que tuviera el pelo largo y negro...*

## Más práctica con el imperfecto del subjuntivo
### *(More practice with the imperfect subjunctive)*

**A. Los favores.** Your boss has been out sick for the past week and wants to know how things are going at the office. Tell him what you asked each employee to do while he was absent, according to the model below.

MODELO: Ana / llamar por teléfono al Sr. Smith
*A Ana le pedí que llamara por teléfono al Sr. Smith.*

1. Pedro / comprar el papel para la impresora
2. Jorge y Luisa / pagar todas las cuentas de esta semana
3. Jaime / entrevistar a los candidatos para el puesto de ayudante
4. Lola y Alejandra / recoger los paquetes en la oficina de correos
5. Manuel / escribir el informe de gastos de este mes
6. Carmen / arreglar la computadora que no funciona
7. Andrés y Bea / visitarlo a Ud. en el hospital
8. Rosa / preparar una fiesta de bienvenida para Ud.
9. Mateo / limpiar la sala de conferencias
10. Miguel / dar la presentación sobre el nuevo producto

**B. Un jefe desagradecido.** Your boss is now back at the office and despite your efforts to keep everything running smoothly, he is complaining about everything you did. Follow the model to figure out what your boss says about each situation below.

MODELO: Pedro / reparar las llantas de mi coche
*Yo quería que Pedro reparara las llantas de mi coche y no las ha reparado.*

1. Jorge y Luisa / visitar a mi esposa en la casa de campo
2. Jaime / pedir información sobre la compañía telefónica
3. Lola y Alejandra / decorar mi oficina
4. Manuel / organizar mis reuniones para el próximo mes
5. Carmen / comprar una computadora portátil
6. Andrés / leer los documentos de los abogados
7. Bea / traerme flores al hospital
8. Rosa / informar a los clientes de mi condición física
9. Mateo / invertir todo mi dinero en la bolsa de valores
10. Miguel / hacer planes para el picnic de verano de la compañía

**C. Las inversiones.** You have become fascinated with the stock market and are reading everything you can about the history and investments of certain companies. Tell a classmate what each of the following people did. Using 20/20 hindsight, your classmate will decide whether or not they made a smart move.

MODELO: Mi tío/comprar muchas acciones de Microsoft.
E1: *Mi tío compró muchas acciones de Microsoft.*
E2: *No fue una buena idea que tu tío comprara muchas acciones de Microsoft.*

1. Mi padre/invertir $3.000 en *America Online* en 1992.
2. Mi abuelo/vender sus acciones de *Coca-Cola* en 1929 por $2.
3. Mi tía/no hacer nada cuando tuvo la oportunidad de invertir en *Viagra.*
4. Unos amigos de mi abuelo/pedir un préstamo del banco para comprar un terreno en el centro de Los Ángeles en 1920.
5. Yo/decir "no" cuando me ofrecieron acciones en *Coca-Cola Nueva.*
6. Nosotros/no invertir en una casa en la playa antes del desastroso huracán.

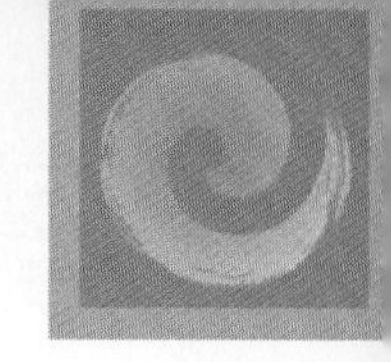

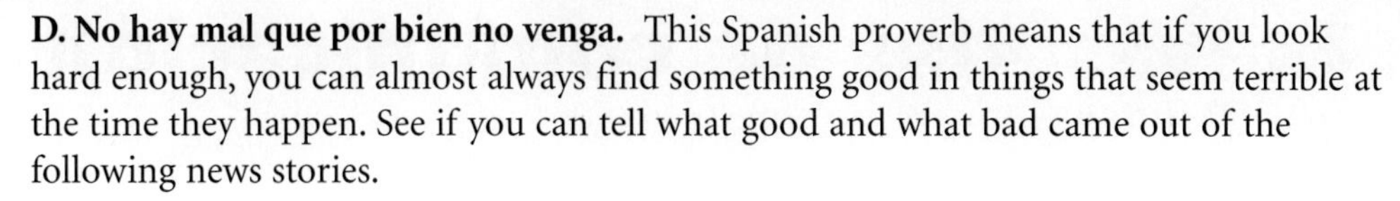

**D. No hay mal que por bien no venga.** This Spanish proverb means that if you look hard enough, you can almost always find something good in things that seem terrible at the time they happen. See if you can tell what good and what bad came out of the following news stories.

MODELO: La muerte de la Princesa Diana
*Me gustó que personas de todas partes la recordaran.*
*No me gustó (Es malo) que hubiera tantos problemas con la prensa.*

1. el problema tecnológico Y2K
2. la posibilidad de hacer clones humanos
3. los desastres naturales en Centroamérica
4. la guerra con Irak
5. las reformas en la asistencia pública (*welfare reform*)
6. el problema de los refugiados de Kosovo
7. el tiroteo (*shooting*) en Colorado
8. el virus informático Melissa
9. los crímenes cometidos por Milosevic
10. los incendios (*fires*) en Florida

**E. Ojalá que no fuera así...** How did you feel about the outcomes of the following events?

MODELO: el juicio de Bill Clinton
*No me gustó que la prensa le prestara tanta atención.*
*Me alegré de que todo se resolviera legalmente.*

1. el personaje de Leonardo di Caprio en el *Titánic*
2. el episodio final del programa *Seinfeld*
3. la final de la Copa Mundial de Fútbol Femenina.
4. la nota que le dio a Ud. el/la profesor/a de español el semestre pasado
5. el anuncio del progreso en la lucha contra el cáncer
6. el regreso de John Glenn al espacio
7. la legalización de marihuana para enfermos en California
8. el acuerdo de la unión de jugadores de la NBA

**F. La clase de español.** As you finish the semester or year of studying Spanish, think back about what you liked about learning the language and what you didn't like to learn. What kinds of activities did you want to do more of, and what kinds of activities did you want to do less of? Work in pairs or groups and compare your thoughts.

MODELO: *No me gustó que hubiera tantos verbos para aprender.*
*Me gustó mucho que pudiéramos trabajar en grupo.*
*¡Quería que tuviéramos más horas de clase!*

# TEMA 4 Nuevas vías de comunicación

## El nuevo milenio

### La programación internacional

*Isabel habla por teléfono con Mary....*

ISABEL: Hola, Mary quisiera...

MARY: ¡Ay, Isabel, estoy sufriendo mucho! Ahora no puedo hablar contigo porque el doctor le acaba de decir a Mónica que su esposo tiene seis meses de vida. ¿Qué harías tú? ¿Se lo dirías a él?

ISABEL: No sé, no sabría qué hacer. ¿Quién es Mónica?

MARY: Es la protagonista de la telenovela *Días perdidos en la oscuridad.* ¿No la ves?

ISABEL: La vería si pudiera, pero no tengo mucho tiempo. Por lo que oigo en el Canal 6, juraría que todo el mundo ve las telenovelas en español. ¿Por qué canal la transmiten?

MARY: Por el Canal 18 de la Ciudad de México. La recibo directamente por satélite. ¿Te gustaría verla conmigo?

ISABEL: No, gracias. Además, hay otras telenovelas en las cadenas hispanas de los Estados Unidos.

MARY: Sí, también las transmiten en muchos países no hispanos, como Rusia, Japón y China, dobladas en sus propias lenguas. Me pregunto qué le aconsejarían a Mónica en Japón.

**Expansion.** Tell about the popularity of soap operas in the Hispanic world. If possible, show a brief clip from one, such as the Eric Estrada show, *Dos mujeres y un camino* (ex-Chips star), Thalía in *María, la del barrio,* Adamari López in *Sin ti,* Adela Noriega in *Guadalupe.* Encourage students to watch a soap because the acting is so melodramatic that they will be able to understand while improving language skills. Mention other popular programs such as *Cristina, Sábado gigante internacional, Onda max.*

**A. ¿Comprende Ud.?** Conteste las siguientes preguntas según el diálogo.

1. ¿Cuál es el problema de Mary?
2. ¿Qué le dijo el doctor a Mónica, la protagonista de *Días perdidos en la oscuridad*?
3. ¿Cómo recibe Mary la telenovela?
4. ¿Dónde se pueden ver las telenovelas?

**Answers for A.** 1) *Está sufriendo mucho.* 2) *Que su esposo tiene seis meses de vida.* 3) *Por satélite.* 4) *En todo el mundo.*

**B. No hay límites.** Termine cada oración con una fantasía, pues no existen los límites. Intercambie ideas con su compañero/a.

MODELO: Con buena salud, mi pareja ideal y mucho dinero...
*Me pasaría los días en la playa tomando el sol, nadando y leyendo libros clásicos.*

1. ...iría a ______________ con ______________ por ______________.
2. ...me compraría ______________ y ______________.
3. ...comería ______________ y bebería ______________.
4. ...(no) le(s) daría mucho dinero a ______________ para ______________.
5. ...buscaría ______________ porque ______________.
6. ...empezaría ______________ para que (no) hubiera ______________.

**C. La información tecnológica.** La tecnología es esencial en el mundo de los negocios. En la última década, los hispanos en los Estados Unidos han aumentado su acceso a las computadoras casi dos veces más que el resto de la nación. Lea el artículo y hable con dos compañeros/as de la importancia de la tecnología. Mencionen ejemplos específicos sobre dónde ven su influencia, en la comunicación, las cuentas bancarias, la preparación de material para las clases, etc.

Se dice que las compañías de dueños hispanos gastarán 9,6 billones de dólares este año en tecnología. Esto representa más de siete veces los ingresos de Microsoft de 1996 de 1,36 billones de dólares. Los negocios que no usen tecnología no estarán aquí al llegar el siglo XXI. Es una necesidad absoluta, no un lujo.

**EL USO DE COMPUTADORAS**

| Población entera de los EE. UU. | 1984 (en miles) | 1993 (en miles) | % de cambio |
|---|---|---|---|
| Acceso a computadoras | 14.999 | 47.988 | 220% |
| Uso de computadoras en el trabajo | 24.172 | 51.106 | 111% |
| Uso de computadoras | 31.099 | 67.397 | 117% |
| **Hispanos** | **1984** | **1993** | **% de cambio** |
| Acceso a computadoras | 372 | 1.954 | 425% |
| Uso de computadoras en el trabajo | 863 | 2.492 | 189% |
| Uso de computadoras | 1.091 | 3.322 | 204% |

Fuente: Censo de los EE. UU. Encuesta de la población de 1993, "Uso de computadoras en los EE. UU."

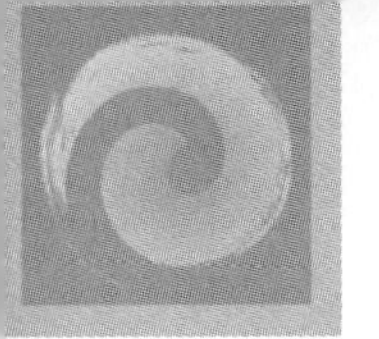

##  La Supercarretera de información

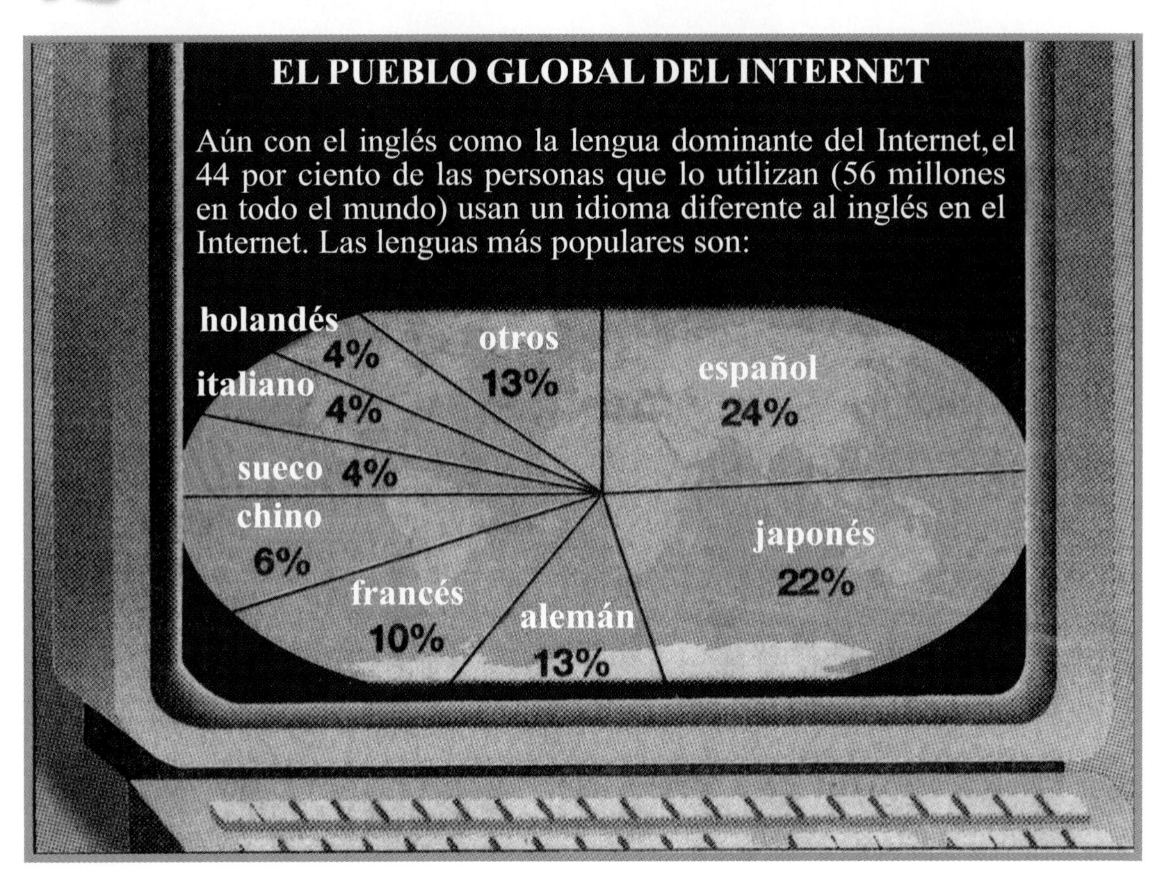


### Las ventajas del Internet

*Ana visita al Prof. Yuja en su oficina....*

ANA: Profesor Yuja, ¿qué haría si le dijera que no podía hacer el examen final?

PROF. YUJA: Si me dijeras cuál es el problema, tal vez lo entendería. Si no tomas el examen, tendrás una mala calificación.

ANA: Mi papá está muy enfermo y tengo que ir a Costa Rica a verlo. Si se muriera sin verme, me sentiría muy mal.

PROF. YUJA: Lo siento, Ana. Tal vez podríamos tener el examen por el Internet. Los dos tenemos salas de charla. Si nos pusiéramos de acuerdo, podríamos hacerlo el mismo día del examen final en la universidad.

ANA: ¡Excelente! Yo ya tengo su dirección de correo electrónico. Le voy a dejar la de mis padres en su buzón.

PROF. YUJA: Perfecto, ¡qué haríamos si no existiera el Internet!

**A. ¿Comprende Ud.?** Conteste las siguientes preguntas según el diálogo.

1. ¿Cuál es el problema de Ana?
2. ¿Qué calificación recibiría ella sin presentar el examen final?
3. ¿Cómo pueden resolver el problema?
4. ¿Qué día será el examen?

**Answers for A.** 1) *Tiene que ir a Costa Rica porque su padre está enfermo.* 2) *Una calificación mala.* 3) *Tomarlo por el Internet.* 4) *El mismo día del examen final.*

**B. ¿Qué haría yo si...?** Termine cada oración con su sueño personal para el futuro. Compare sus ideas con las de su compañero/a.

MODELO: Si fuera rica...*les daría parte de mi dinero a los pobres.*

1. Si tuviera una enfermedad grave...
2. Si hablara español perfectamente...
3. Si fuera presidente/a...
4. Si no tuviera comida...
5. Si ganara mucho dinero en mis inversiones...
6. Si fuera famoso/a...

**C. El nuevo milenio.** Haga una lista de lo que espera ver en cuanto a la tecnología del siglo XXI. ¿Habría periódicos como los de hoy si los tuviéramos electrónicamente? ¿Se puede imaginar un mundo en el que el dinero en efectivo ya no exista y sólo se use plástico para todo? Piense en por los menos cinco cambios probables y escuche las ideas de su compañero/a.

**D. La Supercarretera de información.** Si Ud. tuviera el apoyo financiero de unos amigos (sus compañeros) abriría su propia empresa para proveer servicio de Internet para los miles y miles (millones?) de usuarios (*users*) de computadoras en México. Prepare un presupuesto posible y un plan para ese negocio. ¿Piensa ofrecer el servicio por todo México? ¿en 31 estados? ¿solamente en D. F.? ¿Cuántos empleados necesitará? ¿Habrá sucursales?

Internet

## Enorme potencial de negocios para el país: IMEF

***Por Roxana de la Cruz Zuart***

Como sólo el uno por ciento de las computadoras existentes en México se encuentran conectadas al Internet—en Estados Unidos y Europa la cifra asciende al 32 por ciento—existe "un enorme potencial" para el crecimiento de la promoción empresarial y comercial mexicana en la Supercarretera de la información.

En una sesión auspiciada por el Instituto Mexicano de Ejecutivos de Finanzas (IMEF) se destacó que el comercio en el Internet ofrece innumerables ventajas.

Entre otras, se encuentra la de ofrecer menores costos de insumos, reducción de inventarios, ciclo de producto reducido, servicios al cliente más efectivos y sobre todo nuevas oportunidades de venta.

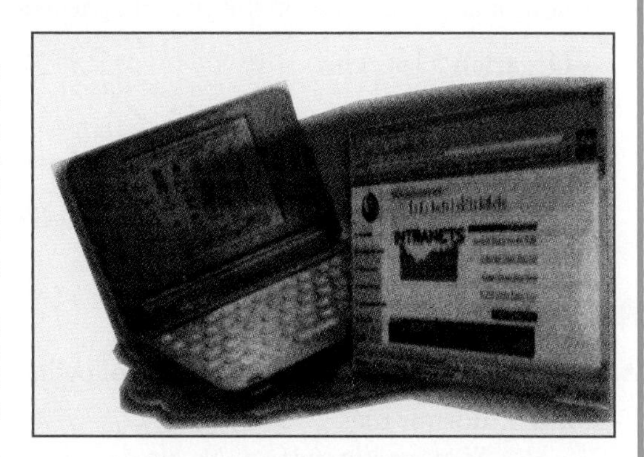

Para el año 2002 se prevé que a través del Internet se comercialicen ventas por encima de los 41.100 millones de dólares, cantidad considerable, si se toma en cuenta el coste reducido que el Internet proporciona a las empresas.

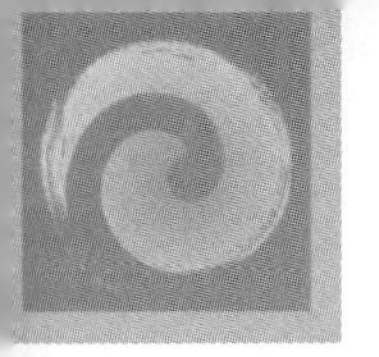

# El condicional
## (*The conditional*)

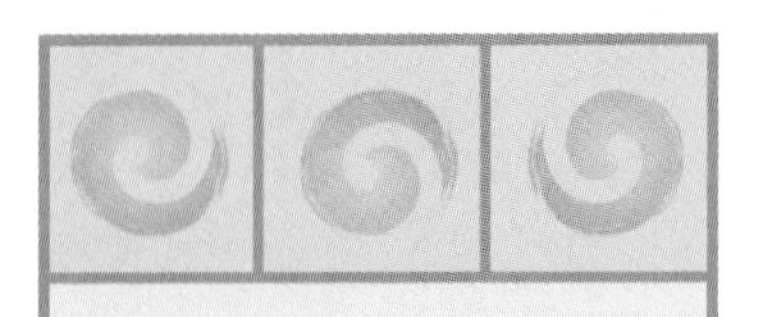

**Para averiguar**

1. How is the conditional generally translated into English?
2. The stem of the conditional is the same as what other tense? What other tense has the same ending?

- Use the conditional to say that someone *would do* something or that something *would happen* under certain conditions. You have already used the conditional in **me gustaría**… to say that you *would like* (to do) something. The conditional is formed using the same verb stem as the future tense with the same endings as those used for the imperfect of **-er**/**-ir** verbs.

| | hablar | comer | vivir | hacer |
|---|---|---|---|---|
| yo | hablar**ía** | comer**ía** | vivir**ía** | har**ía** |
| tú | hablar**ías** | comer**ías** | vivir**ías** | har**ías** |
| él, ella, Ud. | hablar**ía** | comer**ía** | vivir**ía** | har**ía** |
| nosotros/as | hablar**íamos** | comer**íamos** | vivir**íamos** | har**íamos** |
| vosotros/as | hablar**íais** | comer**íais** | vivir**íais** | har**íais** |
| ellos, ellas, Uds. | hablar**ían** | comer**ían** | vivir**ían** | har**ían** |

—Me **encantaría** estar de vacaciones esta semana. — *I would love to be on vacation this week.*
—¿Qué **harías**? — *What would you do?*
—Me **levantaría** tarde, **iría** a la playa y **tomaría** el sol. — *I would get up late, I would go to the beach, and I would sunbathe.*

- The conditional may be used to make polite requests or suggestions.

**¿Podrías** ayudarme? — *Could you help me?*
¿**Me diría** Ud. la hora? — *Would you tell me the time?*
**Deberías** comer mejor. — *You should eat better.*

- The conditional is also used in Spanish to express probability and concession. While the future expresses probability and concession in a present time frame, the conditional expresses probability and concession in the past.

—**Llegarían** a las ocho. — *They probably arrived at eight o'clock.*

—¿Por qué no fue Efrén a la fiesta? — *Why didn't Efrén go to the party?*
—**Tendría** otro compromiso. — *He probably had another engagement.*

—**Sería** joven pero era muy buena escritora. — *She might have been young, but she was a very good writer.*

## A lo personal

**A. Con más tiempo.** Would you do the following things if you had more time?

MODELO: dormir más
*Sí, dormiría más.* o *No, no dormiría más.*

1. mirar más telenovelas
2. trabajar más
3. sacar mejores notas en sus clases
4. visitar más a sus padres
5. hacer más ejercicio
6. cocinar más
7. salir más a bailar
8. ser más feliz
9. ir al parque
10. viajar más

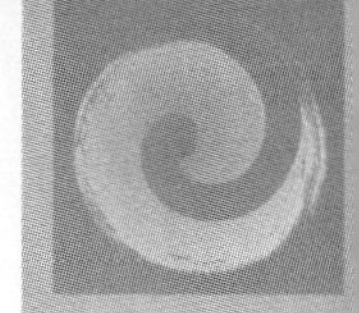

**B. ¿Qué harías?** Ask a classmate what he/she would do if faced with the following choices. Your classmate should provide a reason for his/her selection.

MODELO: vivir en México o en España
E1: *¿Vivirías en México o en España?*
E2: *Viviría en México.*

1. estudiar ruso o japonés
2. ser médico/a o abogado/a
3. comprar un coche norteamericano o uno japonés
4. preferir ser más guapo/a o más inteligente
5. casarse por dinero o sólo por amor
6. comer mejor o hacer más ejercicio para sentirse bien

**C. ¿Lobo o cordero?** Ask a classmate to answer the following questions. Then use the scoring key to find out whether he/she is a wolf (**lobo**) or a lamb (**cordero**) in his/her interpersonal relationships.

# ¿LOBO O CORDERO?

1. ¿Dirías una mentira sobre ti mismo para impresionar a una persona poco conocida?
2. En una tienda, ¿le indicarías un error a favor tuyo al dependiente que te devuelve el cambio?
3. ¿Preferirías pasar las vacaciones sin tu pareja?
4. ¿Te gustaría más tener un gato que otros animales?
5. ¿Volverías con gusto a ver viejas películas que te habían gustado en otros tiempos?
6. ¿Te lanzarías en paracaídas?
7. ¿Tendrías la misma profesión que tus padres?
8. ¿Llevarías ropa muy original y algo vistosa?
9. ¿Aceptarías una invitación de una persona poco conocida?
10. ¿Te gustaría volver a vivir en el pasado?
11. ¿Te describirías como una persona optimista?
12. ¿Te molestaría encontrar a un ex-amor con otra pareja?
13. ¿Saldrías con alguien de la edad de tus padres?
14. ¿Te gustaría ser abogado/a?

**RESULTADOS:**
Suma un punto por cada respuesta que coincida con las siguientes:
1. sí 2. no 3. sí 4. sí 5. no 6. sí 7. no 8. sí 9. sí 10. no 11. sí 12. no 13. sí 14. sí

| | |
|---|---|
| De 1-5 puntos: | Eres un corderito tierno e indefenso. Tímido/a, romántico/a y dulce. |
| De 6-10 puntos: | Eres una persona equilibrada y razonable. |
| De 11-14 puntos: | Eres un verdadero lobo. |

**D. En un mundo perfecto.** First decide if the following statements about the modern world are true. Then, say whether or not they would also be true in a perfect world.

MODELO: Hay mucha gente sin hogar.
*Sí, es verdad que hay mucha gente sin hogar. En un mundo perfecto, no habría gente sin hogar.*

1. Tenemos mucho estrés en la vida diaria.
2. Las mujeres tienen las mismas oportunidades que los hombres.
3. El aire está contaminado.
4. Hay muchas enfermedades.
5. Todos los enfermos pueden ver a un médico.
6. El tratamiento médico cuesta mucho dinero.
7. Es difícil encontrar trabajo.
8. Cada día mucha gente pasa hambre.

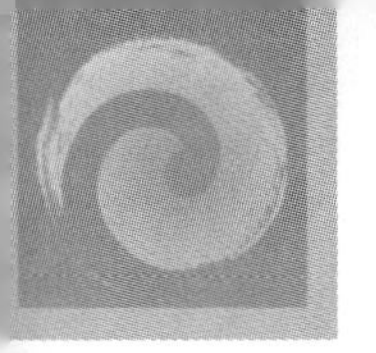

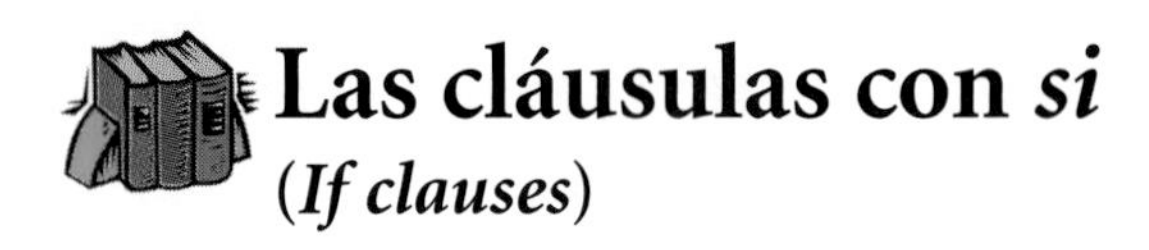

# Las cláusulas con *si*
## (*If clauses*)

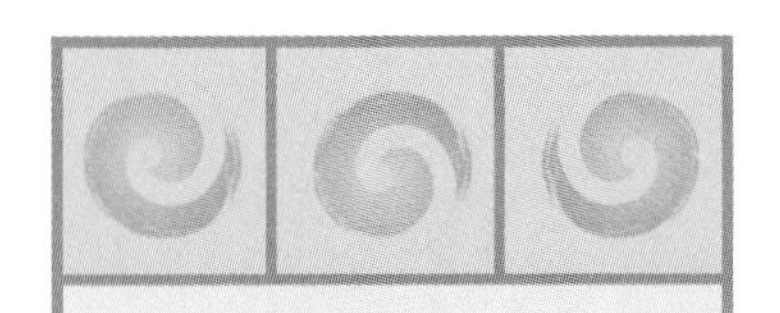

### Para averiguar

1. When an "if" situation is likely to happen, what tenses will you use?
2. If an "if" situation is impossible or unlikely, what tenses will you use?
3. Is it possible to use present subjunctive after "if"?

- Use **si** (*if*) with present and future indicative tenses to talk about situations that are likely to happen.

| | |
|---|---|
| **Si tengo** dinero, **iré** de compras. | *If I have money, I will go shopping.* |
| **Si hago** ejercicio, **bajaré** de peso. | *If I exercise, I will lose weight.* |

- Use **si** followed by the past subjunctive in the *if* clause plus a conditional verb to talk about situations that are highly unlikely, totally impossible, or contrary to fact—even if they refer to the present or future time.

| | |
|---|---|
| **Si** yo **fuera** Ud., **estudiaría** todos los verbos para el examen. | *If I were you, I would study all of the verbs for the test.* (I am not you, nor will I ever be—contrary to fact) |
| **Si** yo **fuera** un gato, **diría** "miau". | *If I were a cat* (which I am not), *I would say "meow."* |
| **Si tuviera** dinero, **iría** de compras mañana. | *If I had money* (which I don't), *I would go shopping tomorrow.* |

- **Si** can also be used with the imperfect subjunctive plus a conditional verb when the outcome of the situation depends on the condition.

| | |
|---|---|
| **Si** me **ayudaras** a limpiar yo te **ayudaría** con las cuentas. | *If you helped me clean I'd help you with the bills.* |
| **Si compraras** fruta fresca yo **prepararía** una ensalada. | *If you bought fresh fruit I'd prepare a salad.* |

- Even though the order of the clauses in the sentence may be reversed, the relationship to the verbs in each individual clause will remain the same in either situation.

| | |
|---|---|
| **Si** me **llamaras** yo **hablaría** contigo. | *If you called me I'd talk to you.* |
| Yo **hablaría** contigo **si** me **llamaras**. | *I'd talk to you if you called me.* |

## A lo personal

**A. Amigos.** You know your friend is not being realistic when she tells you the following things. Reword her statements to show that you know that they will never happen.

MODELO: Si tengo dinero, iré de compras.
*Si tuviera dinero, iría de compras.*

1. Si tengo tiempo mañana, vendré a visitarte.
2. Si tengo energía, haré ejercicio.
3. Si recibo mi cheque mañana, te devuelvo el dinero que te debo.
4. Si salgo con Antonio Banderas, te lo diré.
5. Si gano la lotería, te daré la mitad.
6. Si voy al Caribe esta noche, te mandaré una postal.
7. Si me ofrecen un trabajo fabuloso en México, lo acepto.
8. Si mis padres necesitan dinero, yo se lo prestaré.

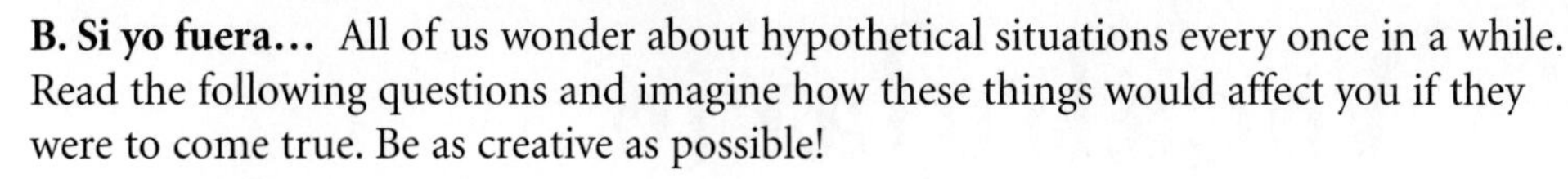

**B. Si yo fuera...** All of us wonder about hypothetical situations every once in a while. Read the following questions and imagine how these things would affect you if they were to come true. Be as creative as possible!

MODELO: Si Ud. fuera un gato, ¿qué diría?
*Si yo fuera un gato, diría "miau".*

1. Si Ud. fuera el/la profesor/a de español, ¿qué tarea daría esta noche?
2. Si Ud. no tuviera que estudiar esta noche, ¿qué haría?
3. Si Ud. no tuviera que preocuparse por su salud ¿qué comería?
4. Si Ud. no tuviera que preocuparse por el dinero, ¿qué compraría?
5. Si Ud. pudiera remediar un problema en el mundo, ¿qué problema sería?
6. Si Ud. tuviera la oportunidad de hablar con el presidente, ¿qué le diría?
7. Si Ud. pudiera tener la identidad de cualquier persona del mundo, ¿a quién escogería?
8. Si Ud. pudiera elegir una nueva profesión, ¿qué profesión sería?
9. Si Ud. encontrara un millón de dólares mañana, ¿cómo lo gastaría?
10. Si Ud. supiera que iba a tener quince hijos, ¿cómo reaccionaría?

**C. Consecuencias.** Work with a classmate to compare the lifestyles of a student and a famous movie star. Make a chain list of 10 items for each.

| MODELO: **Estudiante** | **Estrella de cine** |
|---|---|
| *Si soy estudiante, no tengo dinero.* | *Si fuera estrella del cine, tendría dinero.* |
| *Si no tengo dinero, no como muy bien.* | *Si tuviera dinero, comería bien.* |
| *Si no como bien...* | |

**D. Pretextos.** Your roommate has very high expectations placed on you and hopes you will do everything as he/she would. Answer his/her questions with an appropriate excuse.

MODELO: ¿Por qué no haces más ejercicio?
*Haría más ejercicio si tuviera tiempo.*

1. ¿Por qué no visitas más a tus padres?
2. ¿Por qué no te quedas más en casa?
3. ¿Por qué no trabajas menos?
4. ¿Me puedes prestar tu coche?
5. ¿Me puedes dar 10 dólares?
6. ¿Me puedes ayudar a mudarme mañana?
7. ¿Por qué no aprendes francés?
8. ¿Por qué no estudias todos los fines de semana?
9. ¿Me puedes preparar una cena especial esta noche?
10. ¿Me puedes acompañar a la universidad el domingo?

**E. La herencia.** How would your world change if a rich relative were to leave you millions of dollars? Work with a classmate to describe how different your life would be if you had all that money.

Discuss:
- whether or not you would share with anyone
- if you would invest any of it and if so, how
- what strategy you would adopt to minimize the amount taken by the IRS
- whether this money would change your attitude towards life in general

# Vocabulario

## TEMA 3
### Una entrevista

**Sustantivos**

| | |
|---|---|
| **la autoridad** | *authority* |
| **el donativo** | *donation* |
| **la fluctuación** | *fluctuation* |
| **el grupo** | *group* |
| **el/la joven** | *young man, woman* |
| **la junta directiva** | *board of directors* |
| **el reportaje** | *report* |
| **el seminario** | *seminar* |
| **la tecnología** | *technology* |

**Verbos**

| | |
|---|---|
| **actuar** | *to act* |
| **ahorrar** | *to save* |
| **construir** | *to build* |
| **donar** | *to donate* |
| **observar** | *to observe* |

**Adjetivos**

| | |
|---|---|
| **bajo/a** | *low* |
| **listo/a** | *clever* |
| **mundial** | *worldwide* |
| **pasado/a** | *past* |
| **positivo/a** | *positive* |

**Otras expresiones**

| | |
|---|---|
| **en contacto con** | *in contact with* |
| **generosamente** | *generously* |

## TEMA 4
### Nuevas vías de comunicación

**Sustantivos**

| | |
|---|---|
| **el buzón** | *mailbox* |
| **la cadena** | *chain* |
| **la calificación** | *grade* |
| **la oscuridad** | *darkness* |
| **el/la protagonista** | *leading man, lady* |
| **el salón de charla** | *chat room* |
| **el satélite** | *satellite* |
| **el siglo** | *century* |
| **la telenovela** | *soap opera* |

**Verbos**

| | |
|---|---|
| **existir** | *to exist* |
| **jurar** | *to swear* |
| **presentar** | *to submit* |

**Adjetivos**

| | |
|---|---|
| **doblado/a** | *dubbed* |
| **mismo/a** | *same* |
| **perdido/a** | *lost* |

**Otras expresiones**

| | |
|---|---|
| **directamente** | *directly* |
| **lo que** | *that which* |
| **todo el mundo** | *everybody* |

# Reunión B

**A escuchar.** **¡Vamos a escribir un libro!** La Sra. Martín le pide al Prof. Yuja que colabore en un libro de texto. Conteste las preguntas según la información que escuche.

1. ¿Desde dónde llama Amanda Martín?
2. ¿Qué quería ella?
3. ¿Tendría que ir el profesor Yuja a algún lugar en especial?
4. ¿Cómo podría mandar el material?
5. ¿Qué le mandaría la Sra. Martín?
6. ¿Cuándo no hubieran podido hacer esto?

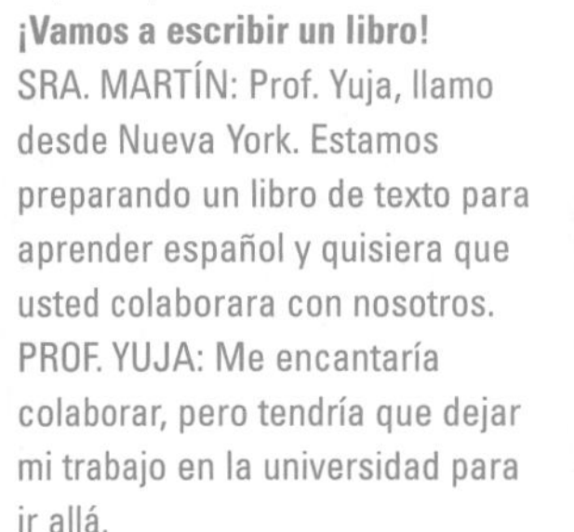

**Tapescript for A escuchar. ¡Vamos a escribir un libro!**
SRA. MARTÍN: Prof. Yuja, llamo desde Nueva York. Estamos preparando un libro de texto para aprender español y quisiera que usted colaborara con nosotros.
PROF. YUJA: Me encantaría colaborar, pero tendría que dejar mi trabajo en la universidad para ir allá.
SRA. MARTÍN: No es necesario. Podría escribir desde su propia casa y mandarnos el material por Internet.
PROF. YUJA: ¿Sí? ¿No tendría que ir a Nueva York?
SRA. MARTÍN: Tal vez tendría que venir una o dos veces, pero podríamos vernos durante las vacaciones de la universidad.
PROF. YUJA: ¿Cómo sabría yo lo que ustedes quieren que haga?
SRA. MARTÍN: Si le interesara este proyecto, le mandaría una guía con toda la información.
PROF. YUJA: Sí, me interesa. ¡Qué maravilla! Si viviéramos en el siglo pasado, no podríamos hacerlo así.

**A conversar.** Uno/a de Uds. es padre o madre y el/la otro/a el/la hijo/a de trece años. El/La padre/madre supo que el/la hijo/a buscaba "cosas sucias" en el Internet. Discutan, entre padre/madre e hijo/a, los usos positivos/negativos del Internet y las consecuencias del mal comportamiento (*behavior*).

MODELO: *Te compraría una computadora nueva si la usaras con buenas metas. Pero si te encuentro otra vez mirando programas así, te la quito completamente.*

## ¿Lo sabía?

**Los recursos del Internet.** Aquí tenemos las direcciones de los periódicos más populares de España. Elijan una sección e investiguen el contenido de una misma sección en todos los periódicos. Rellenen la ficha con cuatro noticias de su sección y proporcionen la información que se les pide de las cuatro noticias seleccionadas.

| Dirección | Periódico |
|---|---|
| http://www.elpais.es/ | EL PAIS DIGITAL |
| http://www2.vanguardia.es/ | LA VANGUARDIA Barcelona |
| http://www.abc.es/ | ABC |
| http://w3.el-mundo.es/index.html | EL MUNDO DEL SIGLO XXI |
| http://www.elperiodico.es/ | el Periódico on line |

| Personas del grupo: |
|---|
| Sección de: |
| Título de la noticia: |
| |
| Encontrada en el periódico: |
| |
| Palabras relevantes de la noticia: |
| |
| Frases relevantes de la noticia: |
| |

VIDAL, N. "La prensa española en Internet" en *Materias 26.* Consejería de Educación. Embajada de España (Washington, DC) 1998.

**A buscar.** Han buscado información en español en el Internet pero, ¿la han buscado con texto bilingüe? Busquen una publicación bilingüe, hagan copias y compartan lo que encuentren con los demás grupos.

**Answers for A escuchar.**
1) *Nueva York.* 2) *Que colaborara en un texto.* 3) *Podría escribir desde su casa.* 4) *Por Internet.* 5) *Una guía.* 6) *El siglo pasado.*

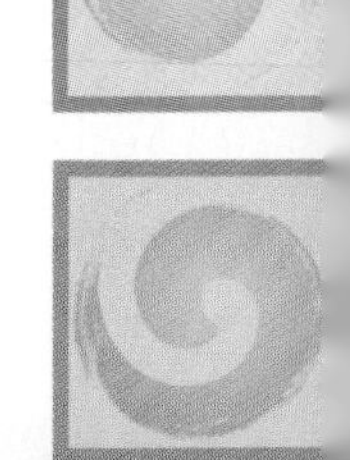

# ¡TRATO HECHO!

## Rincón profesional: El euro

Cierre Ud. los ojos e imagínese por un momento que esta mañana al despertar, el dinero que ha manejado durante toda su vida ha desaparecido. En su lugar, se ha establecido un sistema de dinero compartido con otras naciones y otras economías. ¡Qué sorpresa!

Pues, esto es, con unas pocas diferencias, lo que la mayoría de los bancos y empresas europeos tuvieron que enfrentar el primero de enero de 1999.

Ese día se dieron los primeros pasos hacia lo que será una transformación económica internacional de proporciones y consecuencias enormes. En esa fecha se introdujo oficialmente la nueva moneda *euro* y con ello, las monedas nacionales de Europa—la lira italiana, el franco francés, y claro, la querida peseta española—se borrarán cada vez más hasta que desaparezcan completamente el primero de enero del 2002.

**¿Por qué el *euro*?**

La unidad monetaria en Europa promete prosperidad para todos al:

- apoyar y fortalecer las economías más débiles de Europa.
- reducir los costos de hacer comercio internacional con una moneda sólida en vez de calcular valores equivalentes entre muchas monedas nacionales.
- crear un banco central responsable por las buenas prácticas fiscales.
- estimular la economía de cada país con inversiones del extranjero.
- crear más empleos y más oportunidades.
- ayudar al turista que, hasta ahora, ha tenido que cambiar constantemente el dinero a la moneda local, pagando a cada paso un gran porcentaje en comisiones.

Con tanto como promete el *euro* para la prosperidad de todos, y a pesar de las complicaciones con que se enfrentan los tesoreros de naciones y empresas a la vez, una de las preguntas más comunes que se hacen es:

"Me gusta mucho comprar refrescos y chocolates de las máquinas vendedoras. ¿Las máquinas aceptarán el *euro*?"

**¿Comprende usted?**

1. ¿Qué es el *euro*?
2. ¿Cuándo se hizo efectiva la incorporación del *euro* en los bancos?
3. Describa tres posibles beneficios de la transición al *euro* para la economía.
4. ¿Cuál es uno de los temores del consumidor?

**A escuchar. La educación a distancia.** Escuche el diálogo entre Cecilia y Alejandro y conteste las preguntas según lo que escuche.

1. ¿Que carrera estudió Cecilia?
2. ¿En qué universidad estudió?
3. ¿Desde dónde asistió a las clases?
4. ¿Qué tecnología es necesaria para tomar clases a distancia?

**Tapescript for A escuchar. La educación a distancia.** Cecilia y Alejandro charlan en un café.
ALEJANDRO: Cecilia, ¡felicidades, qué bien que te hayas graduado de psicóloga! No sabía que estuvieras estudiando.
CECILIA: Sí, estudié en la mejor universidad de España.
ALEJANDRO: ¿España? Si hubieras estudiado en Europa, yo lo sabría.
CECILIA: No, mis padres no querían que fuera a Europa. Estudié desde mi casa.
ALEJANDRO: Pero, ¿cómo es posible que pudieras hacerlo?
CECILIA: Lo hice con mi computadora. ¿Sabías de la "Educación a Distancia"?
ALEJANDRO: Claro, nuestro maestro de informática dijo que en el futuro podremos tomar clases, estudiar y buscar información en las mejores bibliotecas del mundo con la computadora.
CECILIA: No, no será en el futuro, ahora puedes hacerlo. Si tuvieras una computadora, podrías estudiar en cualquier universidad del mundo.

**Answers for A escuchar.** 1) *Psicología.* 2) *En España.* 3) *Desde su casa.* 4) *Una computadora y el Internet.*

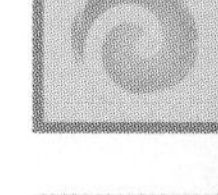
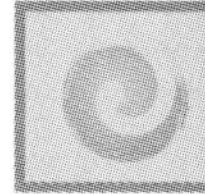

## El buzón de Doña Rosa

Querida Doña Rosa:

El verano pasado fui a Ecuador y conocí a un muchacho maravilloso. Estamos muy enamorados, ¡fue amor a primera vista! Los dos quisiéramos casarnos, pero nuestros padres dicen que todavía somos muy jóvenes. Ellos quieren que terminemos nuestras carreras. De vez en cuando nos llamamos por teléfono, pero el problema es que yo vivo en Florida y las cuentas del teléfono son altísimas. El pasaje de avión es muy caro. ¿Qué puedo hacer? Por favor, no me diga que le escriba cartas, porque tardan mucho tiempo en llegar.

Enamorada

**¿Qué dice Doña Rosa?** Ud. y su compañero/a tienen que ayudar a Dña. Rosa a contestar esta carta con una solución para el problema de "Enamorada". Escriban su respuesta y compártanla con el resto de la clase.

**El instituto.** Dos o tres de ustedes forman la Junta Directiva de su institución. Es su trabajo determinar la dirección que tomará el instituto, decidir qué programas y edificios nuevos habrá y cuáles de los programas y edificios viejos ya no son necesarios. Uno de ustedes es el tesorero/contador del grupo y controlará el dinero. Otro/a es el/la decano/a de programas en humanidades y artes. Otro/a el/la decano/a de programas en ciencias. Otro/a es el/la director/a de programas y equipos atléticos… La junta tiene un millón de dólares para repartir entre los decanos y directores. Cada decano/a y director/a tiene que hacer una lista del equipo (tecnología), personas (secretarios, tutores, profesores) y programas nuevos que sin duda harán famosísima a la institución. Si un millón de dólares no es suficiente, unos decanos o directores pueden recomendar que la mesa directiva quite programas en otras divisiones para obtener más fondos. (Si tuviéramos un estadio…; si quitáramos las clases de biología…)

## A leer

Remember that your own background knowledge in any subject will be the best tool to aid you when faced with an unfamiliar text. In Spanish, as well as many other languages, there are foreign words that are used on a daily basis. Many of those foreign words are English terms or adaptations of them. Keep this in mind when reading the text below, since this is especially true of technological terms.

**Antes de leer.** Do you own a computer, or at least have used one? Are you familiar with the Internet? If your answer is yes, you probably know the most common technical words and that will make it very easy for you to read the following text. Before reading it, circle all the words you already know about computers and the Internet.

### ¡Ya no estamos solos!

La telemedicina llegará a todos los lugares del mundo. En los últimos años hemos tenido una revolución en las comunicaciones con el Internet digital de servicios integrados. Ahora es posible que las imágenes se puedan transmitir, por cable o por satélite con la misma calidad de un televisor. Las posibilidades de estos descubrimientos no tienen límite, pero una de las aplicaciones más importantes es la telemedicina. Ahora los médicos de cualquier país podrán consultar a los mejores especialistas del mundo, desde su propia casa. Lo más interesante es que todo esto sucederá de manera interactiva y en tiempo real. Se podrá tener una videoconferencia: será posible conectarse con distintas personas al mismo tiempo, aunque todos los participantes estén muy lejos.

Si un paciente vive en una zona rural, donde no hay suficientes servicios médicos o especialistas, tendrá los servicios de salud del más alto nivel y la atención más rápida.

¿Su paciente necesita cirugía de emergencia y el doctor no está seguro de cómo hacerla? No hay problema, se puede conectar con un especialista en otro país quien le dirá lo que tiene que hacer. Los radiólogos podrán leer los rayos X y los patólogos las laminillas de las biopsias instantáneamente y desde su casa.

¿Necesita actualizar sus conocimientos médicos, pero trabaja en una zona muy lejana, donde no hay universidades? No importa, la educación a distancia permitirá que estudie y que avance de acuerdo al tiempo que tenga.

¿Qué se necesita? Solamente una computadora, una cámara de televisión y micrófono y podrá tener videoconferencias, charlas, educación a distancia y muchas posibilidades más. La revolución en las comunicaciones solamente está empezando ¡En el siglo XXI habrá muchas otras sorpresas!

**¿Comprende usted?**

1. ¿Puede decir qué palabras relacionadas con la informática encontró?
2. ¿Cómo se pueden transmitir las señales en el Internet?
3. ¿Por qué es importante el Internet para los pacientes?
4. ¿Por qué es importante el Internet para los médicos?
5. ¿Qué equipo se necesita?
6. ¿Cree usted que se puedan salvar vidas por el Internet?

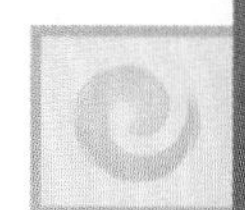

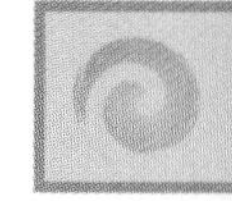

## A escribir

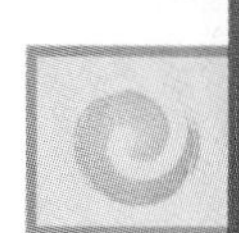

Piense en otras posibilidades para utilizar el Internet en forma global. Después escriba un ensayo corto, explicando sus ideas y presénteselo a sus compañeros/as. ¿Qué se podría hacer para ayudar a los países subdesarrollados? ¿En caso de una catástrofe muy grande? ¿Para alfabetizar, etc...?

# 12 ¡Repaso!

LECCIÓN DOCE

CHECK OUT THE ¡*TRATO HECHO!* WEBSITE AND CD-ROM FOR ACTIVITIES, GAMES, SELF-TESTS, AND MUCH MORE!

## Lección 7

**Tema 1** La vida cotidiana
**Tema 2** Los coches
**Tema 3** Accidentes y emergencias
**Tema 4** Cómo protegerse

## Lección 8

**Tema 1** Los viajes
**Tema 2** El hotel
**Tema 3** Los restaurantes
**Tema 4** Las excursiones

## Lección 9

**Tema 1** La salud
**Tema 2** Póngase en forma
**Tema 3** El bienestar mental
**Tema 4** La sala de urgencias

## Lección 10

**Tema 1** El mundo del trabajo
**Tema 2** Buscando casa
**Tema 3** La casa y las finanzas
**Tema 4** Los negocios

## Lección 11

**Tema 1** El futuro
**Tema 2** ¿Cómo seremos?
**Tema 3** La tecnología
**Tema 4** El nuevo milenio

## Lección 7

# TEMA 1

### La vida cotidiana

*Muchas personas miran al pasado de un modo romántico—todo lo pasado fue mejor. ¿Qué opina Ud.? ¿Prefiere la simplicidad del pasado o la tecnología del presente?*

Answers for A. 1) *Íbamos al banco.* 2) *Escribíamos cartas y las poníamos en el correo.* 3) *Iba a la biblioteca y consultaba la enciclopedia.* 4) *Iba al cine.* 5) *Iba de compras al centro comercial.*

**A. Ahora y entonces.** La tecnología cambia la manera en que hacemos muchas de nuestras actividades diarias. Diga Ud. adónde **iban** las siguientes personas hace diez años para hacer estas cosas.

MODELO: Ahora, para hacer una llamada telefónica cuando no estoy en casa, yo saco mi teléfono celular.
*Hace diez años, para hacer una llamada telefónica cuando yo no estaba en casa, yo* ***iba*** *a un teléfono público.*

1. Ahora si necesitamos cambiar un cheque, vamos al cajero automático.
2. Ahora si les escribe a sus amigos en otro estado, escribe una carta electrónica.
3. Ahora si busco información para un informe, navego por la red.
4. Ahora cuando Ud. quiere ver una película, alquila la película y la ve en casa.
5. Ahora cuando la gente quiere comprar sin salir de casa, mira la televisión.

Answers for B. 1) *Veía/veo.* 2) *Miraba (limpiaba,?)/miro (limpio,?).* 3) *Hacía (estudiaba)/hago (estudio,?).* 4) *Escuchaba/escucho.* 5) *Iba/voy.* 6) *Tomaba/tomo.* 7) *Montaba en (bicicleta)/manejo un (coche).* 8) *Me preocupaba(n)/me preocupa(n).*

**B. Otros cambios.** La tecnología también influye en nuestros gustos, preferencias y costumbres. Cuando era niño/a probablemente Ud. prefería ciertas cosas y ahora prefiere otras. Haga una lista de los cambios de "entonces y ahora" para cada categoría.

MODELO: comida favorita
*Cuando era niño/a* ***comía*** *hamburguesas y pizza. Ahora,* ***como*** *langosta y filete.*

1. programas de televisión
2. actividades del sábado por la mañana
3. la tarea
4. la canción favorita
5. las vacaciones del verano
6. las bebidas favoritas
7. el transporte
8. las preocupaciones principales

**C. Nostalgia.** Escoja Ud. tres de las categorías de la actividad B y escriba un párrafo nostálgico sobre su niñez. Indique lo que le gustaba de la niñez y lo que no le gustaba.

MODELO: Comida favorita, sábado por la mañana, mis amigos
*El sábado por la mañana me levantaba a las seis y veía la televisión....Comía cereal mientras veía El Conejo Bugs. A las ocho llegaban mis amigos para jugar al béisbol....A las doce almorzábamos en casa de Linda.*

**D. Comparaciones.** Escuche el párrafo que su compañero/a escribió para la actividad anterior. ¿Su niñez fue diferente o semejante a la de su compañero/a? Haga una lista de diferencias y semejanzas.

MODELO:

| Yo | Ud. |
|---|---|
| *veía el Conejo Bugs* | *veía Mickey Mouse* |

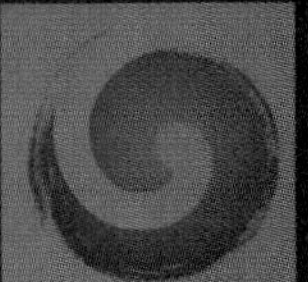

# TEMA 2

## Los coches

*Tener un coche significa independencia, libertad y para muchos, pobreza: seguros, llantas, gasolina... Pero ¿podemos imaginarnos la vida sin el auto? ¡Nunca!*

**A. Crucigrama: El auto.** Lea las definiciones de cosas relacionadas con el auto y escriba la palabra correspondiente en los espacios indicados.

**Vertical**

1. Es peligroso manejar sin ponerse el __________ de seguridad.
2. Es donde pongo la gasolina.
3. Es donde yo voy para llenar el tanque.

**Horizontal**

4. Es necesario cambiar esto cada 3.000 millas.
5. Estos son importantes en caso de un accidente.
6. Hay cuatro y son negras.
7. ¡Ay no! Tenemos una llanta____________.
8. Se usan para parar el coche.
9. Es donde pongo las maletas y otras cosas.

**Answers for A.** 1) *Cinturón.* 2) *Tanque.* 3) *Gasolinera.* 4) *Aceite.* 5) *Seguros.* 6) *Llantas.* 7) *Desinflada.* 8) *Frenos.* 9) *Maletero.*

**B. Lo hice porque...** ¿Cuáles eran las circunstancias que causaron estas acciones?

MODELO: Fui a la gasolinera.
*Fui a la gasolinera porque necesitaba gasolina.*

1. Cambié el aceite.
2. Compré una llanta nueva.
3. Lavé el coche.
4. Puse el aire acondicionado.
5. Choqué con el coche de delante.
6. El policía me multó.

**Answers for B.** 1) *Salía de la ciudad/iba de vacaciones/?.* 2) *La otra era vieja/estaba desinflada/?.* 3) *Estaba sucio.* 4) *Hacía calor.* 5) *Miraba a un/a joven guapo/a /no prestaba atención.* 6) *Manejaba muy rápido.*

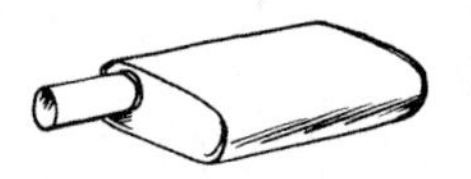

**C. Se me olvidó.** Normalmente Ud. tiene mucho cuidado cuando hace un viaje en coche. Pero ayer Ud. tenía mucha prisa y salió sin tomar las precauciones necesarias. ¡Qué desastre! Diga Ud. lo que no hizo con el coche y el resultado.

MODELO: limpiar el parabrisas
*No limpié el parabrisas y choqué con un coche porque no veía.*

1. revisar los frenos
2. llenar el tanque
3. poner las maletas en el maletero
4. revisar la presión de las llantas
5. abrocharse el cinturón
6. mirar antes de manejar en marcha atrás

**Answers for C.** 1) *No revisé/no pude parar/?.* 2) *No llené/se me acabó.* 3) *No puse/se me quedó la ropa en casa.* 4) *No revisé/tuve una llanta desinflada.* 5) *No me abroché/me pegué.* 6) *No miré/choqué.*

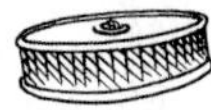

**D. El coche alquilado.** Ud. decidió alquilar un coche nuevo para hacer un viaje. Con un/a compañero/a escriba un diálogo entre el/la dependiente/a de la *Agencia Aquí Alquila* (AAA) y el/la cliente/a. El/La dependiente/a hace preguntas para saber por qué alquila el coche y qué busca en él. El/La cliente/a tiene que explicar los problemas que tenía con el otro coche y el equipo que desea en el coche alquilado.

MODELO: E1 (Cliente): *Necesito alquilar un coche. Iba a salir de la ciudad esta mañana y mi coche se descompuso. Si no encuentro otro, no puedo salir.*
E2 (Dependiente): *¿Adónde iba?*

# Lección 7

## TEMA 3

### Accidentes y emergencias

*Usted está caminando tranquilamente, sin ninguna preocupación cuando—de repente—hay un accidente. En un momento Ud. se transforma en ¡testigo! Aquí tiene la historia de Felipe y Eduardo—testigos.*

Answers for A.
**Dibujo A.** 1) *Caminar/caminaban.* 2) *Escuchar/escuchaban.* 3) *Comer/comía.* 4) *Hacer (calor)/hacía.*
**Dibujo B.** 1) *Ser (bonita)/era.* 2) *Hablar/hablaba.* 3) *Bailar/bailaba.* 4) *Mirarse/se miraba.* 5) *Tomar/tomaba.* 6) *Escuchar/escuchaba.* 7) *Ir/iba.*
**Dibujo C.** 1) *Cambiar/cambiaba.* 2) *Manejar/manejaba.* 3) *Prestar/prestaba.*
**Dibujo D.** 1) *Chocar/chocaba.* 2) *Llover/llovía.* 3) *Correr/corría.* 4) *Gritar/gritaba.* 5) *Mirar/miraba.*

**A. El accidente.** Ayer, Felipe y Eduardo caminaban durante la hora del almuerzo cuando vieron un accidente. Estudie Ud. cada dibujo y después escriba una lista de infinitivos que describa lo que pasa en el dibujo. Después, cambie el infinitivo a una acción en el imperfecto o el pretérito según el dibujo.

MODELO: caminar: *Eduardo y Felipe caminaban por la calle a la hora del almuerzo.*
hacer: *Hacía calor.*

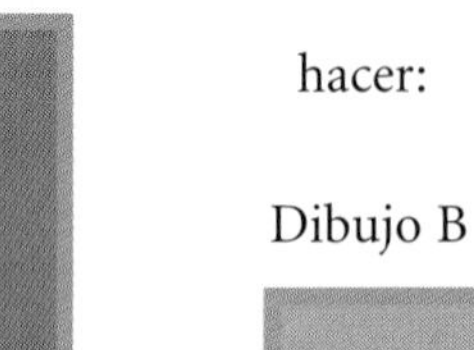

Dibujo A

Dibujo B

Dibujo C

Dibujo D

**B. El informe de los testigos.** Cuando llegó, el policía hizo muchas preguntas acerca de lo que vieron Eduardo y Felipe. En parejas, escriban una lista de las preguntas que hizo el policía para poder escribir su informe. Entonces, con uno/a de ustedes en el papel del policía y con otro/a en el papel de Eduardo y Felipe, creen un diálogo, contestando las preguntas para reportar el accidente.

MODELO: E1 (El policía): *¿Vieron Uds. el accidente?*
E2 (Eduardo/Felipe): *Sí, nosotros lo vimos todo…*

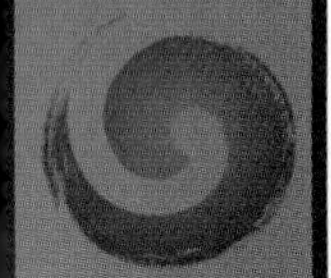

**Lección 7**

# TEMA 4

## Cómo protegerse

*La calle puede ser muy peligrosa. Es importante protegerse cuando se sale. Aquí vamos a repasar algunas normas de tráfico.*

**Las normas de tráfico.** Felizmente nadie se lastimó en el accidente que tuvo Susanita, pero ella tiene que aprender una lección importante. El policía ha escrito aquí una lista de las 10 infracciones que Susanita cometió:

**A. Lecciones para el futuro.** Transforme Ud. todas las infracciones de la lista en frases impersonales que describan las normas de la carretera.

MODELO: Tomaba mientras manejaba.
*No se toma mientras se maneja.*

**Answers for A.** 1) *No se escucha…* 2) *No se baila/se maneja…* 3) *Uno no se pinta ni se peina…* 4) *No se maneja (va) a mucha velocidad…* 5) *Se llevan ropa y zapatos/se maneja…* 6) *Se para.* 7) *No se conduce…* 8) *No se ofrece…* 9) *No se dice…*

**B. Servicio público.** Ahora, Susanita tiene la obligación de ir a una escuela primaria para explicarles a los niños estas normas de seguridad. Escriba cinco ideas que ella puede usar en la clase.

MODELO: *En el coche, siempre se deben abrochar el cinturón de seguridad.*

**C. La seguridad de los niños.** Uno de Uds. es estudiante en la clase primaria y le hace preguntas a Susanita sobre su seguridad personal. Susanita le contesta con una frase impersonal.

MODELO: E1: *¿Puedo aceptar dulces de personas desconocidas?*
E2: *No, no se aceptan dulces de personas desconocidas.*

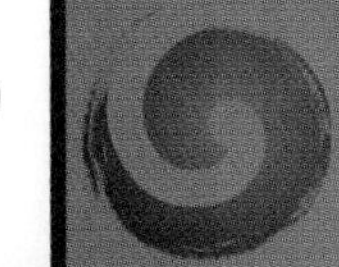

REPASO REPASO REPASO REPASO REPASO REPASO REPASO REPASO REPASO REPASO

# Lección 8

## TEMA 1

### Los viajes

*A veces las preparaciones para un viaje cuestan tanto trabajo que a la hora de salir, Ud. verdaderamente necesita las vacaciones. ¡Vámonos de viaje!*

Answers for A. 1) *Llamamos.* 2) *Conseguimos/sacamos.* 3) *Sacamos/ganamos.* 4) *Consultamos a.* 5) *Sacamos/compramos/pagamos.* 6) *Compramos.* 7) *Leímos.* 8) *Hicimos.*

**A. Preparaciones.** Antes de irse de vacaciones, Ud. y su amigo/a hicieron muchas preparaciones. Explique Ud. qué hicieron con las siguientes cosas.

MODELO: las guías turísticas
*Consultamos las guías turísticas.*

1. el taxi
2. el pasaporte
3. el dinero
4. la agente de viajes
5. los pasajes
6. los rollos de película
7. los folletos de los cruceros
8. las maletas

Answers for B. 1) *Lo llamamos.* 2) *Lo conseguimos/sacamos.* 3) *Lo sacamos/ganamos.* 4) *La consultamos.* 5) *Los sacamos/compramos/pagamos.* 6) *Los compramos.* 7) *Los leímos.* 8) *Las hicimos.*

**B. ¿Cuándo?** Explique Ud. cuándo hicieron estas preparaciones, usando un pronombre de objeto directo. Después, ponga en orden lógico las oraciones.

MODELO: *—Consultamos las guías turísticas. Hace un año las consultamos.*
*—Pedimos un taxi. El día del viaje lo pedimos.*

**C. Un destino para todos.** Ud. y su compañero/a tienen una compañía de publicidad. Uno de sus clientes es el presidente de una línea de cruceros y quiere un anuncio para su barco llamado *Siga Soñando* que explique todo lo que ofrece el crucero para toda la familia. Uds. van a presentarle al cliente un diálogo en forma de preguntas y respuestas con todo lo que los pasajeros puedan soñar en estas vacaciones.

MODELO: E1: *¿Busca Ud.* ***un descanso*** *de las preocupaciones diarias?*
E2: ***Lo*** *va a encontrar en* Siga Soñando.
E1: *¿Desean sus hijos tener* ***discoteca*** *las veinticuatro horas del día?*
E2: *Van a tener****la*** *en* Siga Soñando.

**D. En el futuro.** Uno/a de ustedes acaba de ganar mucho, mucho dinero. El/la otro/a es un/a agente de viajes, experto/a en viajes de lujo. Escriban y presenten a la clase un diálogo en el que los/las dos hacen planes para un viaje extravagante.

Hablen de:
- las fechas del viaje
- el medio de transporte
- los lujos disponibles
- las diversiones posibles

MODELO: Cliente: *¿Agencia* Siga Soñando*? Soy Bill Gates y quiero hacer un crucero a Europa. Necesito hacer una reserva.*

# TEMA 2

## El hotel

*¿Trabaja Ud. o piensa trabajar de cara al público? ¡Prepárese ya para conocer a una gran variedad de personas y costumbres curiosas!*

**A. En el hotel.** Ud. trabaja en un hotel grande y lujoso para turistas. Al regresar del almuerzo, Ud. recibe estos mensajes de clientes que necesitan varios servicios. Déjeles mensajes explicando cuándo van a recibir lo que necesitan.

**Answers for A.** 1) *Les llevo.* 2) *Le consigo/llamo.* 3) *La busco.* 4) *Les doy.* 5) *Puede darme.* 6) *Puedo llevarle.*

MODELO: Mensaje: El Señor Shelton en la habitación 1595 pide más toallas.
*Señor Shelton, le traigo a Ud. más toallas en media hora.*

1. Los señores Durán piden una botella de champán para la medianoche.
2. La señora Vela necesita un taxi para las siete de la tarde.
3. La niña Claudia perdió su muñeca. Está llorando. ¿Puede Ud. buscarla?
4. La familia Vargas quiere información sobre un restaurante elegante.
5. Su jefe quiere saber cuándo puede darle un regalo por su buen servicio.
6. Su madre quiere saber si puede llevarle leche antes de volver a casa.

**B. Las recomendaciones.** El hotel donde trabaja Ud. está en una ciudad enorme con miles de restaurantes de todo tipo. Cuando los clientes le piden recomendaciones, Ud. tiene que hacerles preguntas para saber qué es lo que les gusta. Escriba una lista de seis preguntas para averiguar los gustos de los clientes.

MODELO: *¿Les gusta la comida italiana?*
*¿Les molesta el humo de los cigarros y puros (cigars)?*

**C. Los clientes difíciles.** Trabaje Ud. con un/a compañero/a para inventar un diálogo entre el empleado del hotel y UNO de los siguientes clientes. El empleado va a usar las preguntas que hizo en el ejercicio anterior—y posiblemente otras—también.

MODELO: Dos jóvenes quieren recomendaciones para restaurantes interesantes.

Empleado: *¿Les gusta la comida rápida?*
Jóvenes: *¿Hay música allí?*
Empleado: *¿Qué música les interesa?*

1. una señora mayor con su perrito en un suéter, quiere una recomendación para un restaurante elegante.
2. un profesor pide una recomendación para un restaurante bueno y barato.
3. cinco jóvenes de diecinueve años piden una recomendación para un bar de moda.
4. una señora con su hijo de ocho años quiere una recomendación para un parque de atracciones.

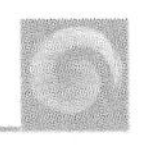



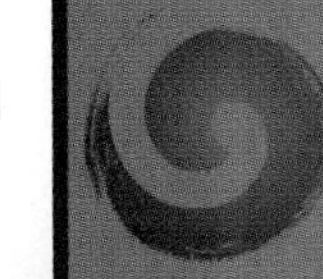

REPASO REPASO REPASO REPASO REPASO REPASO REPASO REPASO REPASO

# Lección 8

## TEMA 3

### Los restaurantes

*Aquí tiene Ud. a otros clientes que necesitan mucha atención. No importa lo que quieran, Ud. debe ofrecerles un buen servicio. Recuerde: ¡El cliente siempre tiene la razón!*

**Answers for A.** 1) *Se la puedo servir.* 2) *Se lo levo.* 3) *Se la busco.* 4) *Se la traigo en dos platos.* 5) *Se la sirvo.* 6) *Se las doy.*

**A. En el restaurante.** Ud. es el mesero de un grupo muy extraño en el comedor de un crucero de lujo. Los pasajeros pagaron mucho dinero por el crucero y si se quejan, Ud. va a perder su trabajo. Conteste estas preguntas con cortesía y con pronombres de objeto directo e indirecto.

MODELO: La señora con el perrito quiere saber si puede traerle champán al perro.
*Sí, señora, se lo traigo enseguida.*

1. Los jóvenes de dieciséis años piden cerveza con el desayuno.
2. Las cinco señoritas piden su desayuno en el camarote al mediodía.
3. La pobre niña, Claudia, perdió su muñeca otra vez. ¿Puede buscarla?
4. El profesor quiere su ensalada en dos platos de colores diferentes.
5. Los padres de tres niños horribles saben que se cierra el comedor a las diez, pero quieren saber si Ud. puede servirles una comida completa a las once.
6. Un niño quiere saber si puede darle sus verduras al perro que toma champán.

**Answers for B.** 1) *¿Se la serviste?/ Sí/No se la serví.* 2) *¿Se lo llevaste?/ Sí/No se lo llevé.* 3) *¿Se la buscaste?/ Sí/No se la busqué.* 4) *¿Se la llevaste?/ Sí/No se la llevé.* 5) *¿Se la serviste?/ Sí/No se las serví.* 6) *¿Se las diste?/ Sí/No se la di.*

**B. ¡El jefe!** El/La jefe/a de camareros quiere saber si los clientes recibieron lo que pidieron. Uno de Uds. va a ser el/la jefe/a. Él/Ella va a transformar cada pedido en una pregunta. El/La otro/a otra va a contestarla.

MODELO: la señora con el perrito quiere saber si puede traerle champán al perro.
Jefe: *El champán, ¿se lo trajiste tú al perro?*
Mesero/a: *Sí/No se lo traje.*

**Answers for C.** 1) *¿Puede comprarme. . . ?/ Sí, se la puedo comprar/puedo comprársela.* 2) *¿Puede prestarme. . . ?/ Sí, se lo puedo prestar/puedo prestárselo.* 3) *¿Puede darme. . . ?/ Sí, se la puedo dar/puedo dársela.* 4) *¿Puede dejarle. . . ?/ Sí, se la puedo dejar/ puedo dejársela.*

**C. El pasajero olvidadizo.** Hay un/a pasajero/a en el crucero que quiere ser amigo/a de Ud. Siempre está a su lado. Este/a pasajero/a no es antipático/a, pero nunca está preparado/a para nada y siempre le pide favores a Ud. Con un compañero/a, use los siguientes favores para inventar diálogos lógicos entre Ud. y el/la pasajero/a.

MODELO: Se me olvidó la cámara fotográfica. (sacar)
E1: *¿Puede sacarme una foto?*
E2: *Sí, se la puedo sacar/Sí, puedo sacársela.*

1. No tengo dinero para comprar cerveza. (comprar)
2. Dejé mi traje de baño en el camarote. (prestar)
3. Quiero escribir unas postales, pero no tengo pluma. (dar)
4. Debo dejarle propina al mesero, pero no tengo dinero. (dejar)

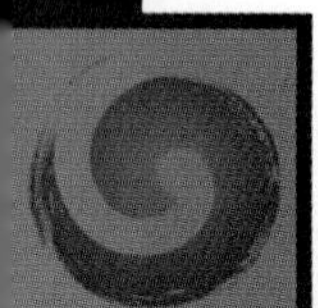

## Lección 8

# TEMA 4

## Las excursiones

*Usted es el guía turístico de un crucero que está en el puerto de Veracruz. Hay muchos lugares de interés que su grupo debe conocer. Pero ¿será posible que todos estos turistas se pongan de acuerdo sobre lo que es un lugar de interés?*

**A. Advertencias.** Hay información importante que los pasajeros necesitan saber. Usted no tuvo tiempo de preparar una lista formal de advertencias. Use estas notas para decirles a los pasajeros lo que deben y no deben hacer.

MODELO: no tomar el agua natural
*No tomen Uds. el agua natural aquí.*

1. tener cuidado con el sol
2. llevar sombrero durante el día
3. ponerse bloqueador de sol
4. no separarse del grupo
5. no sacar fotos en los museos
6. no comer mariscos crudos
7. ir al zócalo para escuchar música
8. siempre salir con un/a compañero/a
9. no llegar tarde al autobús
10. practicar el español con los habitantes de Veracruz

**Answers for A.** 1) *Tengan cuidado...* 2) *Lleven sombrero...* 3) *Pónganse bloqueador...* 4) *No se separen...* 5) *No saquen fotos...* 6) *No coman mariscos...* 7) *Vayan al zócalo...* 8) *Siempre salgan...* 9) *No lleguen tarde...* 10) *Practiquen mucho...*

**B. ¡Qué grupo!** Algunos miembros del grupo le dicen a Ud. lo que quieren hacer. ¡Decida Ud. y después dígales que sí o que no!

**Answers for B.** 1) *Quédese (no se quede)/(no) acompañe.* 2) *(No) pidan.* 3) *Practiquen/(no) vayan de compras.* 4) *Obedezcan.* 5) *No tomen cerveza/presten atención.* 6) *No se quiten las camisas.*

MODELO: La señora con el perro quiere sentarse en el bar. No quiere ir al museo.
*Está bien, señora, siéntese en el bar. No vaya al museo.*

1. El profesor quiere quedarse en el museo. No quiere ir con el grupo a la iglesia.
2. Los jóvenes de dieciséis años quieren los teléfonos de todas las señoritas en la calle.
3. Las cinco señoritas no quieren practicar español. Sólo quieren ir de compras.
4. Los tres niños horribles no quieren obedecer a sus padres.
5. Los padres de los tres niños horribles toman cerveza y no les prestan atención.
6. Los jóvenes quieren quitarse la camisa en el centro para broncearse.

**C. Turismo en mi ciudad.** Usted y su compañero/a quieren abrir un negocio de turismo en su ciudad. Preparen un folleto en español con lugares de interés, atracciones, restaurantes y hoteles. Indiquen en el folleto los precios aproximados para cada lugar. Incluyan un mapa básico de la región.

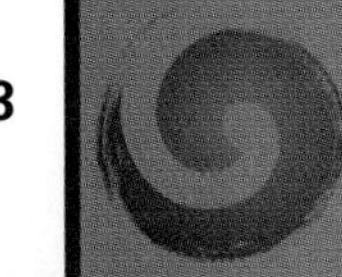

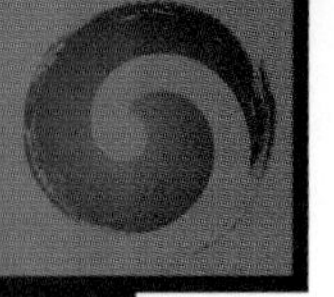

REPASO REPASO REPASO REPASO REPASO REPASO REPASO REPASO REPASO REPASO

## Lección 9

# TEMA 1

### La salud

*Usted acaba de aceptar un empleo en una clínica/hotel, que se llama* **Aguas Milagrosas**, *para celebridades que buscan el equilibrio físico y mental. En realidad, los clientes tienen mucho dinero y pocas ganas de cambiar los placeres que compran el dinero y la fama por una vida tranquila y sana.*

Answers for A. 1) *Nada...* 2) *No te preocupes...* 3) *Recibe...* 4) *Haz...* 5) *Baja...* 6) *Asiste...* 7) *Despiértate...* 8) *Prueba...*

**A. El primer encuentro.** Su primer/a cliente/a celebridad es una amiga suya que se llama Roseanne (o un amigo suyo que se llama Marlon). Explíquele lo que debe hacer en el hotel (con mandatos informales).

MODELO: montar a caballo por las montañas
*Monta a caballo por las montañas.*

1. nadar en la piscina olímpica
2. no preocuparse por nada porque no hay periódicos
3. recibir un masaje profesional todos los días después del ejercicio aeróbico
4. hacer caminatas antes del amanecer
5. bajar de peso sin saberlo
6. asistir a clases de meditación
7. despertarse con los pájaros
8. probar la comida de dieta más rica del mundo

Answers for B. 1) *No comas pastel, come fruta.* 2) *No mires la televisión, haz ejercicio.* 3) *No comas hamburguesas, come ensalada.* 4) *No pidas champán, pide agua mineral.* 5) *No salgas, acuéstate temprano.* 6) *No busques otro hotel, quédate aquí.*

**B. Contradicciones.** Su cliente todavía cree que está en el hotel para descansar y recibir mucha atención. No está preparada/o para lo que usted tiene en mente. Corrija Ud. estas declaraciones que hace su cliente/a.

MODELO: Voy a levantarme mañana a las once. (levantarse a las cinco)
*No te levantes a las once, levántate a las cinco.*

1. Voy a comer pastel de chocolate de desayuno. (comer fruta)
2. Voy a mirar la televisión todo el día. (hacer ejercicio)
3. Voy a comer hamburguesas al mediodía. (ensalada)
4. Antes de cenar voy a pedir una botella de champán. (pedir agua mineral)
5. Por la noche, voy a salir a la cantina a tomar margaritas. (acostarse temprano)
6. Voy a buscar otro hotel. (quedarse aquí)

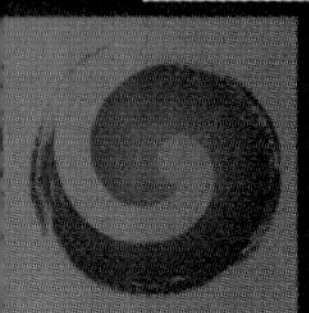

# TEMA 2

## Póngase en forma

*Parte del programa para mantener el equilibrio físico y mental es una sesión con el/la dietista profesional. Usted tendrá que convencer a los clientes de que las dietas y el ejercicio son divertidos.*

**A. El diario de lo consumido.** El dietista quiere que Roseanne o Marlon llenen el diario de la comida antes de la visita. En el papel de Roseanne o de Marlon, imagine lo que ellos comieron durante la semana.

MODELO: lunes: *almuerzo: medio pastel de chocolate y café con crema*

**B. Recomendaciones del dietista.** Analice Ud. el diario de la comida consumida por su compañero/a en el ejercicio anterior. Luego, haga seis sugerencias para una dieta más saludable.

MODELO: *No quiero que comas pastel de chocolate de desayuno. Recomiendo que prepares sopa de tomate, una ensalada de verduras y café solo.*

**C. Clase de cocina.** Cada uno/a de Uds. va a explicar cómo se prepara una de las comidas de dieta que recomendó en el ejercicio B. Pueden usar los mandatos informales y el subjuntivo para sugerir y recomendar.

MODELO: Un almuerzo para Marlon
*Una ensalada grande*
*Una manzana*
*Té*
*Ve a tu tienda favorita y compra lechuga, tomates y pepino. Corta las verduras y ponlas en un plato. No pongas aderezo en la ensalada. Usa limón. Lava la manzana y córtala en cuatro pedazos. Prepara el té sin azúcar.*

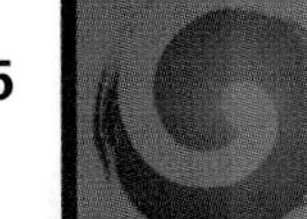

# Lección 9

## TEMA 3

### El bienestar mental

*En el Hotel Aguas Milagrosas, la salud mental es tan importante como la salud física. Una parte importante del régimen aquí es la falta de televisión y periódicos. Hay tantas malas noticias en el mundo que pueden llevarnos fácilmente a la depresión y a la ansiedad.*

**Answers for A.** *Me molesta/No me gusta/Es malo/Es triste que…* 1) *Sufran.* 2) *Haya.* 3) *No estén.* 4) *Haya.* 5) *sSea.* 6) *Gaste.*

**A. Las malas noticias.** Diga Ud. por qué estos problemas mundiales pueden causarle malestar. Use una de las expresiones de emoción: *Temo que… Siento que… No me gusta que… Me molesta que …* etc.

MODELO: Hay mucha violencia en el mundo.
*Me molesta que haya mucha violencia en el mundo.*

1. Muchas personas sufren de pobreza.
2. Hay muchos desastres naturales terribles.
3. Los niños no están seguros en la calle.
4. Hay guerras civiles en muchas naciones.
5. El precio del tratamiento médico es muy alto.
6. El gobierno gasta mucho dinero en tonterías.

**B. Las buenas noticias.** Por cada una de las malas noticias del ejercicio A escriba Ud. una razón para sentirse optimista sobre su propia vida. Use frases de emoción como: *Me alegro de que… , Me gusta que… , Estoy contento/a de que…*

MODELO: Hay mucha violencia en el mundo.
*Me alegro de que mi vecindario sea tranquilo.*

**C. Ojalá que…** Ahora, escriba una lista de cinco deseos para mejorar el mundo y cinco deseos para mejorar su propio bienestar mental.

MODELO: *Ojalá que encuentren pronto una cura para el cáncer.*
*Ojalá que mis profesores no me den tarea esta noche.*

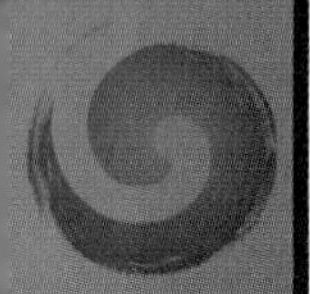

# TEMA 4

## La sala de urgencias

*Usted es estudiante de medicina en la sala de urgencias de un gran hospital metropolitano. Ud. tiene que ver a los pacientes, decidir qué pruebas necesitan y luego hacer un diagnóstico.*

En la sala de urgencias.

| Nombre | Humberto Salazar |
|---|---|
| Edad | setenta y cinco años |
| Familia | esposa María Olga |
| Seguros | Nacionales |
| Síntomas: Después de comer una gran comida italiana, se levantó de la mesa y de repente se cayó. Tenía las manos en el abdomen y se quejaba de un dolor fuerte. Entonces perdió el conocimiento. Durante la cena tomó mucho vino tino. | |
| Pruebas | |
| Diagnóstico | |

**A. El primer paciente.** Usted trabaja con otro estudiante nuevo de medicina que hace las siguientes sugerencias. Diga Ud. si está de acuerdo o no según la información de la ficha anterior.

MODELO: Está borracho.
*No creo que esté borracho. / Dudo que esté borracho. / Sí, creo que está borracho.*

1. Tiene la pierna fracturada.
2. Es una pulmonía.
3. Tiene una infección de oído.
4. Puede ser un infarto (*heart attack*).
5. Le duele la garganta.
6. Va a tener un bebé.

**Answers for A.** *Dudo/no creo/no es verdad que...* 1) *Tenga.* 2) *Sea.* 3) *Haya.* 4) *Pueda.* 5) *Le duela.* 6) *Vaya.* *OR* *Creo/es verdad/es obvio/no dudo que...* 1) *Tiene.* 2) *Es.* 3) *Tiene.* 4) *Puede.* 5) *Le duele.* 6) *Va.*

**B. El médico opina.** Uno/a de ustedes hará el papel de médico en la sala de urgencias y el/la otro/a hará de paciente. Después, para el segundo escenario, pueden cambiar los papeles (*roles*). En cada escenario:

- el médico va a hacerle preguntas al paciente para obtener la información necesaria.
- el médico va a sugerir unas pruebas.
- el paciente puede opinar: *Está bien...* o *No creo que ... sea necesario.*
- el médico escribe su diagnóstico y hace recomendaciones para el tratamiento.

Escenario 1

| Nombre | Anita Meléndez |
|---|---|
| Edad | tres años |
| Familia | Arturo y Melinda Meléndez (padres) |
| Seguros | no |
| Síntomas: Llora constantemente y se toca las orejas. Dejó de comer hace doce horas. No puede dormir. Tose un poco. Tiene diarrea. Fiebre: 39.5 grados. | |
| Pruebas | |
| Diagnóstico | |

Escenario 2

| Nombre | Agustín Amado |
|---|---|
| Edad | veintidós años |
| Familia | En Florida. Viene acompañado por su novia y unos amigos. |
| Seguros | Póliza # 2976456 |
| Síntomas: Estaba esquiando cuando se golpeó contra un árbol. Se cayó y se torció la pierna derecha. No puede caminar. | |
| Pruebas | |
| Diagnóstico | |





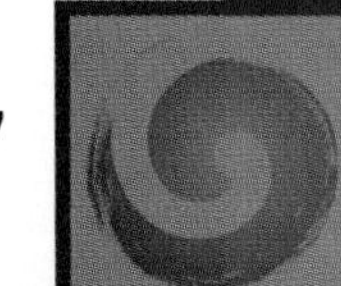

# Lección 10

## TEMA 1

### El mundo del trabajo

*¡Felicidades! Su jefe lo seleccionó a Ud. para ir a Nueva York a recibir entrenamiento especial en una de las compañías más grandes del mundo: La Compañía Prestigiosa. Antes de salir, Ud. le prometió a su jefe que le iba a escribir todos los días con noticias de sus actividades. También les prometió Ud. a sus compañeros un informe detallado de cada día de su viaje a Nueva York.*

Answers for A. 1) *Fácilmente.* 2) *Directamente.* 3) *Tranquilamente.* 4) *Impacientemente.* 5) *Amablemente.* 6) *Inteligentemente.* 7) *Clara.* 8) *Definitivamente.*

**A. La primera carta electrónica al jefe.** Llene el espacio con la forma adverbial correspondiente.

MODELO: Llamé _______ (rápido).
*Llamé rápidamente.*

Estimado Jefe:

Llegué _______ (1) (fácil) a Nueva York y fui _______ (2) (directo) al hotel. Allí me quedé _______ (3) (tranquilo) hasta la mañana. Me desperté a las cinco y tuve que esperar _______ (4) (impaciente) hasta la hora de salir. Fui pronto a *La Compañía Prestigiosa.* Todos los empleados me trataron muy _______ (5) (amable) y me enseñaron los secretos profesionales que les permiten trabajar tan _______ (6) (inteligente). Voy a llegar pasado mañana y le puedo decir _______ (7) y _______ (8) (claro, definitivo) los secretos para mejorar nuestra empresa.

Hasta entonces,
Ricardo

Answers for B. 1) *Se nos acabó.* 2) *Se me olvidó.* 3) *Se me perdieron.* 4) *Se (me) descompuso.* 5) *Se me rompió.* 6) *Se me perdió.*

**B. Y ahora, la carta electrónica para los compañeros.** El viaje, en realidad, no fue tan perfecto. Ud. va a decir la verdad en la carta electrónica que recibieron sus compañeros. Llene los espacios con la forma del verbo.

MODELO: A mí _______ (romperse) los anteojos.
*A mí se me rompieron los anteojos.*

Queridos amigos míos:

Este viaje es todo un desastre. Primero, ayer, cuando mi compañero de cuarto me llevaba al aeropuerto, de repente se paró el coche. —¡Ay de mí!—dijo.—A nosotros _______ (1) (acabarse) la gasolina—. Yo quería mantener la tranquilidad y le dije:—no hay problema. Aquí tengo el teléfono celular en el portafolios. Puedo pedir ayuda—. Pero cuando busqué el portafolios, no estaba.—¡Es el colmo!—le dije. _______ (2) (olvidarse) traer el portafolios. Por lo menos tengo aquí las maletas. Con la ayuda de un chofer simpático, llegué al aeropuerto en el instante en que iban a cerrar la puerta del avión. Todo iba bien hasta que fui a buscar las maletas al llegar a JFK y supe que no habían llegado. A mí _______ (3) (perderse) las maletas. Allí estaba yo, en Nueva York, preparándome para la reunión más importante de mi carrera profesional, sin otra ropa que mis vaqueros. Valientemente, fui al hotel y me acosté temprano. Pero _______ (4) (descomponerse) el despertador y no me desperté hasta las diez de la mañana. Corriendo para vestirme, _______ (5) (romperse) la camisa. En ese momento decidí volver a casa pero no pude porque _______ (6) (perderse) el boleto de vuelta.

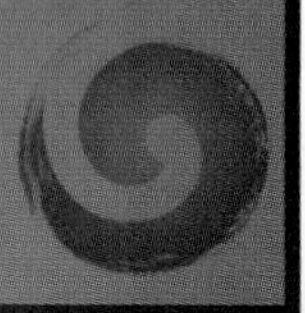

Lección 10

# TEMA 2

## Buscando casa

*Ud. acaba de recibir un telegrama que dice que su compañía le ofrece una promoción enorme, pero esta oportunidad requiere que Ud. se mude a otra ciudad lejos de aquí. ¡Sorpresa! La nueva ciudad es donde vive su hermana favorita. ¡Claro que acepta!*

**A. Seleccionando agente.** Ud. le dice a su hermana las cualidades que busca en un/a agente inmobiliario/a. Aquí está la lista de requisitos.

Answers for A. 1) *Quiera.* 2) *Tenga.* 3) *Conozca.* 4) *Sepa.*

MODELO: Ud. busca a un agente que... vivir en la comunidad
*Yo busco a un agente que viva en la comunidad.*

Yo busco a un agente que...

1. ...no querer una comisión muy alta
2. ...tener buenas referencias de clientes satisfechos
3. ...conocer la comunidad y los precios de las casas
4. ...saber comunicarse con vendedores y otros agentes

**B. La agente perfecta.** Su hermana conoce a la agente perfecta para Ud.: Edith Valdivia. Termine Ud. esta conversación entre Edith y su cliente con la forma indicada del verbo.

Answers for B. 1) *Sea.* 2) *Es.* 3) *Sirva.* 4) *Sirva.* 5) *Tenga.* 6) *Tiene.*

MODELO: Ud.: Busco una casa que _______ (tener) piscina.
*Busco una casa que tenga piscina.*
Edith: Conozco una casa que _______ (tener) una piscina.
*Conozco una casa que tiene piscina.*

1. Ud.: Quiero vivir en una vecindad que _______ (ser) segura.
2. Edith: Hay una vecindad que _______ (ser) muy segura cerca de aquí.
3. Ud.: ¿Hay algún restaurante que _______ (servir) comida española aquí?
4. Edith: No hay ningún restaurante que _______ (servir) comida española.
5. Ud.: Necesito una casa que _______ (tener) un garaje doble.
6. Edith: No, necesita la casa que vimos que _______ (tener) un garaje triple.

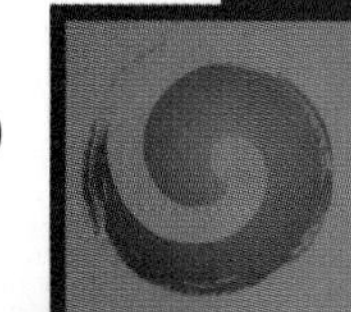



REPASO REPASO REPASO REPASO REPASO REPASO REPASO REPASO REPASO REPASO

## Lección 10

# TEMA 3

### La casa y las finanzas

*La decisión de aceptar la promoción y trasladarse a la ciudad donde vive su hermana está tomada. Ahora, en el momento de decirle adiós a la vida anterior, Ud. se siente muy emocionado/a.*

Answers for A. 1) *Sorprendido/a.* 2) *Firmados.* 3) *Escritos.* 4) *Abiertas.* 5) *Paralizado/a.* 6) *Encantado/a.* 7) *Conocidas.* 8) *Aburrido/a.* 9) *Dichos.* 10) *Abierta.* 11) *Cerrada.*

**A. Un momento de adiós.** Llene los espacios con la forma indicada del participio pasado.

¡Ya llegó el momento de la partida y estoy _________ (1) (sorprender) por la tristeza que siento. Los papeles para la nueva casa están _________ (2) (firmar), los cheques para el enganche están _________ (3) (escribir) y las nuevas cuentas bancarias están _________ (4) (abrir). Pero en vez de sentir entusiasmo por la nueva vida, estoy casi _________ (5) (paralizar) por la emoción. Debo estar _________ (6) (encantar) con el prospecto de ir a una ciudad donde hay muchas personas _________ (7) (conocer) y donde no voy a estar _________ (8) (aburrir) nunca. Bueno. Todos los "adioses" están _________ (9) (decir). La puerta a la nueva vida está _________ (10) (abrir). Y ahora, la puerta de mi vida anterior está _________ (11) (cerrar).

Answers for B. 1) *Están lavadas/cerradas.* 2) *Están abiertas/hechas.* 3) *Están sacudidos/cubiertos.* 4) *Está estacionado/pintado.* 5) *Está apagado/abierto.* 6) *Está pagado/cancelado/suspendido.* 7) *Están lavados/empacados.* 8) *Está envuelta/tirada.*

**B. Antes de salir.** Ud. ha vendido su casa y algunas de sus cosas a una pareja que no va a llegar por dos o tres semanas. Quiere que todo esté bien para los nuevos dueños. Por cada cosa mencionada indique que todo está listo para su salida.

MODELO: Las puertas: cerrar/pintar
*Las puertas están cerradas. Las puertas están pintadas.*

1. Las ventanas: lavar/cerrar
2. Las maletas: abrir/hacer
3. Los muebles: sacudir/cubrir
4. El coche: estacionar/pintar
5. El refrigerador: apagar/abrir
6. El periódico: pagar/cancelar/suspender
7. Los platos sucios: lavar/empacar
8. La basura: envolver/tirar

Answers for C. 1) *La he visto.* 2) *Los he comprado.* 3) *Lo he conocido.* 4) *La he cambiado.* 5) *Las he llamado.* 6) *Lo/la he visto.* 7) *Los he traído.* 8) *Los he resuelto.* 9) *Le he dicho.* 10) *Las he puesto.*

**C. La nueva vida.** Cuando por fin llega a la nueva ciudad, Ud. va directamente a casa de su hermana. Ella está muy entusiasmada con su llegada y tiene muchas preguntas. Uno/a de Uds. es la hermana que hace preguntas, y el/la otro/a inventa las respuestas.

MODELO: vender la casa vieja
E1: *¿Has vendido la casa vieja?*
E2: *Sí, la he vendido.*

1. ver la nueva casa hoy
2. comprar muebles
3. conocer al nuevo jefe
4. cambiar la dirección
5. llamar a las compañías de gas y luz
6. ver al/a la nuevo/a vecino/a guapo/a
7. traer los gatos a la nueva casa
8. resolver los problemas con la hipoteca
9. decirle al nuevo jefe la fecha de su llegada
10. poner las llaves donde las pueda encontrar

**D. Entrevista.** Imaginen que uno/a de ustedes le ha vendido su casa al/a la otro/a. Escriban un diálogo en forma de llamada telefónica entre el/la nuevo/a dueño/a y el/la anterior con información importante de último momento.

MODELO: Nuevo/a dueño/a: *¿Dónde están las llaves?*
Dueño/a anterior: *Están escondidas cerca de la puerta.*

Lección 10

# TEMA 4

## Los negocios

*Usted está encantado/a con su casa, su trabajo y su vida nueva, pero está muy enojado/a porque muchas de las cosas prometidas por el dueño anterior de su casa, el nuevo jefe y la agente inmobiliaria no estaban listas.*

**A. Cuando yo llegué...** Diga Ud. lo que las siguientes personas no habían hecho antes de su llegada.

**Answers for A.** 1) *Habían arreglado.* 2) *Habían puesto.* 3) *Habían quitado.* 4) *Habían limpiado.* 5) *Había preparado.* 6) *Me había traído.* 7) *Había resuelto.* 8) *Había contratado.* 9) *Había escrito.* 10) *Me había buscado.* 11) *Me había preparado.* 12) *Me había dicho.*

MODELO: Cuando yo llegué...
Los dueños anteriores: pintar la casa
*Cuando yo llegué, los dueños anteriores no habían pintado la casa.*

Los dueños anteriores

Cuando yo llegué ellos no...

1. arreglar las ventanas rotas
2. poner una nueva tubería
3. quitar el letrero: SE VENDE ESTA CASA.
4. limpiar la casa

La agente inmobiliaria

Cuando yo llegué a la casa, ella no...

5. preparar los papeles finales
6. traerme el mapa de la ciudad
7. resolver la disputa con el agente del vendedor
8. contratar un arquitecto para remodelar la casa

El nuevo jefe

El primer día de mi nuevo empleo, el nuevo jefe no...

9. escribir mi contrato
10. buscarme secretaria
11. prepararme una oficina
12. decirme el nombre de mi primer cliente

**B. Perdone Ud.** Uno/a de Uds. (E1) ha sufrido las consecuencias de la falta de responsabilidad de otra persona y está furioso/a. Ahora Ud. va a hablar con esta persona. El/La irresponsable (E2) le va a pedir disculpas y va a sugerir la fecha en la que espera que el problema se resuelva.

MODELO: E1: *Me molesta que Ud. no haya pintado la casa.*
E2: *Perdone que no haya pintado la casa. Espero que los pintores la pinten para el sábado.*

**C. Una carta para pedir disculpas.** Escoja Ud. el papel de la agente inmobiliaria, el nuevo jefe o los dueños anteriores de la casa y escriba una carta de disculpas para justificar su negligencia. Cuando la termine, cambie cartas con un/a compañero/a y conteste la carta de disculpas que recibió con otra carta para aceptar las disculpas.

REPASO REPASO REPASO REPASO REPASO REPASO REPASO REPASO REPASO

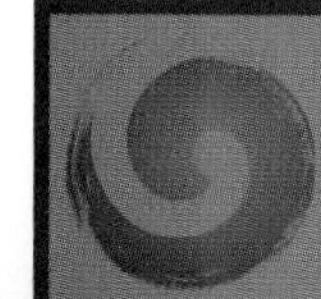

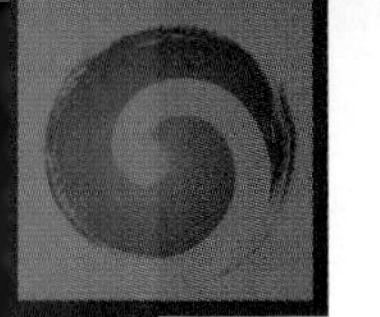



## Lección 11

# TEMA 1

### El futuro

*¡Felicitaciones!. Pronto terminará la clase de español y muchos de ustedes no se verán más. Después de pasar mucho tiempo juntos, será divertido hacer planes para una fiesta de despedida.*

**A. La fiesta de despedida.** Primero, la clase tendrá que tomar las siguientes decisiones.

1. ¿Dónde será la fiesta? ¿Saldrán de la escuela o se quedarán en clase?
2. ¿Cuándo será la fiesta, durante la clase o después de horas escolares?
3. ¿Quiénes vendrán?
4. ¿Habrá invitaciones escritas?
5. ¿Tendrán música?
6. ¿Qué comida habrá? ¿Qué bebidas necesitarán?
7. ¿Querrán música? ¿Qué música escucharán?
8. ¿Qué harán en la fiesta? ¿Habrá juegos o piñatas?
9. ¿Quiénes se encargarán de la limpieza después?
10. ¿Se les ha olvidado algo importante?

**B. Planes para la fiesta.** Cada estudiante escribirá su nombre en un papel y lo pondrá en una caja o sombrero. Cuando todos los nombres estén dentro, cada miembro de la clase escogerá uno. (No podrá ser su propio nombre.) ¿Conoce Ud. bien a la persona que escogió? Use la imaginación para adivinar cómo será la vida de su compañero en cinco años. Todos le escribirán una carta a su compañero/a con sus predicciones y éstas serán reveladas durante la fiesta.

MODELO: *José, tú sacarás la maestría en negocios internacionales y en cinco años serás vicepresidente de Microsoft.*

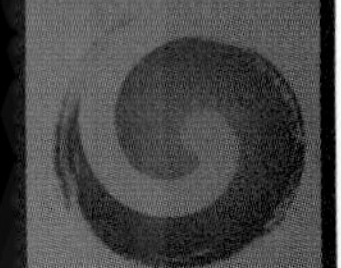

## Lección 11

### ¿Cómo seremos?

*Los miembros de la clase han decidido reunirse en diez años para verse y saber cómo y dónde están todos.*

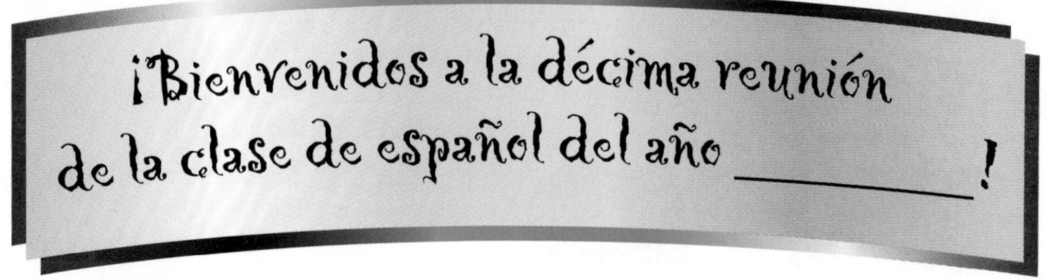


**A. Lo que haremos.** Llene Ud. esta encuesta desde el punto de vista de sus esperanzas y planes actuales.

A. Yo sí vendré a la reunión
   1. porque…
   2. con tal de que…
   3. a menos que…
   4. sin que…

B. Profesión: Yo seré _______,
   1. porque…
   2. con tal de que…
   3. a menos que…
   4. tan pronto como…

C. El amor.
   Estaré casado/a
   Estaré con una persona especial
   Seré soltero/a siempre
   1. hasta que…
   2. después de que…
   3. a menos que…
   4. tan pronto como…

D. Los viajes
   Viajaré
   No viajaré
   Haré viajes internacionales
   1. antes de que…
   2. para que…
   3. tan pronto como…
   4. con tal de que…

E. La educación
   Seguiré estudiando
   No estudiaré más
   Tomaré una clase divertida
   1. con tal de que…
   2. hasta que…
   3. cuando…
   4. a menos que…

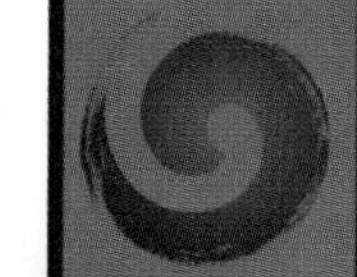

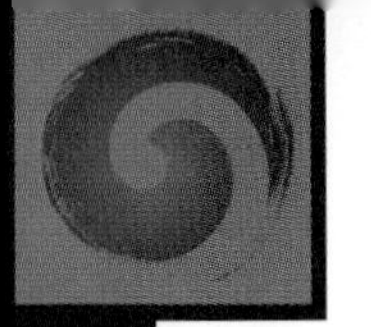

**Lección 11**

# TEMA 3

## La tecnología

*Es muy difícil predecir como será el mundo en quince o veinte años, sobretodo para los niños. ¿Puede Ud. recordar las impresiones que tenía cuando era niño sobre el mundo del futuro?*

**Answers for A.** 1) *Que no existiera.* 2) *Que pudieran escribir.* 3) *Que asistiera/tomara.* 4) *Que viéramos.* 5) *Que pudiéramos ir.* 6) *Que no hubiera.* 7) *Que pudiéramos.* 8) *Que mandáramos.* 9) *Que cocináramos.* 10) *Que hiciéramos.*

**A. ¿Sabía Ud.?** Cuando era niño, ¿se imaginaba Ud. lo siguiente?

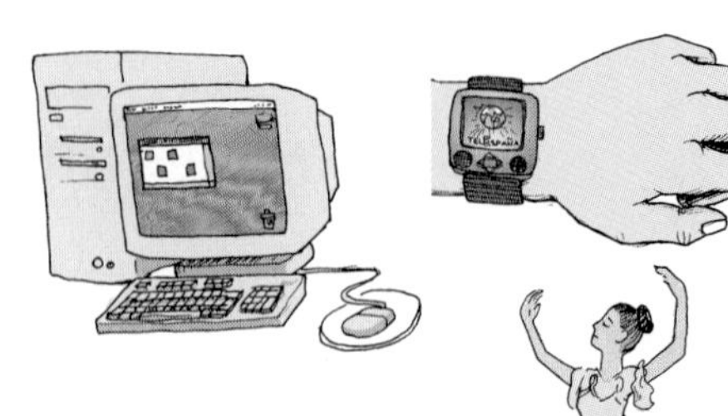

MODELO: nosotros/llegar al planeta Marte
*No me imaginaba que nosotros llegáramos al planeta Marte.*

1. no existir/Santa Claus
2. las personas/poder escribir y entregar cartas instantáneamente por la computadora
3. yo/asistir a la universidad y tomar una clase de español
4. nosotros/ver el nuevo milenio
5. nosotros/poder ir al cine en la sala de nuestra casa
6. no haber muchos empleos para vaqueros, bomberos y bailarines
7. nosotros/poder mirar la televisión en la pantalla de un reloj
8. nosotros/mandar un documento escrito por las líneas de teléfono
9. nosotros/cocinar comidas en dos minutos en un horno microondas
10. nosotros/hacer transacciones bancarias sin salir de casa

**B. Los sueños de los adultos.** Cuando era joven, muchos adultos tenían muchos deseos para Ud. Termine estas oraciones con tres exigencias y planes para cada persona indicada.

MODELO: Mi mamá: quería que yo… , esperaba que yo. . . , deseaba que yo…
*Mi mamá quería que yo me comiera toda la comida.*
*Mi mamá esperaba que yo fuera a la universidad.*
*Mi mamá deseaba que yo llegara a ser presidente de mi país.*

1. Mi maestro favorito
2. Mi mejor amigo/a
3. Mis abuelos
4. Mi peor enemigo/a

**C. Su bienestar emocional.** Usted hizo muchas cosas cuando era niño/a para que otros estuvieran contentos. Diga lo que hizo por estas personas.

MODELO: Mi mamá
*Me cambiaba la ropa todos los días para que mi mamá estuviera contenta.*

1. Mi maestra favorita
2. Mi mejor amigo/a
3. Mi primer amor
4. Mi papá
5. Mi perro/mi gato
6. Mi mamá

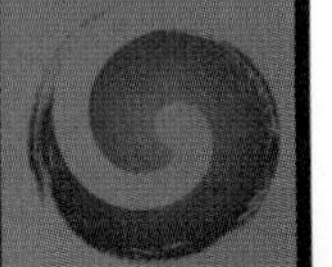

Lección 11

# TEMA 4

## El nuevo milenio

*En un mundo perfecto, no habría hambre. En una clase de español perfecta, no habría tarea. Todos sabemos que el mundo no es perfecto, pero podemos soñar, ¿verdad?*

**A. Buscando la perfección.** Termine estas oraciones para que describan el mundo perfecto según Ud.

MODELO: La clase de español perfecta...
*En una clase de español perfecta, no habría subjuntivo.* o
*En una clase de español perfecta, el/la profesor/a daría más tarea.*

1. El coche perfecto...
2. El hombre o la mujer perfectos...
3. La clase perfecta...
4. Las vacaciones perfectas...
5. El jefe perfecto...
6. La cita perfecta...

**B. ¿Qué pasará? ¿Qué pasaría?** Uno/a de Uds. hará preguntas probables. El/La otro/a las contestará. Después, uno/a de Uds. hará preguntas improbables o imposibles y el/la otro/a las contestará.

MODELO: E1: *¿Qué harás mañana si tienes tiempo?*
E2: *Si tengo tiempo, limpiaré la casa y estudiaré español.*
E2: *¿Qué harías mañana si tuvieras tiempo?*
E1: *Si tuviera tiempo, yo tomaría vacaciones en el Caribe.*

1. ¿Qué harás para prepararte para el examen final de español?
2. ¿Qué harías para sacar una A en la clase?
3. Si recibes un cheque mañana, ¿qué harás con el dinero?
4. Si encontraras una cartera con mil dólares, ¿qué harías con el dinero?
5. ¿Qué le dirás al profesor/a de español cuando termines la clase?
6. ¿Qué le dirías al jefe si tuvieras la oportunidad?

**C. Si yo fuera...** Si Ud. fuera una de las siguientes personas (o animales) ¿qué haría mañana?

MODELO: el/la profesor/a de español.
*Si yo fuera el/la profesor/a de español, yo cancelaría el examen final y les daría a todos una A.*

1. El presidente de la universidad
2. Bill Gates (Guillermo Puertas de Microsuave)
3. La señora con el perro que toma champán
4. George Clooney
5. El chihuahua de Taco Bell
6. La persona más rica del mundo
7. Mi jefe
8. Un/a cantante de fama internacional

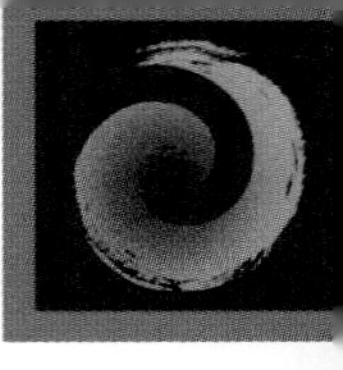

# Verb review

## Regular Verbs: Simple Tenses

| Infinitive<br>Present Participle<br>Past Participle | Indicative | | | | | Subjunctive | | Imperative |
|---|---|---|---|---|---|---|---|---|
| | Present | Imperfect | Preterite | Future | Conditional | Present | Imperfect | |
| hablar<br>hablando<br>hablado | hablo<br>hablas<br>habla<br>hablamos<br>habláis<br>hablan | hablaba<br>hablabas<br>hablaba<br>hablábamos<br>hablabais<br>hablaban | hablé<br>hablaste<br>habló<br>hablamos<br>hablasteis<br>hablaron | hablaré<br>hablarás<br>hablará<br>hablaremos<br>hablaréis<br>hablarán | hablaría<br>hablarías<br>hablaría<br>hablaríamos<br>hablaríais<br>hablarían | hable<br>hables<br>hable<br>hablemos<br>habléis<br>hablen | hablara<br>hablaras<br>hablara<br>habláramos<br>hablarais<br>hablaran | habla tú,<br>no hables<br>hable usted<br>hablemos<br>hablen Uds. |
| comer<br>comiendo<br>comido | como<br>comes<br>come<br>comemos<br>coméis<br>comen | comía<br>comías<br>comía<br>comíamos<br>comíais<br>comían | comí<br>comiste<br>comió<br>comimos<br>comisteis<br>comieron | comeré<br>comerás<br>comerá<br>comeremos<br>comeréis<br>comerán | comería<br>comerías<br>comería<br>comeríamos<br>comeríais<br>comerían | coma<br>comas<br>coma<br>comamos<br>comáis<br>coman | comiera<br>comieras<br>comiera<br>comiéramos<br>comierais<br>comieran | come tú,<br>no comas<br>coma usted<br>comamos<br>coman Uds. |
| vivir<br>viviendo<br>vivido | vivo<br>vives<br>vive<br>vivimos<br>vivís<br>viven | vivía<br>vivías<br>vivía<br>vivíamos<br>vivíais<br>vivían | viví<br>viviste<br>vivió<br>vivimos<br>vivisteis<br>vivieron | viviré<br>vivirás<br>vivirá<br>viviremos<br>viviréis<br>vivirán | viviría<br>vivirías<br>viviría<br>viviríamos<br>viviríais<br>vivirían | viva<br>vivas<br>viva<br>vivamos<br>viváis<br>vivan | viviera<br>vivieras<br>viviera<br>viviéramos<br>vivierais<br>vivieran | vive tú,<br>no vivas<br>viva usted<br>vivamos<br>vivan Uds. |

| ***Vosotros*** **commands** | | | | | |
|---|---|---|---|---|---|
| hablar | hablad<br>no habléis | comer | comed<br>no comáis | vivir | vivid<br>no viváis |

# Regular Verbs: Perfect Tenses

| Indicative | | | | | | | | | | Subjunctive | | | |
|---|---|---|---|---|---|---|---|---|---|---|---|---|---|
| Present Perfect | | Past Perfect | | Preterite Perfect | | Future Perfect | | Conditional Perfect | | Present Perfect | | Past Perfect | |
| he<br>has<br>ha<br>hemos<br>habéis<br>han | hablado<br>comido<br>vivido | había<br>habías<br>había<br>habíamos<br>habíais<br>habían | hablado<br>comido<br>vivido | hube<br>hubiste<br>hubo<br>hubimos<br>hubisteis<br>hubieron | hablado<br>comido<br>vivido | habré<br>habrás<br>habrá<br>habremos<br>habréis<br>habrán | hablado<br>comido<br>vivido | habría<br>habrías<br>habría<br>habríamos<br>habríais<br>habrían | hablado<br>comido<br>vivido | haya<br>hayas<br>haya<br>hayamos<br>hayáis<br>hayan | hablado<br>comido<br>vivido | hubiera<br>hubieras<br>hubiera<br>hubiéramos<br>hubierais<br>hubieran | hablado<br>comido<br>vivido |

# Irregular Verbs

| Infinitive<br>Present Participle<br>Past Participle | Indicative | | | | | Subjunctive | | Imperative |
|---|---|---|---|---|---|---|---|---|
| | Present | Imperfect | Preterite | Future | Conditional | Present | Imperfect | |
| andar<br>andando<br>andado | ando<br>andas<br>anda<br>andamos<br>andáis<br>andan | andaba<br>andabas<br>andaba<br>andábamos<br>andabais<br>andaban | anduve<br>anduviste<br>anduvo<br>anduvimos<br>anduvisteis<br>anduvieron | andaré<br>andarás<br>andará<br>andaremos<br>andaréis<br>andarán | andaría<br>andarías<br>andaría<br>andaríamos<br>andaríais<br>andarían | ande<br>andes<br>ande<br>andemos<br>andéis<br>anden | anduviera<br>anduvieras<br>anduviera<br>anduviéramos<br>anduvierais<br>anduvieran | anda tú,<br>no andes<br>ande usted<br>andemos<br>anden Uds. |
| caer<br>cayendo<br>caído | caigo<br>caes<br>cae<br>caemos<br>caéis<br>caen | caía<br>caías<br>caía<br>caíamos<br>caíais<br>caían | caí<br>caíste<br>cayó<br>caímos<br>caísteis<br>cayeron | caeré<br>caerás<br>caerá<br>caeremos<br>caeréis<br>caerán | caería<br>caerías<br>caería<br>caeríamos<br>caeríais<br>caerían | caiga<br>caigas<br>caiga<br>caigamos<br>caigáis<br>caigan | cayera<br>cayeras<br>cayera<br>cayéramos<br>cayerais<br>cayeran | cae tú,<br>no caigas<br>caiga usted<br>caigamos<br>caigan Uds. |
| dar<br>dando<br>dado | doy<br>das<br>da<br>damos<br>dais<br>dan | daba<br>dabas<br>daba<br>dábamos<br>dabais<br>daban | di<br>diste<br>dio<br>dimos<br>disteis<br>dieron | daré<br>darás<br>dará<br>daremos<br>daréis<br>darán | daría<br>darías<br>daría<br>daríamos<br>daríais<br>darían | dé<br>des<br>dé<br>demos<br>deis<br>den | diera<br>dieras<br>diera<br>diéramos<br>dierais<br>dieran | da tú,<br>no des<br>dé usted<br>demos<br>den Uds. |

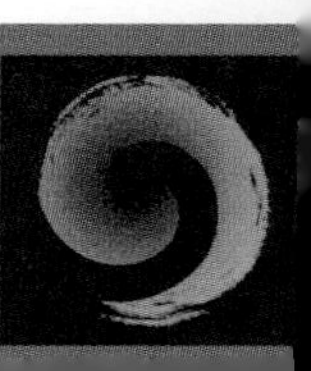

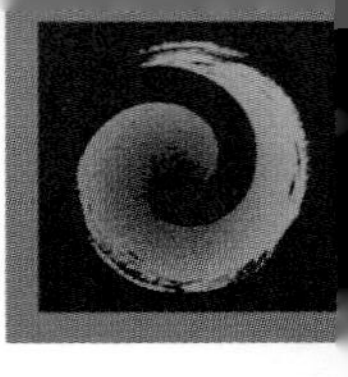

# Irregular Verbs (continued)

| Infinitive<br>Present Participle<br>Past Participle | Indicative | | | | | Subjunctive | | Imperative |
|---|---|---|---|---|---|---|---|---|
| | Present | Imperfect | Preterite | Future | Conditional | Present | Imperfect | |
| decir<br>diciendo<br>dicho | digo<br>dices<br>dice<br>decimos<br>decís<br>dicen | decía<br>decías<br>decía<br>decíamos<br>decíais<br>decían | dije<br>dijiste<br>dijo<br>dijimos<br>dijisteis<br>dijeron | diré<br>dirás<br>dirá<br>diremos<br>diréis<br>dirán | diría<br>dirías<br>diría<br>diríamos<br>diríais<br>dirían | diga<br>digas<br>diga<br>digamos<br>digáis<br>digan | dijera<br>dijeras<br>dijera<br>dijéramos<br>dijerais<br>dijeran | di tú,<br>no digas<br>diga usted<br>digamos<br>digan Uds. |
| estar<br>estando<br>estado | estoy<br>estás<br>está<br>estamos<br>estáis<br>están | estaba<br>estabas<br>estaba<br>estábamos<br>estabais<br>estaban | estuve<br>estuviste<br>estuvo<br>estuvimos<br>estuvisteis<br>estuvieron | estaré<br>estarás<br>estará<br>estaremos<br>estaréis<br>estarán | estaría<br>estarías<br>estaría<br>estaríamos<br>estaríais<br>estarían | esté<br>estés<br>esté<br>estemos<br>estéis<br>estén | estuviera<br>estuvieras<br>estuviera<br>estuviéramos<br>estuvierais<br>estuvieran | está tú,<br>no estés<br>esté usted<br>estemos<br>estén Uds. |
| haber<br>habiendo<br>habido | he<br>has<br>ha<br>hemos<br>habéis<br>han | había<br>habías<br>había<br>habíamos<br>habíais<br>habían | hube<br>hubiste<br>hubo<br>hubimos<br>hubisteis<br>hubieron | habré<br>habrás<br>habrá<br>habremos<br>habréis<br>habrán | habría<br>habrías<br>habría<br>habríamos<br>habríais<br>habrían | haya<br>hayas<br>haya<br>hayamos<br>hayáis<br>hayan | hubiera<br>hubieras<br>hubiera<br>hubiéramos<br>hubierais<br>hubieran | |
| hacer<br>haciendo<br>hecho | hago<br>haces<br>hace<br>hacemos<br>hacéis<br>hacen | hacía<br>hacías<br>hacía<br>hacíamos<br>hacíais<br>hacían | hice<br>hiciste<br>hizo<br>hicimos<br>hicisteis<br>hicieron | haré<br>harás<br>hará<br>haremos<br>haréis<br>harán | haría<br>harías<br>haría<br>haríamos<br>haríais<br>harían | haga<br>hagas<br>haga<br>hagamos<br>hagáis<br>hagan | hiciera<br>hicieras<br>hiciera<br>hiciéramos<br>hicierais<br>hicieran | haz tú,<br>no hagas<br>haga usted<br>hagamos<br>hagan Uds. |
| ir<br>yendo<br>ido | voy<br>vas<br>va<br>vamos<br>vais<br>van | iba<br>ibas<br>iba<br>íbamos<br>ibais<br>iban | fui<br>fuiste<br>fue<br>fuimos<br>fuisteis<br>fueron | iré<br>irás<br>irá<br>iremos<br>iréis<br>irán | iría<br>irías<br>iría<br>iríamos<br>iríais<br>irían | vaya<br>vayas<br>vaya<br>vayamos<br>vayáis<br>vayan | fuera<br>fueras<br>fuera<br>fuéramos<br>fuerais<br>fueran | ve tú,<br>no vayas<br>vaya usted<br>vamos<br>(no vayamos)<br>vayan Uds. |

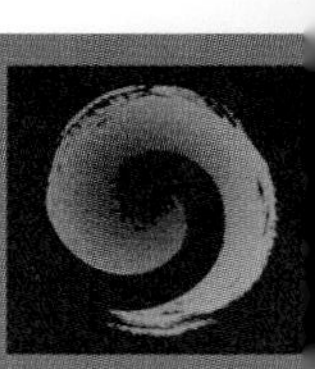

# Irregular Verbs (continued)

| Infinitive<br>Present Participle<br>Past Participle | Indicative | | | | | Subjunctive | | Imperative |
|---|---|---|---|---|---|---|---|---|
| | Present | Imperfect | Preterite | Future | Conditional | Present | Imperfect | |
| oír<br>oyendo<br>oído | oigo<br>oyes<br>oye<br>oímos<br>oís<br>oyen | oía<br>oías<br>oía<br>oíamos<br>oíais<br>oían | oí<br>oíste<br>oyó<br>oímos<br>oísteis<br>oyeron | oiré<br>oirás<br>oirá<br>oiremos<br>oiréis<br>oirán | oiría<br>oirías<br>oiría<br>oiríamos<br>oiríais<br>oirían | oiga<br>oigas<br>oiga<br>oigamos<br>oigáis<br>oigan | oyera<br>oyeras<br>oyera<br>oyéramos<br>oyerais<br>oyeran | oye tú,<br>no oigas<br>oiga usted<br>oigamos<br>oigan Uds. |
| poder<br>pudiendo<br>podido | puedo<br>puedes<br>puede<br>podemos<br>podéis<br>pueden | podía<br>podías<br>podía<br>podíamos<br>podíais<br>podían | pude<br>pudiste<br>pudo<br>pudimos<br>pudisteis<br>pudieron | podré<br>podrás<br>podrá<br>podremos<br>podréis<br>podrán | podría<br>podrías<br>podría<br>podríamos<br>podríais<br>podrían | pueda<br>puedas<br>pueda<br>podamos<br>podáis<br>puedan | pudiera<br>pudieras<br>pudiera<br>pudiéramos<br>pudierais<br>pudieran | |
| poner<br>poniendo<br>puesto | pongo<br>pones<br>pone<br>ponemos<br>ponéis<br>ponen | ponía<br>ponías<br>ponía<br>poníamos<br>poníais<br>ponían | puse<br>pusiste<br>puso<br>pusimos<br>pusisteis<br>pusieron | pondré<br>pondrás<br>pondrá<br>pondremos<br>pondréis<br>pondrán | pondría<br>pondrías<br>pondría<br>pondríamos<br>pondríais<br>pondrían | ponga<br>pongas<br>ponga<br>pongamos<br>pongáis<br>pongan | pusiera<br>pusieras<br>pusiera<br>pusiéramos<br>pusierais<br>pusieran | pon tú,<br>no pongas<br>ponga usted<br>pongamos<br>pongan Uds. |
| querer<br>queriendo<br>querido | quiero<br>quieres<br>quiere<br>queremos<br>queréis<br>quieren | quería<br>querías<br>quería<br>queríamos<br>queríais<br>querían | quise<br>quisiste<br>quiso<br>quisimos<br>quisisteis<br>quisieron | querré<br>querrás<br>querrá<br>querremos<br>querréis<br>querrán | querría<br>querrías<br>querría<br>querríamos<br>querríais<br>querrían | quiera<br>quieras<br>quiera<br>queramos<br>queráis<br>quieran | quisiera<br>quisieras<br>quisiera<br>quisiéramos<br>quisierais<br>quisieran | quiere tú,<br>no quieras<br>quiera usted<br>queramos<br>quieran Uds. |
| saber<br>sabiendo<br>sabido | sé<br>sabes<br>sabe<br>sabemos<br>sabéis<br>saben | sabía<br>sabías<br>sabía<br>sabíamos<br>sabíais<br>sabían | supe<br>supiste<br>supo<br>supimos<br>supisteis<br>supieron | sabré<br>sabrás<br>sabrá<br>sabremos<br>sabréis<br>sabrán | sabría<br>sabrías<br>sabría<br>sabríamos<br>sabríais<br>sabrían | sepa<br>sepas<br>sepa<br>sepamos<br>sepáis<br>sepan | supiera<br>supieras<br>supiera<br>supiéramos<br>supierais<br>supieran | sabe tú,<br>no sepas<br>sepa usted<br>sepamos<br>sepan Uds. |
| salir<br>saliendo<br>salido | salgo<br>sales<br>sale<br>salimos<br>salís<br>salen | salía<br>salías<br>salía<br>salíamos<br>salíais<br>salían | salí<br>saliste<br>salió<br>salimos<br>salisteis<br>salieron | saldré<br>saldrás<br>saldrá<br>saldremos<br>saldréis<br>saldrán | saldría<br>saldrías<br>saldría<br>saldríamos<br>saldríais<br>saldrían | salga<br>salgas<br>salga<br>salgamos<br>salgáis<br>salgan | saliera<br>salieras<br>saliera<br>saliéramos<br>salierais<br>salieran | sal tú,<br>no salgas<br>salga usted<br>salgamos<br>salgan Uds. |

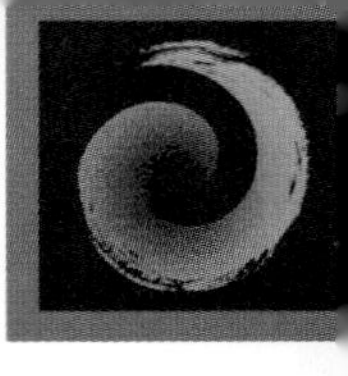

# Irregular Verbs (continued)

| Infinitive<br>Present Participle<br>Past Participle | Indicative | | | | | Subjunctive | | Imperative |
|---|---|---|---|---|---|---|---|---|
| | Present | Imperfect | Preterite | Future | Conditional | Present | Imperfect | |
| ser<br>siendo<br>sido | soy<br>eres<br>es<br>somos<br>sois<br>son | era<br>eras<br>era<br>éramos<br>erais<br>eran | fui<br>fuiste<br>fue<br>fuimos<br>fuisteis<br>fueron | seré<br>serás<br>será<br>seremos<br>seréis<br>serán | sería<br>serías<br>sería<br>seríamos<br>seríais<br>serían | sea<br>seas<br>sea<br>seamos<br>seáis<br>sean | fuera<br>fueras<br>fuera<br>fuéramos<br>fuerais<br>fueran | sé tú,<br>no seas<br>sea usted<br>seamos<br>sean Uds. |
| tener<br>teniendo<br>tenido | tengo<br>tienes<br>tiene<br>tenemos<br>tenéis<br>tienen | tenía<br>tenías<br>tenía<br>teníamos<br>teníais<br>tenían | tuve<br>tuviste<br>tuvo<br>tuvimos<br>tuvisteis<br>tuvieron | tendré<br>tendrás<br>tendrá<br>tendremos<br>tendréis<br>tendrán | tendría<br>tendrías<br>tendría<br>tendríamos<br>tendríais<br>tendrían | tenga<br>tengas<br>tenga<br>tengamos<br>tengáis<br>tengan | tuviera<br>tuvieras<br>tuviera<br>tuviéramos<br>tuvierais<br>tuvieran | ten tú,<br>no tengas<br>tenga usted<br>tengamos<br>tengan Uds. |
| traer<br>trayendo<br>traído | traigo<br>traes<br>trae<br>traemos<br>traéis<br>traen | traía<br>traías<br>traía<br>traíamos<br>traíais<br>traían | traje<br>trajiste<br>trajo<br>trajimos<br>trajisteis<br>trajeron | traeré<br>traerás<br>traerá<br>traeremos<br>traeréis<br>traerán | traería<br>traerías<br>traería<br>traeríamos<br>traeríais<br>traerían | traiga<br>traigas<br>traiga<br>traigamos<br>traigáis<br>traigan | trajera<br>trajeras<br>trajera<br>trajéramos<br>trajerais<br>trajeran | trae tú,<br>no traigas<br>traiga usted<br>traigamos<br>traigan Uds. |
| venir<br>viniendo<br>venido | vengo<br>vienes<br>viene<br>venimos<br>venís<br>vienen | venía<br>venías<br>venía<br>veníamos<br>veníais<br>venían | vine<br>viniste<br>vino<br>vinimos<br>vinisteis<br>vinieron | vendré<br>vendrás<br>vendrá<br>vendremos<br>vendréis<br>vendrán | vendría<br>vendrías<br>vendría<br>vendríamos<br>vendríais<br>vendrían | venga<br>vengas<br>venga<br>vengamos<br>vengáis<br>vengan | viniera<br>vinieras<br>viniera<br>viniéramos<br>vinierais<br>vinieran | ven tú,<br>no vengas<br>venga usted<br>vengamos<br>vengan Uds. |
| ver<br>viendo<br>visto | veo<br>ves<br>ve<br>vemos<br>veis<br>ven | veía<br>veías<br>veía<br>veíamos<br>veíais<br>veían | vi<br>viste<br>vio<br>vimos<br>visteis<br>vieron | veré<br>verás<br>verá<br>veremos<br>veréis<br>verán | vería<br>verías<br>vería<br>veríamos<br>veríais<br>verían | vea<br>veas<br>vea<br>veamos<br>veáis<br>vean | viera<br>vieras<br>viera<br>viéramos<br>vierais<br>vieran | ve tú,<br>no veas<br>vea usted<br>veamos<br>vean Uds. |

# Stem-changing and Orthographic-changing Verbs

| Infinitive<br>Present Participle<br>Past Participle | Indicative | | | | | Subjunctive | | Imperative |
|---|---|---|---|---|---|---|---|---|
| | Present | Imperfect | Preterite | Future | Conditional | Present | Imperfect | |
| incluir (y)<br>incluyendo<br>incluido | incluyo<br>incluyes<br>incluye<br>incluimos<br>incluís<br>incluyen | incluía<br>incluías<br>incluía<br>incluíamos<br>incluíais<br>incluían | incluí<br>incluiste<br>incluyó<br>incluimos<br>incluisteis<br>incluyeron | incluiré<br>incluirás<br>incluirá<br>incluiremos<br>incluiréis<br>incluirán | incluiría<br>incluirías<br>incluiría<br>incluiríamos<br>incluiríais<br>incluirían | incluya<br>incluyas<br>incluya<br>incluyamos<br>incluyáis<br>incluyan | incluyera<br>incluyeras<br>incluyera<br>incluyéramos<br>incluyerais<br>incluyeran | incluye tú,<br>no incluyas<br>incluya usted<br>incluyamos<br>incluyan Uds. |
| dormir (ue, u)<br>durmiendo<br>dormido | duermo<br>duermes<br>duerme<br>dormimos<br>dormís<br>duermen | dormía<br>dormías<br>dormía<br>dormíamos<br>dormíais<br>dormían | dormí<br>dormiste<br>durmió<br>dormimos<br>dormisteis<br>durmieron | dormiré<br>dormirás<br>dormirá<br>dormiremos<br>dormiréis<br>dormirán | dormiría<br>dormirías<br>dormiría<br>dormiríamos<br>dormiríais<br>dormirían | duerma<br>duermas<br>duerma<br>durmamos<br>durmáis<br>duerman | durmiera<br>durmieras<br>durmiera<br>durmiéramos<br>durmierais<br>durmieran | duerme tú,<br>no duermas<br>duerma usted<br>durmamos<br>duerman Uds. |
| pedir (i, i)<br>pidiendo<br>pedido | pido<br>pides<br>pide<br>pedimos<br>pedís<br>piden | pedía<br>pedías<br>pedía<br>pedíamos<br>pedíais<br>pedían | pedí<br>pediste<br>pidió<br>pedimos<br>pedisteis<br>pidieron | pediré<br>pedirás<br>pedirá<br>pediremos<br>pediréis<br>pedirán | pediría<br>pedirías<br>pediría<br>pediríamos<br>pediríais<br>pedirían | pida<br>pidas<br>pida<br>pidamos<br>pidáis<br>pidan | pidiera<br>pidieras<br>pidiera<br>pidiéramos<br>pidierais<br>pidieran | pide tú,<br>no pidas<br>pida usted<br>pidamos<br>pidan Uds. |
| pensar (ie)<br>pensando<br>pensado | pienso<br>piensas<br>piensa<br>pensamos<br>pensáis<br>piensan | pensaba<br>pensabas<br>pensaba<br>pensábamos<br>pensabais<br>pensaban | pensé<br>pensaste<br>pensó<br>pensamos<br>pensasteis<br>pensaron | pensaré<br>pensarás<br>pensará<br>pensaremos<br>pensaréis<br>pensarán | pensaría<br>pensarías<br>pensaría<br>pensaríamos<br>pensaríais<br>pensarían | piense<br>pienses<br>piense<br>pensemos<br>penséis<br>piensen | pensara<br>pensaras<br>pensara<br>pensáramos<br>pensarais<br>pensaran | piensa tú,<br>no pienses<br>piense usted<br>pensemos<br>piensen Uds. |

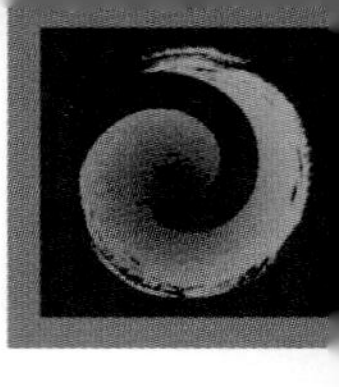

# Stem-changing and Orthographic-changing Verbs (continued)

| Infinitive<br>Present Participle<br>Past Participle | Indicative | | | | | Subjunctive | | Imperative |
|---|---|---|---|---|---|---|---|---|
| | Present | Imperfect | Preterite | Future | Conditional | Present | Imperfect | |
| producir (zc)<br>produciendo<br>producido | produzco<br>produces<br>produce<br>producimos<br>producís<br>producen | producía<br>producías<br>producía<br>producíamos<br>producíais<br>producían | produje<br>produjiste<br>produjo<br>produjimos<br>produjisteis<br>produjeron | produciré<br>producirás<br>producirá<br>produciremos<br>produciréis<br>producirán | produciría<br>producirías<br>produciría<br>produciríamos<br>produciríais<br>producirían | produzca<br>produzcas<br>produzca<br>produzcamos<br>produzcáis<br>produzcan | produjera<br>produjeras<br>produjera<br>produjéramos<br>produjerais<br>produjeran | produce tú,<br>no produzcas<br>produzca usted<br>produzcamos<br>produzcan Uds. |
| reír (i, i)<br>riendo<br>reído | río<br>ríes<br>ríe<br>reímos<br>reís<br>ríen | reía<br>reías<br>reía<br>reíamos<br>reíais<br>reían | reí<br>reíste<br>rio<br>reímos<br>reísteis<br>rieron | reiré<br>reirás<br>reirá<br>reiremos<br>reiréis<br>reirán | reiría<br>reirías<br>reiría<br>reiríamos<br>reiríais<br>reirían | ría<br>rías<br>ría<br>riamos<br>riáis<br>rían | riera<br>rieras<br>riera<br>riéramos<br>rierais<br>rieran | ríe tú,<br>no rías<br>ría usted<br>riamos<br>rían Uds. |
| seguir (i, i)<br>siguiendo<br>seguido | sigo<br>sigues<br>sigue<br>seguimos<br>seguís<br>siguen | seguía<br>seguías<br>seguía<br>seguíamos<br>seguíais<br>seguían | seguí<br>seguiste<br>siguió<br>seguimos<br>seguisteis<br>siguieron | seguiré<br>seguirás<br>seguirá<br>seguiremos<br>seguiréis<br>seguirán | seguiría<br>seguirías<br>seguiría<br>seguiríamos<br>seguiríais<br>seguirían | siga<br>sigas<br>siga<br>sigamos<br>sigáis<br>sigan | siguiera<br>siguieras<br>siguiera<br>siguiéramos<br>siguierais<br>siguieran | sigue tú,<br>no sigas<br>siga usted<br>sigamos<br>sigan Uds. |
| sentir (ie, i)<br>sintiendo<br>sentido | siento<br>sientes<br>siente<br>sentimos<br>sentís<br>sienten | sentía<br>sentías<br>sentía<br>sentíamos<br>sentíais<br>sentían | sentí<br>sentiste<br>sintió<br>sentimos<br>sentisteis<br>sintieron | sentiré<br>sentirás<br>sentirá<br>sentiremos<br>sentiréis<br>sentirán | sentiría<br>sentirías<br>sentiría<br>sentiríamos<br>sentiríais<br>sentirían | sienta<br>sientas<br>sienta<br>sintamos<br>sintáis<br>sientan | sintiera<br>sintieras<br>sintiera<br>sintiéramos<br>sintierais<br>sintieran | siente tú,<br>no sientas<br>sienta usted<br>sintamos<br>sientan Uds. |
| volver (ue)<br>volviendo<br>vuelto | vuelvo<br>vuelves<br>vuelve<br>volvemos<br>volvéis<br>vuelven | volvía<br>volvías<br>volvía<br>volvíamos<br>volvíais<br>volvían | volví<br>volviste<br>volvió<br>volvimos<br>volvisteis<br>volvieron | volveré<br>volverás<br>volverá<br>volveremos<br>volveréis<br>volverán | volvería<br>volverías<br>volvería<br>volveríamos<br>volveríais<br>volverían | vuelva<br>vuelvas<br>vuelva<br>volvamos<br>volváis<br>vuelvan | volviera<br>volvieras<br>volviera<br>volviéramos<br>volvierais<br>volvieran | vuelve tú,<br>no vuelvas<br>vuelva usted<br>volvamos<br>vuelvan Uds. |

# Vocabulary

## Spanish-English

**a** to 1
**a bordo** on board 8
**a la derecha** to the right 7
**a la izquierda** to the left 2
**a menudo** often 4
**a pesar de** in spite of 11
**¿A qué hora?** At what time? 1
**a sus órdenes** at your service 1
**abajo** down there/here 9
**abierto/a** open 1
**abogado/a** attorney/lawyer 5
**abordar** to board, to embark 8
**aborto** abortion *9*
**abrazar** to hug *4*
**abrazarse** to hug one another 4
**abrigo** overcoat 2
**abrir** to open *1*
**abrocharse** to buckle 7
**abuelo/a** grandfather/grandmother 3
**aburrirse** to get bored 7
**acá** here 3
**acabar** to finish 8
**acabar + de + inf.** to have just + -ed 4
**accesorio** accesory 7
**accidente** accident 3
**acciones** shares/stock 10
**aceite** oil 7
**acera** sidewalk 7
**acerca de** about/concerning 3
**acompañar** to accompany 8
**aconsejar** to advise 5
**acostarse (ue)** to go to bed 4
**acreedor/a** creditor 10
**actor** actor *1*, 5
**actriz** actress *1*, 5
**actual** current *2*
**actuar** to act 11
**acudir** to go or to come to *9*
**adelante** ahead *3*
**¡Adelante!** Forward, go on! 4
**adelgazar** to lose weight 9
**además** besides 2, in addition *1*
**Adiós** Goodbye 1
**administración** administration 1
**adoptar** to adopt 3
**adoptado/a** adopted 7
**adoptivo/a** adoptive 7
**aduana** customs 8
**adulto/a** adult 11
**aeropuerto** airport 8
**afeitarse** to shave oneself 4
**aficionado/a** fan 4
**afuera** outside 3
**agencia** agency 1
**agencia inmobiliaria** real estate agency 10
**agitar** to shake 9
**agotar** to use up 9
**agradecer (zc)** to be grateful 9
**agregar** to add 9
**agricultor/a** farmer *7*
**agudo/a** sharp 9
**ahora** now 1
**ahora mismo** right now 8
**ahorrar** to save 11
**ahorro** savings *2*
**aire** air 7
**aire acondicionado** air conditioning 8
**ajustar** to adjust 7
**al contado** in cash 2
**al frente** in front 9
**al mismo tiempo** at the same time 3
**al pie de** at the foot of 7
**alacena** cupboard 3
**alegrarse** to be happy 9
**alegre** happy 2
**alejarse** to move away 7
**alentar (ie)** to encourage 10
**alérgico/a** allergic 7
**alfombra** carpet 3
**alfombrado/a** carpeted *3*
**algo más** something else 2
**alguien** someone 2
**alguno/a** some 3
**alimentarse** to feed oneself 9
**alimento** food 8
**aliviar** to alleviate 9
**allá** there 3
**allí** there 5
**almacén** department store 2
**almohada** pillow 3
**almorzar (ue)** to have lunch 3
**almuerzo** lunch 8
**Aló** Hello 1
**alquilar** to rent 3
**alquiler** rent *2*
**alto/a** tall 2
**altura** altitude, height 8
**alumno/a** student *1*
**amable** kind 5
**amarillo/a** yellow 2
**ambos/as** both 5
**ambulante** traveling 10
**americano/a** American 3
**amigo/a** friend 1
**amistad** friendship 9
**amplio/a** ample 10
**amueblado/a** furnished 10
**analista** analyst 10
**analizar** to analyze 11
**anaranjado/a** orange 2
**anillo** ring 2
**animal doméstico** household pet 9
**año** year 3
**anotar** to make a note of 9
**anteojos** glasses 8
**antepasado** ancestor 3
**anterior** previous 10
**antes** before 7
**antibiótico** antibiotic 9
**anuncio** advertisement 7
**aparecer** to appear 10
**apartamento** apartment 3
**apoyo** support 9
**aprender** to learn *1*, 5
**aprobar** to approve 10
**aprovechar** to take advantage *2*, 9
**apurarse** to hurry 8
**aquí** here 2
**árbol** tree 7
**archivar** to file 5
**arma de fuego** firearm 7
**armario** cupboard/closet 3
**arquitecto/a** architect 10
**arrancar** to start 7
**arreglar** to repair/arrange 4
**arrendador/a** landlord *2*
**arriesgarse** to risk 9
**asaltar** to assault 10
**asar** to roast 3
**ascensor** elevator 8
**asegurado/a** insured 5
**asegurarse** to assure oneself *2*
**asiento** seat 7
**asistir a** to attend 5
**asmático/a** asthmatic 9
**aspirar** to vacuum 3
**asunto** matter 7
**atender (ie) + a** to pay attention to/assist 5
**atentamente** attentively 11
**aterrizar** to land 8
**atrasado/a** delayed 10
**aumentar** to increase 9
**aumentar** to raise *5*
**aunque** even though 11
**auto** car/automobile *1*
**autobús** bus 7
**automóvil** automobile 3
**autoridad** authority 11
**autorizar** to authorize 3
**avena** oatmeal 9
**avenida** avenue *1*, 7
**avergonzado/a** ashamed 9
**avión** airplane 8
**ayudar** to help 2
**azafata** stewardess 8
**azúcar** sugar 8
**azul marino** navy blue 2

**bahía** bay *8*
**bailarín/ina** dancer 4
**bajar** to go down 8
**bajo/a** low 11
**balcón** balcony 3

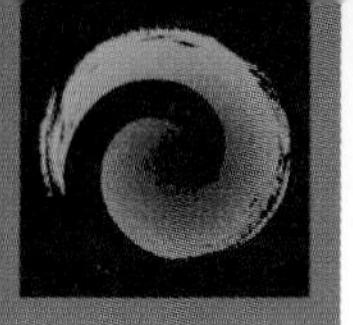

**banana** banana 2
**bañarse** to bathe oneself 4
**banco** bank 7
**bandeja** tray 8
**baño** bathroom 2
**banquero/a** banker 10
**barato/a** inexpensive 2
**barco** boat 8
**barrer** to sweep 3
**bata** robe 2
**batería** battery 7
**beber** to drink 3
**bebida** drink 8
**belleza** beauty *2*
**bello/a** beautiful *2*
**beneficios** benefits *5*
**besarse** to kiss *4*
**biblioteca** library 1
**bichos** bugs 10
**bien** fine 1
**bilingüe** bilingual 5
**billete** bill (currency) 2
**biología** biology 1
**bistec** steak 2
**blanco/a** white 2
**boca** mouth 9
**boda** wedding 4
**bolígrafo** pen 1
**bolsa (de valores)** stock market 10
**bolsa de trabajo** job market 10
**bolso** purse 2
**bombero** fire fighter 5
**bonito/a** pretty 2
**borrador** eraser 1
**borroso/a** blurred 9
**botas** boots 2
**botella** bottle 8
**botón** button 2
**botones** bellboy *8*
**brazo** arm 9
**brevemente** briefly 10
**brindis** toast 4
**brócoli** broccoli 8
**bronceador** tanning lotion 8
**¡Buen provecho! ¡Que aproveche!** Enjoy your meal! 8
**Buenas noches** Good evening/ Good night 1
**Buenas tardes** Good afternoon 1
**Buenos días** Good morning 1
**buscar** to look for 2
**buzón** mailbox 11

**caballo** horse 7
**cabello** hair 9
**cabeza** head 9
**cable** cable 11
**cacahuete** peanut 9
**cachetada** slap 9
**cachete** slap (on the cheek) 9
**cadena** chain 11
**cadera** hip 9
**caer bien/mal** to make a good/bad impression 5
**café** café, coffee 1
**café** brown 2
**cafetería** cafeteria 2
**caja** cashier 2
**cajero automático** automatic teller 8
**cajero/a** cashier 5
**calabaza** squash 9
**calcetines** socks 2
**calculadora** calculator 1
**calefacción** heating 4
**calentamiento** warm-up 9
**calificación** grade *5, 11*
**calle** street 2
**calmante** tranquilizer *9*
**calor** heat 4
**caloría** calorie 9
**calzoncillos** men's undershorts 2
**cama** bed *2, 3*
**camarero/a** maid 8
**camarón** shrimp 2
**camarote** ship's cabin 8
**cambiar** to change 7
**cambiar** to exchange 2
**cambio** change 2
**caminar** to walk 2
**camioneta** pick-up truck 7
**camisón** nightgown 2
**camote** sweet potato 9
**campeón/ona** champion 4
**campeonato** championship 4
**campo** field 11
**canal** channel 11
**candidato/a** candidate 5
**cansado/a** tired 1
**cantante** singer *1*, 5
**cantidad** quantity 2
**cápsula** capsule 9
**cara** face *4*
**cárcel** jail 7
**cargar** to load/charge 7
**carnicería** butcher shop 2
**caro/a** expensive 2
**carrera** career (university studies) 3
**carta** menu 8
**carta de vinos** wine list 8
**cartas** playing cards 4
**casa** house 3
**casa matriz** home office 5
**casado/a** married 3
**casarse (con)** to get married (to) 3
**casero (adj.)** household/home *10*
**casillero** locker *8*
**cebolla** onion 2
**celebrar** to celebrate 4
**cena** dinner 8
**cenar** to eat dinner 8
**cenicero** ashtray 8
**centígrado** centigrade 4
**centro** center *1*, 2
**centro comercial** shopping center 2
**cerámica** ceramic/pottery *1*
**cerca de** near 2
**cercano/a** nearby 8
**cereal** cereal 2
**cerradura** lock 10
**cerrar** to close *1*
**certificado** certificate *3*
**champán** champagne 8
**champú** shampoo 8
**Chao** Ciao 1
**charla** chat 8
**charlar** to chat 3
**cheque** check 2
**chícharo** pea 9
**chocar** to crash 7
**cielo** sky 4
**cine** movie theater *7*
**ciencias** science 2
**cinta** tape 9
**cintura** waist 9
**cinturón** belt 7
**cita** date/appointment 5
**ciudad** city 3
**claro** sure 2
**claro/a** clear/light 7
**cliente/a** client 5
**clima** climate 4
**cobija** blanket 3
**cobrar** to charge 3
**cochera** carport 10
**cocina** kitchen 3
**cocinar** to cook 3
**cocinero/a** cook 5
**codo** elbow 9
**colaborar** to collaborate *11*
**colombiano/a** Colombian 3
**color** color 2
**comedor** dining room 3
**comenzar** to begin *2*
**comenzar (ie)** to begin 9
**comer** to eat 3
**comercial** commercial 2
**comercio** trade 10
**comida** food 3
**¿Cómo está Ud.?** How are you? (formal) 1
**¿Cómo estás?** How are you? (familiar) 1
**¿Cómo se llama Ud.?** What's your name? (formal) 1
**¿Cómo te llamas?** What's your name? (familiar) 1
**cómoda** dresser 3
**cómodo/a** comfortable 3
**compañero/a de clase** classmate, **—de cuarto** roommate 1
**compañía** company 5
**comparar** to compare *7*
**compartir** to share 3
**completamente** completely 10
**completo/a** complete 1
**componente** component *5*
**comportamiento** behavior *9*
**compra** purchase 7
**comprar** to buy 2
**compras** shopping 1, purchases 2
**comprender** to understand 3
**comprobante** claim check 8
**comprometerse** to become engaged 5

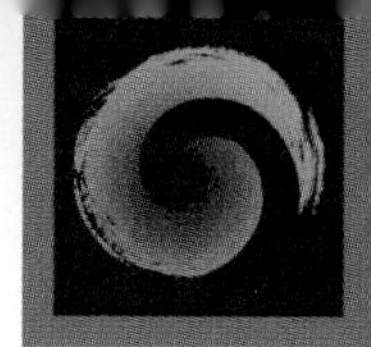

**compromiso** engagement **4**
**computadora** computer **1**
**comunicarse con** to be in touch with **5**
**comunidad** community ***1***
**condado** county **7**
**condominio** condominium **3**
**conducir** to drive **2**
**conductor/a** driver ***7***
**confianza** confidence **2, 7**
**confirmar** to confirm **5**
**congestionado/a** congested **9**
**conmigo** with me **5**
**conocer (a)** to know/be acquainted with **5**
**conocimiento** consciousness **7**
**consciente** conscious ***7***
**concierto** concert ***7***
**conseguir** to obtain/get ***2***
**conseguir (i)** to get/obtain **8**
**consejo** advice **7**
**construir** to build **11**
**consultorio** doctor's office **3**
**contabilidad** accounting **1**
**contacto** contact **11**
**contador/a** accountant **5**
**contable** accountant **5**
**contenido** content **11**
**contento/a** happy **1**
**contestar** to answer ***1*, 5**
**contigo** with you **5**
**continuamente** continuously **10**
**contratar** to hire ***8***
**contratista** contractor **10**
**contrato** contract **5**
**contribuir** to contribute ***5***
**copia** copy ***1***
**corazón** heart **9**
**corredor** corridor **8**
**corredor/a de bolsa** stockbroker **10**
**correo electrónico** e-mail **3**
**correr** to run **3**
**corto/a** short (length) **2**
**costa** coast **4**
**costar (ue)** to cost **2**
**costumbre** custom **7**
**creer** to believe **8**
**crema** cream ***3***
**crepe** crepe **8**
**cromo** chromium **9**
**crucero** cruise ship **8**
**crudo/a** raw **9**
**cuaderno** notebook **1**
**cuadra** block **7**
**cuadro** painting **3**
**cualquier** any ***5***
**cualquier/a** any **9**
**cuando** when **2**
**¿Cuánto/a?** How much? **2**
**¿Cuántos/as?** How many? **1**
**cuarto** quarter **1**
**cuarto de lavado** laundry room **3**
**cubierto/a** covered ***10***
**cubierto** place setting **8**
**cubrir** to cover ***2*, 9**
**cuchara** spoon **8**
**cucharada** spoonful **9**
**cuchillo** knife **8**
**cuello** neck **9**
**cuenta** bill ***2*, 8**
**cuero** leather **7**
**cuerpo** body **4**
**cuestionario** questionnaire **9**
**cuidado/a** cared for **10**
**¡Cuidado!** Careful! **7**
**cuidadosamente** carefully ***10***
**cuidar** to take care of **9**
**culpable** guilty **9**
**cultura** culture **11**
**cumpleaños** birthday **2**
**cumplir** to fulfill **5**
**cuñado/a** brother/sister-in-law **3**
**cuota** installment **10**
**currículum vitae** resumé **5**
**curso** course **5**
**cuyo/a** whose **9**

**dañar** to damage **10**
**daño** damage **7**
**dar** to give **5**
**darse prisa** to hurry **8**
**de** from **1**
**de acuerdo** in agreement/agreed ***1***
**de frente** out in front **3**
**de hecho** as a matter of fact **9**
**De nada.** You're welcome. **1**
**¿De parte de quién?** Who's calling? **5**
**débil** weak **9**
**debilidad** weakness **9**
**decididamente** decidedly **10**
**decidido/a** decided **10**
**decir** to say, tell **2**
**declaración** statement **7**
**dedicarse (a)** to work at/ dedicate oneself to **3**
**dedo** finger **9**
**dejar** to let ***2***, to leave (behind) **5**
**delicioso/a** delicious **8**
**dentro** inside **8**
**departamento** department **11**
**dependiente/a** salesclerk **2**
**deporte** sport **2**
**deportivo/a** sport **2**
**deprimido/a** depressed **9**
**depósito** deposit ***3***
**derecho** right **11**
**derecho/a** right **2,** straight **8**
**desayunar** to eat breakfast **8**
**desayuno** breakfast **8**
**descafeinado/a** decaffeinated **8**
**descansar** to rest **9**
**descender** to descend **3**
**descendiente** descendant **3**
**descomponer** to break down **10**
**descompuesto/a** broken (down) **7**
**desconcertado/a** bewildered **9**
**descuento** discount **2**
**desde** from **1**
**desear** to wish **2**
**desmayarse** to faint **7**
**desobedecer (zc)** to disobey **9**
**desocupado/a** unoccupied ***3***
**desordenado/a** messy **3,** disorganized **9**
**desorganizado** disorganized **3**
**despedir** to fire ***5***
**despegar** to take off **8**
**despejado/a** clear **4**
**despejar** to clear up **10**
**despertarse (ie)** to wake oneself up **4**
**después** afterwards **5**
**destinatario** addressee/payee **5**
**destino** destination **8**
**detalle** detail **5**
**detenerse (g) (ie)** to stop **7**
**detrás** in back **8**
**deuda** debt ***2***
**devolver (ue)** to return (something) **8**
**día** day **1**
**diario** daily **4**
**diario** newspaper **11**
**días hábiles** workdays **5**
**dicho/a** said **10**
**diente** tooth **4**
**dieta** diet **9**
**difícil** difficult **1**
**dilatado/a** prolonged **10**
**dinero** money **1**
**dirección** direction/address **2**
**dirección** direction **7**
**directamente** directly **11**
**director/a** director **5**
**dirigir** to manage/run **5**
**disco** record/(compact disc) ***1***
**Disculpe.** Pardon me. (formal) **1**
**diseñador/a** designer **2**
**diseñar** to design **10**
**diseño** design **10**
**disfrutar** to enjoy **9**
**disponible** available ***3*, 5**
**disquete** floppy disk **5**
**distraído/a** absent-minded/distracted **7**
**distrito** district **11**
**divertido/a** fun/enjoyable **3**
**divertirse (ie)** to enjoy oneself/ have a good time **4**
**divorciarse** to divorce **4**
**doblado/a** dubbed **11**
**doblar** to turn **7**
**doble** double **8**
**docena** dozen **5**
**doctor/a** doctor **5**
**documento** document **5**
**dólar** dollar **2**
**doler (ue)** to hurt **7**
**dolor** pain **9**
**doméstico/a** household related/domestic **3**
**dominar** to have a good command of **5**
**domingo** Sunday **1**
**donar** to donate **11**
**donativo** donation **11**
**dormirse (ue)** to fall asleep **4**
**dormitorio** bedroom/dorm room **1**
**dormitorio** bedroom **3**

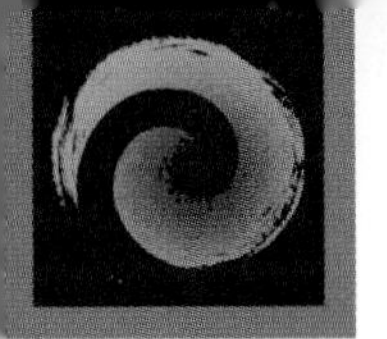

**dos** two **1**
**droga** drug **7**
**ducha** shower **8**
**dueño/a** owner **8**
**duquesa** duchess **8**
**durante** during *11*

**economista** economist **10**
**edad** age *1*
**edificio** building **7**
**editor/a** editor **11**
**efectivamente** indeed **10**
**efecto secundario** side effect **9**
**ejercicio** exercise **1**
**ejercicio aeróbico** aerobic exercise **4**
**ejército** army **7**
**elemental** elementary (school) *1*
**embajada** embassy **7**
**embarazada** pregnant **9**
**embarcar** to board, to embark **8**
**embargo** seizure **10**
**emergencia** emergency *7*
**emocionante** exciting **4**
**empatado/a** tied **4**
**empezar (ie)** to begin **5**
**empleado/a** employee **3**
**empleo** job/employment **2, 5**
**empresa** business **1**
**empujar** to push **9**
**en caso** in case *1*
**en contacto con** in contact with **11**
**en cuanto** as soon as **8**
**en este momento** right now **5**
**¿En qué puedo servirle?** How can I help you? **2**
**en vez de** instead of **9**
**Encantado/a** Pleased to meet you **1**
**encantar** to delight **7**
**encargarse (de)** to take charge of **5**
**encontrar (ue)** to find **2**
**encontrarse (ue)** to meet, bump into **4**
**encuesta** survey **11**
**enfermedad** illness **9**
**enfermería** infirmary/sickbay **3**
**enfermero/a** nurse **3**
**enfermo/a** sick **9**
**enfrente de** in front (of)/across from **2**
**enganche** down payment **10**
**engordar** to gain weight **9**
**enojado/a** angry *7*
**enojarse** to get angry **4**
**enseñar** to show/teach **3**
**ensuciar** to soil/make dirty *1*
**entendido/a** understood **9**
**enterarse** to find out *5*
**entonces** then, next **2**
**entrada** down payment **10**
**entrecejo** space between the eyebrows *9*
**entrega** delivery **10**
**entrenador/a** coach **4**
**entrenamiento** training *5*
**entrenar** to train **11**
**entrevista** interview **5**
**entrevistar** to interview *11*
**enviar** to send **2, 5**
**enyesar** to plaster **7**
**equipaje** luggage **8**
**equipo** equipment **11**
**equipo de sonido** sound system **7**
**escalera** stairs **2**
**escena** scene **7**
**escoger** to choose **10**
**escolar** scholastic **11**
**escondido/a** hidden **9**
**escritor/a** writer **2**
**escritorio** big desk **1**
**escuchar** to listen *1*
**escuela** school **1**
**espacio** space **3**
**espaguetis** spaghetti **8**
**espalda** back **9**
**español** Spanish **1**
**especial** special **2**
**especialista** specialist **11**
**especializarse** to specialize **10**
**especialmente** especially **10**
**espejo** mirror **3**
**esperanza** hope **9**
**esperar** to wait (for)/hope **5**
**esposo/a** husband/wife **3**
**esquí acuático** water skiing **4**
**esquiar** to ski **4**
**esquina** corner **7**
**estación** station **7**
**estacionamiento** parking **7**
**estadísticas** statistics *7*
**estado** state **5**
**Estados Unidos** the United States **3**
**estampilla** stamp **5**
**estante** shelf **1**
**estar de acuerdo** to agree **4**
**éste/a** this one **2**
**estéreo** stereo **2**
**estilo** style **2**
**estiramiento** stretch **9**
**estirarse** to stretch **9**
**estómago** stomach **9**
**éstos/as** these **2**
**estoy...** I am... **1**
**estudiante** student **1**
**estudiar** to study **1**
**estudio** study **3**
**estufa** stove **3**
**etiqueta** label **5**
**evitar** to avoid **7**
**exactamente** exactly **2**
**excursión** excursion **8**
**existir** to exist **11**
**éxito** success *2*, **9**
**expediente** file, dossier **5**
**experiencia** experience **5**
**exportar** to export **5**
**expresarse** to express oneself **11**
**expresión** expression **11**
**extranjero** abroad **10**
**extraño/a** stranger *7*

**fábrica** factory **5**
**fabricar** to manufacture **11**
**fácil** easy **1**
**facturar** to check (luggage) **8**
**falda** skirt **2**
**falta** lack **9**
**faltar** to be missing *1*
**famoso/a** famous *1*
**fantástico/a** fantastic *1*
**farmacéutico/a** pharmacist **9**
**farmacia** pharmacy **2**
**favorito/a** favorite *1*
**felicidad** happiness **4**
**felicidades** congratulations **5**
**felicitar** to congratulate **4**
**feria** fair **10**
**fertilizante** fertilizer *7*
**fideo** noodle **9**
**fiebre del heno** hay fever **9**
**fiesta** party **2**
**fijar** to set (date) **4**
**fijo/a** fixed/set **2**
**final** final/end **5**
**financiamiento** financing **10**
**financiero/a** financial **10**
**finanzas** finance **10**
**firma** signature **11**
**firmar** to sign **2**
**fisioterapia** physical therapy **7**
**flor** flower **3**
**fluctuación** fluctuation **11**
**folleto** brochure/pamphlet **5**
**forma** shape **9**
**foto(grafía)** photo(graph) **3**
**fotocopia** photocopy **5**
**fotocopiadora** copying machine **5**
**fracaso** failure **9**
**fracturarse** to fracture **7**
**francés/esa** French **2**
**frasco** bottle (of medicine) **9**
**frecuentar** to frequent **7**
**freno** brake **7**
**fresco** cool **4**
**fresco/a** fresh **2**
**frío/a** cold **8**
**frondoso/a** leafy **9**
**fruta** fruit **8**
**frutería** fruit stand **2**
**fuente** source *2*
**fuerte** fort *8*, strong **9**
**fuertemente** strongly **10**
**fumar** to smoke *9*
**funcionar** to function/work **4**
**fundar** to establish/found *5*
**furioso/a** angry **1**
**fútbol** soccer **4**

**gafas (de sol)** (sun) glasses **2**
**gallina** hen **7**

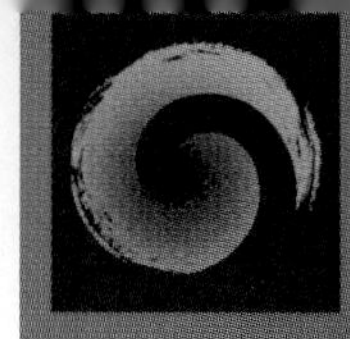

**gana** desire *9*
**ganar** to win 4
**garaje** garage 3
**gas** gas (natural) 3
**gasolinera** gasoline station 7
**gastar** to spend 10
**gasto** expense 7
**gato** cat 3
**general** general 3
**generosamente** generously 10
**gente** people 5
**gerente** manager 1
**gimnasia** gymnastics 4
**gimnasio** gymnasium 4
**gol** goal 4
**golpear** to hit 9
**Gracias** Thank you 1
**grado** degree (temperature) 4
**graduación** graduation *4*
**graduarse** to graduate *4*, 5
**gramática** grammar *1*
**grande** big 1
**granja** farm 7
**gratis** free (of cost) 1
**gratuito/a** free of cost 10
**grave** serious 10
**gripe** flu 9
**gris** grey 2
**grúa** tow truck 7
**grupo** group *1*, 11
**guapo/a** handsome *1*
**guardameta** goalie 4
**guardar** to keep 3
**guardería** childcare 3
**guía** guidebook 8
**guisante** pea 9

**habitación** room 8
**hablador/a** talkative 2
**hacer** to do/to make *1*, 3
**hacia** toward 7
**haga el favor de** please 2
**hallar** to find 9
**¡Hasta la vista!** Be seeing you! 2
**Hasta luego.** See you later. 1
**Hasta mañana.** See you tomorrow. 1
**hay** there is/are 1
**herido/a** wounded 7
**hermanastro/a** stepbrother/sister 3
**hermano/a** brother/sister 3
**hermosísimo/a** very beautiful *8*
**hielo** ice 4
**hijastro/a** stepson/daughter 3
**hijo/a** son/daughter 1
**hipoteca** mortgage *2*, 10
**hipotecario/a** mortgage 10
**hockey sobre hielo** ice hockey 4
**hogar** home 10
**Hola** Hello 1
**hombre de negocios** businessman 5
**hondo/a** deep 9
**horario** schedule 1
**hormigueo** pins and needles 9
**horno (microondas)** oven (microwave) 3
**horóscopo** horoscope *1*
**hospital** hospital 5
**hueso** bone 9
**huésped** guest 8
**huevo** egg 2
**húmedo/a** humid 4

**ídolo** idol *1*
**idioma** language 9
**igual** equal 2
**Igualmente.** Likewise. 1
**imagen** image *2*
**imaginarse** to imagine 8
**imprescindible** indispensable 10
**impresionar** to impress *5*
**impreso/a** printed 10
**impresora** printer 3
**impuesto** tax 2
**incapacidad** inability, disability *1*
**incluir** to include 8
**incómodo/a** uncomfortable 2
**indicación** direction 7
**infantil** related to children 3
**infarto** stroke 9
**información** information *1*
**informal** informal *1*
**informática** computer science 1
**informe** report 7
**ingeniería** engineering *5*
**ingeniero/a** engineer 5
**Inglaterra** England 3
**inglés** English *1*
**ingreso** income *2*, 5
**injusto/a** unjust/unfair *7*
**inquilino/a** tenant 10
**insecticida** insecticide *7*
**inspeccionar** to inspect 10
**inspector/a** inspector 10
**instantáneo/a** instantaneous 11
**inteligente** intelligent 1
**interés** interest 10
**interesante** interesting 10
**interesar** to be interesting *11*
**invertir (ie)** to invest 10
**invierno** winter 4
**inyección** injection 9
**ir** to go *1*, 2
**isla** island *8*
**italiano** Italian *1*
**italiano/a** Italian 8
**itinerario** itinerary 8
**izquierdo/a** left 7

**jabón** soap 8
**japonés/esa** Japanese 2
**jarabe** syrup 9
**jardín** garden 3
**jefe/a** boss 5
**jitomate** (small) tomato 9
**jornada** day/period *2*
**joven** young *1*, 2
**joven** young man, woman 11
**jubilación** retirement *5*
**jubilarse** to retire 7
**juego** game 3
**jueves** Thursday 1
**jugador/a** player 4
**jugo** juice 3
**juicio** judgement 10
**junta directiva** board of directors 11
**juntarse** to get together 5
**junto a** next to 2
**juntos/as** together 1
**jurar** to swear 11

**laboratorio** laboratory *11*
**lacio** straight (hair) *4*
**lado** side 2
**ladrón/ona** thief 10
**lago** lake 7
**lámpara** lamp 8
**lápiz** pencil 1
**largo/a** long 2
**lastimarse** to hurt oneself 9
**lavabo** bathroom sink 8
**lavar** to wash 3
**lavarse** to get washed 4
**leche** milk 2
**lechuga** lettuce 2
**leer** to read *1*, 3
**lengua** language 10
**lentamente** slowly 9
**lenteja** lentil 9
**lento/a** slow 4
**letra** letter (alphabet) 7
**letra de molde** print *2*
**levantar** to lift *1*, 4
**levantarse** to get oneself up 4
**ley** law 7
**libertad** liberty 11
**libra** pound 2
**libre** free 5
**libremente** freely 11
**librería** bookstore 1
**libro** book 1
**licencia** license 7
**licenciado/a** attorney (Mex.) 10
**licenciado/a** graduate (bachelor's) 5
**liga** league 4
**límite** limit 7
**limpiar** to clean 3
**limpio/a** clean 8
**lista** list *1*
**listo/a** ready *3*, clever 11
**lo más pronto posible** as soon as possible 5
**lo que** that which 11

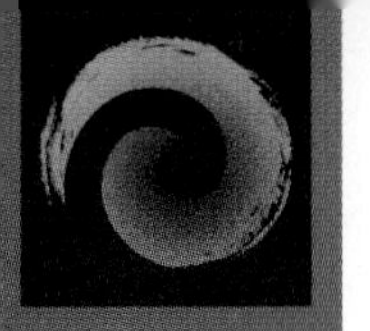

**Lo siento.** I'm sorry. 1
**locutor/a** announcer 4
**lograr** to attain/achieve 11
**lonchera** lunch box 3
**lo demás** the rest 11
**lucha libre** wrestling 4
**lucir** to look good *2*
**lugar** place 1
**lujo** luxury 7
**luna de miel** honeymoon 8
**lunes** Monday 1
**luz** light 1

**llamada** call 4
**llanta** tire 7
**llave** key 8
**llegar** to arrive 5
**llenar** to fill *3, 5*
**lleno/a** full 8
**llevar** to take along/carry 2
**llevarse bien, mal** to get along with, not to get along with 4
**llover (ue)** to rain 4

**madrastra** stepmother 3
**madre** mother 3
**madrugada** dawn *8*
**maestro/a** teacher 1
**maestro/a en prácticas** student teacher 1
**magro/a** lean 9
**maíz** corn 7
**malestar** discomfort 9
**maleta** suitcase 8
**maletero** trunk 7
**mamá** mom 3
**mañana** morning 1
**mancha** spot, stain 2
**mandar** to send 8
**manejar** to drive 4, to operate, run (as in business) 3
**mano** hand *1, 4*
**mantequilla** butter 2
**manzana** apple 8, block 7
**mapa** map 8
**maquillarse** to put on make-up 4
**mar** sea 8
**maravilla** wonder *11*
**marcar** to mark/indicate 8
**mareado/a** nauseous/dizzy 9
**marrón** brown 2
**martes** Tuesday 1
**masaje** massage 9
**mascota** mascot 9
**matar** to kill 9
**material** material *11*
**materno/a** maternal 3

**Me llamo…** My name is… 1
**me parece bien** sounds good to me 3
**mecánico** mechanic 5
**mecánica** mechanics 5
**mediano/a** medium 2
**medianoche** midnight 1
**medias** stockings 2
**médico/a** doctor 3, medical (adj) 7
**medio hermano/a** half brother/sister 3
**medio/a** half 1
**mediodía** noon 1
**medios de comunicación** media 11
**mejor** better 3
**menor** minor 10
**menos** less *1*
**mensaje** message 5
**mentir(ie)** to lie 4
**menú** menu 8
**mercadeo** marketing 10
**mercadotecnia** marketing 11
**mesa** table 1
**mesa de centro** coffee table 3
**mesero/a** waiter/waitress 5
**meta** goal (post) 4
**mi amor** sweetheart 11
**Mi nombre es…** My name is… 1
**miel** honey 9
**millón** million *1*
**mientras** while 7
**miércoles** Wednesday 1
**milanesa** cutlet 8
**millonario/a** millionaire *2*
**mirar** to look (at) 2
**mismo/a** same 11
**mixto/a** mixed 4
**mochila** backpack 2
**modelo** model *1*
**modernizar** to modernize 10
**moderno/a** modern 10
**molestar** to bother 8
**moneda** coin 8
**montaña** mountain 4
**morirse (ue)** to die 7
**mosaico** tile *3*
**mostrar (ue)** to show 8
**motivo** motive, purpose 2
**Mucho gusto** Pleased to meet you 1
**mudarse** to move 5
**muebles** furniture 2
**muelle** pier 8
**muerte** death 9
**muerto/a** dead 3
**mujer** woman 2
**mujer de negocios** business woman 5
**mujer policía** police woman 5
**muletas** crutches 7
**multa** ticket/fine 7
**mundial** worldwide 11
**mundo** world 3
**música** music 2
**musical** musical *1*
**músico** musician 5
**muslo** thigh 9

**nacer** to be born *1, 5*
**nacimiento** birth *2*
**nacionalidad** nationality *3*
**nada** nothing 2
**nadar** to swim 4
**nadie** nobody 2
**nalga** buttock 9
**naranja** orange 2
**nariz** nose 9
**natación** swimming 4
**necesidad** need *1*
**necesitar** to need 2
**negar (ie)** to deny 9
**negocio** business *2, 3*
**negro/a** black 2
**nervioso/a** nervous 1
**nevar (ie)** to snow 4
**nevera** refrigerator 3
**ningún, ninguno/a** none 4
**niño/a** child *1, 2*
**nodriza** nursing (mom) 9
**nombre** name 8
**normalmente** usually 3
**norte** north 7
**Nos vemos** Be seeing you 1
**notar** to notice 10
**noticias** news 5
**noticiero** news program 4
**novela** novel 2
**novio/a** boyfriend/girlfriend 1
**nublado/a** cloudy 4
**nuera** daughter-in-law 3
**nuestro/a** our 5
**nuevo/a** new 1
**número** number *1*
**nunca** never 2

**obra** work (of art, literature) *1*
**obrero/a** worker 5
**observar** to observe 11
**obvio/a** obvious 10
**ocupado/a** busy 1
**oferta** offer 10
**oficina** office 2
**ofrecer (zc)** to offer 10
**¡Ojalá!** I hope so! I wish! 9
**oído** ear 9
**oír** to hear 3
**ojo** eye *4, 9*
**olvidar** to forget 8
**onza** ounce 2
**ordenar** to order 2
**oreja** external ear 9
**organizar** to organize 5
**origen** origin 3
**orinar** to urinate 9
**oscuridad** darkness 11
**oscuro/a** dark 7

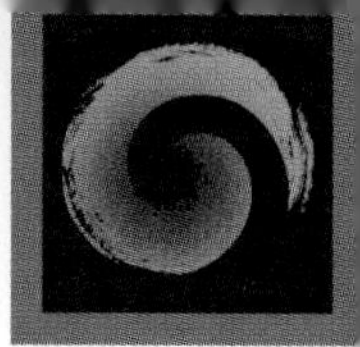

**otoño** fall 4
**otra vez** again 7
**otro/a** other 2

**paciente** patient 9
**padrastro** stepfather 3
**padre** father 3
**pagar** to pay 2
**país** nation, country *5*
**paisaje** landscape 7
**palabra** word 3
**pan** bread 2
**panadería** bakery 2
**papá** dad 3
**papa** potato 2
**papel** paper 1
**papel higiénico** toilet paper 8
**para** for/by *1*, 2
**parabrisas** windshield 7
**parada** stop 7
**paraguas** umbrella 2
**paramédico** paramedic *7*
**parar** to stop 4
**parecer** to seem 10
**pared** wall 3
**pareja** couple/pair 4
**pariente/a** relative *2*
**parrilla** grill/barbecue 3
**parte** part 3
**partido** game, match 4
**pasado/a** past 11
**pasaje** ticket 8
**pasaporte** passport 8
**pasar** to pass *1*
**pasatiempo** pastime 5
**pase** pass 8
**pasillo** corridor/hallway 8
**paso** step *2*
**paso a paso** step by step 10
**pastel** cake 2
**pastelería** bakery (pastries) 2
**pateador/a** kicker 4
**patear** to kick 4
**patrocinador/a** sponsor 10
**patrocinar** to sponsor 4
**patrulla** patrol car *7*
**peatón** pedestrian 7
**pecho** chest 9
**pedagogía** pedagogy 1
**pedir (i)** to order, ask for 4
**pegar** to stick 5
**peinarse** to comb one's hair 4
**pelearse** to fight 4
**peligro** danger 7
**peligroso/a** dangerous 4
**pelo** hair 4
**pelota** ball 4
**peluquería** beauty salon 2
**peluquero/a** hair stylist 5
**pena** grief 9
**pensar (ie)** to think/plan on 4
**peor** worse 7
**pequeño/a** small 1
**perder (ie)** to lose 4
**perdido/a** lost 11
**perdonar** to forgive 2
**perfume** perfume 2
**periódico** newspaper 7
**periodista** journalist 3
**período** period 11
**permitir** to permit/let 8
**perro** dog 3
**personalmente** personally 3
**pertenecer** to belong 2
**pertenencia** belonging 9
**peruano/a** Peruvian 2
**pesas** free weights 4
**pescadería** fish market 2
**pescado** fish 2
**peso** weight 9
**pie** foot 9
**piel** skin *2*, 9
**pierna** leg 7
**piña** pineapple 2
**pintar** to paint 4
**piscina** swimming pool 3
**piso** floor 2
**pizarra** chalkboard 1
**placentero/a** pleasant 8
**planchar** to iron 3
**planear** to plan 8
**planificación** planning 10
**plano** plan 10
**planta baja** ground floor 3
**platillo** course 8
**plato** dish/plate 3
**plazo** installment 10
**plomería** plumbing 10
**plomero/a** plumber 5
**pobrecito/a** poor thing 7
**poder(ue)** to be able/can 3
**policía** police officer 5
**policiaco/a** police (related to) 7
**política** politics 11
**pollo** chicken 2
**polución** pollution *7*
**poner** to put/place 3
**popular** popular 1
**por adelantado** in advance 3
**por ciento** per cent 2
**por cierto** by the way 5
**¡Por Dios!** For Heaven's sake! 9
**por ejemplo** for example 11
**por escrito** in writing 10
**por eso** that's why 10
**por favor** please 2
**por medio de** by means of 5
**por nuestra cuenta** on our own 8
**por qué** why 2
**porcentaje** percentage 11
**porque** because 1
**portarse** to behave 5
**portavoz** spokesperson 10
**portería** goal (post) 4
**portero/a** goalie 4
**positivo/a** positive 11
**postre** dessert 8
**práctica** practice 1
**practicar** to practice 1
**precio** price 2
**precioso/a** lovely 8
**preferir (ie)** to prefer 4
**pregunta** question *5*
**premio** prize *2*
**prensa** press 11
**preocupado/a** worried 7
**preocuparse** to worry 4
**presentar** to submit 11
**préstamo** loan *2*, 10
**presupuesto** budget 5
**primario/a** primary *4*
**primavera** spring 4
**primero** first 1
**primo/a** cousin 2
**principal** main 3
**privado/a** private 3
**probablemente** probably 10
**problema** problem 2
**productor/a** producer 11
**profesor/a** professor/teacher 1
**programa** program 5
**programación** programming 1
**programador/a** programmer 5
**prohibir** to forbid 9
**prometer** to promise 2
**pronto** soon 10
**propiedad** real estate/property 10
**propietario/a** property owner 10
**propina** tip 8
**propio/a** own 3
**proporcionar** to provide 8
**protagonista** leading man/lady 11
**proteger** to protect 7
**próximo/a** next *4*
**prueba** proof 11
**psicología** psychology 1
**psiquiatra** psychiatrist 5
**publicidad** advertising 5
**pueblo** town 7
**puedo** I can 1
**puerto** port *8*
**puesto** job/position 5
**pulgada** inch 3
**pulmón** lung 9
**pulmonía** pneumonia 9
**pulsera** bracelet 2
**punto** point 4
**puntual** punctual 2
**pupitre** student desk 1

**¿Qué?** What? Which? 1
**¿Qué hora es?** What time is it? 1
**¿Qué tal?** How's it going? 1
**quedar en** to agree 5
**quedarse** to stay, remain 7
**quehacer** chore 3
**querer (ie)** to want 4

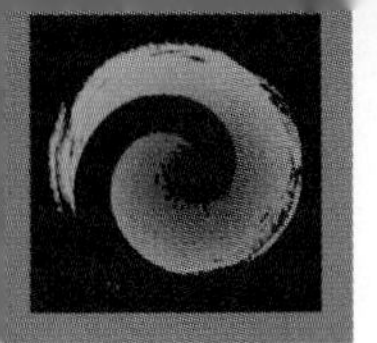

**queso** cheese 2
**¿Quién?** Who? 1
**Quiero presentarle a…** I want you to meet… (formal) 1
**Quiero presentarles a…** I want you to meet… (plural) 1
**Quiero presentarte a…** I want you to meet… (familiar) 1
**químico** chemical *7*
**quiosco** kiosk/stall 7
**quizá(s)** perhaps *10*

**radio** radio 11
**radiografía** X-ray 9
**rápidamente** rapidly 7
**rato** a while 4
**raya** stripe 2
**razonable** reasonable 10
**rebajado/a** reduced 2
**rebajas** sales 2
**recepcionista** receptionist 8
**receta** prescription 9
**recetar** to prescribe 9
**recibo** receipt 2
**recobrar** to regain 7
**recoger** get/obtain 2
**recomendar (ie)** to recommend 8
**reconocer (zc)** to recognize 9
**recordar (ue)** to remember 3
**recorrer** to move through 5
**recto/a** straight *9*, 8
**recuperarse** to recover/get better 7
**redecorar** to redecorate 10
**reflejar** to reflect 9
**refresco** soda 2
**refrigerador** refrigerator 3
**refrigerio** snack 3
**regalar** to give (gift) 8
**regalo** gift 2
**regatear** to bargain 2
**regateo** the act of bargaining *2*
**regresar** to return 2
**regular** so-so 1
**reírse (i)** to laugh 9
**religioso/a** religious 1
**relleno/a** stuffed 8
**reloj** watch/clock 2
**reparación** repair 10
**reparar** to repair 7
**repetir (i)** to repeat *1*
**reportaje** article/report 11
**reportar** to report 7
**reporte** report *3*
**reposo** rest *9*
**representante** representative 8
**requisito** requirement 5
**resolver (ue)** to resolve 10
**respaldar** to back up *2*
**respirar** to breathe 7
**responsable** responsible 3
**restaurante** restaurant *1*, 1
**resuelto** resolved 10
**resultado** result 10
**resumen** summary 11
**resumir** to summarize *11*
**revisar** to check 7
**rodilla** knee 9
**rojo/a** red 2
**romper** to break 7
**ropa** clothing 2
**rosado/a** pink *3*
**ruido** noise 4
**rutina** routine 4

**sábado** Saturday 1
**sábana** sheet 8
**saber** to know 2
**sacar** to get 5
**sacar** to take out *1*
**sacudir** to dust 3
**sala** living room 3
**sala de urgencias** emergency room 7
**salida** exit 5
**salir** to leave/go out 3
**salmón** salmon 2
**salón de charla** chat room 11
**salón de clase** classroom 1
**salud** health 4
**sanar** to heal *9*
**sandalias** sandals 2
**sargento** sargent 7
**satélite** satellite 11
**satisfecho/a** satisfied 10
**secarse** to dry off oneself 4
**secretario/a** secretary 5
**secreto** secret *4*
**seguido** often 3
**seguir (i)** to continue/follow 7
**segundo/a** second 2
**seguridad** safety, security 7
**seguro** insurance *5*, 7
**seguro** *(adj)* sure *2*
**sello** stamp 5
**semáforo** traffic light 7
**semana** week 1
**sembrar (ie)** to sow/plant 7
**semestre** semester 1
**seminario** seminar 11
**señal** sign 9
**sencillo/a** single 8
**señor/a** Mr./Mrs., Sir/Madam 1
**señorita** Miss 1
**sentarse** to sit *1*
**sentirse (ie)** to feel 4
**serio/a** serious 1
**servicio de lavandería** laundry service 8
**servir (i)** to serve 8
**sí** yes 1
**siempre** always 1
**siesta** nap 3
**siglo** century 11
**signo** sign 7
**siguiente** following *2*
**silencio** silence *1*
**silla** chair 1
**silla de ruedas** wheelchair 7
**sillón** armchair 3
**sin embargo** nevertheless 9
**síntoma** symptom 9
**sistema** system *5*
**sitio** place 1
**sobre** envelope 5
**sofá** couch 3
**sofocarse** to suffocate 9
**sol** sun 4
**solamente** only 1
**solicitante** applicant *2*
**solicitud** application 5
**solitario/a** solitary 7
**soltero/a** single *1*
**soltero/a** single 3
**sombrero** hat 2
**sorpresa** surprise 8
**sostén** bra 2
**subir** to go up/get in 8
**súbito/a** sudden *9*
**substancia** substance 7
**sucursal** branch office *5*, 10
**sudadera** sweatshirt 2
**suegro/a** father/mother-in-law 3
**sueldo** salary *5*
**sueño** sleep 9
**suerte** luck *2*, 5
**suéter** sweater 2
**suficiente** sufficient 1
**sufrir** to suffer 9
**sugerir (ie)** to suggest *8*
**supermercado** supermarket 2
**suponer (g)** to suppose 11

**tacón** heel 2
**tal vez** perhaps 9
**talla** size 2
**talón** heel 9
**también** too/also 1
**tanque** tank 7
**tanto/a** so much 3
**tardar** to delay 8
**tarde** late 1
**tarea** homework 1
**tarjeta de crédito** credit card 2
**tasa** valuation 10
**taxímetro** taxi meter 8
**teatro** theater 5
**techo** roof 10
**tecnología** technology 11
**teléfono** telephone 1
**teléfono celular** cell telephone 2
**telenovela** soap opera 11
**televisión** television 11

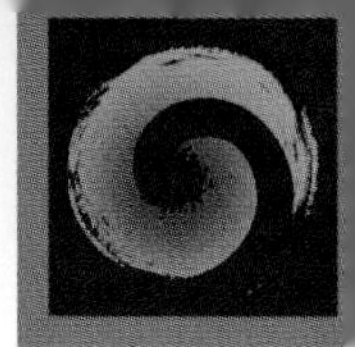

**televisor** television set 2
**temerse** to be afraid of 9
**temperatura** temperature 4
**temporada** season *9*
**temporal** temporary 5
**temprano** early 1
**tenedor** fork 8
**teniente** lieutenant *7*
**tengo** I have 1
**tensión arterial** blood pressure 9
**tercero/a** third 1
**terminar** to end/to finish 1
**término** term 10
**termita** termite 10
**termómetro** thermometer 9
**ternera** veal 8
**terraza** terrace 8
**testamento** will 10
**testigo** witness *7*
**texto** text 1
**tiempo** weather 4
**tienda** store *1*, 2
**tiene** he/she has/you have (formal) 1
**tienes** you have (familiar) 1
**tinto** red (wine) 4
**tío/a** uncle/aunt 3
**típico/a** typical 3
**tirar** to throw away 10
**título** degree/title 5
**tiza** chalk 1
**toalla** towel 8
**tobillo** ankle 9
**tocar** to touch 7
**todavía** still/yet 7
**todo el mundo** everybody 11
**todos** all/everybody 1
**tomar una decisión** to make a decision 5
**tomate** tomato 2
**tortillería** tortilla bakery 2
**tos** cough 9
**total** total 1
**trabajador/a** hard-working *2*, worker 3
**trabajar** to work 1
**traducir** to translate 3
**traer** to bring 3
**traje de baño** bathing suit *8*
**tranquilo/a** peaceful/tranquil 7
**transmisión** broadcast 4
**transmitir** to broadcast 11
**transportar** to transport 8
**transporte** transportation 8
**tratado/a** treated 9
**tratamiento** treatment *2*, 3
**tratar** to mistreat 10
**trato** deal 10
**trigo** wheat 9
**tripulación** crew 8
**triste** sad 7
**trofeo** trophy 4
**tú** you (familiar) 1
**tu** your 2
**turismo** tourism 8
**turístico/a** tourist 8

**último/a** last 1
**un par de** a couple of 7
**universidad** university 1
**unos/as cuantos/as** a few 9
**usted (Ud.)** you (formal) 1
**uva** grape 2

**vaca** cow 7
**vacaciones** vacation *2*
**vacante** vacancy 5
**vacunarse** to be vaccinated 9
**valer (g)** to have value 9
**vaso** glass 8
**vecindario** neighborhood 7
**vecino/a** neighbor 3
**velocidad** speed 7
**vendaje** bandage 9
**vender** to sell *1*, 2
**venir (ie) (g)** to come 3
**venta** sale 5
**ventana** window 1
**ventanilla** window 8
**ver** to see 3
**verano** summer 4
**verdad** true 1
**verdaderamente** truthfully/truly 10
**verde** green 2
**verdura** vegetable 8
**vereda** path 10
**vestíbulo** lobby 8
**vestido** dress 2
**vestirse (i)** to get dressed 4
**vez** time/occasion *2*
**viaje** trip 1
**viajero/a** traveler 8
**vida** life 5, 7
**viento** wind 4
**viernes** Friday 1
**violeta** purple 2
**visitar** to visit 3
**vista** view 3
**vivir** to live *1*, 3
**volar (ue)** to fly 8
**volver (ue)** to return 4
**votar** to vote 11
**vuelo** flight 8

**y** and 1
**ya** already 3
**yerno** son-in-law 3

**zanahoria** carrot 2
**zapatería** shoe store 2
**zapato** shoe 2

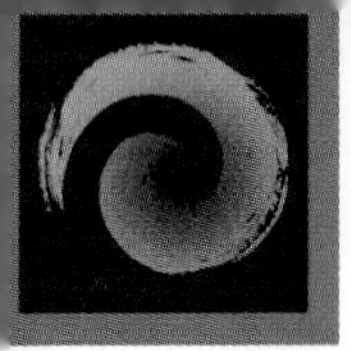

# Vocabulary

## English-Spanish

**a couple of** un par de 7
**a few** unos/as cuantos/as 9
**a while** un rato 4
**abortion** el aborto *9*
**about, concerning** acerca de 3
**abroad** extranjero 10
**absent-minded** distraído/a 7
**accesory** accesorio 7
**accident** accidente 3
**accompany** acompañar 8
**accountant** contador/a, contable 5
**accounting** contabilidad 1
**achieve** lograr 11
**across from** al otro lado de 2
**act** actuar 11
**act** el acto *1*
**act of bargaining** el regateo *2*
**actor** el actor *1*, 5
**actress** actriz 5
**actress** la actriz *1*
**add** agregar 9
**address** dirección 2
**addressee** destinatario/a 5
**adjust** ajustar 7
**administration** administración 1
**adopt** adoptar 3
**adopted** adoptado/a 7
**adoptive** adoptivo/a 7
**adult** adulto/a 11
**advertisement** anuncio 7
**advertising** publicidad 5
**advice** consejo 7
**advise** aconsejar 5
**aerobic exercise** ejercicio aeróbico 4
**afterwards** después 5
**again** otra vez 7
**age** edad *1*
**agency** agencia 1
**agree** estar de acuerdo 4, quedar en 5
**agreed** de acuerdo *1*
**air** aire 7
**air conditioning** aire acondicionado 8
**airplane** avión 8
**airport** aeropuerto 8
**all/everybody** todos 1
**allergic** alérgico/a 7
**alleviate** aliviar 9
**already** ya 3
**also** también 1
**altitude** altura 8
**always** siempre 1
**American** americano/a 3
**ample** amplio/a 10
**analyst** analista 10
**analyze** analizar 11
**ancestor** antepasado 3
**and** y 1
**angry** enojado/a *7*, furioso/a 1
**ankle** tobillo 9
**announcer** locutor/a 4
**answer** contestar *1*, 5
**antibiotic** antibiótico 9
**any** cualquier/a *5*, 9
**apartment** apartamento 3
**appear** aparecer 10
**applicant** solicitante *2*
**application** solicitud 5
**appointment** cita 5
**approve** aprobar 10
**arrange** arreglar 4
**architect** arquitecto/a 10
**arm** brazo 9
**armchair** sillón 3
**army** ejército 7
**arrive** llegar 5
**article** reportaje 11
**as a matter of fact** de hecho 9
**as soon as** en cuanto 8
**as soon as possible** lo más pronto posible 5
**ashamed** avergonzado/a 9
**ashtray** cenicero 8
**ask for** pedir (i) 4
**assault** asaltar 10
**assist** atender (ie) a 5
**assure oneself** asegurarse *2*
**asthmatic** asmático/a 9
**at the foot of** al pie de 7
**at the same time** al mismo tiempo 3
**At what time?** ¿A qué hora? 1
**at your service** a sus órdenes 1, 2
**attain** lograr 11
**attend** asistir a 5
**attentively** atentamente 11
**attorney** abogado/a 5, licenciado/a 10
**aunt** tía 3
**authority** autoridad 11
**authorize** autorizar 3
**automatic teller** cajero automático 8
**automobile** auto 1, automóvil 3
**available** disponible *3*, 5
**avenue** avenida *1*, 7
**avoid** evitar 7

**back** espalda 9
**back up** respaldar *2*
**backpack** mochila 2
**bakery** panadería 2
**bakery (pastries)** pastelería 2
**balcony** balcón 3
**ball** pelota 4
**banana** banana 2
**bandage** vendaje 9
**bank** banco 7
**banker** banquero/a 10
**barbecue** parrilla 3
**bargain** regatear 2
**bathe oneself** bañarse 4
**bathing suit** traje de baño *8*
**bathroom** baño 2
**bathroom sink** lavabo 8
**battery** batería 7
**bay** bahía *8*
**be able** poder(ue) 3
**be acquainted with** conocer (a) (zc) 5
**be afraid of** temerse 9
**be born** nacer *1*, 5
**be grateful** agradecer (zc) 9
**be happy** alegrarse *9*
**be in touch with** comunicarse con 5
**be interesting** interesar *11*
**be missing** faltar *1*
**Be seeing you.** Nos vemos. ¡Hasta la vista! 1
**be vaccinated** vacunarse 9
**beautiful** bello/a *2*
**beauty** belleza *2*
**beauty salon** peluquería 2
**because** porque 1
**become engaged** comprometerse 5
**bed** cama *2*, 3
**bedroom** dormitorio 1, 3
**before** antes 7
**begin** comenzar (ie) *2*, empezar (ie) 5
**behave** portarse 5
**behavior** comportamiento *9*
**believe** creer 8
**bellboy** botones 8
**belong** pertenecer (zc) *2*
**belonging** pertenencia 9
**belt** cinturón 7
**benefits** beneficios *5*
**besides** además 2
**better** mejor 3
**bewildered** desconcertado/a 9
**big** grande 1
**bilingual** bilingüe 5
**bill** cuenta *2*, 8
**bill (currency)** billete 2
**biology** biología 1
**birth** nacimiento *2*
**birthday** cumpleaños 2
**black** negro/a 2
**blanket** cobija 3
**block** cuadra, manzana 7
**blood pressure** tensión arterial 9
**blurred** borroso/a 9
**board of directors** junta directiva 11
**board** abordar/embarcar 8
**boat** barco 8
**body** cuerpo 4
**bone** hueso 9
**book** libro 1
**bookstore** librería 1
**boots** botas 2
**boss** jefe/a 5

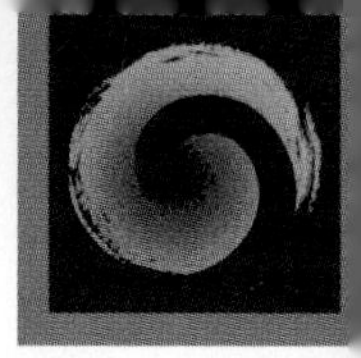

**both** ambos/as 5
**bother** molestar 8
**bottle** botella 8
**bottle (of medicine)** frasco 9
**boyfriend/girlfriend** novio/a 1
**bra** sostén 2
**bracelet** pulsera 2
**brake** freno 7
**branch office** sucursal *5*, 10
**bread** pan 2
**break** romperse 7
**break down** descomponer 10
**breakfast** desayuno 8
**breathe** respirar 7
**briefly** brevemente 10
**bring** traer 3
**broadcast** transmisión 4
**broadcast** transmitir 11
**broccoli** brócoli 8
**brochure** folleto 5
**broken (down)** descompuesto/a 7
**brother** hermano 3
**brother-in-law** cuñado 3
**brown** café/marrón 2
**buckle** abrocharse 7
**budget** presupuesto 5
**bugs** bichos *10*
**build** construir 11
**building** edificio 7
**bump into** encontrarse (ue) 4
**bus** autobús 7
**business** empresa 1, negocio *2*
**businessman/woman** hombre/mujer de negocios 5
**busy** ocupado/a 1
**butcher shop** carnicería 2
**butter** mantequilla 2
**buttock** nalga 9
**button** botón 2
**buy** comprar 2
**by means of** por medio de 5
**by the way** por cierto 5

**cable** cable 11
**café** café 1
**cafeteria** cafetería 2
**cake** pastel 2
**calculator** calculadora 1
**call** llamada 4
**calorie** caloría 9
**can** poder (ue) 3
**candidate** candidato/a 5
**capsule** cápsula 9
**car** auto, carro, coche *1*
**cared for** cuidado/a 10
**career (university studies)** carrera 3
**Careful!** ¡Cuidado! 7
**carefully** cuidadosamente *10*
**carpet** alfombra 3
**carpeted** alfombrado/a *3*
**carport** cochera 10
**carrot** zanahoria 2
**carry** llevar 2
**cashier** caja 2, cajero/a 5
**cat** gato 3
**celebrate** celebrar 4
**cellular telephone** teléfono celular 2
**center** centro *1*, 2
**centigrade** centígrado 4
**century** siglo 11
**ceramic** la cerámica *1*
**cereal** cereal 2
**certain** seguro/a 8
**certificate** certificado *3*
**chain** cadena 11
**chair** silla 1
**chalk** tiza 1
**chalkboard** pizarra 1
**champagne** champán 8
**champion** campeón/ona 4
**championship** campeonato 4
**change** cambio 2
**change** cambiar 2
**channel** canal 11
**charge** cobrar 3, cargar 7
**chat** charla 8
**chat room** salón de charla 11
**check** cheque 2
**check** revisar 7
**check (luggage)** facturar 8
**cheese** queso 2
**chemical** químico *7*
**chest** pecho 9
**chicken** pollo 2, 7
**child** niño/a *1*, 2
**childcare center** guardería 3
**choose** escoger 10
**chore** quehacer 3
**chromium** cromo 9
**city** ciudad 3
**claim check** comprobante 8
**classmate** compañero/a de clase 1
**classroom** salón de clase 1
**clean** limpiar 3
**clean** limpio/a 8
**clear** despejado/a 4, claro/a 7
**clear up** despejar 10
**clever** listo/a 11
**client** cliente/a 5
**climate** clima 4
**clock** reloj 2
**close** cerrar (ie) *1*
**closet** armario 3
**clothing** ropa 2
**cloudy** nublado/a 4
**coach** entrenador/a 4
**coast** costa 4
**coffee** café 1
**coffee table** mesa de centro 3
**coin** moneda 8
**cold** frío/a 8
**collaborate** colaborar *11*
**Colombian** colombiano/a 3
**color** color 2
**comb one's hair** peinarse 4
**come** venir (ie) (g) 3
**comfortable** cómodo/a 3
**commercial** comercial 2
**community** la comunidad *1*
**company** compañía 5
**compare** comparar *7*
**complete** completo/a 1
**completely** completamente 10
**component** el componente *5*
**computer** computadora 1
**computer science** informática 1
**concert** el concierto *7*
**condominium** condominio 3
**confidence** confianza *2*, 7
**confirm** confirmar 5
**congested** congestionado/a 9
**congratulate** felicitar 4
**congratulations** felicidades 5
**conscious** consciente *7*
**consciousness** conocimiento 7
**contact** contacto 11
**content** contenido 11
**continue** seguir (i) (g) 7
**continuously** continuamente 10
**contract** contrato 5
**contractor** contratista 10
**contribute** contribuir *5*
**cook** cocinar 3
**cook** cocinero/a 5
**cool** fresco 4
**copy** copia *1*
**copying machine** fotocopiadora 5
**corn** maíz 7
**corner** esquina 7
**corridor** corredor/pasillo 8
**cost** costar (ue) 2
**couch** sofá 3
**cough** tos 9
**county** condado 7
**country** país *5*
**couple** pareja 4
**course** curso 5, platillo 8
**cousin** primo/a 2
**cover** cubrir *2*, 9
**covered** cubierto/a *10*
**cow** vaca 7
**crash** chocar 7
**cream** crema *3*
**credit card** tarjeta de crédito 2
**creditor** acreedor/a 10
**crepe** crepe 8
**crew** tripulación 8
**cruise ship** crucero 8
**crutches** muletas 7
**culture** cultura 11
**cupboard** alacena, armario 3
**current** actual *2*
**custom** costumbre 7
**customs** aduana 8
**cutlet** milanesa 8

**dad** papá 3
**daily** diario 4
**damage** dañar 10
**damage** daño 7
**dancer** bailarín/bailarina 4

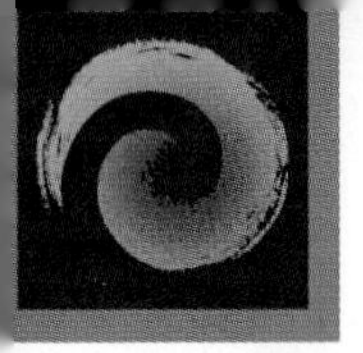

**danger** peligro 7
**dangerous** peligroso/a 4
**dark** oscuro/a 7
**darkness** oscuridad 11
**date** cita 5
**daughter-in-law** nuera 3
**dawn** madrugada *8*
**day** día 1, jornada *2*
**dead** muerto/a 3
**deal** trato 10
**death** muerte 9
**debt** deuda *2*
**decaffeinated** descafeinado/a 8
**decided** decidido/a 10
**decidedly** decididamente 10
**dedicate oneself to** dedicarse (a) 3
**deep** hondo/a 9
**degree (temperature)** grado 4
**degree** título 5
**delay** tardar 8
**delayed** atrasado/a 10
**delicious** delicioso/a 8
**delight** encantar 7
**delivery** entrega 10
**deny** negar (ie) 9
**department** departamento 11
**department store** almacén 2
**deposit** depósito *3*
**depressed** deprimido/a 9
**descend** descender 3
**descendant** descendiente 3
**design** diseñar 10
**design** diseño 10
**designer** diseñador/a 2
**desire** gana *9*
**dessert** postre 8
**destination** destino 8
**detail** detalle 5
**detain** detenerse (g) (ie)
**die** morirse (ue) 7
**diet** dieta 9
**difficult** difícil 1
**dining room** comedor 3
**dinner** cena 8
**direction** dirección 2, indicación 7
**directly** directamente 11
**director** director/a 5
**disability** incapacidad *1*
**discomfort** malestar 9
**discount** descuento 2
**dish** plato 3
**disobey** desobedecer (zc) 9
**disorganized** desorganizado 3, desordenado/a 9
**distracted** distraído/a 7
**district** distrito 11
**divorce** divorciarse 4
**dizzy** mareado/a 9
**do** hacer *1*, 3
**doctor** médico/a 3, doctor/a 5
**doctor's office** consultorio 3
**document** documento 5
**dog** perro 3
**dollar** dólar 2
**domestic** doméstico/a 3
**donate** donar 11
**donation** donativo 11
**double** doble 8
**dorm room** dormitorio 1
**dossier** expediente 5
**down payment** enganche/entrada 10
**down there/here** abajo 9
**dozen** docena 5
**dress** vestido 2
**dresser** cómoda 3
**drink** beber 3
**drink** bebida 8
**drive** conducir (zc) *2*, manejar 4
**driver** el/conductor/a 7
**drug** droga 7
**dry off oneself** secarse 4
**dubbed** doblado/a 11
**duchess** duquesa 8
**during** durante *11*
**dust** sacudir 3

**ear** oído/oreja 9
**early** temprano 1
**easy** fácil 1
**eat** comer 3
**eat breakfast** desayunar 8
**eat dinner** cenar 8
**economist** economista 10
**editor** editor/a 11
**egg** huevo 2
**elbow** codo 9
**elementary (school)** elemental *1*
**elevator** ascensor 8
**e-mail** correo electrónico 3
**embark** abordar/embarcar 8
**embassy** embajada 7
**emergency** emergencia *7*
**emergency room** sala de urgencias 7
**employee** empleado/a 3
**employment** empleo *2*, 5
**encourage** alentar (ie) 10
**end** final 5
**end** terminar *1*
**engagement** compromiso 4
**engineer** ingeniero/a 5
**engineering** ingeniería *5*
**England** Inglaterra 3
**English** inglés *1*
**enjoy** disfrutar 9
**enjoy oneself** divertirse (ie) 4
**Enjoy your meal!** ¡Buen provecho! ¡Que aproveche! 8
**enjoyable** divertido/a 3
**envelope** sobre 5
**equal** igual 2
**equipment** equipo 11
**eraser** borrador 1
**especially** especialmente 10
**establish** fundar *5*
**even though** aunque 11
**everybody** todo el mundo 11
**exactly** exactamente 2
**exchange** cambiar 2
**exciting** emocionante 4
**excursion** excursión 8
**exercise** ejercicio *1*
**exist** existir 11
**exit** salida 5
**expense** gasto 7
**expensive** caro/a 2
**experience** experiencia 5
**export** exportar 5
**express oneself** expresarse 11
**expression** expresión 11
**eye** el ojo *4*, 9

**face** cara *4*
**factory** fábrica 5
**failure** fracaso 9
**faint** desmayarse 7
**fair** feria 10
**fall** otoño 4
**fall asleep** dormirse (ue) 4
**famous** famoso/a *1*
**fan** aficionado/a 4
**fantastic** fantástico/a *1*
**farm** granja 7
**farmer** agricultor/a *7*
**father** padre 3
**father/mother-in-law** suegro/a 3
**favorite** favorito/a *1*
**feed oneself** alimentarse 9
**feel** sentirse (ie) 4
**fertilizer** el fertilizante *7*
**field** campo 11
**fight** pelearse 4
**file** archivar 5, expediente 5
**fill** llenar *3*, 5
**final** final 5
**finance** finanzas 10
**financial** financiero/a 10
**financing** financiamiento 10
**find** encontrar (ue) 2
**find** hallar 9
**find out** enterarse *5*
**fine** bien 1
**fine** multa 7
**finger** dedo 9
**finish** terminar *1*, 5, acabar 8
**fire** despedir *5*
**fire fighter** bombero 5
**firearm** arma de fuego 7
**first** primero/a 1
**fish** pescado 2
**fish market** pescadería 2
**fixed** fijo/a 2
**flight** vuelo 8
**floor** piso 2
**floppy disk** disquete 5

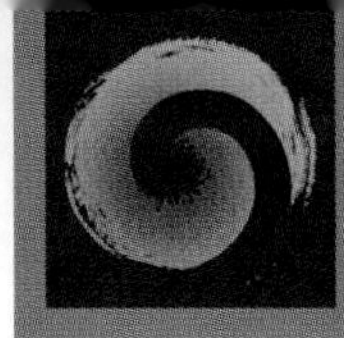

**flower** flor **3**
**flu** gripe **9**
**fluctuation** fluctuación **11**
**fly** volar (ue) **8**
**follow** seguir (i) **7**
**following** siguiente ***2*, 9**
**food** comida **3**, alimento **8**
**foot** pie **9**
**for** para, por **2**
**for example** por ejemplo **11**
**For Heaven's sake!** ¡Por Dios! **9**
**for, by** para ***1***
**forbid** prohibir **9**
**forget** olvidar **8**
**forgive** perdonar **2**
**fork** tenedor **8**
**fort** fuerte ***8***
**forward** adelante **4**
**found** fundar ***5***
**Forward, go on!** ¡Adelante! **4**
**fracture** fracturarse **7**
**free** libre **5**
**free (of cost)** gratis **1**, gratuito/a **10**
**free weights** pesas **4**
**freely** libremente **11**
**French** francés/esa **2**
**frequent** frecuentar **7**
**fresh** fresco/a **2**
**Friday** viernes **1**
**friend** amigo/a **1**
**friendship** amistad **9**
**from** de/desde **1**
**fruit** fruta **8**
**fruit stand** frutería **2**
**fulfill** cumplir **5**
**full** lleno/a **8**
**fun** divertido/a **3**
**function** funcionar **4**
**furnished** amueblado/a **10**
**furniture** muebles **2**

**gain weight** engordar **9**
**game** juego ***2***, partido **4**
**garage** garaje **3**
**garden** jardín **3**
**gas (natural)** gas **3**
**gasoline station** gasolinera **7**
**general** general **3**
**generously** generosamente **10**
**get** conseguir (i) ***2*, 8**
**get along with** llevarse bien **4**
**get angry** enojarse **4**
**get better** recuperarse **7**
**get bored** aburrirse **7**
**get dressed** vestirse (i) **4**
**get in** subir **8**
**get married (to)** casarse (con) **3**
**get oneself up** levantarse **4**
**get out** sacar **5**
**get together** juntarse **5**
**get washed** lavarse **4**
**gift** regalo **2**
**give** dar **5**
**give (gift)** regalar **8**
**glass** vaso **8**
**glasses** anteojos/gafas **8**
**go** ir ***1*, 2**
**go down** bajar **8**
**go out** salir **3**
**go to bed** acostarse (ue) **4**
**go up** subir **8**
**goal** gol **4**
**goal (post)** meta/portería **4**
**goalie** guardameta/portero/a **4**
**Good afternoon** Buenas tardes **1**
**Good evening** Buenas noches **1**
**Good morning** Buenos días **1**
**Good night** Buenas noches **1**
**Goodbye** Adiós **1**
**grade** calificación ***5***
**graduate** graduarse ***4*, 5**
**graduate (bachelor's)** licenciado/a **5**
**graduation** graduación ***4***
**grammar** gramática ***1***
**grandfather** abuelo **3**
**grandmother** abuela **3**
**grape** uva **2**
**green** verde **2**
**grey** gris **2**
**grief** pena **9**
**grill** parrilla **3**
**ground floor** planta baja **3**
**group** grupo ***1*, 11**
**guest** huésped **8**
**guidebook** guía **8**
**guilty** culpable **9**
**gymnasium** gimnasio **4**
**gymnastics** gimnasia **4**

**hair** pelo **4**, cabello **9**
**hair stylist** peluquero/a **5**
**half** medio/a **1**
**half brother/sister** medio hermano/a **3**
**hallway** pasillo **8**
**hand** mano ***1*, 4**
**handsome** guapo/a ***1***
**happiness** felicidad **4**
**happy** contento/a **1**, alegre **2**
**hard-working** trabajador/a **2**
**hat** sombrero **2**
**have a good command of** dominar **5**
**have a good time** divertirse (ie) **4**
**have just + -ed** acabar + de + inf. **4**
**have lunch** almorzar (ue) **3**
**have value** valer (g) **9**
**hay fever** fiebre del heno **9**
**he/she has** tiene **1**
**head** cabeza **9**
**heal** sanar ***9***
**health** salud **4**
**hear** oír **3**
**heart** corazón **9**
**heat** calor **4**
**heating** calefacción **4**
**heel** tacón **2**
**Hello.** Aló, Hola. **1**
**help** ayudar **2**
**hen** gallina **7**
**here** aquí **2**, acá **3**
**hidden** escondido/a **9**
**hip** cadera **9**
**hire** contratar ***8***
**hit** golpear **9**
**home** hogar **10**
**home office** casa matriz **5**
**homework** tarea **1**
**honey** miel **9**
**honeymoon** luna de miel **8**
**hope** esperar **5**
**hope** esperanza **9**
**horoscope** horóscopo ***1***
**horse** caballo **7**
**hospital** hospital **5**
**house** casa **3**
**household pet** animal doméstico **9**
**household related** doméstico/a **3**
**household (adj.)** casero ***10***
**How are you? (familiar)** ¿Cómo estás? **1**
**How are you? (formal)** ¿Cómo está Ud.? **1**
**How can I help you?** ¿En qué puedo servirle? **2**
**How many?** ¿Cuántos/as? **1**
**How much?** ¿Cuánto/a? **2**
**How's it going?** ¿Qué tal? **1**
**hug** abrazar ***4***
**hug one another** abrazarse **4**
**humid** húmedo/a **4**
**hurry** apurarse, darse prisa **8**
**hurt** doler (ue) **7**
**hurt oneself** lastimarse **9**
**husband** esposo **3**

**I am** soy, estoy **1**
**I'm sorry.** Lo siento. **1**
**I can** puedo **1**
**I have** tengo **1**
**I hope so!** ¡Ojalá! **9**
**I want you to meet... (familiar)** Quiero presentarte a ... **1**
**I want you to meet... (formal)** Quiero presentarle a... **1**
**I want you to meet... (plural)** Quiero presentarles a... **1**
**I wish!** ¡Ojalá! **9**
**ice** hielo **4**
**ice hockey** hockey sobre hielo **4**
**idol** ídolo ***1***
**illness** enfermedad **9**
**image** imagen ***2***
**imagine** imaginarse **8**
**impress** impresionar ***5***
**in addition** además ***1***

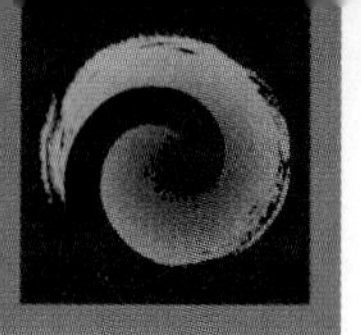

**in advance** por adelantado **3**
**in agreement** de acuerdo ***1***
**in back** detrás **8**
**in cash** al contado **2**
**in contact with** en contacto con **11**
**in front** adelante ***3***
**in front (of)** enfrente de **2**
**in spite of** a pesar de **11**
**in writing** por escrito **10**
**inability** incapacidad ***1***
**inch** pulgada **3**
**include** incluir **8**
**income** ingreso ***2*, 5**
**increase** aumentar **9**
**indeed** efectivamente **10**
**indicate** indicar/señalar **8**
**indispensable** imprescindible **10**
**inexpensive** barato/a **2**
**infirmary** enfermería **3**
**informal** informal ***1***
**information** información ***1***
**injection** inyección **9**
**insecticide** insecticida ***7***
**inside** dentro **8**
**inspect** inspeccionar **10**
**inspector** inspector/a **10**
**installment** cuota/plazo **10**
**instantaneous** instantáneo/a **11**
**instead of** en vez de **9**
**insurance** seguro **5, 7**
**insured** asegurado/a **5**
**intelligent** inteligente **1**
**interest** interés **10**
**interesting** interesante **10**
**interview** entrevista **5**
**interview** entrevistar ***11***
**invest** invertir (ie) **10**
**iron** planchar **3**
**island** isla ***8***
**Italian** italiano/a ***1*, 8**
**itinerary** itinerario **8**

**jail** cárcel **7**
**Japanese** japonés/esa **2**
**job market** bolsa de trabajo **10**
**job** empleo ***2***, puesto **5**
**journalist** periodista **3**
**judgement** juicio **10**
**juice** jugo **3**

**keep** guardar **3**
**key** llave **8**
**kick** patear **4**
**kicker** pateador/a **4**
**kill** matar **9**
**kind** amable **5**
**kiosk, stall** quiosco **7**
**kiss** besar(se) ***4***
**kitchen** cocina **3**
**knee** rodilla **9**
**knife** cuchillo **8**
**know** saber **2**
**know** conocer (a) **5**

**label** etiqueta **5**
**laboratory** laboratorio ***11***
**lack** falta **9**
**lake** lago **7**
**lamp** lámpara **8**
**land** aterrizar **8**
**landlord** el/la arrendador/a ***2***
**landscape** paisaje **7**
**language** idioma **9**, lengua **10**
**last** último **1**
**late** tarde **1**
**laugh** reír(se) (i) **9**
**laundry room** cuarto de lavado **3**
**laundry service** servicio de lavandería **8**
**law** ley **7**
**lawyer** abogado/a, licenciado/a **5**
**leading man/lady** protagonista **11**
**leafy** frondoso/a **9**
**league** liga **4**
**lean** magro/a **9**
**learn** aprender ***1*, 5**
**leather** cuero **7**
**leave (behind)** dejar **5**
**leave** salir(g) **3**
**left** izquierdo/a **7**
**leg** pierna **7**
**lentil** lenteja **9**
**less** menos ***1***
**let** dejar **2**, permitir **8**
**letter (alphabet)** letra **7**
**lettuce** lechuga **2**
**liberty** libertad **11**
**library** biblioteca **1**
**license** licencia **7**
**lie** mentir(ie) **4**
**lieutenant** teniente **7**
**life** vida ***5*, 7**
**lift** levantar ***1*, 4**
**light** luz **1**
**light (adj.)** claro/a **7**
**Likewise** Igualmente **1**
**limit** límite **7**
**list** lista ***1***
**listen** escuchar ***1***
**live** vivir ***1*, 3**
**living room** sala **3**
**load** cargar **7**
**loan** préstamo ***2*, 10**
**lobby** vestíbulo **8**
**lock** cerradura **10**
**locker** casillero ***8***
**long** largo/a **2**
**look (at)** mirar **2**
**look around** recorrer con la mirada ***5***
**look for** buscar **2**
**look good** lucir ***2***
**lose** perder (ie) **4**
**lose weight** adelgazar **9**
**lost** perdido/a **11**
**lovely** precioso/a **8**
**low** bajo/a **11**
**luck** suerte ***2*, 5**
**luggage** equipaje **8**
**lunch** almuerzo **8**
**lunch box** lonchera **3**
**lung** pulmón **9**
**luxury** lujo **7**

**maid** camarero/a **8**
**mailbox** buzón **11**
**main** principal **3**
**make** hacer ***1*, 3**
**make a decision** tomar una decisión **5**
**make a good/bad impression** caer bien/mal **5**
**make a note of** anotar **9**
**manage** dirigir **5**
**manager** gerente **1**
**manufacture** fabricar **11**
**map** mapa **8**
**mark** marcar **8**
**marketing** mercadeo **10**, mercadotecnia **11**
**married** casado/a **3**
**mascot** mascota **9**
**massage** masaje **9**
**match** partido **4**
**material** material ***11***
**maternal** materno/a **3**
**matter** asunto **7**
**mechanic** mecánico **5**
**mechanics** mecánica **5**
**media** medios de comunicación **11**
**medical** médico/a **7**
**medium** mediano/a **2**
**meet** encontrarse (ue) **4**
**menu** menú/carta **8**
**message** mensaje **5**
**messy** desordenado/a **3**
**midnight** medianoche **1**
**milk** leche **2**
**million** millón ***1***
**millionaire** millonario/a ***2***
**minor** menor **10**
**mirror** espejo **3**
**Miss** señorita **1**
**mistreat** tratar mal **10**
**mixed** mixto/a **4**
**model** modelo ***1***
**modern** moderno/a **10**
**modernize** modernizar **10**
**mom** mamá **3**
**Monday** lunes **1**
**money** dinero **1**
**morning** mañana **1**

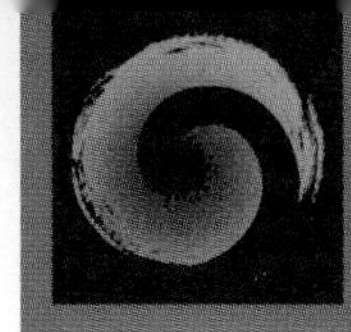

**mortgage** hipoteca **10**
**mortgage** hipotecario/a **10**
**mother** madre **3**
**motive** motivo **2**
**mountain** montaña **4**
**mouth** boca **9**
**move** mudarse **5**
**move away** alejarse **7**
**movie theater** cine *7*
**Mr./Mrs.** señor/a **1**
**music** música **2**
**musical** musical *1*
**musician** músico **5**
**My name is…** Me llamo … **1**
**My name is…** Mi nombre es … **1**

**name** nombre **8**
**nap** siesta **3**
**nation** nación, país *5*
**nationality** nacionalidad *3*
**nauseous** mareado/a **9**
**navy blue** azul marino **2**
**near** cerca de **2**
**nearby** cercano/a **8**
**neck** cuello **9**
**need** necesidad *1*
**need** necesitar **2**
**neighbor** vecino/a **3**
**neighborhood** vecindario **7**
**nervous** nervioso/a **1**
**never** nunca **2**
**nevertheless** sin embargo **9**
**new** nuevo/a **1**
**news** noticias **5**
**news program** noticiero **4**
**newspaper** periódico **7,** diario **11**
**next** próximo/a *4*
**next to** junto a **2**
**nightgown** camisón **2**
**nobody** nadie **2**
**noise** ruido **4**
**none** ningún, ninguno/a **4**
**noodle** fideo **9**
**noon** mediodía **1**
**north** norte **7**
**nose** nariz **9**
**not to get along** llevarse mal **4**
**notebook** cuaderno **1**
**nothing** nada **2**
**notice** notar **10**
**novel** novela **2**
**now** ahora **1**
**number** número *1*
**nurse** enfermero/a **3**
**nursing (mom)** nodriza **9**

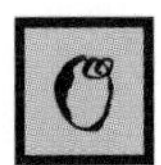

**oatmeal** avena **9**
**observe** observar **11**
**obtain** conseguir (i) ***2*, 8**
**obvious** obvio/a **10**
**occasion** vez *2*
**offer** oferta **2,** ofrecer **10**
**office** oficina **2**
**often** seguido **3,** a menudo **4**
**oil** aceite **7**
**on board** a bordo **8**
**on our own** por nuestra cuenta **8**
**onion** cebolla **2**
**only** solamente **1**
**open** abierto/a **1**
**open** abrir *1*
**operate** manejar **3**
**orange** naranja, anaranjado/a **2**
**order** ordenar **2,** pedir (i) **4**
**organize** organizar **5**
**origin** origen **3**
**other** otro/a **2**
**ounce** onza **2**
**our** nuestro/a **5**
**out in front** en frente **3**
**outside** afuera **3**
**oven (microwave)** horno (microondas) **3**
**overcoat** abrigo **2**
**own** propio/a ***2*, 3**
**owner** dueño/a **8**

**pain** dolor **9**
**paint** pintar **4**
**painting** cuadro **3**
**pair** pareja **4**
**pamphet** folleto **5**
**paper** papel **1**
**paramedic** paramédico/a *7*
**Pardon me. (formal)** Disculpe. **1**
**parking** estacionamiento **7**
**part** parte **3**
**party** fiesta **2**
**pass** pasar *1*
**pass** pase **8**
**passport** pasaporte **8**
**past** pasado/a **11**
**pastime** pasatiempo **5**
**path** vereda **10**
**patient** paciente **9**
**patrol car** patrulla *7*
**pay** pagar **2**
**pay attention to** atender (ie) + a **5**
**payee** destinatario/a **5**
**pea** guisante/chícharo **9**
**peaceful** tranquilo/a **7**
**peanut** cacahuete **9**
**pedagogy** pedagogía **1**
**pedestrian** peatón **7**
**pen** bolígrafo **1**
**pencil** lápiz **1**
**people** gente **5**
**per cent** por ciento **2**
**percentage** porcentaje **11**
**perfume** perfume **2**
**perhaps** quizá *10*
**perhaps** tal vez **9**
**period** jornada ***2*,** período **11**
**permit** permitir **8**
**personally** personalmente **3**
**Peruvian** peruano/a **2**
**pharmacist** farmacéutico/a **9**
**pharmacy** farmacia **2**
**photo(graph)** foto(grafía) **3**
**photocopy** fotocopia **5**
**physical therapy** fisioterapia **7**
**pick-up truck** camioneta **7**
**pier** muelle **8**
**pillow** almohada **3**
**pineapple** piña **2**
**pink** rosado/a *3*
**pins and needles** hormigueo **9**
**place** lugar/sitio **1**
**place** poner(g) **3**
**place setting** cubierto **8**
**plan** planear **8**
**plan (floor)** plano **10**
**plan on** pensar **5**
**planning** planificación **10**
**plaster** enyesar **7**
**plate** plato **3**
**player** jugador/a **4**
**playing cards** cartas **4**
**pleasant** placentero/a **8**
**please** haga el favor de, por favor **2**
**Pleased to meet you.** Encantado/a, Mucho gusto. **1**
**plumber** plomero/a **5**
**plumbing** plomería **10**
**pneumonia** pulmonía **9**
**point** punto **4**
**police (related to)** policiaco/a **7**
**police officer** policía **5**
**police woman** mujer policía **5**
**politics** política **11**
**pollution** la polución *7*
**poor thing** pobrecito/a **7**
**popular** popular **1**
**port** puerto *8*
**position** puesto **5**
**positive** positivo/a **11**
**potato** papa **2**
**pottery** cerámica *1*
**pound** libra **2**
**practice** práctica **1**
**practice** practicar **1**
**prefer** preferir (ie) **4**
**pregnant** embarazada **9**
**prescribe** recetar **9**
**prescription** receta **9**
**press** prensa **11**
**pretty** bonito/a **2**
**previous** anterior **10**
**price** precio **2**
**primary** primario/a *4*
**print** letra de molde *2*
**printed** impreso/a **10**
**printer** impresora **3**
**private** privado/a **3**
**prize** premio *2*
**probably** probablemente **10**

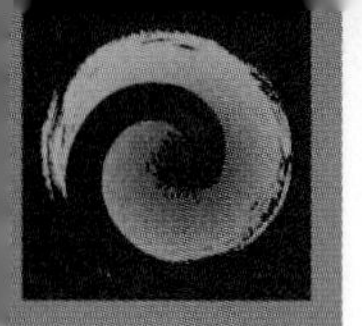

**problem** problema 2
**producer** productor/a 11
**professor** profesor/a 1
**program** programa 5
**programmer** programador/a 5
**programming** programación 1
**prolonged** dilatado/a 10
**promise** prometer *2*, 8
**proof** prueba 11
**property owner** propietario/a 10
**protect** proteger 7
**provide** proporcionar 8
**psychiatrist** psiquiatra 5
**psychology** psicología 1
**punctual** puntual 2
**purchase** compra 7
**purchases** compras 2
**purple** violeta 2
**purpose** motivo 2
**purse** bolso 2
**push** empujar 9
**put on make-up** maquillarse 4
**put** poner 3

**quantity** cantidad 2
**quarter** cuarto 1
**question** pregunta *5*
**questionnaire** cuestionario 9

**radio** radio 11
**rain** llover (ue) 4
**raise** aumentar *5*
**rapidly** rápidamente 7
**raw** crudo/a 9
**read** leer *1*, 3
**real estate/property** propiedad 10
**real state agency** agencia inmobiliaria 10
**reasonable** razonable 10
**receipt** recibo 2
**receptionist** recepcionista 8
**recognize** reconocer (zc) 9
**recommend** recomendar (ie) 8
**record, (compact) disc** disco compacto *1*
**recover** recuperarse 7
**red** rojo/a 2
**red wine** vino tinto 4
**redecorate** redecorar (ue) 10
**reduced** rebajado/a 2
**reflect** reflejar 9
**refrigerator** refrigerador, nevera 3
**regain** recobrar 7
**related to children** infantil 3
**relative** pariente/a *2*
**religious** religioso/a 1
**remain** quedarse *7*
**remember** recordar (ue) 3
**rent** alquilar 3
**rent** alquiler *2*
**repair** reparación 10
**repair** arreglar 4, reparar 7
**repeat** repetir (i) *1*
**report** reportar 7
**report** reporte *3*, informe 7, reportaje 11
**representative** representante 8
**requirement** requisito 5
**resolve** resolver (ue) 10
**resolved** resuelto 10
**responsible** responsable 3
**rest** descansar 9
**rest** reposo *9*
**restaurant** restaurante *1*
**result** resultado 10
**resumé** currículum vitae 5
**retirement** jubilación *5*
**return** regresar 2, volver (ue) 4
**return (something)** devolver (ue) 8
**right** derecho/a 2, derecho 11
**right now** en este momento 5, ahora mismo 8
**ring** anillo 2
**risk** arriesgarse 9
**roast** asar 3
**robe** bata 2
**roof** techo 10
**room** habitación 8
**roommate** compañero/a de cuarto 1
**routine** rutina 4
**run** correr 3, dirigir 5

**sad** triste 7
**safety** seguridad 7
**said** dicho/a 10
**salary** sueldo *5*
**sales** rebajas 2, 5
**salesperson** dependiente/a 2
**salmon** salmón 2
**same** mismo/a 11
**sandals** sandalias 2
**sargent** sargento 7
**satellite** satélite 11
**satisfied** satisfecho/a 10
**Saturday** sábado 1
**save** ahorrar 11
**savings** ahorros *2*
**say** decir (i) (g) 2
**scene** escena 7
**schedule** horario 1
**scholastic** escolar 11
**school** escuela 1
**science** ciencias 2
**sea** mar 8
**season** la temporada *9*
**seat** asiento 7
**second** segundo/a 2
**secret** secreto *4*
**secretary** secretario/a 5
**security** seguridad 7
**see** ver 3
**See you later** Hasta luego 1
**See you tomorrow** Hasta mañana 1
**seem** parecer (zc) 10
**seizure** embargo 10
**sell** vender *1*, 2
**semester** semestre 1
**seminar** seminario 11
**send** enviar *2*, 5
**serious** serio/a 1, grave 10
**serve** servir (i) 8
**set (date)** fijar 4
**set** juego *2*,
**set** fijo/a 2
**shake** agitar 9
**shampoo** champú 8
**shape** forma 9
**share** compartir 3
**shares** acciones 10
**sharp** agudo/a 9
**shave oneself** afeitarse 4
**sheet** sábana 8
**shelf** estante 1
**ship's cabin** camarote 8
**shoe** zapato 2
**shoe store** zapatería 2
**shopping** las compras *1*
**shopping center** centro comercial 2
**short (length)** corto/a 2
**show** enseñar 3, mostrar (ue) 8
**shower** ducha 8
**shrimp** camarón 2
**sick** enfermo/a 9
**sickbay** enfermería 3
**Sir/Madam** señor/a 1
**sister** hermana 3
**sister-in-law** cuñada 3
**side** lado 2
**side effect** efecto secundario 9
**sidewalk** acera 7
**sign** firmar 2
**sign** señal 9
**signature** firma 11
**silence** el silencio *1*
**singer** cantante 5
**singer** el/la cantante *1*
**single** sencillo/a 8
**single** soltero/a *1*
**sit** sentarse *1*
**size** talla 2
**ski** esquiar 4
**skin** piel *2*, 9
**skirt** falda 2
**sky** cielo 4
**slap** cachetada/cachete 9
**sleep** sueño 9
**slow** lento/a 4
**slowly** lentamente 9
**small** pequeño/a 1
**smoke** fumar *9*
**snack** refrigerio 3
**snow** nevar (ie) 4
**so much** tanto/a 3
**soap** jabón 8

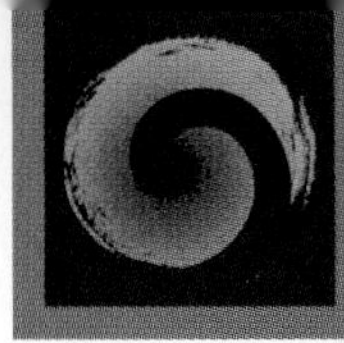

**soap opera** telenovela **11**
**soccer** fútbol **4**
**socks** calcetines **2**
**soda** refresco **2**
**soil, make dirty** ensuciar ***1***
**solitary** solitario/a **7**
**some** alguno/a **3**
**someone** alguien **2**
**something else** algo más **2**
**son/daughter** hijo/a **1**
**son-in-law** yerno **3**
**soon** pronto **10**
**so-so** regular **1**
**sound system** equipo de sonido **7**
**sounds good to me** me parece bien **3**
**source** la fuente ***2***
**sow** sembrar (ie) **7**
**space** espacio **3**
**space between the eyebrows** el entrecejo ***9***
**spaghetti** espaguetis **8**
**Spanish** español **1**
**special** especial **2**
**specialist** especialista **11**
**specialize** especializarse **10**
**speed** velocidad **7**
**spend** gastar **10**
**spokesperson** portavoz **10**
**sponsor** patrocinador/a **10**
**sponsor** patrocinar **4**
**spoon** cuchara **8**
**spoonful** cucharada **9**
**sport** deporte/ deportivo/a **2**
**spot** mancha **2**
**spring** primavera **4**
**squash** calabaza **9**
**stairs** escalera **2**
**stamp** estampilla/sello **5**
**start** arrancar **7**
**state** estado **5**
**statement** declaración **7**
**station** estación **7**
**statistics** estadísticas ***7***
**stay** quedarse **7**
**steak** bistec **2**
**step** paso ***2***
**step by step** paso a paso **10**
**stepbrother/sister** hermanastro/a **3**
**stepfather** padrastro **3**
**stepmother** madrastra **3**
**stepson/daughter** hijastro/a **3**
**stereo** estéreo **2**
**stewardess** azafata **8**
**stick** pegar **5**
**still** todavía **7**
**stock** acción **10**
**stock market** bolsa (de valores) **10**
**stockbroker** corredor/a de bolsa **10**
**stockings** medias **2**
**stomach** estómago **9**
**stop** parar **4**
**stop** parada **7**
**store** la tienda ***1*****, 2**
**stove** estufa **3**
**straight** derecho/a, recto/a **8**
**straight (hair)** lacio ***4***
**stranger** extraño/a **7**
**street** calle **2**
**stretch** estirarse **9**
**stretch** estiramiento ***9***
**stripe** raya **2**
**stroke** infarto **9**
**strong** fuerte **9**
**strongly** fuertemente **10**
**student** alumno/a ***1*****,** estudiante **1**
**student desk** pupitre **1**
**student teacher** maestro/a en prácticas **1**
**study** estudiar **1**
**study** estudio **3**
**stuffed** relleno/a **8**
**style** estilo **2**
**submit** presentar **11**
**substance** substancia **7**
**succeed** lograr ***9***
**success** éxito ***2*****, 9**
**sudden** súbito/a ***9***
**suffer** sufrir **9**
**sufficient** suficiente **1**
**suffocate** sofocarse **9**
**sugar** azúcar **8**
**suggest** sugerir (ie) ***8*****, 10**
**suitcase** maleta **8**
**summarize** resumir ***11***
**summary** resumen **11**
**summer** verano **4**
**sun** sol **4**
**sun glasses** gafas (de sol) **2**
**Sunday** domingo **1**
**supermarket** supermercado **2**
**support** apoyo ***9***
**suppose** suponer (g) **11**
**sure** seguro ***2*****,** claro **2**
**surprise** sorpresa **8**
**survey** encuesta **11**
**swear** jurar **11**
**sweater** suéter **2**
**sweatshirt** sudadera **2**
**sweep** barrer **3**
**sweet potato** camote **9**
**sweetheart** mi amor **11**
**swim** nadar **4**
**swimming** natación **4**
**swimming pool** piscina **3**
**symptom** síntoma **9**
**syrup** jarabe **9**
**system** el sistema ***5***

**table** mesa **1**
**take advantage** aprovechar ***2***
**take advantage of** aprovecharse de **9**
**take along** llevar **2**
**take care of** cuidar **9**
**take charge of** encargarse (de) **5**
**take off** despegar **8**
**take out/off** sacar ***1*****, 5**
**talkative** hablador/a **2**
**tall** alto/a **2**
**tank** tanque **7**
**tanning lotion** bronceador **8**
**tape** cinta **9**
**tax** impuesto **2**
**taxi meter** taxímetro **8**
**teach** enseñar **3**
**teacher** maestro/a, profesor/a **1**
**technology** tecnología **11**
**telephone** teléfono **1**
**television** televisión **11**
**television set** televisor **2**
**tell** decir (i) (g) **2**
**temperature** temperatura **4**
**temporary** temporal **5**
**tenant** inquilino/a **10**
**term** término **10**
**termite** termita **10**
**terrace** terraza **8**
**text** texto **1**
**Thank you.** Gracias. **1**
**that which** lo que **11**
**that's why** por eso **10**
**the rest** los demás **11**
**theater** teatro **5**
**then** entonces **2**
**there** allá ***3***
**there** allí **5**
**there is/are** hay **1**
**thermometer** termómetro **9**
**these** éstos/as **2**
**thief** ladrón, ladrona **10**
**thigh** muslo **9**
**think** pensar (ie) **5**
**third** tercero **1**
**this one** éste/a **2**
**throw away** tirar **10**
**Thursday** jueves **1**
**ticket** multa **7,** pasaje **8**
**tied** empatado/a **4**
**tile** mosaico ***3***
**time** hora **1,** vez ***2***
**tip** propina **8**
**tire** llanta **7**
**tired** cansado/a **1**
**title** título **5**
**to** a **1**
**toast** brindis **4**
**together** juntos/as **1**
**toilet paper** papel higiénico **8**
**tomato** tomate **2**
**tomato (small)** jitomate **9**
**too** también **1**
**tooth** diente **4**
**tortilla bakery** tortillería **2**
**total** total **1**
**touch** tocar **7**
**tourism** turismo **8**
**tourist (adj.)** turístico/a **8**
**tow truck** grúa **7**
**toward** hacia **7**
**towel** toalla **8**
**town** pueblo **7**
**trade** comercio **10**

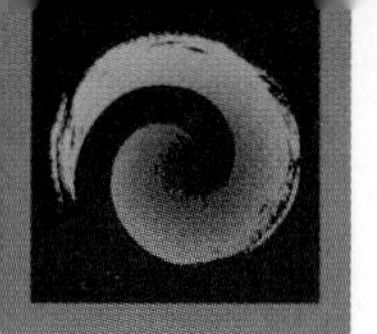

**traffic light** semáforo 7
**train** entrenar 11
**training** el entrenamiento *5*
**tranquil** tranquilo/a 7
**tranquilizer** el calmante *9*
**translate** traducir 3
**transport** transportar 8
**transportation** transporte 8
**traveler** viajero/a 8
**traveling** ambulante 10
**tray** bandeja 8
**treated** tratado/a 9
**treatment** tratamiento *2*, 3
**tree** árbol 7
**trip** viaje 1
**trophy** trofeo 4
**true** verdad 1
**truly** verdaderamente 10
**trunk** maletero 7
**truthfully** verdaderamente 10
**Tuesday** martes 1
**turn** doblar 7
**two** dos 1
**typical** típico/a 3

**umbrella** paraguas 2
**uncle** tío 3
**uncomfortable** incómodo/a 2
**undershorts (men's)** calzoncillos 2
**understand** comprender 3
**understood** entendido/a 9
**United States** Estados Unidos 3
**university** universidad 1
**unfair** injusto/a *7*
**unjust** injusto/a *7*
**unoccupied** desocupado/a *3*
**urinate** orinar 9
**use up** agotar 9
**usually** normalmente 3

**vacancy** vacante 5
**vacation** las vacaciones *2*
**vacuum** aspirar 3
**valuation** tasa 10
**veal** ternera 8
**vegetable** verdura 8
**very beautiful** hermosísimo/a *8*
**view** vista 3
**visit** visitar 3
**vote** votar 11

**waist** cintura 9
**wait (for)** esperar 5
**waiter** mesero 5
**waitress** mesera 5
**wake oneself up** despertarse (ie) 4
**walk** caminar 2
**wall** pared 3
**want** querer (ie) 4
**warm-up** calentamiento 9
**wash** lavar 3
**watch** reloj 2
**water skiing** esquí acuático 4
**weak** débil 9
**weakness** debilidad 9
**weather** tiempo 4
**wedding** boda 4
**Wednesday** miércoles 1
**week** semana 1
**weight** peso 9
**What time is it?** ¿Qué hora es? 1
**What?** ¿Qué? 1
**What's your name? (familiar)** ¿Cómo te llamas? 1
**What's your name? (formal)** ¿Cómo se llama Ud.? 1
**wheat** trigo 9
**wheelchair** silla de ruedas 7
**when** cuando 2
**Which?** ¿Cuál?, ¿Qué? 1
**while** mientras 7
**white** blanco/a 2
**Who?** ¿Quién? 1
**Who's calling?** ¿De parte de quién? 5
**whose** cuyo/a 9
**why** por qué 2
**wife** esposa 3
**will** testamento 10
**win** ganar 4
**wind** viento 4
**window** ventanilla 8
**window** ventana 1
**windshield** parabrisas 7
**wine list** carta de vinos 8
**winter** invierno 4
**wish** desear 2
**with me** conmigo 5
**with you** contigo 5
**without** sin *1*
**witness** testigo 7
**woman** mujer 2
**wonder** la maravilla *11*
**word** palabra 3
**work** trabajar 1, funcionar 4
**work (of art, literature)** la obra *1*
**work at** dedicarse (a) 3
**workdays** días hábiles 5
**worker** obrero/a 5
**worker** trabajador/a 3
**world** mundo 3
**worldwide** mundial 11
**worried** preocupado/a 7
**worry** preocuparse 4
**worse** peor *7*
**wounded** herido/a 7
**wrestling** lucha libre 4
**writer** escritor/a 2

**X-ray** radiografía 9

**year** año 3
**yellow** amarillo/a 2
**yes** sí 1
**yet** todavía 7
**you (familiar)** tú 1
**you (formal)** usted (Ud.) 1
**you have (familiar)** tienes 1
**you have (formal)** tiene 1
**You're welcome.** De nada. 1
**young** joven *1*, 2
**young man, woman** joven 11
**your** tu 2

# Credits

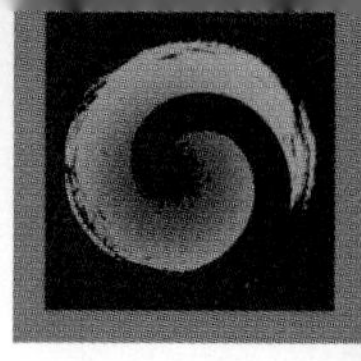

## Text Credits

**Page 5:** "Un jaguar toma jugo en la jungla" © Roger Paré y la courte échelle, © 1992 Susaeta Ediciones; **page 39**: Richard Newsham, Publications Supervisor/Westpark (Ventura, CA); **page 47:** reprinted by permission of La Nación, S.A.; **page 53:** ¿En qué nos equivocamos? reprinted by permission of BUENA SALUD Magazine, Editores Asociados, S.A., Buenos Aires, Argentina; **page 97:** "Residencial Santa Fé" reprinted by permission of UBICA; **page 101:** cover of *GeoMundo* reprinted by permission of *GeoMundo*; cover of *TV y novelas* reprinted by permission of Editorial America, S.A., d/b/a Editorial Televisa; cover of *Medix* reprinted by permission of Editorial America, S.A., d/b/a Editorial Televisa; cover of *Balón* reprinted by permission of *Balón*; cover of *Mundo 21* reprinted by permission of Editorial America, S.A., d/b/a Editorial Televisa; cover of *Casa y Estilo* reprinted by permission of Casa y Estilo Internacional; **page 107:** reprinted by permission of La Nación, S.A.; **page 109:** reprinted by permission of Sears, Roebuck and Co.; **page 117:** cover of *Ser Padres* reprinted by permission of Gruner & Jahr; cover photo reprinted by permission of Augutus Butera; **page 159:** Table of Contents reprinted by permission of *Panorama Deportivo*; **page 169:** *L. A. Times*, June 28, 1998; **page 189:** "Buscando personal multicultural" and "Hispanic Online" reprinted by permission of HISPANIC Magazine; **page 204:** Table of Contents reprinted by permission of *Clara mensual con mil ideas,* Mexico; **page 207:** reprinted by permission of HISPANIC Magazine; **page 245:** reprinted by permission of Grupo Sílaba; **page 269:** reprinted by permission of Automobile Club of Southern California; **page 271:** reprinted by permission of CA DMV; **page 272:** reprinted by permission of Marion County Sheriff's Office, Salem, OR; **page 275:** reprinted by permission of *El País* and Rosa Montero; **page 281:** reprinted by permission of Port of Portland; **page 313:** recipe reprinted by permission of Editorial America, S.A., d/b/a Editorial Televisa; **page 407:** reprinted by permission of BUENA SALUD Magazine, Editores Asociados, S.A., Buenos Aires, Argentina; **page 293:** reprinted by permission of *Revista Mía de México*; **page 337:** reprinted by permission of March of Dimes Birth Defects Foundation; **page 339:** reprinted by permission of Eli Lilly and Company; **page 341:** reprinted by permission of National Domestic Violence Hotline; **page 349:** reprinted by permission of Eli Lilly and Company; **page 353:** reprinted by permission of *Vanidades*; **page 355:** reprinted by permission of *Clara mensual con mil ideas*, Barcelona, España; **page 363:** Ford advertisement Courtesy Ford Motor Co.; **page 379:** reprinted by permission of People Weekly © 1998 Time Inc.; **page 380:** Barnett Bank article reprinted by permission of Vista Magazine, January/February 1997; **page 381:** Guía de Ayuda Financiera reprinted by permission of Wells Fargo; **page 383:** article on Tanya Pages reprinted by permission of *Latina Style* Magazine; **page 389:** "Cuán Seguro Es el Hogar," by R. Cores, reprinted by permission of Vista Magazine, June 1998; **page 389:** Allstate advertisement reprinted by permission of Allstate Insurance Company; **page 391:** "Conexion de Cliente" reprinted by permission of Southern California Edison; **page 391:** Home Depot/ACE article, by Michael D. White, reprinted by permission of World Trade Magazine; **page 397:** "Citicorp y Travelers" article republished by permission of Dow Jones, Inc. via Copyright Clearance Center, Inc. © 1998, Dow Jones and Company, Inc. All Rights Reserved Worldwide; **page 405:** reprinted by permission of Airtouch Cellular; **page 411:** reprinted with permission of Corporate Media Partners d/b/a americast; **page 413:** reprinted by permission of Pacific Bell; **page 415:** Sensormatic advertisement reprinted by permission of Sensormatic Electronics Corp.; **page 417:** reproduced with permission of AT&T; page 421: "Esta es su oportunidad…" © 1999 The Arbitron Company; **pages 423 and 425:** reprinted by permission of HISPANIC BUSINESS INC., 425 Pine Ave., Santa Barbara, CA 93117; **page 430:** "El futuro es nuestro"; artist: Laura Rodríguez; **page 431:** reprinted by permission of HISPANIC BUSINESS INC., 425 Pine Ave., Santa Barbara, CA 93117; **page 433**: reprinted by permission of Ocho Columnas; **page 405:** "¿Lobo o cordero?" reprinted by permission of *Clara mensual con mil ideas*, Barcelona, España; **page 439:** reprinted by permission of Embajada de España, Consejería de Educación.

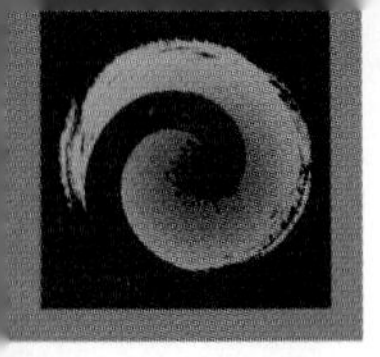

# Photo Credits

**Page 2:** Bob Daemmrich/Stock Boston; **page 9 (left):** Jack Messler/D. Donne Bryant Stock Photography; **page 9 (right):** Steven Ferry; **page 21:** Laura Luongo/Shooting Star International Photo Agency; **page 40:** Walter Hodges/Westlight/Corbis; **page 43:** Benainous-Duclos/Liaison Agency, Inc.; **page 44:** Chad Ehlers/Tony Stone Images; **page 48:** Patricia Rush; **page 83:** Mark Richards/PhotoEdit; **page 84:** Peter Menzel/Stock Boston; **page 86:** Scott Barrow/International Stock Photography Ltd.; **page 88:** Walter Hodges/Westlight/Corbis; **page 91:** Patricia Rush; **page 103:** Deborah Davis/ PhotoEdit; **page 117:** Augustus Butera; **page 124 (top and bottom)** and **page 125 (top and bottom):** Patricia Rush; **page 128:** Robert Frerck/Odyssey Productions; **page 130: (top left)** Tom McCarthy/Southern Stock/Index Stock Imagery, Inc.; **page 130 (top right):** Glenn Wilson; **page 130 (bottom right):** Frank White/Liaison Agency, Inc.; **page 133:** Patricia Rush; **page 143:** Bruno Luca/AP/Wide World Photos; **page 147:** Zade Rosenthal/Photofest; **page 150:** Bill Bachmann/Southern Stock/Index Stock Imagery, Inc.; **page 157 (top, left to right):** Clive Bunskill/Allsport Photography (USA), Inc., Mark Thompson/Allsport Photography (USA), Inc., Al Bello/Allsport Photography (USA), Inc., Jonathan Daniel/Allsport Photography (USA), Inc.; **page 157 (bottom, left to right):** Mike Powell/Allsport Photography (USA), Inc., Elsa Hasch/Allsport Photography (USA), Inc., Rick Stewart/Allsport Photography (USA), Inc.; **page 159:** Jonathan Daniel/Allsport Photography (USA), Inc.; **page 166:** Richard R. Renaldi/Impact Visuals Photo & Graphics, Inc.; **page 167:** Robert Frerck/Odyssey Productions; **page 170:** Bruce Ayres/Tony Stone Images; **page 193 (top left):** John Waterman/Tony Stone Images; **page 193 (top right):** Sung Park/Austin American Statesman/Sygma Photo News; **page 193 (bottom):** Peter Krinninger/International Stock Photography Ltd.; **page 207:** Frank Curry; **page 208:** Michael Newman/PhotoEdit; **page 209:** Steve Agricola/Stock Boston; **page 212 (top to bottom):** Bob Daemmrich/Stock Boston; Chad Ehlers/Tony Stone Images; Scott Barrow/International Stock Photography Ltd.; Robert Frerck/Odyssey Productions; Bruce Ayres/Tony Stone Images; **page 234:** EFE News Services, Inc.; **page 239 (top):** Patricia Rush; **page 239 (bottom):** Doug Armand/ Tony Stone Images; **page 254:** Pete Saloutos/Photographic Resources; **page 256:** ATC Productions/Photographic Resources; **page 262:** EFE News Services, Inc.; **page 264:** Tomas del Amo/Profiles West/Index Stock Imagery, Inc.; **page 272:** Mark Richards/PhotoEdit; **page 273:** EFE News Services, Inc.; **page 276:** Dennis Hallinan/FPG International LLC; **page 280:** Comstock; **page 287:** Patricia Rush; **page 298:** Pete Seaward/Tony Stone Images; **page 307 (top left):** Jan Stephan; **page 307 (top right):** Berenholtz/The Stock Market; **page 307 (bottom left):** D. Donne Bryant Stock Photography; **page 307 (bottom right):** Rick Strange/Index Stock Imagery, Inc.; **page 314 (top):** David Sutherland/Tony Stone Images; **page 314 (bottom):** IKAN (Simion)/Peter Arnold, Inc.; **page 315 (top):** Kelvin Aitken/Peter Arnold, Inc.; **page 314 (bottom):** John Kieffer/Peter Arnold, Inc.; **page 317:** Berenholtz/The Stock Market; **page 318:** Donna Binder/Impact Visuals Photo & Graphics, Inc.; **page 322:** David R. Frazier Photolibrary, Inc.; **page 327:** Henley/The Stock Market; **page 335 (left):** Ken Tannenbaum/The Image Bank; **page 335 (right):** Steve Niedorf/The Image Bank; **page 346:** Patricia Rush; **page 351 (left and right):** Agencia EFE; **pages 356 and 357 (all):** Miraval Life in Balance ™ Resort and Spa; **page 360:** Don and Pat Valenti/Tony Stone Images; **page 379:** Rex Rystedt/People Weekly Syndication; **page 398 (top):** Bachmann/PhotoEdit; **page 398 (bottom):** Peter Menzel/Stock Boston; **page 402:** Ulrike Welsch/Stock Boston; **page 404:** Michael Newman/PhotoEdit; **page 406:** David Young-Wolff/PhotoEdit; **page 422:** Robert Frerck/Odyssey Productions; **page 425:** David Chambers/Tony Stone Images; **page 440 (top):** EFE News Services Inc.; **page 440 (bottom):** Agencia EFE.

# Index

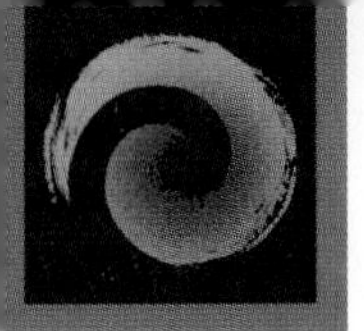

Mar del Caribe
Océano Atlántico
Océano Pacífico
TRINIDAD Y TOBAGO
Port-of-Spain
Barranquilla
Cartagena
Maracaibo
Caracas
VENEZUELA
R. Orinoco
Georgetown
Paramaribo
GUAYANA
Cayena
SURINAM
GUAYANA FRANCESA
Medellín
Manizales
Bogotá
Cali
COLOMBIA
Quito
ECUADOR
Guayaquil
CORDILLERA DE LOS ANDES
R. Amazona
Iquitos
Manaus
R. Amazonas
Belém
Cajamarca
R. Madeira
BRASIL
Recife
PERÚ
Macchu Picchu
Lima
Ayacucho
Cuzco
Salvador
Arequipa
L. Titicaca
La Paz
BOLIVIA
Brasilia
Arica
Sucre
Iquique
Potosí
Belo Horizonte
PARAGUAY
Antofagasta
Rio de Janeiro
São Paulo
Santos
Salta
Asunción
Tucumán
CORDILLERA DE LOS ANDES
CHILE
R. Paraná
R. Uruguay
Porto Alegre
Córdoba
Rosario
URUGUAY
Valparaíso
Mendoza
Santiago
Buenos Aires
Montevideo
La Plata
Río de la Plata
Concepción
Bahía Blanca
ARGENTINA
Puerto Montt
América del Sur
Islas Malvinas
0 200 400 600 800 millas
Estrecho de Magallanes
0 200 400 600 800 kilómetros
Punta Arenas
TIERRA DEL FUEGO
Cabo de Hornos